MW00993719

STUDIO CERAMICS

STUDIO CERAMICS

BRITISH STUDIO POTTERY 1900 TO NOW

ALUN GRAVES

CONTENTS

Previous. Bernard Leach, bottle, stoneware, 1931 (cat. 532)

Opposite. Bryan Newman at Aller Pottery, Somerset, 1982

FOREWORD BY TANYA HARROD

Studio ceramics emerged in Britain as a new and engaging art form in the early 20th century. But it did not feature in the standard histories of British art, or, for that matter, of British design, even though a handful of critics writing before the Second World War had recognized the sculptural qualities of thrown pots, seeing them as an exceptionally pure form of abstraction. By the 1950s handmade ceramics became one of the pleasures of peacetime and, as a greatly expanded discipline, operated independently in parallel to the art world.

Institutionally, studio ceramic practice came to be allied with modern craft, which in Britain by 1971 was supported by its own government body, the Crafts Council, whose status until 1999 was equal to that of the Arts Council. Significantly, ceramics were not collected by the Tate Gallery, London, or subsequently by its successor institution for British art, Tate Britain. It was the Victoria and Albert Museum which valorized studio ceramics, chiefly through acquisitions made by the museum's Circulation Department until that Department's closure in 1977. Subsequently the museum's Ceramics Department continued to collect with commitment and insight.

This magnificent new catalogue of the Victoria and Albert Museum's collection builds on Oliver Watson's groundbreaking 1990 publication *British Studio Pottery: The Victoria and Albert Museum Collection*. Considerably expanded, it reflects the growth in the collection over three decades. It registers the current turn towards ceramics within the fine-art world, represented by works by Richard Deacon, Laura Ford and Nicholas Pope, as well as the rather younger Aaron Angell and Jesse Wine. They join earlier acquisitions of works by Barry Flanagan, Bruce McLean and John Piper, these 'fine artist' ceramicists now being fully integrated into the catalogue rather than treated separately.

Alun Graves has also redrawn the boundaries of the catalogue, including in it Bloomsbury ceramic experimentation and the figure-makers at work in Chelsea during the 1920s and 1930s. Admired in their day, but now largely forgotten, these Chelsea figurines sit alongside more recent acquisitions of figurative work by artists such as Claire Curneen, Philip Eglin and Rachel Kneebone. Underlining this enlarged field of ceramics, meanwhile, are acquisitions from performative events orchestrated by artists such as Clare Twomey and Keith Harrison.

Despite this welcome expansion, at the heart of this catalogue are the multitude of men and women identified firmly with the studio ceramic movement – who until recently have remained outliers of the British art scene. Great artists such as Gillian Lowndes, Magdalene Odundo and Gwyn Hanssen Pigott made their own way, undisturbed by the need for endorsement by the fine-art world. A sense of having taken the road less travelled was to energize figures as different as Richard Batterham and Ewen Henderson. And if studio ceramics emerged in part as a critique of industrial ceramics, in the later work of Neil Brownsword its role has shifted, memorializing a depleted culture of making as the manufacture of industrial wares moved from its epicentre in the six towns of Stoke-on-Trent to South-East Asia and East Asia.

This book is a celebration both of individuals and of brave purpose. I knew, and know, most of the ceramicists whose careers began in the 1950s and later, and I have researched in detail the lives of the generations who worked in the early 20th century. This invaluable catalogue is a record of responsible and imaginative collecting by a great museum. The practice of ceramics as an art and as a craft is honoured – in an introductory essay followed by an impressive photographic sequence and by the individual biographical entries. The complexity and beauty of ceramics made in studio are set out for our pleasure and as an aid to future scholarship.

PREFACE

This book is both an introduction to British studio ceramics and a catalogue of the Victoria and Albert Museum's collection. Its format follows that of Oliver Watson's earlier catalogue, first published in 1990,[1] and I am indebted to Oliver for allowing me to use his text as a starting point; indeed, Oliver's words resound in a number of the entries. The catalogue takes an inclusive approach to British studio ceramics, encompassing work made by international artists while in the UK, and that made by British artists while working overseas. Essentially concerned with objects made by the artists themselves, the catalogue largely omits items (including tiles) decorated using bought-in ceramic blanks, and excludes ventures into industrial design. It does, however, include work made collaboratively and pieces that appropriate found objects.

An important and defining feature of the V&A collection is its contemporariness.[2] The collection is as old as the discipline itself, and their histories are entwined. The earliest pot recorded in this book is a slipware bowl by Reginald Wells, made in 1909. Given by Herman Hart in 1917, this work was arguably the V&A's first acquisition of studio pottery (at the same time Hart gave several pieces by the Martin Brothers, whose eclectic wares are more often seen in the context of art pottery and are not catalogued here). Hart's gift was followed in 1919 by the donation of a further 14 pots by Wells, presented by the artist's friend Victor Ames, and a vase by Dora Lunn, selected by the museum and given by Lt-Col. Kenneth Dingwall. A stockbroker with considerable interest in ceramics, Dingwall was a beneficent donor to the museum and gave it a number of important studio pots, including its first piece by Bernard Leach (in 1921). The V&A's first purchases of studio pottery were meanwhile made in 1923: a pot by William Staite Murray, bought from the artist for 7 guineas (£7.7s.), and a slipware bowl by Hamada Shōji, bought at Paterson's Gallery, London, for £2.15s.

In the first two decades of the museum's collecting in this field, studio pots were acquired by both the Ceramics Department and the Circulation Department, which organized travelling exhibitions to museums and art schools. The principal authority in the museum was Bernard Rackham, Keeper of Ceramics from 1914 to 1938, who advised upon acquisitions for both departments. But Circulation would firmly take the lead in contemporary collecting, such that by 1950 the Department's contemporary holdings were 'much more extensive than those of the main Museum'.[3] Acquisitions of studio ceramics by Circulation were driven by its Keeper, Peter Floud, and Hugh Wakefield, who succeeded him in 1960, alongside curators including Carol Hogben and David Coachworth. In 1975 Circulation was incorporated into a Department of Regional Services, but in 1977 was closed and its collections dispersed to the curatorial departments. The Ceramics Department then seized the initiative on contemporary collecting under John Mallet, Keeper from 1976 to 1989, most notably through the activities of Assistant Keeper Oliver Watson, who succeeded Mallet in the redefined role of Chief Curator. My own collecting activities began in the late 1990s, continuing from 2001 within an amalgamated Department of Sculpture, Metalwork, Ceramics and Glass.

For the most part, the collection has been formed through the acquisition of single objects or small groups, often purchased directly from the artists or from (mostly London-based) galleries. Significant groups of material have also been added with the absorption of the British Institute of Industrial Art's collection in 1934, and the distribution of items from the Contemporary Art Society in the 1930s and '40s. Judiciously selected gifts have enriched the collections, while financial support from donors has been vital. Particular thanks must go to Gerard and Sarah Griffin, whose generosity has supported many 21st-century acquisitions. In a letter to Kenneth Dingwall drafted in 1919, following his gift of Dora Lunn's vase, Rackham noted: 'We are the more grateful as with the slender sum at our disposal for purchases we find it difficult ourselves to buy for the Museum examples of present-day craftsmanship, and yet we feel that the best contemporary work should not go unrepresented; so when friends like yourself come forward to aid us are glad to take advantage of this help.'[4] A century on, the realities of funding an active programme of contemporary collecting remain remarkably unchanged.

1 Watson (1993).

2 On the development of the collection, see J.V.G. Mallet, 'Collecting for the Victoria and Albert Museum', *CR*, 70 (1981); Watson (1990); 'Growth of the Collection', in Watson (1993), pp.36–40; and Alun Graves, 'Room 138', *CR*, 201 (2003).

3 Victoria and Albert Museum, *V&A Museum Circulation Department: Its History and Scope* (London, 1950), p.3.

4 V&A Archive, nominal file, MA/1/D1185/6.

STUDIO CERAMICS IN BRITAIN

Potter, sculptor, craftsman, artist – what does it matter what you call me. What's in a name? I use the ceramic processes. I shape clay in some way and then fire it![1]

So wrote Bryan Newman in 1963 in a short article that railed against the list of 'should nots' for potters that marked the factionalized world of studio ceramics. For Newman, an artist whose work encompassed both domestic pottery and abstract ceramic sculpture (fig.1), it was as defensible to make pots that learned something from the past as it was to make sculpture that responded to the avant-garde, or indeed to find a route in between: 'why should pottery be always pure pottery, sculpture pure sculpture – there is a whole range of interesting forms using elements of both.'[2] Newman sits at the midpoint of studio ceramics, both chronologically and conceptually; its history now extends for comfortably more than a century, and those four equally valid descriptors he offered for his activity – 'potter', 'sculptor', 'craftsman', 'artist' – indicate some of its possibilities. Within its sphere lies an interrelated series of artistic practices concerned with the making of objects that range from tableware to individual vessels, from small-scale figures to large-scale sculpture, and which increasingly might extend into the realms of installation art or performance. The extent to which these activities can be construed as a single discipline is a matter of debate, but they are bound together by the use of a common material, clay, and its multifarious associated processes. The technical complexities of the medium are a unifying factor for diverse practitioners, and must account for the fact that – for better or worse – so much discussion of ceramics is expended on technique.

In her introduction to Peter Dormer's survey *The New Ceramics* in 1986, the potter Alison Britton observed ceramics'

FIG.1 Bryan Newman, sculpture, stoneware, 1969 (cat. 722)
FIG.2 Alison Britton, *Flat-backed Jug with Stork*, high-fired earthenware, 1978 (cat. 87); *Flat-backed Jug with Stork, red version*, high-fired earthenware, 1978 (cat. 88)

ability to deal with both design and art as being distinctive of the discipline. Adopting a literary allusion, she wrote: 'There is prose and there is poetry. In pottery there seems to remain a possibility for providing both, sometimes in the same object.'[3] Of those objects that might straddle design and art (or prose and poetry) in this way, Britton perhaps had in mind the complex, self-conscious and brilliant pots of her own circle (fig.2), as well as certain more mannered historical precedents that performed playful visual tricks. But poetry can also be found in objects of less ambiguous utility. In recognizing this, it is tempting to note the collapsing of the gap between poetry and prose that has occurred in literature since the 1990s, exemplified strongly by the new nature writing – the creative non-fiction – of Roger Deakin, Robert Macfarlane and others, in which lyrical storytelling becomes the means of communicating the natural world. A comparable lyricism can be found in the best domestic studio pottery, in which incident and gesture combine in forms that are in essence functional. In the case of such works, understanding artistic intent gets us only so far; their makers often do not set out to be commentators, and might actively resist artist status. But aesthetic appreciation and engagement are subjective. In his single written statement, the potter Hans Coper described what he claimed was the only pot that had really fascinated him: 'a pre-dynastic Egyptian pot, roughly egg-shaped, the size of my hand ... It conveys no comment, no self-expression, but seems to contain and reflect its maker and the human world it inhabits ... It was not the cause for my making pots, but it gave me a glimpse of what man is.'[4] Is it fanciful to suggest that, say, a Richard Batterham teapot (fig.3) might similarly give us a glimpse of what it is to be human? If it does, it is not because of its perfect utility, nor because of Batterham's undeniable technical facility. Rather, it is the outcome of the innumerable aesthetic decisions made and enacted by him that influence how we perceive the object through multiple senses; decisions which ensure that Batterham – like Britton – never made *exactly* the same object twice.

This individuality is an essential attribute of studio ceramics, present then both in consciously artistic 'individual pieces' and in repetition making by hand, where it offers a counter to the uniformity of industrial production. Studio ceramics is, in essence, an anti- or at least non-industrial practice, the studio or small workshop being the primary site for making, and the work that of a single person or perhaps small team, made without division of labour. In such a model, 'the brain which conceives the pot controls the making of it also', as the potter and educator Dora Billington succinctly expressed it.[5] The motivation for seeking such independence might be the opportunities it affords in terms of artistic expression, or it might be underpinned by a more philosophical or ethical stance – these are concurrent and interwoven strands in the history of studio ceramics, as we will see. Or it might simply be the desire for a different kind of life, something which was a factor for many in the decades after the Second World War.

FIG.3 Richard Batterham, teapot, stoneware, 1984 (cat. 56)

The earliest precedent for the more consciously independent practice that would come to define studio ceramics can perhaps be found in the sibling potters the Martin Brothers, who worked collaboratively making salt-glazed stoneware in London from 1873.[6] Robert Wallace Martin – the eldest of the four brothers – acted as designer and modeller, drawing upon his training as a sculptor to transform thrown jars into the caricatured birds for which the Martins are best known. Walter and Edwin Martin were both throwers, Walter being also a skilled technician and glaze chemist, and Edwin an accomplished decorator; Charles Martin, meanwhile, dealt with sales and ran their shop. In the 1900s, probably through the hands of Edwin Martin, they began to explore gourd-like vase forms that showed a degree of Japanese influence. These exhibited, as a commentator in *The Studio* – most likely Charles Holmes – enthused, 'features which are essentially characteristic of the potter's craft – the manipulation of clays of varied texture and of coloured glazes, and of such decorative treatment as essentially belongs to the potter's art, and bears no resemblance to that of other crafts'. Such progress was enough to suggest that there was 'no reason why the potter should not in the future, as he has done upon rare occasions in the past, rise to the greatest distinction as an artist'.[7] Nevertheless, aside from the enthusiasms of Sidney Greenslade[8] and Ernest Marsh[9] – passionate collectors of Martinware who would go on to become important supporters of the new studio potters – the Martin Brothers lacked direct connection with, and did not have any great influence upon, the fledgling studio pottery movement. Indeed, for the young Michael Cardew, they seemed part of the 'stuffy ... cobwebby' world of arts and crafts from which he sought fresh air.[10]

Cardew's antipathy to the work of the Martin Brothers is indicative of the distinct, if varied, tastes of the new studio potters, which tended to favour simple, essential forms and surfaces. His own interests lay in English slip-decorated earthenware, a tradition which had also inspired Reginald Wells, perhaps the first artist who would become firmly associated with the new movement. A young sculptor, Wells had by 1903 gained recognition for his realist small-scale bronzes.[11] Enterprising and resourceful, he did his own casting, and, before long, began also to experiment with pottery. By 1908 he had built a kiln at Coldrum Farm, Wrotham, Kent, and set about making slipware, drawing heavily upon local traditions.[12] Surviving pieces from this period present various technical deficiencies and appear inexpertly thrown – problems that would be resolved when Wells moved his pottery to Chelsea, London, about 1909, and employed as a thrower Edward J. Baker, a potter from Hoo, Kent.[13] At Chelsea, Wells retained the Coldrum name and initially continued with slipware. However, the focus of his output would soon shift in response to the growing interest in early Chinese stoneware, which he was emulating by 1913.[14] Wells continued production at Chelsea until 1914, when he turned his attention to aircraft manufacture for the duration of the First World War.

Another pioneer was Denise Wren (then Tuckfield), who had come to England from Australia as a child.[15] The daughter of an inventor, Wren shared family traits of invention and self-reliance. At Kingston School of Art she discovered clay through modelling classes, and with the encouragement of her teacher Archibald Knox, began about 1911 to visit a local flowerpot maker, Mr Mercer, from whom she absorbed the rudiments of throwing. The following year she co-founded the Knox Guild of Design and Craft and set about making handbuilt and thrown pottery in their shared studio in Kingston upon Thames, using a kick-wheel bought from Mercer and firing the work in his kiln.

The early careers of Wells and Wren reflect the times; neither was yet fully independent as a potter. Tuition in throwing was, meanwhile, hard to come by, and at first might not even have been seen as necessary. Given the emphasis placed upon it from the 1920s through to the 1960s, this seems surprising. But it was only in the 1910s that throwing began to be recognized as a creative rather than an artisanal act. This distinction – which had much to do with class – was reflected in the art schools. The first course that covered all stages of pottery production was taught by Richard Lunn at the Royal College of Art, London, from 1903, but this dealt with casting and moulding rather than throwing, which was carried out where required by a professional potter working from the students' drawings. At Camberwell School of Arts and Crafts, pottery was taught along similar lines from 1907, again by Lunn. Only with the appointment of his successor, Alfred Hopkins, in 1915 was throwing taught at Camberwell, but at first only to male students, much to the anger of Dora Lunn and Gwendolen Parnell, who briefly studied there.[16] Both women became successful early studio potters: Lunn (the daughter of Richard) founded the Ravenscourt Pottery in 1916, initially producing mould-made ware; Parnell began making pottery figures in Chelsea about 1917. Other pioneering women include Frances Richards and Lois Glover, both of whom produced moulded pottery in this early period. Another was Dora Billington, who had been a student of Richard Lunn at the Royal College of Art at the time of his death in 1915. Already knowledgeable and with experience in the Staffordshire Potteries, Billington began teaching at the College, and later also at the Central School of Arts and Crafts, becoming one of the century's most important ceramic educators.

Among the first to recognize the creative significance of throwing was the painter and critic Roger Fry. Known for his championing of Post-Impressionist art, Fry established the Omega Workshops in 1913 with the aim of bringing its aesthetics and sensibilities into domestic life through objects and interiors designed and decorated by young artists. After initially painting on commercially made pottery, Fry in late 1913 began throwing his own pots for Omega, under the guidance of George Schenck, an elderly flowerpot maker in Mitcham, Surrey. In the Omega Workshops catalogue issued the following year, Fry set out his ethos:

> *Of all crafts none has suffered more than pottery from the application of scientific commercialism. We now use almost entirely articles which have lost all direct expressiveness of surface modelling. Our cups and saucers are reduced by machine turning to a dead mechanical exactitude and uniformity. Pottery is essentially a form of sculpture, and its surface should express directly the artist's sensibility both of proportion and surface. The Omega pottery is made on the wheel by artists and is not merely executed to their design. It therefore presents, as scarcely any modern pottery does, this expressive character.*[17]

Fry continued his exploration of pottery from 1914, working in a corner of the factory of Carter & Co. in Poole, Dorset, where he made austere but spirited tableware (fig.4) in monochrome white tin glaze or occasionally intense blue or metallic black glazes, most of which he seems himself to have thrown. Though Omega

FIG.4 Omega Workshops, sauce boat, earthenware, *c.* 1914–15 (cat. 748); plate, earthenware, *c.* 1914–15 (cat. 745); tureen and cover, earthenware, *c.* 1914–15 (cat. 744)

was a short-lived venture, its pottery had influence. For Quentin Bell, reflecting on the products of the Omega Workshops 50 years on, in 1964, it was Fry's ceramics that stood out. His sauce boat was 'a prototype of the ceramics of our century. From it a generation has learned to avoid fussiness and indecision'.[18]

Significant in Fry's Omega statement was his assertion that pottery was a form of sculpture – an essentially formalist reading that positioned pottery within the developing discourse of abstraction in art. Such an association was underpinned by the reappraisal that was taking place among collectors, curators and critics of a range of historic ceramic types, most particularly early Chinese wares of the Song (960–1279) and Yuan (1279–1368) dynasties.[19] Previously disregarded by European collectors in favour of the richly decorated porcelain of the late Ming (1368–1644) and Qing (1644–1911) dynasties, these earlier wares had begun to receive greater attention as new examples came to light through the excavation of tombs in China. An exhibition of *Early Chinese Pottery and Porcelain* at the Burlington Fine Arts Club, London, in 1910 did much to generate interest. Fry reviewed the exhibition enthusiastically, and in the years following Song pottery was increasingly held as an exemplar of aesthetic perfection. In his theory of significant form, published in 1914, Clive Bell asserted: 'No one ever doubted that a Sung pot or a Romanesque church was as much an expression of emotion as any picture that ever was painted.'[20] A similar critical reappraisal took place of early English earthenware, particularly of the medieval period, with later vernacular slipwares also gaining renewed interest among collectors, furthered by publications including Charles Lomax's *Quaint Old English Pottery* of 1909. This redrawing of the ceramic canon around more austere or essential forms had a stimulating effect on studio potters, who, like Wells, began to reinterpret them in their work.

•••

The years 1919 and 1920 brought an extraordinary concentration of activity, as studio potters sought to re-establish themselves after the First World War. Reginald Wells resumed potting in Chelsea in 1919, concentrating both on stonewares of Chinese inspiration, and on realist animal and human figures, some developed from his earlier bronzes. In the same year Charles and Nell Vyse established a studio there, and embarked on the making of pottery figures. Fellow figure-maker Gwendolen Parnell was already working nearby, establishing Chelsea as an important centre for pottery figure-making in the 1920s.[21] The technically accomplished Vyses would later turn also to the emulation of early Chinese stonewares, but they were not in the vanguard; only about 1926 did their experiments begin.[22] Meanwhile, Denise Wren and her husband, Henry, bought a plot of land in Oxshott, Surrey, in 1920, and set about building a house and pottery. And alongside this activity, workshops were established by the two most prominent studio potters of the interwar years: William Staite Murray and Bernard Leach.

Born in Deptford, London, in 1881, Murray had dabbled in painting before following his family into employment in the seed and bulb trade. He continued to harbour artistic ambitions, however, and became interested in pottery, studying briefly at Camberwell. About 1915 he established a pottery in Yeoman's Row, Kensington, with the Vorticist painter Cuthbert Hamilton, making thrown earthenware dishes with vibrant abstract painting. But in 1919, at a new workshop in Rotherhithe, he turned his attention to stoneware. Despite limited experience, he quickly gained an impressive degree of technical control, making by the early 1920s thrown pots with rich, monochrome glazes (fig.5) or brush decoration. A report of an exhibition organized by the Arts League of Service in 1924 shows the measure of his achievement. His pots 'represented the results of experiments made with oil firing for the first time in this country and ... some very fine specimens' had been obtained. He had 're-discovered a great number of the old Chinese glazes' and was 'considered by connoisseurs as the first [leading] potter in this country.'[23]

Bernard Leach came to ceramics by an altogether different route. Born in Hong Kong in 1887, he spent his early childhood in East Asia before travelling to England in 1897 to attend school. Artistically inclined, he studied at the Slade School of Fine Art and later at London School of Art, where he was taught etching by Frank Brangwyn. Romantic and nostalgic ideas of Japan then drew him to return in 1909 to that country, where he became part of an intellectual and artistic circle that included the future artist–potter Tomimoto Kenkichi and Yanagi Sōetsu, founder of the *mingei* (folkcraft) movement. His first experience of pottery-making came in 1911, at a party where pots were being decorated and raku-fired. He was, he recalled in his memoirs, 'on the spot seized with the desire to take up this craft.'[24] Thus begins the story of an extraordinary life's work, enriched in its telling by Leach himself. He subsequently found a teacher in the elderly Urano Shigekichi, sixth in a line of traditional potters, and went on to establish his first kiln in Tokyo in 1913. After a period in China, he set up a workshop on Yanagi's land at Abiko in 1916, moving again after a disastrous fire in 1919. At a new pottery in Tokyo – his last in Japan – Leach gained technical advice from Hamada Shōji, a young potter working at Kyoto City Ceramic Research Institute, who chose to accompany him to England when he returned the following year.

FIG.5 William Staite Murray, pot, stoneware, 1924 (cat. 691); pot, stoneware, 1924 (cat. 692)

The Leach Pottery in St Ives, Cornwall, would become the most famous of all studio pottery workshops. Such is its renown – and that of St Ives as the artistic centre it would become – its location now seems unsurprising. But its limited resources of clay, and of wood for fuel, together with its distance from major centres, made it a challenging place to start a pottery. Leach's decision to set up his workshop there had been prompted by an offer of financial assistance from Frances Horne, founder of the St Ives Handicraft Guild. Together with Hamada, he built an Asian-style climbing kiln and began making slipware, stoneware and raku. While its location at the western tip of Cornwall offered an alternative to the metropolitan dominance of other studio potteries – an aspect that would be of lasting influence – the Leach Pottery was nevertheless planned around 'the individuality of the artist' and its economics based 'on the studio and not on the country workshop'. 'Hamada and I regarded ourselves as being on the same basis as Murray in London, Decoeur in Paris and Tomimoto in Japan', Leach asserted. His values were informed by those of the designer and reformer William Morris and were profoundly anti-industrial: 'this is the counter-revolution, the refusal of the slavery of the machine.'[25] In the early years production at St Ives was beset with technical problems, some of which were overcome by the Japanese potter and ceramic engineer Matsubayashi Tsurunosuke, who worked there in 1923 and 1924. Matsubayashi redesigned and rebuilt the climbing kiln and gave lectures on technical matters to the pottery team, which by then included Leach's first students, Michael Cardew and Katharine Pleydell-Bouverie. Both would go on to become important studio potters: Cardew re-established the production of slipware at Winchcombe Pottery, Gloucestershire, a former country workshop; Pleydell-Bouverie made stoneware with wood-ash glazes at Coleshill, Berkshire, working for a time with Norah Braden, another exceptional Leach pupil.

Late in 1923, after three years in St Ives, Hamada returned to Japan. The first significant solo exhibitions of studio pottery had been his, held at Paterson's Gallery on London's Old Bond Street in May and November 1923.[26] These had proved highly successful and gained positive critical attention,[27] doing much to establish the name of the Leach Pottery as well as furthering the interests of studio potters more widely. Both Leach and Murray would exhibit regularly at Paterson's throughout the remainder of the 1920s. By this time studio pottery had coalesced as an identifiable movement, and an albeit short-lived Guild of Potters had been formed. The Guild's first exhibition, at the Gieves Art Gallery on Old Bond Street in 1924, was split evenly between figures and pots, which were intermixed in the displays. It was judged 'a good beginning in the organization of this very important art', by *The Times*' critic, Charles Marriott, who noted the attractions of the 'ornamental figures of the Chelsea type' by Parnell and others, but held as more serious the pots of Murray, Leach, Wells and Lunn. 'In pottery, of all the arts, what really counts is mastery of materials, in simple forms and colours arising out of the actual means of production', he opined.[28] Not all critics dismissed ceramic figures so readily, but they would broadly be seen as a more popular art, and attract less critical discussion.

While Leach's concerns were underscored by moral conviction, Murray's were primarily aesthetic. In 'Pottery and the Essentials in Art' – a short text of about 1924 – he outlined his position, addressing the central issues of abstraction and the relationship of pottery with painting and sculpture:

> *Pottery is perhaps more readily enjoyed as a pure aesthetic expression than either Sculpture or Painting. ... A finely proportioned Pot is accepted as beautiful without the disturbing question of the meaning of its form. It is an abstraction, and once we experience pleasure in contemplating it as such, we shall be ready to discard the literary element and discover the underlying principles of beauty ... in Sculpture and Painting. Pottery may be considered the connecting link between Sculpture and Painting, for it incorporates both. ... But the first aesthetic importance of Pottery is form, for it is plastic Sculpture, fundamental, of primitive dignity and power.*[29]

Murray's views were closely aligned with those articulated by Bernard Rackham and Herbert Read in their pioneering survey, *English Pottery*, published in 1924, in which they asserted: 'Sculpture ... had from the first an imitative intention, and is to that extent less free for the expression of the aesthetic sense than pottery, which may be regarded as plastic art in its most abstract form.'[30] The same year, Rackham wrote on Murray's work for *The Studio*, prefacing his remarks with the same assertion.[31] Murray was firmly on the ascendant. In 1925 he was appointed as Pottery Instructor at the Royal College of Art in preference to Leach. Increasingly, he became associated with the development of British modernism, exhibiting alongside the painters Christopher Wood, Ben Nicholson and Winifred Nicholson. He was elected a member of the 7 & 5 Society, a group of painters and sculptors, and his work was owned by H.S. Ede – known today as the founder of Kettle's Yard house and collection, Cambridge – who wrote lyrically of his work. In 1930 Murray held the first of a series of solo exhibitions at the prestigious Lefevre Galleries in London; Herbert Read contributed the introduction to the catalogue, revisiting the words of *English Pottery* to emphatically state: 'pottery is plastic art in its most abstract essence.'[32]

Alongside Murray, Reginald Wells was the potter who garnered the greatest critical acclaim in the 1920s. Frank Rutter, art critic for the *Sunday Times*, was particularly fulsome in his praise, declaring that Wells had 'not only raised himself to the head of his profession', but had lifted pottery 'to the level of the fine arts'. His exhibition at the Beaux Arts Gallery in 1927, Rutter suggested, 'surpasses any other one-man show of pottery that has yet taken place'.[33] Similarly effusive was the sculptor Frederick Lessore, who contributed an article on Wells to the journal *Artwork* in 1926/27. Wells had by then moved his studio from Chelsea to Storrington in Sussex, and was clearly throwing his own work: 'a sculptor's mind ... dictates the ever-varying forms and proportions of his pots, as they grow on the wheel, and a sculptor's skilful fingers fashion the clay.'[34] But Lessore's appreciation betrayed its elitism. 'The scale of aesthetic values is so high', he suggested, 'that only the artist or the practised connoisseur can hope to readily appreciate its real merit; such art can never become a popular art.'[35]

If Lessore's views unfairly reflect the breadth of appeal of Wells' work, they perhaps indicate the limits of its reach. Such was becoming an increasing concern for Leach, who had grown conscious of 'the chasm which a century of factories had torn between ordinary life and hand crafts such as mine'.[36] In a polemic pamphlet of 1928, *A Potter's Outlook*, he railed against the failure of individual potters to offer an alternative to the 'wretched' shapes, 'harsh' colours and 'banal' decoration of commercial pottery:

> *What have the artist-potters been doing all this while? Working by hand to please ourselves as artists first, and therefore producing only limited and expensive pieces, we have been supported by collectors, purists, cranks, or 'arty' people, rather than by the normal man or woman. In so far we have tended ourselves to become abnormal, and consequently most of our pots have been*

still-born: they have not had the breath of reality in them: it has been a game.[37]

Leach's solution was to 'counterbalance the exhibition of expensive personal pots by a basic production of domestic ware'.[38] He had for some time attempted at St Ives to make slipware that might be taken into daily use – as had Cardew rather more industriously at Winchcombe. And in 1927 Leach had held a parallel exhibition of modestly priced domestic ware at Dorothy Hutton's gallery, The Three Shields, in Kensington to coincide with a select show of stoneware at Paterson's, a model he repeated in 1928 at the New Handworkers' Gallery, which published *A Potter's Outlook*. But he had concluded that slipware did not fit with modern life, and aspired instead to make a range of semi-porcellaneous stoneware for household use. Only in the late 1930s was this successfully achieved at St Ives, through the interventions of Leach's son David. But Bernard Leach's vision for a model of production that balanced domestic ware with 'individual pieces' would become commonplace among studio potters after the Second World War. The advent of galleries such as New Handworkers', which opened in 1927, and Muriel Rose's The Little Gallery, opened in 1928, meanwhile marked a changing retail landscape for studio craft in London, offering carefully selected, high-quality handmade objects intended for domestic use, often presented in relation to the domestic interior and other craft objects.[39]

FIG.6 Bernard Leach, jar, stoneware, 1931 (cat. 533)

Despite his declared interest in domestic ware – and the precarious state of the Leach Pottery's finances – Leach made some of his finest individual pieces in the years around 1930, before he removed himself temporarily to work and teach at the progressive Dartington Hall estate in Devon. Among these is the original in a series of bottles brush-decorated with fish motifs (frontispiece p.2 and cat. 532), which – along with his famous *Leaping Salmon* vase[40] – was glazed with a creamy-white bracken-ash glaze, the qualities of which Leach felt he never equalled. Their decoration demonstrates the fluency of Leach's brushwork, a facility matched by his graphic skills with incised, sgraffito designs (fig.6) – abilities which have sometimes been celebrated at the expense of his capabilities as a maker. Leach was not the most skilled of throwers, and would regularly have the most proficient members of his team throw basic shapes to his design, which he then finished and decorated. Yet Leach's sensitivity to form was considerable, and the refined elegance of his shapes was matched in the period only by the work of Katharine Pleydell-Bouverie and Norah Braden. As the painter Patrick Heron observed, a continuously curving, lyrical outline was typical of Leach's work, in contrast to the 'sculptural, architectural approach' of Murray, whose pots had a '*carved* aspect', their silhouettes defined by a succession of planes.[41] Murray's largest pots became increasingly statuesque in the 1930s, and often had a pronounced anthropomorphism. It was perhaps this tendency that Charles Marriott objected to when he wrote that Murray 'has lately been in some danger of forgetting that a pot is after all a pot'.[42] The special status of ceramics in the interwar years was, after all, dependent on the interpretation of pottery *as* sculpture, based on its essential, abstract qualities. It was not the result of pottery absorbing the representational conventions of sculpture. Murray's monumental pots of the 1930s were perhaps only fully appreciated after 1958, when they had once again been exhibited in London.[43] By then an entirely new appreciation of sculptural form in ceramics was developing. But Murray had long ceased potting, after the outbreak of the Second World War had caught him in Rhodesia (now Zimbabwe) and he had made the country his home.

•••

As Murray's career began to wane in the late 1930s, a talented group of his Royal College of Art students started to make names for themselves. Margaret Rey, Sam Haile, Robert Washington and Henry Hammond all followed Murray in making vigorously thrown individual stoneware pots, often with lively painted surfaces. Haile, who was also a Surrealist painter, was perhaps the most inventive: Patrick Heron considered him to have made 'the first modern pots which bore any relation to contemporary painting'.[44] But tragically Haile was killed in a motor accident in 1948. The momentum of the others was diminished in the post-war years, though Hammond in particular maintained an important career as an educator. Heber Mathews, another talented pupil, developed more strongly contemporary work during the 1950s, but his career ended abruptly with his unexpected death in 1959.

Leach's influence in the post-war years was, in contrast, considerable. In large part this was due to the publication in 1940 of *A Potter's Book*, which he had worked on at length in the late 1930s. Part manual, part polemic, *A Potter's Book* offered an impassioned statement on the role of the contemporary potter and of Leach's aesthetic values. Reasoning that Chinese Tang (AD 608–906) and Song dynasty wares had become widely recognized as the 'noblest achievement' in ceramics,[45] Leach advocated – somewhat dogmatically – for potters to accept 'without hesitation' what he called the 'Sung standard'.[46] This, he advised, meant not the imitation of individual Song pieces, but a 'striving towards unity, spontaneity and simplicity of form', achieved by using natural materials to obtain the best qualities of body and glaze.[47] Alongside this were chapters detailing the materials and processes of making ceramics. Perhaps most compelling, however, was Leach's attempt to convey 'the actual life of a potter' through an imagined series of letters describing the cycle of making in a pottery workshop.[48] Detailing both successes and failures, this reads like a quest, offering an enticing vision of an independent creative life. Many would-be potters were inspired by its call, some seeking training at St Ives as a result: Alexander Sharp travelled from Scotland in the hope of being taken on; Warren and Alix MacKenzie came from the USA.

Others who had worked at the Leach Pottery in the 1920s and '30s moved further afield. Harry Davis, who had been the mainstay of the pottery while Leach was in Japan in 1934–35, went to the Gold Coast (now Ghana) in 1937 to teach and set up a pottery at Achimota College. His work formed part of a colonial initiative to develop new industries based on traditional crafts.[49] Returning to England in 1946, Davis established Crowan Pottery in Cornwall with his wife, May, aiming to develop a rural workshop that was both 'creatively alive' and had 'economic vitality'.[50] Their well-designed and well-executed domestic stoneware (fig.7) balanced concerns for performance with those for beauty. It owed something to Leach's aesthetic, but reflected their sophisticated technical knowledge and pragmatism in the use of machinery: Crowan Pottery was based in an old watermill, which they adapted to provide power. In 1962 Harry and May emigrated to New Zealand, establishing Crewenna Pottery, which they ran along similar lines. Michael Cardew, meanwhile, followed Harry Davis to the Gold Coast in 1942, taking over his post at Achimota College. Without Davis' scientific knowledge the pottery floundered, but after its closure in 1945 Cardew stayed on independently, drawn romantically to the possibilities of West Africa. In the village of Vume Dugame he established a pottery where for three years he struggled to make stoneware, producing nonetheless some sublimely beautiful pots that showed the imprint of local styles, before ill health forced his return to England. At his new pottery at Wenford Bridge in Cornwall, Cardew was joined by the Australian potter Ivan McMeekin in 1949, and for a short period they worked productively and creatively, before Cardew returned to West Africa to take up the post of Pottery Officer, employed by the colonial government of Nigeria. He established at Abuja (now Suleja) a Pottery Training Centre, where he successfully produced stoneware inflected by Nigerian pottery traditions, working with trainees and talented Gwari

FIG.7 Harry and May Davis, teapot, stoneware, 1951 (cat. 266); bowl, stoneware, 1950 (cat. 264); coffee pot, stoneware, 1950 (cat. 265)

FIG.8 Ladi Kwali, pot, stoneware, 1957

women potters including Ladi Kwali (fig.8). Cardew's earlier experiences in Africa had impressed on him the need for a detailed technical understanding of raw materials and processes, and communicating this became a mission. At Wenford Bridge in 1959 he ran a two-week course entitled 'Fundamental Pottery with Emphasis on Geology and Raw Materials', which in time formed the basis of his book *Pioneer Pottery*, published in 1969.

...

The 1950s brought a new, contemporary spirit to studio ceramics, as they did to art and design more broadly. The first glimpses of this came in 1951 at the Festival of Britain, where studio pottery appeared in a variety of contexts in the pavilions of the South Bank Exhibition in London. Domestic wares from the Leach Pottery and Crowan Pottery were widely shown, as were tiles by Steven Sykes, and pots and tableware by the Austrian potter Lucie Rie, who had arrived in London before the war. Both Rie and Sykes were among 'The Younger English Potters' subsequently featured by Dora Billington in a pivotal article for *The Studio* in 1953. 'After some years of increasing production and decreasing inspiration', she wrote, studio pottery 'now shows welcome signs of coming to life again.'[51] After briefly reviewing the history she identified the problem: 'stoneware had gone stale, and no one seemed able to do anything about it. The critics were bored, the public was bored and complained about drab colours, even potters were bored and went on mechanically improving their technique and refining their aesthetic formula, oblivious of the trends in contemporary design in other crafts and materials.'[52] But there were 'signs at last that a few younger potters are beginning to work and think in a more contemporary way'.[53] Billington praised the exquisite refinement of Rie's porcelain bowls, and the rich decoration of Sykes' tiles and pots, ornamented with stamps and sprigs. But she gave greatest prominence to three potters associated with the Institute of Education, University of London, and the Central School of Arts and Crafts: William Newland, Margaret Hine and Nicholas Vergette. In a further article devoted to them, she began: 'To all who saw the work of these three potters so admirably displayed at the Crafts Centre ... it must have been apparent that English studio pottery is at last acquiring a "New Look", more in tune with current ideas in house decoration and design generally. Gay, amusing, colourful ... an exciting mixture of sculpture, painting and potting.'[54] These potters were eclectic, their work influenced by travel, by ancient and contemporary art, and – specifically – by Picasso, whose ceramics had made an impact when they were first seen in Britain in the 1950 Arts Council exhibition *Picasso in Provence*. Picasso's playful manipulation of thrown shapes for sculptural purposes suggested possibilities that Newland, Hine and Vergette enthusiastically explored.[55] A strongly Mediterranean flavour infused their work, discernible in their chosen imagery of doves, bulls and harlequins (fig.9), and their frequent use of tin glaze.

The three artists formed a close group. Newland – a New Zealander who had remained in London to study art following war service – discovered pottery while training for the Art Teacher's Diploma at the Institute of Education, and attended further classes with Billington at the Central School. Charismatic and talented, he was soon appointed to teach pottery at the Institute, where Hine and Vergette were among his students. The three shared a studio in London's Bayswater in the early 1950s, and Newland and Hine married. They collaborated on commissions for coffee bars and restaurants, and held joint exhibitions. There was a sense that these young potters were together finding their way: James Tower, another of Newland's students, developed with him, while training at the Institute, their distinctive technique of incising decoration through a contrasting second layer of tin glaze. A prodigious talent, Tower was making tin-glazed ceramic vessels of unrivalled sculptural purity by the mid-1950s, employing this technique in the

FIG.9 William Newland, figure of a harlequin, earthenware, 1954 (cat. 717)

decoration of their surfaces. Kenneth Clark – like Newland, a New Zealander who had made London his home – and Ann Wynn Reeves, who he married, were also notable for their strongly contemporary work.

But the 'New Look' in ceramics would not last. Overtly stylized and fashionably contemporary, it was perhaps inevitable that it would be short-lived. Yet other factors contributed to its demise. Vergette moved in 1958 to the USA, where he concentrated increasingly on public commissions for murals and sculpture. Tower abandoned glazed ceramics in 1959, working instead with unglazed sculptural ceramic forms and casting in bronze. Newland, meanwhile, increasingly devoted time to teaching to the exclusion of making. And significantly, in terms of its effacing from the collective ceramic memory, was the omission of its leading protagonists from the first important surveys of studio pottery: George Wingfield Digby's *The Work of the Modern Potter in England* (1952) and Muriel Rose's *Artist-Potters in England* (1955). Reviews of these books by Newland and Billington, respectively, emphasize the partiality of their coverage: 'As a survey of the development of English pottery between the wars', Newland wrote of Wingfield Digby's book, 'it would have been excellent, but ... there is little in it that is post-war in spirit, or of our day.' Of particular issue for Newland was the author's bias towards stoneware, 'with which he maintains all English potters are primarily concerned', while ignoring entirely modern ceramic sculpture and tin-glazed earthenware.[56] Billington raised similar objections in her review of Rose's book, observing that 'she has set her own limits', and left out 'a number of potters today who choose to work in a more English, or in a contemporary European idiom', largely in favour of Leach's pupils.[57]

...

While Newland and his circle were overlooked in Rose and Wingfield Digby's books, two potters who came to represent post-war studio pottery in Britain were better served: Lucie Rie and Hans Coper. Both had also been included at the 1952 exhibition at Dartington Hall, which Leach and Rose had initiated alongside an international conference of pottery and textiles.[58] There, according to one critic, their work alone had seemed 'outside the prevailing atmosphere of rural quietism' and demonstrated that 'the artist craftsman is not necessarily an anachronism in our time'.[59] Rie had established a successful potting career in Vienna before the war, but her work was little known in Britain when she arrived in 1938, having fled the Nazi regime. For a time she survived primarily by making ceramic buttons, but like other studio potters who were successful in gaining a licence to work, she was able to take advantage of the continuing restrictions imposed on the sale of factory-made pottery, and found a receptive market for her tableware in the years after the war. The arrival of fellow émigré Hans Coper, who joined Rie as an assistant in 1946, was significant for them both. Bernard Leach had advised Rie to throw heavier forms, but Coper dissuaded her, encouraging her instead to follow her own instincts and to draw upon her Viennese work. The path towards the refined, modern tableware and pottery for which Rie is celebrated was set.

Rie's work shows a powerful unity in its conception. Fired once only, with glazes applied to raw clay, it demonstrates an intimate association between form and surface. Linear sgraffito patterns (fig.10) incised through glaze reveal the underlying fabric; stains added to the clay body blush colour into glazes during firing, as do lines of inlaid coloured clay; rich textures arise from both surface markings and the qualities of glazes. Flaring shapes and spiralling bands of colour, meanwhile, capture the energy of the potter's wheel. Historical sources for forms and decoration are sometimes apparent – typically from the ancient Mediterranean, as well as Neolithic Britain – but are filtered through a refined modernism. Rie was nevertheless almost completely silent about her own work, leaving a critical space that has not altogether been filled. Discussion has largely

FIG.10 Lucie Rie, bowl, porcelain, *c.* 1960–65 (cat. 860)

FIG.11 Hans Coper, 'Large flat bottle', stoneware, 1958 (cat. 228)

focused on her biography, her making techniques and her metropolitanism. Though far from being the first urban studio pottery, Rie's compact London workshop, located within her home and equipped with an electric kiln, has offered a compelling model for urban practice. Rie's exploration of the possibilities of electric-kiln firing is also significant, forging an aesthetic that was developed and codified by Emmanuel Cooper, another avowedly urban potter. Rie's metropolitanism has also been equated with a sophisticated modernity. George Wingfield Digby, for example, wrote effusively of her work's 'sparkle of sophistication', suggesting it 'looked best in a modern setting in a London room'.[60] Rie and Coper were certainly urban and urbane, and had a sense of how their work related to architecture and the interior. Yet there is a danger here of a casual dialecticism suggesting false polarities between urban and rural practice. Urban workshops typically have certain features and depend upon particular technologies, but they do not hold a monopoly on these or upon sophistication. The work of John Ward, which shares the formalist character and refinement of Rie's, is a case in point. Ward studied under Rie at Camberwell School of Art and Crafts, but since 1979 has worked in rural Pembrokeshire, absorbing the colour and light of the landscape in his work. And Coper himself moved in 1967 to rural Somerset, making there some of his most celebrated pots.

More intensely than Rie, Hans Coper evolved an archaicized modernism. Having sought tuition in throwing from Heber Mathews at Rie's suggestion, he soon began assisting Rie in the production of her tableware, and set about making his own individual pieces. Round-bellied jugs, pots and deep dishes carried bold, abstract, linear decoration cut through manganese glaze. Abraded and incised layers of white slip and manganese produced dry, textured surfaces on pots with increasing sculptural presence. In the later 1950s, while still sharing Rie's studio, Coper began assembling complex, composite forms from thrown elements, most notably his flattened bottle (fig.11) and 'thistle' forms that placed thrown discs face to face on pedestal-like feet. These were shown in a solo exhibition at Henry Rothschild's influential gallery Primavera, in London, in 1958, the final year in which Coper shared Rie's studio. The following January he took up studio and living accommodation with Digswell Arts Trust in Hertfordshire to concentrate on architectural ceramics. Working with a group of architects, he had as his brief: 'To develop forms and techniques, from tiles and reliefs to free sculptural features, both decorative and to meet certain technical and functional needs of contemporary building (both unique features and prototypes for production)'.[61] In his first years at Digswell, Coper concentrated on the development of cladding tiles and bricks for use in schools and public buildings constructed using prefabricated systems. He then turned his attention to a series of major architectural commissions, including mural schemes and the monumental candlesticks made for Basil Spence's Coventry Cathedral, arguably Coper's greatest achievement. Returning to London in the mid-1960s, Coper concentrated on a restricted series of composite sculptural forms; distinctive, inventive and poised, they held a sense of ritual or ceremony. They also embodied a certain restraint, reflecting Coper's understanding of pottery as 'an accumulation of sensations and not an expression of emotion'.[62] This period of work culminated in a major exhibition with the weaver Peter Collingwood at the V&A in 1969, for which Coper – against his inclinations – contributed his single, near-legendary, artist statement.[63] This brief, concentrated text offers a distillation of his thinking, detailing his concern 'with extracting essence rather than with experiment', and his countering of the 'absurdity' of an aesthetically driven craft through the discipline of work. It also demonstrates his understanding of human creativity as a continuum: the enigmatic 'pre-dynastic Egyptian pot' that had so fascinated him was: 'An object of complete economy made by MAN; Giacometti man; Buckminster Fuller man. A constant.' Pottery, it seems, provided Coper with a means to be both contemporary and connected with the deep past.

...

While Hans Coper evolved sculptural form through the discipline of the wheel, others found greater freedom in handbuilding. In stimulating these new approaches and the sculptural possibilities they offered, the Central School of Arts and Crafts and Goldsmiths' College in London played significant roles.[64] At the Central throwing began to lose its dominance under Gilbert Harding Green, who took over from Dora Billington as head of pottery in 1956, after working as her assistant. Harding Green encouraged experiment and supported creative students such as Gordon Baldwin, who studied there from 1951 to 1954. Students at the Central also benefited from the teaching of Basic Design – led by the sculptor William Turnbull – which encouraged an analytical and experimental approach to materials and processes. Other fine artists, including Eduardo Paolozzi, were also influential teachers. Billington and Harding Green, meanwhile, fostered the development of promising students and young artists by appointing them to technical and teaching postions, which added to the progressive and creative atmosphere of pottery at the Central. Baldwin was appointed as technical assistant in 1956, succeeding Ian Auld and Nicholas Vergette. The following year he was promoted to a teaching position to allow Harding Green to appoint Dan Arbeid to the role.[65] Auld also took up a teaching post in 1957. Ruth Duckworth and Gillian Lowndes both studied at the Central in the later 1950s and began teaching there soon after. By the mid-1960s Baldwin, Auld, Arbeid, Duckworth and Lowndes were all recognized as leading handbuilders, all working with sculptural ambition and all save Baldwin working in stoneware. A handsome survey, *The Art of the Modern Potter* (1967), by Tony Birks gave extensive coverage to their work, alongside that of Rie, Coper, Robin Welch – who like Birks himself had also studied at the Central – and Bryan Newman, who had trained at Camberwell. Together their work represented an extraordinary range of formal invention and artistic expression, and demonstrated an increasing freedom in drawing ideas and influence from beyond the realm of ceramics, particularly from architecture and natural forms.

A progressive school of handbuilt pottery also developed at Goldsmiths' College, where Baldwin taught during his final year as a student at the Central and again from 1956. David Garbett, who began as a technician at Goldsmiths' in 1953, also became an influential teacher there. Notable students included Alan Wallwork, Bernard Rooke and Betty Blandino. The enterprising Wallwork established his own gallery in Forest Hill, London, in the late 1950s, but the most significant retail support for the new generation of potters came from Henry Rothschild's gallery Primavera.[66] Located in London's Sloane Street, Primavera showed a range of craft and design objects, including pots by Bernard Leach and Katharine Pleydell-Bouverie. Hans Coper, as we have seen, exhibited there in 1958, while the new handbuilders gained exhibitions in the subsequent years: Dan Arbeid in 1959; Ruth Duckworth in 1960; a group show from Goldsmiths' College in 1961; Ian Auld and Bryan Newman together in 1961–62. Further shows at Primavera maintained Rothschild's support for these progressive studio potters, giving coverage also to Gillian Lowndes, Ian Godfrey, Gwyn and Louis Hanssen, and Janet Leach, among others. Ken Stradling at the Bristol Guild of Applied Art was another important early supporter, devoting exhibitions to Arbeid in 1961 and Lowndes in 1963.

...

A second important survey of contemporary practice was published in 1967: Michael Casson's *Pottery in Britain Today*. Altogether more encompassing than Birks', it presented the work of 70 potters or workshops, subdivided into three sections covering handbuilding, individual wheel-made pottery, and repetition production of domestic ware. Casson's book reflects the remarkable growth in studio ceramics that had occurred since the war: what had been the province of a small number of pioneering artists had become a substantial movement. It was taught increasingly widely and supported by a growing number of organizations. Casson made the point that potters who held teaching posts – who were economically shielded but had limited time – were represented in the first two sections of his book, which dealt with individual pieces, but were largely precluded from the last. But the potters of his final section were for Casson the 'life-blood of the movement, for it will be their work that is in everyday use in the home'.[67] 'Functionally sound and aesthetically rewarding', the best domestic pottery, he maintained, 'radiates its own particular kind of life'.[68] Two potters were held up as exemplars: Richard Batterham, who had established a pottery in Durweston, Dorset, in 1959, after apprenticing at the Leach Pottery; and Ray Finch, who had taken over Winchcombe Pottery from Cardew, and established a production of exemplary domestic stoneware in the late 1950s. Both were remarkable potters who showed an extraordinary dedication to their craft. Reviewing Batterham's work for the American journal *Craft Horizons* in 1972, Tony Hepburn – a radical sculptor–potter and perhaps unlikely supporter – found him to be 'out-Leaching Leach',[69] an observation accurate in reflecting his single-mindedness in making functional wares with uniformly high aesthetic values, without preciousness, and without separation between repetition ware and individual work.

Unlike Batterham, who preferred to work alone, Ray Finch embraced a workshop ethos, making Winchcombe – like the Leach Pottery – an important training ground for potters. Other workshops established in the mid-1950s were run along similar lines, with teamworking and opportunities for apprentices: David Leach's Lowerdown Pottery in Devon and Alan Caiger-Smith's Aldermaston Pottery in Berkshire – which was exceptional in producing highly decorative tin-glazed earthenware (fig.12) – are notable examples. Geoffrey Whiting also established his Avoncroft Pottery near Droitwich in Worcestershire in this period, a small but significant workshop making domestic ware. With the public appetite for handmade domestic pottery growing and the number of potteries increasing, opportunities for a workshop training became more widely available, though expansion was not always a straightforward matter. After five years of running his own workshop, the slipware potter John Solly noted that he had 'arrived now at what must be a tricky spot for all one-man craft businesses. There is at present all the work that is physically possible for one person, but not enough for two.'[70] Workshop experience was nevertheless invaluable, and for some it represented the only real way to assimilate the craft. Others advocated for art-school study, the two positions forming strongly opposing camps. This situation was exacerbated in the early 1960s with the advent of the new Diploma of Art and Design

FIG.12 Alan Caiger-Smith, pebble bottle, earthenware, 1968 (cat. 126); teapot, earthenware, 1968 (cat. 125)

(DipAD), which liberalized art education and – in contrast to the earlier centrally examined National Diploma in Design – gave new freedom to art colleges to design their own courses and examine their own students.[71] Ceramics – now often preferred to Pottery as the course title – found a place within Three-Dimensional Design, one of five overarching areas of art-school study. For teachers such as Henry Hammond at Farnham School of Art, Surrey, the new Diploma gave students 'an opportunity to develop imaginative powers as well as technical skills', while benefiting from the breadth of teaching in the school.[72] Against these changes, however, a radically different course emerged, which offered something closer to a workshop training. Established by Victor Margrie and Michael Casson in 1963, the Studio Pottery Course at Harrow School of Art was a two-year vocational course with production throwing at its heart.[73] Designed to be narrow and deep, it set out to equip students with the necessary skills to establish and run their own workshops, including building kilns and wheels. With its ethos of self-sufficiency, the Harrow course chimed with the mood of the counterculture, attracting students who were drawn to the possibilities of a more independent life. It produced a school of heavily thrown domestic stoneware that remained fashionable for a time, but also had lasting impact in encouraging the creative exploration of wood-firing and salt-glazing in studio pottery. Colin Pearson – who had trained with Ray Finch – and Walter Keeler were among its influential staff. Its students included Janice Tchalenko, Micki Schloessingk, Peter Starkey, Sarah Walton and Jane Hamlyn.

•••

The independent nature of practice for the growing number of studio potters called for new ways to work collectively and share information. The first specialist journal, *Pottery Quarterly*, edited by the potter Murray Fieldhouse, was launched in spring 1954 in response to 'the need for a specialised forum to which studio potters – a widely scattered fraternity having few opportunities for personal meetings – could have ready recourse'.[74] Lively and engaging, *Pottery Quarterly* was in its early years devoted to 'Pottery as Art in the widest sense', though during the 1960s became increasingly partisan in favour of craft pottery of the Leach school, and irregular in its publication. Support for studio potters and small workshops, meanwhile, came from the Rural Industries Bureau, and it was the Bureau that brought together a group of potters in 1956 to discuss collective opportunities for exports. Out of this came the greater ambition to establish an association of potters, which led in 1958 to the foundation of the Craftsmen (later Craft) Potters Association (CPA).[75] Rosemary Wren and Eileen Lewenstein were members of its first Council, and David Canter – who would go on to found Cranks vegetarian restaurant – was appointed as its Honorary Secretary. The energetic Canter was instrumental in the establishment of the first Craftsmen Potters Shop in Lowndes Court, off Carnaby Street, London, which opened in 1960 with an inaugural exhibition of stoneware by Ray Finch. Managed until 1972 by Mick Casson's sister Pan Henry, the shop was an immediate commercial success, providing many potters with a significant outlet for sales. Outgrowing its original site, the shop moved in 1967 to nearby Marshall Street, where it continued a lively programme of exhibitions of members' work. Since 2010 it has operated as the Contemporary Ceramics Centre in Great Russell Street, Bloomsbury. Perhaps the most significant of the CPA's activities, however, has been its publication of *Ceramic Review*, which launched in January 1970 under the editorship of Emmanuel Cooper and Eileen Lewenstein.

Opportunities to exhibit and sell work were increasing. Throughout the 1950s and '60s the Crafts Centre of Great Britain, in Hay Hill (later moving to Earlham Street), London, offered an important outlet and exhibition space for studio ceramics.[76] A membership organization with a somewhat complicated history, the Centre received a modest grant from the UK government's Board of Trade, but remained in this period financially precarious. The Centre merged with a further organization that had come to represent the crafts – the Crafts Council of Great Britain[77] – to form the British Crafts Centre in 1972, by which time it was receiving an annual grant from the newly formed Crafts Advisory Committee (CAC). In 1987 the British Crafts Centre became Contemporary Applied Arts, continuing with its important programme of solo and group exhibitions under the directorship of Tatjana Marsden. Crafts also formed an active strand of the Commonwealth Art Gallery's exhibition programme during the 1960s and '70s. Part of the Commonwealth Institute in Kensington, London, the Gallery provided an important showcase for the work of artists from countries of the Commonwealth, and gave solo exhibitions to the Guyanese ceramic and mixed-media sculptor Donald Locke and the Nigerian potter Danlami Aliyu, both then working in the UK. Potters without direct Commonwealth ties also found a place in the programme, including Eric Mellon, Marianne de Trey and Betty Blandino. A growing number of specialist craft galleries and shops, meanwhile, provided wider opportunities for studio potters to sell and exhibit work, among them Bluecoat Display Centre, Liverpool, opened 1959; Peter Dingley Gallery, Stratford-upon-Avon, Warwickshire, opened 1966; Joan Crossley-Holland's Oxford Gallery, Oxford,[78] opened 1968; and David Canter's Craftwork, in Guildford, Surrey, opened 1971. Museums also played an increasing role in promoting contemporary studio ceramics: the V&A's Circulation Department organized the exhibition *Five Studio Potters* (Dan Arbeid, Alan Caiger-Smith, Tony Hepburn, Gillian Lowndes and Lucie Rie), which toured from 1969. A further exhibition, *Six Studio Potters* (Gordon Baldwin, Michael Casson, Hans Coper, Ian Godfrey, Jacqueline Poncelet and Peter Simpson), toured from 1977.[79]

Significant government support for the crafts came in 1971 with the formation of the Crafts Advisory Committee, the forerunner of the Crafts Council.[80] Instigated by Lord Eccles – the minister responsible for the arts, delegated from the Department of Education and Science – the CAC forged a new identity for the crafts, aligned more closely with fine art than with design. The CAC supported the crafts in an impressive variety of ways: providing grants to craftspeople and financial support to other organizations, including the Crafts Centre of Great Britain; establishing a national collection of craft; instigating a selected 'Index of Craftsmen', as a reference resource; staging exhibitions at its Waterloo Place Gallery, London, and organizing national and international touring exhibitions; and launching in 1973 the magazine *Crafts*. The potter Victor Margrie was appointed as the CAC's Secretary in 1971, and, from the outset, studio ceramics gained significant support. At the landmark CAC exhibition, *The Craftsman's Art*, held at the V&A in 1973, ceramics were generously represented, the wide-ranging selection of work shown encompassing late pots by Bernard Leach through to bone-china forms and vessels by Glenys Barton and Jacqueline Poncelet, two young graduates of the Royal College of Art.[81] The following year an international touring exhibition organized with the British Council further signalled the CAC's support for an emerging generation concerned more with conceptual and formal enquiry than serving the requirements of function: *Ceramic Forms* presented work by Glenys Barton, Jacqueline Poncelet, Paul

FIG.13 Elizabeth Fritsch, pot, stoneware, 1975 (cat. 360)

Astbury, Elizabeth Fritsch, Jill Crowley, Geoffrey Swindell and the more long-established Gordon Baldwin.[82]

...

With the exception of Baldwin, all the artists represented in *Ceramic Forms* had studied at the Royal College of Art. This reflected significant changes at the College, which from 1948 until about 1964 had focused almost entirely on design for the pottery industry. Under David Queensberry, Professor of Ceramics, however, the College opened up to a wide range of approaches and began accepting students with an interest in studio practice,[83] Mo Jupp being the first.[84] In support of this broadening agenda, Queensberry made a number of significant appointments to his teaching staff, among them Eduardo Paolozzi and Hans Coper, who taught one day a week from 1966. Coper's impact on the new generation of students would be profound. Elizabeth Fritsch, who began studying at the College in 1968, was among the earliest and most important of those to come under his influence (fig.13). When she initially applied to the course, Queensberry had considered her 'in a completely different category' to most students 'from an intellectual and spiritual point of view', despite her then-limited technical understanding. From the start she explored pinched and coiled vessel forms, with a particular interest in 'warm yet celestial colours' and matt, fresco-like surfaces.[85] Like other students, she found Coper's teaching 'rigorous and searching but also tolerant and amusing', and drew inspiration from the 'austere metaphysical quality' of his work.[86] In 1974, three years after graduating, she was given a solo exhibition at the CAC's Waterloo Place Gallery, by which time she had developed a fascination with what she described as the 'paradoxical movement away from the substantial (clay pot) towards the insubstantial (air and music)'. Increasingly, she explored 'spatial games' in the rhythmic, geometric painting of her surfaces and through foreshortened forms, which inhabited 'the shadowy space half-way between two and three dimensions'.[87] The work of Glenys Barton and Jacqueline Poncelet – shown together at Waterloo Place the previous year, while the gallery was under the management of the British Crafts Centre – was equally refined and hardly less surprising. Both worked in bone china, Barton producing precise geometrical sculptures with correspondingly exact graphic decoration, and Poncelet making exquisite, translucent vessels with delicately patterned or carved geometrical surfaces. Barton and Poncelet would later be given solo exhibitions by the CAC (or Crafts Council), as would Jill Crowley and fellow Royal College of Art graduates Alison Britton and Carol McNicoll. This promotion and support from the Crafts Council served to reinforce the ties of shared studios and overlapping periods of study, forging an identifiable grouping of progressive women potters within a wider, developing urban community of craft practice. It would be Britton, however, who would articulate the concerns of a core group whose work explored vessel forms. In a seminal essay written as one of 14 selectors for the Crafts Council exhibition *The Maker's Eye*, she wrote: 'I would say that this group is concerned with the outer limits of function; where function, or an idea of possible function, is crucial, but is just one ingredient in the final presence of the object, and is not its only motivation.' Such objects, she suggested, had a 'double presence': they performed a function (albeit perhaps one as intrinsic as containing), but also provided commentary on their own purpose and being. Often made in light of the experience of observing forms of representation in modern painting, they were 'about life and still life at once'.[88] Her selection of objects – hybrids to varying degrees of the ordinary and the metaphorical – included work by Britton herself, Poncelet, Fritsch, McNicoll, Janice Tchalenko and, at the outer 'magical' limit, Andrew Lord.

In the late 1970s Britton made slab-built jugs, with jaunty, asymmetric forms and symbolic pictorial decoration. But after her Crafts Council exhibition in 1979, she developed tougher, more ambiguous jar and bowl forms with bold abstract painting, slab-building pieces in a way that was part-planned, part-improvised, and decorating both before and after assembly of the slabs. The interplay between form and painted surface is significant, as is her concern with the relationship between function and decoration. This conscious exploration of the ornamental is also strongly present in the work of Poncelet, McNicoll and other notable potters of Britton's wider peer group, including Angus Suttie, Richard Slee and Henry Pim. Allied with this is a decorative eclecticism: these artists drew freely from a broad range of sources, both within and beyond the history of ceramics. Slee – adept at the art of quotation – looked to Sèvres porcelain, art pottery and Disney animation, his work a witty and joyful riposte to the sobriety of the stoneware potters. Suttie, meanwhile, drew inspiration from the bold patterning of African textiles and Greek pottery for his colourful, decorative pots. The new generation nevertheless attracted the ire of some critics, who objected to their free cultural borrowing and seemingly decadent disregard for function.[89] Branding them 'bureaucratically endorsed whizz-kids', Christopher Reid, for example, protested at their 'speciousness and flippancy' and suggested Pim's work in particular was based on 'a culture of doodles'.[90] But their enquiring and provocative work had already shifted the agenda for ceramics, and exposed the narrowness of established standards and conventions.

By the mid-1980s the one-off, largely non-functional vessel had become the prevalent form in studio ceramics. A number of significant artists who have remained primarily committed to the vessel form established careers in this period, including Magdalene Odundo, Jennifer Lee, Kate Malone and Ken Eastman. The publication in 1986 of Peter Dormer's international survey *The New Ceramics* might be seen as the high-point of this dominance, Dormer noting unapologetically that 'the emphasis rests heavily upon the ceramic vessel – in all its variety'.[91] Ceramics was, for Dormer, primarily 'about pots', while 'ceramic sculpture should usually be considered alongside other sculpture'. Modern pottery was, 'in any case, rich and surprising enough to merit its own discussion'. Underlying this was perhaps the assumption, made earlier by Dormer, that 'Contemporary pottery's role tends to be domestic', its function being to provide 'delight, solace, and a thickening of the visual texture of the home'.[92] This period also marked the peak of interest in the 'vessel' as a conceptual entity, a distinct art form spanning multiple craft disciplines. In 1987 a Gulbenkian Craft Initiative called 'The Vessel Forum' sought to explore these themes, but Henry Pim, reporting on the event, found it limiting:

> *Somehow ... the emphasis was that vessels no matter how unsuited to practical use, should remain within the scope of the domestic, the intimate, the world of things enjoyed at close quarters. We had lost track of that other traditional aspect of craft which is to enhance large public spaces, to create things that can be large, public and monumental.*[93]

Pim had anticipated a number of the directions that ceramics would take in subsequent decades – developments that would see artists such as Felicity Aylieff and Kate Malone working at increased scale, making ceramics that suited the public realm. And by the time a revised edition of *The New Ceramics* was published in 1994, Dormer had added a new chapter exploring 'The Sculptural Ambitions of Potters', in which he noted the 'steady emergence of the ceramic sculptor' as part of ceramics' continued progression into a form of fine art.[94]

But sculpture had never really gone away. The art-orientated group assembled by the CAC in 1974 for *Ceramic Forms* pursued predominantly sculptural paths: Glenys Barton – who showed geometrical sculptural pieces in *Ceramic Forms* – turned to figurative sculpture, as did Jill Crowley; Paul Astbury continued to develop sculpture around science-fiction inflected themes, often using found objects. Gordon Baldwin's work of the period explored the intersection between painting, sculpture and ceramics, while Geoffrey Swindell's porcelain vessels and containers were a form of sculpture in miniature, suggesting organic or technological forms. Further exhibitions gave prominence to the highly individual work of these and other sculptor–potters: *New Ceramics* at the Ulster Museum, Belfast, in 1974; *Towards Ceramic Sculpture* at the Oxford Gallery, Oxford, in the same year; and *Seven in 76* at Portsmouth City Museum and Art Gallery, which alongside Baldwin, Poncelet and Swindell, presented work by Peter Simpson, Tony Hepburn, Graham Burr and Alan Barrett-Danes. A new edition of Tony Birks' *Art of the Modern Potter* in 1976, meanwhile, extended its coverage to include Hepburn, Barrett-Danes, Andrew Lord, Ian Godfrey and Janet Leach – a selection that foregrounded sculptural concerns. Perhaps most radical and exploratory, however, was Sunderland Arts Centre's 1978 touring exhibition *State of Clay*, which set out 'to demonstrate a much broader and freer approach to the medium of clay', recognizing the artists' 'need to experiment and transcend the boundaries'.[95] Among the works shown were psychologically intense, part-figurative sculptures by Ruth and Alan Barrett-Danes (Ruth's contribution to their collaborative work belatedly being recognized) and innovative sculptural forms by Gillian Lowndes, in which she began to explore the firing of clay in combination with other materials. Astbury, Baldwin and Barton were among the other artists represented, the exhibition being recognized by the fine art critic William Varley as going 'a long way towards persuading us that the objects shown are objects of meaning and not merely of sensual or retinal charm'.[96]

Such recognition was not always forthcoming. Paul Astbury was among those who felt a deep frustration with the status of ceramic sculpture, writing earlier that:

> *Working in such a material as clay does offer a few problems to the Sculptor. Apart from all the other sculptors in the world he is called a 'Ceramic' Sculptor and in the eyes of the public may have associations with the Craft world. It is very discouraging to think that people may see sculpture made from clay as some kind of freak divergence or part of Craft pottery. Sculpture is sculpture, no matter what it is made of.*[97]

Participating in the debates around ceramic sculpture, Gordon Baldwin noted that the arguments 'seem to grow out of the fact that the sculpture may be fired in the same kiln as a pot and even be made by the same person that made the pot'. Some ceramic sculpture, he observed, was low on content, but the problem was that all work done in ceramic was lumped together irrespective of its quality, in a way that would not be done with oil paint on canvas. He was not, he asserted: 'interested in objects just because they are made of ceramic. ... [but] I am intensely interested in the pot being a vehicle for other layers of meaning as well as that of being a container and I am intensely interested in painting and sculpture.'[98] For Baldwin, concerns with sculpture and concerns with the 'vessel' became enmeshed. For others, however, the vessel became a constraint. Jacqueline Poncelet began moving beyond her fine bone-china vessels in 1976 with a series of angular slab-built pots. Softer slab-built forms followed, of increasing size and complexity, and with textured and patterned surfaces. A landmark solo exhibition at the Whitechapel Art Gallery, London, in 1985 presented these sculptural forms – by now reminiscent of limbs, claws, horns and tentacles – lying on the gallery floor or propped against walls. Ewen Henderson – an artist with a radical and exploratory approach to material comparable to Lowndes' – also moved beyond the confines of the vessel during the late 1980s, making standing forms akin to megaliths and sculptures that recalled skulls. Sara Radstone, Henry Pim and Angus Suttie – contemporaries who studied under Henderson and Ian Auld at Camberwell School of Art and Crafts in the late 1970s – all moved from handbuilt vessels towards sculpture. Martin Smith followed a similar trajectory with his architectonic vessel forms.

Two important exhibitions of the 1990s affirmed the potential of clay as sculpture: *The Raw and the Cooked* at the Barbican Art Gallery, London, and Museum of Modern Art, Oxford, in 1993–94;[99] and *Pandora's Box* at the Crafts Council, London, in 1995.[100] Curated by Ewen Henderson, *Pandora's Box* sought to identify a tradition of material exploration in clay – work of a powerful, more rugged aesthetic – proposing a canon that largely circumnavigated artists trained at the Royal College of Art and endorsed by the CAC. At its core was the work of Baldwin, Lowndes and Henderson himself, positioned between an earlier generation that included Dan Arbeid, Ian Auld, Ruth Duckworth, Mo Jupp and Colin Pearson, and a subsequent one, including Radstone, Pim, Suttie and Lawson Oyekan. *The Raw and the Cooked* was much broader in its coverage, though also reflected the communities surrounding its curators: Alison Britton and the writer and critic Martina Margetts, who, like Britton, taught at the Royal College of Art. Writing in its catalogue, Margetts stated

> *The coming of age of ceramic art in Britain ... is the subject of this exhibition. Here clay is not a craft material but an authentic medium for sculpture. The works take myriad forms, in concept, scale and meaning: the continuing exploration of the vessel form ... is balanced by works concerned with the ironic re-presentation of ceramic traditions; with figuration; with landscape (physical, mythological, metaphorical); and with identity.*[101]

FIG.14 Nicholas Pope, *Hermaphroditic Font*, earthenware, 1995 (cat. 809)

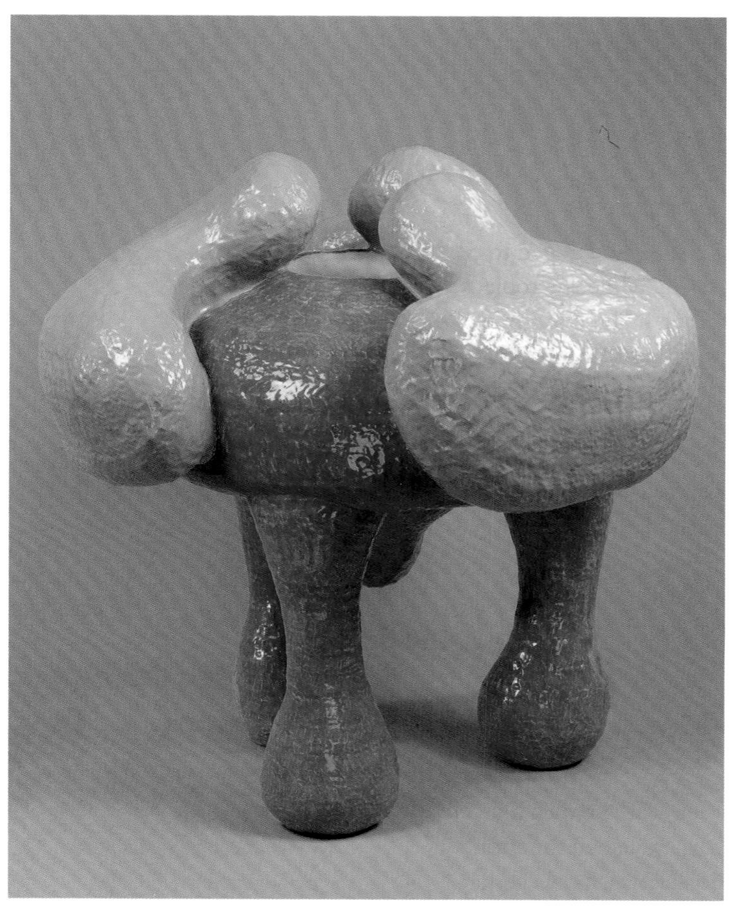

The Raw and the Cooked was a bold, optimistic and inclusive statement of clay's potential to produce work to lift the human spirit. Its alignment of the vessel with sculpture – which *Pandora's Box* similarly did – represented a conceptual shift from the mid-1980s, when some writers had, not altogether convincingly, sought to reinforce their separation.[102] Such writing had helped to identify attributes of ceramic vessels that were particular to them: the relationship of internal volume to exterior form; the planar characteristics of the three-dimensional ceramic surface. But it demands a peculiarly inelastic definition of sculpture to assert that these are not sculptural concerns. Also significant in *The Raw and the Cooked* was its inclusion of work by sculptors from outside the discipline of ceramics, including Tony Cragg, Antony Gormley and Bruce McLean. This reflected an important and developing trend, fuelled in part by organizations such as the European Ceramic Work Centre (EKWC) in the Netherlands, which offered residencies to artists who wished to explore the medium (fig.14). Alongside these substantial surveys and institutional initiatives, the focused presentation of studio ceramics in commercial galleries also developed significantly in this period, with the establishment in London by Anita Besson of Galerie Besson off Old Bond Street in 1988,[103] and the founding of Barrett Marsden (later Marsden Woo) Gallery by Tatjana Marsden and Julianna Barrett in Clerkenwell in 1998.

...

Before we leave behind the developments of the 1970s and '80s that led to the art-orientated ceramic scene of the early 1990s, it is important to recognize the continued influence of Bernard Leach. Encouraged to concentrate on his own pots by Janet Leach, while she took over the running of the Leach Pottery, Leach had made some of his most impressive work in the late 1950s and '60s. Failing eyesight, however, led him to cease potting about 1972. Instead, he focused on writing, publishing several books, including his memoirs, *Beyond East and West*. Meanwhile, a major retrospective at the V&A in 1977 asserted his importance. Following his death in 1979, his ideas continued to be foregrounded, not least by Michael Cardew. Like Alison Britton, Cardew was chosen in 1981 as a selector for *The Maker's Eye*,[104] a pairing that reinforced the sense in the 1980s that the main line of demarcation lay between two types of vessels: those of the 'New Ceramics' and those of the Leach school. In his essay for *The Maker's Eye*, Cardew wrote: 'We do not want to make Chinese, or Korean, or primitive pots. But we have seen clearly what they have which our own so badly lack, and having seen it we are not likely to lose sight of it again.'[105] In addition to established functional potters such as Ray Finch and Richard Batterham, a new generation had by then seen clearly what those pots had, and pursued it with dedication in their own work: Mike Dodd, Jim Malone, Phil Rogers, Clive Bowen, Svend Bayer and Edward Hughes were among them. This school of Leach-influenced potters remained robust through the first two decades of the 21st century.

The 1990s, however, saw a different type of functional potter take centre stage, and throwing make a resurgence as a creative force. The 'New Ceramics' had been dominated by handbuilding, but throwing had remained a vehicle for expressive and inventive form in the hands of some potters during the 1980s, notably Walter Keeler and Takeshi Yasuda. Keeler had begun to develop complex, sharply defined teapots and jugs assembled from thrown elements, while Yasuda threw generous dishes and platters that retained a sense of the softness and plasticity of the clay in the fired pieces. Although these inventive objects have unimpaired function, they are nevertheless not 'everyday' pots. For Yasuda in particular, the suggestion of significance and ritual that they might bring to the dining table is important. Joanna Constantinidis, another maker of inventive, thrown, one-off pots, meanwhile began in the late 1980s a parallel small-scale production of porcelain tableware, made in slowly evolving series. Informed by the early porcelain of Tomimoto Kenkichi and the tableware of Lucie Rie, these austere white forms reflected a modernist sensibility and presented a fresh and compelling aesthetic. Julian Stair also sailed against the prevailing wind during the 1980s, becoming increasingly preoccupied by making pottery for use; by 1990 he had, like Constantinidis, established a series production of spare, elegant tableware in porcelain and stoneware. For Edmund de Waal, meanwhile, porcelain provided an opportunity for reappraisal and renewal. After an unfulfilling start making domestic stoneware in rural Herefordshire,[106] he found liberation in softly dented, thrown celadon porcelain pots, working from 1993 in an urban London studio. Making porcelain that might be handled allowed, he suggested, for 'a breadth in intention – the pots can live in the domestic realm ... and also in the sacramental realm of things put aside, looked after, cared for, placed in special places, given in particular ways'.[107] Through the 1990s this new, gentle functionalism – with its associated tendencies of decorative restraint, a preference for porcelain, the expression of the plasticity of clay, and a commitment to throwing – gathered momentum. A number of makers were drawn to work in the style, and the studio in Vanguard Court, Camberwell, that de Waal and Stair shared from 1995 became an important urban training ground. Chris Keenan, de Waal's first apprentice, and Carina Ciscato, who worked as an assistant to Stair, would both become exceptional makers of refined, thrown porcelain, sharing a nearby studio. Rupert Spira – whose work underwent a similar reappraisal to de Waal's – meanwhile turned from robust functional wares,

FIG.15 Richard Slee, *Drunk Punch*, earthenware, 1991 (cat. 923)

made under the influence of Michael Cardew, to finely thrown, minimal forms, richly decorated with monochrome glazes. A succession of group exhibitions reflected the mood: *Soft Clay* in 1996 and *Contemporary Pots* in 1998, both at Contemporary Applied Arts, and *The New White* in 1999 at the V&A, which offered – Alison Britton suggested – 'evidence of the high cool edge of contemporary throwing in Britain, that fits so beautifully into current moves towards minimalism in the interior'.[108] A more closely mediated relationship with architecture would, however, come to define de Waal's subsequent practice. Stair, meanwhile, remained committed to function. Determined to assert the status of objects for use, he began raising them on ceramic 'grounds', and embarked upon a series of funerary ceramics that explored the containment of the body after death.

...

Alongside the resurgence of the creative potential of throwing, the 1990s saw the continued emergence of artists concerned with narrative and commentary, figuration and representation. Building on the work of Jill Crowley and Mo Jupp, the exploration of the sculptural figure in ceramics gathered in strength and relevance in the hands of Christie Brown, Stephen Dixon, Philip Eglin, Susan Halls and Claire Curneen, among others.[109] In 1996 Eglin won the Jerwood Prize for Applied Arts for his large, graffiti-splashed glazed earthenware nudes, providing a marker of the increased recognition of figural work. Richard Slee, meanwhile, had begun to ease away from vessels and develop figurative and sculptural forms. In the early 1990s he explored social and cultural tropes through Toby jug characters (fig.15), and later embarked upon a series of landscape forms that incorporated found objects with both humour and tenderness. When Slee won the next ceramics-focused Jerwood Prize in 2001, it seemed to the curator and writer Oliver Watson that 'the ceramic world had finally caught up with him'.[110] Greater recognition still of the ascendancy of narrative ceramics – which might take the form of vessels with pictorial imagery or modelled figurative elements, as well as self-contained figurative sculptures – came in 2003, when the Turner Prize was awarded to Grayson Perry. The fine-art trained Perry employed 'guerrilla tactics': his ceramic vases provided a means of introducing by decorative stealth his potent commentary on gender, sexuality and class. Perry, like Slee, was ambivalent about craft, but his Turner Prize win had a seismic impact upon ceramics, allowing greater scope for its acceptance as an art medium.

The narrative potential of ceramics has remained a rich vein, providing a means to explore issues of identity and place, to question and challenge societal and political norms, and to confront humanitarian or environmental issues. An associated trait has been an interest in bricolage or collage, the appropriation and subversion of found objects and images opening up possibilities for narrative and commentary. Artists have approached this through a variety of means. In works that explored the social culture of the Staffordshire Potteries, Neil Brownsword cast objects from appropriated factory moulds, which he then manipulated and assembled as figurative sculpture. In later installations he composed elements salvaged from the factory floor and reworked, presenting them as a form of industrial archaeology. Paul Scott employs the visual language of blue-and-white transfer-printed earthenware to develop politically charged, collaged imagery on found ceramics. In an equivalent way, Carol McNicoll assembles polemic domestic objects from elements cast from found ceramic ornaments and figures she has herself modelled, adding layers of pattern and imagery; sometimes found objects make their way directly into her work. Barnaby Barford composed satirical tableaux that commented on social mores, using found and manipulated ceramic figurines. Matt Smith creates uncanny composite sculptural objects using casts taken from found objects and historic moulds, in order to destabilize established narratives

60 George Wingfield Digby, 'Introduction', in Arts Council, *Lucie Rie: A Retrospective Exhibition of Earthenware, Stoneware and Porcelain 1926–1967* (London, 1967), p.6.

61 Quoted in Alun Graves, 'Hans Coper: Sculpture in Architecture', *Interpreting Ceramics*, ejournal, 14 (2012). Several drafts of Coper's 'Programme of Research' for Digswell exist. Hertfordshire Archives and Local Studies, DE/DAT/5/1/10.

62 Birks (1967), p.31.

63 V&A (1969), cited in endnote 4.

64 On the Central School, see Alison Britton, 'Central Ceramics: Dora Billington and Gilbert Harding Green', in Backemeyer (2000), pp.82–90, and Harrod (1999), pp.232–6; on Goldsmiths' College, see Cowley (1993).

65 Baldwin reveals this detail in his Crafts Lives interview in the British Library, London, sound archive (C960/38).

66 On Primavera, see Greg (1995), and Barker and Buckley (2015).

67 Casson (1967), p.1.

68 *Ibid.*, section 3, no page number.

69 Tony Hepburn, 'Letter from London', *Craft Horizons*, 32:6 (1972), p.57.

70 John Solly, 'The First Five Years', *Pottery Quarterly*, 6:23 (1959), p.86.

71 On art schools in the 1960s, see Harrod (1999), pp.238–43.

72 'Evening Meeting: Training the Potter', in Craftsmen Potters Association (1966), p.25.

73 On the Harrow Studio Pottery Course, see Michael Casson, 'Ceramics and Education', *Ceramic Review*, 21 (1973); Northern Centre for Contemporary Art (1989); Harrod (1999), pp.240–1; and Peters (2012).

74 *Pottery Quarterly*, 1:1 (1954).

75 On the history of the Craftsmen Potters Association, see Cooper (2007b), in particular Rosemary Wren, 'The Early Years', pp.6–13, and Michael Casson, 'On the Move', pp.14–25.

76 The Crafts Centre of Great Britain was established in 1946 by a joint council representing: the Arts and Crafts Exhibition Society; the Red Rose Guild; the Society of Scribes and Illuminators; the Senefelder Club; and the Society of Wood Engravers. A separate Scottish Crafts Centre was established in Edinburgh in 1949. On the Crafts Centre of Great Britain, see Harrod (1999), pp.207–8 and 211–20.

77 Formed in 1964 and distinct from the later Crafts Council, which was created by the renaming of the Crafts Advisory Committee in 1979.

78 The records of the Oxford Gallery are at the Crafts Study Centre, Farnham (OXG).

79 V&A (1977).

80 On the Crafts Advisory Committee / Crafts Council, see Harrod (1999), pp.369–93.

81 Crafts Advisory Committee (1973), pp.40–4.

82 Crafts Advisory Committee (1974). See also 'Seven British Ceramists', *Crafts*, 10 (1974), pp.18–21. The exhibition initially toured in Austria and Switzerland.

83 Queensberry was appointed Professor of Ceramics at the Royal College of Art in 1959. On the changes he instigated, see David Queensberry, 'Liz Fritsch', in Leeds Art Galleries, *Elizabeth Fritsch: Pots about Music*, exh. cat. (Leeds, 1978), no page number.

84 'Evening Meeting: Training the Potter', in Craftsmen Potters Association (1966), pp.27–8.

85 Elizabeth Fritsch, 'Pots about Music', in Leeds Art Galleries (1978), cited in endnote 83.

86 'Hans Coper', tributes, *Crafts*, 54 (1982), pp.34–5.

87 Fritsch (1978), cited in endnote 85.

88 Crafts Council (1981), pp.16–19.

89 On contrasting critical positions on the 'new crafts', see Rosemary Hill, 'Writing about the Studio Crafts', in Dormer (1997), pp.196–201.

90 Christopher Reid, 'A Culture of Doodles', *Crafts*, 64 (1983), p.11.

91 Dormer (1986), p.12.

92 Peter Dormer, 'Familiar Forms', in ICA (1985), p.5.

93 Henry Pim, 'Views on the Vessel', *Crafts*, 91 (1988), pp.13–14.

94 Dormer (1994), p.194.

95 'Foreword', in Sunderland Arts Centre (1978), no page number.

96 William Varley, 'State of Clay', exh. review, *Crafts*, 35 (1978), p.46.

97 Paul Astbury, in Rothschild (1972), no page number.

98 'Sculptors in Limbo?', *Crafts*, 33 (1978), pp.33–4.

99 See Museum of Modern Art, Oxford (1993). The exhibition was organized by the Museum of Modern Art, Oxford, but was shown first at the Barbican Art Gallery, London. After Oxford, it toured to Taipei Fine Arts Museum; Glynn Vivian Art Gallery, Swansea; Shigaraki Ceramic Cultural Park, Japan; and Musée d'Art Contemporain de Dunkerque, France.

100 Crafts Council (1995b).

101 Martina Margetts, 'Metamorphosis: The Culture of Ceramics', in Museum of Modern Art, Oxford (1993), p.15.

102 See for example Alison Britton, 'The Modern Pot', and Tanya Harrod, 'Pots and Fine Art', both in ICA (1985), which explore ideas put forward by George Woodman and Garth Clark respectively.

103 The records of Galerie Besson are at the Crafts Study Centre, Farnham (BES).

104 The potter Emmanuel Cooper was also a selector.

105 Crafts Council (1981), p.20.

106 On this first workshop, see Edmund de Waal, *The White Road* (London, 2015), pp.93–6.

107 Edmund de Waal, 'White Porcelain Tablewares', *Studio Pottery*, 18 (1995), p.46.

108 Britton (2001). See also, for example, Windsor (1997).

109 For a contemporary account, see Stephen Dixon, 'The Contemporary British Figure: Narrative, Metaphor and Tradition', in Stair (2000), pp.162–7.

110 Tate St Ives, *Richard Slee: Grand Wizard*, exh. cat. (St Ives, 2003), p.9.

111 Edmund de Waal, 'Signs & Wonders', in V&A, *Signs & Wonders: Edmund de Waal and the V&A Ceramics Galleries* (London, 2009), p.30.

112 See Dahn (2011) and Alun Graves, 'You Gotta Make It Happen!: Curating Clay's Expanded Field', The Peter Dormer Lecture, Royal College of Art, London, online video (2017), https://vimeo.com/245210032

113 Presented first at the World Ceramic Biennial, Korea, 2001, and then in the Crafts Council exhibition *Approaching Content*, 2003.

114 Twomey (2009).

115 Originally coined by Rosalind Krauss, the term 'expanded field' was taken up by the Ceramics Research Centre (CRC-UK) at the University of Westminster in connection with a three-year, Arts and Humanities Research Council (AHRC)-funded research project exploring the relationship between contemporary ceramic practice and museum culture. See Brown, Stair and Twomey (2016).

116 Made for the Woman's Hour Craft Prize (which Cummings subsequently won) and exhibited at the V&A.

117 AWARD exhibition text.

118 'Roots and Resonances: Magdalene Odundo and Ben Okri', in *Magdalene Odundo: The Journey of Things*, exh. cat. (London, 2019), no page number.

119 *Jennifer Lee: The Potter's Space*, Kettle's Yard, Cambridge, 2019, and *Magdalene Odundo: The Journey of Things*, The Hepworth Wakefield, 2019, touring to Sainsbury Centre, Norwich.

TIMELINE OF CERAMICS

Left. **PL.1** Denise Wren, pot, earthenware, 1913 (cat. 1120)

Below. **PL.2** Reginald Wells, handled bowl, earthenware, 1909 (cat. 1076); handled pot, earthenware, *c.* 1909 (cat. 1077)

Opposite. **PL.3** Bernard Leach, vase, raku, 1913 (cat. 513)

Left. **PL.4** Omega Workshops, vase, earthenware, *c.* 1914 (cat. 737)

Below left. **PL.5** Cuthbert Hamilton, dish, earthenware, *c.* 1919 (cat. 410)

PL.6 Dora Lunn, pot, earthenware, *c.* 1916–28 (cat. 635); vase, earthenware, *c.* 1919 (cat. 632)

PL.7 Charles and Nell Vyse, *The Balloon Woman*, earthenware, 1920 (cat. 1015); *The Lavender Girl*, earthenware, 1920 (cat. 1017)

Below left. **PL.8** Stella Crofts, *Giraffes*, earthenware, 1923 (cat. 238)

Below right. **PL.9** Madeline Raper, perfume burner: *Round Thatched Cottage*, earthenware, 1924 (cat. 817)

Opposite. **PL.10** Bernard Leach, large dish, earthenware, 1923 (cat. 518)

Right. **PL.11** Hamada Shōji, bowl, earthenware, 1922–23 (cat. 404)

Below right. **PL.12** Hamada Shōji, bottle, stoneware, 1923 (cat. 408)

ME
CLAY BUT
COME THIS WAY
PUNCH (OR BEER)
ALL THE

Opposite. **PL.13** Michael Cardew, harvest jug, earthenware, 1925 (cat. 133)

Below. **PL.14** Bernard Leach, bowl, stoneware, 1925–26 (cat. 523)

Opposite. **PL.15** Reginald Wells, bowl, stoneware, *c.* 1925 (cat. 1098); pot, stoneware, *c.* 1924 (cat. 1097)

Below. **PL.16** William Staite Murray, bowl, stoneware, 1924 (cat. 694); pot, stoneware, *c.* 1926–28 (cat. 701); bowl, stoneware, 1930 (cat. 708)

Left. **PL.17** William Staite Murray, bottle, stoneware, 1928 (cat. 702)

Opposite. **PL.18** Bernard Leach, bowl: *Korean washerwoman*, porcelain, 1931 (cat. 535)

PL.19 Norah Braden, jar, stoneware, 1929 (cat. 79); pot, stoneware, 1929 (cat. 80)

PL.20 Katharine Pleydell-Bouverie, bottle: *Roc's Egg*, stoneware, 1929–30 (cat. 781)

Below. **PL.21** Duncan Grant and Phyllis Keyes, vase, earthenware, *c.* 1932 (cat. 501); Vanessa Bell and Phyllis Keyes, vase, earthenware, *c.* 1932 (cat. 502)

Opposite. **PL.22** William Staite Murray, pot: *Eterne* (later *Wheel of Life*), stoneware, 1933–34 (cat. 712)

Below. **PL.23** Michael Cardew, bowl, earthenware, *c.* 1936 (cat. 140)

Opposite. **PL.24** Michael Cardew, cider jar, earthenware, 1938 (cat. 150)

Below left. **PL.25** Margaret Rey, bowl, stoneware, 1936–37 (cat. 823)

Below right. **PL.26** Henry Hammond, bowl, stoneware, 1938 (cat. 415)

Opposite. **PL.27** Robert Washington, tall pot, stoneware, 1938 (cat. 1063); tall pot, stoneware, 1938 (cat. 1064)

Opposite. **PL.28** Lucie Rie, pot, earthenware, 1936–37 (cat. 836); lidded pot, earthenware, 1936–37 (cat. 835)

Below. **PL.29** Lucie Rie, tea set, earthenware, *c.* 1936 (cat. 834)

PL.30 Leach Pottery, jug, stoneware, 1940 (cat. 583); jug, stoneware, 1940 (cat. 582)

Right. **PL.31** Sam Haile, jug, earthenware, *c.* 1946 (cat. 396)

Below right. **PL.32** Marianne de Trey, dish, earthenware, 1950 (cat. 276); '½pt mug', earthenware, 1950 (cat. 278); dish, earthenware, 1950 (cat. 277)

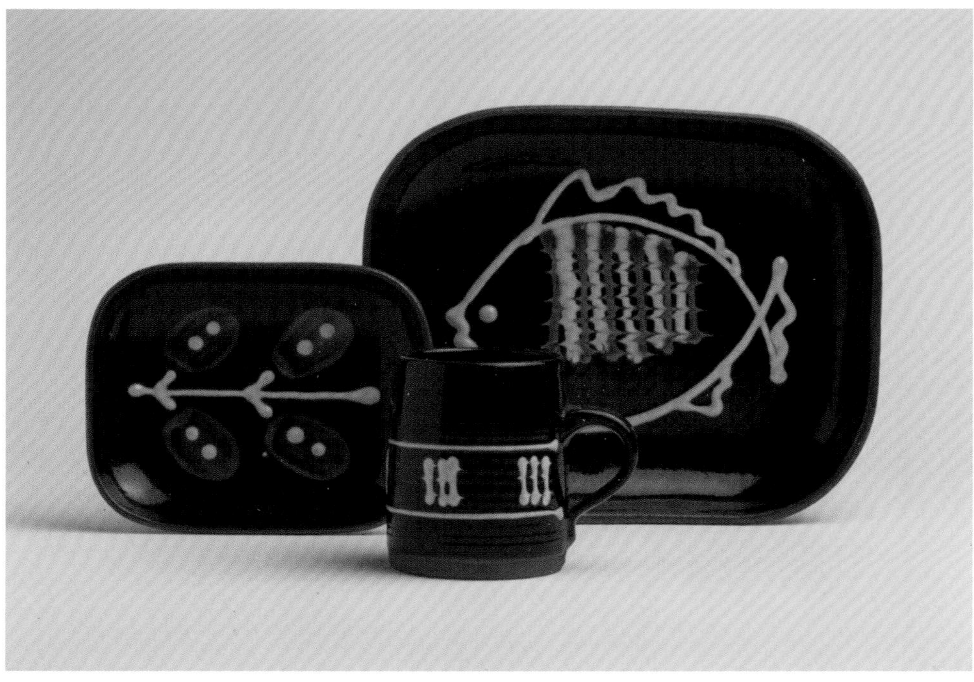

PL.33 Lucie Rie, bowl, stoneware, 1950 (cat. 844); bowl, porcelain, 1950 (cat. 846); bowl, porcelain, 1950 (cat. 845)

PL.34 Hans Coper, handled pot, stoneware, 1951 (cat. 225)

Below left. **PL.35** Margaret Hine, dish, earthenware, *c.* 1954 (cat. 448)

Below right. **PL.36** Margaret Hine, figure of a mounted harlequin, earthenware, *c.* 1953–54 (cat. 446)

Opposite. **PL.37** William Newland, figure on a donkey, earthenware, *c.* 1954 (cat. 718)

NEWLAND

Opposite. **PL.38** James Tower, 'Grey Blue Form', earthenware, 1957 (cat. 999)

Below. **PL.39** Hans Coper, bowl, stoneware, *c.* 1955 (cat. 227)

PL.40 Bernard Leach, pilgrim bottle, stoneware, 1956 (cat. 547)

PL.41 Michael Cardew, jar with screw stopper, stoneware, *c.* 1957 (cat. 163); dish, stoneware, *c.* 1957 (cat. 164)

Opposite top. **PL.42** Alan Caiger-Smith, bowl, earthenware, 1959 (cat. 121)

Opposite bottom. **PL.43** Gwyn Hanssen, punch set, stoneware, *c.* 1961 (cat. 429)

Right. **PL.44** Henry Hammond, tall pot: *Cow Parsley*, stoneware, 1959 (cat. 421)

Opposite. **PL.45** Helen Pincombe, pot, stoneware, 1958 (cat. 772); pot, stoneware, 1958 (cat. 773)

Below left. **PL.46** Ruth Duckworth, pot, stoneware, 1959 (cat. 306)

Below right. **PL.47** Dan Arbeid, 'Tall white bottle', stoneware, 1961 (cat. 6)

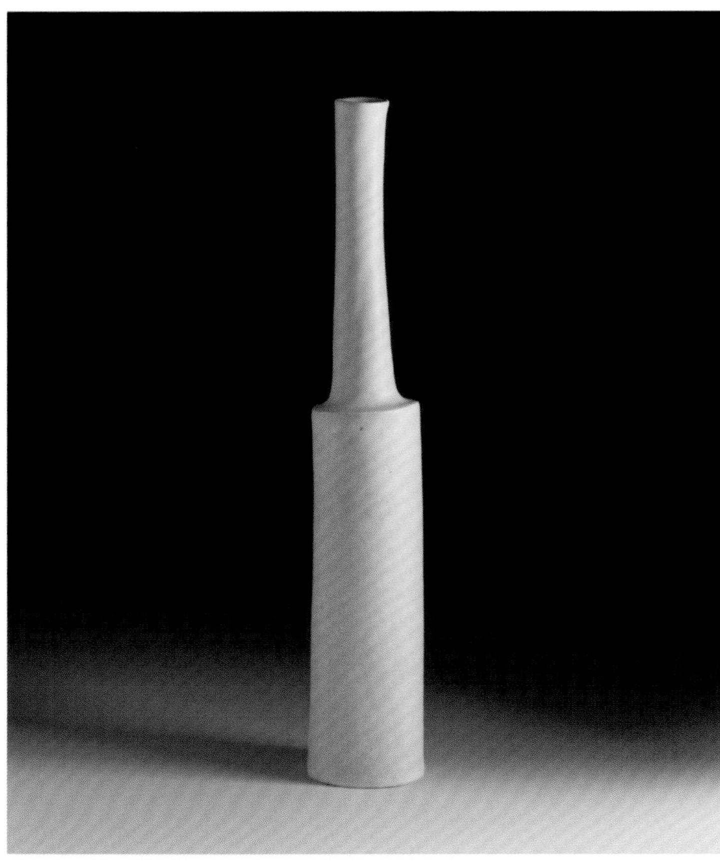

Below left. **PL.48** Janet Leach, large vase, stoneware, 1965 (cat. 566)

Below right. **PL.49** Ruth Duckworth, *Weed Pot (will not hold water)*, stoneware, 1966 (cat. 309)

Opposite. **PL.50** Louis Hanssen, pot, stoneware, 1965 (cat. 428)

Opposite. **PL.51** Gillian Lowndes, three standing pipes, stoneware, 1967 (cat. 625)

Right. **PL.52** Ian Auld, pot, stoneware, 1965 (cat. 17)

Below right. **PL.53** Robin Welch, 'Cylinder with Split Centre', stoneware, 1968 (cat. 1073)

Below. **PL.54** Lucie Rie, 'Large bowl', stoneware, 1967 (cat. 866); 'High bowl', stoneware, 1967 (cat. 867)

Opposite. **PL.55** Lucie Rie, 'Tall-necked bottle', stoneware, 1967 (cat. 862)

Opposite. **PL.56** Hans Coper, 'Large oval-bodied pot narrowing to an elliptical top', stoneware, 1968 (cat. 230)

Below. **PL.57** Hans Coper, 'Bud-shaped pot', stoneware, 1968 (cat. 234)

Below. **PL.58** Tony Hepburn, *Box with tubes*, stoneware, 1968 (cat. 445)

Opposite. **PL.59** Gordon Baldwin, *Reptilian Black*, earthenware, 1969–70 (cat. 25)

Opposite. **PL.60** Ian Godfrey, *Large white chest of drawers*, stoneware, 1969–70 (cat. 371)

Below. **PL.61** Bryan Newman, *Houses with motorway*, stoneware, 1973 (cat. 723)

PL.62 Alan and Ruth Barrett-Danes, *Fungi Form with Frogs*, porcelain, 1975 (cat. 41)

Below. **PL.63** Denise Wren, elephant, stoneware, 1971 (cat. 1128)

Right. **PL.64** Mo Jupp, helmet, stoneware, 1972 (cat. 474)

Below right. **PL.65** Donald Locke, *Standing Bottle with Sternum*, stoneware, 1976 (cat. 622)

Below. **PL.66** Colin Pearson, pot, porcelain, 1971 (cat. 761)

Opposite. **PL.67** Michael Casson, footed bowl, stoneware, 1975 (cat. 190)

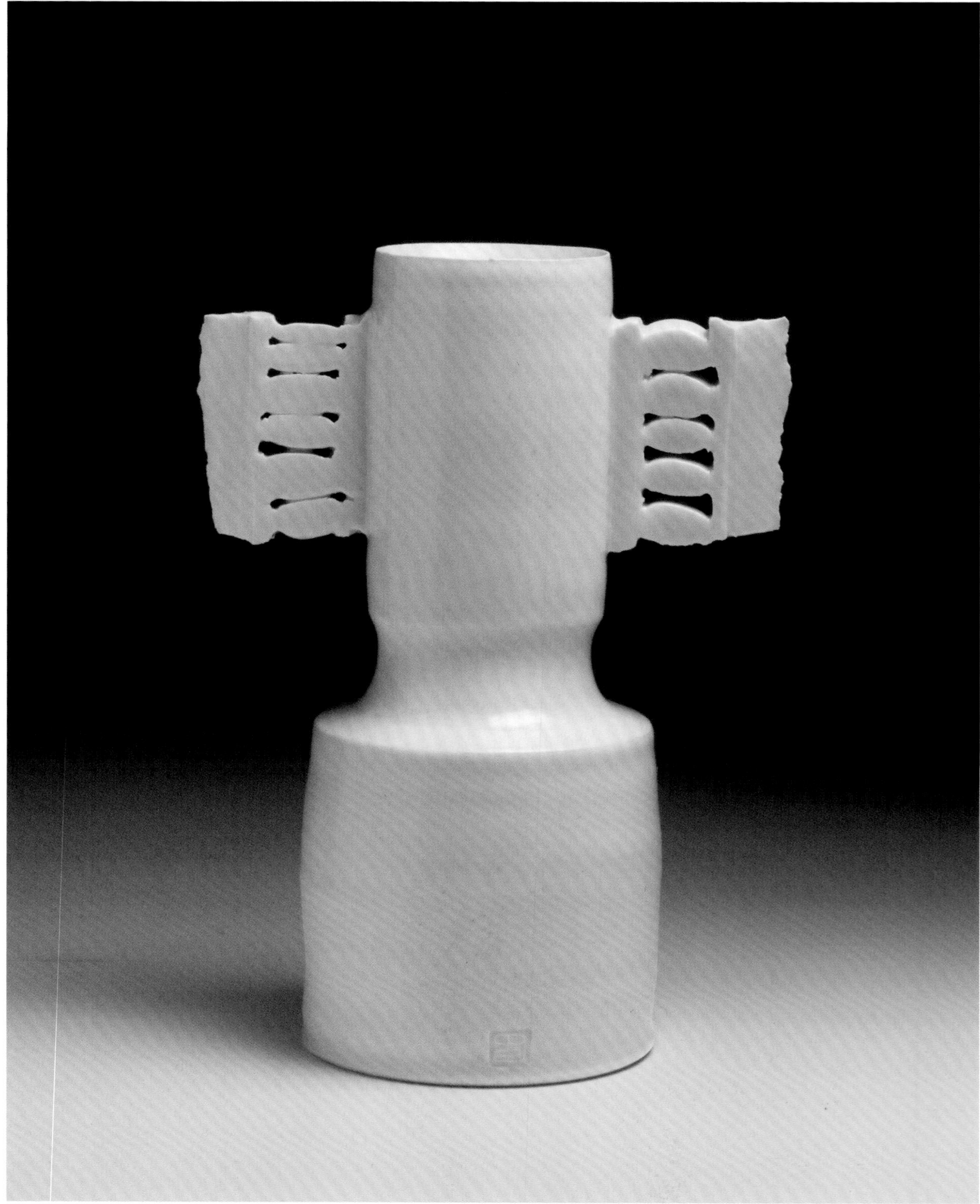

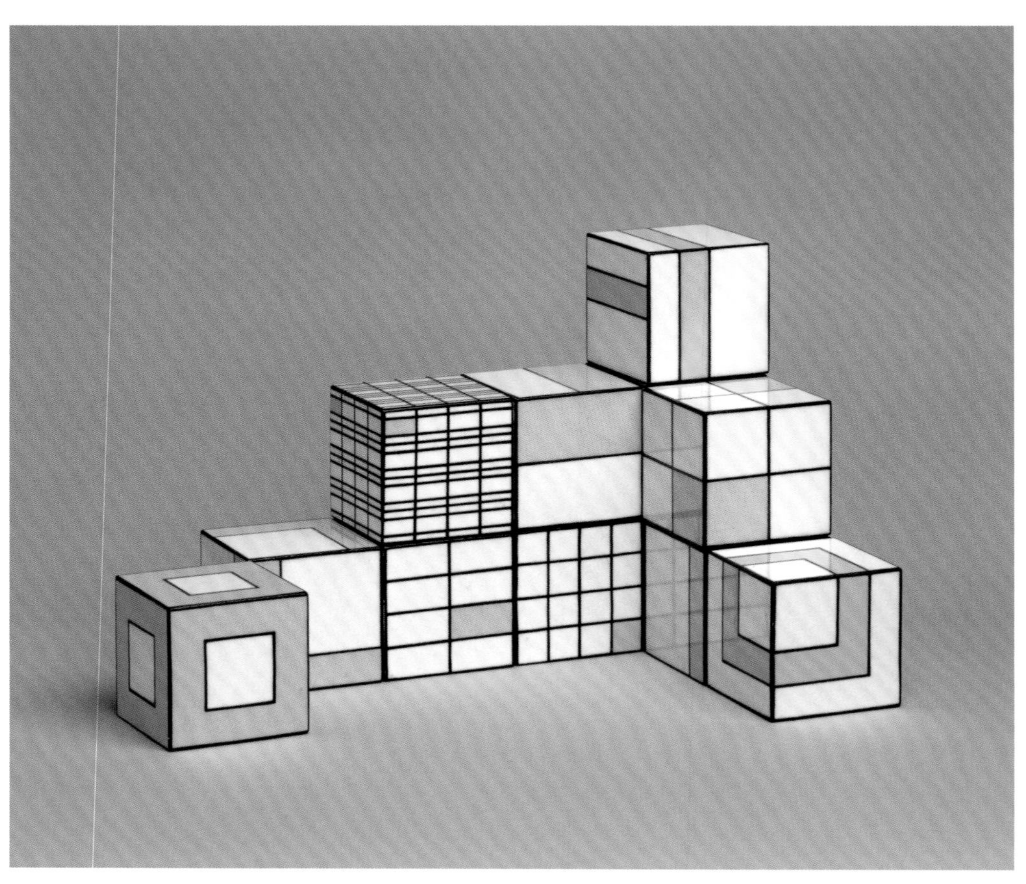

Opposite top. **PL.68** Glenys Barton, *Graphic Permutations*, bone china, 1971 (cat. 52)

Opposite bottom. **PL.69** Jacqui Poncelet, *Tilted form*, bone china, 1976 (cat. 799); *Oval form with a half foot*, bone china, 1976 (cat. 798)

Below. **PL.70** Andrew Lord, *Vase and dish. Cubist black set*, earthenware, 1978 (cat. 624)

Above. **PL.71** Alison Britton, *Yellow Triangles*, high-fired earthenware, 1981 (cat. 89)

Above right. **PL.72** Janice Tchalenko, jug, stoneware, 1980 (cat. 987)

Opposite. **PL.73** Elizabeth Fritsch, *Optical pot*, stoneware, 1980 (cat. 362)

Opposite. **PL.80** Joanna Constantinidis, flattened bottle, stoneware, 1983 (cat. 214)

Below. **PL.81** Walter Keeler, teapot, stoneware, 1984 (cat. 486); 'Angular teapot', stoneware, 1982 (cat. 484)

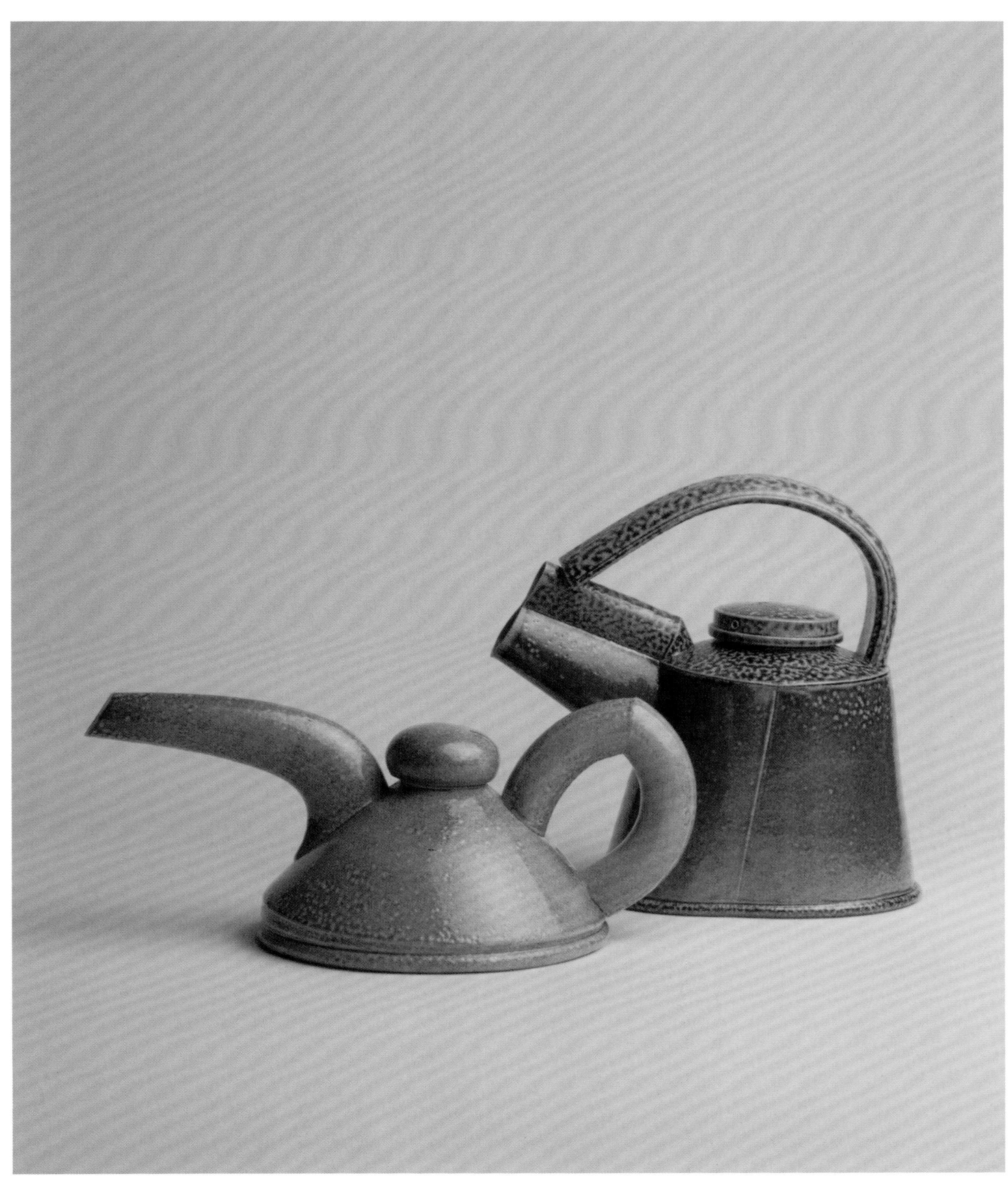

Above left. **PL.82** Richard Slee, *Cornucopia*, earthenware, 1983 (cat. 917)

Above right. **PL.83** Carol McNicoll, bowl, earthenware, 1985 (cat. 674)

PL.84 Jacqueline Poncelet, *Sculpture in 3 Parts*, earthenware, 1986 (cat. 808)

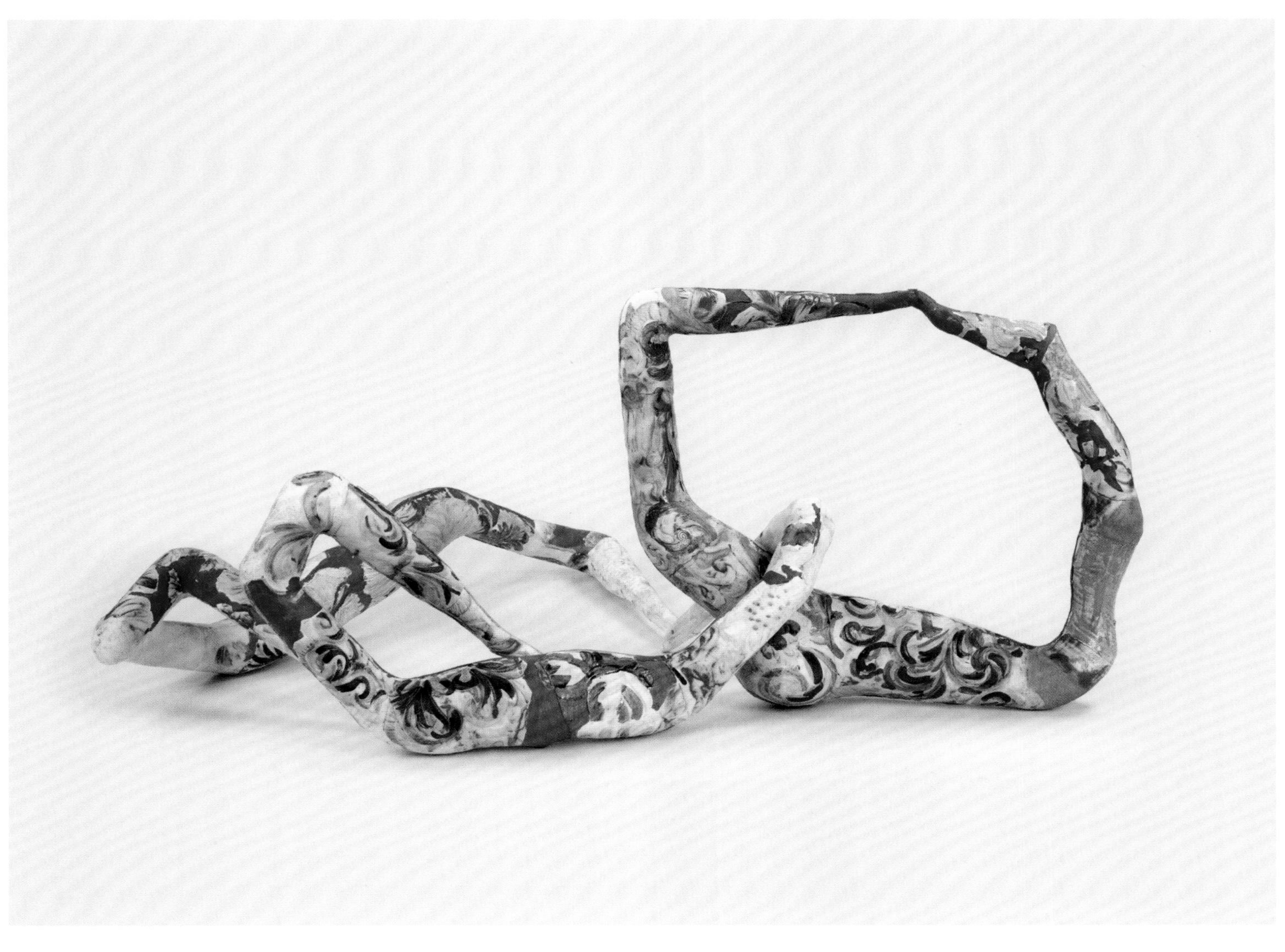

Opposite. **PL.85** Sandy Brown, platter, stoneware, 1987 (cat. 112)

Below. **PL.86** Elspeth Owen, *Menopause Pot*, earthenware, 1987 (cat. 750)

Below. **PL.87** John Ward, 'Green and white banded oval bowl with double groove', stoneware, 1985 (cat. 1060)

Opposite. **PL.88** Magdalene Odundo, *Symmetrical ribbed pot*, earthenware, 1983 (cat. 733)

PL.89 Ewen Henderson, sculpture from the series *Skull Mountain*, bone china and porcelain laminated to stoneware, 1988 (cat. 441)

PL.90 Gordon Baldwin, *Large Round Vessel from an Inscape*, earthenware, 1988–89 (cat. 31)

Opposite. **PL.91** Angus Suttie, *Large Blue Form*, earthenware, 1988 (cat. 973)

Below left. **PL.92** Henry Pim, *Pleated Pot*, stoneware, 1983 (cat. 768)

Below right. **PL.93** Sara Radstone, pot, stoneware, 1983 (cat. 812)

Above. **PL.94** Alison Britton, *White and Brown Pot, Big Spout*, high-fired earthenware, 1990 (cat. 98)

Opposite top. **PL.95** Gillian Lowndes, *Scroll*, bone china, fibreglass, stainless-steel rope, 1996 (cat. 631)

Opposite bottom. **PL.96** Martin Smith, *Fact & Expectation No.1*, red earthenware, 1992 (cat. 933)

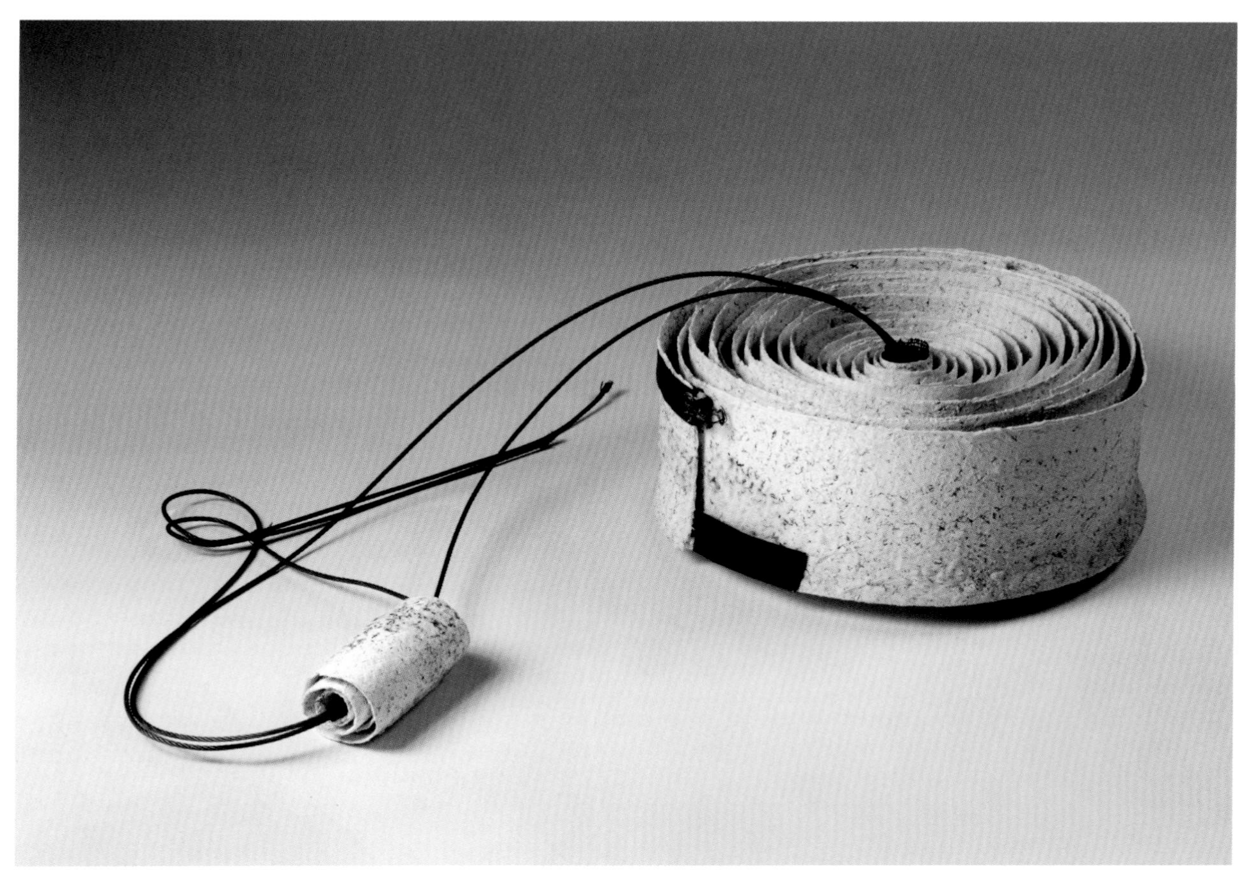

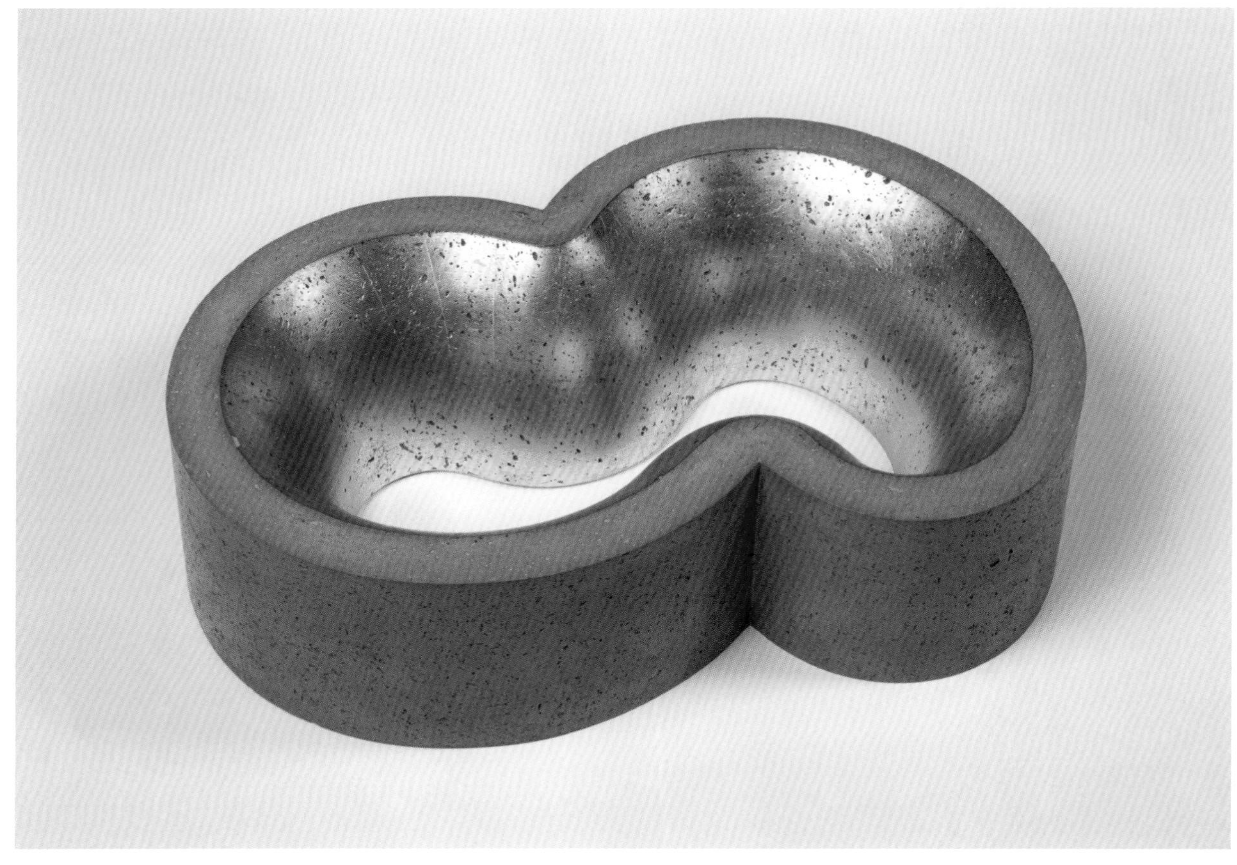

PL.97 Takeshi Yasuda, small dish with a handle, stoneware, 1996 (cat. 1145); cream jug, earthenware, 1996 (cat. 1144)

PL.98 Edmund de Waal, teapot, porcelain, 1996 (cat. 289); beaker, porcelain, 1996 (cat. 290)

Above left. **PL.99** Jim Malone, bottle, stoneware, 1998 (cat. 644)

Above right. **PL.100** Mike Dodd, pot, stoneware, 1989 (cat. 299)

Below left. **PL.101** Jane Hamlyn, *Bell jar*, stoneware, 1997 (cat. 414)

Below right. **PL.102** Phil Rogers, bottle, stoneware, 1999 (cat. 887)

Opposite. **PL.103** Neil Brownsword, *She Wants Your Junk*, ceramic collage with found elements on steel armature, 1999 (cat. 114)

Below. **PL.104** Grayson Perry, *My Heroes*, earthenware, 1994 (cat. 766)

Opposite. **PL.105** Philip Eglin, *Venus et Amour*, earthenware, 1990 (cat. 322)

Above. **PL.106** Stephen Dixon, *Family of Nations*, stoneware, 1992 (cat. 297)

Below. **PL.107** Susan Halls, figure of a dog: *Little Horror*, raku, 1997 (cat. 403)

Opposite. **PL.108** Christie Brown, *Brick Stone Mother* from the series *The Cast of Characters*, high-fired earthenware (brick clay), 1997 (cat. 110)

Below. **PL.109** Felicity Aylieff, *Oval Rotation*, white earthenware with porcelain and glass aggregates, 1999 (cat. 18)

Opposite. **PL.110** Lawson Oyekan, sculpture: *Coming Up For Air* series, red earthenware, 2001 (cat. 751)

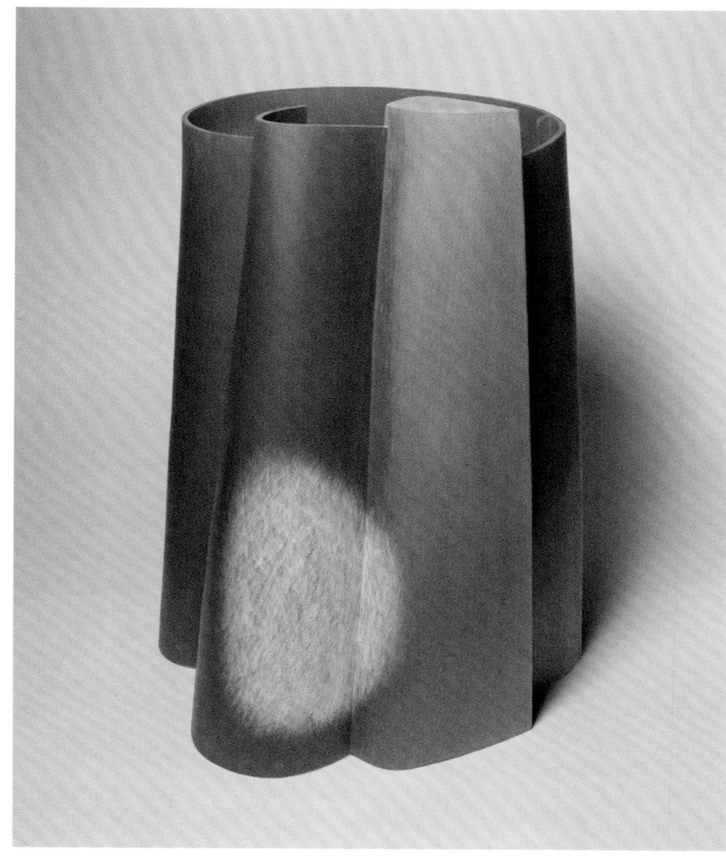

Left. **PL.111** Alison Britton, *Container*, high-fired earthenware, 2001 (cat. 103)

Below. **PL.112** Ken Eastman, *November Night*, stoneware, 2002 (cat. 314)

Opposite top. **PL.113** Emmanuel Cooper, bowl, porcelain, *c.* 2000–10 (cat. 223); jug, stoneware, *c.* 2000–10 (cat. 224)

Opposite bottom. **PL.114** Walter Keeler, 'Cut branch dish', earthenware, 2005 (cat. 492)

PL.115 Keith Harrison, *Transformer*, domestic electric heater, Egyptian paste, portable cassette player, cassette recording, timer switches, 2002 (cat. 435)

PL.116 Laura Ford, *Headthinker III*, stoneware, steel, plaster, clothing, plinth, 2003 (cat. 352)

Below. **PL.117** Richard Slee, *Sausage*, earthenware, workbench, elastic straps, 2006 (cat. 927)

Opposite top. **PL.118** Hans Stofer, *Robin Day*, porcelain bowl, gold leaf, removeable porcelain figure, steel, magnets, 2006 (cat. 968)

Opposite bottom. **PL.119** Barnaby Barford, *She'll Need More than a Makeover*, found porcelain or earthenware objects, enamel paint, other media, 2008 (cat. 39)

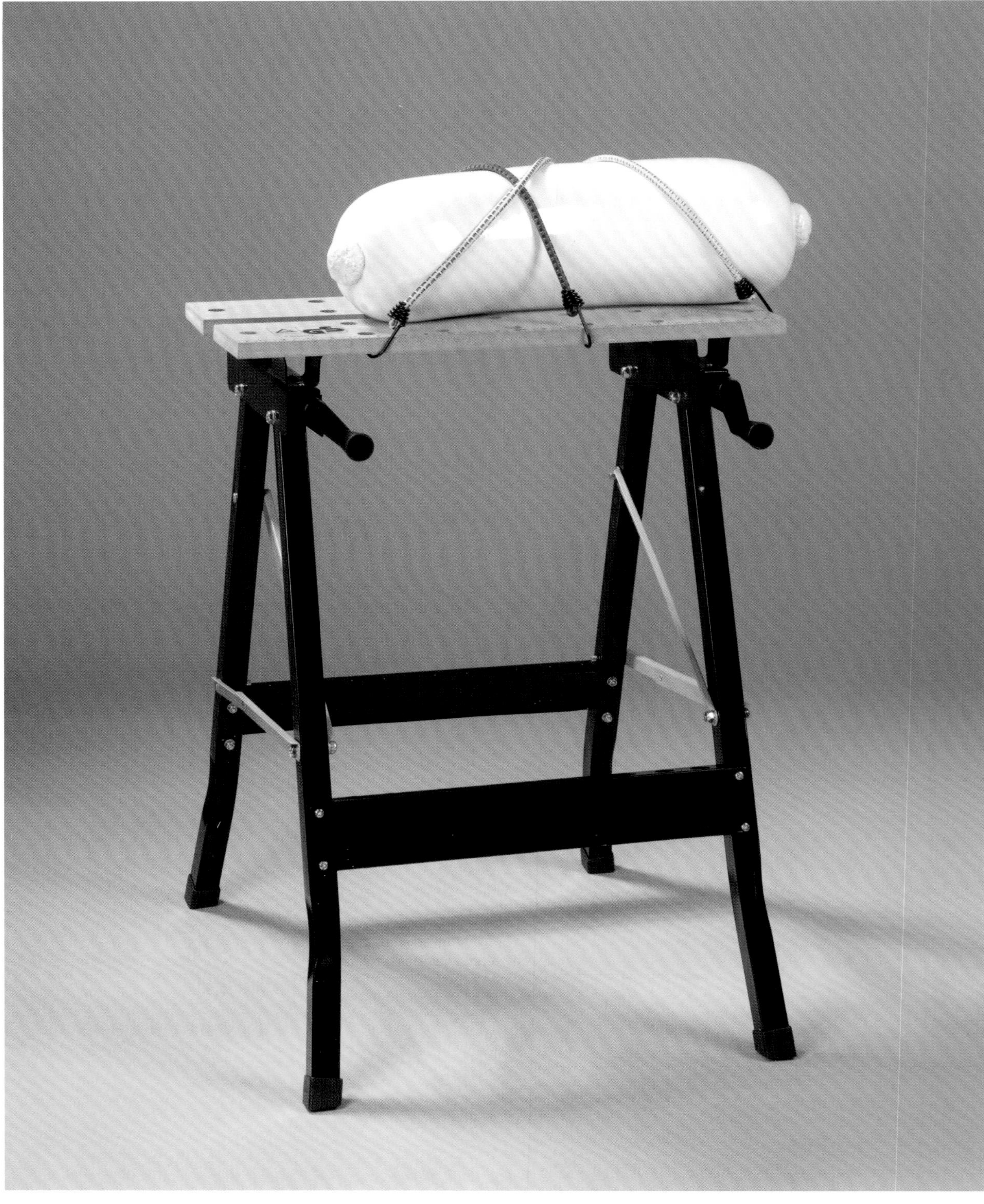

Above. **PL.120** Simon Carroll, basin, earthenware, *c.* 2000–03 (cat. 174)

Left. **PL.121** Danlami Aliyu, dish, stoneware, 2008 (cat. 2)

Opposite. **PL.122** Svend Bayer, jar, stoneware, 2005 (cat. 64)

Opposite. **PL.123** Jennifer Lee, *Pale, haloed granite traces, bronze specks*, coloured stoneware, 2007 (cat. 612)

Below. **PL.124** Halima Cassell, *Dark Trivalve*, stoneware, 2008 (cat. 186)

PL.125 Felicity Aylieff, *Chasing Black*, porcelain, 2006 (cat. 19)

PL.126 Julian Stair, *Monumental Jar IX*, red stoneware, 2012 (cat. 964)

PL.127 Kate Malone, *Snow Lady Gourd*, stoneware, 2008 (cat. 647)

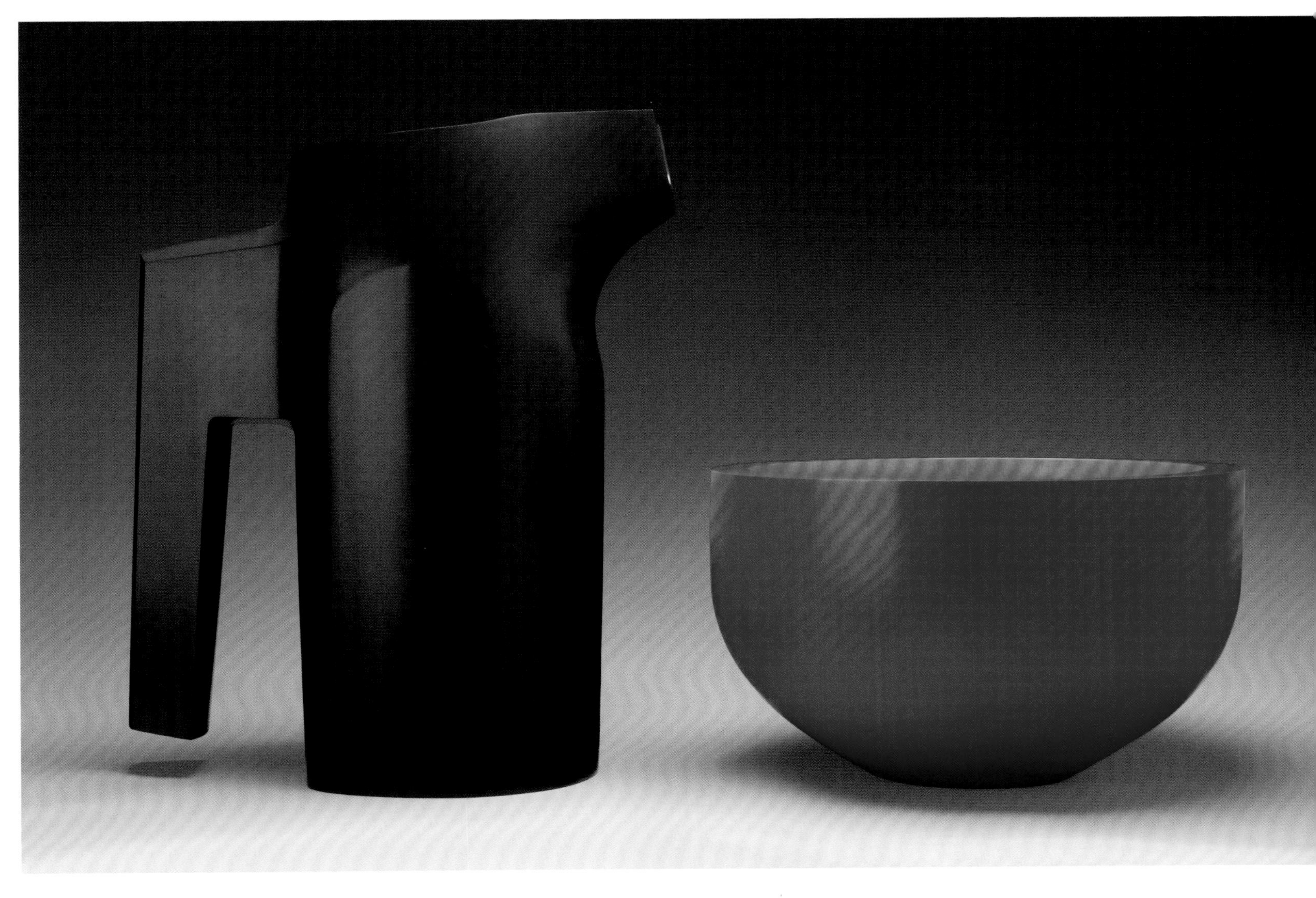

PL.128 Nicholas Rena, *The Given's the Given*, earthenware, painted and polished, 2008 (cat. 821); *Red Bowl*, earthenware, painted and polished, 2009 (cat. 822)

Above. **PL.129** Martin Smith, *Serial Dialogue in Fifteen Parts*, earthenware and platinum leaf, 2007 (cat. 937)

Opposite. **PL.130** Richard Deacon, *Bottle Green Republic*, ceramic, wood, rubber, 2009 (cat. 295)

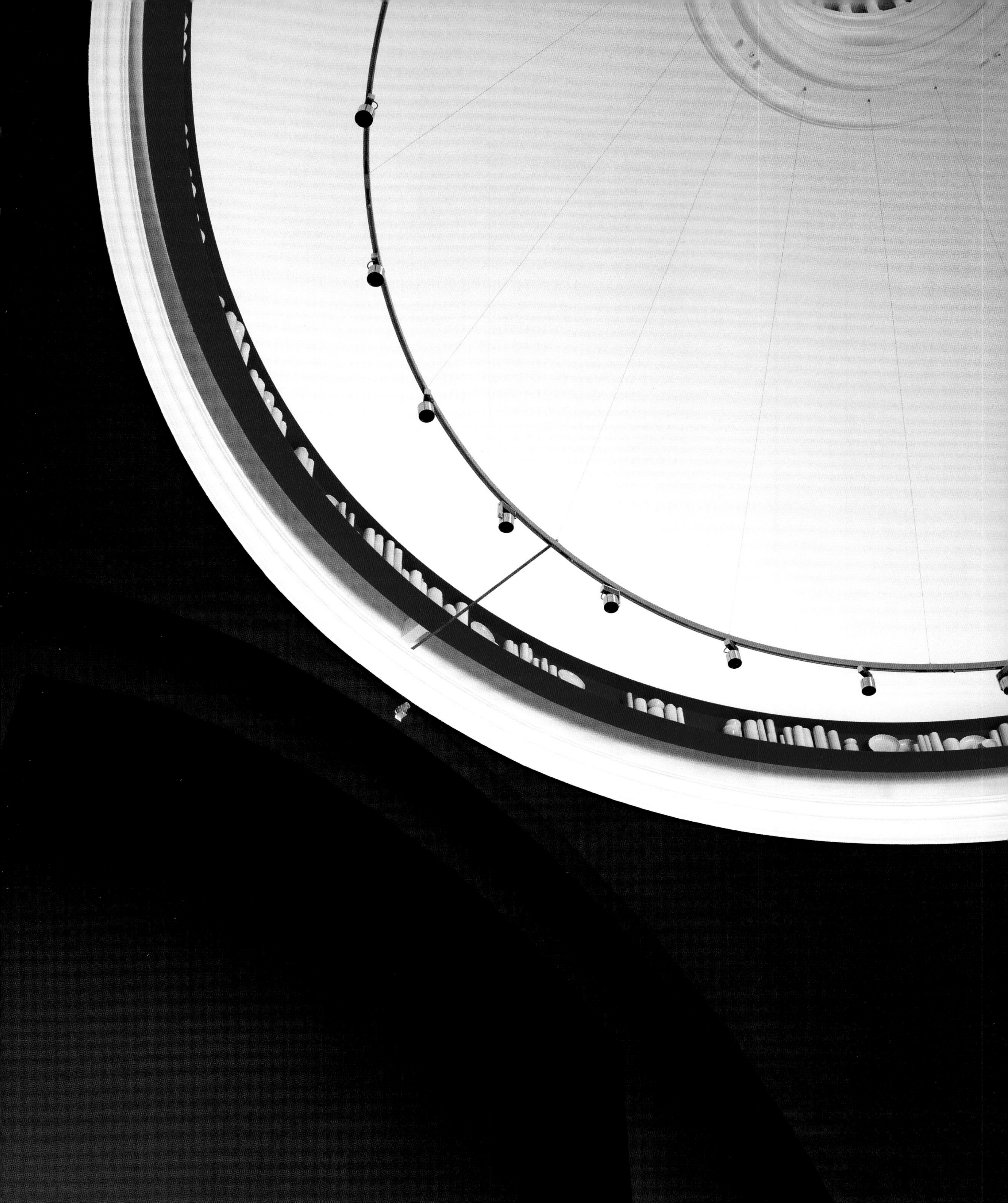

Opposite. **PL.131** Edmund de Waal, *Signs & Wonders*, porcelain and powder-coated aluminium, 2009 (cat. 293)

Above. **PL.132** Gwyn Hanssen Pigott, *Kinder Trail*, porcelain, 2010 (cat. 432)

PL.133 Carol McNicoll, *Home Sweet Home*, earthenware and found earthenware plate, 2011 (cat. 677)

PL.134 Paul Scott, *Scott's Cumbrian Blue(s), Hedgerow No. 6*, in-glaze transfer collage and gold lustre on Copeland earthenware platter, 2012 (cat. 901)

PL.135 Edmund de Waal, *the collector (for Paul)*, 17 porcelain vessels in a wood and acrylic cabinet, 2015 (cat. 294)

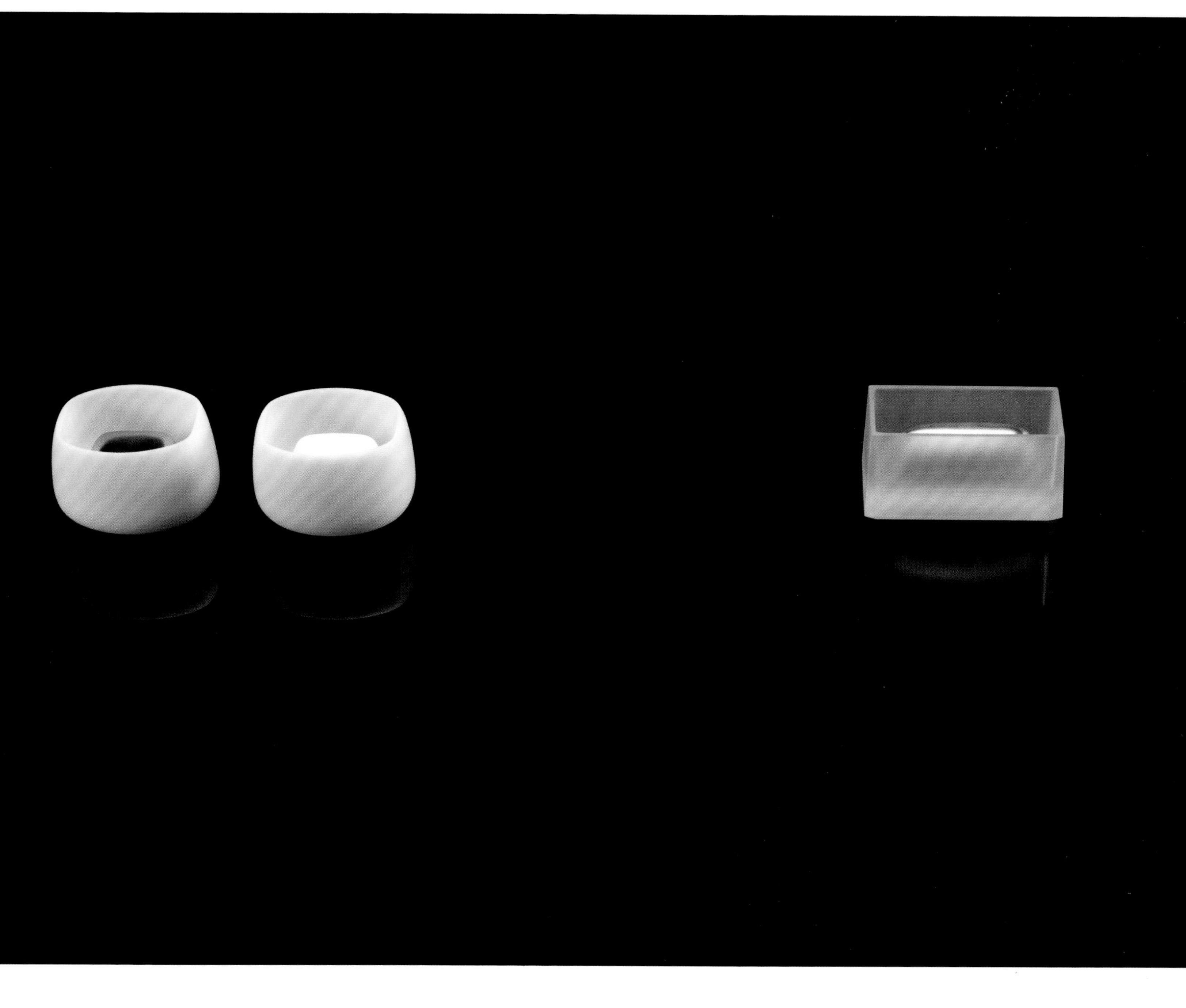

PL.136 Andrea Walsh, *Collection of Contained Boxes*, lost-wax cast glass, bone china, 22ct burnished gold and platinum, 2018 (cat. 1056)

Below. **PL.137** Nao Matsunaga, *Busy Signal*, high-fired black earthenware and carved wood, 2012 (cat. 671)

Opposite top. **PL.138** Jesse Wine, *Jesse show passion III*, earthenware, 2014 (cat. 1117)

Opposite bottom. **PL.139** Aaron Angell, *Caterpillar Engine*, stoneware, 2017 (cat. 4)

PL.143 Neil Brownsword, installation: *Relic*, bone china, lead, wood, 2016 (cat. 116)

Opposite. **PL.144** Claire Partington, *Cub*, earthenware, 2018 (cat. 760)

Below. **PL.145** Matt Smith, *Wunderkammer 2*, black Parian porcelain, 2017 (cat. 938)

Opposite. **PL.146** Akiko Hirai, large moon jar: *Eclipse Night*, stoneware with 'landscape inclusions', 2019 (cat. 452)

Below. **PL.147** Fernando Casasempere, *Natura Morta 8*, porcelain with steel mount, 2018 (cat. 184)

PL.148 Grayson Perry, *Matching Pair*, ceramic, 2017 (cat. 767)

PL.149 Vicky Lindo, *Swimming in Coolree Reservoir (Platter)*; pot: *Yearning for some facts*; *The Green Man (Platter)*; pot: *Wexford People*; from *Dead Dad Book*, earthenware, 2019 (cat. 618 I–L)

A–Z OF ARTISTS

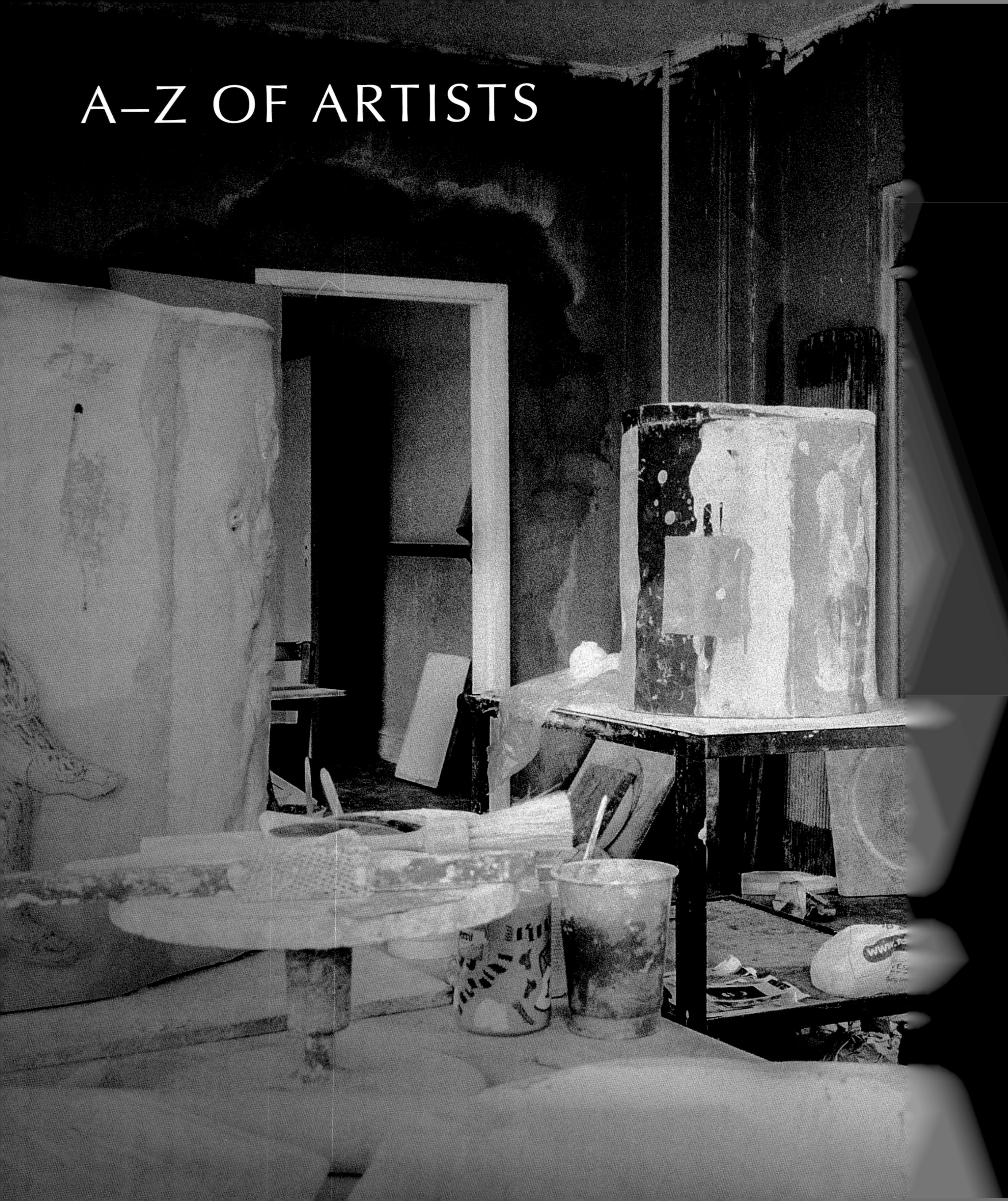

Happy faxing
love Phil x.

This catalogue is arranged alphabetically by name of artist or, in some instances, pottery. Japanese artists who have worked predominantly in their home country are referred to following Japanese naming convention, with family name followed by given name (for example Hamada Shōji). Artists of Japanese heritage based in the UK are, however, referred to according to British convention. Cross-references between entries are indicated by (qv).

The entries follow a standard format:

Biography: chronology and commentary:
A short biography is given in the form of a tabulated chronology, followed by a brief commentary on the artist's work.

Exhibition history is generally limited to major or key shows, such as retrospectives, exhibitions in public institutions, or the earliest solo exhibitions.

Bibliography:
The bibliography for each artist lists first their own writing, where such exists, followed by publications and texts relevant to their work. Each of these two groups is ordered by date.

Exhibition catalogues normally appear under the name of the host institution, unless a specific author is named.

Abbreviated references are given for publications of wider relevance, which are listed in full in the main bibliography at the end of the book (*see* pp.408–11). The widely referenced journal *Ceramic Review* is abbreviated as *CR*.

Catalogue of works:
The catalogue entries for the ceramics are usually in date order for each artist. Deviations from this are sometimes made in order to group related objects or acquisitions.

The entry records the work's title in *italics*, where one is known, followed by its date. For works that are untitled but where an original description from the artist, gallery or exhibition catalogue is of interest, this is given in quotation marks.

The entry then records the date, a simple technical description – all vessels can be assumed to be thrown, unless stated otherwise – followed by a transcript or description of any maker's marks. The place of making is given only where it cannot be inferred from the chronology. The work's dimensions are recorded in centimetres (cm) and are usually given for overall height (h.) and greatest horizontal depth or diameter (d.). For tiles and similar objects, height (h.) and width (w.) are given.

The V&A accession number (which gives the year of acquisition) and the source from which the work was obtained is then given, along with the price paid and any credit for support.

Abbo, Jerome 1934–2016

1934	born Netherlands, the son of Jussuf Abbo, a Jewish Palestinian Ottoman sculptor who had made a career in Germany and who was fleeing the Nazi regime with Jerome's mother, Ruth
1935–	arrives in England, the family initially living in London, later moving to Sussex
1960s	works as set designer and painter for Cambridge Arts Theatre; meets Dan Arbeid (qv)
1963–67	shares house and studio with Arbeid in Wendens Ambo, Essex; learns ceramics
1965	group exhibition, *Viewpoint*, Primavera, Cambridge
1966–71	ceramic technician and part-time lecturer, Central School of Arts and Crafts, London; moves to Brighton following appointment in London
c. 1970–72	solo and group exhibitions, Forum Gallery, Brighton
1971–	teaches on Studio Pottery Course at Harrow School of Art; course director from 1974
1984	retires; ceases making ceramics

A largely self-taught potter, Jerome Abbo was introduced to ceramics by Dan Arbeid (qv), whose studio and house he and his family shared for a time. Abbo was a charismatic and influential teacher, who preserved the vocational ethos of the Studio Pottery Course at Harrow, while broadening its focus from production pottery. His own work comprised ceramic beaded jewellery and handbuilt vases, goblets and containers, but he made and exhibited little as his teaching commitments increased.

1

Barbara Harding, 'CPA Potters Camp', *CR*, 23 (1973)
Paisley Museum and Art Galleries (1984), p.11
Danny Killick, 'The Harrow Pottery Course', in Northern Centre for Contemporary Art (1989), pp.51–2, 62
Christie Brown, 'Anxiety of Endeavour', in Peters (2012), pp.42, 52

Exhibition reviews: Eileen Lewenstein, 'Three Potters', *CR*, 7 (1971); *CR*, 19 (1973)

1 Pot, *c.* 1970–73
Stoneware, slab-built, mottled beige glaze; marks: 'Abbo' and '119', painted; h.29.7cm, d.17.8cm
C.307-1993. Source: John Lloyd, Brighton, £200
The vendor, John Lloyd, had earlier sold Abbo's pots in his gallery, Forum Gallery, Brighton.

Aesthetic Sabotage *see* Robert Dawson

Aldermaston Pottery *see* Alan Caiger-Smith

Aliyu, Danlami 1952–2012

1952	born Minna, Nigeria
1966–70	apprenticeship at Pottery Training Centre, Abuja (now Suleja), under Michael OBrien (qv)
1970–75	works at small demonstration pottery at Jos Museum
1975–76	comes to England, works at Wenford Bridge Pottery, Cornwall, under Michael Cardew (qv)
1976–79	studies ceramics and photography at West Surrey College of Art and Design, Farnham, under Henry Hammond (qv)
1977	solo exhibition, Commonwealth Art Gallery, London
1979–	returns to Minna, works as photographer, later establishes local government-funded pottery
1985–	establishes Maraba Pottery, near Kaduna, with OBrien, and his brother, Umaru Aliyu

1988–	sets up Al Habib Pottery in Minna, making earthenware colourfully decorated with oil-based paints; returns periodically to make stoneware at OBrien's pottery in Surrey

Danlami Aliyu began his career at the Pottery Training Centre in Abuja (now Suleja), Nigeria, founded by Michael Cardew (qv) and then run by Michael OBrien (qv). He later trained directly with Cardew at Wenford Bridge. His restrained, fluently decorated stonewares represent the highly distinctive school of practice that emerged around Cardew's African excursions, which overlaid African influence upon the developing traditions of the studio pottery movement.

Danlami Aliyu, 'Nigerian Pottery Tradition and New Technique', *Pottery Quarterly*, 13:52 (1980)

— 'Traditional Matters', interview by Moria Vincentelli, *Ceramic Archive Bulletin* (*University of Wales, Aberystwyth*), 4 (2000)

Commonwealth Art Gallery, *Danlami Aliyu: Pottery*, exh. pamphlet (London, 1977)

Michael OBrien, exh. review, *Crafts*, 31 (1978)

Tanya Harrod, obituary, *The Guardian* (25 May 2012)

Harrod (2012), pp.364–81

Michael OBrien, letter, *CR*, 257 (2012)

2 Dish, 2008 (pl.121)
Stoneware, incised decoration through a dark slip under a white-flecked 'Jun' glaze; marks: 'DA' in monogram, impressed; made at the workshop of Michael OBrien, Epsom, Surrey; h.5.8cm, d.36.9cm
C.157-2009. Source: given by Michael OBrien

The museum also holds a jug made by Danlami Aliyu while training at Abuja, not catalogued here (C.57-2008).

Aller Pottery *see* Bryan Newman

Angell, Aaron 1987–

1987	born London
2007–11	studies fine art at Slade School of Fine Art, London
2014	establishes Troy Town Art Pottery at Open School East, London
2016–	moves Troy Town to Hoxton Street, London
2017	co-curates exhibition, *That Continuous Thing*, Tate St Ives; residency at Tate St Ives and Leach Pottery, St Ives
2018	visits Japan and Korea with Grizedale Arts
2020–	launches Hoxton Gardenware, a community project at his workshop teaching business and making skills
2021–	begins wood-firing sculpture at Oxford Anagama Project, Wytham; plans River Eden Anagama, a private studio in Edenbridge, Kent

Aaron Angell is an artist who works primarily with ceramics, and a protagonist in a movement that has drawn non-ceramic artists to clay. He established Troy Town Art Pottery as a 'radical and psychedelic' studio for artists to explore ceramics as a sculptural medium, as well as a space in which to work and develop his own knowledge of glaze chemistry and firing techniques. His sculptures and tableaux draw upon hobbyist cultures, folk art, and handbuilt ceramics of the 1960s and '70s.

Aaron Angell, 'The Plant: Notes on Troy Town Art Pottery', in Matson and Thorne (2016), pp.108–15

— 'A Radical Vision', *CR*, 285 (2017)

Ryan Gander, 'Aaron Angell', *Art Review* (March 2011)

Tom Morton, 'Aaron Angell', interview, *Frieze*, 156 (2013)

Fanny Singer, 'Studio Visit: Aaron Angell', interview, *Art Papers*, 38:4 (2014)

Tanya Harrod, 'Meet the New Table-top Radicals', *Crafts*, 252 (2015)

Claire Shea, 'Throwing Shapes', *Elephant*, 26 (2016)

Amy Sherlock, 'In Two Places', *Frieze*, 179 (2016)

Elderton and Morrill (2017), pp.26–7

Imogen Greenhalgh, 'The Spirit of Clay', interview, *Crafts*, 265 (2017)

Amy Sherlock, 'Making Good', *Frieze*, 210 (2020)

Exhibition reviews: Noemi Smolik, *Artforum International*, 54:9 (2016); James Clegg, *Art Review* (March 2018); Christina Jansen, *Crafts*, 271 (2018)

3 *Swan Pedalo One* (*I remember John Barleycorn*), 2013
Stoneware, handbuilt, coloured glazes; marks: 'AAA 2013', incised; h.26.8cm, d.46cm
C.5-2018. Source: Rob Tufnell, London, £4000; acquired through the generosity of Gerard and Sarah Griffin

4 *Caterpillar Engine*, 2017 (pl.139)
Stoneware, handbuilt, ash, rutile and barium glazes; marks: 'AAA 17', incised; h.38.7cm, d.67.5cm
C.4:1,2-2018. Source: *see* 3, £4160

3

Shown in the exhibition *That Continuous Thing: Artists and the Ceramics Studio, 1920 – Today*, Tate St Ives, 2017.

Arbeid, Dan 1928–2010

1928	born Stepney, London
1942–55	works in clothing factory
1955	travels to Israel, works on a kibbutz
1956–57	works at Harsa ceramics factory, Beersheba
1957–	returns to England; appointed technical assistant at Central School of Arts and Crafts, London; studio at Abbey Art Centre, New Barnet, Hertfordshire
1959|63	solo exhibitions, Primavera, London
1961	solo exhibition, Bristol Guild of Applied Art
1963–83	moves to Wendens Ambo, Essex, sets up studio with oil-fired kilns; shares house and studio for a time with Jerome Abbo (qv)
1966–85	teaches at Central School of Arts and Crafts
1969–	touring exhibition *Five Studio Potters*, organized by V&A
1983–	moves to Brighton, Sussex, establishes studio
1998–	buys house in south of France, establishes studio, divides time between homes

Dan Arbeid was a pioneer of handbuilding in the post-war period and regarded as working on the extremes of pottery-making. His work shows an imaginative and inventive approach to form, a willingness to experiment, and a delight in extremes of texture. His output reduced considerably as his teaching commitments increased, but he continued to develop new work in later years, characterized by vivid use of colour.

5

7

9 / 8

10 / 13 / 12 / 11

Decorative Art (1960/61), (1961/62)
Birks (1967), pp.109–24, (1976), pp.156–67
Casson (1967), p.5, pls.1–2, 71–2
Potters (1972) to (1977)
Paisley Museum and Art Galleries (1984), pp.11–12
Crafts Council (1995b), pp.22–3
Ken Stradling Collection/Bristol Guild of Applied Art, *Dan Arbeid: A Retrospective* (Bristol, 2011)

Exhibition reviews: *Pottery Quarterly*, 6:23 (1959), pp.104–5, pls.5–7; *Pottery Quarterly*, 8:29 (1963), pp.33–4, pls.10–11; illustration, *Crafts*, 56 (1982), p.52; Andy Christian, *Ceramics: Art and Perception*, 88 (2012)

Obituaries: Emmanuel Cooper, *The Guardian* (22 November 2010); *The Times* (27 November 2010); Tony Birks, *Ceramics: Art and Perception*, 88 (2012)

An artist statement written for the *Five Studio Potters* exhibition is in the manuscripts collection, National Art Library, V&A, London (MSL/1969/3560).

5 Vase, 1959
Stoneware, coil-built, thin ash-glaze exterior, grey glaze interior; marks: 'Arbeid', painted; h.21.4cm, d.21cm
Circ.157-1959. Source: Primavera, London (solo exhibition, 1959, no.41), £8.8s.
Illustrated in Birks (1967), pl.81, where Arbeid comments: 'I remember it looked beautiful with cornflowers in it, but I wish I had it back now, in a plastic state, to alter that terrible rim.'

6 'Tall white bottle', 1961 (pl.47)
Stoneware, grey-white matt glaze; marks: 'Arbeid', painted; h.42cm, d.7.2cm
Circ.297-1961. Source: Bristol Guild of Applied Art (solo exhibition, 1961, no.34), £10.10s.
Illustrated in Birks (1967), pl.80; Casson (1967), pl.2; and Crafts Council (1995b), p.23.

7 Large pot, 1968
Stoneware, slab- and coil-built, thick pitted grey-green ash glaze; h.38.4cm, d.38.5cm
Circ.837-1968. Source: the artist, £45 (acquired for the V&A travelling exhibition *Five Studio Potters*, beginning 1969)

8 Pot, 1968
Stoneware, coil-built, thick pitted grey-green ash glaze; marks: 'DA', impressed; h.33.9cm, d.19.5cm
Circ.836-1968. Source: *see* 7, £25

9 Bowl, 1968
Stoneware, coil-built, thick pitted grey ash glaze; marks: 'DA', impressed; h.10cm, d.23.6cm
Circ.838-1968. Source: *see* 7, £15

10 'Pin pot', 1968
Stoneware, handbuilt, thick pitted grey ash glaze; marks: 'DA', impressed; h.35.2cm, d.8.5cm
Circ.839-1968. Source: *see* 7, £12
So-called because the pot was initially formed around a rolling pin.

11 'Pin pot', 1968
Stoneware, handbuilt, thick pitted grey ash glaze; marks: 'DA' in a circular monogram, impressed; h.32.4cm, d.7.4cm
Circ.840-1968. Source: *see* 7, £12

12 'Pin pot', 1968
Stoneware, handbuilt, thick pitted grey ash glaze; marks: 'DA', impressed; h.33.3cm, d.8.2cm
Circ.841-1968. Source: *see* 7, £12

13 'Pin pot', 1968
Stoneware, handbuilt, thick pitted grey ash glaze; marks: 'DA', impressed; h.25.6cm, d.8.5cm
Circ.842-1968. Source: *see* 7, £10

Arden Pottery *see* Barbara Cass

Astbury, Paul 1945–

1945	born Cheshire
1960–68	studies at Stoke-on-Trent College of Art
1968–71	studies ceramics at Royal College of Art, London
1968–	successive studios in Shepherd's Bush, London
1972–	teaches part-time at Hornsey College of Art (later Middlesex Polytechnic), London
1978	solo exhibition, *Marked Surfaces*, British Crafts Centre, London
1989–2004	Head of Ceramics, Middlesex University

Paul Astbury has used clay to create sculpture with a strong conceptual basis, exploring themes of fragmentation, transition and obsolescence. Earlier work in stoneware and porcelain made much use of cast and press-moulded forms taken from found objects, as well as modelled elements. Works of the late 1970s reassembled from shards were followed by found, obsolete objects covered with ceramic pieces. In a further series, begun in 1992, Astbury took casts of domestic ceramic objects, maintaining them in a wet clay condition in sealed vitrines.

Paul Astbury, 'Fragmentations', *CR*, 17 (1972)
— statement, in Rothschild (1972)
— *Document: A Body of Raw Clay Sculpture* (London, 1999)
— 'Other States', *CR*, 200 (2003)
Crafts Advisory Committee (1974), pp.9–12
Oxford Gallery (1974)
Ulster Museum (1974)
Crafts Advisory Committee (1976), p.75
Sunderland Arts Centre (1978)
Crafts Council (1980), p.52
Speight (1983), pp.159–60, 191
Crafts Council (1985), pp.24–5
Museum of Modern Art, Oxford (1993), pp.16–17, 80, 93
Emmanuel Cooper, 'Fired Earth: The Art of Paul Astbury', *Ceramics: Art and Perception*, 21 (1995)
London Institute (1998), pp.12–13, 25
Charlotte F. Speight and John Toki, *Hands in Clay* (Mayfield, 1999), pp.166–7
Del Vecchio (2001), pp.179–81, 192
Clark, Strauss and others (2012), pp.284–5, 356–7, 421
Breen (2019)

Exhibition reviews: Emmanuel Cooper, 'Marked Surfaces', *Art & Artists*, 13:3 (1978); William Varley, 'State of Clay', *Crafts*, 35 (1978)

14

15

14 *Wendy House, Dragon and Machine*, 1971
Semi-porcelain, toys and models cast from press-moulds and attached to base, iron oxide and dolomite glaze; marks: 'P.J.A.', impressed, and '71.', incised; h.16.8cm, d.28.4cm
C.146-1993. Source: Christie's, London, £223.50

15 Box: *Untitled*, 1980
Cardboard, stoneware, paper, custom-tinted 'Araldite' adhesive, screws, Sellotape, felt-tip pen, paint; marks: 'P.J.A' and two curvilinear motifs, impressed, and 'Paul Astbury / 1980', in pen; h.27.2cm, d.27cm
C.8-2010. Source: the artist, £6800

Auld, Ian 1926–2000

1926	born Hove, East Sussex
1947–48	studies at Brighton College of Arts and Crafts
1948–51	studies painting and printmaking at Slade School of Fine Art, London
1951–52	teacher training at Institute of Education, University of London, where learns pottery under William Newland (qv); spends six months at Odney Pottery, Berkshire, under John Bew (qv)
1952–54	technical assistant, Central School of Arts and Crafts, London
1954–57	teaches at art school in Baghdad, Iraq; travels in Middle East
1957–	returns to England; establishes studio at Wimbish, Essex, with oil-fired kiln; teaches at Central and Camberwell schools of art
1961–62	exhibition with Bryan Newman (qv) at Primavera, London
1965–74	appointed senior lecturer at Bath Academy of Art in succession to James Tower (qv); later moves to Bristol Polytechnic
1966–74	establishes studio at Grittleton, Wiltshire, shared with Gillian Lowndes (qv)
1970–72	travels with Lowndes to Nigeria to take up research post at Ife University
1974–85	appointed Head of Ceramics at Camberwell School of Art and Crafts; moves to Camberwell, initially dividing time between there and Wiltshire; teaching takes over from making
1977	exhibition with Lowndes at British Crafts Centre, London, his last major show
1988	moves with Lowndes to Toppesfield, Essex
1996	marries Gillian Lowndes

Ian Auld was an important early exponent of handbuilding. His earliest work was of press-moulded, tin-glazed earthenware dishes. After his return from the Middle East, he began working in stoneware and his pots became concerned with form – mostly simple slab-built architectonic shapes with dry glazes and restrained, integrated decoration. A distinguished educationist, Auld presided over the ceramics course at Camberwell during a period of great influence. He also formed an important collection of African sculpture, and from the 1970s ran a shop dealing in this and other artefacts in Camden Passage, Islington, London.

Arts and Crafts Exhibition Society (1954)
Decorative Art (1961/62), (1962/63), (1965/66), (1967/68), (1970/71)
Biographical notes, *Pottery Quarterly*, 8:30 (1963), p.2, pl.2
Birks (1967), pp.45–60, (1976), pp.168–81
Casson (1967), p.5, pls.3–6
Fiona Bird, 'Potting it Together', *The Times* (21 August 1969)
Rose (1970), p.50, pl.80
Potters (1972), (1974), (1975)
Sue Harley, 'Ian Auld and Gillian Lowndes', *CR*, 44 (1977)
Paisley Museum and Art Galleries (1984), pp.12–13
Rosemary Hill, 'Dealer in African Art', *Crafts*, 90 (1988)
Paul Rice, 'Ian Auld', *Studio Pottery*, 6 (1993)
Crafts Council (1995b), pp.24–5
Nottingham City Museums and Galleries (2017), p.15

16

Exhibition reviews: *Pottery Quarterly*, 7:28 (1962), pp.146–7, pls.10–11; Elaine and Emanuel Benson, *Craft Horizons*, 26:6 (1966); J.D.H. Catleugh, *CR*, 29 (1974), and 45 (1977); Lavinia Learmont and Louise Collis, *Art & Artists*, 12:1 (1977)

Obituaries: Emmanuel Cooper, *The Independent* (29 February 2000); David Whiting, *Crafts*, 164 (2000); *The Guardian* (14 March 2000)

16 Bottle, 1959
Stoneware, slab-built, applied decoration, yellow-brown glaze; marks: 'IA' in square monogram, impressed; h.41.8cm, d.12.5cm
Circ.240-1960. Source: the artist, £8

17 Pot, 1965 (pl.52)
Stoneware, slab-built, matt yellow-brown glaze; marks: 'IA' in rectangular seal, impressed; h.33.9cm, d.22cm
Circ.351-1965. Source: Crafts Centre of Great Britain, London, £12.12s.

Aylieff, Felicity 1954–

1954	born Edlesborough, Bedfordshire
1972–78	studies ceramics and textiles at Bath Academy of Art
1981–93	teaches at Goldsmiths' College, London
1989–2001	teaches at Bath Spa University College; awarded Professorship in 2001
1993–96	postgraduate ceramic research at Royal College of Art, London
2000–20	studio in Larkhall, Bath, shared with Takeshi Yasuda (qv)
2001	shortlisted for Jerwood Applied Arts Prize
2001–	teaches at Royal College of Art; awarded Professorship in 2019
2002–03	solo exhibition, *Sense and Perception*, Manchester Art Gallery, and tour
2003	marries Takeshi Yasuda
2006–	begins making work in Jingdezhen, China, on annual residencies
2007–09	solo exhibition, *Out of China*, Canary Wharf, London, and tour
2011–	co-founds Red House Ceramics Studio, Jingdezhen, with Takeshi Yasuda and Baixu Xiong

A central figure in the world of studio ceramics, Felicity Aylieff is a respected educator as well as a maker of great accomplishment, recognized in particular for her development of large-scale works. Her practice has also led trends towards collaborative, international working, which have redefined ideas of how and where 'studio' ceramics might be made. Her work has proceeded in distinct phases, beginning with handbuilt vessels in coloured porcelain with unglazed, polished surfaces. During her period of research at the Royal College of Art, she developed a terrazzo-like clay body, with which she went on to produce a series of large, press-moulded, abstract sculptures. Since 2006 she has worked regularly in China, collaborating with specialist factories on the production of porcelain vases of monumental scale, which she decorates using a range of historically informed techniques.

Felicity Aylieff, 'Larger than Life', *CR*, 165 (1997)
— 'Chinese Whispers', *CR*, 221 (2006)
Potters/The Ceramics Book (1989) to (2012)
Victoria Art Gallery, *Felicity Aylieff: The Elusive Body*, exh. cat. (Bath, 1996)
Loes and Reinier, *Dashed, Speckled, Brushed*, exh. cat. (Deventer, 1998)
Waller (1998), pp.118–21
Scottish Gallery, *Felicity Aylieff: New Work, An Evolution*, exh. cat. (Edinburgh, 2000)
Crafts Council (2001), pp.10–11, 30
Penny Smith, 'Integration of Colour and Form', *Ceramics: Art and Perception*, 46 (2001)
Manchester Art Gallery, *Sense and Perception*, exh. cat. (2002)
Liz Mitchell, 'Significant Space', *CR*, 197 (2002)
Perryman (2004), pp.155–61
Ann Elliott (ed.), *Out of China: Monumental Porcelain: Felicity Aylieff*, exh. cat. (Plumpton Green, 2007)
Tony Birks, 'Felicity Aylieff', *Revue de la Céramique et du Verre*, 158 (2008)
Contemporary Applied Arts, *Felicity Aylieff*, exh. cat. (London, 2009)
Carlano (2010), pp.34–5
Colin Martin, 'Felicity Aylieff at Royal Delft', in *Brandpunt Terra 2011* (Delft, 2011), pp.152–61
Porcelain City – Jingdezhen, exh. cat. (London, 2011)
Corinne Julius, 'Ceramics of Epic Scale', *Craft Arts International*, 91 (2014)
Colin Martin, 'Monumental Vases', *CR*, 269 (2014)
Paul Bailey, 'Someone of Her Time', *Ceramics: Art and Perception*, 108 (2018)
Thormann (2018)

Exhibition reviews: Larry Berryman, *Crafts*, 90 (1988); Jane Norrie, *Crafts*, 98 (1989); Nicki Jarvis, *Studio Pottery*, 24 (1996); John Colbeck, *CR*, 163 (1997); David Whiting, *Crafts*, 180 (2003); Maev Kennedy, *Crafts*, 209 (2007); Robert James Turner, *CR*, 229 (2008)

18 *Oval Rotation*, 1999 (pl.109)
White earthenware with porcelain and glass aggregates, press-moulded; h.60cm, d.100cm
C.3-2000. Source: the artist, £2000; gift of Adrian Sassoon, Esq.
Shown in the exhibition *Felicity Aylieff: New Work, An Evolution*, The Scottish Gallery, Edinburgh, 2000.

19 *Chasing Black*, 2006 (pl.125)
Porcelain, thrown in sections, painted with cobalt and iron oxides; made in Jingdezhen, China; h.193cm, d.67cm
C.127-2009. Source: the artist, £3825; acquired through the generosity of Gerard and Sarah Griffin

20

Made during a residency with the Pottery Workshop Experimental Factory, Jingdezhen, working at Mr Yu's Big Ware Factory. Shown in the exhibition *Out of China: Monumental Porcelain by Felicity Aylieff* at One Canada Square, Canary Wharf, London, 2007, and tour.

20 *Still Life with Books and Bird*, 2012
Porcelain, painted in *fencai* overglaze enamels; marks: 'F. Aylieff / CHINA', inscribed in blue; made in Jingdezhen, China; h.46cm, d.31.1cm
C.76-2013. Source: Adrian Sassoon, £4800; acquired through the generosity of Gerard and Sarah Griffin

---

Bakewell, Sam 1983–

1983	born Yeovil, Somerset
2002–05	studies ceramics at University of Wales Institute, Cardiff
2009–11	studies ceramics at Royal College of Art, London
2014–	joins Studio Manifold, Haggerston, London
2015	wins British Ceramics Biennial AWARD, Stoke-on-Trent
2017	Jerwood Makers Open commission
2018–19	residency, V&A, London
2019|21	solo exhibitions, Corvi-Mora, London

Sam Bakewell makes sculptures that explore clay as both material and metaphor. He identifies clay as chthonic – or associated with the underworld – and implicitly connected with death and creation. Some pieces are worked obsessively – the tiny porcelain hairball, *Of beauty reminiscing*, was carved with a needle over a two-year period – while others are made rapidly and intuitively. Most works are produced within distinct ongoing series.

Sam Bakewell, 'Drying Ceramics', *CR*, 251 (2011)
Cardiff School of Art and Design, *Prospect: Ten Artists in Clay*, exh. cat. (Cardiff, 2006)
Jerwood Visual Arts, *Jerwood Makers Open 2017*, exh. cat. (London, 2017)
Teleri Lloyd-Jones, 'Jerwood Makers Open', exh. review, *Crafts*, 268 (2017)
Bornholm Art Museum, *European Ceramic Context 2018*, exh. cat. (Gudhjem, 2018), p.45
Alison Britton, 'Dark Materials', *V&A Magazine*, 49 (2019)
Imogen Greenhalgh, 'Imaginations at Work', *CR*, 297 (2019)
Meşher (2019), pp.42–62
Jameela Thurloway, 'Artist to watch: Sam Bakewell', Contemporary Art Society, online (30 May 2019)

21 *Imagination Dead Imagine*, 2004–15
11 works, with individual plaster plinths. Dimensions stated refer to works only.
C.70 to 80-2019. Source: the artist, £10,000; acquired through the generosity of Gerard and Sarah Griffin
Made as 'personal talismans' over more than a decade, these works were collectively exhibited as *Imagination Dead Imagine* at the British Ceramics Biennial in 2015, housed in a structure described by Bakewell as a 'pseudo-shaman's mud hut'.

A *Of beauty reminiscing*, 2013–15 (pl.142)
Porcelain; h.2cm, d.4.7cm
C.70:1,2-2019

B *Host*, 2015 (pl.142)
Parian porcelain; h.10cm, d.5.6cm
C.71:1,2-2019

C *Whom do I owe regret?*, 2009–15 (pl.142)
Parian porcelain; h.5.3cm, d.3.4cm
C.72:1,2-2019

D *Here neither*, 2012 (pl.142)
Parian porcelain; h.8.3cm, d.5.2cm
C.73:1,2-2019

E *Thynge*, 2011
Porcelain, glaze; h.18.2cm, d.7.7cm
C.74:1,2-2019

F *as yet undone*, 2010
Parian porcelain; h.45cm, d.3.3cm
C.75:1,2-2019

G *what it is*, 2010
Glass, cork, bird and insect remains; h.4.8cm (bird vial); h.4.5cm (insect vial)
C.76:1 to 3-2019

H *between touch and ethics*, 2010
Parian porcelain; h.9.5cm, d.13.3cm
C.77:1,2-2019

I *untitled (toad)*, 2010
Parian porcelain; h.3.4cm, d.7.5cm
C.78:1,2-2019

J *Cup*, 2009
Porcelain, glaze; h.5.8cm, d.7.9cm
C.79:1,2-2019

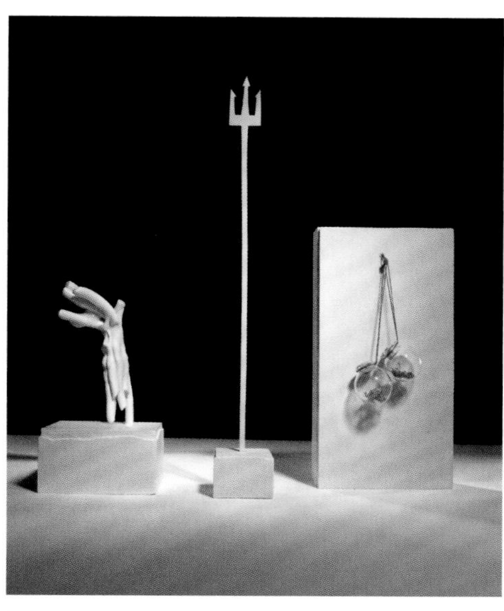

21 E / F / G

21 H / I / J / K

K *Black Sun*, 2004
Porcelain, glaze; d.2.8cm
C.80:1,2-2019

Baldwin, Gordon 1932–

1932	born Lincoln
1949–51	studies painting at Lincoln Art School, introduced to pottery
1951–54	studies ceramics at Central School of Arts and Crafts, London; teaches ceramics part-time at Goldsmiths' College, London, during final year
1954–56	National Service in Royal Artillery
1956–63	resumes teaching part-time at Goldsmiths'
1956–87	technical assistant at Central School for a year, thereafter teaches part-time
1957–96	teaches ceramics at Eton College, Berkshire, lives and maintains a studio there
1958–	marries Nancy Chandler, a painter

1970	solo exhibition, Crafts Centre of Great Britain, London
1972–84	house in Market Drayton, Shropshire
1974	exhibition with Peter Simpson (qv) at British Crafts Centre
1983	retrospective touring exhibition, organized by Cleveland County Museum, Middlesbrough
1986–	new house in Market Drayton
1989	solo exhibition, Contemporary Applied Arts, London; retrospective exhibition, Museum Boijmans Van Beuningen, Rotterdam
1992	awarded OBE
1996–	retires from Eton College; thereafter lives and works full-time in Market Drayton
1999–2013	regular solo exhibitions at Barrett Marsden (later Marsden Woo) Gallery, London
2012	touring retrospective exhibition, York Art Gallery

Gordon Baldwin is among the most significant ceramic sculptors. In common with other pioneers of handbuilt and constructed form, he benefited from the enlightened teaching of the Central School, and himself became an influential teacher there, at Goldsmiths' College and at Eton College. His early work was overtly figurative, showing the influence of contemporary post-war sculpture, but through the 1960s he worked on progressively more abstract forms. He subsequently became increasingly interested in the vessel as a concept, exploring contained space and the relationship between form and painted surface. His influences lie primarily outside the world of ceramics, in landscape, Surrealist art, music, chance and systems.

Gordon Baldwin, statement, in Portsmouth City Museum and Art Gallery (1976), pp.2–3, reproduced in V&A (1977), pp.2–3 and elsewhere
— 'Sculptors in Limbo?', *Crafts*, 33 (1978)
Arts and Crafts Exhibition Society (1957)
Charles S. Spencer, 'The Experimental Work of Gordon Baldwin', *The Painter and Sculptor*, 2:3 (1959)
Birks (1967), pp.61–76, (1976), pp.194–207
Casson (1967), p.5, pls.7–13
V&A (1972), p.105
Crafts Advisory Committee (1974), pp.29–32
Oxford Gallery (1974)
Jeannie Lowe, 'Gordon Baldwin', *CR*, 31 (1975)
Crafts Advisory Committee (1976), p.75
Crafts Council (1980), p.52
Potters (1980), (1983)
Tony Birks, 'Upstart Forms', *Crafts*, 51 (1981)
Cleveland County Museum Service, *Gordon Baldwin: A Retrospective View*, exh. cat., text by John Houston (1983)
Oxfordshire County Museum Services (1984), pp.12–13
Paisley Museum and Art Galleries (1984), pp.13–14
Crafts Council (1985), pp.26–7
Contemporary Applied Arts, *Gordon Baldwin*, exh. pamphlets, text by Alison Britton (London, 1989) and (1993)
Tanya Harrod, 'Sources of Inspiration', *Crafts*, 96 (1989)
Dorris Kuyken-Schneider (ed.), *Gordon Baldwin: Mysterious Volumes*, exh. cat. (Rotterdam, 1989)
Museum of Modern Art, Oxford (1993), pp.18–19, 80–1, 93
Crafts Council (1995b), pp.26–9
— (1996b), pp.12–13
— (1996c), pp.104, 123
Emmanuel Cooper, 'Special Silences', *CR*, 158 (1996)
Annabel Freyberg, 'Art Master', *World of Interiors* (April 1996)
Galerie Besson, *Gordon Baldwin*, exh. pamphlet, text by David Whiting (London, 1996)
Christie's, *The Mrs Liliana L. Epstein Studio Pottery Collection* (London, 27 April 1998), lots 289–330
Scottish Gallery, *Gordon Baldwin*, exh. pamphlet, text by David Whiting (Edinburgh, 1998)
Barrett Marsden Gallery, *Gordon Baldwin*, exh. pamphlet, text by Anne-Carole Chamier (London, 1999)
— *Gordon Baldwin: Sensual Pleasures*, exh. pamphlet, text by Emmanuel Cooper (London, 2001)
Hannah Wingrave, 'Modernist Inspiration', *Ceramics in Society*, 46 (2001)
Alison Britton, 'Gordon Baldwin', exh. essay, Barrett Marsden Gallery (2003)
Ruthin Craft Centre (2004), pp.30–3, 66
Anthony Ray, 'Pottery as Sculpture: The Work of Gordon Baldwin', *English Ceramic Circle Transactions*, 19:1 (2005)
Emmanuel Cooper, 'Pillow Talk', *CR*, 233 (2008)
Whiting (2009), pp.64–9
Carlano (2010), pp.36–7
Clark, Strauss and others (2012), pp.358, 422
David Whiting (ed.), *Gordon Baldwin: Objects for a Landscape* (York, 2012)

Exhibition reviews: 'Potters from the Central School', *Pottery Quarterly*, 1:3 (1954); Audrey Blackman, *CR*, 2 (1970); Tony Hepburn, *CR*, 6 (1970), and *Craft Horizons*, 31:1 (1971); Emmanuel Cooper, *CR*, 22 (1973); David Reeves, *Crafts*, 9 (1974); Richard Wentworth, *Crafts*, 34 (1978); Tanya Harrod, *Crafts*, 123 (1993); Deborah Norton, *Studio Pottery*, 3 (1993); Robert Silver, *Studio Pottery*, 21 (1996); Amanda Fielding, *CR*, 180 (1999); David Whiting, *Crafts*, 174 (2002)

An interview with Gordon Baldwin is in the Crafts Lives sound archive at the British Library, London (C960/38). Essays issued alongside exhibitions at Marsden Woo Gallery, London, offer further useful texts.

22 Cup, saucer and further cup, 1954
Red earthenware, greyish tin glaze, painted in blue or brown; marks: 'Gordon Baldwin / 54', incised (saucer); h.7.6cm (cups), d.16cm (saucer)
C.136:1,2-2013 (illustrated); C.137-2013. Source: Mallams, Oxford, £558
These items date from Baldwin's diploma show at the Central School. Formerly in the collection of Kenneth and Ann Clark.

23 Figure, 1957–58
Earthenware, handbuilt, matt black glaze, metal; marks: 'GB', painted; made at Eton; h.75cm, d.43cm

22

23

24

26

27

28

29

30

C.32-2016. Source: Erskine, Hall & Coe, London, £8000; purchased in memory of Annabel Freyberg through the generosity of her friends

24 *Torso pot*, 1964
Earthenware, handbuilt, incised, decorated with slips and glazes; marks: 'GB', painted; made at Eton; h.57.8cm, d.27cm
C.33-2016. Source: *see* **23**, £5400

25 *Reptilian Black*, 1969–70 (pl.59)
Earthenware, handbuilt, lustrous black glaze; marks: 'GB 69', incised; made at Eton; h.33.5cm, d.48.8cm
Circ.461-1970. Source: Crafts Centre of Great Britain, London (solo exhibition: *Objects from an Inscape*, 1970, no.3), £24.15s.
This piece was started about September 1969 but not completed until July 1970, Baldwin noting: 'For a long time it stood in my studio waiting to be glazed.'

26 *Seascape*, 1969
Earthenware, handbuilt, lustrous black glaze; made at Eton; h.64.3cm (standing form), d.60.3cm (lying form)
Circ.466&A-1970. Source: given by the artist (from solo exhibition: *Objects from an Inscape*, Crafts Centre of Great Britain, London, 1970, no.27)

27 *Larger porcelain bowl on base about painting and sculpture*, 1974
Porcelain, thrown, turned and assembled, blue colouring in a matt white glaze; marks: 'GB 74', painted; made at Eton; h.19.8cm, d.19cm
Circ.486-1974. Source: British Crafts Centre, London (exhibition with Peter Simpson, 1974, no.10), £22.05
One of four pieces so described in the exhibition handlist.

28 *Fragments of painting in the form of a dish*, 1976
Stoneware, press-moulded, pink, blue, yellow and green painting in a white glaze; marks: 'GB 76', painted; h.9.7cm, d.46.5cm
Circ.530-1976. Source: the artist, £25

29 *Extended dish: Seferis Series No. 1*, 1980
Earthenware, press-moulded and slab-built, decorated with slips and pigments; marks: 'GB 80', painted; h.35.9cm, d.40.7cm
C.25-1980. Source: Craftsmen Potters Association, London (exhibition with Nick Homoky, Ruth and Alan Barrett-Danes, and Peter Simpson, 1980, no.24), £250
From a series of pieces inspired by a poem of the Greek poet George Seferis about boats on the Nile.

30 *Avis II*, 1984
Earthenware, handbuilt, mottled blue matt surface; marks: 'GB 3/84', incised; h.58.8cm, d.53.8cm
C.155-1984. Source: British Crafts Centre, London (exhibition: *8 Ceramicists*, 1984, no.4), £775.80

32

33

34

35

31 *Large Round Vessel from an Inscape*, 1988–89 (pl.90)
Earthenware, coil-built, black glaze inside with green patches outside; marks: 'GB 88', incised; h.58.4cm, d.48.4cm
C.40-1989. Source: Contemporary Applied Arts, London (solo exhibition, 1989, no.9), £1620

32 *Dark Rocking Piece*, 1992
Earthenware, handbuilt, painted in matt blue and black with incised lines; marks: '92 / GB', painted; h.72cm, d.53.5cm
C.206-1993. Source: Contemporary Applied Arts, London (solo exhibition, 1993), £2070

33 *Venus Love Trap Vessel II*, 2003–04
Earthenware, handbuilt, matt yellow surface; marks: 'GB / 2003' in a circle, incised, and '03/04', handwritten label; made at Market Drayton; h.32cm, d.52.5cm
C.81-2005. Source: Barrett Marsden Gallery, London; given by the artist

34 *Vessel from a Quartet II*, 2004–05
Earthenware, handbuilt, matt white surface, abraded and incised; marks: 'GB / 2004' in a circle, incised, and '20/05', handwritten label; made at Market Drayton; h.50cm, d.50.5cm
C.82-2005. Source: Barrett Marsden Gallery, London (solo exhibition: *Gordon Baldwin: Vessels and Drawings*, 2005); given by the artist

35 *Vessel in the Form of an Ancient Sound I*, 2007
Earthenware, handbuilt, reddish-brown matt surface; marks: 'GB / 2007', incised, and '22/07', handwritten label; h.50cm, d.46cm
C.18-2009. Source: Barrett Marsden Gallery, London (solo exhibition: *Gordon Baldwin: Drawings and Vessels*, 2008), £3118.72; given in memory of Philip McGuinness

Ballantyne, David 1913–1990

1913	born London
1919	family moves to Liverpool
1932–35	studies painting at Liverpool School of Art
1936	teacher training at Institute of Education, University of London, attending classes in ceramics at Central School of Arts and Crafts under Dora Billington (qv)
1946–50	teaches at Bridgnorth Grammar School, Shropshire
1950–78	teaches ceramics at Bournemouth College of Art, retiring as senior lecturer in ceramics and environmental design
c. 1955–67	workshop in Highcliffe, Dorset, producing domestic ware and individual pieces in saltglaze; designs kilns and wheels as SAVIAC Workshops (an acronym for Striving After Values In an Age of Crisis)
1968–	moves to new house and workshop in Highcliffe; abandons saltglaze; works in stoneware, porcelain and other materials

A potter, teacher and designer noted for the breadth of his abilities, David Ballantyne became an early exponent of salt-glazing in the post-war period, making domestic ware and individual pieces. He also designed pottery kilns and wheels. Stimulated by a reorganization at Bournemouth College of Art that brought pottery into a department of Environmental Design, Ballantyne became interested in a wider range of outputs from the 1960s onwards, including door furniture, ceramic lettering and architectural components. This led him to explore materials such as concrete and wood, while continuing to work in porcelain and stoneware.

David Ballantyne, 'Some Techniques Associated with Handbuilt Pottery', *Pottery Quarterly*, 2:6 (1955)
— '1060°C. and All That', *Pottery Quarterly*, 3:9 (1956)
— 'The Anatomy of Kick-wheels', *Pottery Quarterly*, 4:15 (1957)
— 'Non-potting', *Pottery Quarterly*, 8:29 (1963)
— 'Decorative Ventilator Bricks', *CR*, 82 (1983)
— 'Architectural Ceramics', *Artists Newsletter* (September 1984)
Smithsonian Institution (1959)
'Art Teacher Who Cuts Out the Frills', *Bournemouth Times* (13 March 1971)
Dorset Craft Guild, *Retrospect and Prospect*, exh. pamphlet (1988)

Peter Stoodley, 'Renaissance Man of Clay', *CR*, 128 (1991)
— letter, *CR*, 205 (2004)
Pearson (2005), pp.85, 87
Nottingham City Museums and Galleries (2017), pp.16–17

Exhibition reviews: 'Heal's New Designs', *Pottery Quarterly*, 3:10 (1956); Frederick Laws, *Crafts*, 12 (1975); Richard Grasby, *Dorset Craft Guild Newsletter*, 43 (1989); Emmanuel Cooper, *CR*, 204 (2003)

Obituaries: Emmanuel Cooper, *The Independent* (25 July 1990); Peter Stoodley, *CR*, 125 (1990)

36 Pot: *Meteorite*, 1962
Stoneware, coil-built, non-vitreous slip, saltglaze; h.58cm, d.17.4cm
Circ.487-1962. Source: the artist, £21

37 Lidded potpourri jar: *Seabird*, 1962
Stoneware, thrown and assembled, saltglaze; h.12.5cm, d.12.2cm
Circ.488&A-1962. Source: the artist, £3.10s.

36

37

Bam, Ranti 1982–

1982	born Lagos, Nigeria; grows up in London
2006–08	MA Research by Project (Art, Design and Visual Culture), The Cass, London Metropolitan University
2013–15	studies ceramics at City Lit, London
2018	Catinca Tabacaru Gallery/Dzimbanhete Arts Interactions residency, Harare, Zimbabwe
2020–21	residency, Cité Internationale des Arts, Paris

Ranti Bam explores the narrative, metaphorical and haptic possibilities of clay. She is known for her colourful handbuilt vessels, collaged from monoprinted and painted slabs, which in their construction and patterning are reminiscent of fabrics. Bam works between London and Lagos, her socially engaged practice including frequent workshops and international residencies.

Annie Le Santo, 'Curative Clay', *CR*, 305 (2020)
Samantha Manton, 'In Conversation with Ranti Bam', *V&A Blog*, online (12 April 2021)

38 *Itari*, 2019
Terracotta, handbuilt, monoprinted and painted with slips and stains; marks: 'RANTI / BAM / 19', inscribed; h.43cm, d.20cm
C.28-2020. Source: 50 Golborne at Collect 2020, £3000

38

Barford, Barnaby 1977–

1977	born Redhill, Surrey
1997–2000	studies 3D Design at University of Plymouth, Exeter
1999	exchange to ISIA (Istituto Superiore per le Industrie Artistiche), Faenza, Italy
2000–02	studies ceramics at Royal College of Art, London
2004–	teaches at Central Saint Martins, London
2005–	regular solo exhibitions at David Gill Gallery, London
2008	animated film, *Damaged Goods*, commissioned by Animate Projects
2011	solo exhibition, *The Big Win*, Laing Art Gallery, Newcastle upon Tyne
2013	solo exhibition, MOCA Virginia, USA
2015	installation, *The Tower of Babel*, V&A, London
2016	h.Club 100 award in Art, Design & Craft

Barnaby Barford is known for his puckish satire and incisive social commentary. His work exposes human frailties, prejudices and desires, or – increasingly – confronts societal ills driven by insatiable greed, inequality and the loss of community. His earlier pieces grouped reworked found ceramic figurines as witty, satirical tableaux; sculptures and installations developed from the 2010s utilize bespoke ceramic components outsourced from specialist manufacturers. These works typically draw narratives and symbolism from mythology and religion, as in his monumental *Tower of Babel*, and his exploration of the theme of the apple. Barford returns regularly to ceramics, though works across a range of media, including drawing and painting based on repeated words.

Barnaby Barford, *The Tower of Babel*, exh. cat. (London, 2015)
Shipley Art Gallery (2003b), pp.19–20
Emma Maiden, 'Figure it Out', *Crafts*, 201 (2006)
Hanaor (2007), pp.72–5
David Gill Galleries, *Barnaby Barford: Private Lives*, exh. cat. (London, 2008)
— *Damaged Goods*, exh. cat. (London, 2010)
— *Love Is ...*, exh. cat. (London, 2011)
Carlano (2010), pp.38–9
Veiteberg (2011), pp.74–5
Clark, Strauss and others (2012), pp.268–9, 288–9, 358, 418, 422
Garcia (2012), pp.40–1, 158–9
Grant Gibson, 'Original Sin', *Crafts*, 240 (2013)
Becky Sunshine, 'Porcelain Provocateur', *Sunday Times Style Magazine* (17 March 2013)

40

40

40

Virginia Museum of Contemporary Art, *Barnaby Barford*, exh. cat. (Virginia Beach, 2013)
Mark Brown, 'Tower of London', *The Guardian* (9 September 2015)
Andy Christian, 'Tower of Clay', *CR*, 275 (2015)
Dahn (2015), pp.136–40
Marcus Field, 'Let's Talk Shops', *Evening Standard* (3 September 2015)
Clare (2016), pp.118–20
David Gill Gallery, *Barnaby Barford: Me Want Now*, exh. cat. (London, 2016)
— *More More More: Barnaby Barford*, exh. cat. (London, 2019)
Eline De Mont, 'Barnaby Barford', *Imagicasa Art* (2019)
Charlotte Vannier and Véronique Pettit Laforet, *Ceramique: 90 Artistes Contemporains* (Paris, 2019), pp.216–19

Exhibition reviews: Emma Maiden, *Crafts*, 179 (2002); Joanna Howells, *CR*, 199 (2003); Ralph Turner, *CR*, 232 (2008); Helen Moore, *CR*, 251 (2011); Jessica Hemmings, *Crafts*, 234 (2012)

39 *She'll Need More than a Makeover*, 2008 (pl.119)
Found porcelain or earthenware objects, enamel paint, other media; marks: 'BARNABY BARFORD 2008', engraved, and 'OH MY GOD! LOOK AT HER – SHE HASN'T GOT A CHANCE', written in gold (earlier title); h.21.7cm, d.32cm
C.15-2010. Source: David Gill Galleries, £3375; acquired through the generosity of Gerard and Sarah Griffin
Shown in the exhibition *Barnaby Barford: Private Lives*, David Gill Galleries, London, 2008.

40 Twenty-two shops from *The Tower of Babel*, 2015 (*see also* fig.17)
Bone china, slip-cast, transfer-printed; made for the artist by 1882 Ltd, Stoke-on-Trent; marks: 'THE TOWER OF BABEL / BARNABY BARFORD|2015 / V&A / DAVID GILL / 1882', printed; each signed by hand: 'B. Barford' and marked with its unique number; h.12cm, d.11cm (nos. 0005, 0022, 0337, 2780), h.12cm, d.6.5cm (nos. 0083, 0377, 0491, 0541, 0656, 2581, 2583, 2629, 2818), h.12.5cm, d.6cm (nos. 0794, 1784, 1822, 2243), h.10.7cm, d.6cm (nos. 0947, 1406, 2457, 2740, 2760)
C.34 to 55-2016. Source: the artist, £6172.92; acquired through the generosity of Gerard and Sarah Griffin
The Tower of Babel was a 6m-high installation made up of 3000 individual bone china buildings, each depicting a London shop photographed by the artist. It represented a hierarchy, with the most exclusive shops at its top. The *Tower* was exhibited at the V&A 8 September – 1 November 2015, during which the shops were individually retailed at prices that reflected the status of the premises depicted, ranging from £95 for a derelict shop to £6000 for a fine art gallery.

Barrett-Danes, Alan 1935–2004 and **Ruth** (née **Long**) 1940–

Alan

1935	born Rainham, Kent
1950–54	studies ceramics at Maidstone College of Art
1956–57	studies ceramics at Stoke-on-Trent College of Art
1957–60	staff designer for Crown Clarence, Stoke-on-Trent
1960–61	teaches at Nuneaton School of Art
1962–67	teaches at Slough College of Further Education
1967–91	teaches ceramics at Cardiff College of Art

Ruth

1940	born Plymouth, Devon
1956–60	studies ceramics and illustration at Plymouth College of Art
1960–61	trains as art teacher at Brighton College of Arts and Crafts
1961–68	various teaching posts and design work
1969–94	teaches practical media in School of Occupational Therapy, University of Wales College of Medicine
1962	Ruth and Alan marry
1968–	together establish workshop near Cardiff, Ruth assisting Alan in production of domestic ware
1974–	move to Abergavenny, Monmouthshire, establish workshop
1982–	Ruth establishes own studio at Abergavenny
2006–	Ruth moves to Liss, Hampshire

Alan Barrett-Danes came from a line of Kent potters working at Hoo and Upchurch. Rather than join the family workshop, he went to art college and for a period worked in the ceramics industry before establishing his own studio. He also became an inspirational teacher. From about 1974 he worked in collaboration with his wife, Ruth, creating part-figurative sculptural pieces. Alan was responsible for the basic form and technical aspects; Ruth modelled the human and animal figures, and developed ideas and narratives. These drew on fantasy literature as well as her experience of working within mental health settings. Working independently from 1982, Ruth continued to model figures, while Alan returned to individual wheel-made vessels. Since Alan's death, Ruth has returned to her first love, printmaking.

Earlier accounts of Alan and Ruth Barrett-Danes' practice give limited recognition of Ruth's contribution.

Alan and Ruth Barrett-Danes, interview, in Cameron and Lewis (1976), pp.8–17, 165
Ruth Barrett-Danes, 'A Continuing Tradition', *CR*, 210 (2004)
V&A (1972), p.105
Oxford Gallery (1974)
Tony Birks, 'Alan Barrett-Danes – Narrative Potter', *CR*, 36 (1975)
Birks (1976), pp.146–55
Crafts Advisory Committee (1976), p.76
Portsmouth City Museum and Art Gallery (1976), pp.3–4
Sunderland Arts Centre (1978)
Crafts Council (1980), p.52
Lane (1980), pp.53, 117–19
Potters (1980) to (1989)
Lane (1983), pp.124–6
Malcolm Cook, 'Ruth Barrett-Danes – Ambiguities of Identity', *CR*, 113 (1988)
Bergesen (1993)
Vincentelli (2000), pp.154–5
Jeffrey Jones, obituary, *Interpreting Ceramics*, ejournal, 6 (2005)
Llantarnam Grange Arts Centre, *Barrett-Danes: A Continuing Tradition* (Cwmbran, 2009)

Exhibition reviews: Craig Raine, *Crafts*, 30 (1978); Janet Hamer, *CR*, 239 (2009)

41 *Fungi Form with Frogs*, 1975 (pl.62)
Porcelain, thrown (fungus forms) and modelled, sprayed slips, lustres; h.20.1cm, d.30.8cm
C.20-2020. Source: given by Ruth Barrett-Danes
Illustrated in Birks (1976), pl.151.

42 *Cabbage Kingdom*, 1974–76
Porcelain, moulded and modelled, lustre; h.14cm, d.23.5cm
C.21-2020. Source: *see* **41**

43 *Armchair Struggles*, 1978–79
Porcelain, moulded and modelled, sprayed slip; h.15cm, d.21.2cm
C.22-2020. Source: *see* **41**

44 *Anthropomorphic Frog Pot*, 1980
Porcelain, thrown and modelled, body stains, lustre; h.9cm, d.10.5cm
C.24&A-1980. Source: Craftsmen Potters Association, London (exhibition with Nick Homoky, Gordon Baldwin and Peter Simpson, 1980, no.10), £140

Items **45** and **46** were made by Ruth Barrett-Danes alone.

45 *Sacrificial Sheep*, 1988
Porcelain, coil-built and modelled, body stains, terra sigillata and vitreous slip; marks: 'RBD', incised; h.16.2cm, d.19.1cm
C.14-1989. Source: Contemporary Applied Arts, London, £561.60

46 *Fish out of Water*, 1997–98
Porcelain, coil-built and modelled, body stains, vitreous slip; marks: 'RBD', incised; h.21.5cm, d.18cm
C.23-2020. Source: given by Ruth Barrett-Danes

42

43

44

45

46

Barron, Paul 1917–1983

1917 born Wantage, Berkshire; grows up in Brighton, Sussex
1937–39 studies pottery at Brighton School of Art, under Norah Braden (qv)
1940–46 war service
1946–49 studies ceramics at Royal College of Art, London, under Helen Pincombe (qv)
1949–54 studio at Runwick House, Hampshire
1949–82 teaches at Farnham School of Art (later West Surrey College of Art and Design) with Henry Hammond (qv)
1954–83 studio at Bentley, Hampshire, shared with Henry Hammond

Paul Barron, a colleague and friend of Henry Hammond (qv), is best remembered for his role as a teacher at Farnham. He worked mainly in reduced stoneware, making individual pieces or working in short series. Barron developed a deep knowledge of ash glazes, learnt from Katharine Pleydell-Bouverie (qv).

Paul Barron, 'A Glaze Spectrum using Wood Ash', *Pottery Quarterly*, 10:38 (1971)
— 'Glazes', *CR*, 20 & 21 (1973)
Arts and Crafts Exhibition Society (1950) to (1957)
Dartington Hall (1952)
Wingfield Digby (1952), p.82, pl.58
Rose (1955), p.23, pl.67, (1970), p.44, pl.69
Lewis (1956), pls.339–40
Illustration, *Pottery Quarterly*, 6:23 (1959), pl.9
Casson (1967), p.5, pls.73–7
Potters (1972) to (1983)
Crafts Advisory Committee (1976), p.76
Crafts Council (1980), p.53
Paisley Museum and Art Galleries (1984), p.16

Obituaries: Sebastian Blackie, *Crafts*, 67 (1984); Henry Hammond, *CR*, 85 (1984)

47 Jug, 1950
Earthenware, wiped decoration in white over dark slips; marks: 'B', in a square, impressed; h.31.7cm, d.20.4cm
Circ.277-1950. Source: Arts and Crafts Exhibition Society (Twenty-second Exhibition, V&A, 1950, no.191), £3.13s.6d.

48 Jug, 1950
Earthenware, wiped decoration in dark over white slips; marks: 'B', in a square, impressed; h.28cm, d.15.3cm
Circ.276-1950. Source: *see* 47 (no.185), £2.12s.6d.

48 / 47

49

49 Pot, *c.* 1965
Stoneware, incised decoration, bluish glaze; h.28cm, d.28cm
C.37-1989. Source: bequest of Kathleen Stickland

Barry, Val (née **Fox**) 1937–2018

1937 born Barnsley, Yorkshire
1967–70 studies ceramics at Sir John Cass School of Art, London
1970– establishes studio in Crouch End, London
1970–74 teaches pottery at South Lambeth Institute, London
1971– solo exhibition, Gallery 273, Queen Mary College, London; exhibits widely thereafter
1975 wins Gold Medal at International Ceramics Competition, Faenza
1978 visits China on trip organized by Craftsmen Potters Association
1984 receives Crafts Council grant to study bronze techniques; subsequently abandons clay to work in bronze

Val Barry made thrown or handbuilt individual sculptural pieces in stoneware and porcelain. Notably these included flattened slab-built forms based on the sails of Chinese junks or jade blades. Her work in bronze, exhibited under the name Valerie Fox, explored similar forms on a larger scale.

'CPA New Members', *CR*, 31 (1975)
Potters (1975) to (1983)
Crafts Advisory Committee (1976), p.77
Emmanuel Cooper, 'The Pots of Val Barry', *CR*, 57 (1979)
Crafts Council (1980), p.53
Lane (1980)
Windhorse Trust, *Feeling Through Form: Eight Contemporary British Sculptors*, exh. cat. (1986)
Frankel (2000), pp.152–3
Nottingham City Museums and Galleries (2017), p.18
Bearnes Hampton and Littlewood, *20th Century and Contemporary*, sale cat., including works from Val Barry's estate (Exeter, 11 June 2019), lots 120–58

Exhibition reviews: Jonathan Sidney, *CR*, 13 (1972); *The Times* (6 November 1975); Jon Catleugh, *Crafts*, 39 (1979); Emmanuel Cooper, *Art & Artists*, 14:3 (1979)

50 *Sword Form*, 1981
Porcelain, slab-built; marks: 'VaB', impressed; h.23cm, d.14.8cm
C.44-1981. Source: Craftsmen Potters Association, London (exhibition with Peter Meanley, Peter Beard and Dorothy Feibleman, 1981, no.23), £115.20

51 *Abstract Form*, 1981
Stoneware, slab-built; marks: 'VaB', impressed;

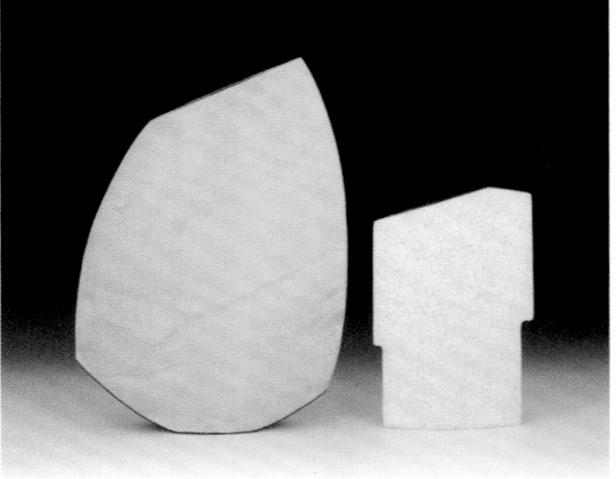

51 / 50

68 / 69

70

Bew, John 1897–1954 *see also* Odney Pottery

1897	born Camberwell, London
c. 1922	studies pottery at Camberwell School of Arts and Crafts, under Alfred Hopkins (qv)
1930–36	workshop at Farleigh, Surrey
1938	works at Leach Pottery, St Ives; with wife, Grace Bew, a weaver, moves to Maes-yr-haf educational settlement, Trealaw, Wales, and establishes pottery, providing employment for six workers; becomes a supplier to the retailer John Lewis Partnership about 1939
1942–	invited by the John Lewis Partnership to establish pottery at Odney, Cookham, Berkshire, to supply products and provide training for people exempt or discharged from service on medical grounds; after conversion of derelict farm in 1943, seven staff taken on
1944–	exhibits regularly with Arts and Crafts Exhibition Society, becoming Craft Member of the Society by 1952
1954	November: dies, apparently suicide by drowning

John Bew was a principled potter who sought fulfilment through the making of functional wares in accordance with his own standards and ideals. Primarily a slipware potter, he ran successful small production potteries while making his own pots. Much of his enterprise was concerned with social rehabilitation.

John Bew, 'Slip Methods at Odney', with biographical notes, *Pottery Quarterly*, 1:1 (1954)
— 'The Nature of the Crafts', letter, *Pottery Quarterly*, 1:2 (1954), pp.44–5
— 'Making and Selling', *Pottery Quarterly*, 1:4 (1954)
British Institute of Industrial Art (1933), p.62
Brygos Gallery (1937a), (1937b)
Arts and Crafts Exhibition Society (1944), (1946), (1950), (1952), (1954)
Obituary, *Pottery Quarterly*, 2:5 (1955), p.35
'John Bew Pots Acquired for the Collection', *Ceramic Archive Bulletin* (*University of Wales, Aberystwyth*), 1 (1997)

An account of the history of Odney Pottery is in the archives of the John Lewis Partnership, John Lewis Partnership Heritage Centre, Cookham.

70 Pot, 1950
Earthenware, dark splash under an amber glaze; marks: 'J', painted, 'ODNEY', impressed; h.23.3cm, d.17.7cm
Circ.335-1955. Source: bequest of the artist
The pot was selected from those held by Grace Bew, following her husband's death.

Billington, Dora M. 1890–1968

1890	born Tunstall, Staffordshire
1907–10	studies at Tunstall School of Art
1910–12	studies at Hanley School of Art; works as a decorator for Bernard Moore
1912–17	studies at Royal College of Art, London, specializing in embroidery and pottery; receives diploma in 1915
1915–	takes over teaching of pottery at Royal College of Art following death of Richard Lunn, father of Dora Lunn (qv), while continuing her studies
1919–55	teaches pottery at Central School of Arts and Crafts, London, becoming Head of Pottery in 1938
1925	ceases teaching at Royal College of Art following appointment of William Staite Murray (qv) as Pottery Instructor by William Rothenstein, Principal of the College
mid-1930s–	maintains small studio at her home in Kingston upon Thames, Surrey
1949–53	President of the Arts and Crafts Exhibition Society

Dora Billington played an important part in the development of studio pottery in Britain, primarily through her role as a teacher. Born into a family of pottery workers, she had a knowledge of industrial production and worked for a time as a pottery decorator. However, it was her appreciation of the aesthetic potential of ceramics in the developing context of studio practice that would have the greater impact. In this she was non-partisan, recognizing the importance of throwing, but championing a range of styles and approaches beyond the dominant Anglo-Asian stoneware aesthetic. Under Billington and her colleague Gilbert Harding Green, teaching at the Central School became a progressive force in the post-war era, and she promoted the work of artists such as William Newland (qv), Margaret Hine (qv), James Tower (qv) and Nicholas Vergette (qv), who embraced a contemporary spirit. Her own work was highly varied, ranging from thrown stoneware to decoration for factory-made tableware.

Dora Billington, *The Art of the Potter* (London, New York and Toronto, 1937)
— 'The Younger English Potters', *The Studio*, 145:720 (1953)
— 'The Arts and Crafts Exhibition Society', with biographical notes, *Pottery Quarterly*, 1:3 (1954)
— 'The New Look in British Pottery', *The Studio*, 149:742 (1955)
— book review of 'Artist-Potters in England', *The Studio*, 150:750 (1955)
— *The Technique of Pottery* (London, 1962)
British Institute of Industrial Art (1922), (1927), (1929)
Decorative Art (1926), (1929)
Arts and Crafts Exhibition Society (1928) to (1952)
British Council (1942)
John Farleigh, *The Creative Craftsman* (London, 1950), pp.187–95
Wingfield Digby (1952), p.80, pl.53
Julian Stair, 'Dora Billington', *Crafts*, 154 (1998)
Alison Britton, 'Central Ceramics: Dora Billington and Gilbert Harding Green', in Backemeyer (2000), pp.82–90
Marshall Colman, 'Dora Billington: From Arts and Crafts to Studio Pottery', *Interpreting Ceramics*, ejournal, 16 (2015)

Obituaries: *The Times* (14 August 1968); Gilbert Harding Green, *Pottery Quarterly*, 9:35 (1969)

71

72

73

71 Tobacco jar, 1923
Earthenware, tin glaze, painted in blue; marks: 'DMB' in monogram, incised and painted; h.20.8cm, d.12.3cm
C.502&A-1934. Source: British Institute of Industrial Art (given by the artist, 1923)

72 Panel of six tiles, *c.* 1937
Earthenware, pinkish-grey glaze, painted win brown and blue; h.25.4cm, w.38.1cm
C.19-1946. Source: given by the artist

73 Coffee set, 1950
Stoneware, tenmoku glaze; marks: 'DB' in monogram, impressed; h.23.2cm, d.13.8cm (coffee pot), h.10.2cm, d.12.7cm (sugar basin and cover), h.7.9cm (each of two cups), d.13.5cm (each of two saucers)
Circ.434&A, 436&A, 437&A, 438&A-1950. Source: Arts and Crafts Exhibition Society (Twenty-second Exhibition, V&A, 1950), £8.8s. William Newland (qv) suggested that he may have made this coffee set to Billington's design when he trained under her at the Central School of Arts and Crafts. The set includes an identical second coffee pot (Circ.435&A-1950).

The museum also holds a Bernard Moore 'rouge flambé' vase decorated by Billington (C.177-1984) and a number of pieces of factory-made tableware with her hand-painted designs (C.503 to 505-1934 and Circ.341 to 345-1954), not catalogued here.

Blandino, Betty 1927–2011

1927	born London
1957–58	studies painting and ceramics at Goldsmiths' College, London
1961–67	Assistant Director of Upper Gallery, Whitechapel Art Gallery, London; Director from 1963
1967–71	Art Advisor to East Sussex Educational Committee
1971–73	studies art education at Institute of Education, University of London
1973	marries G.O. Jones, Director of National Museum of Wales
1973–78	sets up studio in St Hilary, Vale of Glamorgan
1978–87	studio in St Briavels, Gloucestershire
1988–	studio in Summertown, Oxford
2005	ceases potting

A leading exponent of coiling and pinching techniques, Betty Blandino produced thin-walled, sculptural vessels with decoration that emphasized the surface traces left from the making process.

Betty Blandino, *Coiled Pottery: Traditional and Contemporary Ways* (London, 1984)
— *The Figure in Fired Clay* (London, 2001)
Commonwealth Art Gallery, *Betty Blandino*, exh. pamphlet (London, 1975)
Crafts Advisory Committee (1976), p.80
Oriel, *Betty Blandino, Alistair Crawford*, exh. pamphlet (Cardiff, 1976)
Crafts Council (1980), p.54
Obituary, *The Times* (15 October 2011)

74

Exhibition reviews: Rosemarie Pitts, *Crafts*, 48 (1981); Larry Berryman, *Crafts*, 90 (1988)

74 Pot, 1981
Stoneware, coiled and pinched, painted with oxides under a tin glaze; marks: 'BB' in monogram, impressed; h.35.2cm, d.34.5cm
C.70-2005. Source: given by Dasha Shenkman

Bowen, Clive 1943–

1943	born Cardiff
1959–63	studies painting and etching at Cardiff College of Art
1965–69	apprentice to Michael Leach (qv) at Yelland Pottery, north Devon
1970	works as thrower at Brannam Pottery, north Devon; assists Michael Cardew (qv) at Wenford Bridge at weekends; builds small experimental wood-fired kiln
1971–	establishes pottery at Shebbear, north Devon, in former farm buildings; builds catenary-arch wood-fired kiln
1976	builds large double-chambered wood-fired kiln
2009–	makes first of several visits to Japan, potting at Masaaki Shibata's workshop in Sasayama

Clive Bowen has stood as the foremost maker of wood-fired domestic slipware since the 1970s. He works in response to English slipware traditions – in particular those of north Devon – reinventing them for a contemporary audience. His work has

great vitality and fluency of gesture, notably in the abstract decoration of large individual pieces including platters, jars and tall jugs. Bowen remains committed to the idea of function, wanting his pots to enhance the enjoyment of everyday life and the serving of food.

Clive Bowen, contribution, in York City Art Gallery (1983), see also nos.70–82, pls.20–2 and biography
Potters/The Ceramics Book (1983) to (2012)
David Briers, *Clive Bowen*, Aberystwyth Arts Centre: Ceramic Series 4 (1984)
Stephen Course, 'Clive Bowen – Slip Decorated Earthenware', *CR*, 91 (1985)
Crafts Council (1985), p.31
Wren (1990), pp.68–9
Contemporary Applied Arts, *Clive Bowen*, exh. pamphlet, text by Alison Britton (London, 1991)
Emmanuel Cooper, 'Beginning to Lose Your Tail', *CR*, 131 (1991)
Geraldine Norman, 'Beautiful Pots for Daily Life', *Resurgence*, 165 (1994), reprinted as 'Country Potter', *CR*, 149 (1994)
Crafts Council (1996c), pp.85, 125
Alan Powers, 'Still Small Voice', *Crafts*, 147 (1997)
Eden and Eden (1999), pp.24–8
Galerie Besson, *Clive Bowen*, exh. pamphlet, text by David Whiting (London, 2002)
David Whiting, 'Sources of Inspiration', *Crafts*, 174 (2002)
Paul Vincent, 'Clive Bowen', *Ceramics in Society*, 51 (2003)
Peter Davies, *5 Devon Potters* (London, 2004)
Goldmark Gallery, *Clive Bowen: New Pots*, exh. cat., text by David Whiting (Uppingham, 2006) – see also cats. from 2009, 2014 and 2019
Ruthin Craft Centre (2006), pp.28–31, 75
Whiting (2009), pp.18–23
Carlano (2010), pp.46–7
Ian Howie, 'With Great Pleasure', *CR*, 260 (2013)
Scottish Gallery, *Clive Bowen: The Devon Potter*, exh. pamphlet (Edinburgh, 2017)
Andy Christian, 'Honest Pottery', *CR*, 299 (2019)
Scottish Gallery, *Clive Bowen, Masaaki Shibata: Masters of Slipware: East and West*, exh. cat., texts by Clive Bowen (Edinburgh, 2020)

Exhibition reviews: Eileen Lewenstein, *Crafts*, 114 (1992); Paul Vincent, *Studio Pottery*, 3 (1993); Alison Britton, *CR*, 198 (2002); Jack Doherty, *CR*, 201 (2003); Giles Sutherland, *CR*, 244 (2010)

76 / 77

A recorded interview with Clive Bowen is in the Potters of the Bernard Leach Legacy collection at the British Library, London (C1330/04). A documentary film, *Clive Bowen: Born, Not Made*, was made by Goldmark and released on DVD in 2014.

75 Dish, 1982 (pl.77)
Earthenware, slip-trailed in white on black; marks: 'CB' in a circle, impressed; h.7.3cm, d.55cm
C.68-1984. Source: given by the Friends of the V&A (purchased at the Craftsmen Potters Association exhibition, *Studio Ceramics Today*, V&A, 1983, no.16, £80.50)

76 Jug, 1988
Earthenware, slip-trailed in black on white; h.28.2cm, d.18.9cm
C.7-1989. Source: Contemporary Applied Arts, London, £48.60

77 Lidded 'store jar', 1991
Earthenware, wiped decoration through white slip and slip-trailed in green; h.34.1cm, d.26.4cm
C.232:1,2-1991. Source: Contemporary Applied Arts, London (solo exhibition, 1991), £108

Braden, Norah (D.K.N.) 1901–2001

1901	born Margate, Kent
1918–20	studies at Central School of Arts and Crafts, London
1921–23	studies painting at Royal College of Art, London
1923–25	post-diploma studies in pottery at Royal College of Art, under Dora Billington (qv)
1925–27	joins Leach Pottery, St Ives, as secretary and pupil
1927–	moves with parents to West Hoathly, Sussex
1928–36	works with Katharine Pleydell-Bouverie (qv) at Coleshill, Berkshire, for part of each year
1930|32	joint exhibitions with Pleydell-Bouverie at Paterson's Gallery, London
1936–	returns to Sussex to care for mother; virtually ceases to pot; teaches at Brighton School of Art until 1949
1945–66	teaches part-time at Bishop Otter College, Chichester
1950–55	teaches part-time at Camberwell School of Arts and Crafts
1966–67	teaches full-time at Chichester Technical College

Norah Braden was a potter of great ability, considered by Bernard Leach (qv) as the most sensitive of all his students. For nine years she worked alongside Katharine Pleydell-Bouverie at Coleshill, producing reduction-fired stoneware and experimenting with wood-ash glazes. The work of both is markedly similar, yet Ernest Marsh observed Braden's to be the 'more virile' in shape and decoration. She was later obliged by personal circumstances to turn to teaching, and all but ceased making after Coleshill. Self-effacing, she was largely omitted from George Wingfield Digby's *The Work of the Modern Potter in England* (1952) – the first detailed survey of studio pottery – at her own insistence.

British Institute of Industrial Art (1927), (1929), (1933), pp.80–1
Arts and Crafts Exhibition Society (1928), (1931), (1938)
Colnaghi (1928), (1929)
Decorative Art (1929), (1930)
Paterson's Gallery, *Stoneware by D.K.N. Braden and K. Pleydell-Bouverie*, exh. cat. (London, 1930)
W.A. Thorpe, 'English Stoneware Pottery by Miss K. Pleydell-Bouverie and Miss D.K.N. Braden', *Artwork*, 6:24 (1930)
Paterson's Gallery, *Stoneware by K. Pleydell-Bouverie and D.K.N. Braden*, exh. cat. (London, 1932)
Zwemmer (1933)
Brygos Gallery (1936)
V&A (1936), pls.39–40, 46, 49
British Council (1942)
Ernest Marsh, 'Studio Potters of Coleshill, Wilts', *Apollo*, 38 (December 1943)
Cooper (1947), p.*i*, pls.1–2
Wingfield Digby (1952), pp.*x*, 37, 78–9
Rose (1955), p.19, pls.52–5, (1970), pp.36–7, pls.56–9
Leach (1978), p.155
Isabelle Anscombe, *A Woman's Touch* (London, 1984), pp.160, 163–5
Paisley Museum and Art Galleries (1984), p.18
Vincentelli and Hale (1986)
Cardew (1988), see esp. pp.53–4
Birks and Wingfield Digby (1990), pp.153–5

Riddick (1990), p.28
Gaze (1997), pp.310–11
Vincentelli (2000), pp.143–7
Cooper (2003), pp.161–2
Emmanuel Cooper, biography, in *Oxford Dictionary of National Biography* (Oxford, 2009)
Harrod (2012), pp.93–4
Nottingham City Museums and Galleries (2017), p.22

Exhibition reviews: *The Times*, 'Stoneware Pottery' (22 May 1930), 'Stoneware Pottery' (23 May 1932), 'Pots for Bulbs' (30 September 1933)

Obituaries: Adrian Lewis-Evans, *CR*, 189 (2001); Paul Rice, *Crafts*, 170 (2001)

The papers of Norah Braden are at the Crafts Study Centre, Farnham (NBR).

78 Bowl, 1925–27
Stoneware, greyish ash glaze; marks: 'NB' and 'SI' in monogram, impressed; made at Leach Pottery, St Ives; h.5.3cm, d.9cm
C.59-1973. Source: given by Dr Mildred Creak and Mrs Falchikov

79 Jar, 1929 (pl.19)
Stoneware, mottled green-brown ash glaze, painted in green; marks: 'NB' in monogram, painted; h.17.5cm, d.15.6cm
C.959-1935. Source: given by the Pottery and Crafts Fund of the Contemporary Art Society (purchased from The Little Gallery, London, 1929)
A paper label gives the price, £2.2s. A stoneware bowl by Braden (C.961-1935), acquired from the same source, was destroyed during air raids in 1940–41 while on loan to Sheffield College of Arts and Crafts.

80 Pot, 1929 (pl.19)
Stoneware, ash glaze, green-grey streaked with rust; marks: 'NB' in monogram, painted; h.14.8cm, d.12.7cm
C.960-1935. Source: *see* 79

81 Covered pot, 1931
Stoneware, grey-green ash glaze, painted in brown; marks: 'NB' in monogram and '[?]. XLIV.', painted; h.7.5cm, d.11cm
Circ.765&A-1931. Source: the artist (shown at the Fifteenth Exhibition of the Arts and Crafts Exhibition Society, Royal Academy, London, 1931, no.364a), 15s.

82 Jar, *c.* 1933–34
Stoneware, ribbed, dark grey-green box-ash glaze with rust splashes; marks: 'NB' in monogram, painted; h.20.4cm, d.19.3cm
C.31-1943. Source: given by the Pottery and Crafts Fund of the Contemporary Art Society (purchased from Artificers' Guild, London, 1935, £2.2s.)
Illustrated in Rose (1955), pl.55. The pot bears Contemporary Art Society paper labels inscribed: 'C.A.S.', '148' and 'Norah Braden'.

83 Pot, 1935
Stoneware, unglazed, painted in brown, with ash flashing; marks: 'NB' in monogram, impressed; h.19.8cm, d.20cm
Circ.333-1935. Source: The Little Gallery, London, £3.3s.

84 Chocolate jar, *c.* 1936–37
Stoneware, unglazed, painted in brown on a speckled body; marks: 'MADE BY / N. BRADEN / FOR / BENDICKS KENSINGTON', painted; h.19.3cm, d.16.2cm
C.247&A-1976. Source: Sotheby's Belgravia, £77
One of a series of jars commissioned from Braden by London chocolatiers Bendick's to fit their standard boxes, and offered as an 'aide to hospitality', with options for weekly refills.

81 / 78

83

82

84

85

85 Bowl, 1938
Stoneware, grey-green pearwood-ash glaze with iron splashes; marks: '97', incised; h.14.8cm, d.23.4cm
Circ.304-1938. Source: Arts and Crafts Exhibition Society (*Fiftieth Anniversary Exhibition*, Royal Academy, London, 1938), £7.7s. Illustrated in Rose (1955), pl.52.

Britton, Alison 1948–

1948	born Harrow, Middlesex
1966–67	foundation studies at Leeds College of Art
1967–70	studies ceramics at Central School of Art and Design, London
1970–73	studies ceramics at Royal College of Art, London
1973–75	shares studio with Carol McNicoll (qv) at 401½ Workshops, London; works mostly on commissions for tiles
1975–86	studio at King's Cross, London, shared with Jacqueline Poncelet (qv) until 1977, then Prue Venables
1976	first solo exhibition, Amalgam, London
1979	solo exhibition, Crafts Council, London
1981	selector for Crafts Council exhibition, *The Maker's Eye*
1984–2018	teaches at Royal College of Art; Research Coordinator, 2005–15
1986–	studio in Stamford Hill, London, shared first with Prue Venables, later Bryan Illsley (qv)
1990	touring retrospective exhibition organized by Aberystwyth Arts Centre, concluding at Museum Boijmans Van Beuningen, Rotterdam; made Fellow of Royal College of Art; awarded OBE
1998–2018	gallery artist with regular exhibitions, Barrett Marsden (later Marsden Woo) Gallery, London
2001	shortlisted for Jerwood Applied Arts Prize
2014–	Chair of Trustees, Crafts Study Centre, Farnham, Surrey
2016	retrospective exhibition, *Content and Form*, V&A, London; gives Peter Dormer Lecture, Royal College of Art
2017	Woman's Hour Craft Prize finalist
2018–	gallery artist, Corvi-Mora, London (first solo exhibition, 2020)
2019	awarded Honorary Doctorate, Royal College of Art

One of the leading ceramic artists of her generation, Alison Britton rose to prominence as part of the group of women potters trained at the Royal College of Art – including Jacqueline Poncelet (qv), Carol McNicoll (qv) and Elizabeth Fritsch (qv) – who formed the core of the 'New Ceramics' movement. Sculptural and painterly, Britton's ceramics took function and ornamentation as subjects to explore rather than qualities to necessarily exhibit directly, an approach that shifted the agenda for craft practice. Her pots are marked by ambiguity and contradiction, sitting between the sculptural and the everyday, between representation and reality. She has consistently explored container forms, manipulating and disrupting the formal elements of jug, jar or bowl in predominantly slab-built pieces. Bold abstract mark-making replaced earlier pictorial decoration during the 1980s, the angular forms of that period themselves giving way to more contoured shapes in the 1990s as part of a complex, ongoing evolution of form and surface. The spontaneity of poured rather than painted slips and glazes became a particular focus of the 2010s.

Britton has also had a distinguished teaching career, and is a prolific and perceptive critical writer on the crafts. An anthology of her writing, *Seeing Things*, was published by Occasional Papers in 2013 (revised 2022).

Alison Britton, essay, in Crafts Council (1981), pp.16–19
— 'Sèvres with Krazy Kat', *Crafts*, 61 (1983)
— 'The Modern Pot', in ICA (1985), pp.11–14
— introduction, in Dormer (1986)
— 'The Manipulation of Skill on the Outer Limit of Function', in Crafts Council (1991), pp.4–9
— 'The Story So Far', *CR*, 129 (1991)
— 'The Urban Potter', in British Council (1991), pp.65–7
— 'Use, Beauty, Ugliness and Irony', in Museum of Modern Art, Oxford (1993), pp.9–12
— 'The Open-minded Eye', *Crafts*, 150 (1998)
— 'The Fiction of Form', *Journal of Modern Craft*, 2:1 (2009)
— *Seeing Things* (2013), revised (2022)
— 'Past and Present', *Crafts*, 259 (2016)
Marigold Coleman, 'Public and Private', *Crafts*, 21 (1976)
Crafts Advisory Committee (1976), p.81
Crafts Council, *The Work of Alison Britton*, exh. cat. (London, 1979)
Elizabeth Fritsch, 'Juggling into Jugs', *Crafts*, 41 (1979)
Houston (1979), pp.46–51
John Russell Taylor, 'Playing with Clay', *CR*, 60 (1979)
Crafts Council (1980), p.54
Oxfordshire County Museum Services (1984), pp.16–25
Paisley Museum and Art Galleries (1984), p.19
Crafts Council (1985), pp.32–3
Peter Dormer, *Alison Britton in Studio* (London, 1985)
ICA (1985), p.43
Contemporary Applied Arts, *Alison Britton*, exh. pamphlet, text by Oliver Watson (London, 1987)
Angus Suttie, 'Alison Britton', *CR*, 107 (1987)
Aberystwyth Arts Centre, *Alison Britton: A Retrospective*, exh. cat. (1990)
Contemporary Applied Arts, *Alison Britton*, exh. pamphlet, text by Tanya Harrod (London, 1990)
Tanya Harrod, *Alison Britton: Ceramics in Studio* (London, 1990)
Houston (1991)
Victor Margrie, 'Alison Britton', *Studio Pottery*, 4 (1993)
Museum of Modern Art, Oxford (1993), pp.22–3, 81–2, 93
Oliver Watson, 'Alison Britton: Artiste et Potière', *Revue de la Céramique et du Verre*, 82 (1995)
Crafts Council (1996c), pp.106, 125–6
Barrett Marsden Gallery, *Alison Britton: Poetry and Prose*, exh. pamphlet, text by Thimo te Duits (London, 1998)
Edmund de Waal, 'Thinking Aloud', *CR*, 173 (1998)
Edward Lucie-Smith, 'Sources of Inspiration', *Crafts*, 167 (2000)
Linda Sandino, *Complexity and Ambiguity: The Ceramics of Alison Britton* (London, 2000)
Crafts Council (2001), pp.12–13, 30
Barrett Marsden Gallery, *The Ed Wolf Collection of Alison Britton Pots* (London, 2005)
Carlano (2010), pp.48–9
Clark, Strauss and others (2012), pp.360, 424
Crafts Study Centre, *Life and Still Life*, exh. cat. (Farnham, 2012)
Teleri Lloyd-Jones, 'Pouring and Pairing', *Crafts*, 235 (2012)
'Woman's Hour Craft Prize', supplement, *Crafts*, 268 (2017)
Thorpe (2021), pp.27–38

Exhibition reviews: Emmanuel Cooper, *Art & Artists*, 14:9 (1980); William Packer, *Crafts*, 105 (1990); Griselda Gilroy, *Crafts*, 115 (1992); Oliver Watson, *CR*, 153 (1995), and 202 (2003); Edward Lucie-Smith, *Crafts*, 154 (1998); David Whiting, *Crafts*, 169 (2001); Shane Enright, *Crafts*, 197 (2005); Amanda Game, *CR*, 255 (2012); Tim Andrews, *Ceramics: Art and Perception*, 91 (2013); Emma Crichton-Miller, *Crafts*, 259 (2016); Charlotte Dew, *CR*, 279 (2016); Sebastian Blackie, *Ceramics: Art and Perception*, 106 (2017)

86

90

91

92

93

94

Essays issued alongside exhibitions at Marsden Woo Gallery, London, offer further useful texts.

86 *Rabbit Jug*, 1976
High-fired earthenware, slab- and coil-built, painted and sprayed underglaze pigments and crayon under a clear matt glaze; marks: 'Alison / Britton', incised; h.23.2cm, d.43.7cm
C.347-2018. Source: Oxford Ceramics Gallery, £1400; acquired through the generosity of Gerard and Sarah Griffin
Shown in solo exhibition, Amalgam, London, 1976.

87 *Flat-backed Jug with Stork*, 1978 (fig.2)
High-fired earthenware, slab-built, painted underglaze pigments and crayon under a clear matt glaze; marks: 'Alison Britton 78', incised; h.24.5cm, d.21.4cm
C.99-1979. Source: the artist, £80
Shown with **88** in the exhibition *Jugs and Aprons* (joint with Stephanie Bergman), Aberdeen Art Gallery, 1979.

88 *Flat-backed Jug with Stork, red version*, 1978 (fig.2)
High-fired earthenware, slab-built, painted and sprayed underglaze pigments and crayon under a clear matt glaze; marks: 'Alison Britton 78', incised; h.27.5cm, d.28.3cm
C.100-1979. Source: *see* **87**, £90

89 *Yellow Triangles*, 1981 (pl.71)
High-fired earthenware, slab-built, painted with slips and underglaze pigments under a clear matt glaze; marks: 'Alison Britton 1981', incised; h.27.8cm, d.21.5cm
C.87-1981. Source: Prescote Gallery, Cropredy (solo exhibition, 1981, no.5), £315

90 *Green Circle, Green Square*, 1983
High-fired earthenware, slab- and coil-built, painted with slips and underglaze pigments under a clear matt glaze; marks: 'Alison Britton 83', incised (on both pieces); h.17.5cm (pot), d.37.6cm (dish)
C.322&A-1983. Source: Aspects, London (exhibition with Floris van den Broecke, 1983), £630
Listed in the exhibition handlist as 'Green vessels set'.

91 *Big White Jug*, 1987
High-fired earthenware, slab-built, painted with slips and underglaze pigments under a clear matt glaze; marks: 'Alison Britton 87', incised; h.38.2cm, d.39cm
C.233-1987. Source: Contemporary Applied Arts, London (solo exhibition, 1987, no.10), £882

92 *Leaning Blue and White Pot*, 1987
High-fired earthenware, slab-built, painted with slips and underglaze pigments under a clear matt glaze; marks: 'Alison Britton / 87', incised; h.46.1cm, d.37.5cm

95 / 96 / 97

C.248-2014. Source: gift of Ed Wolf
Shown in solo exhibition, Contemporary Applied Arts, London, 1987.

93 *Double Pot, Brown and White*, 1987
High-fired earthenware, slab-built, painted with slips under a clear matt glaze; marks: 'Alison Britton / 87', incised; h.37.1cm, d.41.4cm
C.249-2014. Source: *see* **92**
Shown in solo exhibition, Contemporary Applied Arts, London, 1987.

94 *High Spouted Pot*, 1988
High-fired earthenware, slab-built, painted with slips and underglaze pigments under a clear matt glaze; marks: 'Alison Britton / 88', painted; h.37.6cm, d.44.7cm
C.250-2014. Source: *see* **92**
Shown in solo exhibition, Crafts Council of NSW, Sydney, Australia, 1988.

95 *Pink Dish*, 1990
High-fired earthenware, slab-built, painted with slips and underglaze pigments under a clear matt glaze; marks: 'Alison Britton 90', incised; h.7.4cm, d.39.7cm
C.251-2014. Source: *see* **92**
Shown in solo exhibition, Contemporary Applied Arts, London, 1990.

96 *Small Brown Jug*, 1990
High-fired earthenware, slab-built, painted with slips and underglaze pigments under a clear matt glaze; marks: 'Alison Britton 90', incised; h.15.7cm, d.30.2cm
C.252-2014. Source: *see* **92**
Shown in solo exhibition, Contemporary Applied Arts, London, 1990.

97 *Blue and White Tilted Pot*, 1990
High-fired earthenware, slab-built, painted with slips and underglaze pigments under a clear matt glaze; marks: 'Alison Britton 90', incised; h.32cm, d.36.5cm
C.253-2014. Source: *see* **92**
Shown in solo exhibition, Aberystwyth Arts Centre, 1990.

98 *White and Brown Pot, Big Spout*, 1990 (pl.94)
High-fired earthenware, slab-built, painted with slips and underglaze pigments under a clear matt glaze; marks: 'Alison Britton 90', incised; h.47.1cm, d.33cm
C.1-1992. Source: Aberystwyth Arts Centre (solo exhibition, 1990), £1800

99 *Yellow Pot*, 1990, repainted and refired 1991
High-fired earthenware, handbuilt, painted with slips and underglaze pigments under a clear matt glaze; marks: 'Alison Britton / 90', incised; h.19.8cm, d.57.5cm
C.254-2014. Source: gift of Ed Wolf

100 *Pot with Handles*, 1994
High-fired earthenware, slab-built, painted with slips and underglaze pigments under a clear matt glaze; marks: 'Alison Britton 94', incised; h.43.3cm, d.32.8cm
C.74-1995. Source: the artist (from solo exhibition: *Form and Fiction*, Galerie für englische Keramik Marianne Heller, Sandhausen, Germany, 1995), £1800

101 *Green and Brown Pot*, 1996; repainted, refired and lid added 1998
High-fired earthenware, handbuilt, painted with slips and underglaze pigments under a clear matt glaze, painted wooden lid; the lid made by Bryan Illsley; marks: 'Alison Britton / 1996', incised; h.51cm (with lid), d.34cm
C.255:1,2-2014. Source: gift of Ed Wolf
Shown in solo exhibition, Barrett Marsden Gallery, London, 1998.

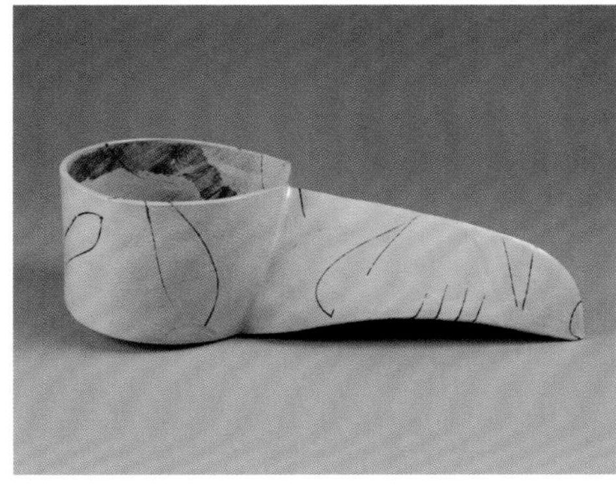

99

100

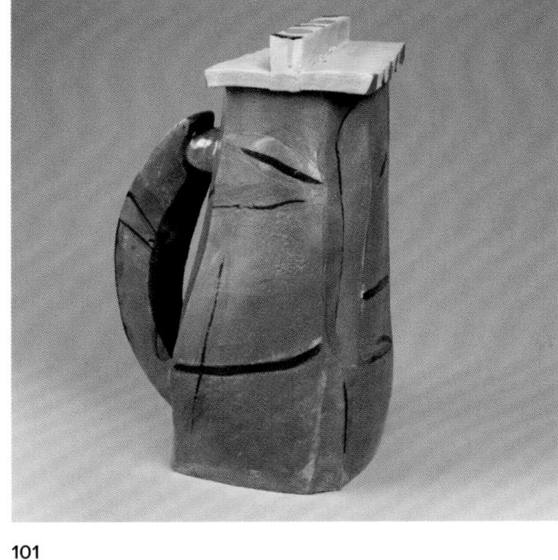

101

102

104

105 / 106

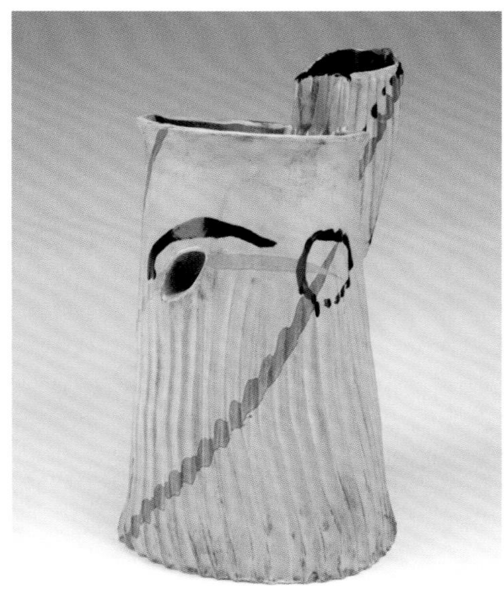

107

102 *Jar with Handles*, 1998
High-fired earthenware, handbuilt, painted with slips and underglaze pigments under a clear matt glaze; marks: 'Alison Britton 98', incised; h.48.3cm, d.38.7cm
C.10-1999. Source: Barrett Marsden Gallery, London (exhibition: *Alison Britton: Poetry and Prose*, 1998), £2340

103 *Container*, 2001 (pl.111)
High-fired earthenware, handbuilt, painted with slips and underglaze pigments under a clear matt glaze; marks: 'Alison Britton / 2001', incised; h.46.9cm, d.33.9cm
C.256-2014. Source: gift of Ed Wolf
Shown in the *Jerwood Applied Arts Prize*, Crafts Council, London, 2001.

104 *Columns and Boxes*, 2006–07
High-fired earthenware, handbuilt, with poured and painted slips and glazes; marks: 'Alison Britton 2006', incised; h.40.1cm, d.42.3cm
C.98-2007. Source: Barrett Marsden Gallery (solo exhibition: *Containing*, 2007); gift of Ed Wolf
From a series that, in Britton's words, 'played with aspects of classical form and gender, and the idea of division, looking at the capital as head and column as body'.

105 *Outpour*, 2012
High-fired red earthenware, handbuilt, with poured and painted slips and glazes; marks: 'Alison Britton / 2012', incised; h.51cm, d.33.5cm
C.132-2013. Source: given by the artist
Shown in solo exhibition, *Standing and Running*, Marsden Woo Gallery, London, 2012.

106 *Ruse*, 2012
High-fired red earthenware, handbuilt, with poured slips and glazes; marks: 'Alison Britton / 2012', inscribed in pencil; h.12.5cm, d.46.5cm
C.27-2016. Source: Marsden Woo Gallery, London, £3706.82; acquired through the generosity of Gerard and Sarah Griffin
Shown in solo exhibition, *Life and Still Life*, Crafts Study Centre, Farnham, 2012.

107 *Outcrop*, 2015
High-fired earthenware, handbuilt, with poured and painted slips and glazes; marks: 'Alison Britton / 2015', incised; h.46.8cm, d.36.8cm
C.28-2016. Source: *see* 106, £4448.18
From a group of new work shown in the retrospective *Alison Britton: Content and Form*, V&A, 2016.

Brown, Christie 1946–

1946	born Shipley, Yorkshire
1966–69	studies arts at Manchester University
1970–75	works as television researcher
1975–77	freelance propmaker; tours with community theatre; begins life-drawing and pottery classes at Sir John Cass School of Art, London
1978–79	domestic-ware thrower at Elephant Pottery, London
1979–	sets up studio at Kingsgate Workshops, London
1980–82	studies ceramics at Harrow College of Higher Education
1988	exhibition with Imogen Margrie at Michaelson and Orient, London
1989–91	moves studio to Hebden Bridge, Yorkshire
1991–	returns to Kingsgate Workshops
1993–2012	teaches ceramics at University of Westminster
1995	solo exhibition, The Scottish Gallery, Edinburgh
1996	shortlisted for Jerwood Prize for Applied Arts
2000	solo exhibition, *Fragments of Narrative*, Wapping Hydraulic Power Station, London
2001–16	Professor of Ceramics, University of Westminster
2012	solo exhibition, *DreamWork*, Freud Museum, London
2015–	moves studio to Neasden, London

Christie Brown is a leading artist working with figural sculptural ceramics, an interest which she developed while studying at Harrow and which followed a short period making domestic ware. Earlier work was of large, flattened, slab-built torsos. She began press-moulding figures during the 1990s, using the process as a way to explore archetypes. In the 2000s Brown became increasingly interested in parallels between archaeology and psychoanalysis, and in exploring human-animal hybrids, her work sometimes responding directly to specific sites and museum collections. She has also played an important role as a teacher and researcher at the University of Westminster.

Christie Brown, 'Figurative Forms', *CR*, 121 (1990)
— 'Assembling a Cast of Characters', *Ceramics: Art and Perception*, 26 (1996)
— 'Clay Bodies', in Stair (2000), pp.154–61
— 'Embodying Transformation', *Interpreting*

Ceramics, ejournal, 8 (2006), repro. in Dahn and Jones (2013), pp.148–59
— 'Anxiety of Endeavour: Personal Recollections of Harrow', in Peters (2012), pp.40–53
— 'Casting About: Re-researching Through Drawing Practice', University of Westminster Ceramics Research Centre – UK, online essay series 14 (2016)
Brown, Stair and Twomey (2016)
'British Figurative Expression', *Ceramics Monthly*, 35:6 (1987)
Lionel Phillips, 'Christie Brown', *Studio Pottery*, 16 (1995)
Scottish Gallery, *Christie Brown: The Cast of Characters*, exh. cat., text by Janice West (London: University of Westminster, 1995)
Crafts Council (1996b), pp.14–15
Ruth Pavey, 'Character Studies', *Crafts*, 142 (1996)
Katie Bevan, 'Under Control', *CR*, 180 (1999)
Christie Brown: Fragments of Narrative, exh. cat. (London, 2000), text by Edmund de Waal repro. in *Ceramics: Art and Perception*, 46 (2001)
Babette Martini, 'Between the Dog and the Wolf', *Interpreting Ceramics*, ejournal, 5 (2004)
Institute of Archaeology, *Christie Brown: Collective Traces: A Response to the Petrie Museum*, exh. cat., text by James Putnam (London, 2006)
Hanaor (2007), pp.106–7
Carlano (2010), pp.52–3
Garcia (2012), pp.42–5, 162–5
Bird (2013), pp.77–8
Liz Farrelly, 'Family, Home and Soane', *Crafts*, 241 (2013)
Arthouse1, *Rara Avis*, exh. leaflet, text by Tessa Peters (London, 2016)
Grant Gibson, 'Animal Instinct', *Crafts*, 259 (2016)
Tessa Peters, 'Narrative Strategies', *New Ceramics*, 1 (2017)
Glen R. Brown, 'Anti-Hierarchical Hybridity', *Ceramics: Art and Perception*, 110 (2018)
Meşher (2019), pp.110–35
Natalie Baerselman le Gros, 'Theatre of Lives', *CR*, 309 (2021)

Exhibition reviews: Emma Maiden, *Crafts*, 166 (2000); Alun Graves, *CR*, 212 (2005); Tony Birks, *Ceramics: Art and Perception*, 84 (2011); Shane Enright, *Crafts*, 240 (2013), and 'Marking the Line', *Crafts*, 242 (2013); Amanda Game, *CR*, 260 (2013); Colin Martin, 'Marking the Line', *Craft Arts International*, 88 (2013)

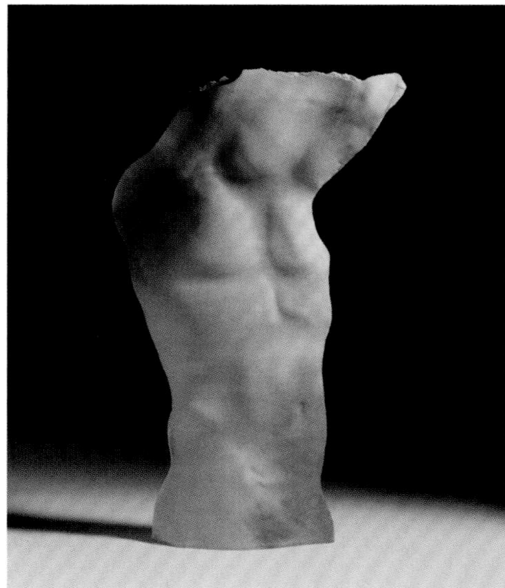

108

109

108 *Red Man Raised Arms*, 1988
Stoneware, slab-built and modelled, painted vitreous slip, smoked; marks: 'CB', incised; h.77.4cm, d.46.3cm
C.3-1989. Source: Michaelson and Orient, London (exhibition with Imogen Margrie, 1988), £472.50

109 Head from the series *The Cast of Characters*, 1995
Stoneware, press-moulded, vitreous slip, rolled in grog; h.16.6cm, d.17.5cm
C.24-1996. Source: gift of Adrian Sassoon, Esq.

110 *Brick Stone Mother* from the series *The Cast of Characters*, 1997 (pl.108)
High-fired earthenware (brick clay), press-moulded, vitreous slip; h.79.8cm, d.33.5cm
C.19-1998. Source: the artist, £1050; gift of Adrian Sassoon, Esq.
According to the artist, this work – one of the *Stone Mother* series from *The Cast of Characters*, made 1995–98 – represents one aspect of the female. The use of moulds in the production of the series refers to ideas about cloning, archetypes and mimesis.

Brown, Paul 1921–2000

1921 born Bournemouth, Dorset; grows up in south-east London
1937 foundation studies at Woolwich Polytechnic
1949–53 studies ceramics at Royal College of Art, London
1954–63 teaches ceramics at Leeds College of Art; develops and exhibits pottery alongside his wife, Yvette Brown
1964– moves to Scotland with Yvette, establishing a hotel and becoming founder members of Balnakeil Craft Village, Sutherland
1975– moves to Aysgarth Falls, North Yorkshire, establishes Yore Mill Craft Centre; returns to active potting from 1977 to about 1986
1998– moves to Ariège, France

Working alongside his wife, Yvette, who turned for a time to potting having previously studied textiles, Paul Brown developed bold, asymmetric handbuilt pots, often thin-necked, with colourful painterly or textured surfaces. Their work was shown with the Craftsmen Potters Association and elsewhere. Brown was known for his forthright opinions and his questioning of the traditions forged by Bernard Leach (qv). Accepting of modern art and technology, if not all aspects of modern life, he wrote in 1962: 'I am happy ... to be living in this 20th century Western Society. I positively like plastics, fast cars and motorways ... but ... I also cherish the threatened values of quietness and privacy, contact with nature, working with natural materials ... and the preservation of those things which are the product of the passage of time ... or the loving hand of men long dead.'

Paul Brown, 'Towards a New Standard', *Pottery Quarterly*, 6:23 (1959), with reply from Bernard Leach, *Pottery Quarterly*, 6:24 (1959)
— letter, *CPA Newsletter*, 10 (1962)
'The Art of the Potter, Wakefield Art Gallery', exh. review, *Pottery Quarterly*, 6:23 (1959), pp.105–6, pl.12
Decorative Art (1961/62), (1962/63), (1963/64)
Michael Casson, 'Ceramics by Paul and Yvette Brown', *Pottery Quarterly*, 8:29 (1963)
Neophyte, comments on a talk by Paul Brown, *CPA Newsletter*, 12 (1964)
Obituary, *CR*, 183 (2000)

111

111 Tall pot: *Noctulid*, 1958
Earthenware, handbuilt, coloured glazes; h.54cm, d.13.8cm
Circ.1-1959. Source: the artist, £18.18s.

Brown, Sandy 1946–

1946	born Tichborne, Hampshire
1968–	arrives in Japan
1970–73	discovers ceramics; trains at Daisei Pottery, Mashiko
1973–75	returns to England with Takeshi Yasuda (qv), who she later marries; establishes studio at Monk Sherborne, Hampshire
1975–81	moves to Meshaw, Devon; shares studio with Yasuda
1981–93	successive studios in South Molton, Devon; separates from Yasuda in 1990
1994–	successive studios in Appledore, Devon

Sandy Brown is an exuberant potter whose bold, gestural decoration in strong colours made a considerable impact on the domestic pottery scene. Alongside functional wares, Brown has developed expressive figural and abstract sculptures, working on an increasingly architectural scale.

Sandy Brown, 'A Potter in Japan', *CR*, 96 (1985)
— 'A Theatre of Colour', *CR*, 99 (1986)
— 'Bold, Wild and Dangerous', *CR*, 116 (1989)
— 'A Potter's Day', *CR*, 124 (1990)
— 'The Grand Opera of Pots and Food', *CR*, 131 (1991)
— 'A Potter's Move', *CR*, 149 (1994)
— 'Wodges, Splodges, Swooshes and Squiggles', *Studio Potter*, 28:1 (1999)
— *Sandy Brown* (Yeovil, 2003)
— 'What If ...', *CR*, 237 (2009)
David Briers, *Sandy Brown*, Aberystwyth Arts Centre: Ceramic Series 16 (1986)
Potters/The Ceramics Book (1986) to (2012)
Tanya Fields, 'Leading Questions: Sandy Brown', *ArtsWest* (June 1987)
Oriel 31, *Sandy Brown: The Complete Picture*, exh. cat. (Welshpool, 1987)
Tony Birks, 'Sandy Brown and Takeshi Yasuda', *Ceramics Monthly*, 40:5 (1992)
Lionel Phillips, 'Sandy Brown: The Sculptures', *Ceramics: Art and Perception*, 30 (1997)
Emmanuel Cooper, 'Sources of Inspiration', *Crafts*, 152 (1998)
Rufford Craft Centre, *The Exhilaration of Life: New Ceramics by Sandy Brown*, exh. cat. (Nottinghamshire, 2000)
Dewar (2002), pp.59–61
Julia Beyer, 'On Fertile Ground', *CR*, 204 (2003)
Ritual: The Still Point and The Dance: Sandy Brown, exh. cat., text by David Whiting (2006)
Simon Olding, 'Symbolic Visions', *CR*, 221 (2006)
David Whiting, 'The Still Point and the Dance', *Ceramics: Art and Perception*, 66 (2007)
Whiting (2009), pp.40–5
Andy Christian, 'Sandy Brown', *Ceramics: Art and Perception*, 87 (2012)
— 'A Sanctuary of Colour', *CR*, 276 (2015)
Dahn (2015), pp.120–2
Simon Olding, 'A Temple for the Self', *Resurgence and Ecologist*, 292 (2015)
Morris (2018), pp.68–73

Exhibition reviews: David Briers, *Crafts*, 89 (1987), and 107 (1990); Gwen Heeney, *Arts Review* (31 July 1987); Patrick Sargent, *Studio Pottery*, 1 (1993); Margot Coatts, *Crafts*, 128 (1994); Lionel Phillips, *Studio Pottery*, 19 (1996); Paul Vincent, *Studio Pottery*, 30 (1997); Tony Birks, *CR*, 171 (1998); Ian Wilson, *Crafts*, 166 (2000)

112 Platter, 1987 (pl.85)
Stoneware, painted in blue, brown and red; h.2.9cm, d.47.9cm
C.60-1988. Source: Contemporary Applied Arts, London, £242.10

Browne, Irene M. 1882–1943

1882	born Islington, London
1900s	studies at Croydon School of Art and Westminster Technical Institute
1906–11	studies modelling at Chelsea Polytechnic, under Charles Hartwell
c. 1911–	studio at Stamford Bridge Studios, Wandon Road, London
1919	studies pottery at Putney School of Art
1920–	makes earthenware figures, fired at Fulham Pottery
1927	purchases own electric kiln

A figure-maker, Irene Browne began working in pottery in 1919, having earlier produced and exhibited plaster and bronze figures and portraits.

British Institute of Industrial Art (1922), (1923), (1929)
Arts and Crafts Exhibition Society (1923)
Royal Academy of Arts (1923)
Guild of Potters (1924)
Vincentelli and Hale (1986)
Vincentelli (2000), pp.239–40
'Miss Irene Mary Browne', *Mapping the Practice and Profession of Sculpture in Britain and Ireland 1851–1951*, University of Glasgow History of Art and HATII, online database (2011)

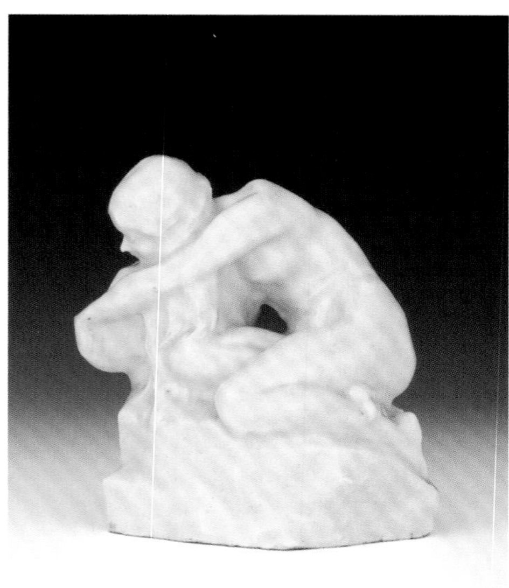

113

113 Figure: *Grief*, 1923
Glazed earthenware; marks: 'I M Browne', incised; h.13cm, d.12cm
C.439-1934. Source: British Institute of Industrial Art (given by the artist)

Brownsword, Neil 1970–

1970	born Stoke-on-Trent
1987–89	trainee modeller and graphic

	designer, Josiah Wedgwood and Sons, Stoke-on-Trent
1990–93	studies ceramics at Cardiff Institute of Higher Education
1993–95	studies ceramics at Royal College of Art, London
1995–2018	teaches ceramics at Buckinghamshire New University, High Wycombe; Professor from 2015
1996	solo exhibition, City Museum and Art Gallery, Stoke-on-Trent
1999	residency at European Ceramic Work Centre (EKWC), 's-Hertogenbosch, Netherlands
1999–2006	practice-based PhD, Brunel University, London
2005	solo exhibition, *Collaging History*, Potteries Museum and Art Gallery, Stoke-on-Trent
2011	wins British Ceramics Biennial AWARD (One-off category), Stoke-on-Trent
2011–	Professor, KHiB / University of Bergen, Norway
2015	Grand Prize at Gyeonggi International Ceramic Biennale, South Korea
2017	Woman's Hour Craft Prize finalist
2017	solo exhibition, *Factory*, Icheon World Ceramic Centre, South Korea
2017–18	residency (with Juree Kim), V&A, London
2019–	Professor, Staffordshire University
2021	solo exhibition, *Alchemy and Metamorphosis*, Potteries Museum and Art Gallery, Stoke-on-Trent

Neil Brownsword's diverse, expansive and highly influential practice uses ceramics, film and performance to explore the industry and heritage of his native Staffordshire, and the impact of globalization. His early work was figurative, moving from autobiographical themes to those based on social observation. These sculptures collaged randomly made elements, thrown, handbuilt or cast from obsolete industrial moulds. This use of collage persisted as Brownsword began making installations that referenced industrial archaeology, incorporating elements salvaged from ceramic manufacturing processes. From the mid-2010s, he has made work in collaboration with former industry artisans, with Brownsword framing and choreographing their practice, emphasizing their skills and the cultural value of embodied knowledge.

Neil Brownsword, 'Action – Reflection: Tracing Personal Developments', *Interpreting Ceramics*, ejournal, 2 (2002)
— 'Nature Needs its Vultures', in Muthesius Kunsthochschule, *Beyond Site*, exh. cat. (Kiel, 2013)
— 'Resurrecting the Obsolete', *CR*, 259 (2013)
— 'Marrying the Hand with the Hi-tech', *Crafts*, 247 (2014)
— 'Obsolescence and Renewal', *PMC Notes*, 17 (2021)
— **(ed.)**, *Topographies of the Obsolete: Rhizomatic Trajectories* (Stoke-on-Trent, 2020)
— *Alchemy and Metamorphosis: Neil Brownsword*, exh. publication, texts by Laura Breen and others (Stoke-on-Trent, 2021)
— **and Anne Helen Mydland (eds)**, *Topographies of the Obsolete: Vociferous Void*, exh. publication (Stoke-on-Trent, 2013)
— *Topographies of the Obsolete: Site Reflections* (Stoke-on-Trent, 2015)
— *Topographies of the Obsolete: Ashmolean Papers* (Stoke-on-Trent, 2017)
City Museum and Art Gallery, *Neil Brownsword: The Fine Line – Revelations in Clay*, exh. pamphlet (Stoke-on-Trent, 1996)
Crafts Council (1996c), pp.116, 126
— *Close*, exh. cat. (London, 2000)
Alun Graves, 'Traditional Elements', *CR*, 183 (2000)
Seisbøll (2000)
Crafts Council (2003), pp.13–16
Shipley Art Gallery (2003b), pp.23–4
Potteries Museum and Art Gallery, *Neil Brownsword: Collaging History*, exh. cat. (Stoke-on-Trent, 2005)
Glenn Adamson, 'Up From the Ashes', *Ceramics: Art and Perception*, 73 (2008)
Galerie Besson, *Neil Brownsword: Poet of Residue*, exh. pamphlet (London, 2008)
Grant Gibson, 'The Kilning Fields', *Crafts*, 211 (2008)
Twomey (2009), pp.8–9, 37–55, 125
Whiting (2009), pp.128–33
Carlano (2010), pp.54–5
WCC-BF (2010), pp.70–1, 92
Veiteberg (2011), pp.76–7
Dahn (2015), pp.65–70
Korea Ceramic Foundation, *The 8th Gyeonggi International Ceramic Biennale 2015*, exh. cat. (2015), pp.18–23, 254–69
— *Factory: Neil Brownsword*, exh. cat. (2017)
'Woman's Hour Craft Prize', supplement, *Crafts*, 268 (2017)
Ezra Shales, 'Soil So Good: Neil Brownsword's Reinventions', in Harrod (2018), pp.135–41
Roddy Clarke, 'Spode Ceramics', *Hole & Corner*, 19 (2019)
Sue Herdman, 'Made in Stoke', *CR*, 300 (2019)
Laura Breen, 'Making Cities: Places, Production, and (Im)material Heritage', in Nick Cass, Gill Park and Anna Powell (eds), *Contemporary Art in Heritage Spaces* (Abingdon, 2020)
Isabella Smith, 'Breaking the Mould', *Crafts*, 291 (2021)
Thorpe (2021), pp.183–90

Exhibition reviews: Paul Vincent, *Studio Pottery*, 22 (1996); Emma Maiden, 'Figuratively Speaking', *Crafts*, 147 (1997); Pamela Johnson, '3Up:Close', *Crafts*, 167 (2000); Richard Noyce, *CR*, 192 (2001); Matthew Partington, *CR*, 216 (2005); David Whiting, *Crafts*, 196 (2005), and 249 (2014); Teleri Lloyd-Jones, 'Possibilities and Losses', *Crafts*, 219 (2009)

114 *She Wants Your Junk*, 1999 (pl.103)
Ceramic collage with found elements on steel armature; h.47.2cm, d.42.5cm
C.66-2002. Source: the artist, £2250
Shown in the Crafts Council exhibition *Decadence*, 1999.

115

115 Installation: *Elegy*, 2009
Glazed ceramic, looped video projection (60 mins); for installation on plinth: h.12cm, w.220cm, d.120cm
C.123:1 to 17, 124-2011. Source: the artist, £15,000; acquired through the generosity of Gerard and Sarah Griffin

116 Installation: *Relic*, 2016 (pl.143)
Bone china, modelled, lead, wood; made in collaboration with china flower-maker Rita Floyd; h.9cm, l.300cm, w.45cm
C.29:1,2-2016. Source: New Art Centre, Salisbury, £15,000; acquired through the generosity of Gerard and Sarah Griffin

Buck, Steve 1949–2021

1949	born Leeds, Yorkshire
1979–81	studies ceramics at Harrow College of Higher Education
1982–	studio at Kingsgate Workshops, London
1986–89	solo exhibitions at Anatol Orient (later Michaelson and Orient), London
1989	wins Unilever Prize, Portobello Contemporary Art Festival; residency in Tokoname, Japan
1995–2012	teaches ceramics at University of Westminster
2008	residency at Fuping Art Village, Shaanxi, China
2009	solo exhibition, *Parallel Worlds*, National Centre for Craft and Design, Sleaford, Lincolnshire

Steve Buck consistently explored abstract sculptural form through distinct series of objects of other-worldy or alien character. Early small-scale, finely worked pieces in bright colours and metallic finishes led to larger, richly textured biomorphic sculptures. From the 1990s onwards he developed works with geometrical forms and surfaces, including pieces based on grid-like structures.

Tanya Harrod, 'Rococo Buck', *Crafts*, 93 (1988)
Angel Row Gallery, *Steve Buck: New Sculpture*, exh. pamphlet, text by Marina Vaizey (Nottingham, 1991)
Kingsgate Gallery, *Not Awake, Not Asleep*, exh. cat., text by John Houston (Harrow, 2001)
Tessa Peters, 'Points of Departure', *CR*, 190 (2001)
John Houston, 'Hollow Forms and Inner Space', *Ceramics: Art and Perception*, 52 (2003)
Hub, *Parallel Worlds: New Work by Steve Buck*, exh. pamphlet, text by Tessa Peters (Sleaford, 2009)
Peters (2012)

Exhibition reviews: Alison Britton, 'Six Ways', *Crafts*, 92 (1988); Marina Vaizey, *Crafts*, 100 (1989); John Houston, *Crafts*, 111 (1991); David Whiting, *Crafts*, 173 (2001)

117

117 *Untitled*, 1987
Earthenware, handbuilt, matt glazes and underglaze colours; h.39.6cm, d.33cm
C.83-1987. Source: Anatol Orient, London, £360

Burnett, Deirdre 1939–2022

1939	born Shimla, India
1962–63	studies painting and sculpture at St Martin's School of Art, London
1964–67	studies ceramics at Camberwell School of Art and Crafts
1967–	establishes workshop in East Dulwich, at first supporting individual work with tableware production
1974–	workshop in Gipsy Hill, London
1975–79	solo exhibitions at Peter Dingley Gallery, Stratford-upon-Avon; Amalgam, London; and elsewhere
1980s–	ceases exhibiting and works at reduced capacity due to carpal tunnel syndrome
1999–	resumes full-time potting after successful surgery
2017	solo exhibition, Stour Gallery, Shipston-on-Stour, Warwickshire

Deirdre Burnett became known in the 1970s for her fine, thrown and pinched porcelain bowls, recalling organic forms. She continued to make individual vessels in oxidized stoneware and porcelain, thrown, turned and altered, or handbuilt, using oxides and materials in the body to achieve glaze colour and volcanic texture.

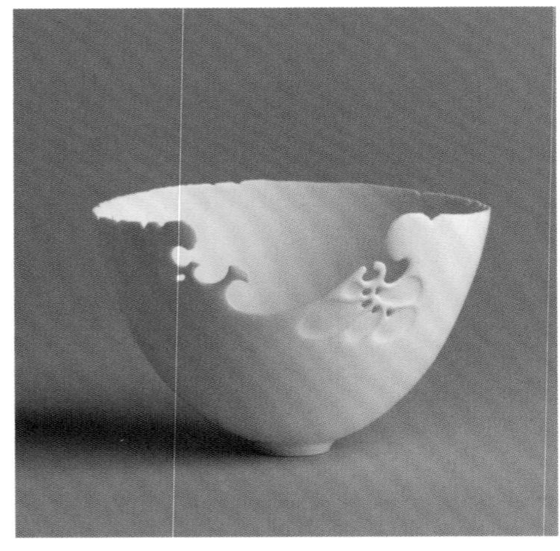
118

V&A (1972), p.106
'CPA New Members', *CR*, 29 (1974)
Potters/The Ceramics Book (1975), (1977), (1980), (1997) to (2012)
Crafts Advisory Committee (1976), p.82
Crafts Council (1980), p.54
Sainsbury Centre (1990)
Frankel (2000), pp.154–5

Exhibition reviews: J.D.H. Catleugh, *CR*, 13 (1972); Murray Fieldhouse, *Crafts*, 22 (1976)

118 Bowl, 1980
Porcelain, carved decoration, matt glaze; marks: 'DB', applied seal; h.7.9cm, d.11.9cm
C.40-1981. Source: Craft Shop, V&A, £153.72

Burr, Graham 1929–2003

1929	born Roxwell, Essex
1952–54	studies at Chelmsford School of Art, where learns pottery under Joanna Constantinidis (qv)
1954–57	studies ceramics at Camberwell School of Arts and Crafts
1957–65	studio in Camberwell, London, initially concentrating on painting but working increasingly with clay; teaches part-time at Camberwell, Beckenham and Oxford schools of art
1963|75	solo exhibitions at British Crafts Centre, London
1965–88	teaches ceramics full-time at Ravensbourne College of Art, Kent
1965–89	studio in Greenwich, London
1972	awarded diploma at *International Ceramics 1972* exhibition, V&A

Graham Burr reacted against the aesthetics and philosophies of Bernard Leach (qv) and the Anglo-Asian school, instead looking towards painting and sculpture and seeking to make work of contemporary relevance. Having initially made domestic ware, he increasingly explored form and surface, his work gradually abandoning any semblance of function. From about 1970 he developed a notable series of enclosed, geometrical, press-moulded ceramic sculptures with rich, painterly surfaces.

Arts and Crafts Exhibition Society (1954), (1957)
Decorative Art (1959/60), (1961/62)
Illustrations, *Pottery Quarterly*, 8:30 (1963), pls.6–7
Casson (1967), p.5, pls.16–17, 79
Potters (1972) to (1983)
V&A (1972), p.106
Eileen Lewenstein, 'Graham Burr', *CR*, 32 (1975)
J.D.H. Catleugh, exh. review, *CR*, 34 (1975)
Crafts Advisory Committee (1976), p.82
Portsmouth City Museum and Art Gallery (1976), with text by W.A. Ismay, p.4
Crafts Council (1980), p.54

Obituaries: Emmanuel Cooper, *CR*, 202 (2003), and *The Independent* (12 May 2003)

119

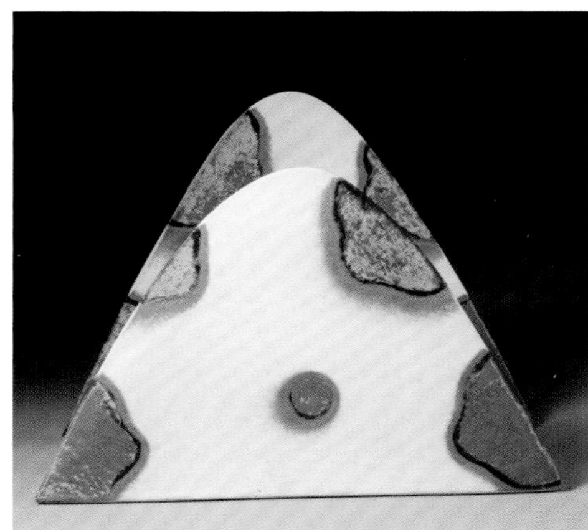

120

119 *Double-Curved Slab*, 1965
Stoneware, slab-built, ash glaze; marks: 'GB' in monogram, painted; h.31.8cm, d.31.2cm
C.6-2005. Source: given by Joan Burr
Illustrated in Casson (1967), pl.16.

120 *Double Image*, 1974
Stoneware, press-moulded, grey slip and copper oxide under matt white glazes, reduction fired; h.40cm, d.54.5cm
C.7:1,2-2005. Source: given by Joan Burr
Shown in the exhibition *Ceramic Sculpture by Graham Burr*, British Crafts Centre, London, 1975.

Caiger-Smith, Alan 1930–2020

1930	born Buenos Aires, Argentina
1933	family returns to England
1947	studies painting and drawing at Camberwell School of Arts and Crafts
1949–52	studies history and English at King's College, Cambridge
1954–55	evening classes in ceramics at Central School of Arts and Crafts, London, with Dora Billington (qv)
1955–	establishes pottery at Aldermaston, Berkshire
1956–61	Geoffrey Eastop (qv) joins Caiger-Smith at Aldermaston
1956–63	studio in Homer Street, London, run concurrently with pottery
1958	pottery shown at Heal's, London
1961	begins experiments with reduced lustre; work begins on first wood-fired kiln
1963	first major London exhibition, at Primavera
1968	first major international exhibition, Matsuya Gallery, Tokyo
1969–	touring exhibition, *Five Studio Potters*, organized by V&A
1973–78	Chairman of the British Crafts Centre
1985	retrospective touring exhibition, Stoke-on-Trent City Museum and Art Gallery
1988	awarded MBE
1989–91	major commission for large lustre pots for the headquarters of Pearl Assurance, Peterborough
1993–	Aldermaston Pottery closes; premises continue to be shared by Caiger-Smith, Andrew Hazelden and others, working independently
2006	workshop finally closes

Alan Caiger-Smith devoted himself to the production of tin-glazed earthenware with painted decoration in colours or reduced lustre, pioneering the revival of these techniques in studio ceramics. His workshop at Aldermaston was run with little division of labour, each of about seven potters sharing in all aspects of the work. Most pots were decorated by the potter who threw them. Repeat designs made up the greater part of production, alongside commissions and individual pieces for exhibition, but no catalogue was issued, allowing a degree of freedom. Caiger-Smith's artistic fluency and technical mastery were matched by his historical knowledge, and he became a recognized authority in his field.

Alan Caiger-Smith, 'Notes on Tin-glaze Earthenware', *Pottery Quarterly*, 9:35 (1969)
— 'Workshop/Aldermaston Pottery', *CR*, 5 (1970)
— *Tin-glaze Pottery in Europe and the Islamic World* (London, 1973)
— interview, in Cameron and Lewis (1976), pp.30–46, 165
— 'Why Decorate Pots?', *Crafts*, 52 (1981)
— *Lustre Pottery: Technique, Tradition and Innovation in Islam and the Western World* (London, 1985)
— 'A Potter's Day', *CR*, 118 (1989)
— *Alan Caiger-Smith and Aldermaston Pottery, 1955–1993: Selective Catalogue of the Final Exhibition 1993* (Aldermaston, 1993)
— 'Big Pots', *CR*, 141 (1993)
— 'Ending with a Flourish', *Crafts*, 122 (1993)
— *Pottery, People and Time: A Workshop in Action* (Shepton Beauchamp, 1995)
— 'Tin Glaze Earthenware, Past and Present Manufacture', *English Ceramic Circle Transactions*, 20:3 (2009)
— 'What If ...', *CR*, 238 (2009)
— and R. Lightbown (eds), *The Three Books of the Potter's Art* (London, 1980)
Arts and Crafts Exhibition Society (1957)
Decorative Art (1961/62)
Casson (1967), p.5, pls.80–2, 186–8
Potters (1972) to (1994)
V&A (1972), p.106
Ulster Museum (1974)
Lucie-Smith (1975), pp.49–57
Crafts Advisory Committee (1976), p.83

Thomas Shafer, *The Professional Potter* (London, 1978), pp.10–29

Aldermaston Pottery: Notes on the Pottery, pottery booklet (Aldermaston, 1980)

Crafts Council (1980), p.55

George and Nancy Wettlaufer, 'England's Alan Caiger-Smith', *Ceramics Monthly*, 28:1 (1980)

Neal French, 'Lustre and light', *CR*, 90 (1984)

Paisley Museum and Art Galleries (1984), p.21

Crafts Council (1985), pp.34–5

Stoke-on-Trent City Museum and Art Gallery, *Tin-glaze and Smoked Lustre: Pottery by Alan Caiger-Smith and Aldermaston Pottery, 1955–1985*, exh. cat. (1985)

Lois Hicks, 'Alan Caiger-Smith and Aldermaston Pottery', *CR*, 138 (1992)

Colin Martin, 'The Potter and the Plantsman', *CR*, 277 (2016)

Nottingham City Museums and Galleries (2017), pp.23–4

Jane White, *Alan Caiger-Smith and the Legacy of Aldermaston Pottery* (Oxford, 2018)

Exhibition reviews: Murray Fieldhouse, *Pottery Quarterly*, 5:20 (1958); Richard Dunning, *CR*, 2 (1970); J.D.H. Catleugh, *CR*, 25 (1974); W.A. Ismay, *CR*, 40 (1976); Margot Coatts, *Studio Pottery*, 18 (1995)

Obituaries: Tanya Harrod, *The Guardian* (18 March 2020); *The Times* (27 March 2020); *The Telegraph* (3 April 2020)

An interview with Alan Caiger-Smith is in the Crafts Lives sound archive at the British Library, London (C960/32). An artist statement written for the *Five Studio Potters* exhibition is in the manuscripts collection, National Art Library, V&A, London (MSL/1969/3560).

All works made at Aldermaston Pottery, Berkshire, unless stated otherwise.

121 Bowl, 1959 (pl.42)
Earthenware, tin glaze, painted in bronzy-green and pink; marks: 'ACS' in monogram, painted; made at Homer Street, London; h.13cm, d.40.9cm
Circ.59-1959. Source: the pottery, £7.7s.

122 Large bowl, 1968
Earthenware, tin glaze, painted in blue and orange lustre; marks: 'ACS' in monogram, painted; h.12.8cm, d.44.3cm
Circ.592-1968. Source: Primavera, Cambridge (solo exhibition, 1968, no.6), £18

123 Potpourri jar, 1968
Earthenware, tin glaze, painted in lustre; marks: 'ACS' in monogram, painted; h.34cm, d.31.5cm
Circ.820&A-1968. Source: the pottery, £18

124 Onion form, 1968
Earthenware, tin glaze, painted in orange lustre; h.25.8cm, d.21.2cm
Circ.821-1968. Source: *see* **123**, £10

125 Teapot, 1968 (fig.12)
Earthenware, tin glaze, painted in grey and blue-green; marks: 'ACS' in monogram, painted; h.16.3cm, d.20.8cm
Circ.822&A-1968. Source: *see* **123**, £8

126 Pebble bottle, 1968 (fig.12)
Earthenware, tin glaze, painted in blue and green; marks: 'ACS' in monogram, painted; h.9.8cm, d.14.8cm
Circ.823-1968. Source: *see* **123**, £5

127 Large bowl, 1976
Earthenware, tin glaze, painted in tawny-grey lustre; marks: 'ACS' in monogram, painted; h.18.3cm, d.49.5cm
C.79-1976. Source: given by Morley College Ceramic Circle in memory of their Chairman, James Cross
Shown in solo exhibition, British Crafts Centre, 1976, no.60.

128 Bowl, 1987
Earthenware, painted in lustre over a dark blue slip and transparent glaze; marks: 'ACS' in monogram, painted; h.9.1cm, d.28.6cm
C.2-1989. Source: given by the Contemporary Art Society

129 Bowl, 1993
Red earthenware, tin glaze, painted in lustre; marks: 'ACS' in monogram and 'WA', painted; date cypher for 1993; h.8.5cm, d.27cm
C.229-1993. Source: Aldermaston Pottery (final exhibition, 1993), £250

122

123

124

127

128

129

Campavias, Estella 1918–1990

1918	born Istanbul, Turkey, of Spanish heritage
1947	moves to London
1955–	attends pottery course at Chelsea Pottery (qv) under David Rawnsley; begins making ceramics
1956–61	solo exhibition at Ansons Gallery, London, followed by regular solo exhibitions at Gallery One, London
1961	ceases potting
1974–	works in sculpture

Estella Campavias began potting without formal training. Initially she worked in earthenware, but focused on stoneware after experimenting with stoneware glazes in 1957. At that time she worked from a studio in Fulham Road, London. Her work

130 / 131

comprised individual plates, dishes and bowls with bright glazes, and altered forms. A sizeable group of pieces was selected for the Smithsonian Institution exhibition *British Artist Craftsmen*, which toured in the USA and Canada from 1959.

'The Art of the Potter, Wakefield Art Gallery', exh. review, *Pottery Quarterly*, 6:23 (1959), pp.105–6
Smithsonian Institution (1959)
Geneviève Couteau, *Estella Campavias* (Paris, 1981)
Paisley Museum and Art Galleries (1984), p.21

130 Bowl, 1957
Stoneware, pale blue glaze; marks: indistinct seal; h.10.4cm, d.21.8cm
Circ.131-1958. Source: the artist, £15.15s.

131 Bowl, 1958
Stoneware, bright yellow-green glaze; h.13cm, d.14.2cm
Circ.6-1959. Source: the artist (following an exhibition at Gallery One, London), £16.16s.

Cardew, Michael 1901–1983

1901	born Wimbledon, London
1919–23	studies Classics at Exeter College, Oxford
1921	learns pottery from William Fishley Holland at Braunton Pottery, Devon, during summer
1923–26	works with Bernard Leach (qv) at St Ives
1926–	establishes Winchcombe Pottery, Gloucestershire, at former Greet Potteries, assisted by Elijah Comfort, making slipware
1927–	Sidney Tustin joins pottery
1928	first solo exhibition, New Handworkers' Gallery, London
1933	marries Mariel Russell
1934	son Seth Cardew (qv) born
1936–	Ray Finch (qv) joins pottery
1938	works briefly at Copelands, Stoke-on-Trent, making prototypes intended for industrial production
1939–41	establishes pottery at Wenford Bridge, Cornwall, leaving Finch to run Winchcombe; makes small amount of earthenware
1941–42	returns to work at Winchcombe
1942–45	appointed by Colonial Office (a government department) to go to Achimota College, Gold Coast (now Ghana), to develop pottery at Alajo, taking over from Harry Davis (qv)
1945–48	establishes Volta Pottery at Vume, Gold Coast
1946	sells Winchcombe business to Finch
1948	returns to England due to ill health; works briefly at Kingwood Design and Craftsmanship, Wormley, Surrey
1949–50	builds down-draught kiln for stoneware at Wenford Bridge, and works there assisted by Ivan McMeekin, who is taken into partnership
1950–	appointed Pottery Officer to the government in Nigeria, returns to Africa
1951–65	establishes Pottery Training Centre, Abuja (now Suleja), Nigeria; returns periodically to Wenford Bridge on leave
1959	runs 'Fundamental Pottery' course at Wenford Bridge
1964	awarded MBE
1965–	returns to Wenford Bridge
1967	visits USA, teaches at University of Wisconsin, works at Kent Benson's studio, Venice Beach, California
1968	visits New Zealand and Australia, works with McMeekin on training project at Bagot Aboriginal Reserve (now Bagot Community), Darwin; returns via Nigeria, visiting Abuja
1969	publishes *Pioneer Pottery*
1969–	Svend Bayer (qv) joins pottery
1972	tours USA with Ladi Kwali and Clement Kofi Athey
1973	travels to Nigeria and Ghana with Alister Hallum to film *Mud and Water Man*; Michael OBrien (qv) left in charge at Wenford Bridge
1974–	Seth Cardew joins pottery

1975–78 visits to Canada and USA
1976 retrospective exhibition, Museum Boymans-van Beuningen, Rotterdam, and tour
1981 visits New Zealand and Australia; awarded CBE

Michael Cardew was a pioneer of studio pottery, a maker of purposeful, beautiful, unprecious, yet often magnificent objects that responded to regional traditions and utilized locally sourced materials. He was the first student at the Leach Pottery, St Ives, attracted there by a love of slipware formed in childhood. He subsequently established his own pottery at Winchcombe, run as a productive country workshop, making earthenware. A romantic attachment to Cornwall, and a desire – realized only later – to make stoneware, prompted a move before the Second World War to Wenford Bridge, where he worked briefly before temporarily abandoning the enterprise. A combination of opportunity and circumstance then took Cardew to Africa, first to Ghana and later Nigeria, the experiences of which fundamentally shaped his work and outlook. Though a colonial servant, he was fiercely critical of British overseas policy. He became motivated as much by the making of potters as of pots, and his path was determined by his complex and sometimes fraught professional and personal relationships, not least his love for his protégé Clement Kofi Athey (*see* 167). In later life he became an inspirational countercultural figure, performing internationally through demonstrations and lectures, and drawing a stream of talented students to Wenford Bridge.

Michael Cardew, 'Modern English Potters', lecture (1938), transcript, *Interpreting Ceramics*, ejournal, 6 (2005)
— 'Industry and the Studio Potter', *Crafts: The Quarterly of the Red Rose Guild*, 2:1 (1942)
— 'Raw Materials for Pottery', *Athene*, 7:1/2 (1955)
— 'Potting in Northern Nigeria', *Pottery Quarterly*, 3:11 (1956)
— 'Bernard Leach – Recollections', in Barrow (1960)
— 'Training Potters in Abuja', *Pottery Quarterly*, 7:26 (1961)
— 'Chün Glazes', *Pottery in Australia*, 7:1 (1968)
— *Pioneer Pottery* (London, 1969)
— 'Potters and Amateur Potters', *Pottery Quarterly*, 10:38 (1971)
— 'A View of African Pottery', *Ceramics Monthly*, 22:2 (1974)
— 'What Pots Mean to Me', *CR*, 32 (1975)
— interview, in Cameron and Lewis (1976), pp.47–53, 165
— 'Michael Cardew at 75', compiled by Len Dutton, *CR*, 40 (1976)
— 'Why Make Pots in the Last Quarter of the 20th Century?', *Studio Potter*, 7:1 (1978)
— 'The Fatal Impact', *CR*, 55 (1979)
— selector's essay, in Crafts Council (1981), pp.21–3
— 'Michael Cardew', in conversation with Patrick Heron, *Crafts*, 50 (1981)
— 'An Essay on Pottery', *Ceramics Monthly*, 30:8 (1982)
— contribution, in York City Art Gallery (1983)
— 'Traditions', *Ceramics Monthly*, 32:1 (1984)
— *A Pioneer Potter: An Autobiography* (London, 1988)
Decorative Art (1927), (1930)
Arts and Crafts Exhibition Society (1928) to (1941)
British Institute of Industrial Art (1929)
Colnaghi (1932)
V&A (1936), pls.7, 43
Brygos Gallery, *Slipware Pottery by Michael Cardew*, exh. cat. (London, 1937)
British Council (1942)
Ernest Marsh, 'Michael Cardew, Potter, of Winchcombe, Gloucestershire', *Apollo*, 37 (May 1943)
Cooper (1947), p.*i*, pls.4–6
Michael Cardew: Stoneware Pottery made in West Africa, exh. pamphlet, text by Michael Cardew (London, 1948)
Berkeley Galleries, *Stoneware Pottery by Michael Cardew*, exh. pamphlet, text by Michael Cardew (London, 1950) – see also pamphlets from 1958, 1959 and 1962
Dartington Hall (1952)
Wingfield Digby (1952), pp.35–7, 73–5, pls.28–35
Rose (1955), pp.16–19, pls.C, 40–51, (1970), pp.32–6, pls.D, 40–53
Lewis (1956), pls.328–30
Casson (1967), p.5, pls.83–9
Charles Counts, 'Michael Cardew', *Craft Horizons*, 32:1 (1972)
Dave Enna, 'Michael Cardew', *Ceramics Monthly*, 20:3 (1972)
Potters (1972) to (1980)
Katharine Pleydell-Bouverie, 'Michael Cardew', *CR*, 20 (1973)
Crafts Advisory Committee (1976), p.83
— *Michael Cardew: A Collection of Essays* (London, 1976)
Ray Finch, 'Cardew at Winchcombe', *Crafts*, 23 (1976)
Ronn Hartviksen, 'A Cardew Workshop', *Ceramics Monthly*, 24:7 (1976)
— 'A Day in the Field with Michael Cardew', *CR*, 45 (1977)
Garth Clark, *Michael Cardew: A Portrait* (London, 1978)
Crafts Council (1980), p.55
Peter Dick, 'Michael Cardew and Pupils', *CR*, 80 (1983)
W.A. Ismay, 'Kindred Pots', *Crafts*, 63 (1983)
York City Art Gallery (1983), see nos.4–42, pls.2–12 and biography, for Cardew's own work
'Michael Cardew – Pioneer Potter', tributes, *CR*, 81 (1983)
Obituary, *The Times* (16 February 1983)
Paisley Museum and Art Galleries (1984), p.22
Crafts Council (1985), p.35
Tate Gallery (1985), pp.232–3
Vincentelli and Hale (1986)
W.A. Ismay, 'Michael Cardew – A Pioneer Potter', *CR*, 111 (1988)
Tanya Harrod, 'The Breath of Reality', *Journal of Design History*, 2:2/3 (1989)
Birks and Wingfield Digby (1990), pp.121–37
Riddick (1990), pp.29–33
Doug Fitch, 'Sidney Tustin Recalls the Early Days of Winchcombe Pottery', *Studio Pottery*, 9 (1994)
Tanya Harrod, 'Michael Cardew', *Crafts*, 126 (1994)
Jane Herold, 'Cardew's Legacy', with contributions from Svend Bayer, Ray Finch, Seth Cardew, Michael OBrien and others, *Studio Potter*, 22:2 (1994)
Garth Clark, 'Thinking of Cardew and Africa', *Studio Pottery*, 13 (1995)
Michael OBrien, 'Michael Cardew in Africa', *CR*, 192 (2001)
Papers from 'Michael Cardew Centenary Symposium', University of Wales, Aberystwyth, *Interpreting Ceramics*, ejournal, 3 (2001)
J.V.G. Mallet, 'The "Gentleman" Potters Part 2, Michael Cardew and Katharine Pleydell-Bouverie', *English Ceramic Circle Transactions*, 18:3 (2004)
Ron Wheeler and John Edgeler, *Sid Tustin: Winchcombe Potter: A Celebration* (Winchcombe, 2005)
John Edgeler, *Michael Cardew and the West Country Slipware Tradition* (Winchcombe, 2007)
— *Michael Cardew and Stoneware: Continuity and Change* (Winchcombe, 2008)
Clark, Strauss and others (2012), pp.100–5, 361–2, 425
Tanya Harrod, *The Last Sane Man: Michael Cardew, Modern Pots, Colonialism and the Counterculture* (New Haven/London, 2012)
John Edgeler, *Michael Cardew and Winchcombe Pottery 1926–1939* (Winchcombe, 2014)
Nottingham City Museums and Galleries (2017), pp.26–7
Edgeler (2019)

132

134

136

Exhibition reviews: *The Times*, 'Stoneware Pottery' (3 November 1928), 'Winchcombe Pottery' (11 June 1931), 'Two Potters' (10 November 1933), (10 November 1938), (25 February 1958); P.B., 'Winchcombe Pottery', *Journal of the Royal Society of Arts*, 79:4099 (12 June 1931); *Pottery Quarterly*, 6:24 (1959); Susan Peterson and Bernard Kester, *Craft Horizons*, 28:3 (1968); W.A. Ismay, *CR*, 34 (1975)

The papers of Michael Cardew are in the V&A Archive of Art and Design, London (AAD/2006/2), and at the Crafts Study Centre, Farnham (MAC).

All works made as marked at Winchcombe Pottery, Gloucestershire; Wenford Bridge Pottery, Cornwall; or the Pottery Training Centre, Abuja, Nigeria, unless stated otherwise.

132 Dish, *c.* 1923–24
Earthenware, incised decoration through white slip, galena glaze with green splashes; marks: 'MC' and 'SI' in monogram, impressed; made at Leach Pottery, St Ives; h.4.7cm, d.17.3cm
C.60-1985. Source: Paul Rice Gallery, London, £270

133 Harvest jug, 1925 (pl.13)
Earthenware, incised decoration through white slip, galena glaze; marks: 'MC' and 'SI' in monogram, impressed; made at Leach Pottery, St Ives; h.19.2cm, d.20cm
C.81-2008. Source: Bonhams, London (sale: *Under a Western Sky: The Art of Newlyn and St Ives*, 19 November 2008, lot 49), £7657; purchased with the assistance of the Horn Bequest
This jug was shown in the British Pavilion of the 1925 Paris International Exhibition, where it was commended by the critic Frank Rutter (1925, pp.136–7). Its inscription reads: 'DESPISE ME NOT BECAUSE I'M MADE / OF CLAY – BUT MAKE ME WELCOME WHEN / I COME THIS WAY – MY BELLY FILL WITH GOOD / STRONG PUNCH (OR BEER) – & I WILL MAKE YOU MERRY / ALL THE YEAR'. The 'MC' seal is a rare scrolling version that Cardew made using his signet ring.

135

134 Tobacco jar, 1929
Earthenware, slip-trailed and painted in brown on a white slip, galena glaze; marks: 'WP' in monogram, impressed; h.17.5cm, d.12cm
C.424&A-1934. Source: British Institute of Industrial Art (given by the artist, 1929)

135 Jar with handles, 1929–30
Earthenware, slip-trailed in brown under a green galena glaze; marks: 'MC' and 'WP' in monogram, impressed; h.19.5cm, d.16.6cm
C.956-1935. Source: given by the Pottery and Crafts Fund of the Contemporary Art Society (purchased from Cotswold Gallery, London, 1930, 15s.6d.)

137 / 148

136 Bowl, 1929–30
Earthenware, wiped decoration through a white slip, galena glaze; marks: 'MC' and 'WP' in monogram, impressed; h.8.3cm, d.24.5cm
C.957-1935. Source: *see* **135** (10s.6d.)

137 Cider jar, *c.* 1930
Earthenware, painted in brown on a white slip, galena glaze; marks: 'MC' and 'WP' in monogram, impressed; h.25.5cm, d.18.3cm
Misc.2(153)-1934. Source: given by Margaret Armitage (née Bulley)
Paper label on base gives the original price: 8s.6d.

138 Vase, 1933
Earthenware, slip-trailed in white on a black slip, galena glaze; marks: 'MC' and 'WP' in monogram, impressed; h.32cm, d.20.2cm
Circ.346-1939. Source: given by the Pottery and Crafts Fund of the Contemporary Art Society

139 / 138

144

142 / 141

145

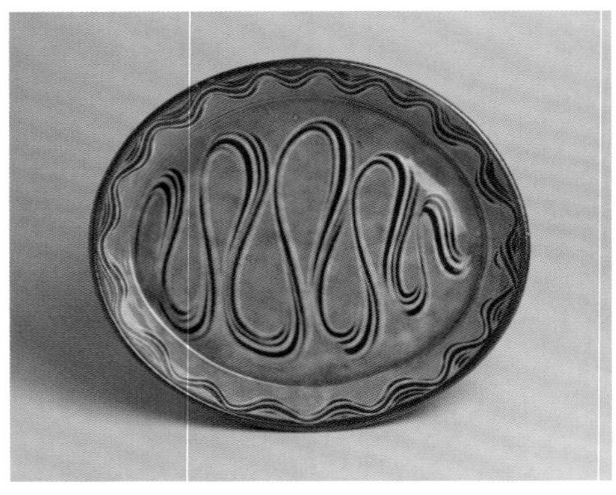

143

146

(purchased from The Little Gallery, London, 1933, probably from solo exhibition, £1.10s.)

139 Bowl, 1933–34
Earthenware, slip-trailed in white on a black slip, galena glaze; marks: 'MC' and 'WP' in monogram, impressed; h.7cm, d.31.8cm
Circ.347-1939. Source: given by the Pottery and Crafts Fund of the Contemporary Art Society (purchased from The Little Gallery, London, 1934, £1.10s.)

140 Bowl, *c.* 1936 (pl.23)
Earthenware, slip-trailed in white on a black slip, galena glaze; marks: 'MC' and 'WP' in monogram, impressed; h.13.5cm, d.35cm
Circ.37-1938. Source: given by Henry Bergen (shown in the British Pavilion at the Paris International Exhibition, 1937)
Illustrated in Wingfield Digby (1952), pl.30.

141 Jug, 1938
Earthenware, slip-trailed in white on a black slip, galena glaze; marks: 'MC' and 'WP' in monogram, impressed; h.28.5cm, d.22.7cm
Circ.310-1938. Source: The Brygos Gallery, London (solo exhibition, 1938, no.251), £1.11s.6d.

142 Jug, 1938
Earthenware, slip-trailed in white on a black slip, galena glaze; marks: 'MC' and 'WP' in monogram, impressed; h.24cm, d.21.2cm
Circ.311-1938. Source: *see* **141** (no.336), 15s.

143 Dish, 1938
Earthenware, combed decoration through a white slip, galena glaze; h.6.3cm, d.43cm
Circ.312-1938. Source: *see* **141** (no.351), £1.5s.

144 Large jar, 1938
Earthenware, banded and painted in white slip, galena glaze; marks: 'MC' and 'WP' in monogram, impressed; h.35.8cm, d.32.7cm
Circ.313-1938. Source: *see* **141** (no.111), £3.3s.
Illustrated in Wingfield Digby (1952), pl.29, and Rose (1955), pl.46.

145 Breakfast dish and cover, 1938
Earthenware, slip-trailed in white on a black slip, galena glaze; marks: 'WP' in monogram, impressed; h.11.4cm, d.25.4cm
Circ.314&A-1938. Source: *see* **141** (no.48), 10s.6d.
Cardew suggested in 1981 that the base was thrown by himself and the lid by Elijah Comfort. This was revealed by the thick profile of the lid's flange – 'lazy throwing', which was, according to Cardew, the 'sign of a true professional'.

146 Large plate, 1938
Earthenware, slip-trailed in white, galena glaze; marks: 'MC' and 'WP' in monogram, impressed; h.6.5cm, d.35.5cm
Circ.315-1938. Source: *see* **141** (no.343), £1.11s.6d.

147 Plate, 1938
Earthenware, slip-trailed in white on a black slip, galena glaze; h.2.8cm, d.24.4cm
Circ.316-1938. Source: *see* **141** (no.149), 6s.6d.

148 Quart bottle, 1938 (illustrated p.191)
Earthenware, incised decoration through a black slip, galena glaze; marks: 'MC' and 'WP' in monogram, impressed; h.20.4cm, d.13.6cm
Circ.317-1938. Source: *see* **141** (no.254), £1.10s.

149 Jug, 1938
Earthenware, slip-trailed in white on partial black slip, galena glaze; marks: 'MC' and 'WP' in monogram, impressed; h.29.5cm, d.23.2cm
Circ.318-1938. Source: *see* **141** (no.88), £1.1s.

150 Cider jar, 1938 (pl.24)
Earthenware, incised decoration through a black slip, galena glaze, wooden tap; marks: 'MC' and 'WP' in monogram, impressed; h.45cm, d.27.5cm
Circ.319-1938. Source: *see* **141** (no.325), £5.5s.
Illustrated in Wingfield Digby (1952), pl.28.

151 Covered bowl, 1947–48
Stoneware, dark green glaze, painted in iron-brown; marks: 'MC' in monogram and Volta Pottery seal, impressed, 'MC' painted; made at Volta Pottery, Vume; h.12.5cm, d.17.5cm
Circ.33&A-1950. Source: the artist, £3.3s.
This bowl had apparently been omitted from Cardew's 1948 exhibition *Stoneware Pottery Made in West Africa*, as it had been a favourite of Mariel Cardew. Having failed to acquire work from the exhibition, the museum negotiated its acquisition in 1950. Cardew noted that the bowl was imperfect due to a crack caused by the compression strains of the glaze on the body, but observed that 'African enterprize [*sic*] has always been costly, and this is one of the few survivors'. Illustrated in Wingfield Digby (1952), pl.31.

152 Soup tureen, 1950
Stoneware, grey glaze, painted in blue and brown; marks: 'MC' in monogram and Wenford Bridge seal, impressed; h.18.6cm, d.26.9cm
Circ.423&A-1950. Source: Berkeley Galleries, London (solo exhibition, 1950), £5.5s.

153 Casserole, 1950
Stoneware, grey glaze, painted in brown; marks: 'MC' in monogram and Wenford Bridge seal, impressed; h.24.5cm, d.23.2cm
Circ.424&A-1950. Source: *see* **152**, £5.5s.

154 Dish: *Pheasant and Palm* pattern, 1950
Stoneware, grey glaze, painted in dark grey; marks: 'MC' in monogram and Wenford Bridge seal, impressed; h.4.3cm, d.27.2cm
Circ.425-1950. Source: *see* **152**, £3.3s.

147

149

157 / 153 / 155 / 156 / 158

151

152

154

159 / 160

165

169

161

167 / 166 / 168

170

162

155 Cider jar, 1950
Stoneware, celadon glaze, painted in brown; marks: 'MC' in monogram and Wenford Bridge seal, impressed; h.31.5cm, d.20.4cm
Circ.426-1950. Source: *see* **152**, £6.6s.

156 Jug, 1950
Stoneware, celadon glaze, painted in brown; marks: 'MC' in monogram and Wenford Bridge seal, impressed; h.27.5cm, d.25cm
Circ.427-1950. Source: *see* **152**, £7.7s.

157 Bowl, 1950
Stoneware, grey glaze blushed pink, painted in brown; marks: 'MC' in monogram and Wenford Bridge seal, impressed; h.12.5cm, d.26.5cm
Circ.428-1950. Source: *see* **152**, £4.10s.

158 Bowl, 1950
Stoneware, grey glaze, painted in brown; marks: 'MC' in monogram and Wenford Bridge seal, impressed; h.12.3cm, d.24cm
Circ.429-1950. Source: *see* **152**, £4.4s.

159 Covered bowl, 1950
Stoneware, grey glaze, painted in brown; marks: 'MC' in monogram and Wenford Bridge seal, impressed; h.12.9cm, d.19.7cm
Circ.430&A-1950. Source: *see* **152**, £2.2s.

160 Soup bowl, 1950
Stoneware, grey glaze, painted in brown; marks: 'MC' in monogram and Wenford Bridge seal, impressed; h.6cm, d.16.4cm
Circ.431-1950. Source: *see* **152**, 17s.6d.

161 Teapot, 1950
Stoneware, unglazed, painted in brown; marks: 'MC' in monogram and Wenford Bridge seal, impressed; h.22.8cm, d.21.5cm
Circ.432&A-1950. Source: *see* **152**, £4.10s.

162 Vase: *Vume* pattern, 1950
Stoneware, incised decoration, grey glaze; marks: 'MC' in monogram and Wenford Bridge seal, impressed; h.24.3cm, d.19.4cm
Circ.433-1950. Source: *see* **152**, £5.5s.

163 Jar with screw stopper, *c.* 1957 (pl.41)
Stoneware, sgraffito decoration through a black slip, 'jun' glaze; marks: 'MC' in monogram and Abuja seal, impressed; h.31.9cm, d.24.7cm
Circ.112&A-1958. Source: Berkeley Galleries, London (exhibition: *Stoneware Pottery … Made at Abuja*, 1958), £12.12s.

164 Dish, *c.* 1957 (pl.41)
Stoneware, combed decoration through a black

187

189

192

188

191

W.A. Ismay, 'Pots from Three Kilns', *CR*, 84 (1983)
Paisley Museum and Art Galleries (1984), p.23
Crafts Council (1985), pp.35–6
Tanya Harrod, 'Sources of Inspiration', *Crafts*, 99 (1989)
W.A. Ismay, 'Michael Casson', *Studio Pottery*, 9 (1994)
David Whiting, *Michael and Sheila Casson*, Aberystwyth Arts Centre: Ceramic Series 84 (1997)
Minogue and Sanderson (2000), pp.44–6
Cochrane (2001), pp.65–7
Nick Lees, 'Integrity and Interpretation', *CR*, 189 (2001)
Rogers (2002), pp.126–30
Tributes, *CR*, 206 (2004)
Emmanuel Cooper and Amanda Fielding, *Michael Casson* (Ruthin, 2010)
Simon Ford, 'Function and Expression', *Ceramics: Art and Perception*, 82 (2010)
Nottingham City Museums and Galleries (2017), p.29

Exhibition reviews: *Pottery Quarterly*, 6:22 (1959); Tony Hepburn, *Craft Horizons*, 33:1 (1973); W.A. Ismay, *CR*, 19 (1973), 25 (1974), and 58 (1979); David Leach, *Crafts*, 7 (1974); Lionel Phillips, *Crafts*, 19 (1976); Walter Keeler, *Crafts*, 46 (1980); Eileen Lewenstein, *Crafts*, 103 (1990); Paul Vincent, *Studio Pottery*, 9 (1994); David Whiting, *Studio Pottery*, 17 (1995); Stephen Woodruff, *CR*, 156 (1995)

Obituaries: Emmanuel Cooper, *The Independent* (17 December 2003); *The Times* (20 December 2003); Walter Keeler, *The Guardian* (27 December 2003); David Whiting, *Crafts*, 187 (2004)

Interviews with Michael Casson are in the Recording the Crafts video archive at UWE Bristol (also held in the National Art Library, V&A, London, 704.AA.0011 to 704.AA.0014) and the Ceramic Archive, Aberystwyth University, a summary of which was published in *Interpreting Ceramics*, ejournal, 6 (2005), alongside other transcripts. An interview with Sheila Casson is in the Crafts Lives sound archive at the British Library, London (C960/104).

187 Plate: 'Tenmoku landscape', 1973
Stoneware, wiped decoration through red slip, tenmoku glaze; marks: 'MC' in monogram, painted in black enamel; h.6.7cm, d.40cm
Circ.4-1974. Source: Craftsmen Potters Association, London (solo exhibition, 1973, no.145), £20

188 Large jug, 1974
Stoneware, wiped decoration through red slip, tenmoku glaze; marks: impressed seal; h.43cm, d.32.5cm
Circ.517-1974. Source: the artist, £30

189 Dish, 1975
Porcelain, incised decoration, pale blue-green glaze; marks: 'MC' in monogram, painted; h.9.5cm, d.37.6cm
Circ.8-1976. Source: Casson Gallery, London (solo exhibition, 1975), £45

190 Footed bowl, 1975 (pl.67)
Stoneware, porcelain inlay, dry clay-ash glaze exterior, tenmoku interior; marks: 'MC' in monogram, painted; h.16.5cm, d.18.7cm
Circ.9-1976. Source: *see* **189**, £25

191 Bowl, 1976
Stoneware, grey glaze, painted in blue and grey; marks: 'MC' in monogram, painted; h.11cm, d.15cm
Circ.531-1976. Source: the artist, £6

192 Large jug, 1984
Stoneware, mottled brown saltglaze; marks: 'MC' in monogram, impressed; h.50.4cm, d.22.2cm
C.151-1984. Source: British Crafts Centre, London (exhibition: *8 Ceramicists*, 1984, no.19), £108.90

193

194

193 Pot: *Swimmers*, *c.* 1990
Stoneware, painted in blue and brown slips, salt-glazed; marks: 'MC' in monogram, impressed; h.26.8cm, d.25.8cm
C.45-1991. Source: Contemporary Ceramics: Craftsmen Potters Shop and Gallery, London (solo exhibition, 1990), £496.72

Chambers, Matthew 1975–

1975	born London
1993–99	apprentice and assistant to Philip Wood, Somerset
1999–2002	studies ceramics at Bath Spa University College
2002–04	studies ceramics at Royal College of Art, London
2004–15	studio at Quay Arts, Newport, Isle of Wight
2011–18	regular solo exhibitions at Campden Gallery, Chipping Campden, Gloucestershire, and New Craftsman Gallery, St Ives
2015–	studio at St Lawrence, Isle of Wight
2018	solo exhibition, Contemporary Ceramics Centre, London

Matthew Chambers is known for his precise stoneware sculptures built up from concentric hemispherical thrown sections. Inspired by Constructivism and Optical Art, these draw upon the skills that he attained through working as a production thrower.

Matthew Chambers, 'A Potter's Practice', *CR*, 236 (2009)
— 'Matthew Chambers', *Ceramics Monthly*, 61:6 (2013)
Fiona Hackney, exh. review, *CR*, 272 (2015)
Katherine Caddy, 'Closing the Circle', *CR*, 282 (2016)

194 *Red Fade Spiral*, 2018
Stoneware coloured with iron oxide, thrown and assembled; marks: 'M Chambers 2018', incised; h.32.5cm, d.34cm
C.31-2019. Source: Cavaliero Finn at Collect 2019, £3000; purchase funded by Christopher M. Gorman-Evans

Chappell, John 1931–1964

1931	born Ealing, London
1947–50	works in laboratory of Regent Oil Company while studying chemistry and mathematics part-time at London University
1950–52	begins potting in his spare time with Murray Fieldhouse (qv) at Pendley Manor; subsequently joins Fieldhouse as full-time apprentice
1952–53	serves one-month prison term as conscientious objector to national service; travels to Algeria to teach children
1953–55	establishes Coldharbour Pottery at Berkhamsted Common, Hertfordshire, with Bernard Devine, making salt-glazed stoneware
1955	moves workshop to Wilstone, Hertfordshire; travels to France
1956–59	works as a cook and English teacher in Sweden, in order to save enough money to travel to Japan
1959–60	arrives in Japan; works with Uchida Kunio in Kyoto
1960–61	visits Australia and New Zealand
1961–62	returns to Kyoto, establishing workshop in Gojo
1962–	establishes workshop and kilns at Do-mura, Shiga, Japan
1964	travels to Australia with Japanese potter Kawai Takéichi for an exhibition tour there and in New Zealand; killed in a motorcycle accident in Sydney

John Chappell was a talented and exacting young potter who was gaining increasing international recognition at the time of his tragic death. An early exponent of saltglaze in studio pottery, Chappell assimilated influences from both England and Japan.

John Chappell, 'Making Salt Glaze Stoneware', *Pottery Quarterly*, 1:2 (1954)
— 'Letter from Vallauris', with biographical notes, *Pottery Quarterly*, 2:7 (1955)
— 'The Swedish Illusion: A Warning', *Pottery Quarterly*, 4:13 (1957)
— 'Letter from Saigon', *Pottery Quarterly*, 6:23 (1959)
— 'Potting in Japan', *New Zealand Potter*, 4:1 (1961)
— 'A Visitor's Views [on New Zealand]', *Pottery Quarterly*, 7:27 (1962)
Helen Mason, 'John Chappell', *New Zealand Potter*, 3:2 (1960)
— 'The Visit of John and Anja Chappell', *New Zealand Potter*, 4:1 (1961)
— 'John Chappell: Potter 1931–1964', *New Zealand Potter*, 7:1 (1964)
Dominion Museum, *Takeichi Kawai, John Chappell*, exh. cat. (Wellington, 1964)

195 Bottle, *c.* 1963
Stoneware, mottled brown saltglaze; marks: 'JC', impressed; h.18.3cm, d.11.5cm
Circ.47-1966. Source: Anja Chappell (the artist's widow), £4
Selected with **196** and **197** from John Chappell's final, posthumous exhibition.

196 / 195

197

198 / 199

196 Wine jar, *c.* 1963
Stoneware, green glaze on rim, ash flashings; marks: possibly 'JC', incised; h.27.4cm, d.21cm
Circ.46-1966. Source: *see* **195**, £8

197 Bottle, *c.* 1963
Porcelain, painted in underglaze blue; h.14.6cm, d.9.3cm
Circ.45-1966. Source: *see* **195**, £3

Chelsea Pottery

Chelsea Pottery was established in Radnor Walk, Chelsea, London, by David and Mary Rawnsley in 1952 as an 'open studio' where subscribing members could come and work. It developed into a two-sided business: classes for amateur potters and a commercial studio pottery. This produced thrown earthenwares decorated in a distinctive technique termed 'inlay and overlay', which involved incising the design onto the piece before spraying on an oxide and painting with coloured glazes. Daphne Corke and Joyce Morgan worked at the pottery from the outset, decorating wares and on occasion signing their work. Corke left to work at Lexden, Colchester, Essex, in 1955; Morgan continued at Chelsea Pottery for 40 years, working with Brian Hubbard, who took over its running following the Rawnsleys' departure in 1959. The painter and tile-decorator Christina Sheppard – examples of whose later tiles are in the V&A (C.72 to 75-1994) – worked at Chelsea Pottery from 1958 to 1964. Frank Spindler joined as a thrower and modeller after leaving Odney Pottery (qv). Chelsea Pottery moved to Ebury Mews, Belgravia, in 1994 but closed in 1997.

The four pieces in the V&A are marked 'EIIR 1953' in commemoration of the coronation of Elizabeth II in that year.

201 / 200

'Pottery Revival in Chelsea', *The Times* (16 June 1952)
Marita Ross, 'New Pottery in Old Chelsea', *Everybody's Weekly* (15 October 1955)
'The Chelsea Pottery', *The Guardian* (3 June 1961)
Rebecca Luffman, 'Graphic Variety and Christina Sheppard at the V&A', *Glazed Expressions*, 84 (2019)
Joan Witham, 'Chelsea c1952–1997', *Antiques Info*, undated

198 Dish: *Fossil Fish* series, 1953
Earthenware, incised and painted in coloured glazes; marks: 'EIIR Chelsea Pottery 1953', incised; h.6.3cm, d.19.7cm
C.73-1953. Source: given by David Rawnsley of the Chelsea Pottery
Decorated by Daphne Corke.

199 Bowl, 1953
Earthenware, incised and painted in coloured glazes; marks: 'EIIR Chelsea Pottery 1953', incised; h.7.7cm, d.19.4cm
Circ.406-1953. Source: *see* **198**
Decorated by Daphne Corke.

200 Dish, 1953
Earthenware, incised and painted in coloured glazes; marks: 'EIIR Chelsea Pottery 1953', incised; h.4.2cm, d.19.8cm
Circ.407-1953. Source: *see* **198**
Decorated by John Drummond. Drummond was associated with Chelsea Pottery only briefly.

201 Dish, 1953
Earthenware, incised and painted in coloured glazes; marks: 'EIIR Chelsea Pottery 1953', incised, and 'Jem' in monogram, inscribed; h.3.5cm, d.19.5cm
C.74-1953. Source: *see* **198**
Decorated by Joyce Morgan.

Ciscato, Carina 1970–

1970	born São Paulo, Brazil
1988–92	studies industrial design at Fundação Armando Alvares Penteado, São Paulo
1992–93	introduced to ceramics through apprenticeship with Marietta Cremer, Krefeld, Germany
1993–99	apprenticed to Lucia Ramenzoni, São Paulo
1999–	moves to London
2000–03	assistant to Julian Stair (qv), London
2003–	establishes own studio in Camberwell, London, shared with Chris Keenan (qv)
2003	solo exhibition, Egg, London
2011|14	solo exhibitions, Beaux Arts, Bath
2014	solo exhibition, *The Arris, Interpreted*, Messum's, London
2017	residency at Mashiko Museum of Ceramic Art, Tochigi, Japan

Carina Ciscato's thrown and altered porcelain vessels demonstrate her own distinctive formal and structural language, being almost architectural, while also capturing the plasticity of the raw material. Works are individual but form part of interrelated groups.

Carina Ciscato, 'Masterclass', *CR*, 273 (2015)
— statement, in Bendavid and Lalumia (2017), pp.14, 37
Caroline Wheater, 'A Fine Edge', *Homes & Antiques* (October 2003)
Diana Woolf, 'Lookout', *Crafts*, 187 (2004)
Amanda Fielding, 'Subverting Form', with technical notes, *CR*, 227 (2007)
Whiting (2009), pp.74–7
The Ceramics Book (2012)
Bird (2013), pp.77–8
Liz Farrelly, 'Family, Home and Soane', *Crafts*, 241 (2013)
Morris (2018), pp.99–103

202

Exhibition reviews: Frances Priest, *CR*, 195 (2002); Lindsey Brown, *CR*, 252 (2011); Shane Enright, 'Marking the Line', *Crafts*, 242 (2013); Colin Martin, 'Marking the Line', *Craft Arts International*, 88 (2013); Abraham Thomas, 'Marking the Line', *CR*, 262 (2013)

202 Pot: *Double wall*, 2007
Porcelain, thrown and altered; marks: indistinct mark, painted in blue; h.16.4cm, d.22.2cm
C.19-2008. Source: Joanna Bird Pottery, London, £600; acquired through the generosity of Gerard and Sarah Griffin

Clark, Ann *see* Ann Wynn Reeves

Clark, Kenneth 1922–2012

1922	born Wellington, New Zealand
1945–48	after service in Royal Navy, studies painting at Slade School of Fine Art, London, on scholarship from New Zealand government; introduced to pottery under Dora Billington (qv) at Central School of Arts and Crafts, London
1949–87	teaches at Central School
1951–58	teaches at Goldsmiths' College, London
1952–	establishes studio in Old Gloucester Street, London; Ann Wynn Reeves (qv) joins him in 1953
1954–	marries Ann; Kenneth Clark Pottery moves to Howland Street
1957–	pottery moves to Clipstone Street
1966–	pottery moves to Dryden Street, Covent Garden
1980–	pottery relocates to Lewes, Sussex, trading as Kenneth Clark Ceramics
1981–84	President of the Society of Designer Craftsmen
1990	awarded MBE
1997–	retires from company; continues working as freelance designer-maker

Kenneth Clark worked in partnership with his wife, Ann Wynn Reeves (qv). At first they made individual studio pieces marked with their own initials, but gradually moved towards the semi-industrial production of colourfully decorated tiles and dishes, mostly designed by Ann. They also worked to commission on architectural ceramic panels and tile murals. Kenneth Clark also wrote a number of practical manuals of ceramics.

Kenneth Clark, 'Potters Must Eat', *Pottery Quarterly*, 7:28 (1962)
— *Practical Pottery and Ceramics* (London, 1964)
— *The Potter's Manual* (London, 1983)
— *The Tile: Making, Designing and Using* (Marlborough, 2002)
Decorative Art (1953/54), (1954/55), (1955/56)
Lewis (1956), pls.377–8
Arts and Crafts Exhibition Society (1957)
Profile, *Pottery Quarterly*, 5:19 (1958), pl.13
Helen Mason, 'The Kenneth Clark Pottery, London', *New Zealand Potter*, 5:1 (1962)
Casson (1967), p.5, pls.98–100, 195
Crafts Advisory Committee (1976), p.85
Crafts Council (1980), p.55
Margot Coatts, 'Kenneth and Ann Clark – Designers in Clay', *Studio Pottery*, 29 (1997)

Obituaries: *The Times* (30 June 2012); Sarah Hosking, *The Guardian* (18 July 2012); *Daily Telegraph* (6 August 2012)

The museum holds various tiles and a dish from the Kenneth Clark Pottery not catalogued here (C.157 to 171-1980, C.84 to 86, 90 to 101-2014), as well as tableware designed by Clark for Denby and Pountney & Co. (C.87, 88-2014).

203 Dish, 1952
Earthenware, slip-trailed decoration on a dark ground; marks: 'K.C. / 52.', painted; made at the Central School or at William Newland's studio; h.5.2cm, d.29.5cm
C.77-2014. Source: given by Ann Clark

204 Vase in the form of a coal scuttle, 1956
Earthenware, painted in black and turquoise on a tin glaze; made by Kenneth Clark, designed and decorated by Paul Gell; marks: 'KC / 56', painted; h.25.2cm, d.16.2cm
C.81-2014. Source: *see* **203**

205 Bowl, 1998
Earthenware, painted in lustre; marks: 'KC / 98', painted in black; h.7.7cm, d.21cm
C.89-2014. Source: *see* **203**

See also **1139** *under* Ann Wynn Reeves.

203

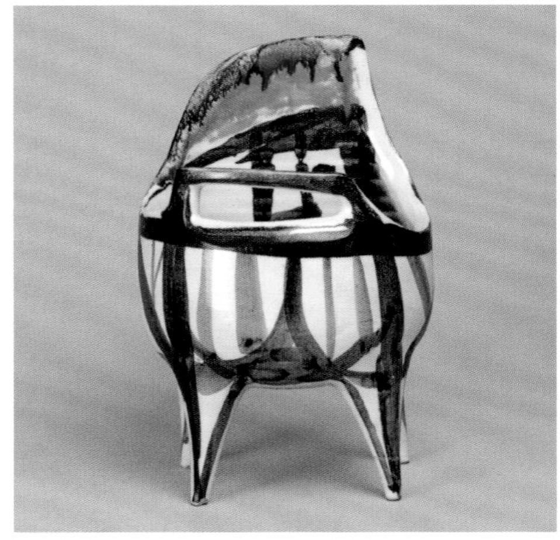

204

205

Clarkson, Derek 1928–2013

1928	born Bacup, Lancashire, and remains a lifelong resident there
1944–47	studies at Manchester School of Art
1949–61	teaches at Stockport, Bolton and Burnley schools of art
1959–61	studies at Burnley School of Art
1961–65	teaches at Stafford College of Art
1965–79	teaches at Mather College and City of Manchester College of Higher Education
1980–	pots full-time

Derek Clarkson specialized in refined, narrow-necked bottles and small bowls, often with brush decoration, working initially in reduced stoneware and later porcelain. He also became an expert in crystalline glazes, with which he began experimenting in 1989.

Derek Clarkson, 'Thrown and Turned Bottles', *CR*, 88 (1984)
— 'Light Fantastic', *CR*, 107 (1987)
— 'The Crystal Maze', *CR*, 137 (1992)
— 'Electric Crystalline Firing', *Studio Potter*, 25:1 (1996)
Decorative Art (1966/67), (1968/69)
Casson (1967), p.5, pls.18, 101–3
Potters (1972) to (2000)
David Whiting, 'Crystalline Ceramics', exh. review, *Crafts*, 125 (1993)
Lane (1995)
Alex McErlain, 'Passing It On', *NPA News* (March–April 2014)

Clarkson's glaze notes are held by Manchester Metropolitan University Special Collections Museum (CLA/1–CLA/5).

206 Bottle, 1982
Stoneware, wood-ash glaze, painted in cobalt and iron; marks: 'DC' in a rectangle, impressed; h.24.3cm, d.16cm
C.69-1984. Source: given by the Friends of the V&A (purchased at the Craftsmen Potters Association exhibition, *Studio Ceramics Today*, V&A, 1983, no.27, £32.25)

207 Bottle, 1994
Porcelain, crystalline glaze; marks: 'DC' in monogram, and dot and triangle (year symbol for 1994), impressed; h.25.4cm, d.8cm
C.58-1995. Source: Craft Potters Association, London (exhibition: *Studio Ceramics 94*, V&A, 1994), £212

206

207

Clinton, Margery 1931–2005

1931	born Glasgow
1949–53	studies painting at Glasgow School of Art
1960s	begins working in ceramics
1969–	moves to London
1973–74	researches reduction lustres at Royal College of Art, London
1978–	returns to Scotland, establishes workshop at Haddington, East Lothian, working with one or two assistants
1995–	moves to Dunbar, works alone

Margery Clinton concentrated on in-glaze reduction lustres, adding copper or silver compounds to her glazes or painting them onto the glaze before the glaze firing. This contrasts with the clay-paste reduction lustres used by Alan Caiger-Smith (qv), which require a further firing. Clinton used the technique on a range of pottery and tiles, mainly in earthenware, but also porcelain and bone china. She also fulfilled many commissions for tilework.

208

Margery Clinton, 'Elusive lustres', *CR*, 103 (1987)
— *Lustres* (London, 1991)
— 'A Physic Garden Mural', *CR*, 159 (1996)
'CPA New Members', *CR*, 41 (1976)
Potters (1977) to (2000)
Obituary, *The Scotsman* (9 June 2005)

208 Bottle, 1979
Earthenware, matt black glaze with poured in-glaze lustre glazes; marks: 'MC JW Feb 79', painted; h.38cm, d.23.6cm
C.117-1979. Source: the artist, £18.50
The initials 'JW' stand for Jan Williamson, with whom Clinton worked in partnership for a short period.

The museum also holds four tiles with silkscreened lustre decoration based on designs from 13th-century tiles from Iran (C.116 to C-1979).

Cohen, David 1932–2018

1932	born Milwaukee, Wisconsin, USA
1957	studies at Layton Art School, Milwaukee
1958–62	studies sculpture and ceramics at Edinburgh College of Art
1962–63	fellowship at Scripps College, California, with Paul Soldner
1963–	returns to Scotland, establishes studio at Juniper Green, Edinburgh
1965–86	teaches ceramics at Edinburgh College of Art
1973	solo exhibition, Scottish Craft Centre, Edinburgh Festival
1975–	establishes studio near North Berwick, East Lothian
1986–91	Head of Ceramics at Glasgow School of Art

209

David Cohen specialized in raku, making large, individual pieces. He later developed modular compositions and installations based on plate forms, for interiors and gardens.

David Cohen, *The Basics of Throwing* (London, 2008)
— and Scott Anderson, *A Visual Language: Elements of Design* (London, 2006)
Illustration and biographical note, *CR*, 21 (1973), p.9
Paisley Museum and Art Galleries (1984), pp.23–4
Potters (1989)
Cordelia Oliver, 'The Critic's Eye', *Crafts*, 105 (1990)
Paul Nesbitt, 'Fired with Enthusiasm', exh. review, *Crafts*, 144 (1997)
Scott Anderson, obituary, *The Scotsman* (11 July 2018)

A documentary film on Cohen was made for the BBC Scotland arts programme *Scope*, *c.* 1974.

209 Pot, 1988
Raku, unglazed body with green-gold neck and foot, gold interior; h.46.2cm, d.35.4cm
C.34-1989. Source: given by Agi Katz, Boundary Gallery, London

Cole, John R. (Jack) 1907–1988

1907	born Woolwich, London
c. 1926	trains as woodwork and metalwork teacher at Shoreditch Training College
1930–31	attends pottery evening classes at Woolwich Polytechnic
1931	granted sabbatical from teaching to study at Central School of Arts and Crafts, London
1931–	with brother, Walter Cole (qv), builds kiln at Plumstead, London, making stoneware
1933–	with Walter, builds kiln at New Barn, Longfield, Kent, making stoneware and later also tin-glazed earthenware
c. 1936	teaches pottery at Camberwell School of Arts and Crafts
1936–67	teaches at Beckenham School of Art, becoming Principal in 1945; later appointed Principal of Ravensbourne College of Art
1947–	with Walter, reopens Rye Pottery, Sussex
1968	retires

In the 1930s John Cole shared pottery kilns with his brother Walter Cole (qv) and exhibited regularly with him. According to John, the name of their workshop, The Earth Potteries, 'arose from a desire that unless more natural materials were used in the making we did not think good pottery would result'. The brothers later reopened Rye Pottery. While John's teaching commitments prevented him playing a major part in its day-to-day running, he was involved in decisions on policy and improvements until the late 1960s. Although little-known today, John Cole exhibited alongside some of the major potters and artists of the 1930s. Cecilia Sempill – co-founder of the design and craft retailer Dunbar Hay, and an authority on ceramics – in 1944 listed him among those who 'have played a very real part in ... a revival of the true art of pottery in this country'.

Zwemmer (1933)
Arts and Crafts Exhibition Society (1935), (1941)
Brygos Gallery (1936)
— *Stoneware and Earthenware by John R. Cole and W. Vivian Cole*, exh. cat. (London, 1937)
'Stoneware', exh. review, *The Times* (19 March 1937)
British Council (1942), p.23
Sempill (1944), p.44

See also bibliography for Walter Cole.

210 Pot, 1936–37
Stoneware, speckled grey glaze, painted in brown; marks: 'EARTH', impressed; h.7.7cm, d.6.7cm
C.74-1937. Source: given by Lt-Col. K. Dingwall, DSO, through Art Fund
Acquired with **211**, a bowl by Walter Cole. Both had probably been exhibited at The Brygos Gallery in 1937.

210 / 211

Cole, Walter Vivian (Wally) 1913–1999

1913	born Woolwich, London
1930–31	studies sculpture, pottery and drawing at Woolwich Polytechnic
1931–36	studies sculpture, pottery and animal drawing at Central School of Arts and Crafts, London
1931–38	shares pottery kilns with John Cole (qv) at Plumstead, London, and Longfield, Kent
1936–38	works on architectural carvings for John Skeaping and Eric Kennington
1937	exhibition with John Cole at The Brygos Gallery, London, showing stoneware and, for the first time, tin-glazed earthenware
1940–46	serves in camouflage unit, Royal Engineers
1946–47	works for Council of Industrial Design; teaches at Central School
1947–	with John Cole, reopens Rye Pottery, Sussex, making production wares (mainly tin-glazed earthenware) and some individual pieces
1962	Silver Medal, International Ceramics Exhibition, Prague
1978	retires from management of Rye Pottery
1982	awarded MBE

During the 1930s Walter (known then as Vivian) Cole worked primarily as a sculptor, his work influenced by John Skeaping, who taught him at Woolwich and the Central School. Walter also made and exhibited studio pottery with his brother John Cole (qv). The impetus for their later interest in production pottery came from W.B. Honey, then Assistant Keeper of Ceramics at the V&A, who suggested at their Brygos Gallery exhibition in 1937 that the individual pieces were generally too expensive to use on the table, and that it would be

good if they could make some less expensive ware that could be used as such. This idea was realized in 1947, when they acquired and reopened the former Bellevue Pottery in Rye, setting up a team on small-scale industrial lines to produce modestly priced tableware.

Zwemmer (1933)
Arts and Crafts Exhibition Society (1935)
Brygos Gallery (1936)
— *Stoneware and Earthenware by John R. Cole and W. Vivian Cole*, exh. cat. (London, 1937)
Decorative Art (1961/62), (1962/63)
Casson (1967), p.5, pls.104–5
Rye Pottery 1869–1969, pottery booklet (1969)
Potters (1972) to (1977)
Crafts Council (1980), p.55
Tanya Harrod, 'Sources of Inspiration', *Crafts*, 123 (1993)
Rye Art Gallery, *Wally Cole: Sculptor/Potter*, exh. cat. (1993)
New Century, *Rye Pottery*, exh. cat. (London, 1996)

Exhibition reviews: 'Stoneware', *The Times* (19 March 1937); Colin Pearson, *Crafts*, 42 (1980); Arda Lacey, *Studio Pottery*, 5 (1993)

Obituaries: Emmanuel Cooper, *The Independent* (28 January 1999); David Whiting, *Crafts*, 158 (1999); *The Times* (19 February 1999)

211 Bowl, 1936–37
Stoneware, tenmoku glaze; marks: 'WV' in monogram, incised; h.3.7cm, d.8cm
C.73-1937. Source: *see* **210**

The museum also holds examples of the standard production of Rye Pottery, not catalogued here (C.242 to 245-1991 and C.112-1993).

Constantinidis, Joanna (née **Connell**) 1927–2000

1927	born York
1946–49	studies at Sheffield College of Art, where introduced to pottery
1951–89	teaches ceramics at Chelmsford Technical College and School of Art, and makes there in spare time
1959–	moves to Great Baddow, Essex
1969|73	solo exhibitions, Peter Dingley Gallery, Stratford-upon-Avon
1976	solo exhibition, Craftsmen Potters Shop, London
1982–	regular solo exhibitions at Crafts Council Shop at the V&A and elsewhere
1989–	retires from teaching; makes full-time at Great Baddow
1995	touring retrospective exhibition, University of Derby

Joanna Constantinidis worked in a modernist idiom, making thrown and altered vessels that were both austere and sensual. Her work shows great sensitivity and expression in form and line, her shapes enhanced by subtle matt or lustred surfaces. Constantinidis also produced an influential and highly regarded range of white porcelain tableware.

Joanna Constantinidis, 'Some Techniques', *Pottery Quarterly*, 11:42 (1974)
— 'Joanna Constantinidis', *CR*, 90 (1984)
— 'White Porcelain Tablewares', *Studio Pottery*, 18 (1995)
Lewis (1956), pls.362, 364
Decorative Art (1960/61), (1971/72)
Casson (1967), pp.5–6, pls.106–8
Potters (1972) to (1997)
V&A (1972), p.108
Crafts Advisory Committee (1976), p.87
Crafts Council (1980), p.56
Paisley Museum and Art Galleries (1984), pp.24–5
Crafts Council (1985), pp.36–8
Bonhams, *Contemporary Ceramics*, including the Sharman Collection (London, 27 February 1989), lots 138–59
Cooper (1990)
The Ballantyne Collection, *Joanna Constantinidis: Ceramics from Twenty Five Years*, exh. cat. (Derby, 1995)
Josie Walter, 'Joanna Constantinidis', *CR*, 152 (1995)
David Whiting, 'Sources of Inspiration', *Crafts*, 149 (1997)
V&A (1999)
Bonhams, *International Contemporary Ceramics*, including selected works from the estate of Joanna Constantinidis (London, 18 May 2004), lots 158–66
David Whiting, biography, in *Oxford Dictionary of National Biography* (Oxford, 2004)
Carlano (2010), pp.56–7
Nottingham City Museums and Galleries (2017), pp.30–1

Exhibition reviews: Richard Dunning, *CR*, 21 (1973); W.A. Ismay, *CR*, 42 (1976); Tanya Harrod, *Crafts*, 96 (1989); Paul Vincent, *Studio Pottery*, 9 (1994); Julian Stair, *Studio Pottery*, 15 (1995); David Whiting, *Crafts*, 135 (1995); Robert S. Silver, *Studio Pottery*, 38 (1999)

Obituaries: Edmund de Waal, *Crafts*, 167 (2000); David Whiting, *The Guardian* (3 August 2000); *The Times* (5 August 2000)

The papers of Joanna Constantinidis are at the Crafts Study Centre, Farnham (CON).

212 Bowl, 1976
Porcelain, brown glaze with irregular spiral dark lines; marks: 'C', impressed; h.11.8cm, d.12.6cm
C.292-1976. Source: Craftsmen Potters Association, London (solo exhibition, 1976, no.26), £22.56
The metallic, lustrous surface of this bowl and other works in the same exhibition represented a new direction for the artist.

213 Pot, *c.* 1980
Porcelain, with iron and manganese lines, semi-transparent brown glaze; marks: 'C' in a circle, impressed; h.19.6cm, d.9.2cm
C.77-1996. Source: gift of Adrian Sassoon, Esq.

212

213

219 / 217 / 215 / 216 / 218

214 Flattened bottle, 1983 (pl.80)
Stoneware, saggar-fired, lustred surface; marks: 'C', impressed; h.52cm, d.25.5cm
C.211-1983. Source: Henry Rothschild Associates, Cambridge (group exhibition, Kettle's Yard, no.31), £225

215 Teacup and saucer, *c.* 1996
Porcelain, clear semi-matt glaze; marks: 'C' in a circle, impressed on saucer; h.6.8cm (cup), d.16.4cm (saucer)
C.47:1,2-1996. Source: Crafts Council Shop at the V&A, £54

216 Plate, *c.* 1996
Porcelain, clear semi-matt glaze; marks: 'C' in a circle, impressed; d.28.7cm
C.82-1996. Source: Contemporary Applied Arts, London (exhibition: *Soft Clay*, 1996), £52.20

217 Beaker, *c.* 1996
Porcelain, clear semi-matt glaze; marks: 'C' in a circle, impressed; h.16.5cm, d.7.5cm
C.83-1996. Source: *see* **216**, £45.45

218 Bowl, *c.* 1996
Porcelain, clear semi-matt glaze; marks: 'C' in a circle, impressed; h.11.1cm, d.14.9cm
C.84-1996. Source: *see* **216**, £57.82

219 Spoon, *c.* 1996
Porcelain, thrown and cut, clear semi-matt glaze; marks: 'C' in a circle, impressed; h.5.2cm, d.13.2cm
C.85-1996. Source: *see* **216**, £43.42

Cook, George Frederick 1919–1982

1919	born Preston, Lancashire
c. 1938	studies pottery at Blackpool School of Art
1940s	studies pottery at Central School of Arts and Crafts, London, under Dora Billington (qv); course interrupted by war service but completed after the war
1948–66	establishes workshop, The Potter's Wheel Studio, Ambleside, Westmorland
1966–68	teaches part-time at Harris College, Preston, Lancashire, and Ulster School of Art
1968–82	teaches full-time at Ulster School of Art

220

George Frederick Cook produced domestic earthenware and stoneware from his pottery in Ambleside. He is known for his slip-trailed earthenware, decorated in blue and other colours, and for his later sgraffito designs in a mid-century style.

Arts and Crafts Exhibition Society (1948) to (1957)
Decorative Art (1950/51), (1954/55), (1957/58), (1958/59), (1959/60)
Notice of group exhibition at Crafts Centre, London, *Pottery Quarterly*, 3:12 (1956), p.158, pl.11
Paisley Museum and Art Galleries (1984), p.25

220 Jug, 1950
Earthenware, slip-trailed decoration over dark and light slips; marks: 'COOK / AMBLESIDE', incised; h.33.7cm, d.22.3cm
Circ.273-1950. Source: Arts and Crafts Exhibition Society (Twenty-second Exhibition, V&A, 1950, no.180), £5.5s.

Cooper, Emmanuel 1938–2012

1938	born Pilsley, Derbyshire
1958–60	studies at Dudley Teacher Training College
1960–61	studies at Bournemouth College of Art, taking pottery under David Ballantyne (qv)
1961–62	attends pottery classes at Hornsey College of Art, while working full-time as an art teacher
1963	turns to pottery; works with Gwyn Hanssen (qv)
1964	works with Bryan Newman (qv)
1965–	establishes workshop in Notting Hill, London
1970–2010	co-editor of *Ceramic Review* with Eileen Lewenstein (qv); editor from 1998
1971–97	teaches part-time at Middlesex Polytechnic
1972–80	teaches at Camberwell School of Art and Crafts, London
1972	solo exhibition at British Crafts Centre, London
1973–	establishes Fonthill Pottery, Finsbury Park, London
1976–	moves pottery to Primrose Hill, London
1981	selector for *The Maker's Eye*, Crafts Council, London
1988–	ceases production of domestic ware; henceforth works alone
1996	awarded PhD, Middlesex University
1996–2002	touring solo exhibition, Ruthin Crafts Centre
2000–11	Visiting Professor, Royal College of Art, London
2002	awarded OBE
2003	solo exhibition, Fine Art Society, London; biography of Bernard Leach (qv) published
2012	biography of Lucie Rie (qv) published
2013–14	touring retrospective exhibition, Ruthin Crafts Centre

An accomplished potter recognized in particular for his development of vibrant and dramatic glazes for electric kilns, Emmanuel Cooper was a pivotal figure in the world of studio ceramics who played an influential role as an editor, writer and teacher. His long-standing editorship of *Ceramic Review* was of particular importance. He was also an activist for LGBTQ rights and a champion of folk art. For more than 20 years he ran his workshop as a small urban production pottery, making thrown domestic stoneware and individual pots. Despite misgivings about abandoning functional ware, he later turned exclusively to individual pieces,

concentrating increasingly on a restricted range of forms, notably conical bowls and flattened jugs. As a writer he was enormously prolific, publishing almost 30 books alongside a vast body of critical writing in journals and exhibition catalogues.

The following bibliography reflects Cooper's own practice and his broader writing on ceramics. Texts concerning individual artists are listed elsewhere. *See* main bibliography (pp.408–11) for full references. For a broader account of his writing, see Horbury (2019), below.

Emmanuel Cooper (1970), (1972a), (1972b), (1976), (1980), (1981), (1982), (1987), (1990), (1992), (2000), (2002), (2003), (2007a), (2007b), (2009), (2012)
— 'Nickel Glazes', *CR*, 55 (1979)
— essay, in Crafts Council (1981), pp.24–7
— 'Amazing Glaze', *CR*, 105 (1987)
— 'Bodies, Surfaces and Texture', *CR*, 160 (1996)
— 'Subject and Object: A Potter and His Life', in Johnson (1998), pp.173–7
— 'Cool, Calm and Collected', *CR*, 194 (2002)
Cooper and Royle (1978)
Lewenstein and Cooper (1974)
Decorative Art (1968/69), (1969/70), (1971/72)
Potters/The Ceramics Book (1972) to (2012)
Lucie-Smith (1975), pp.56–9
Crafts Advisory Committee (1976), p.88
Edelman (1976), Part II
Crafts Council (1980), p.56
Edward Lucie-Smith, *Emmanuel Cooper*, Aberystwyth Arts Centre: Ceramic Series 56 (1992)
Ruthin Craft Centre, *Emmanuel Cooper*, exh. cat. (1996)
Hanaor (2007), pp.142–3
Beaux Arts, *Emmanuel Cooper: Abundance: Form Texture Colour*, exh. cat. (Bath, 2008)
'Simply Emmanuel', *CR*, 245 (2010)
Ruthin Craft Centre, *Emmanuel Cooper OBE: Retrospective 1938–2012*, exh. cat. (2013)
Charles Darwent, 'Fired by Alchemy', *World of Interiors*, 33:2 (2014)
Leach Pottery, *Emmanuel Cooper: Connections and Contrasts*, exh. cat. (St Ives, 2015)
David Horbury (ed.), *Making Emmanuel Cooper: Life and Work from his Memoirs, Letters, Diaries and Interviews* (London, 2019)

Exhibition reviews: Anthony Hepburn, *Craft Horizons*, 31:1 (1971); Gordon Baldwin, *Crafts*, 7 (1974); Margot Coatts, *Crafts*, 143 (1996); Jack Doherty, *CR*, 162 (1996); Alison Britton, 'Glazed Ceramics', *Crafts*, 149 (1997); Felicity Aylieff, *CR*, 184 (2000); Colin Martin, *Craft Arts International*, 92 (2014); Ian Wilson, *CR*, 267 (2014)

Obituaries: *The Times* (26 January 2012); Jeffrey Weeks, *The Guardian* (30 January 2012); Julian Treuherz, *The Independent* (31 January 2012); *The Telegraph* (6 February 2012); Bonnie Kemske, *Ceramics: Art and Perception*, 87 (2012); *CR*, 254 (2012)

An interview with Emmanuel Cooper is in the Crafts Lives sound archive at the British Library, London (C960/44).

221 Bowl, 1970
Stoneware, wax-resist decoration in black over white slips, bone-ash glaze; marks: impressed device; h.7.5cm, d.35cm
Circ.490-1970. Source: Crafts Centre of Great Britain, London (solo exhibition, 1970), £10

222 Bowl, 1981
Porcelain, green glaze, metallic rim; h.13.2cm, d.16cm
C.51-1982. Source: the artist, £74.75

221

222

Considered by Cooper to have been one of his most successful pieces of the time.

223 Bowl, *c.* 2000–10 (pl.113)
Porcelain, yellow glaze specked with gold, red and green, bronze rim; marks: impressed seal; h.9.5cm, d.26.7cm
C.2-2019. Source: given by the Estate of Emmanuel Cooper

224 Jug, *c.* 2000–10 (pl.113)
Stoneware, thrown and altered, volcanic white glaze, tinged with blue, red and green; h.20.7cm, d.26cm
C.3-2019. Source: *see* **223**

Coper, Hans 1920–1981

1920	born Chemnitz, Germany
1939	emigrates to England
1940	arrested as enemy alien, sent to Canada
1941–43	returns to England, serving in Pioneer Corps
1946–58	meets Lucie Rie (qv), joins her workshop in Albion Mews, London
1950–56	shared exhibitions with Rie, Berkeley Galleries, London
1954	wins Gold Medal at Milan Triennale
1956	solo exhibition, Bonniers, New York
1958	solo exhibition, Primavera, London
1959–65	takes studio and accommodation at Digswell Arts Trust, Hertfordshire
1962	commission for Coventry Cathedral candlesticks
1963–	moves to Princedale Road, London
1963–72	teaches at Camberwell School of Art and Crafts
1966–75	teaches at Royal College of Art, London
1967–	moves to Frome, Somerset, establishes workshop
1975–	final UK solo exhibition at Robert Welch, Chipping Camden, Gloucestershire; amyotrophic lateral sclerosis diagnosed, pots with increasing difficulty

Hans Coper is among the most internationally significant ceramic artists of the post-war era. His importance lies both in his formidable body of work, which shows wheel-thrown clay as a vehicle for sculptural expression of the highest order, and through his impact as a teacher. Coper joined the workshop of fellow émigré Lucie Rie (qv) without practical experience of ceramics, but quickly assimilated the rudiments of pottery, aided in part by classes in throwing at Woolwich Polytechnic

with Heber Mathews (qv). After a period assisting Rie with button-making and tableware, Coper began to make individual pieces. Working with a restricted set of materials, he went on to develop a highly individual vocabulary of forms, which appeared poised between the contemporary and the ancient. He also extended studio pottery into the realm of architecture, fulfilling important commissions for murals and monumental candleholders, and developing designs for acoustic bricks and other building components. Reticent in discussing his own work, his one written statement – made for his joint exhibition with the weaver Peter Collingwood at the V&A – succinctly characterizes the disciplined nature of his enquiry, identifying his concern with 'extracting essence rather than with experiment and exploration'. His influence was perhaps most strongly felt on a generation of potters at the Royal College of Art, including Alison Britton (qv) and Elizabeth Fritsch (qv), who sensed the possibilities of pottery's 'ambiguous reference to purpose and function'.

See also bibliography for Lucie Rie, where shared publications are listed.

Dartington Hall (1952)
Wingfield Digby (1952), p.84, pls.61, 64
Fennemore (1953)
Rose (1955), p.24, pls.76–85, (1970), pp.45–8, pls.104–17
Lewis (1956), pls.372–3
Smithsonian Institution (1959)
Decorative Art (1959/60), (1961/62), (1965/66)
Birks (1967), pp.29–44, (1976), pp.70–87
Casson (1967), p.6, pls.109–14
Tony Birks, 'Purist Potter', *Design*, 247 (1969)
V&A, *Collingwood/Coper: Rugs and Wall-hangings by Peter Collingwood, Pots by Hans Coper*, exh. picture-book, statement by Hans Coper, photographs by Jane Gate (London, 1969)
— *Collingwood Coper Exhibition: Catalogue*, leaflet (London, 1969)
— (1972), p.108
Lucie-Smith (1975), pp.62–71
Crafts Advisory Committee (1976), p.88
V&A (1977), pp.4–6
Hetjens Museum, *Hans Coper*, exh. cat. (Düsseldorf, 1980)
'Hans Coper', tributes, *Crafts*, 54 (1982)
Tony Birks, *Hans Coper* (London, 1983), revised (Catrine, 2013)
Emmanuel Cooper, 'Hans Coper – Artist Potter', *CR*, 84 (1983)
Alison Britton, 'Hans Coper 1920–1981', *American Craft*, 44:2 (1984)
Paisley Museum and Art Galleries (1984), pp.27–8
Serpentine Gallery, *Hans Coper, 1920–1981*, exh. leaflet (London, 1984)
Crafts Council (1985), pp.38–41
ICA (1985), p.43
Louise Campbell (ed.), *To Build a Cathedral: Coventry Cathedral 1945–1962* (Warwick, 1987), nos.141–3
Sainsbury Centre for Visual Arts (1990)
David Whiting, 'Coper at Coventry', *Studio Pottery*, 20 (1996)
Frankel (2000), pp.14–63
Hans Coper Retrospective: Innovation in 20th Century Ceramics, exh. cat. (Tokyo, 2009)
Cooper (2012)
Alun Graves, 'Hans Coper: Sculpture in Architecture', *Interpreting Ceramics*, ejournal, 14 (2012)
Geraint Franklin, 'On the Tiles', *C20: The Magazine of the Twentieth Century Society*, 1 (2014)
Nottingham City Museums and Galleries (2017), pp.33–4
Ashmolean Museum, *Hans Coper 100*, exh. cat., text by David Whiting, photographs by Jane Coper (Oxford, 2020)

Exhibition reviews: Robert Melville, *Architectural Review*, 112 (November 1952), and 116 (September 1954); *Pottery Quarterly*, 3:12 (1956); *Architectural Review*, 124 (October 1958); *Pottery Quarterly*, 5:18 (1958); Anthony Hepburn, *Craft Horizons*, 29:3 (1969); L.R. Rogers, *CR*, 7 (1971); Ian Bennett, *Crafts*, 17 (1975); Bob Rogers, *CR*, 36 (1975); Christopher Reid, *Crafts*, 65 (1983); Max Wykes-Joyce, *Art & Artists*, 214 (July 1984)

225 Handled pot, 1951 (pl.34)
Stoneware, incised design through manganese oxide under a yellowish glaze; marks: 'HC' in monogram, impressed; h.26.6cm, d.19.9cm
Circ.54-1951. Source: the artist, £6.10s.

226 Bottle, 1954
Stoneware, layered white slips and manganese oxide over a textured body with incised design, interior with manganese glaze; marks: 'HC' in monogram, impressed; h.43cm, d.19cm
Circ.337-1955. Source: the artist, £12.12s.

227 Bowl, *c.* 1955 (pl.39)
Stoneware, incised decoration through manganese oxide under a white glaze, the exterior with layered white slips and manganese oxide over a textured body; marks: 'HC' in an oval, impressed; h.12.4cm, d.37.6cm
C.15-2016. Source: Phillips, London, £92,292.14; purchased in memory of Annabel Freyberg through the generosity of her friends

228 'Large flat bottle', 1958 (fig.11)
Stoneware, layered white slips and manganese oxide over a textured body, interior with manganese glaze; marks: 'HC' in monogram, impressed; h.49.2cm, d.38.1cm
Circ.154-1958. Source: Primavera, London (exhibition: *Stoneware Pots by Hans Coper*, 1958, no.27), £36.15s.

229 Large bowl, 1958
Stoneware, greyish-white glaze with brown flecks; marks: 'HC' in monogram, impressed; h.10.2cm, d.39.1cm
Circ.155-1958. Source: *see* **228** (no.39), £12.12s.

230 'Large oval-bodied pot narrowing to an elliptical top', 1968 (pl.56)
Stoneware, layered white slips over a textured, incised body, interior with manganese glaze; marks: 'HC' in monogram, impressed; h.54cm, d.42cm

226

229

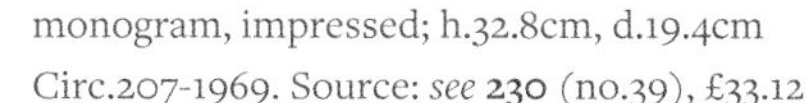

Circ.204-1969. Source: the artist (exhibition: *Collingwood/Coper*, V&A, 1969, no.17), £84

231 'Bottle form with ridged shoulders and wide rim', 1968
Stoneware, layered white slips and manganese oxide over a textured, striated body, interior and rim with manganese glaze; marks: 'HC' in monogram, impressed; h.19.2cm, d.14.9cm
Circ.205-1969. Source: *see* **230** (no.45), £24.10s.

232 'Flat spade-shaped pot', 1968
Stoneware, metallic black manganese oxide over a textured, incised body; marks: 'HC' in monogram, impressed; h.19.4cm, d.12.8cm
Circ.206-1969. Source: *see* **230** (no.38), £20.6s.

233 'Flat spade-shaped pot', 1968
Stoneware, abraded layered white slips and oxides over a textured, incised body, interior with manganese glaze; marks: 'HC' in monogram, impressed; h.32.8cm, d.19.4cm
Circ.207-1969. Source: *see* **230** (no.39), £33.12s.

234 'Bud-shaped pot', 1968 (pl.57)
Stoneware, layered white slips and manganese oxide over a textured, striated body, interior with manganese glaze; marks: 'HC' in monogram, impressed; h.30.4cm, d.22.2cm
Circ.208-1969. Source: *see* **230** (no.87), £28

235 'Bud-shaped pot', 1968
Stoneware, layered white slips and manganese oxide over a textured body, interior with manganese glaze; marks: 'HC' in monogram, impressed; h.18cm, d.12.8cm
Circ.767-1969. Source: given by J.M.W. Crowther (from *Collingwood/Coper* exhibition, V&A, 1969, no.86)

236 'White pot on high foot', 1975
Stoneware, layered white slips over a textured, incised body, interior with manganese glaze; marks: 'HC' in monogram, impressed; h.24cm, d.14.3cm
Circ.398-1976. Source: the artist, £108
Illustrated in Birks (1976), pl.90.

237 'Black form on square foot', 1975
Stoneware, metallic black manganese oxide over a textured, incised body; marks: 'HC 'in block script, impressed; h.27.5cm, d.8.1cm
Circ.399-1976. Source: the artist, £122
Illustrated in Birks (1976), pl.75.

231

232 / 233

235 / 236

237

Crofts, Stella R. 1898–1964

1898	born Nottingham
1916–22	studies at Central School of Arts and Crafts, London
1922–23	studies sculpture and pottery at Royal College of Art, London
1923–	establishes studio in Ilford, Essex
1925–29	wins Bronze Medal at Paris International Exhibition; exhibits widely and internationally
1932–	studio at Norsey Wood, Billericay, Essex

Stella Crofts was a successful and prolific maker of pottery figures. She is known particularly for her detailed, naturalistic representations of animals and birds, which reflect her lifelong interest in zoology.

British Institute of Industrial Art (1922), (1923), (1927), (1929)
Arts and Crafts Exhibition Society (1923), (1926), (1928), (1938) to (1950)
Royal Academy of Arts (1923)
Florence Davies, 'British Handcraft in Detroit', *American Magazine of Art*, 15:2 (1924), pp.74–5
Guild of Potters (1924), (1925), (1926)
Decorative Art (1925), (1926), (1927), (1931), (1951/52)
Redfern Gallery, *Early English Water-colours Dated 1828–1829 and Pottery by Stella Crofts*, exh. pamphlet (London, 1926)
Colnaghi (1927), (1929)
Redfern Gallery, *Oils by Tom Nash and Pottery Groups by Stella Crofts*, exh. pamphlet (London, 1929)
Beaux Arts Gallery, *Fine China Statuettes by the Worcester Royal Porcelain Co. Ltd*, exh. pamphlet (London, 1931)
Hawkins Opie (1985), p.345
Vincentelli and Hale (1986)
Albert Gallichan, 'Stella Crofts 1898–1964: Potter and Ceramic Sculptor', *Journal of the Decorative Arts Society*, 20 (1996)

239

240

241

242

Paul Hughes, *Stella's Ark: Stella Crofts: Studio Potter, Animal Modeller and Designer* (High Wycombe, 2015)
Knott (2021)

Exhibition reviews: S.B.W., 'The Guild of Potters', *The Studio*, 91 (1926), pp.34–5; R.R. Tatlock, *Daily Telegraph* (18 October 1929); *The Times* (22 October 1929)

238 *Giraffes*, 1923 (pl.8)
Earthenware, slip-cast, greenish glaze, painted in black; marks: 'Stella R Crofts / ENGLAND', incised; h.17.1cm, d.18.3cm
C.427-1934. Source: British Institute of Industrial Art (given by the artist, 1923)

239 *Donkey Stealing Carrots*, introduced 1923
Earthenware, slip-cast, painted in colours; marks: 'Stella R Crofts', incised; h.17.5cm, d.19cm
C.131-1977. Source: Richard Dennis, London, £30

240 'Sea Lion Knife Rest', introduced 1924
Earthenware, slip-cast, painted in colours; marks: 'Stella R Crofts', incised; h.15.6cm, d.14.9cm
C.130-1977. Source: *see* **239**, £10

241 *Cheetah family*, 1927
Earthenware, slip-cast, painted in colours; marks: 'Stella R Crofts / 1927', incised; h.17cm, d.21.5cm
C.482-1927. Source: given by J.F. Wilson, Esq.

242 *Motherhood (Antelope Group)*, 1928 (introduced 1923)
Earthenware, slip-cast, mauve glaze; marks: 'Stella R Crofts', incised; h.16cm, d.10cm
C.431-1934. Source: British Institute of Industrial Art (given by the artist)

Crowan Pottery *see* Harry and May Davis

Crowley, Jill 1946–

1946	born Cork, Ireland
1966–69	studies ceramics at Bristol Polytechnic
1969–72	studies ceramics at Royal College of Art, London
1970–2017	teaches ceramics at Morley College, London
1972	travelling scholarship to Greece, and to USA, where she attends summer school with Paul Soldner, working in raku
1972–	founder member of 401½ Workshops, Lambeth, London
1977	solo exhibition, Crafts Council Gallery, London
1981–	workshop in Brixton, London
1996	shortlisted for Jerwood Prize for Applied Arts

Jill Crowley is one of the group of women artists, including Glenys Barton (qv), Alison Britton (qv), Carol McNicoll (qv) and Jacqueline Poncelet (qv), who emerged from the Royal College of Art in the early 1970s and went on to revolutionize ceramic practice. She achieved early success, and during the 1980s was the foremost figurative sculptor in clay working in the UK. She is known in particular for her human and cat portrait heads, mermaid figures, and sculptures of hands and arms, the last initially modelled after those of her own baby. Her work is immediate and appealing, with a stimulating wit and sense of caricature, underpinned by detached but tender observation.

Crafts Advisory Committee (1974), pp.21–4
— (1976), p.89
Crafts Council, *Jill Crowley*, exh. cat. (London, 1977)
Houston (1979), pp.22–9
Ulster Museum, *Jill Crowley: Ceramic Sculptor*, exh. cat. (Belfast, 1979)
Crafts Council (1980), p.56
Christopher Reid, 'Jill Crowley', *Crafts*, 55 (1982)
Speight (1983), pp.92–3
Oxfordshire County Museum Services (1984), pp.26–7
Paisley Museum and Art Galleries (1984), p.28
David Briers, *Jill Crowley*, Aberystwyth Arts Centre: Ceramic Series 9 (1985)
Crafts Council (1985), pp.41–3
Tanya Harrod, 'Jill Crowley', *CR*, 114 (1988)
Wren (1990), pp.62–3
Contemporary Applied Arts, *Jill Crowley*, exh. pamphlet (London, 1992)
Pamela Johnson, 'Sources of Inspiration', *Crafts*, 118 (1992)
Eileen Lewenstein, 'Hands On', *CR*, 136 (1992)
Museum of Modern Art, Oxford (1993), pp.26–7, 83, 93–4
Crafts Council (1995b), pp.30–1
— (1996b), pp.16–17

Exhibition reviews: Lavinia Learmont and Louise Collis, *Art & Artists*, 12:1 (1977); Sheila Ross, *Crafts*, 34 (1978); Tanya Harrod, *Crafts*, 75 (1985); Peter Dormer, 'Clay Bodies', *Crafts*, 102 (1990); Victor Margrie, *Studio Pottery*, 2 (1993); Julia Pitts, *CR*, 181 (2000)

243

244

An interview with Jill Crowley is in the Crafts Lives sound archive at the British Library, London (C960/124).

243 *Cat Portrait*, 1980
Raku, handbuilt; marks: 'J Crowley', incised; h.35.4cm, d.10.9cm
C.116-1980. Source: British Crafts Centre, London (exhibition: *Raku and Saltglaze*, 1980, no.15), £230

244 *Portrait of a Darts Player*, 1981
Stoneware, handbuilt, low-fired coloured glazes; h.23.5cm, d.30.8cm
C.84-1982. Source: Oxford Gallery, Oxford, £508.10

245 *Hand*, 1988
Stoneware, handbuilt, pink, yellow, green and cream matt glazes; marks: 'J. Crowley', incised; h.38.4cm, d.36.6cm

245

C.4-1989. Source: Michaelson and Orient, London, £715.50

Cummings, Phoebe 1981–

1981	born Walsall, West Midlands
1999–2002	studies 3D Crafts at University of Brighton
2003–05	studies ceramics at Royal College of Art, London
2006	solo exhibition, *Fragments*, Corn Exchange Gallery, Edinburgh
2008	residency, John Michael Kohler Arts Center, Wisconsin, USA
2010	residency, V&A, London
2011	wins British Ceramics Biennial AWARD, Stoke-on-Trent
2012–13	Ceramics Fellowship, Camden Arts Centre, London
2013	solo exhibition, University of Hawai'i Art Gallery, Honolulu
2017	wins Woman's Hour Craft Prize
2017–	Research Associate, University of Westminster

Phoebe Cummings creates intricately detailed temporary sculptures and installations in raw clay, responding to the natural world and its interpretation through historic art and design. Her radical and innovative practice developed in the absence of a permanent studio space and with minimal equipment. Instead, Cummings began working peripatetically around residencies and other opportunities to make work directly on site. Left unfired, her works last only the duration of the exhibition or residency, after which they are broken down and the clay reclaimed, their ephemerality adding to their poetic charge. Since 2012 she has increasingly made sculptural components at home in preparation for building works on site.

Phoebe Cummings, 'Elsewhere, Here', in Newlyn Art Gallery, *Down There Among The Roots*, exh. cat. (2011)
— 'An Island Aside', University of Westminster Ceramics Research Centre – UK, online essay series 7 (2013)
— 'Peripatetic Making: A Borrowed Space, Time Continuum', *Journal of Modern Craft*, 8:3 (2015)
— 'Collected Activity: Making in the Museum', in Brown, Stair and Twomey (2016), pp.146–53
Hanaor (2007), pp.108–9
Jerwood Visual Arts, *Formed Thoughts*, exh. cat. (London, 2012)
Camden Arts Centre, *Phoebe Cummings*, File Note 78, text by Zoe Laughlin (London, 2013)
Ann Christie, 'Mind and Matter', *CR*, 263 (2013)
Robert Preece, 'Material Performance', interview, *Sculpture*, 32:10 (2013)
Dahn (2015), pp.16, 90–4
Visual Arts Centre, *Épisode: 2nd Virginia McClure Ceramic Biennale*, exh. cat. (Montréal, 2016)
Elderton and Morrill (2017), pp.64–7
Imogen Greenhalgh, 'Disappearing Acts', *Crafts*, 269 (2017)
'Woman's Hour Craft Prize', supplement, *Crafts*, 268 (2017)
Rachael Chambers, 'Craft in the Spotlight', *CR*, 289 (2018)
Morris (2018), pp.258–61
Meşher (2019), pp.136–54

Exhibition reviews: Tony Franks, *CR*, 221 (2006); Stephen Knott, 'Formed Thoughts', *CR*, 255 (2012); Imogen Greenhalgh, 'Material Language', *Crafts*, 262 (2016)

246 *After the Death of the Bear*, 2010
Unfired porcelain, sieve; h.18.5cm, d.20.6cm
C.51-2019. Source: given by the artist

246

247

Made during Cummings' V&A residency, this landscape is modelled on top of a sieve found in the studio. The scene derives from a 19th-century transfer-printed design.

247 Fragments of *Triumph of the Immaterial*, 2017–19 (*see also* fig.18)
Earthenware; h.28.5cm, w.102cm (overall)
C.52:1 to 16-2019. Source: given by the artist
Made for the Woman's Hour Craft Prize in 2017, *Triumph of the Immaterial* was a fountain modelled in raw clay, which enacted its own destruction. Fragments of the fountain were fired following its exhibition at the V&A, these being displayed on the subsequent tour. The composition of the group held by the museum was determined by the artist at the time of acquisition.

Cummins, Paul 1977–

1977	born Chesterfield, Derbyshire
2003–05	studies architecture and environmental design at Sheffield Hallam University
2007–10	studies craft at University of Derby
2011–	establishes Paul Cummins Ceramics, Derby
2012	series of six installations, *The English Flower Garden*, for London 2012 Cultural Olympiad
2014	installation, *Blood Swept Lands and Seas of Red*, Tower of London
2015	awarded MBE
2015–18	tour of *Wave* and *Weeping Window* elements of *Blood Swept Lands and Seas of Red*

Paul Cummins makes landscape installations incorporating ceramic flowers. He is best known for creating *Blood Swept Lands and Seas of Red*, an installation of 888,246 poppies at the Tower of London, staged in collaboration with the theatre designer Tom Piper, marking the centenary of the start of the First World War.

'Floral Arrangement', *Crafts*, 223 (2010), p.11
Corinne Jones, 'Paul Cummins', interview, *The Observer* (14 December 2014)
Mark Brown, 'Blood-swept Lands', *The Guardian* (28 December 2014)
Holly Goring, 'Blood Swept Lands', *Ceramics Monthly*, 63:2 (2014)
'Flowers at the Tower', *Crafts*, 250 (2014), p.9
Harriet Baker, 'Helping Hands', *CR*, 281 (2016)
'Expert Eyes', *CR*, 285 (2017)
Jenny Kidd and Joanne Sayner, 'Unthinking remembrance? Blood Swept Lands and Seas of Red and the Significance of Centenaries', *Cultural Trends*, 27:2 (2018)
John Richardson, 'Sentimental Witnesses: Modern War Representation and the Eighteenth Century', *Mosaic*, 51:2 (2018)

248 16 poppies from the installation *Blood Swept Lands and Seas of Red*, 2012–14
Glazed earthenware, steel, plastic, rubber; h.variable, d.13cm (each poppy)
C.9 to 25-2015. Source: Historic Royal Palaces, £400
Conceived by Cummins and made under his direction in Derby, Tunstall and Whichford, the 888,246 poppies that formed the installation represented every British or colonial military fatality of the First World War. Sixteen poppies were acquired in memory of the sixteen V&A staff members who lost their lives.

248

Curneen, Claire 1968–

1968	born Tralee, County Kerry, Ireland
1986–90	studies ceramics at Crawford College of Art and Design, Cork
1990–91	studies ceramics at University of Ulster, Belfast
1991–92	studies ceramics at Cardiff Institute of Higher Education
1993–	studio in Cardiff
1999	wins *Ceramics Monthly* international competition, sculpture category
2001	Gold Medal in Craft and Design, National Eisteddfod of Wales
2003–	teaches ceramics at Cardiff Metropolitan University
2012	Creative Wales Ambassador Award
2017	Crafts Council Collect Open Award for *Tending the Fires*

One of the foremost figurative ceramic sculptors working today, Claire Curneen emerged in the 1990s during a resurgence of activity in the field. She is known for her lyrical and affecting figures reflecting aspects of the human condition, informed by mythology and Christian iconography. Sensitively modelled with particular emphasis on the hands, her figures are handbuilt in porcelain, terracotta or black stoneware, with touches of gilding or printed decoration.

Ruthin Craft Centre, *Claire Curneen: New Work*, exh. cat. (Ruthin, 1997)
Emmanuel Cooper, *Claire Curneen*, Aberystwyth Arts Centre: Ceramic Series 91 (1998)
Sarah James, 'Searching for Answers', *Ceramics: Art and Perception*, 38 (1999)
Nicholas Lees, 'A Melancholy Beauty', *CR*, 195 (2002)
Natasha Mayo, 'The Role of Narrative in Claire Curneen's Ceramics', *Kerameiki Techni*, 42 (2002)
Ruthin Craft Centre, *Claire Curneen: Succour*, exh. cat. (Ruthin, 2003)
Shipley Art Gallery (2003b), pp.25–6
Ian Wilson, 'Contemplation', *Keramik Magazin*, 4 (2003)
Amanda Fielding, 'Claire Curneen', *New Ceramics*, 5 (2005)
Alex McErlain, 'Thoughtful Sadness', *Ceramics: Art and Perception*, 62 (2005)

Ruthin Craft Centre (2006), pp.32–5, 75
Hanaor (2007), pp.78–81
Whiting (2009), pp.122–7
Carlano (2010), pp.62–3
Garcia (2012), pp.74–5
Laura Gray, 'To This I Put My Name', *Craft Arts International*, 91 (2014)
Catherine Roche, 'An In-between Space', *CCQ Magazine*, 3 (2014)
— 'Shifting States: Liminal Narratives in the Work of Claire Curneen', *New Ceramics*, 5 (2014)
Ruthin Craft Centre, *Claire Curneen: To This I Put My Name*, exh. cat. (Ruthin, 2014)
Andy Christian, 'Emotional Metaphors', *CR*, 286 (2017)
Emma Crichton-Miller, 'Body of Evidence', *Crafts*, 265 (2017)
Richard Davey, 'Beauty in Brokenness: The Sculpture of Claire Curneen', *Image: Art, Faith, Mystery*, 97 (2018)
Yinka Shonibare, *Criminal Ornamentation*, exh. cat. (London: Hayward Publishing, 2018), p.42
Kay Whitney, 'About to Happen', *Ceramics Monthly*, 68:9 (2020)

Exhibition reviews: Mick Casson, 'Master's Exhibiton in Cardiff', *Ceramics Monthly*, 41:6 (1993); Roger Berthoud, *Studio Pottery*, 24 (1996); Emmanuel Cooper, *CR*, 167 (1997); David Whiting, *Crafts*, 144 (1997); Cynthia Rose, *Crafts*, 187 (2004); Alex McErlain, *CR*, 212 (2005); Liz Mitchell, *CR*, 270 (2014); Mella Shaw, *Crafts*, 247 (2014)

249 *Untitled*, 2002
Porcelain, handbuilt, with gilt floral transfers, on stoneware base; marks: 'Untitled', inscribed on inside of base; h.53.6cm, d.28.9cm
C.67-2002. Source: the artist, £1070; gift of Adrian Sassoon, Esq.
Shown in the exhibition *Claire Curneen: Figurative Ceramics*, Contemporary Applied Arts, London, 2002.

249

250 *Tending the Fires*, 2016 (pl.141)
Porcelain, handbuilt, transparent and blue glazes, gilding; h.50cm, d.221cm
C.23:1 to 39-2018. Source: given by the artist
Shown at Collect Open, Collect 2017.

Dalton, William Bower 1868–1965

1868	born Wilmslow, Cheshire
1888–92	studies at Manchester School of Art, where introduced to pottery
1892–98	studies at National Art Training School, London (Royal College of Art from 1896)
1898–99	lecturer at Huddersfield School of Art
1899–	appointed Principal of the recently established Camberwell School of Arts and Crafts, and Curator of the South London Art Gallery
1909	designs and builds house and studio at Longfield, Kent
1919–	retires from Camberwell to concentrate on own work, mainly pottery and watercolours; continues as Curator until 1931
1924	President of Guild of Potters
1941	moves to USA after home bombed during war; establishes pottery workshop at Stamford, Connecticut
1965	returns to England

An influential educator, W.B. Dalton played an important role in the development of studio ceramics through his establishment of a pottery course at Camberwell School of Arts and Crafts, where he was Principal. Dalton appointed Richard Lunn as tutor, who was succeeded by Alfred Hopkins (qv). Early students included Reginald Wells (qv), William Staite Murray (qv), Charles Vyse (qv) and Roger Fry (qv). Dalton began making his own pottery about 1916, initially earthenware with painted decoration. In the early 1920s he modelled figures, but increasingly concentrated on Chinese-influenced stoneware and porcelain, achieving restrained and subtle glaze effects. Until 1925 he used the kilns at Camberwell, finally installing an electric kiln at Longfield in 1928. He continued potting after moving to the USA, and went on to write several practical manuals.

W.B. Dalton, *Craftsmanship and Design in Pottery* (London, 1957)
— *Notes from a Potter's Diary* (London, 1960)
— *Just Clay* (Bristol, 1962)
Arts and Crafts Exhibition Society (1916) to (1938)
British Institute of Industrial Art (1922), (1927)
Royal Academy of Arts (1923)
Guild of Potters (1924), (1925), (1926)
Colnaghi (1927), (1928), (1929), (1932)
Decorative Art (1930)
V&A (1936), pl.41
Riddick (1990), p.34
Jane Bailey, 'William Bower Dalton ARCA 1868–1965', *Journal of the Decorative Arts Society*, 35 (2011)
Lily Crowther, 'William Bower Dalton: Potter and Teacher', *V&A Online Journal*, 4 (2012)

251 Figure of a man, *c.* 1920–29
Glazed stoneware, modelled; marks: 'WBD' in monogram, painted; h.12.5cm, d.5.1cm
C.167-2014. Source: bequeathed by Mme. Renée Collinson

252 Vase, *c.* 1930–39
Stoneware, blue pigment and celadon glaze; marks: 'WBD' in monogram, incised; h.10.6cm, d.9.4cm
C.171-2014. Source: *see* **251**

251

252 / 254 / 253

255 / 256

253 Lidded jar, *c.* 1930–39
Stoneware, red glaze; marks: 'WBD' in monogram, incised; h.12cm, d.7.4cm
C.172:1,2-2014. Source: *see* **251**

254 Bottle, *c.* 1930–39
Porcelain, pale blue glaze; marks: 'WBD' in monogram, incised; h.14cm, d.9.5cm
C.179-2014. Source: *see* **251**

255 Bowl, 1933
Stoneware, brown and green-grey mottled glaze; marks: 'WBD' in monogram, incised; h.6.4cm, d.17.2cm
C.412-1934. Source: British Institute of Industrial Art (given by the artist, 1933)

256 Bowl, 1933
Stoneware, brown and grey mottled glaze; marks: 'WBD' in monogram, impressed; h.11.2cm, d.16.9cm
C.413-1934. Source: *see* **255**

Dart Pottery (also **Dartington Pottery**)

Dart Pottery began as the Dartington Pottery Training Workshop, established with support from the Crafts Advisory Committee and Dartington Hall Trust in 1975. The original idea for a training workshop was taken forward by David Leach (qv) and David Canter, assisted by Michael Casson (qv) and Marianne de Trey (qv). Peter Starkey (qv) was appointed as manager, and the pottery was established at Shinners Bridge, Devon, in time taking over the workshops formerly occupied by Bernard Leach (qv) and de Trey. A range of domestic ware designed to be easily made by trainees was introduced by Starkey and Peter Cook. In 1984 Janice Tchalenko (qv) was engaged to develop a new range of shapes and patterns, and the pottery was bought by its then management – Peter Cook, Stephen Course and Peter Hazell. Renamed Dart Pottery, the workshop continued to take apprentices, but ran with increased commercial emphasis. Tchalenko's colourful designs ensured popular success, and in 1988 Dart won the BBC Radio Times Enterprise Award, for Small Business of the Year. It reverted to its former name, Dartington Pottery, in 1992, but finally closed in 2005, the business being acquired by Grayshott Pottery, Surrey, which continued a limited production of its designs.

Murray Fieldhouse, 'The Dartington Pottery Training Workshop', *CR*, 58 (1979)
Potters (1980) to (2000)
'Britain's New Domestic Pottery', *Ceramics Monthly*, 33:6 (1985)
'Animating Space', editorial, *CR*, 111 (1988)
Stephen Course, 'Dart Pottery – Colour from the Quarry', *CR*, 116 (1989)
Tanya Harrod, 'Design and Production: Janice Tchalenko and Dart Pottery', in Northern Centre for Contemporary Art (1989), pp.74–6
Whiting (1993) – see esp. Stephen Course, 'Dartington Pottery: 1984 to the Present'
Stephen Brayne, 'A Tradition of Change', *CR*, 150 (1994)
Richard Dennis Gallery, *Modern Antiques*, exh. cat., text by Malcolm Haslam (London, 1996)
Simon Olding, 'Joining Forces', *CR*, 229 (2008)

Exhibition reviews: Paul Barron, *Crafts*, 36 (1979); Emmanuel Cooper, 'Modern Antiques', *Crafts*, 143 (1996)

257 Teapot and mug: *Black Rose* pattern, 1989
Stoneware, painted coloured glazes; marks: 'DP' in monogram, impressed; h.16.2cm, d.21.3cm (teapot); h.7.7cm, d.11.6cm (mug)
C.22&A, 23-1989. Source: Craftsmen Potters Association, London, £46.55 (teapot), £6.20 (mug)
Designed by Janice Tchalenko.

258 Jug and plate: *Poppy* pattern, 1989
Stoneware, painted coloured glazes; marks: 'DP' in monogram, impressed; h.15.8cm, d.14.7cm (jug); h.3.4cm, d.27cm (plate)
C.24, 25-1989. Source: *see* **257**, £11 (jug), £13.15 (plate)
Designed by Janice Tchalenko.

259 Vase: *Leopard* pattern, 1989
Stoneware, painted coloured glazes; h.19.8cm, d.14.2cm

257

258

259 / 260

C.26-1989. Source: *see* **257**, £11.40
Designed by Janice Tchalenko.

260 Plate: *Peacock* pattern, 1989
Stoneware, painted coloured glazes; h.3cm, d.22.2cm
C.27-1989. Source: *see* **257**, £24.20
Designed by Clare Woodhall. On Woodhall, see Whiting (1993), p.89.

261 *Fish bowl*, 1996
Stoneware, thrown, applied relief mouldings, reduction glazes; marks: 'DP' in monogram, impressed; numbered '13/100' in pen, and

261

262

signed 'Roger Law', 'Janice Tchalenko' and in monogram 'PB' [Pablo Bach]; h.12cm, d.31.2cm
C.75-1996. Source: Richard Dennis, London (exhibition: *Modern Antiques*, 1996), £235
Designed by Roger Law and Janice Tchalenko, the moulded decoration cast from models by Pablo Bach. Glazes developed by Stephen Course. From an edition of 100.

262 Dish, 2001
Stoneware, painted decoration on a white glaze; marks: 'ROGER LAW / AT / DARTINGTON / 2001', inscribed, and 'DP' in monogram, impressed; d.48cm, w.38.3cm
C.126-2001. Source: given by Roger Law
Designed and painted by Roger Law, after drawings made in Australia. The shape designed by Tavs Jorgensen, *c.* 1997.

Davis, Derek 1926–2008

1926	born London
1945–49	studies painting at Central School of Arts and Crafts, London
1952–55	establishes artist community at Hillesden, Buckinghamshire, with Eric James Mellon (qv); John Clarke, from whom he learns rudiments of potting; Ruth Lambert, whom he later marries; and others; produces press-moulded slip-decorated earthenwares
1955–	moves to Arundel, Sussex, establishes workshop
1965	solo exhibition, Primavera, Cambridge; frequent solo exhibitions thereafter
1967	artist-in-residence, University of Sussex
c. 1994	ceases potting; returns to painting

Derek Davis' output as a potter is highly varied. From the 1960s he became known for his use of *sang de boeuf* and other Chinese glazes on thrown stoneware and porcelain. By the late 1970s he was concentrating on handbuilt forms. His later work became increasingly painterly, often boldly abstract, or at times figurative and offering contemporary social comment.

Derek Davis, statement, in Rothschild (1972)
— 'Copper Red Glazes in Reduction', *CR*, 66 (1980)
Arts and Crafts Exhibition Society (1957)
Biographical notes, *Pottery Quarterly*, 8:30 (1963), p.4, pl.9
Decorative Art (1970/71)
Potters (1972) to (1992)
Crafts Council (1980), p.56
Paisley Museum and Art Galleries (1984), pp.29–30
'Pots and Potters', *CR*, 117 (1989)
Carolyn Genders, *Derek Davis: Painter/Potter* (Ford, 2003)

Exhibition reviews: Richard Dunning, *CR*, 7 (1971); Anthony Hepburn, *Craft Horizons*, 31:1 (1971); Tony Garnett, *CR*, 20 (1973); Margot Coatts, *Crafts*, 165 (2000)

Obituaries: *The Times* (10 September 2008); Emmanuel Cooper, *The Independent* (13 September 2008); Carolyn Genders, *The Guardian* (9 October 2008)

263 Dish, 1982
Stoneware, painted in brown and black; marks: 'Davis', painted in black; h.5.5cm, d.34cm
C.70-1984. Source: given by the Friends of the V&A (purchased at the Craftsmen Potters

263

Association exhibition, *Studio Ceramics Today*, V&A, 1983, no.43, £64.50)

Davis, Harry (**H.C.**) 1910–1986 and **May** (née **Scott**) 1914–1995

Harry	
1910	born Cardiff; educated in England and Switzerland
1927–33	studies briefly at Bournemouth School of Art; works at Broadstone Potters, Dorset, where becomes a skilled thrower, trained by a potter whose last name was Bean
1933–37	taken on at Leach Pottery, St Ives, after demonstrating throwing skills to Bernard Leach (qv) at Dartington; runs Leach Pottery with Laurie Cookes during absence of Bernard and David Leach (qv), 1934–35
1937–42	teaches and establishes pottery at Achimota College, Gold Coast (now Ghana); Michael Cardew (qv) takes over in 1942
May	
1914	born Manchester
1933	studies briefly at Salford School of Art; works with Muriel Bell at her pottery in Malvern, Worcestershire
1934	sets up pottery workshop at parents' home in Wilmslow, Cheshire
1936–37	joins Leach Pottery as paying pupil; meets Harry
1937–38	establishes pottery studio in South Kensington, London; exhibits at The Brygos Gallery
1938	Harry and May marry in London
1939–40	May joins Harry at Achimota College, providing unpaid assistance
1941–	May travels to Paraguay to join Bruderhof community, a pacifist

	Christian community recently relocated from England
1942–46	Harry joins May in Paraguay; together they leave community; later they move to Patagonia
1946–62	return to England; together establish Crowan Pottery, Praze, Cornwall, in converted watermill
1959|63	exhibitions at Crafts Centre of Great Britain, London
1962–72	emigrate to New Zealand; establish Crewenna Pottery, Wakapuaka, Nelson
1972–79	join aid project at Izcuchaca, Peru, establishing a pottery
1979–	return to Crewenna Pottery, New Zealand

Harry and May Davis are important figures in the history of studio pottery. Practical, indefatigable and socially motivated, Harry Davis was a pioneer who advocated the use of local materials and for intermediate technologies that offered economic self-sufficiency. His embrace of machinery within the context of a studio pottery workshop helped the Crowan and Crewenna potteries to produce wares at affordable prices, while his detailed knowledge of materials helped attain a standard of technical excellence in their domestic stoneware and porcelain. His achievements were made in collaboration with May, herself an accomplished potter. Crowan or Crewenna pots were practical and functional, and, on principle, not personally marked. Harry became the main production thrower at Crowan, working with apprentices, with May doing much glazing and decorating of pots. Initially May also threw pots, and at Crewenna again shared both throwing and decorating, as did their daughter Nina. Most Crowan pots were decorated with brushwork or wax-resist. At Crewenna incised decoration was also used.

Harry Davis, 'In Defence of the Rural Workshop', *Pottery Quarterly*, 6:24 (1959)
— 'An Historical Review of Art, Commerce and Craftsmanship', *Pottery in Australia*, 9:2 (1970)
— 'Art Identity and Anonymity', *Pottery in Australia*, 11:2 (1972)
— 'Some Thoughts on Attitudes', *CR*, 13 (1972)
— 'An Historical Review of Art, Commerce and Craftsmanship', *Studio Potter*, 6:1 (1977)
— 'The Craft Movement Assessed Historically', *Studio Potter*, 9:1 (1980)
— 'An Assessment of the Craft Movement', *CR*, 67 (1981)
— 'Handcraft Pottery: Whence and Whither', *Studio Potter*, 13:1 (1984)
— 'Handcraft Pottery – Whence and Whither', *CR*, 93 (1985)
— 'Chip Resistant Pots', letter, *CR*, 95 (1985)
— 'Potters, Zombies and Others', *Ceramics Monthly*, 33:7 (1985)
— *The Potter's Alternative* (North Ryde, 1987)
May Davis, 'Crewenna Pottery', *New Zealand Potter*, 6:1 (1963)
— 'Harry Davis', *CR*, 109 (1988)
— *May: Her Story* (Nelson, 1990)
Harry and May Davis, 'Crewenna Pottery', *New Zealand Potter*, 7:1 (1964)
— letter from Crewenna, in Craftsmen Potters Association (1966), pp.73–5
Cooper (1947), p.*i*, pl.8
Arts and Crafts Exhibition Society (1952), (1954)
Dartington Hall (1952)
Wingfield Digby (1952), pp.81–2, pls.56–7
Decorative Art (1954/55), (1956/57), (1958/59), (1960/61)
Rose (1955), p.14, pl.25B, (1970), p.39
Lewis (1956), pls.347–8
Helen Mason, 'Crowan Pottery in New Zealand', *New Zealand Potter*, 5:1 (1962)
Peter Cape, *Artists and Craftsmen in New Zealand* (Auckland, 1969), pp.37–9
Alan Peascod, 'An Impression of the Seminar and Master Classes Conducted by Harry Davis', *Pottery in Australia*, 9:2 (1970)
Dennis Pile, 'Harry and May Davis', *Pottery in Australia*, 9:2 (1970)
Janet Mansfield, 'Harry and May Davis in Australia, 1972', *Pottery in Australia*, 11:2 (1972)
Victor Margrie, exh. review, *CR*, 13 (1972)
Caroline Pearce-Higgins, 'Harry Davis in Peru', *Crafts*, 43 (1980), p.11
Doreen Blumhardt, *Craft New Zealand: The Art of the Craftsman* (Wellington, 1981)
Michael Buckley, 'The Handworked Machine', *CR*, 67 (1981)
Paisley Museum and Art Galleries (1984), p.30
Tate Gallery (1985), p.237
Michael Cardew, tribute, *CR*, 109 (1988)
Arthur Griffiths, 'Working at Crowan in the Early 50s', *CR*, 109 (1988)
Harry Horlock Stringer, 'Harry and May Davis – Pots from Crewenna', *CR*, 115 (1989)
Riddick (1990), p.35
Harrod (1999)
Vincentelli (2000), pp.148–54
Cooper (2003), pp.178–9, 199–202, 226
Whybrow (2006), pp.100–1 and elsewhere
Harrod (2012)

Obituaries (Harry Davis): Seth Cardew, *Crafts*, 82 (1986); Harry Horlock Stringer, *CR*, 101 (1986)

A film produced and directed by Stan Jenkins, *Harry and May Davis: Potters*, was released on VHS video in 1987.

All works made at Crowan Pottery, Cornwall.

264 Bowl, 1950 (fig.7)
Stoneware, incised decoration, tenmoku glaze; marks: 'CP' in monogram, impressed; h.6.8cm, d.15.5cm
Circ.61-1951. Source: Primavera, London, 6s.

265 Coffee pot, 1950 (fig.7)
Stoneware, grey-green glaze, painted in iron; marks: 'CP' in monogram, impressed; h.15.7cm, d.18.2cm
Circ.62&A-1951. Source: *see* **264**, 12s.

266 Teapot, 1951 (fig.7)
Stoneware, tenmoku glaze; marks: 'CP' in monogram, impressed; h.16.6cm, d.19.8cm
Circ.19&A-1952. Source: Primavera, London, £1.1s.6d.

267 Dish, 1958
Stoneware, greenish-brown glaze, painted in iron; marks: obscured seal; h.3.8cm, d.34.6cm
Circ.42-1959. Source: the pottery, £4

267

268

268 Crock and cover, 1958
Stoneware, oatmeal glaze, wax-resist decoration in iron; marks: 'CP' in monogram, impressed; h.32.6cm, d.34.7cm
Circ.18&A-1959. Source: Primavera, London, £16.10s.
Paper labels on the base read: 'Restricted sale. See Mr Rothschild' and 'Museum only. £16/10/–'. This large pot has remarkably thin walls and base, showing Davis' considerable skill as a thrower. When supplying it to the museum, Henry Rothschild described it as 'quite unique'.

Dawson, Robert 1953–

1953	born New York City
1986–	studio in West Norwood, London
1990–93	studies ceramics and fine art at Camberwell College of Arts
1997–99	studies ceramics at Royal College of Art, London
2008	solo exhibition, *Ornament and Crime*, The Scottish Gallery, Edinburgh
2021	exhibition with Richard Slee (qv), Musée Ariana, Geneva

Robert Dawson – who works under the name Aesthetic Sabotage – is known for his use of manipulated decorative patterns and motifs as printed imagery on industrially sourced plates and tile panels. Often appropriating historic ceramic designs, he typically uses variations in clarity or changes in perspective to create feelings of uncertainty or a sense of the unexpected. Works are produced as short editions or architectural commissions, or occasionally as designs for industrial production. Since 2015 Dawson has concentrated on painterly works, applying raw clay to canvas.

Sally Howard, 'Robert Dawson and the Willow Pattern Plate', *Ceramics: Art and Perception*, 27 (1997)
Paul Vincent, 'Robert Dawson', *Studio Pottery*, 26 (1997)
London Institute (1998), pp.22–3, 27
Lesley Jackson, 'Robert Dawson: Aesthetic Sabotage', *Ceramics in Society*, 57 (2004)
Lucia van der Post, 'Retro Tableware', *The Times Magazine* (30 October 2004)
Marcus Fairs, *21st Century Design* (London, 2006), pp.278–9
Hanaor (2007), pp.190–3
Bonnie Kemske, 'Tilted and Skewed', *CR*, 236 (2009)

269

Tessa Peters and Janice West (eds), *The House of Words*, exh. cat. (London: Dr Johnson's House Trust, 2009), pp.14–15
Jerwood Visual Arts, *Jerwood Contemporary Makers*, exh. cat. (London, 2010)
WCC-BF (2010), pp.72–3, 93
Veiteberg (2011), pp.84–5
Clark, Strauss and others (2012), pp.366, 419, 428
Alison Syme, *Willow* (London, 2014), pp.120–3

Exhibition reviews: Tony Franks, *CR*, 233 (2008); Helen Carnac, 'The House of Words', *Journal of Modern Craft*, 3:2 (2010)

269 Plate: *In Perspective Willow 1*, 1996
Overglaze enamel print on bone china plate; marks: 'AESTHETIC SABOTAGE / LONDON' and 'edition no.', printed in blue, with '99/100' and 'RD', inscribed in black; d.27.4cm
C.18-2008. Source: given by the artist
The screen-printed transfer derives from a photograph of an original Willow-pattern tissue transfer, taken at an angle.

The museum also holds Dawson's *After Willow Pattern* and *After Landscape Pattern* designs for Wedgwood, not catalogued here (C.294 to 305-2009).

de Trey, Marianne 1913–2016

1913	born London, of Swiss parents
1932–36	studies textile design at Royal College of Art, London
1938	marries Sam Haile (qv)
1939	moves with Haile to USA
1941–42	learns to make pottery, while Haile teaches ceramics at Alfred University, New York State
1942–43	moves with Haile to Ann Arbor, Michigan; takes over as pottery instructor at University of Michigan in 1943 when Haile inducted (drafted) into US Army
1944	helps to start School for American Craftsmen at Dartford, New Hampshire
1945	returns to England; sets up workshop with Haile at Bulmer Brickyard, Sudbury, Suffolk
1947	moves with Haile to Shinners Bridge, Dartington, Devon, to cabin and studio previously occupied by Bernard Leach (qv)
1948–	Haile killed in motor accident; de Trey starts production at Shinners Bridge Pottery with help of her sister, Judy de Trey
1955–	founder member of Devon Guild of Craftsmen
1957	Shinners Bridge Pottery destroyed by fire
1958–	rebuilds pottery, converting production from earthenware to oxidized stoneware, with small oil-fired kiln for own work
1961	solo exhibition, Crafts Centre of Great Britain, London
1964	Collin Kellam, apprenticed to de Trey since 1962, builds wood-fired kiln, which de Trey subsequently uses for individual stoneware pots
1965	exhibition with John Reeve at Primavera, London
1980	ceases domestic ware production at Shinners Bridge Pottery, the pottery name going out of use; continues to make individual pieces, concentrating on thrown porcelain
1983–	moves to new, smaller workshop on site; Dartington Pottery Training Workshop takes over main workshop
1995	retrospective at High Cross House, Dartington
2006	awarded CBE

Marianne de Trey ran a well-organized pottery workshop producing domestic ware, one of the first to do so in the post-war period. Her earliest production was of slip-decorated or tin-glazed earthenware. Later, following a fire at the pottery, this was replaced by oxidized stoneware. To facilitate production, de Trey employed three or four assistants and established an apprentice scheme. She also developed her own individual work, in particular forms for flower arranging,

using a small oil-fired kiln and later also a wood-fired kiln. She ceased production potting in 1980, but continued to make individual pieces until her early nineties, mostly in thrown porcelain, introducing colour through a range of techniques.

Marianne de Trey, brief statement and biographical notes, *Pottery Quarterly*, 8:30 (1963), p.8, pl.34, and 8:32 (1965), p.108, pl.11
— 'Workshop', *CR*, 10 (1971)
— statement, in Rothschild (1972)
— '35 Years a Potter', *CR*, 83 (1983)
— 'Shinners Bridge from the 40s to the 80s', in Whiting (1993), pp.33–6
— 'A Memoir', in *De Trey at Dartington* (Dartington, 1995), pp.8–12
Arts and Crafts Exhibition Society, textiles (1938), pottery (1948) to (1954)
Cooper (1947), p.*iv*, pls.46–8
Decorative Art, (1950/51), (1951/52), (1954/55), (1956/57), (1962/63), (1967/68)
Dartington Hall (1952)
Wingfield Digby (1952), p.84, pls.59, 62
Lewis (1956), pls.333–4
Casson (1967), p.8, pls.236–41
Eileen Lewenstein, 'Marianne de Trey', *Ceramics Monthly*, 19:7 (1971)
Commonwealth Art Gallery, *Marianne de Trey*, exh. cat. (London, 1972)
Potters (1972) to (1992)
Crafts Advisory Committee (1976), p.90
Edelman (1976), Part II
Crafts Council (1980), p.56
Paisley Museum and Art Galleries (1984), p.32
Margot Coatts, 'Sources of Inspiration', *Crafts*, 135 (1995)
Emmanuel Cooper, exh. review, *Crafts*, 136 (1995)
De Trey at Dartington, exh. cat., text by Margot Coatts (Dartington, 1995)
Sophie Heath, 'The Inspiration of Marianne de Trey', Crafts Study Centre, online essay (2004)
Bristol Guild of Applied Art, *Marianne de Trey: Retrospective Exhibition*, text by David Whiting (Bristol, 2006)
Marianne de Trey, published following an exhibition at the Devon Guild of Craftsmen (Shepton Beauchamp, 2007)

Obituaries: David Whiting, *The Guardian* (19 October 2016); *The Telegraph* (25 October 2016); *The Times* (16 November 2016)

An interview with Marianne de Trey is in the Recording the Crafts video archive at UWE Bristol (also held in the National Art Library, V&A, London, 704.AA.0015 to 704.AA.0024).

270 Bowl, 1950
Earthenware, tin glaze, incised decoration through dark pigment; marks: 'de T' in a rectangular seal; h.8.3cm, d.29cm
Circ.278-1950. Source: Arts and Crafts Exhibition Society (Twenty-second Exhibition, V&A, 1950, no.194), £2.2s.

270

272 / 273 / 274

279 / 280

271

275

281

282

284 / 287 / 285

283

286

271 Flat bowl, 1950
Earthenware, tin glaze, painted in colours; marks: scallop shell seal, impressed; h.5cm, d.28cm
Circ.14-1951. Source: the artist, £1.10s.

272 Butter dish, 1950
Earthenware, tin glaze, painted in blue; marks: scallop shell seal, impressed; h.2cm, d.12.6cm
Circ.5-1951. Source: *see* **271**, 5s.

273 '½pt jug', 1950
Earthenware, tin glaze, painted in colours; marks: scallop shell seal, impressed; h.10cm, d.11.5cm
Circ.6-1951. Source: *see* **271**, 7s.6d.

274 '1pt mug', 1950
Earthenware, tin glaze, painted in colours; marks: scallop shell seal, impressed; h.11.7cm, d.12.9cm
Circ.11-1951. Source: *see* **271**, 10s.6d.

275 Jam pot, 1950
Earthenware, tin glaze, painted in colours; marks: scallop shell seal, impressed; h.8.2cm, d.9.5cm
Circ.10&A-1951. Source: *see* **271**, 12s.6d.

276 Dish, 1950 (pl.32)
Earthenware, slip-trailed in white and green on a black slip; h.2.4cm, d.16.2cm
Circ.7-1951. Source: *see* **271**, 5s.

277 Dish, 1950 (pl.32)
Earthenware, slip-trailed in white and green on a black slip; marks: scallop shell seal, impressed; h.3.2cm, d.24.6cm
Circ.8-1951. Source: *see* **271**, 2s.6d.

278 '½pt mug', 1950 (pl.32)
Earthenware, slip-trailed in white on a black slip; marks: scallop shell seal, impressed; h.9.6cm, d.11.2cm
Circ.9-1951. Source: *see* **271**, 7s.6d.

279 '1pt jug', 1950
Earthenware, slip-trailed in white and green on a black slip; marks: scallop shell seal, impressed; h.12.4cm, d.12.8cm
Circ.15-1951. Source: *see* **271**, 10s.6d.

280 'Quart jug', 1950
Earthenware, incised decoration through a dark slip; marks: scallop shell seal, impressed; h.17.6cm, d.27.8cm
Circ.12-1951. Source: *see* **271**, £1.5s.

281 Bowl, 1950
Stoneware, applied decoration, brown saltglaze; h.10.5cm, d.15cm
Circ.13-1951. Source: *see* **271**, £1.10s.

282 Bowl, 1961
Stoneware, fluted, white glaze; marks: scallop shell seal, impressed; h.11cm, d.18.5cm
Circ.256-1961. Source: Crafts Centre of Great Britain, London (exhibition: *Stoneware Pottery for Flower Arrangements by Marianne de Trey*, 1961, no.84), £2.2s.

283 Set of three bowls ('J' type), 1961
Stoneware, fluted and scraped, oatmeal glaze; marks: scallop shell seal, impressed; h.9.9cm, d.12.6cm (largest bowl)
Circ.255 to B-1961. Source: *see* **282** (no.52), £2.12s.6d.

284 Bowl, *c.* 1985–2003
Porcelain, wax-resist, slip and sgraffito decoration; marks: 'deT' in monogram, impressed rectangular seal; h.5.3cm, d.17.1cm
C.139-2013. Source: given by the artist

285 Bowl, *c.* 1985–2003
Porcelain, wax-resist, slip and sgraffito decoration; marks: 'deT' in monogram, impressed triangular seal; h.6.4cm, d.14.6cm
C.140-2013. Source: *see* **284**

286 Bowl, *c.* 1985–2003
Porcelain, thrown with coloured clays; marks: 'deT' in monogram, impressed triangular seal; h.8.6cm, d.15cm
C.141-2013. Source: *see* **284**

287 Five-sided bowl, *c.* 1988–94
Porcelain, wax-resist, slip, incised and painted decoration under a barium glaze; marks: 'deT' in triangular monogram, impressed rectangular seal; h.5.1cm, d.9.5cm
C.142-2013. Source: *see* **284**

de Waal, Edmund 1964–

1964	born Nottingham
1981–83	apprenticeship with Geoffrey Whiting (qv), Canterbury, Kent
1983–86	studies English Literature, University of Cambridge
1986–88	workshop in Herefordshire
1988–92	studio in Sheffield
1991–92	studies Japanese Language, University of Sheffield

1992–93	Daiwa Anglo-Japanese Foundation Scholarship, Sheffield and Japan
1993–95	studio in Woolwich, London
1995–2005	studio in Camberwell, London, shared with Julian Stair (qv)
1999	first architectural intervention, High Cross House, Dartington, Devon
2006–12	studio in Tulse Hill, London
2007	solo exhibition, Kettle's Yard, Cambridge, and mima, Middlesbrough
2009	installation, *Signs & Wonders*, V&A, London
2011	awarded OBE
2012	made Senior Fellow of Royal College of Art, London
2013–	studio in West Norwood, London
2013–16	honorary doctorates, University of Sheffield; University of the Arts, London; Canterbury Christ Church University; University of Nottingham; University of York
2016	exhibition *During the Night*, Kunsthistorisches Museum, Vienna
2019	exhibition *elective affinities*, Frick Collection, New York
2019–20	installation *psalm / library of exile*, Museo Ebraico and Ateneo Veneto, Venice; Japanisches Palais, Dresden; and British Museum, London

Among the most prominent and influential ceramic artists of the 21st century, Edmund de Waal is known for his installations of porcelain vessels and his parallel work as an author. Initially a maker of domestic stoneware following a workshop training, de Waal turned to porcelain, consolidating its use during study in Japan. He subsequently developed pared-back yet gestural celadon porcelain for kitchen or table, leading a fashion for more coolly minimal ceramics. In the late 1990s he began grouping pieces as 'cargoes' – reflecting porcelain's history as a traded commodity – and making works for specific sites. A further evolution came with his use of bespoke shelves or cabinets, positing ceramic display as a form of sculpture. Subsequent work has focused on the vitrine as a module for display, increasingly presenting porcelain alongside other materials. Often work is developed in response to museum collections, as de Waal collaborates internationally with major institutions. As a writer, de Waal is important in a number of ways: he has advocated for potters to write about their work; he has produced an important body of critical writing, including his revisionist monograph on Bernard Leach (qv); he has combined memoir with history in the acclaimed *The Hare with Amber Eyes* and later works. His writing and ceramics share concerns with materiality and the memorial power of objects.

Edmund de Waal, 'White Porcelain Tablewares', *Studio Pottery*, 18 (1995)
— 'Kitchen Porcelain', *CR*, 158 (1996)
— *Bernard Leach* (London, 1997)
— 'Parts of a Journal, December 1997 – May 1998', in Johnson (1998), pp.28–30
— 'Speak for Yourself', *CR*, 182 (2000)
— 'Making in the City', *Resurgence*, 209 (2001)
— 'Radical Pots', *Interpreting Ceramics*, ejournal, 2 (2002)
— *20th Century Ceramics* (London, 2003)
— *The Parade of Objects: Rethinking Twentieth Century Ceramics*, Peter Dormer Lecture (London: Royal College of Art, 2003)
— 'Terra Incognita', in Tate Liverpool (2004)
— 'No Ideas but in Things', in Clark (2006), pp.350–61
— *The Hare with Amber Eyes* (London, 2010)
— *The Pot Book* (London, 2011)
— 'A local history', text to accompany an installation, University of Cambridge (2012)
— 'From Head to Hand', *Studio Potter*, 41:1 (2013)
— *Edmund de Waal*, with texts by Emma Crichton-Miller, Edmund de Waal and others (London, 2014)
— *The White Road* (London, 2015)
— *Letters to Camondo* (London, 2021)
— 'This Living Hand: Henry Moore and Touch', in Henry Moore Foundation, *This Living Hand*, exh. pamphlet (2021)
Margot Coatts, 'Sense and Sensibility', *Crafts*, 134 (1995)
Crafts Council (1996c), pp.80, 129
Galerie Besson, *Edmund de Waal*, exh. pamphlet (London, 1997)
Potters (1997)
Rob Barnard, 'Julian Stair and Edmund de Waal', interview, *Ceramics: Art and Perception*, 38 (1999)
Gabi Dewald, 'Fruits of the Spirit: Porcelain by Edmund de Waal', *Ceramics: Art and Perception*, 35 (1999)
High Cross House, *Modern Home: An Intervention by Edmund de Waal at High Cross House*, exh. cat., texts by Edmund de Waal and others (Totnes: Dartington Hall Trust, 1999)
V&A (1999)
Crafts Council (2001), pp.28–9, 31
Julia Pitts, 'Opposites Attract', *CR*, 198 (2002)
Contemporary Applied Arts, *Edmund de Waal*, exh. pamphlet (London, 2003)
Emmanuel Cooper, 'Hidden Depths: The Ceramics of Edmund de Waal', *Ceramics: Art and Perception*, 54 (2003)
Blackwell, The Arts and Crafts House, *Edmund de Waal: A line around a shadow*, exh. cat., texts by Edmund de Waal and Edward King (Bowness-on-Windermere, 2005)
National Museums and Galleries of Wales, *Edmund de Waal: Arcanum: Mapping 18th-century European Porcelain*, exh. cat., texts by Edmund de Waal and others (Cardiff, 2005)
Kettle's Yard, *Edmund de Waal at Kettle's Yard, mima and elsewhere*, exh. cat., texts by Michael Harrison and others (Cambridge, 2007)
V&A, *Signs & Wonders: Edmund de Waal and the V&A Ceramics Galleries*, texts by Glenn Adamson, Alun Graves and Edmund de Waal (London, 2009)
Alan Cristea Gallery, *Edmund de Waal: From Zero*, exh. cat., text by A.S. Byatt (London, 2010)
— *Edmund de Waal: a thousand hours*, exh. cat., text by Colm Tóibín (London, 2012)
Waddesdon Manor, *Edmund de Waal at Waddesdon*, exh. cat., texts by Juliet Carey and Edmund de Waal (Aylesbury, 2012)
Emma Crichton-Miller, 'Porcelain Stories', *Apollo*, 178:614 (2013)
Fitzwilliam Museum, *Edmund de Waal: On White: Porcelain Stories from the Fitzwilliam Museum*, exh. pamphlet, text by Edmund de Waal (Cambridge, 2013)
Gagosian, *Atemwende: Edmund de Waal*, exh. cat., text by Adam Gopnik (New York, 2013)
atmosphere: Edmund de Waal, published for an installation at Turner Contemporary, Margate, Kent, text by Edmund de Waal (London, 2014)
Shane Enright, 'Edmund de Waal', book review, *Crafts*, 249 (2014)
Grant Gibson, 'Edmund de Waal in Black and White', interview, *Crafts*, 257 (2015)
Pier Arts Centre, *wavespeech: Edmund de Waal / David Ward*, exh. pamphlet, text by Michael Tooby (Stromness, 2015)
Royal Academy, *Edmund de Waal: white*, exh. pamphlet, text by Edmund de Waal (London, 2015)
Juliet Carey, 'Edmund de Waal at Waddesdon', in Brown, Stair and Twomey (2016), pp.186–95
Gagosian, *Edmund de Waal: ten thousand things*, exh. cat., text by Joan Simon (New York, 2016)
Galerie Max Hetzler, *Edmund de Waal: Irrkunst*, exh. cat., text by Edmund de Waal (Berlin, 2016)
Kunsthistorisches Museum, *Edmund de Waal: During the Night*, exh. cat., texts by Edmund de Waal and others (Vienna, 2016)
Universalmuseum Joanneum, *Kneaded Knowledge: The Language of Ceramics: Edmund de Waal, Ai Weiwei*, exh. cat., texts by Peter Pakesch and Edmund de Waal (Graz, 2016)

288

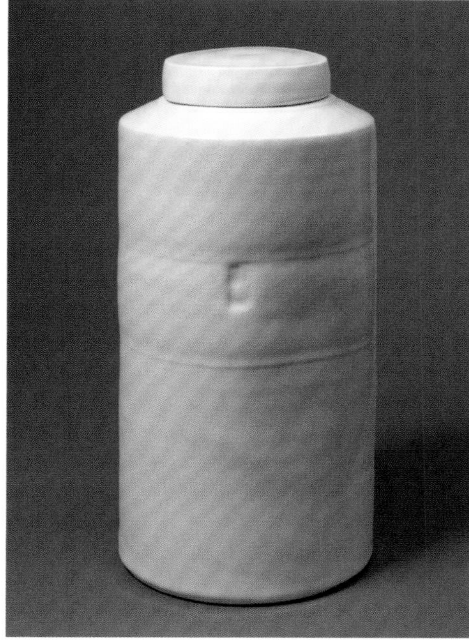

291

292

Artipelag, *Edmund de Waal, Giorgio Morandi*, exh. cat., texts by Jorunn Veiteberg and others (Stockholm, 2017)
Espace Muraille, *Lettres de Londres*, exh. cat. (Geneva, 2017)
wavespeech, exh. publication, Pier Arts Centre, Stromness (Bath, 2018)
Museu d'Art Contemporani d'Eivissa, *white island*, exh. pamphlet (Ibiza, 2018)
Frick Collection, *elective affinities: Edmund de Waal at The Frick Collection*, exh. cat., texts by Edmund de Waal and Charlotte Vignon (New York, 2019)
Gagosian and Ca' Foscari University of Venice, *Edmund de Waal: psalm*, exh. cat., texts by Edmund de Waal, Ben Okri, David Grossman and others (Venice, 2019)
Japanisches Palais, Staatliche Kunstsammlungen, *library of exile*, exh. pamphlet (Dresden, 2019)
Janet McKenzie, 'Edmund de Waal', interview, *Studio International*, ejournal (14 November 2019)
MAK Center, *--one way or other--: Edmund de Waal at the Schindler House*, exh. pamphlet (Los Angeles, 2019)
Museo Ebraico, *psalm*, exh. pamphlet (Venice, 2019)
British Museum, *Edmund de Waal: library of exile*, exh. cat., texts by Edmund de Waal, Hartwig Fischer and Elif Shafak (London, 2020)

Exhibition reviews: Paul Vincent, *Studio Pottery*, 15 (1995); Malcolm Haslam, *Crafts*, 149 (1997); David Whiting, *CR*, 168 (1997), and 'The New White', *Crafts*, 160 (1999); Lesley Jackson, *Crafts*, 162 (2000); Kate McIntyre, *Crafts*, 180 (2003); Edward Lucie-Smith, *Crafts*, 186 (2004); David Briers, *Crafts*, 199 (2006); Michael Tooby, *Ceramics: Art and Perception*, 70 (2007); Tony Birks, *Ceramics: Art and Perception*, 82 (2010); Shane Enright, *Crafts*, 237 (2012); Michael McTwigan, *CR*, 266 (2014); Jennifer Piejko, *Crafts*, 275 (2018); Colin Martin, *CR*, 298 (2019); Veronica Simpson, *Studio International*, ejournal (2 June 2019); Isabella Smith, *Crafts*, 285 (2020)

288 Bowl, *c.* 1995
Porcelain, thrown, white crackle glaze exterior, celadon interior, blue rim; marks: impressed seal; h.16.5cm, d.32.5cm
C.48-1996. Source: Crafts Council Shop at the V&A, £283.50

289 Teapot, 1996 (pl.98)
Porcelain, white crackle glaze, wire handle; marks: impressed seal; h.23.3cm, d.20.1cm
C:80:1,2-1996. Source: Contemporary Applied Arts, London (exhibition: *Soft Clay*, 1996), £134.10

290 Beaker, 1996 (pl.98)
Porcelain, white crackle glaze exterior, celadon interior; marks: impressed seal; h.9.7cm, d.8.6cm
C.81-1996. Source: *see* **289**, £41.40

291 Lidded jar, 2001
Porcelain, celadon glaze; marks: impressed seals on neck and front; h.38cm, d.19.1cm
C.40:1,2-2004. Source: Adrian Sassoon, £2232.50

292 Pot, 2001–02
Porcelain, celadon glaze, red pigment; marks: impressed seal; h.15.8cm, d.11.8cm
C.136-2006. Source: given by the Friends of the V&A
From a limited edition made for the Friends of the V&A (see *V&A Magazine*, January–April 2002, p.25).

293 *Signs & Wonders*, 2009 (pl.131)
Glazed porcelain and powder-coated aluminium; marks: 'Edmund de Waal Signs & Wonders 2009' and the V&A logo, printed label on each pot; h.40cm, d.11.64m (overall)
C.277-2009. Source: the artist; made possible through the generosity of Art Fund, Nicholas and Judith Goodison, Gerard and Sarah Griffin, Blackburn Associates Limited, Mr and Mrs Charles Booth-Clibborn
Signs & Wonders was a site-specific commission for the new V&A Ceramics Galleries, opened in 2009. It comprises 425 porcelain pots placed on a circular lacquer-red aluminium shelf installed in the dome of Room 141. Most of the pots were thrown and glazed in de Waal's London studio. The flat dishes were made by Hartley Greens & Co. at the Leeds Pottery, Stoke-on-Trent, but were subsequently glazed at the artist's studio. The powder-coated aluminium shelf was fabricated by Aspinalls in Heysham, Lancashire.

294 *the collector (for Paul)*, 2015 (pl.135)
17 glazed porcelain vessels in a wood and acrylic cabinet; h.90cm, w.50cm, d.15cm
C.26:1 to 19-2015. Source: given by the artist in honour of Sir Paul Ruddock

Deacon, Richard 1949–

1949	born Bangor, Caernarfonshire
1968–69	studies at Somerset College of Art, Taunton
1969–72	studies at St Martin's School of Art, London
1974–77	studies Environmental Media at Royal College of Art, London
1977–2000	married to Jacqueline Poncelet (qv)
1977–91	studio in Acre Lane, Brixton, London
1978	studies art history part-time at Chelsea School of Art

1978–79	travels to USA with Poncelet, makes ceramic pots and associated series of drawings
1987	wins Turner Prize
1991–	studio in Herne Hill, London
1999	at suggestion of sculptor Thomas Schütte, produces first ceramic sculptures, working with Anna Zimmerman at the studio of Niels Dietrich, Cologne, Germany
1999	awarded CBE
1999–2009	Professor at École Nationale Supérieure des Beaux-Arts, Paris
2005	solo exhibition, *Out of Order*, Tate St Ives
2007	represents Wales at Venice Biennale
2009–15	Professor at the Kunstakademie, Düsseldorf, Germany
2014	retrospective exhibition, Tate Britain, London

One of the leading sculptors of his generation, Richard Deacon came to prominence in the 1980s as part of the group termed New British Sculptors. He describes himself as a 'fabricator', his abstract sculptures emphasizing construction and the manipulation of materials. He has worked primarily in wood, metal and – since 1999 – clay, often collaborating with specialist studios in the production of works. His ceramics are made in Cologne in the studio of Niels Dietrich, where he works with skilled handbuilders or sometimes directly manipulates the material himself, as in the *Republic* series, in which lengths of clay are cut like timber. In contrast to the open, modular forms characteristic of his sculpture in wood or metal, his ceramic works exhibit a unity and fixedness, and a formal interest in the possibilities of colour.

Richard Deacon, 'The Inside', *CR*, 244 (2010)
— 'Integrated Artwork', *Architects' Journal*, 240:22 (2014)
— *So, And, If, But. Writings 1970–2012* (Düsseldorf, 2014)
— and Niels Dietrich, *About The Size Of It* (Cologne/Düsseldorf, 2005)
Jon Thompson and others, *Richard Deacon* (London, 2000)
Dundee Contemporary Arts, *Richard Deacon: Sculpture*, exh. cat. (Dundee, 2001)
Nicholas Rena, 'Wise Enough to Play the Fool', *CR*, 196 (2002)
Gerhard Kolberg, 'Like You Know: Richard Deacon's Ceramic Sculptures', in Museum Ludwig, *AC: Richard Deacon: Made in Cologne*, exh. cat. (Cologne, 2003)
Clarrie Wallis, 'Richard Deacon', in Judith Nesbitt and Jonathan Watkins (eds), *Days Like These*, exh. cat. (London: Tate Publishing, 2003), pp.74–9
Tate St Ives, *Richard Deacon: Out of Order*, exh. cat. (St Ives, 2005)
Arts Council of Wales, *Richard Deacon: Artists from Wales at the 52nd International Art Exhibition La Biennale di Venezia*, exh. cat. (Cardiff, 2007)
Ikon Gallery, *Richard Deacon: Personals*, exh. cat. (Birmingham, 2007)
Lisson Gallery, *Richard Deacon: Association*, exh. cat. (London, 2012)
John Routledge, 'Trying the Combinations', interview, *Sculpture*, 33:2 (2014)
Clarrie Wallis, *Richard Deacon*, exh. cat., interviews by Penelope Curtis (London: Tate Publishing, 2014)
Kunstmuseum Winterthur, *Richard Deacon: On the Other Side*, exh. cat. (Düsseldorf, 2015)
Thomas Schütte Foundation, *Richard Deacon: Under The Weather*, exh. cat. (Düsseldorf, 2016)
Elderton and Morrill (2017), pp.76–9
Rajesh Punj, 'Fluidity and Fixedness', interview, *Sculpture*, 37:2 (2018)
Interview, in Racz (2020), pp.85–95

Exhibition reviews: Carmine Iannaccone, *Art Issues*, 67 (2001); Christopher Knight, *Los Angeles Times* (11 June 2004); Martin Coomer, *Modern Painters* (March 2006); Linda Sandino, *CR*, 269 (2014)

A documentary film, *Richard Deacon: In Between*, directed by Claudia Schmid, was released in 2014.

295 *Bottle Green Republic*, 2009 (pl.130)
Glazed ceramic, wood, rubber; h.34cm, d.59cm, h.65cm (plinth)
C.75, 76-2014. Source: Lisson Gallery, London, £40,000; acquired through the generosity of Gerard and Sarah Griffin
Shown in solo exhibition, *Association*, Lisson Gallery, London, 2012.

Dernbach, Josef (**Jupp**) (later **Dernbach-Mayen**) 1908–1990

Jupp Dernbach was a versatile artist who worked primarily as a painter, printmaker, mosaicist and sculptor. Born in Mayen, Germany, he studied art in Berlin, before moving to Paris in 1937, and was in London by 1939. He was a lifelong friend of Hans Coper, who he met while they were interned during the Second World War. They met again in 1946 at Lucie Rie's (qv) studio, where both had sought work. They assisted in button-making, and helped design and build Rie's top-loading kiln. Jupp continued to work as her assistant until 1950, experimenting with the decoration of large dishes in his free time. He went on to make a mosaic for the Dome of Discovery at the Festival of Britain in London in 1951, and produced public sculpture.

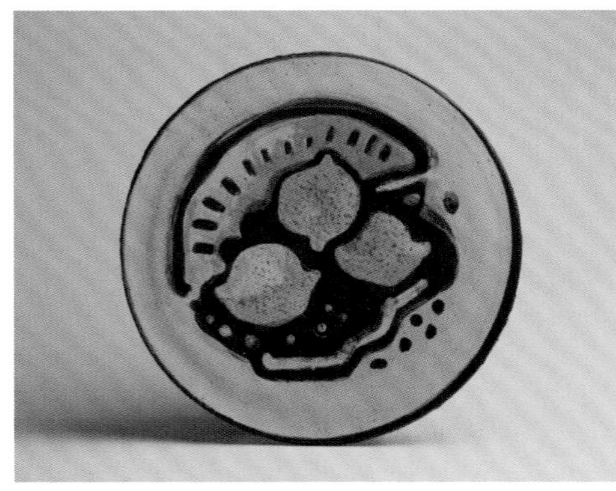
296

Tony Birks, *Hans Coper* (London, 1983), pp.13, 15, 20–1
Harrod (1999), pp.205, 271
Cooper (2012), pp.146, 152
York Art Gallery, *Lucie Rie: Ceramics and Buttons* (York, 2018), pp.27–9

296 Dish, *c.* 1949
Stoneware, white glaze, painted in yellow and brown; marks: 'JD' in monogram, painted; made in Lucie Rie's studio; h.4cm, d.35.6cm
Circ.60-1951. Source: the artist, £15.15s.

Dixon, Stephen 1957–

1957	born Peterlee, County Durham
1976–80	studies fine art at University of Newcastle upon Tyne
1983–86	studies ceramics at Royal College of Art, London
1987	first solo exhibition, Anatol Orient, London
1998–	Research Fellow in Contemporary Crafts, Manchester Metropolitan University; Senior Research Fellow from 2003; Professor from 2007
2000	Arts Council 'Year of the Artist' award for collaborative project with Amnesty International and Kosovan refugees
2005	retrospective exhibition, *The Sleep of Reason*, Manchester Art Gallery and tour
2006	travels to Australia on research project investigating impact of dislocation on production of cultural artefacts
2009–10	ceramics residency, V&A
2014	Arts Council 'Reimagine India' residency, Bapugaon, Maharashtra

2021 wins British Ceramics Biennial AWARD, Stoke-on-Trent

Stephen Dixon's work is infused with social and political narratives, and marked by a strong sense of satire. Typically utilizing vessel forms, Dixon makes extensive use of expressive figurative elements, either modelled or set within a graffiti-like graphic surface. Since 2006 he has also explored intervention and installation art, and made political portrait heads. His studio practice has increasingly been complemented by a range of public and community arts projects and commissions.

Stephen Dixon, 'A Potter's Day', *CR*, 127 (1991)
— 'A Partisan Self-portrait', *CR*, 139 (1993)
— 'The Contemporary British Ceramic Figure', in Stair (2000), pp.162–7
— 'Ceramics of Substance', *Ceramics in Society*, 57 (2005)
— 'The Sleep of Reason', *Ceramics: Art and Perception*, 59 (2005)
— 'Monopoly and the Truth', interview, *Crafts*, 220 (2009)
— interview, in Peters and West (2011), pp.36–43
— 'Why Clay?', *Interpreting Ceramics*, ejournal, 14 (2012)
— 'Fragments and Narratives: Reflections on a Residency at the V&A', University of Westminster Ceramics Research Centre – UK, online essay series 11 (2014)
— 'Ceramics, Narrative and Commemoration', *Craft Research*, 10:1 (2019)
Pamela Johnson, 'Subversive Ceramics', *Crafts*, 95 (1988)
Rosemary Hill, 'Six of the Best', *Crafts*, 106 (1990)
Reginal Gant, 'Stephen Dixon's Carnival of Clay', *Ceramics: Art and Perception*, 9 (1992)
Manchester Art Gallery, *The Levantine Chess Set*, exh. guide (1995)
Barbican Centre (1998)
Claudia Clare, 'An Alternative Voice', *CR*, 209 (2004)
Lesley Jackson, 'War Paint', *Crafts*, 188 (2004)
'Stephen Dixon – 21 Countries', *Ceramics in Society*, 57 (2004)
Liz Mitchell (ed.), *The Sleep of Reason*, exh. cat. (Manchester Art Gallery, 2005)
Hanaor (2007), pp.194–5
Jeremy Theophilus, 'Guerrilla Ceramics', *Art and Architecture*, 68 (2009)
Carlano (2010), pp.64–5
Winch (2010), pp.14–19
Clark, Strauss and others (2012), pp.368, 431
Laura Mitchell, 'Material Memory', *CR*, 257 (2012)
Teleri Lloyd-Jones, 'Peace Talks', *Crafts*, 242 (2013)

298

Exhibition reviews: Rosemary Hill, *Crafts*, 122 (1993); Pamela Johnson, *Crafts*, 135 (1995); Emmanuel Cooper, *CR*, 187 (2001); Lesley Jackson, *Crafts*, 168 (2001); Alex McErlain, *CR*, 208 (2004); Robin Emmerson, *CR*, 214 (2005); Alfred Hickling, *The Guardian* (23 March 2005)

297 *Family of Nations*, 1992 (pl.106)
Stoneware, handbuilt, with applied and impressed decoration, coloured slips and glazes; inscribed 'FAMILY / OF / NATIONS' and 'ANNUS HORRIBILIS'; marks: 'DECEMBER 9|2', impressed; h.22.6cm, d.20.4cm
C.97:1,2-2012. Source: given by the artist
According to Dixon, 'the piece is about the United Nations, and its inability to act together to prevent the break-up of Yugoslavia and the ensuing civil wars. The animals are representatives of the major nations of the security council, Britain, France, America and Russia.'

298 *Laocoön*, 2001–02
Earthenware, slab-built, with slips and hand-drawn transfers; marks: 'STEPHEN DIXON', impressed; h.68cm, d.41cm
C.21:1,2-2005. Source: Adrian Sassoon, £2643.75

Dodd, Mike 1943–

1943 born Sutton, Surrey
1957–61 attends Bryanston School, Dorset, where taught pottery by Donald Potter
1962–65 studies medicine at Cambridge University
1966–67 studies ceramics at Hammersmith College of Art
1968–71 workshop at Edburton, Sussex
1971–75 workshop at Whatlington, Sussex
1975–79 establishes Cider House Pottery at Breage, Cornwall; begins making glazes from local materials
1979 spends six months at Oxapampa, Peru, constructing wood-fired kiln as part of project for Amuesha community
1981–86 teaches ceramics at Cumbria College of Art
1986–94 establishes Wellrash Pottery at Boltongate, Cumbria
1995–99 workshop at Cheddington, Dorset
1999– establishes Butleigh Pottery, Butleigh, Somerset

Mike Dodd makes reduction-fired stoneware and porcelain, working broadly within the Anglo-Asian school of practice established by Bernard Leach (qv). While responding to tradition, Dodd's work shows much invention, notably through his exploratory use of locally available materials and a certain daring in developing form. This is evident in his 'textured' pots, the broken surfaces of which result from powdered clay applied to still-wet forms, which are then worked from within to open up a network of fissures. Dodd balances domestic ware production with making individual pieces, remaining committed to the idea of function in a broader sense of enrichment to everyday life.

Mike Dodd, 'In Defence of Tradition', *Pottery Quarterly*, 11:43 (1974)
— 'Confused Ramblings', *Artists Newsletter* (April 1983)
— 'A Pottery in Oxapampa, Peru', *CR*, 81 (1983)
— 'Makers or Breakers', *Artists Newsletter* (March 1984)
— 'Studio Pottery, Cumbria College of Art and Design', *Real Pottery* (*Pottery Quarterly*), 14:56 (1985)
— contribution, in 'Bernard Leach – A Living Tradition', *CR*, 108 (1987)
— 'Healthy Roots', *Artists Newsletter* (June 1987)
— 'A Potter's Day', *CR*, 147 (1994)
— 'Function and Dysfunction', *Ceramics: Art and Perception*, 34 (1998)
— *An Autobiography of Sorts* (Brook, 2004) – reproduces a number of earlier texts
'New Members', *CR*, 5 (1970)
Potters/*The Ceramics Book* (1972) to (2012)
Tim Proud, 'Mike Dodd – Unambiguous Potter', *CR*, 107 (1987)
Tanya Harrod, 'Mike Dodd', *Ceramics Monthly*, 39:1 (1991)
Rogers (1991), pp.100–7, (2003), pp.114–18
'An Interview with Mike Dodd', *Studio Pottery*, 8 (1994)
David Whiting, 'Spirit in Action', *CR*, 195 (2002)

Goldmark Gallery, *Mike Dodd: Recent Pots*, exh. cat., text by Mike Dodd (Uppingham, 2007) – see also cats. from 2009, 2011, 2015 and 2018
Alex McErlain, 'Spirited Pots', *CR*, 309 (2021)

Exhibition reviews: W.A. Ismay, *CR*, 18 (1972), and 32 (1975); Paul Vincent, *Studio Pottery*, 1 (1993); Emma Clegg, *CR*, 187 (2001)

A recorded interview with Mike Dodd is in the Potters of the Bernard Leach Legacy collection at the British Library, London (C1330/02). A documentary film, *Mike Dodd: Potter*, was made by Goldmark and released on DVD in 2011.

299 Pot, 1989 (pl.100)
Stoneware, incised and textured, green-brown ash glaze; marks: 'MD' in a square monogram, impressed; h.25.7cm, d.21.5cm
C.38-1989. Source: Contemporary Applied Arts, London, £135.45

Doherty, Micky *see* Micki Schloessingk

Dring, James (C.J.) 1905–1985

1905 born Wandsworth, London
1920–27 studies at Clapham School of Art
1927–31 studies at Royal College of Art, London, originally in School of Painting; attends pottery classes under William Staite Murray (qv) from second year, and transfers to School of Design in third year, gaining diploma in 1930
1931–46 married to the graphic designer and textile artist Lilian Dring
1932– workshop in London, producing decorated tiles, plates and dishes
1937 exhibition with Sam Haile (qv) at The Brygos Gallery, London
c. 1938–40 workshop in Teddington, Middlesex
1947– ceases producing ceramics; continues to work as a painter

Primarily a painter, James Dring was drawn to William Staite Murray's (qv) pottery department while at the Royal College of Art. His ceramic production utilized factory-made blanks, upon which he fired painted decoration. He seems not to have made his own pottery. He largely abandoned ceramics after his Teddington workshop was destroyed by bombing during the Second World War, and it is not known where his final pieces, made about 1947, were fired. Dring was a close friend of Sam Haile (qv), and the two exhibited together in the 1930s. Several of Haile's pots were beqeathed to the V&A by Dring, including a loving cup (397) made as a gift to commemorate Dring's second marriage to the watercolourist Olive Dring (née Stacey). James Dring was the younger brother of the artist William Dring.

Arts and Crafts Exhibition Society (1935), (1938), (1941), (1948)
Brygos Gallery, *Stoneware Pottery by T.S. Haile and Decorated Plates and Tiles by C.J. Dring*, exh. cat. (London, 1937)
Wertheim Gallery, *Contemporary Georgian Exhibition*, exh. cat. (London, 1937)
Decorative Art (1950/51) – illustrates work made earlier

300 Two tiles, 1929
Earthenware, painted in blue and red; marks: 'J DRING / May 29', painted; 'J DRING / 1929', painted; h.14.7cm (each)
C.420 & 421-1934. Source: British Institute of Industrial Art (given by the artist, 1929)

301 Tile, *c.* 1938
Earthenware, grey glaze, painted in colours; marks: 'JAMES / DRING' enclosing a device, painted; h.32.3cm, w.31.8cm
C.20-1946. Source: given by the artist
Shown in the exhibition *Tiles and Tilework*, V&A, 1939, organized in collaboration with the Council for Art and Industry.

302 Plate, *c.* 1947
Painted decoration on factory-made earthenware blank; marks: 'J. DRING' and a device, painted; h.2.3cm, d.25.6cm
C.83-1986. Source: bequeathed by the artist

303 Cup and saucer, 1947
Painted decoration on factory-made earthenware blanks; marks: 'JAMES / DRING / 47' and a device, painted; h.6cm (cup), d.14.7cm (saucer)
C.81&A-1986. Source: *see* **302**

304 Plate, 1947
Painted decoration on factory-made earthenware blank; marks: 'JAMES / DRING / 47' and a device, painted; h.4.3cm, d.25.6cm
C.82-1986. Source: *see* **302**

300

302

301

304 / 303

Duckworth, Ruth (née Windmüller)
1919–2009

1919	born Hamburg, Germany
1936	moves to England
1936–40	studies drawing, painting and sculpture at Liverpool School of Art
1946	learns stone carving at Kennington School of Art, London
1949	marries Aidron Duckworth, a sculptor and designer
1955	studies ceramics at Hammersmith College of Art, but finds teaching doctrinaire
1956–58	studies ceramics at Central School of Arts and Crafts, London
1959–64	teaches part-time at Central School; establishes studio at Kew, London, with Aidron
1960	first solo exhibition of ceramics, Primavera, London
1964–	accepts teaching post at University of Chicago, USA
1966	returns briefly to England, making work at Kew and teaching; returns permanently to USA
1977	retires from teaching at University of Chicago
1982–	converts former pickle factory into studio in Chicago
2005–06	major retrospective, Museum of Arts and Design, New York, and tour

Ruth Duckworth played a significant role in the development of ceramic sculpture in Britain, her work challenging traditional thinking about pottery. Having fled Nazi Germany, she practised at first as a sculptor in stone and wood. Interested in the possibilities of ceramics, she followed the suggestion of Lucie Rie (qv) and began study, first at Hammersmith and then at the Central School, where she subsequently became an influential teacher. While in London, Duckworth made rugged, handbuilt stoneware pots and delicate, organic porcelain sculptures, as well as crisply thrown stoneware tableware. After moving to Chicago, she developed larger-scale work, including murals, alongside refined, abstract porcelain forms.

Ruth Duckworth, statement, in Rothschild (1972)
— interview by Judith Raphael, *Art Journal*, 53:1 (1994)
— 'The Fullness of Form', *Studio Potter*, 26:1 (1997)
— **and Aidron Duckworth**, 'Potting in a Vacuum', *Pottery Quarterly*, 7:26 (1961), pp.55–6, 70
— **and Alice Westphal**, *Ruth Duckworth* (Evanston: Exhibit A, 1977)

Arts and Crafts Exhibition Society (1957)
Decorative Art (1960/61), (1962/63), (1963/64), (1965/66), (1968/69)
Biographical notes, *Pottery Quarterly*, 8:30 (1963), p.4, pls.10–11, and 8:32 (1965), p.106, pl.16
Birks (1967), pp.141–60, (1976), pp.22–39
Casson (1967), p.6, pls.21–6
Rose (1970), pp.50–1, pls.83–4
V&A (1972), p.108
Emmanuel Cooper, 'A Great Original', *CR*, 25 (1974)
Alice Westphal, 'The Ceramics of Ruth Duckworth', *Craft Horizons*, 37:4 (1977)
Museum Boymans-van Beuningen, *Ruth Duckworth*, exh. cat. (Rotterdam, 1979)
Emmanuel Cooper, 'Artist Potter', *CR*, 68 (1981)
Paisley Museum and Art Galleries (1984), pp.32–3
Garth Clark and Oliver Watson, *American Potters Today* (London: V&A, 1986)
Tanya Harrod, 'Free Spirit', *Crafts*, 85 (1987)
Michael McTwigan, 'Ruth Duckworth', *American Ceramics*, 10:2 (1992)
Crafts Council (1995b), pp.32–3
Gaze (1997), pp.470–1
Janet Koplos, 'Sources of Inspiration', *Crafts*, 160 (1999)
Jo Lauria and Tony Birks, *Ruth Duckworth: Modernist Sculptor*, with detailed chronology (Aldershot, 2004)
Ruthin Craft Centre, *Ruth Duckworth: Duckworth at Ninety*, exh. cat. (Ruthin, 2009)
Carlano (2010), pp.66–7
Clark, Strauss and others (2012), pp.302–3, 368–9, 431

Exhibition reviews: Ann Philipp, *Arts Review*, 14:18 (1962); Julian Stair, *Art in America*, 93:5 (2005), and *Crafts*, 195 (2005); Emmanuel Cooper, *Crafts*, 220 (2009); Tony Birks, *Ceramics: Art and Perception*, 91 (2013)

Obituaries: Emmanuel Cooper, *The Guardian* (30 October 2009); Polly Ullrich, *Studio Potter*, 38:1 (2009); Tony Birks, *Ceramics: Art and Perception*, 80 (2010)

Ruth Duckworth's papers are in the Archives of American Art at the Smithsonian Institution, Washington, DC (AAA.duckruth).

305 Dish, 1959
Stoneware, green glaze, painting in black; marks: 'RWD', impressed; h.9.2cm, d.40cm
Circ.241-1959. Source: A & R Duckworth Ltd, £7

306 Pot, 1959 (pl.46)
Stoneware, coil-built, green glaze at lip; h.24.5cm, d.23.8cm
Circ.242-1959. Source: *see* 305, £6

307 'Tile Mask', 1962
Stoneware, matt black mask on a mottled-green glazed tile; h.15cm, d.15cm
Circ.617-1962. Source: Primavera, London (exhibition: *Ruth and Aidron Duckworth*, 1962, no.105), £4

308 'Small Porcelain Sculpture', 1966
Porcelain, handbuilt, greenish glaze with metallic black; h.11.8cm, d.12.6cm
Circ.763-1967. Source: Primavera, London (exhibition: *Stoneware by Ruth Duckworth a nd Glass by Sam Herman*, 1967, no.25), £8
Illustrated in Birks (1967), pl.114.

309 *Weed Pot (will not hold water)*, 1966 (pl.49)
Stoneware, handbuilt, spattered black and

305

307

308

green glaze; h.31.4cm, d.34cm
Circ.764-1967. Source: *see* **308** (no.50), £20

The museum also holds later work by Duckworth made in the USA, catalogued in Clark and Watson (1986), cited above.

Dunn, Constance E. (née **Wade**) 1904–1976

1904	born Dorking, Surrey
1921–24	studies at Cambridge School of Art
1924–28	studies pottery at Royal College of Art, London, initially under Dora Billington (qv), then under William Staite Murray (qv)
1928	marries John Dunn, a trained chemist
c. 1930–32	teaches at Constantine College, Middlesbrough
c. 1933–	sets up own workshop at Billingham, Durham, working on high-temperature wares with her husband, who assists on technical side; work interrupted by war
1946–	resumes potting; builds new oil-fired kiln to her own design

Constance Dunn was an accomplished potter, who worked with technical command in stoneware and porcelain with rich glazes or brush decoration. An early student of William Staite Murray (qv), she was well represented at the exhibition of *Recent Examples of British Pottery* organized by the British Institute of Industrial Art and held at the V&A in 1927. She continued to exhibit in London after establishing her workshop in County Durham, showing at The Brygos Gallery in the late 1930s, and after the Second World War supplying work to the Crafts Centre of Great Britain and to The Heffer Gallery in Cambridge.

British Institute of Industrial Art (1927)
Decorative Art (1929), (1950/51), (1958/59)
Brygos Gallery (1936), (1937b)
Arts and Crafts Exhibition Society (1948) to (1957)
Dartington Hall (1952)
Wingfield Digby (1952), pp.80–1, pl.54
Lewis (1956), pls.358–9
Paisley Museum and Art Galleries (1984), p.33
Nottingham City Museums and Galleries (2017), p.35

310 Bowl, 1931
Stoneware, incised and painted, mottled grey glaze; marks: 'W' in a triangle, impressed; h.7cm, d.12.3cm
C.415-1934. Source: British Institute of Industrial Art (purchased through the Spielmann Memorial Fund, 1931)

310

312 / 311

311 Bowl, 1947
Stoneware, green-black 'hare's fur' glaze, iron rim; marks: 'W' in a triangle, impressed; h.7.8cm, d.17.2cm
Circ.339-1955. Source: the artist, £6.6s.

312 Bowl, 1954
Stoneware, painted in iron, transparent glaze; marks: impressed seal; h.12cm, d.15.2cm
Circ.338-1955. Source: *see* **311**, £4.4s.

Eastman, Ken 1960–

1960	born Watford, Hertfordshire
1979–83	studies ceramics at Edinburgh College of Art
1984–87	studies ceramics at Royal College of Art, London
1987–91	studio in St Pancras, London
1990–	solo exhibition, Contemporary Applied Arts, London; thereafter frequent solo exhibitions in UK and internationally, including at Galerie De Witte Voet, Amsterdam; Pro-Art Gallery, St Louis, Missouri, USA; Nancy Margolis Gallery, New York; Galerie Marianne Heller, Heidelberg, Germany
1992–98	studio in Kimbolton, Herefordshire
1995	wins Premio Faenza at International Ceramics Competition, Faenza
1996	shortlisted for Jerwood Prize for Applied Arts
1998	awarded Arts Foundation Fellowship
1998–2011	Research Lecturer, Glasgow School of Art
1999–	studio in Hamnish, Herefordshire
2000–19	gallery artist with regular exhibitions, Barrett Marsden (later Marsden Woo) Gallery, London
2001	wins Gold Medal at World Ceramic Exposition, Korea
2007–10	designs range of bone-china vessels for Royal Crown Derby

Ken Eastman's practice is centred on non-functional, slab-built vessels. While taking certain visual cues from landscape or architecture, his work is essentially abstract, reflecting a desire to express what has not previously been seen. Painted slips and oxides bring rich, nuanced colour to the contours of spatially complex forms.

Ken Eastman, 'On Making Pots', exh. essay, Barrett Marsden Gallery (London, 2007)
Alison Britton, 'The Critic's Eye', *Crafts*, 98 (1989)
Contemporary Applied Arts, *Ken Eastman*, exh. pamphlets, texts by Alison Britton (London, 1990) and (1995)
Tanya Harrod, 'Towers of Strength', *Crafts*, 106 (1990)
Houston (1991)
Museum of Modern Art, Oxford (1993), pp.32–3, 83–4, 94
Patricia Degener, 'Architectural Form', *Ceramics: Art and Perception*, 18 (1994)
Crafts Council (1995a), p.38
Jane McCabe, 'Lares and Penates', *CR*, 153 (1995)
Crafts Council (1996b), pp.18–19
Jane McCabe, 'Pots in Place: Ken Eastman's Ceramics', *Ceramics: Art and Perception*, 26 (1996)
Angel Row Gallery, *Ken Eastman: New Works*, exh. cat., text by Alison Britton (Nottingham, 1998)
Barrett Marsden Gallery, *Ken Eastman*, exh. pamphlet, text by Tanya Harrod (London, 2000)
Seisbøll (2000)
Jane McCabe, *Ken Eastman: Behind the Gates of Clay* (London, 2004)
David Whiting, 'Ken Eastman', exh. essay, Barrett Marsden Gallery (London, 2005)
Glen R. Brown, 'Actual and Allusive: The Vessels of Ken Eastman', *Ceramics Monthly*, 55:2 (2007)
Hanaor (2007), pp.168–9

Liz Hoggard, 'And the Winner Is ...', *Crafts*, 205 (2007)
Glenn Adamson, 'Ken Eastman', exh. essay, Marsden Woo Gallery (London, 2009)
Nicholas Oddy, 'Factory Formed', *CR*, 237 (2009)
Whiting (2009), pp.102–7
Carlano (2010), pp.68–9
WCC-BF (2010), pp.76–7, 94
Flaminio Gualdoni, 'The Shape of Things', *La Ceramica in Italia e nel Mondo*, 33 (2017)
David Whiting, 'The Cut of the Light', *Ceramics Monthly*, 67:10 (2019)
Peter Schmitt, 'Covering Ground', exh. essay, Galerie Marianne Heller (Heidelberg, 2020)
Thorpe (2021), pp.147–54

Exhibition reviews: Pamela Johnson, *Crafts*, 136 (1995); Paul Vincent, *Studio Pottery*, 16 (1995); David Whiting, *Crafts*, 154 (1998); Edmund de Waal, *Crafts*, 167 (2000); Tony Franks, *Ceramics: Art and Perception*, 70 (2007); Andy Christian, *Ceramics: Art and Perception*, 81 (2010)

313 Pot, 1989
Stoneware, slab-built, painted with coloured slips and oxides; marks: 'Eastman Sept 89. 3989.', painted; h.23.8cm, d.46cm
C.51-1990. Source: Contemporary Applied Arts, London, £407.70

314 *November Night*, 2002 (pl.112)
Stoneware, slab-built, painted with coloured slips and oxides; marks: 'Eastman 2002', painted; h.70cm, d.49cm
C.15-2003. Source: Barrett Marsden Gallery, £3000; purchased through the James Yorke-Radleigh bequest

315 *Border Country*, 2015
Stoneware, slab-built, painted with coloured slips and oxides; marks: 'Eastman 2015', painted; h.53.1cm, d.31.9cm
C.68-2015. Source: Marsden Woo Gallery, London (solo exhibition, 2015), £2763.33; acquired through the generosity of Gerard and Sarah Griffin

316 *On My Way*, 2015
Stoneware, slab-built, painted with coloured slips and oxides; marks: 'Eastman 2015', painted; h.51.8cm, d.29.7cm
C.69-2015. Source: *see* **315**, £2763.33

The museum also holds a collection of bone china vessels, designed by Ken Eastman for Royal Crown Derby, not catalogued here (C.310 to 319-2009).

313

315 / 316

Eastop, Geoffrey 1921–2014

1921	born Norbury, London
1940–46	war service
1949–52	studies painting at Goldsmiths' College, London, takes pottery as subsidiary subject in final year
1952–53	in France, studies at Académie Ranson, Paris
1953–54	joins Odney Pottery, Cookham, Berkshire, assisting John Bew (qv); begins teaching pottery part-time at Reading Technical College
1956–61	joins Alan Caiger-Smith (qv) at Aldermaston Pottery, working in tin-glazed earthenware
1962–	teaches full-time at Reading Technical College, later moving to Berkshire College of Art and Design
1962–69	sets up workshop at Padworth, Berkshire, making reduced stoneware
1968	meets John Piper (qv)
1969–84	establishes workshop at Fawley Bottom farmhouse, Piper's home near Henley-on-Thames, Berkshire; produces own work in oxidized stoneware and porcelain, also making earthenware dishes and pots for himself and Piper to decorate
1984–	moves to Ecchinswell, Berkshire, establishing workshop and showroom; begins working with painted vitreous slips on stoneware
1986	retires from teaching
1992	retrospective exhibition organized by Portsmouth City Museum

Trained as a painter, Geoffrey Eastop sought to cross perceived boundaries between craft and art through his work. His output was technically diverse, exploring painterly surfaces as well as the sculptural qualities of altered thrown forms. For a number of years he collaborated with the painter John Piper (qv), with whom he also undertook several architectural commissions. In later years he concentrated on handbuilt forms.

Geoffrey Eastop, 'Aesthetic Boundaries', *CR*, 65 (1980)
— 'Painting with Vitreous Slips', *CR*, 121 (1990)
— 'Plotting your Path', *CR*, 131 (1991)
— 'On Crossing Over', *CR*, 204 (2003)
— 'If Only ...', *CR*, 233 (2008)
— *The Piper Years: A Memoir* (Greenwich, 2011)
Arts and Crafts Exhibition Society (1957)
Decorative Art (1961/62), (1972/73)
Potters/The Ceramics Book (1972) to (2012)
Bohun Gallery, *Geoffrey Eastop: The Hollow Vessel*, exh. cat. (Henley-on-Thames, 1980)
Portsmouth City Museum, *Geoffrey Eastop: 40 Years of Change in Studio Pottery*, exh. cat. (1992)
Margot Coatts, 'Sources of Inspiration', *Crafts*, 125 (1993)
'Geoffrey Eastop', *Ceramics Monthly*, 44:3 (1996)
Margot Coatts, 'Geoffrey Eastop: The Definition of an Artist Potter', *Studio Pottery*, 36 (1999)
— *Geoffrey Eastop: A Potter in Practice* (Ecchinswell, 1999)
Berkeley Square Gallery, *Geoffrey Eastop: The Hollow Dimension*, exh. cat. (London, 2001)
River and Rowing Museum, *Geoffrey Eastop: Retrospective: Looking Forward*, exh. pamphlet (Henley-on-Thames, 2005)
Carlano (2010), pp.70–1
Ben Eastop, obituary, *CPA News*, 160 (2015)
Jane White, *Alan Caiger-Smith and the Legacy of Aldermaston Pottery* (Oxford, 2018), pp.20–3, 27–9

317

318

Exhibition reviews: W.A. Ismay, *CR*, 24 (1973); Paul Vincent, *Studio Pottery*, 1 (1993); Nicki Jarvis, *Studio Pottery*, 26 (1997); Emmanuel Cooper, *CR*, 174 (1998); Felicity Aylieff, *CR*, 195 (2002); Carolyn Genders, *Ceramics Monthly*, 52:5 (2004); Simon Olding, *CR*, 215 (2005)

An interview with Geoffrey Eastop is in the Crafts Lives sound archive at the British Library, London (C960/68).

317 Pot, *c.* 1980
Porcelain, thrown and cut, reactive glazes; marks: 'GE' in monogram, painted, '36' printed label; h.18.3cm, d.16.6cm
C.259-1993. Source: the artist, £200

318 *Garden Ornament*, 1981
Porcelain, thrown and altered, reactive glazes; marks: 'GE' in monogram, painted; h.20.3cm, d.9cm
C.77-2004. Source: given by the artist
In a letter to the museum Eastop commented: 'I have always been interested in the possibility that a piece of work can imply a significance beyond its direct formal appearance, as in the *Garden Ornament*, where the urn has become a flower.'

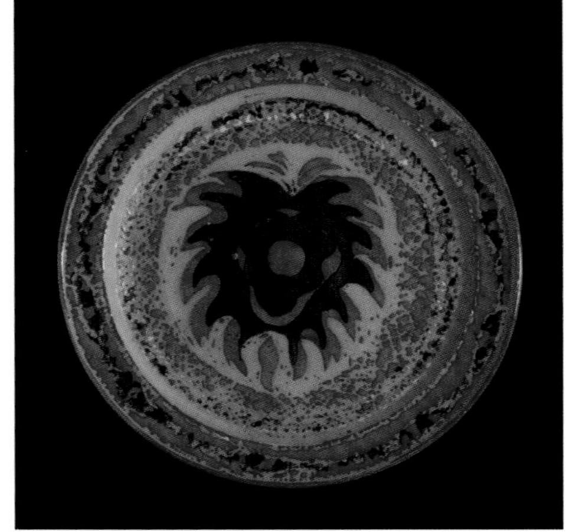

319

320

319 Dish: *Oriental*, *c.* 1983
Red earthenware, thrown, painted coloured glazes with wax-resist; marks: 'GE' in monogram, painted, '52' printed label; d.50cm
C.260-1993. Source: private sale, £250
Originally purchased from Eastop's solo exhibition at Bohun Gallery, Henley-on-Thames, 1983.

320 Jar, 1992
Stoneware, thrown and altered, sprayed and painted slips; marks: 'G', painted; h.35.1cm, d.17.6cm
C.106-2007. Source: given by the artist

321

321 *Dry Stone Wall*, 2004
Stoneware, handbuilt, painted with coloured slips; marks: 'G', painted; h.39.6cm, d.37.1cm
C.107-2007. Source: the artist, £350

Eglin, Philip 1959–

1959	born Gibraltar
1979–82	studies ceramics at North Staffordshire Polytechnic
1983–86	studies ceramics at Royal College of Art, London
1987–92	studio in Mucklestone, Staffordshire
1990–	solo exhibition, Stafford Art Gallery; thereafter frequent solo exhibitions in UK and internationally, including regular shows at The Scottish Gallery, Edinburgh, and Garth Clark Gallery, New York
1992–2003	studio in Newcastle-under-Lyme, Staffordshire
1993	awarded Arts Foundation Fellowship
1996	wins Jerwood Prize for Applied Arts
2001	solo exhibition, V&A, London
2001–	gallery artist with regular exhibitions, Barrett Marsden (later Marsden Woo) Gallery, London
2003–11	studio in Shelton, Stoke-on-Trent
2011–	moves to Wales, establishes studio near Abercraf, Powys

Philip Eglin draws upon eclectic sources, from ceramic tradition and art history to religion,

sport and consumer culture. At times incisive and subversive, his work is typified by wit and humour, and an expressive freedom of gesture. He gained early recognition for his nude female figures, which recall the paintings of the early 16th-century artist Lucas Cranach. He has since explored figures of the Madonna or Madonna and Child, Christ, and Popes, referencing Northern European Gothic woodcarvings, as well as making a variety of vessel forms, notably generously proportioned buckets and diminutive jugs presented in groups. His work is handbuilt, sometimes using slabs press-moulded with details from disposable packaging. Larger pieces typically carry graffiti-like text and collaged printed or painted imagery. His exploration of the ceramics collection at Aberystwyth University during the 2010s has meanwhile prompted work in slipware.

Rosemary Hill, 'The Venus of Harlow New Town', *Crafts*, 102 (1990)
— 'Six of the Best', *Crafts*, 106 (1990)
Tanya Harrod, 'Beauty of Continuities', *CR*, 131 (1991)
Houston (1991)
John Houston, 'Philip Eglin', *Studio Pottery*, 3 (1993)
Museum of Modern Art, Oxford (1993), pp.34–5, 84, 94
Sister Wendy Beckett, 'Ways of Seeing', *CR*, 148 (1994)
Crafts Council (1996b), pp.20–1
— (1996c), pp.117, 132
Scottish Gallery, *Philip Eglin*, exh. cat., texts by Oliver Watson and Alison Britton (Edinburgh, 1997)
Crafts Council, *Only Human*, exh. cat. (London, 1999), pp.12–13, 24–5, 54–5
Barrett Marsden Gallery, *Philip Eglin*, exh. pamphlet, text by Tanya Harrod (London, 2001)
V&A, *Philip Eglin*, exh. pamphlet, texts by Alun Graves and Paul Williamson (London, 2001)
Nottingham Castle Museum and Art Gallery, *Borrowings: Philip Eglin*, exh. cat. (2007)
Amanda Game, 'The Sacred and the Profane', *CR*, 239 (2009)
Scottish Gallery, *Popes, Pin-ups and Pooches: Philip Eglin*, exh. cat. (Edinburgh, 2009)
Whiting (2009), pp.140–5
Carlano (2010), pp.72–3
Lakeland Arts Trust, *Philip Eglin: Mixed Marriage(s)*, exh. cat., text by David Whiting (Kendal, 2011)
Clark, Strauss and others (2012), pp.369, 432
Alison Britton, 'Philip Eglin', in Britton (2013), pp.192–5
Aberystwyth Arts Centre, *Philip Eglin: Slipping the Trail* (2015)
Emma Crichton-Miller, 'Celebrating the Playful Potential of Clay', *Crafts*, 267 (2017)
Scottish Gallery, *Philip Eglin: Unfinished Business*, exh. cat., text by Sara Roberts (Edinburgh, 2017)
Taste Contemporary, *Philip Eglin: Ajar*, exh. cat., text by Alison Britton (Geneva, 2019)

Exhibition reviews: Peter Dormer, 'Clay Bodies', *Crafts*, 102 (1990); Jane Norrie, *Arts Review*, 43:5 (1991); *Studio Pottery*, 12 (1994); Roger Berthoud, *Studio Pottery*, 24 (1996); William Packer, *Financial Times* (29 October 1996); David Whiting, *Crafts*, 144 (1997), and 202 (2006); Oliver Watson, *CR*, 191 (2001); Emma Clegg, *CR*, 221 (2006); Judy Adams, *CR*, 225 (2007); Alison Britton, *CR*, 234 (2008); Glenn Adamson, *Crafts*, 227 (2010); Jo Dahn, *CR*, 277 (2016)

Essays issued alongside exhibitions at Marsden Woo Gallery, London, offer further useful texts.

322 *Venus et Amour*, 1990 (pl.105)
Earthenware, soft-slab built, white slip and painted oxides, honey glaze; h.82cm, d.29cm
C.128-1991. Source: Oxford Gallery, Oxford (solo exhibition, 1991), £985.50

323

324

325

323 *Mother and child*, 1993
Earthenware, soft-slab built, white slip, painted oxides and body stains, transparent glaze; h.36.8cm, d.54.2cm
C.45-1993. Source: the artist, £1200

324 *Bucket*, 1995
Earthenware, slab-built, white slip, painted oxides, transparent glaze, on-glaze transfer-prints; h.41.3cm, d.34.8cm
C.108-1998. Source: Contemporary Applied Arts, London (from their 50th anniversary exhibition, *A View of Clay*, curated by Alison Britton, 1998), £2520

325 *Microwave Oven Safe Madonna*, 2001
Porcelain, handbuilt using press-moulded sections, gilded; marks: 'Eglin / S.O.T. / 2001', incised on back; 'MICROWAVE OVEN SAFE', moulded on back; h.36cm, d.14.5cm
C.8-2002. Source: Barrett Marsden Gallery, £2880; purchase funded by the Friends of the V&A
Shown in the exhibition *Philip Eglin*, V&A, 2001. The form of the figure derives from a medieval woodcarving of the Virgin in the V&A (A.8-1912).

El Nigoumi, Siddig 1931–1996

1931	born near Kassala, Sudan
1948–50	teacher training at Dilling Institute of Education, Kordofan
1950–52	works as calligrapher for Publications Bureau, Khartoum

1952–55	studies at Khartoum School of Art
1957–60	wins scholarship to study ceramics at Central School of Arts and Crafts, London
1960–67	teaches ceramics at Khartoum School of Art
1967	returns to England
1968–95	teaches at West Surrey College of Art and Design, Farnham

Siddig El Nigoumi's work reflects his Sudanese heritage, demonstrating in particular his mastery of Arabic calligraphy and his love of traditional Nubian house decoration. He often applied his lively sense of line and pattern to contemporary British themes, in a seemingly effortless merging of cultures. Although a skilled thrower, he concentrated on press-moulded dishes and handbuilt vessels, working initially in stoneware with slip-trailed decoration, but increasingly in the low-fired, burnished, incised and smoked earthenware for which he is most celebrated.

Siddig El Nigoumi, 'Press Moulded Dishes', *CR*, 33 (1975)
— interview, in Cameron and Lewis (1976), pp.119–25, 167
V&A (1972), p.114
Paul Barron, 'Siddig A El Nigoumi', *CR*, 24 (1973)
Potters (1974) to (1983)
Moira Vincentelli, *Siddig El'Nigoumi*, Aberystwyth Arts Centre: Ceramic Series 11 (1985)
Sebastian Blackie, 'Siddig El Nigoumi', *Ceramics Monthly*, 37:1 (1989)
Perryman (1995), pp.26–8, (2008), pp.32–6
Alan Windsor, *Siddig el Nigoumi: A Sudanese Potter in England* (London, 2015)
— 'The Potter from the Nile', *CR*, 276 (2015)
Nottingham City Museums and Galleries (2017), pp.36–7
Sebastian Blackie, 'Siddig el Nigoumi: A Potter in Exile', *Ceramics: Art and Perception*, 113 (2019)

Exhibition reviews: Guy Burn, *Arts Review* (14 April 1978); Paul Barron, *Crafts*, 39 (1979)

Obituaries: Khalid Al Mubarak, *The Guardian* (28 October 1996); Emmanuel Cooper, *The Independent* (2 November 1996) and *Crafts*, 144 (1997); Sebastian Blackie, *CR*, 163 (1997)

326 *Ibreeq* (water vessel), 1980 (pl.75)
Earthenware, burnished and incised; marks: 'Nigoumi 80' and a scorpion, incised; h.22.4cm, d.20.5cm
C.56-1980. Source: Craftsmen Potters Association, London (*Jugs* exhibition, 1980, no.92), £126

327

327 Dish: *The Great Royal Wedding*, 1981
Earthenware, burnished, incised and smoked; marks: 'Nigoumi 1981', a scorpion and 'THE GREAT ROYAL WEDDING 1981', incised on reverse; h.6.4cm, d.38cm
C.77-1984. Source: given by the Friends of the V&A (purchased at the Craftsmen Potters Association exhibition, *Studio Ceramics Today*, V&A, 1983, no.126, £183.75)
The Arabic inscription reads 'al-zawwaj al-maliki al-kabir 1981' ('The Great Royal Wedding 1981').

Epton, Charlotte (later Bawden)
1902–1970

1902	born Lincoln
1921–25	studies at Royal College of Art, London, in School of Design, taking classes in pottery
1925–29	teaches art at Cheltenham Ladies' College; makes and, on occasion, exhibits pottery
c. 1928–	meets Michael Cardew (qv), becoming friends and a regular visitor to Winchcombe
1929–31	works at Leach Pottery, St Ives, as secretary to Bernard Leach (qv); makes own work in evenings
1931	leaves Leach Pottery in frustration after much of her work is destroyed when firefighters flood a hot kiln while extinguishing a fire
1931–*c.* 1933	works for Muriel Rose at The Little Gallery, London
1932–	marries the artist Edward Bawden, moves to Great Bardfield, Essex; ceases potting
early 1950s	makes pots at Chelmsford School of Art, with support of Joanna Constantinidis (qv)

Charlotte Epton made stoneware and slipware pots at Leach Pottery while working as Bernard Leach's (qv) secretary. Her surviving work shows her to have been a potter of subtlety and sensitivity. Muriel Rose, gallerist and author, has noted that while her marriage to Edward Bawden and raising their children gave no opportunity for making ceramics for many years, Epton never lost her deep interest in pots and commitment to pottery education. In later years she organized pottery courses for the Women's Institute's Denman College, Berkshire (now Oxfordshire), and was a pottery examiner for colleges in the Cambridge area.

'Cotswold Handicrafts', *Gloucester Citizen* (4 May 1927)
Arts and Crafts Exhibition Society (1931)
Muriel Rose, 'Charlotte Epton of St Ives', letter, *CR*, 42 (1976)
Tate Gallery (1985), p.236
Cooper (2003), pp.174–5
Whybrow (2006), pp.96–7
Helen Brown, 'Charlotte Epton, Potter, Artist and Teacher', in Edgeler (2019), pp.50–9

328 Lidded jar, 1930–31
Stoneware, pale grey crackled glaze; marks: 'EP' and 'SI' in monogram, impressed; made at Leach Pottery, St Ives; h.17.7cm, d.10.4cm
Circ.766&A-1931. Source: the artist (shown at the Fifteenth Exhibition of the Arts and Crafts Exhibition Society, Royal Academy, London, 1931), £3.3s.

329 Bowl, 1930–31
Stoneware, pale grey glaze with green flush; marks: 'EP' and 'SI' in monogram, impressed; made at Leach Pottery, St Ives; h.14cm, d.16cm

328 / 329

C.417-1934. Source: British Institute of Industrial Art (purchased through the Spielmann Memorial Fund, 1931)

Evans, James 1964–

1964	born Romford, Essex
1984–87	studies ceramics at Central School of Art and Design, London
1987–89	studies fine art at University of Colorado, USA
1990	solo exhibition at Museum of Contemporary Art, Roskilde, Denmark
1994–2001	studio in Kennington, London
2001	shortlisted for Jerwood Applied Arts Prize
2001–03	studio in Tulse Hill, London
2003–	studios in Waterloo, London, and Helhoughton, Norfolk
2017–	teaches at Morley College, London
2021	solo virtual exhibition, Marsden Woo, London

James Evans creates abstract ceramic sculptures that carry ambiguous references to familiar forms, most notably suggesting the human body or architecture. His work combines a characteristic economy of form and line with rich surface qualities achieved through crackle or lustrous glazes, or a range of metallic or rust-like finishes. Work of the late 2010s and 2020s has used fragmentary forms and aged surfaces to evoke the passage of time.

Potters (1997)
Barbican Centre (1998)
Kate Bevan, 'Ripe and Raw', *CR*, 182 (2000)
Crafts Council, *Ripe*, exh. cat. (London, 2000)
Crafts Council (2001), pp.16–17, 31
Alun Graves, 'James Evans' Myriad Forms', *Ceramics: Art and Perception*, 61 (2005)
Freddie Robins, 'Open Frequency 2006: James Evans', *axisweb*, online essay (2006)
Tessa Peters, 'James Evans: Abugation', exh. essay, Marsden Woo Gallery (London, 2012)

Exhibition reviews: Edward Lucie-Smith, 'Ripe', *Crafts*, 164 (2000); Emma Clegg, *CR*, 215 (2005); Rob Kesseler, *CR*, 257 (2012); Matthew Kangas, *Ceramics Monthly*, 61:1 (2013)

330

330 *Dondurma*, 2004
Earthenware, handbuilt, crackle glaze; h.26.4cm, d.42.7cm
C.41-2004. Source: cosa at Collect 2004, £1000

Feibleman, Dorothy 1951–

1951	born Indianapolis, Indiana, USA
1969–73	studies ceramics at Rochester Institute of Technology, New York
1973	moves to England
1973–75	studio in Retford, Nottinghamshire
1975–	studio in London
1993	wins INAX Design Prize, Tokoname, Japan
1997–	begins travelling regularly to Japan, making work
2002	Gold Prize, 6th International Ceramics Competition, Mino, Japan

Dorothy Feibleman is known for her fine 'agate' porcelain, which she was inspired to develop through a desire to replicate the patterning of millefiori glass beads. Different coloured clays are laminated and rolled, from which thin sections are cut and used to build delicate bowls or elements for jewellery. Since 1995 she has also developed laminated white porcelain forms using clays of varying translucency.

Dorothy Feibleman, 'Precious Forms', *CR*, 101 (1986)
'CPA New Members', *CR*, 35 (1975)
Crafts Advisory Committee (1976), p.92
Potters (1977) to (2000)
Fiona Adamczewski, exh. review, *Crafts*, 40 (1979)
Crafts Council (1980), p.57
John Catleugh, 'Dorothy Feibleman's Agate Porcelain', *CR*, 68 (1981)
Oxfordshire County Museum Services (1984), pp.30–1
Gibson (1987), pp.78–87
Waller (1998), pp.80–2
Henry Pim, 'Dorothy Feibleman's Patterns of Thought', *Ceramics: Art and Perception*, 46 (2001)
Perryman (2004), pp.167–8
Jo Connell, *Colouring Clay* (London, 2007), pp.22–3
Cate McQuaid, 'Dorothy Feibleman', *Ceramics: Art and Perception*, 79 (2010)
Naomi Miyake (ed.), *Collected Works of Dorothy Feibleman*, texts by Jo Lauria and others (Tokyo, 2023)

331 / 332

331 Bowl: *Lunar II*, 1981
Porcelain, handbuilt, laminated coloured clays; h.7.1cm, d.11.5cm
C.43-1981. Source: Craftsmen Potters Association, London (exhibition with Val Barry, Peter Meanley and Peter Beard, 1981, no.161), £288

332 Bowl, 1983
Porcelain, handbuilt, laminated coloured clays; h.8cm, d.9.8cm
C.161-1984. Source: the artist, £575

The museum also holds a necklace of gold and porcelain beads by Feibleman, not catalogued here (M.127-1984).

Fieldhouse, Murray 1925–2018

1925	born Birmingham
1945	decides to take up a craft when demobbed from the Royal Air Force
1946–47	works with Harry Davis (qv) in Cornwall
1947–48	works at Kingwood Design and Craftsmanship, Wormley, Surrey
1948–	joins Pendley Manor Centre of Adult Education, Tring, Hertfordshire, sets up pottery and teaches pottery courses
1954–90	edits and produces *Pottery Quarterly* (later *Real Pottery*)
1959–60	edits and produces *Crafts Review*
1962–	establishes new workshop, Pitstone Hill Pottery, at Northfield, Tring, Hertfordshire; continues to run events at Pendley

333 / 334

1974	founds Dacorum and Chiltern Potters Guild
1985–	pots only occasionally

Murray Fieldhouse became interested in the crafts from reading philosophy and through pacifism, only later electing to be a potter. Appointed resident potter and instructor at Pendley Manor, he soon established a range of standard ware, though his energies were progressively taken up by teaching, lecturing and publishing. He is of importance for his editorship of the pioneering journal *Pottery Quarterly* and the short-lived *Crafts Review*.

Murray Fieldhouse, *Pottery* (London, 1952)
— 'Real Pottery', *Studio Potter*, 20:2 (1992)
E.E. Gilbert, 'Pendley Pottery', *The Studio*, 141 (1951), pp.86–7
Decorative Art (1952/53) to (1955/66), (1960/61), (1961/62), (1966/67)
Arts and Crafts Exhibition Society (1954)
Casson (1967), p.6, pls.119–20
Potters (1972) to (1980)

An interview with Murray Fieldhouse is in the Crafts Lives sound archive at the British Library, London (C960/24).

333 Bowl, 1958
Stoneware, white glazed interior, unglazed exterior; marks: 'mf' in monogram, impressed; h.8.4cm, d.15.4cm
Circ.40-1959. Source: the artist, £4.14s.6d. (with 334)

334 Bowl, 1958
Stoneware, white glazed interior, unglazed exterior; marks: 'mf' in monogram, impressed; h.6.4cm, d.12.4cm
Circ.41-1959. Source: *see* 333

Finch, Ray (Raymond) 1914–2012

1914	born Streatham, London
1935	asks to join Michael Cardew (qv) at Winchcombe after seeing his pots; Cardew advises him to get some experience; briefly attends Central School of Arts and Crafts, London
1936	joins Cardew at Winchcombe Pottery, Gloucestershire
1939	Cardew moves to Cornwall, leaving Finch in charge of the pottery
1941	Cardew returns briefly before leaving for Africa
1943	joins National Fire Service
1946	purchases pottery business from Cardew; Sidney Tustin rejoins pottery after war service, remaining until 1978; production resumes
1952	purchases workshops; begins experiments with stoneware
1959	builds oil-fired kiln, moves largely to stoneware production
1960	inaugural solo exhibition at Craftsmen Potters Shop, London
1961–	gains contract to supply Cranks restaurant in London
1964	discontinues earthenware production
1970–71	spends six months running Kolonyama Pottery, Lesotho
1974	large wood-fired kiln built
1979–	hands pottery management to Michael Finch, but continues to work into his nineties
1980	awarded MBE

Ray Finch ran Winchcombe Pottery for more than three decades, and remained a guiding presence after passing its management to his son Michael. Winchcombe's basic product remained the same throughout – well-designed, well-crafted tableware. Finch developed Michael Cardew's wood-fired earthenware into a more durable stoneware range that gained popular success, and alongside that of the Leach Pottery set the standard for domestic ware. Finch placed much value on teamwork, and Winchcombe became a destination for potters seeking a workshop training.

Ray Finch, 'Winchcombe Pottery', *CR*, 3 (1970)
— statement, in Rothschild (1972)
— 'Cardew at Winchcombe', *Crafts*, 23 (1976)
— contribution, in York City Art Gallery (1983), see also nos.106–20, pls.32–5 and biography
— 'Making Teapots', *CR*, 99 (1986)
British Council (1942)
Wingfield Digby (1952), p.82, pl.59
Lewis (1956), pls.343–4
Decorative Art (1965/66)
Casson (1967), p.6, pls.199–201
Rose (1970), p.36, pls.70–1
Potters/The Ceramics Book (1972) to (1992), (1997) to (2006)
V&A (1972), p.109
Marigold Coleman, 'Ray Finch's Workshop', *Crafts*, 11 (1974)
Norval Kern, 'Winchcombe Pottery', *Ceramics Monthly*, 23:4 (1975)
Crafts Advisory Committee (1976), p.92
— (1977), p.12
Michael Cardew, 'Ray Finch', *CR*, 59 (1979)
Crafts Council (1980), p.57
Kathleen Wilson Mechali, 'A Conversation with Ray Finch', *Ceramics Monthly*, 30:5 (1982)
Crafts Council (1985), pp.44–5, 87
Eileen Lewenstein, 'Ray Finch and Winchcombe Pottery', *CR*, 125 (1990)
David Whiting, 'Sources of Inspiration', *Crafts*, 143 (1996)
Wheeler (1998)
W.A. Ismay, 'In Production', *CR*, 176 (1999)
Minogue and Sanderson (2000), pp.22–4
Matthew Partington, 'Ray Finch and Functional', *Interpreting Ceramics*, ejournal, 1 (2000)
John Edgeler (ed.), *Ray Finch: Craftsman Potter of the Modern Age* (Winchcombe, 2006)
Alex McErlain, 'Seventy Years a Potter', *CR*, 220 (2006)
John Edgeler, 'The Country Potter', *CR*, 279 (2016)
Nottingham City Museums and Galleries (2017), pp.40–1

Exhibition reviews: W.A. Ismay, *CR*, 31 (1975); Tanya Harrod, 'Heroes with Feats of Clay', *The Independent* (26 November 1990)

Obituaries: David Whiting, *The Guardian* (31 January 2012) and *Crafts*, 235 (2012); *The Times* (9 February 2012); Ron Wheeler, *The Independent* (20 February 2012)

Recorded interviews with Ray Finch are at the British Library, London, in the Crafts Lives sound archive (C960/18) and the Bernard Leach Legacy collection (C1330/22).

335 Jug, 1941
Earthenware, white slip, greenish glaze; marks: 'RF' and 'WP' in monogram, impressed; h.15.8cm, d.14cm
Circ.11-1941. Source: Heal & Son Ltd, London, 3s.9d.

335 / 336

339 / 337 / 338

341 / 342

336 Jug, *c.* 1950
Earthenware, wiped decoration through white slip, brownish glaze; marks: 'WP' in monogram, impressed; h.20.4cm, d.18.2cm
Circ.419-1950. Source: the pottery, £1.1s.

337 Bowl, *c.* 1950
Earthenware, trailed white slip, mottled greenish glaze; marks: 'WP' in monogram, impressed; h.7.4cm, d.12.6cm
Circ.420-1950. Source: *see* **336**, 15s.

338 Bowl, 1950
Earthenware, combed decoration through dark over light slip; marks: 'WP' in monogram, impressed; h.8cm, d.12.7cm
Circ.421-1950. Source: *see* **336**, 15s.

339 Baking dish, 1950
Earthenware, trailed white slip, amber glaze; marks: 'WP' in monogram, impressed; h.3.5cm, d.19cm
Circ.422-1950. Source: *see* **336**, 7s.6d.

340 Teapot, 1982 (pl.78)
Stoneware, incised decoration, tenmoku glaze; h.17.7cm, d.20.6cm
C.71&A-1984. Source: given by the Friends of the V&A (purchased at the Craftsmen Potters Association exhibition, *Studio Ceramics Today*, V&A, 1983, no.60, £41.40)

341 Lidded soup pot, 1988
Stoneware, ash flashings; marks: 'WP' in monogram, impressed; h.11.6cm, d.15cm
C.18&A-1989. Source: David Mellor shop, London, £5.27
Items **341** and **342** represent Winchcombe Pottery's standard range of domestic stoneware.

342 Casserole, 1988
Stoneware, ash flashings; marks: 'WP' in monogram, impressed; h.9.8cm, d.20.9cm
C.21&A-1989. Source: *see* **341**, £8.66

Finnemore, Sybil (later **Parsons**) 1906–1977

1906	born Croydon, Surrey
1923–28	studies pottery at Central School of Arts and Crafts, London, under Dora Billington (qv); there meets future husband, Tom Raymond Parsons
1927–28	Parsons appointed teacher at Bembridge School, Isle of Wight; gains permission to build his own workshop, Yellowsands Pottery, on school grounds
1929	Finnemore and Parsons marry, setting up home nearby and jointly running pottery
1931	pottery destroyed by fire
1932–39	workshop rebuilt adjacent to their home in Bembridge; production continues until wartime
c. 1949–65	pottery reopens; renamed Bembridge Pottery *c.* 1954

Sybil Finnemore gained recognition for her work while still a student at the Central School of Arts and Crafts. Her pottery was sold through Elspeth Little's pioneering shop Modern Textiles, and acquired for the permanent collection of the British Institute of Industrial Art (now at the V&A). While at the Central she met her future husband, T.R. Parsons, with whom she ran the Yellowsands Pottery at Bembridge on the Isle of Wight. Until 1931 both stoneware and painted tin-glazed earthenware were made, but subsequently earthenware only. Finnemore also modelled some animal figures.

'The L.C.C. Central School Exhibition', *The Studio*, 92 (1926), pp.88–91
British Institute of Industrial Art (1927), (1929)
Arts and Crafts Exhibition Society (1928), (1931), (1938)
Decorative Art (1928), (1930), (1932)
'Miss Sybil Finnemore's Pottery', *The Studio*, 95 (1928), pp.32–3
Brygos Gallery (1936)
Vincentelli and Hale (1986)
Lisa and Andrew Dowden, *A Century of Ceramics: A Selection of 20th Century Potters and Potteries in the Isle of Wight* (Sandown, 2005), pp.57–68

343 Pot, 1928
Stoneware, incised design through black slip, greyish-white glaze; marks: 'S. FINNEMORE / 1928', incised; h.21.8cm, d.16.2cm
C.416-1934. Source: British Institute of Industrial Art (purchased through the Spielmann Memorial Fund)

343

Fisher, Daniel 1973–

1973 born Norwich, Norfolk
1994–97 studies ceramics at Camberwell College of Arts
1997–99 studies ceramics at Royal College of Art, London
2000– establishes studio in Stroud, Gloucestershire
2001 solo exhibition, Galerie Besson, London
2010s discontinues making for several years

Daniel Fisher is known for his thrown and manipulated porcelain and stoneware vessels, which intensely explore the qualities of his materials in the pursuit of works of elemental beauty. The fragile, translucent walls of his 'flame bowls' are achieved by squeezing and pulling the sides of a thrown porcelain cylinder while suspending it upside down.

Daniel Fisher, 'Opening Doors', *CR*, 183 (2000)
Alison Britton, exh. review, *CR*, 189 (2001)
Galerie Besson, *Daniel Fisher*, exh. pamphlet, text by David Whiting (London, 2001)
David Whiting, 'White Fire', *Crafts*, 179 (2002)
Whiting (2009), pp.91–5
Game (2016), pp.106–7, 204–5

344 *Flame Bowl*, 2004
Porcelain, thrown, hung and pinched; h.37.5cm, d.38.5cm
C.3-2005. Source: gift of Nicholas and Judith Goodison through Art Fund
Shown by Joanna Bird at Collect 2005, V&A.

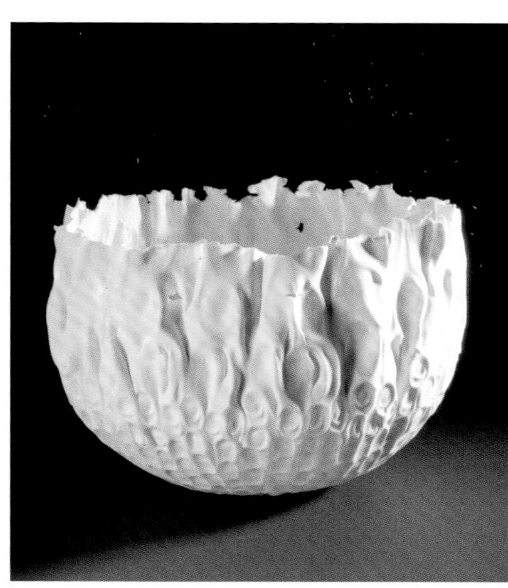

344

Flanagan, Barry 1941–2009

1941 born Prestatyn, North Wales
1964–66 studies sculpture at St Martin's School of Art, London
1974 visits Ann Stokes (qv) in Hampstead, London, to learn pottery techniques, and with her makes some coiled pots
1975 moves to Aston-le-Walls, Northamptonshire, living there for 18 months; builds wood-fired kiln with Peter Briggs; solo exhibition, *Coil, Pinch and Squeeze Pots*, Art & Project, Amsterdam
1992 visits Llorens Artigas Foundation, Gallifa, Spain, makes ceramics

Best known for his later large-scale bronze hares, Barry Flanagan was a significant figure in the development of British sculpture from the 1960s onwards. His exploratory and influential earlier work experimented with unorthodox sculptural materials, including fabric, sand and rope, used simply to emphasize their inherent properties. Flanagan made ceramics in the mid-1970s, coiling and pinching pots, and firing them in a wood-fired kiln. His handling of clay reflects his earlier exploration of soft materials, while also reflecting an interest in the spiral as a geometrical figure. Flanagan returned briefly to ceramics in 1992, working with similar forms but adding glazes.

Barry Flanagan, 'Sculptors in Limbo?', *Crafts*, 33 (1978)
'Barry Flanagan', *Art & Project Bulletin*, 93 (1975)
British Council, *Barry Flanagan: Sculpture*, exh. cat. (London, 1982), pp.26, 70–1, 84–5
Waddington Galleries, *Barry Flanagan*, exh. cat. (London, 1994)
Enrique Juncosa (ed.), *Barry Flanagan: Sculpture 1965–2005* (Dublin: Irish Museum of Modern Art, 2006), pp.44–8
Clarrie Wallis and Andrew Wilson (eds), *Barry Flanagan: Early Works 1965–1982* (London: Tate Publishing, 2011), pp.102–3, 144–5

345 *Coil pot*, 1975–76
Earthenware, coil-built, unglazed; h.19.3cm, d.13cm
C.171&A-1984. Source: Anthony Stokes, London, £1437

345

Flynn, Michael 1947–

1947 born Germany, of Irish parents
1963–65 studies painting at Birmingham College of Art
1975–78 studies ceramics at Cardiff College of Art
1985–86 studies fine art at Cardiff College of Art
1991–94 teaches at Koninklijke Academie voor Kunst en Vormgeving, 's-Hertogenbosch, Netherlands
1994–2002 teaches at Institut für Künstlerische Keramik, Höhr-Grenzhausen, Germany

Michael Flynn is known for his freely modelled, spirited, figurative sculpture, which he develops around themes associated with folklore, mythology and belief systems. He has divided his time between studios in Cardiff and Germany, also travelling widely, teaching and making work on residencies.

Michael Flynn, 'The Domestic Icon', *CR*, 118 (1989)
— 'Bewegung und Freiheit', *Neue Keramik*, 12 (1995)
— *Ceramic Figures: A Directory of Artists* (London, 2003)
Oriel 31, *Michael Flynn: Running the Dog*, exh. cat. (Welshpool, 1989)
Peter Dormer, 'Myth and Mischief', *Crafts*, 109 (1991)
Paul Greenhalgh, *Michael Flynn*, Aberystwyth Arts Centre: Ceramic Series 52 (1992)
Alison Smith, 'Michael Flynn', *CR*, 140 (1993)
Angelika Gause, 'Death of the Dancer', *Ceramics: Art and Perception*, 26 (1996)
Paul Greenhalgh, 'Still Life With Attitude', *Crafts*, 149 (1997)
Alison Smith, 'Restless Spirit', *CR*, 172 (1998)
— 'Michael Flynn's Backward Glance', *Ceramics: Art and Perception*, 50 (2002)
Ruthin Craft Centre (2006), pp.36–9, 76

346

347 / 348

349

Whiting (2009), pp.110–15
BWA Wrocław, *Michael Flynn: Bez Powrotu/No Return*, exh. cat., texts by Michael Flynn, Agnieszka Kurgan and Paul Greenhalgh (Wrocław, 2010)
Paul Greenhalgh, 'Michael Flynn', *Ceramics: Art and Perception*, 95 (2014)
Monika Patuszyńska, 'Tracing Michael Flynn', *Ceramics Ireland*, 33 (2014)
Michael Robinson, 'Michael Flynn', *Perspective: Journal of Royal Society of Ulster Architects*, 24:4 (2015)
Frank Nievergelt, *Passionnément Céramique: Collection Frank Nievergelt*, exh. cat., Musée Ariana, Geneva (Milan, 2016)
Galerie de l'Ancienne Poste, *Michael Flynn: Le Spectacle de la Vie*, exh. cat., texts by Isabelle Naef Galuba and Guillaume Morel (Toucy, 2017)
Mels Boom, 'Dansend door het leven', *De Kleine K*, 57 (2019)
Messums Wiltshire, *Michael Flynn*, exh. cat. (Tisbury, 2020)
Greenhalgh (2021), pp.470–1

Exhibition reviews: Angus Suttie, 'Fire and Smoke', *Crafts*, 65 (1983); Louisa Buck, *Crafts*, 101 (1989); Emmanuel Cooper, *Crafts*, 117 (1992); Frank Nievergelt, *Keramos*, 178 (2002); Jo Dahn, *Crafts*, 204 (2007)

346 *Angel / Flight*, 1988
Terracotta and sculpting marl (angel) and porcelain (running figure), modelled and raku-fired, with white crackle glaze and lustre, assembled on concrete base; h.75cm, d.78cm
C.40A, B-1990. Source: The Black Bull Gallery, London (group exhibition: *Casting, Carving and Modelling*, 1990), £1850

347 Figure of a pig, 1991
Sculpting marl, modelled, painted with copper oxide and salt solution onto wet clay and immediately raku-fired; made at Koninklijke Academie voor Kunst en Vormgeving, 's-Hertogenbosch, Netherlands; h.20cm, d.37.9cm
C.183-1991. Source: the artist, £235
Made as a demonstration to students that a simple kiln can be constructed and work fired immediately, even while the clay remains wet.

348 Figure of a pig, 1991
Sculpting marl, modelled, biscuit-fired, painted with copper oxide and salt solution, raku-fired, further painting with cobalt oxide and salt solution, refired in electric kiln; made at Koninklijke Academie voor Kunst en Vormgeving, 's-Hertogenbosch, Netherlands; h.16.2cm, d.32.2cm
C.184-1991. Source: the artist, £235

349 *Heroic Deeds*, 2001
Porcelain, modelled, painted in blue, yellow and red; h.29.8cm, d.35.6cm
C.23:1,2-2005. Source: given by the artist

Flynn, Sara 1971–

1971	born Cork, Ireland
1989–92| 97–98	studies ceramics at Crawford College of Art and Design, Cork
2000–	establishes studio in Kinsale, County Cork
2005–	moves studio to Leap, County Cork
2012–	regular solo exhibitions at Erskine, Hall & Coe, London
2015–	moves to Belfast, sets up studio
2017	Loewe Foundation Craft Prize finalist
2017	three-person exhibition, *Chance Encounters III*, Loewe Miami Design District store, Florida, USA
2019	solo exhibition, Sokyo Gallery, Kyoto, Japan

Sara Flynn makes sculptural porcelain vessels with a keen sense of line and volume. Thrown and altered, their rippling and sharp-edged forms are enhanced by a rich spectrum of complex, yet muted glazes. Flynn also makes small-scale abstract sculpture in bronze.

Sarah Foster, 'Sara Flynn's Porcelain Vessels', *Ceramics: Art and Perception*, 77 (2009)
Erskine, Hall & Coe, *Sara Flynn*, exh. cat., text by Sebastian Blackie (London, 2012) – see also catalogues from 2014, 2016, 2018 and 2020
Frances McDonald, 'Turning Points', *Irish Arts Review*, 29:4 (2012)
Angus Stewart, 'Irish Charm', *CR*, 259 (2013)
Andy Christian, exh. review, *CR*, 272 (2015)
Morris (2018), pp.122–5
Galerie de l'Ancienne Poste, *Sara Flynn*, exh. cat., text by Guillaume Morel (Toucy, 2021)

350 / 351

350 *Flection Vessel*, 2018
Porcelain, thrown and altered, metallic brown glaze; marks: 'F' with three dots, impressed; h.31.3cm, d.13.5cm
C.345-2018. Source: Erskine, Hall & Coe, London (solo exhibition, 2018), £8500; purchase funded by Christopher M. Gorman-Evans

351 *Flection Vessel*, 2018
Porcelain, thrown and altered, cream glaze exterior, metallic brown interior; marks: 'F' with three dots, impressed; h.27.3cm, d.17.4cm
C.346-2018. Source: *see* 350, £8500

Ford, Laura 1961–

1961	born Cardiff
1978–82	studies at Bath Academy of Art, with period at Cooper Union School of Art, New York
1982–83	studies sculpture at Chelsea School of Art
c. 1998–	teaches, and begins making ceramics, at Middlesex University
c. 1999–	installs kiln in studio at Kentish Town, London
2003	solo exhibition, *Headthinkers*, Houldsworth, London
2005	represents Wales at Venice Biennale
2017–	moves kiln to studio in West Sussex

Laura Ford is a sculptor known for her poignant, enigmatic figures, which often take the form of human-animal hybrids. Her work conveys a strong sense of narrative, and typically has an unsettling, dream-like quality. Ford develops work in a range of media, often mixed, and frequently incorporating fabric. She works sporadically in ceramics, usually making small-scale sculptures, though notably also the donkey heads of her *Headthinkers* series.

Camden Arts Centre, *A Stranger Here Myself: Laura Ford and Jacqueline Poncelet*, exh. cat., texts by Jenni Lomax and Penelope Curtis (London, 1998)
Hayward Gallery, *The British Art Show 5*, exh. cat. (London, 2000)
Aldrich Contemporary Art Museum, *Into My World: Recent British Sculpture*, exh. cat., texts by Jessica Hough and Stephen Hepworth (Ridgefield, 2004)
Arts Council of Wales, *Somewhere Else: Artists from Wales at the Venice Biennale*, exh. cat. (Cardiff, 2005)
Museum Sinclair-Haus, *Laura Ford*, exh. cat., text by Mark Gisbourne (Bad Homburg, 2009)
Schaezlerpalais Augsburg, *Laura Ford*, exh. cat., text by Christof Trepesch (Augsburg, 2013)
Sculpture by Laura Ford, published to accompany an exhibition at Strawberry Hill House, Twickenham, London, texts by Stephen Feeke and Judith Collins (Salisbury: New Art Centre, 2015)
Kunstverein Schwetzingen, *Laura Ford: A Foot in Each World*, exh. cat., text by Dietmar Schuth (Schwetzingen, 2017)
Interview, in Racz (2020), pp.245–55

Exhibition reviews: Will Bennett, 'Object of the Week', *Daily Telegraph* (10 March 2003); Rachel Withers, 'Critic's Picks', *Artforum International*, ejournal (8 April 2003); Ian Wilson, *Crafts*, 180 (2003); David Whiting, 'Breakers', *Crafts*, 202 (2006)

Laura Ford was the subject of a short film in the BBC series *Contemporary Visions*, 2004.

352 *Headthinker III*, 2003 (pl.116)
Stoneware, handbuilt, glaze, steel, plaster, clothing, plinth; h.91cm, d.128cm
C.22:1 to 3-2008. Source: Houldsworth, London, £8000; acquired through the generosity of Gerard and Sarah Griffin
Shown in solo exhibition, *Headthinkers*, Houldsworth, London, 2003.

Fournier, Sheila (née Cook, previously Lord) 1930–2000

1930	born Filey, Yorkshire
1949–50	teacher training at Goldsmiths' College, London; meets Robert Fournier, who has recently established a pottery department at Goldsmiths'
1961	marries Robert Fournier
1962–65	workshop in Greenwich, London, renting space from Alan Wallwork (qv)
1965–71	Sheila and Robert move workshop to Brenchley, Kent
1971–87	establish pottery at The Tanyard, a former workhouse in Lacock, Wiltshire
1987	Sheila and Robert retire from potting

353

Sheila Fournier (previously Lord) learned pottery from Robert Fournier (1915–2008), who she met at Goldsmiths' College and later married. Together they formed a potting team, making oxidized domestic stoneware and their own individual pieces, fired in electric kilns. Sheila Fournier is particularly known for her press-moulded stoneware bowls of swelling form with cracked, multi-layered rims, and later, delicate work in inlaid porcelain.

Sheila Fournier, 'Built-in Decoration', *CR*, 6 (1970)
Sheila Lord and Robert Fournier, 'Rolled Inlay', *Pottery Quarterly*, 3:10 (1956)
Casson (1967), p.6
Fiona Bird, 'Potting it Together', *The Times* (21 August 1969)
Potters (1972) to (1986)
V&A (1972), p.109
Barbara Harding, 'CPA Potters Camp', *CR*, 23 (1973) – describes and illustrates a demonstration by Sheila Fournier
Edelman (1976), Parts II and III
Emmanuel Cooper, 'Robert Fournier', obituary, *The Independent* (12 March 2008)

Exhibition reviews: Murray Fieldhouse, *CR*, 9 (1971); Richard Dunning, *CR*, 13 (1972); Peter Thompson, *Crafts*, 21 (1976)

An interview with Robert Fournier is in the Crafts Lives sound archive at the British Library, London (C960/62).

353 Bowl, 1969
Stoneware, press-moulded and handbuilt in red and buff clays, blue copper glaze; marks: 'SF' in a circle, impressed; h.16cm, d.35.5cm
Circ.661-1969. Source: Primavera, London, £16

Fox-Strangways, Sylvia ('Jane') 1890–1975

1890	born Jubbulpore (now Jabalpur), India
c. 1920–22	attends classes at Central School of Arts and Crafts, London
1923–24	studies at Royal College of Art, London
c. 1926–27	works at Leach Pottery, St Ives

1927–29 arrives at Dartington Hall, Devon; sets up pottery workshop and kiln; teaches pottery, painting and drawing
1929– retires from pottery and active work at Dartington through ill health; remains a close friend of Dorothy Elmhirst

Sylvia Fox-Strangways exhibited 'hand-made pottery including stoneware, majolica, slipware, coloured glazes and underglaze painting' at Shoolbred's department store, London, in 1924, having learned pottery at art-school classes. She subsequently joined Bernard Leach (qv) at St Ives, and showed earthenware, stoneware and raku made there at the Guild of Potters' exhibition in 1926. On Leach's recommendation she was invited by Leonard and Dorothy Elmhirst to establish a pottery at Dartington Hall, Devon, and there committed herself to introducing art into the life of the estate community, teaching and organizing exhibitions. She made pottery and tiles, some of which were installed in fireplaces at Dartington Hall. After leaving Dartington, she maintained close connections with the estate, also writing poetry and painting watercolours.

British Institute of Industrial Art (1923), (1927), (1929)
Guild of Potters (1925), (1926)
Arts and Crafts Exhibition Society (1926)
Colnaghi (1927), (1928)
Whiting (1993), p.59
Jeremiah (1997)
— (1998)
Cooper (2003), p.161
Whybrow (2006), pp.34, 230

Exhibition reviews (and notices): 'The Arts and Crafts Student', *The Studio*, 84:354 (1922), p.138; 'Court and Society', *Daily Mail* (1 November 1924), p.8; S.B.W., 'The Guild of Potters', *The Studio*, 91 (1926), pp.34–5; illustration, *The Studio*, 95 (1928), p.44; 'English Pottery', *The Times* (30 November 1928)

Papers of Jane Fox-Strangways, including correspondence with Leonard and Dorothy Elmhirst, are in the Dartington Hall Trust archive at the Devon Heritage Centre, Exeter. See also 'The Arts' in Victor Bonham-Carter, *Dartington Hall, 1925–56: A Report*, held with the archive.

354 Tile, 1926
Stoneware, cream glaze, painted in red, yellow and black; made at Leach Pottery, St Ives; h.10.5cm, w.10.3cm
C.418-1934. Source: British Institute of Industrial Art (given by Bernard Leach, 1926)

355 / 354

355 Tile, 1926
Stoneware, buff glaze, painted in red, green and black; marks: 'S.F.S.' in monogram, and '1926', painted; made at Leach Pottery, St Ives; h.10.5cm, w.10.2cm
C.419-1934. Source: *see* 354

Franklin, Ruth 1948–

1948 born London
1972–73 studies ceramics at Croydon School of Art
1973–75 studies ceramics at Harrow School of Art
1975–84 studio with Barbican Arts Group, London
1984–2002 teaches at Camberwell College of Arts
1996–98 studies printmaking at Camberwell College of Arts
2002– teaches at City Lit, London

Ruth Franklin produced porcelain and earthenware pots with rims cut in relation to their figurative surface decoration, and later slab-built figurative forms, exploring themes of London life. During the 1980s she began making sculpture in other materials and discontinued ceramics, returning on occasion in the 2000s after a period of printmaking.

'CPA New Members', *CR*, 60 (1979)
Crafts Council (1980), p.57
Potters (1980), (1983)
Paisley Museum and Art Galleries (1984), p.36
Crafts Council (1985), p.45
Sunderland Arts Centre, *Ruth Franklin: Ladies and Chairs*, exh. pamphlet (1985)

356

Exhibition reviews: Peter Dormer, *Crafts*, 54 (1982), and correction, 55 (1982), p.11; 'Katharine House Gallery', *Arts Review* (30 September 1983)

356 Cup: *Arsenal*, 1980
Porcelain, painted in underglaze colours; marks: 'R. Franklin', painted; h.14.3cm, d.12.5cm
C.69-1980. Source: Craft Shop, V&A, £31

Frith, David 1943–

1943 born Ashton-under-Lyne, Lancashire
1947– family moves to North Wales
1961–62 studies industrial ceramics at Wimbledon School of Art
1962–63 studies pottery, under Derek Emms, and weaving at Stoke-on-Trent College of Art
1963 sets up workshop in Denbigh, Wales, making slip-decorated earthenware
1966– Margaret Seddon, his future wife, joins the pottery full-time; develops range of oxidized stoneware
c. 1969–75 workshop expands, employing a number of assistants
1971– solo exhibition at Bluecoat Display Centre, Liverpool; regular solo and joint exhibitions in UK and overseas thereafter
1974 installs gas-fired kiln, switching to production of reduction-fired stoneware
1975 begins conversion of nearby semi-derelict mill to new home and workshop, naming it Brookhouse Pottery
1980– regular summer schools at the pottery

1997	retrospective exhibition, Rufford Craft Centre, Nottinghamshire
1999	builds large wood-fired kiln
2000	spends month working in Mashiko, Japan; exhibitions in Mashiko and Tokyo
2013	50-year celebratory exhibition, Ruthin Craft Centre, Denbighshire

David Frith, who works alongside his wife, Margaret Frith (1943–), is a technically accomplished potter of the Anglo-Asian Leach school, working in reduction-fired stoneware. Very much a workshop potter, he has earned his living primarily through sales of his pots. Increasingly he has made individual pieces, often of substantial size, though these remain informed by his experience of repetition potting. Strong decorative motifs in wax-resist or trailed pigment are characteristic.

Crafts Advisory Committee (1977), p.13
Potters/The Ceramics Book (1980) to (2012)
Emmanuel Cooper, *David Frith*, Aberystwyth Arts Centre: Ceramic Series 3 (1984)
— 'David Frith – Potter', with section on workshop practice by David Frith, *CR*, 97 (1986)
Philip Hughes, 'The Definite Article', *CR*, 164 (1997)
Ruthin Craft Centre, *David and Margaret Frith* (Ruthin, 2003)
— *David Frith. Margaret Frith* (Ruthin, 2013)
Sue Herdman, 'Of Pots and Partnership', *CR*, 289 (2018)

Exhibition reviews: Brian Starkey, *Crafts*, 53 (1981); Judy Adams, *CR*, 166 (1997); Norman Makinson, *CR*, 206 (2004); Alex McErlain, *CR*, 265 (2014)

357 Lidded jar, 1982
Stoneware, cut sides, tenmoku glaze, green glazed interior; marks: 'df' in monogram and a device, impressed; h.19cm, d.15.8cm
C.14&A-1982. Source: Craftsmen Potters Association, London (solo exhibition, 1982, no.154), £27

358 Square dish on four feet, 1982
Stoneware, celadon glaze, wax-resist decoration through blue wash, trailing in iron; marks: 'df' in monogram and a device, impressed; h.8.6cm, d.38.8cm
C.72-1984. Source: given by the Friends of the V&A (purchased at the Craftsmen Potters Association exhibition, *Studio Ceramics Today*, V&A, 1983, no.66, £96.75)

357

358

Fritsch, Elizabeth (née Hughes) 1940–

1940	born Oswestry, Shropshire
1958–64	studies at Birmingham School of Music and Royal Academy of Music, London
1968–71	studies ceramics at Royal College of Art, London; awarded Silver Medal and Herbert Read Memorial Prize
1972–73	works at Bing & Grøndahl factory, Copenhagen; prize-winner in Royal Copenhagen Porcelain Jubilee Competition
1973–76	studio at Gestingthorpe, Suffolk
1974	solo exhibition, Waterloo Place Gallery (Crafts Advisory Committee), London
1976–85	studio at Digswell House, Hertfordshire
1978–79	touring solo exhibition, *Pots About Music*, Leeds Art Galleries
1980	receives Crafts Council/Guild of St George John Ruskin Craft Award, to develop 'Fictional Archaeology' project
1985–	studio in east London
1987	selected for Post Office commemorative stamp issue marking Bernard Leach centenary
1993–95	touring solo exhibition, *Vessels from Another World*, Northern Centre for Contemporary Art, Sunderland
1995	awarded CBE; made Senior Fellow of Royal College of Art
1996|2001	shortlisted for Jerwood Applied Arts Prize
2008	solo exhibition, Fine Art Society, London
2010	retrospective exhibition, National Museum Cardiff

Perhaps the most influential potter of the late 20th century, Elizabeth Fritsch was the first of the progressive 'New Ceramics' group to emerge from the Royal College of Art in the 1970s. Her work anticipated many of the approaches that would be widely taken up in the 1970s and 1980s: handbuilding; focus on the 'vessel'; spatial games with perspective; attention to painted surface and colour. Her placing of forms in assemblages also foreshadowed later trends. Fritsch works between two and three dimensions. Her pots occupy the space between illusion and reality, their flattened forms appearing as fully rounded vessels when seen from a particular viewpoint. The surreal and insubstantial character of her pots is furthered by their rhythmic and geometric painted surfaces of fresco-like colour, which have a correspondence with music – a major theme for Fritsch. Seascapes and architectural structures meanwhile provide inspiration for distinct series from 1998 to 2000. Throughout, her work is underpinned by formidable technical proficiency, which facilitates the improvisation inherent in the forming and painting of her pots.

Elizabeth Fritsch, interview, in Cameron and Lewis (1976), pp.62–9, 166
— 'Pots from Nowhere', *Crafts*, 71 (1984)
— 'Notes on Time in Relation to the Making and Painting of Pots', *Crafts*, 97 (1989)
— **and Jane Hamlyn**, 'Metaphysical Vessels', *CR*, 148 (1994)
Crafts Advisory Committee (1974), pp.17–20
John Houston, 'Traps to Fill Emptiness', *Crafts*, 10 (1974)
Oxford Gallery (1974)
Decorative Art (1975/76), (1977)
Lucie-Smith (1975), pp.71–8
Crafts Advisory Committee (1976), p.93
Leeds Art Galleries, *Elizabeth Fritsch: Pots About Music*, exh. cat. (1978)
John Russell Taylor, 'Pots about Music', *CR*, 58 (1979)
Crafts Council (1980), p.58
'News: Bursary Boom', *Crafts*, 45 (1980)

Paisley Museum and Art Galleries (1984), pp.37–8
Royal College of Art, *Pots from Nowhere*, exh. leaflet (London, 1984)
Crafts Council (1985), pp.46–9
Peter Dormer, *Elizabeth Fritsch in Studio* (London, 1985)
ICA (1985), p.43
Houston (1991)
Edward Lucie-Smith, *Elizabeth Fritsch: Vessels from Another World: Metaphysical Pots in Painted Stoneware*, exh. cat. (London, 1993)
Museum of Modern Art, Oxford (1993), pp.36–7, 84, 94
Crafts Council (1996b), pp.22–3
Gaze (1997)
Crafts Council (2001), pp.18–19, 31
Ruthin Craft Centre (2002), pp.30–5, 77
Perryman (2004), pp.16–21
Joanna Bird, 'Colour, Form and Rhythm', *Ceramics: Art and Perception*, 74 (2008)
Fine Art Society, *Elizabeth Fritsch*, exh. cat., text by Andrew Lambirth (London, 2008)
National Museum Wales, *Dynamic Structures: Painted Vessels by Elizabeth Fritsch*, exh. cat., text by Andrew Renton (Cardiff, 2010)
Clark, Strauss and others (2012), pp.176–7, 375, 435
Nottingham City Museums and Galleries (2017), p.43
Who's Who 2020 (2019)

Exhibition reviews: Eileen Lewenstein, 'Diploma Students', *CR*, 4 (1970); J.D.H. Catleugh, *CR*, 30 (1974), and 44 (1977); Ian Bennett, *Crafts*, 25 (1977); Peter Inch, *Crafts*, 35 (1978); Emmanuel Cooper, *Art & Artists*, 14:3 (1979), *Crafts*, 156 (1999), and *CR*, 247 (2011); Philip Rawson, *Crafts*, 73 (1985); Shane Enright, *Studio Pottery*, 6 (1993); Marina Vaizey, *Crafts*, 129 (1994); Amanda Fielding, *CR*, 175 (1999), and 236 (2009); Emma Crichton-Miller, *Crafts*, 216 (2009); Laura Gascoigne, *The Spectator* (30 October 2010)

An interview with Elizabeth Fritsch is in the Crafts Lives sound archive at the British Library, London (C960/25).

359 Pot, 1971
Stoneware, handbuilt, painted coloured slips; made at Royal College of Art, London; h.9cm, d.6.7cm
C.427-2017. Source: given by David Queensberry

360 Pot, 1975 (fig.13)
Stoneware, handbuilt, painted slips and oxides; h.22.8cm, d.11.6cm
Circ.408-1975. Source: Primavera, Cambridge (exhibition: *Ceramic Form*, Kettle's Yard, Cambridge, 1975, no.113), £72

359

361

361 *Saxophone and Piano Duo*, 1978
Stoneware, handbuilt, painted slips and oxides; h.26cm, d.10.3cm
C.160&A-1979. Source: Leeds City Art Galleries (solo exhibition: *Pots About Music*, 1978), £420

362 *Optical pot*, 1980 (pl.73)
Stoneware, handbuilt, painted slips and oxides; h.31.1cm, d.23.2cm
C.13-1981. Source: given in memory of Robert Kennedy, Assistant Keeper of the National Art Library, by a group of colleagues and friends

363 *Funeral Urn: Windblown*, 1984
Stoneware, handbuilt, painted slips and oxides; h.31.3cm, d.22.1cm
C.51-1985. Source: Queensberry Hunt, London (solo exhibition: *Pots from Nowhere*, Royal College of Art, London, 1984), £1800

363

Fry, Roger *see* Omega Workshops

Fuller, Geoffrey 1936–2022

1936	born Chesterfield, Derbyshire
1953–65	librarian in Sheffield
1965–66	foundation course at Chesterfield College of Art and Design
1966–70	studies ceramics at West Surrey College of Art and Design, Farnham, continuing as technical assistant for 18 months
1972–88	workshop in Chesterfield
1975–87	teaches ceramics part-time and later full-time at Chesterfield College of Art and Design
1988–	purchases and runs 17th-century inn, Three Stags' Heads, Wardlow Mires, Derbyshire, with his wife, Patricia, also a potter; establishes workshop
2012–	stages annual Wardlow Mires Pottery and Food Festival

Geoffrey Fuller was a highly individual potter who brought an original vision to traditional forms, responding in particular to English country pottery of the 17th and 18th centuries and popular Staffordshire figures. After initially working in salt-glazed stoneware, he concentrated on earthenware, making vessels and figures intended for domestic life. His work is notable for his fluid handling of clay, capturing a sense of movement and spontaneity, and his use of soft, translucent colours that reflect the landscape.

364

365

366

'Potters', *CR*, 10 (1971)
Potters (1972) to (1977), (1989)
Peter Lane, 'A British Potters' Festival', *Ceramics Monthly*, 33:8 (1985)
Gabrielle Pertt, 'Geoffrey Fuller – Folk Potter', *CR*, 110 (1988)
Josie Walter, *Geoffrey Fuller*, Aberystwyth Arts Centre: Ceramic Series 45 (1991)
Paul Vincent, 'Geoffrey Fuller', *Studio Pottery*, 4 (1993)
Eden and Eden (1999), pp.38–41
Victoria Eden, 'A World Apart', *CR*, 196 (2002)
Hannah Wingrave, 'Innocent Eye', *Studio Pottery*, 48 (2002)
Whiting (2009), pp.152–7
David Whiting, obituary, *The Guardian* (19 May 2022)

Exhibition reviews: Mike Dodd, *Crafts*, 82 (1986); Mary Sara, *Studio Pottery*, 16 (1995); Julian Stair, *Studio Pottery*, 18 (1995); Emmanuel Cooper, 'Soft Clay', *Crafts*, 143 (1996)

364 Lidded jar, 1988
Earthenware, white slip, greenish glaze; h.15.1cm, d.14.3cm
C.8&A-1989. Source: Contemporary Applied Arts, London, £77.40

Garbett, David 1928–2014

1928	born Epsom, Surrey
1940s	takes classes in pottery at Kingston School of Art, Surrey, under Dora Billington (qv)
1949–51	studies painting and sculpture at Camberwell School of Arts and Crafts
1952–53	one-year non-diploma course in painting at Slade School of Fine Art, London
1953–84	teaches ceramics at Goldsmiths' College, London, working initially as a technician; later becomes Head of Ceramics (succeeded by Ken Bright in 1977)
1961	exhibits in *Handbuilt Pottery from Goldsmiths' College*, Primavera, London

David Garbett taught ceramics at Goldsmiths' College for 30 years, working for a time alongside Gordon Baldwin (qv), with whom he advocated new approaches, including handbuilding and sculptural form.

Arts and Crafts Exhibition Society (1957)
Paisley Museum and Art Galleries (1984), p.38
Cowley (1993)

365 Form, 1960
Earthenware, handbuilt, incised, dark brown glaze; made at Goldsmiths' College, London; h.42.6cm, d.53cm
C.101-1994. Source: given by Doug Jones

Garland, David 1941–

1941	born Kettering, Northamptonshire
1946–61	grows up in New Zealand
1961–64	trains at London College of Printing
1972–	establishes small pottery workshop in Oxford; largely self-taught as a potter
1975–	moves to Chedworth, Gloucestershire, sets up pottery and painting studios, builds wood-fired kiln
1987	Crafts Council touring exhibition, *David Garland: Ceramics*
2000	solo exhibition, Kate Ganz USA, New York
2006	solo exhibition, Galerie Besson, London

David Garland, a painter and graphic artist, turned to pottery while working as a designer for the Oxford University Press. Much acclaimed for his brushwork, he makes a variety of domestic pottery forms and individual pieces of generous size, decorated boldly in slips and oxides. He has gradually turned from wood-firing to the use of an electric kiln.

Pamela Johnson, 'Singing the Blues', *Crafts*, 70 (1984)
Crafts Council (1985), p.49
Henry Pim, 'Finding a Voice', *CR*, 105 (1987)
'Pot and Potter', editorial, *CR*, 106 (1987)
Pamela Johnson, 'David Garland', *Ceramics Monthly*, 36:6 (1988)
Galerie Besson, *David Garland*, exh. leaflet, text by Gillian Darley (London, 2006)
Timothy Wilcox, 'Homage to Mankind', *CR*, 219 (2006)

Exhibition reviews: Tanya Harrod, *Crafts*, 88 (1987); Emmanuel Cooper, *Crafts*, 106 (1990); Timothy Wilcox, *Crafts*, 118 (1992)

366 Bowl, 1984
Earthenware, painted in blue on a white slip; marks: 'Garland', incised, and 'Garland 84', painted; h.11.3cm, d.36cm
C.187-1984. Source: Amalgam, London, £128

Gaunce, Marian 1945–2019

1945	born Stratton, Cornwall
1969–70	foundation course at Worthing School of Art
1970–71	studies ceramics at West Surrey College of Art and Design, Farnham
1978–81	studies ceramics at Croydon College of Art, winning Marlow Award in final year
1980–	sets up studio at home in South Croydon, London
1981–88	group exhibitions at Queensberry Hunt, London, and elsewhere
1989–95	discontinues potting
1991–	moves to West Bagborough, Somerset
1996–	establishes studio at West Bagborough
c. 2000–	ceases potting

367 / 368

Marian Gaunce made geometrically patterned, press-moulded porcelain vessels using a painstaking process of laminating together strips of clay stained with different colours. Her output was necessarily small, as the work was slow to make and difficult to fire.

Kenneth Clark, 'Marian Gaunce – Colour in Clay', *CR*, 91 (1985)
Peter Lane, *Ceramic Form* (London, 1988), pp.151, 157 (illustrations)

367 Pot, 1982
Porcelain, press-moulded, laminated pink, grey, black and white clays, unglazed; h.18.6cm, d.18.6cm
C.148-1982. Source: Christopher Wood Gallery, London, £500

368 Dish, 1984
Porcelain, press-moulded, laminated white and blue-grey clays, unglazed; marks: 'MG', impressed; h.5.9cm, d.27.9cm
C.186-1984. Source: Queensberry Hunt, London, £250

Glebe Pottery *see* Madeline Raper

Glover, Lois Mary (née Moore) 1886–1963

c. 1915–	attends pottery classes at Camberwell School of Arts and Crafts, under Alfred Hopkins (qv); studio in Chelsea, London
1917	marries Richard Sydney Glover, later editor of *Apollo* magazine (1925–29)
c. 1918–26	moves to Blyth House, Southwold, Suffolk, the house of Ann Darwin 'Nancy' Fox; kiln in basement
1927–32	moves to Watford, Hertfordshire; becomes sole breadwinner after husband loses job
1932–35	lives in Essex; no workshop, not making
1935–	moves to Glastonbury, Somerset, to establish pottery after responding to an advert for a potter
c. 1937–38	ceases potting

369 / 370

An elusive figure, Lois Glover must number among the earliest studio potters. She is said to have worked in Chelsea in the 1910s, and to have exhibited at the British Industries Fair (held annually in London from 1915). A report in *The Bazaar, Exchange and Mart* – undated but certainly not before 1917 – praised her stand at an unknown exhibition for its variety of ashtrays, bowls and vases in a range of colours. Glover threw some of her shapes, though others, including pentagonal and square-sectioned vases, must have been moulded. She is said to have also made figures, night-light stands in the form of cottages, and coffee cups, as well as ceramic beads, which the retailer Liberty sold in the late 1920s. Her biographical details were supplied by her son, John Glover.

369 Vase, *c.* 1915–17
Red earthenware, uneven blue glaze; h.20.6cm, d.10.5cm
C.149-1991. Source: given by John Glover Esq., in memory of his mother, Lois M. Glover

370 Bowl, *c.* 1935–38
Red earthenware, iridescent glaze; marks: 'G' and 'Copy/Glastonbury/bowl', incised; h.6.5cm, d.10.5cm
C.148-1991. Source: *see* **369**

Produced as souvenirs, Glover's copies of the well-known bronze bowl excavated from Glastonbury Lake Village were sold mainly through the Copper Kettle Tearooms, Glastonbury.

Godfrey, Ian 1942–1992

1942	born Ely, Cambridgeshire; spends childhood in London
1957–62	studies painting at Camberwell School of Art and Crafts, where also begins study of ceramics under Dick Kendall, taught also by Lucie Rie (qv) and Ian Auld (qv)
1962–67	workshop in City Road, Islington, London
1962–75	teaches part-time at Camberwell School of Art and Crafts
1965	first solo exhibition, Primavera, London
1967–68	works at Royal College of Art, London, on pottery fellowship
1968–76	workshop in Goswell Road, Islington, London
1972|74	solo exhibitions at Crafts Centre of Great Britain (later British Crafts Centre), London
1974	wins Gold Medal at International Ceramics Competition, Faenza
1976–80	sets up and runs domestic pottery workshop for Hans Jørgen Grum in Denmark
1980–	returns to London; establishes workshop in Highgate

Ian Godfrey created a stylized and individual world of stoneware pottery forms, richly adorned with animals and buildings forming landscapes in miniature. His work is imbued with archaic references, and suggestive of ritual. Highly personal, it appears other-worldly, mystical and magical. Much of his ornament was carved with a penknife, and applied to thrown stoneware forms along with other modelled details, before glazing. After enjoying great success in the early 1970s, Godfrey largely retreated from exhibition. He finally ceased potting due to the onset of AIDS-related illnesses.

Ian Godfrey, interview, in Cameron and Lewis (1976), pp.70–7, 166
— statement and biography, in V&A (1977), pp.6–7
Peter Crotty and Rosemary Wren, 'The Secret Life of Ian Godfrey', *CR*, 16 (1972)
Decorative Art (1973/74)
Potters (1974) to (1983)

373 / 372

375

374

376

Jacquey Visick, 'Potman in a Fragile Landscape', *Design*, 303 (1974)

Notice of bursary, *Crafts*, 14 (1975), p.9

Birks (1976), pp.88–103

Crafts Advisory Committee (1976), p.96

Paisley Museum and Art Galleries (1984), p.39

Crafts Council (1985), p.49

Galerie Besson, solo exhibition pamphlets (London, 1989 and 1993)

Bill Ismay, 'Ian Godfrey: A Celebration', *Studio Pottery*, 2 (1993)

'Ian Godfrey Retrospective', *Ceramics Monthly*, 41:5 (1993)

Frankel (2000), pp.142–5

Bonhams, *International Contemporary Ceramics*, including a group of museum deaccessioned works by Ian Godfrey (London, 18 May 2004), lots 167–82

Nottingham City Museums and Galleries (2017), pp.44–5

Oxford Ceramics Gallery, *Ian Godfrey: An Enchanted Landscape*, exh. cat. (Oxford, 2019)

Peter Warren, 'Ian Godfrey', *Anglian Potters Newsletter* (Autumn 2019)

David Whiting, 'An Enchanted Vision', *CR*, 297 (2019)

Exhibition reviews: *Pottery Quarterly*, 8:29 (1963), pl.15; Rosemary Wren, *CR*, 7 (1971); Tony Hepburn, *Craft Horizons*, 32:4 (1972); *The Times* (17 May 1972); *Pottery Quarterly*, 39:10 (1972), pls.8–11; J.D.H. Catleugh, *CR*, 28 (1974); Tony Hepburn, *Crafts*, 9 (1974)

Obituaries: Emmanuel Cooper, *Crafts*, 119 (1992), and *The Independent* (28 August 1992); *The Times* (10 September 1992)

371 *Large white chest of drawers*, 1969–70 (pl.60)
Stoneware, handbuilt, matt off-white glaze; h.31cm, d.23.8cm
Circ.57 to DD-1970. Source: Primavera, London (group exhibition: *25 Years in Association with Primavera – An Exhibition of Ceramics*, 1970, no.52), £20

372 'Black dish', 1972
Stoneware, cut and incised decoration, matt black glaze; h.6.8cm, d.25.7cm
Circ.423-1972. Source: Crafts Centre of Great Britain, London (solo exhibition, 1972, no.19), £12.15

373 Lidded pot, 1972
Stoneware, thrown, with carved and modelled elements, matt white and yellow-brown glaze; h.20.2cm, d.14.5cm
Circ.422&A-1972. Source: Crafts Centre of Great Britain, London, £16.20

374 *Grey Fox Box*, 1974
Stoneware, thrown, with carved and modelled elements, thin buff glaze; h.27cm, d.28.5cm
Circ.491&A-1974. Source: British Crafts Centre, London (solo exhibition, 1974, no.99), £55.12

375 *Anxiety Bowl*, 1976
Stoneware, thrown, with modelled elements, matt black glaze; h.8.8cm, d.35.9cm
Circ.532-1976. Source: British Crafts Centre, London, £21.27

376 *Barrel Pot*, 1976
Stoneware, modelled, thick pitted grey-green glaze; h.13.5cm, d.25cm
Circ.533-1976. Source: the artist, £42.50
The barrel contains loose pellets of clay to make it rattle when shaken.

Gordon, William 1905–1996

1905	born St Petersburg, Russia, to Scottish and Russian parents
1913	family returns to Scotland, moving to London in 1917
1930s	works as sculptor and designer of decorative ironwork, having studied history and languages at Oxford University
1939	experiments at small saltglaze factory in Brampton, Chesterfield, Derbyshire, owned by Plowright Brothers Ltd; work interrupted by war
1946–56	establishes saltglaze workshop at Old Whittington, Chesterfield, trading as Walton Pottery Co. Ltd
1958	designs abstract tile mural for Basildon bus station, Essex, made by Carter & Co., Poole, Dorset
1958–59	tile mural for St Aidan's Church, Leicester
c. 1960–70	rents workshop at Oxshott, Surrey, from Denise Wren (qv), sets up own kiln
1963	ceramic sculpture for New Zealand House, London

Noted for his revival of salt-glazed stoneware, William Gordon produced figures, lampstands, vases and dishes, using a white clay body enhanced by coloured slips. His enterprise was seen as an intermediate between studio and factory production; his wares were slip-cast from models he made himself, and his output small enough for him to retain personal control. He later concentrated on architectural ceramics, fulfilling commissions for Modern Movement architects

377

378 / 383

including Basil Spence and Robert Matthew, with whom he was closely associated.

British Council (1942), pp.24, 32, 47–8
Sempill (1944), pp.46–8
Royal Scottish Museum, *Living Traditions: 1951 Festival Exhibition of Scottish Architecture and Crafts*, exh. cat. (1951)
Hugh Wakefield, 'William Gordon's Saltglaze', *The Studio*, 141 (1951), pp.114–15
Dartington Hall (1952)
Wingfield Digby (1952), pp.84–5, pl.63
Decorative Art (1952/53)
Lewis (1956), pls.365–7
'Walton Pottery Closure', *Derbyshire Times* (13 January 1956)
'Tiled Church Wall', *Architectural Review*, 126 (1959), p.287
Pearson (2005)

379

382 / 381 / 380

377 *Harlequin*, 1950
Stoneware, slip-cast, grey slip, saltglaze; h.36cm, d.7cm
Circ.186-1950. Source: the pottery, £2.10s.
A version of this model was made before the Second World War, *see* British Council (1942).

378 Lampstand, 1950
Stoneware, slip-cast, blue-black slip, saltglaze; marks: 'O' with a stroke through, incised; h.41cm, d.11.6cm
Circ.188-1950. Source: *see* 377, £2.4s.

379 Bowl, 1950
Stoneware, slip-cast, incised decoration and brown painting, saltglaze; h.6.3cm, d.13cm
Circ.189-1950. Source: *see* 377, £1.10s.

380 *Seagull*, 1950
Stoneware, slip-cast, black slip, saltglaze; h.16.2cm, d.20.8cm
Circ.187-1950. Source: *see* 377, £1.10s.

381 *Quail*, 1951
Stoneware, slip-cast, cream slip, saltglaze; marks: 'O' with a stroke through, painted, and 'MADE IN ENGLAND', printed; h.17cm, d.20.3cm
Circ.76-1952. Source: Story & Co., London, £2.2s.

382 *Duck*, 1955
Stoneware, slip-cast, black slip, saltglaze; h.16.6cm, d.16.7cm
Circ.116-1956. Source: given by the pottery

383 Lampstand, 1955
Stoneware, slip-cast, grey slip, saltglaze; marks: 'O' with a stroke through, painted, and 'MADE IN ENGLAND', printed; h.21.2cm, d.13.4cm
Circ.117-1956. Source: *see* 382

Gorry, Colin 1952–

1952	born Staffordshire
1979–82	studies ceramics at Camberwell School of Art and Crafts
1982–85	studio in West Kensington, London
1984	first solo exhibition, Anatol Orient, London
1985–92	successive studios in Brixton, London
1993–99	studio in Walton-on-Thames, Surrey
2020–	establishes studio in Margate, Kent

Colin Gorry is recognized for his thrown and assembled sculptural jugs and bottles with richly textured glazes. Of great vigour and poise, these garnered him acclaim in the late 1980s. Gorry later ceased potting for a lengthy period, concentrating on a parallel career in special effects for TV and film.

384

Martina Margetts, 'Pot Au Feu', *Crafts*, 100 (1989)
Rice and Gowing (1989)
Rice (2002)

Exhibition reviews: Tanya Harrod, *Crafts*, 84 (1987); Marina Vaizey, *Sunday Times* (20 December 1987)

384 Jug, 1990
Stoneware, thrown and assembled, bubbled white glaze; marks: 'CG' in a circle, impressed; h.81cm, d.15.9cm
C.26-1991. Source: the artist (from exhibition: *Colin Gorry, Dan Kelly, Colin Pearson*, Michaelson & Orient, London, 1990), £495

Grant, Duncan 1885–1978

See 501 and 505 *under* Phyllis Keyes and 736 *under* Omega Workshops

Gregory, Ian 1942–2021

1942 born Eastcote, London
1960s works as an actor in film, TV and theatre, initially alongside study at St Martin's School of Art, London
1972– establishes pottery at Ansty, Dorset; builds wood-fired kiln; makes terracotta flowerpots while learning to throw efficiently
1975– begins salt-glazing
1977– Visiting Lecturer at Bath Academy of Art, and Cardiff, Medway and Harrow schools of art
1980– moves to Suffolk for short period, later returning to Ansty

A self-taught potter, Ian Gregory worked with a pioneering spirit, becoming an early exponent of saltglaze in studio pottery and an innovator in kiln-building, notably through his development of portable and improvised kilns. He initially became known for his slab-built saltglaze model furniture and large-scale sculptures of buildings, made alongside domestic ware. He later pioneered the use of paperclay, making figurative sculpture, in particular dogs. Gregory also worked in bronze and was an accomplished watercolourist.

Ian Gregory, *Kiln Building* (London, 1977), revised (2003)
— *Sculptural Ceramics* (London, 1992)
— 'Pack up your Kiln', *CR*, 172 (1998)
— *Alternative Kilns* (London, 2005)

385

386

'CPA New Members', *CR*, 36 (1975)
Potters/The Ceramics Book (1977) to (2012)
Phil Rogers, *Ian Gregory*, Aberystwyth Arts Centre: Ceramic Series 79 (1996)
Rogers (2002), pp.143–7
Where I Fell in Love Gallery, *Ian Gregory*, exh. cat., text 'Vitality and Essence' by Ashley Howard (2006)
Brian Moore, 'Dorset Lives', *Dorset Life* (May 2011)

385 *Chest of Drawers*, 1980
Stoneware, brown saltglaze; h.13.8cm, d.7cm
C.180-1980. Source: Casson Gallery, London, £11.50

386 *Hound Dog*, 1994
Earthenware, handbuilt, grey-pink raku glaze; h.51cm, d.91cm
C.59-1995. Source: Craft Potters Association, London (exhibition: *Studio Ceramics 94*, V&A, 1994), £600

Groves, Lewis A. ('Loo') 1903–1975

1903 born London
1944 joins Taena Community, a pacifist Christian community at Taena Farm, Aylburton, Gloucestershire, after working in an insurance office for 25 years; his sister Connie and her husband, George Ineson, are founder members
1947–49 trains with Margaret Leach (qv) at The Barn Pottery, Brockweir, Gloucestershire
1949– establishes pottery at Taena Farm
1950– Margaret Leach joins him
1952 Taena Community relocates to Whitley Court, Upton St Leonards, Gloucestershire; visits Bernard Leach (qv) for help designing new kiln
1960s Taena Pottery continues after community dissolves
1975 passes running of Taena Pottery to Sean and Vici Casserley

387 / 388

A student of Margaret Leach, Lewis Groves concentrated on slip-decorated earthenware, working from the pottery he established within the Taena Community. The community managed a farm, and engaged in a range of art and craft activities, of which pottery was the first.

George Ineson, *Community Journey* (London, 1956)
Whybrow (2006), p.108
John Edgeler, 'Low Tech, High Skill', *CR*, 237 (2009)

387 Dish, 1950
Earthenware, black slip trailed on white, under amber glaze; marks: cross in a double circle, impressed; h.3.8cm, d.28.5cm
Circ.156-1950. Source: the artist, £1.5s.

388 Jug, 1950
Earthenware, amber glaze; marks: cross in a double circle, impressed; h.10.5cm, d.12cm
Circ.157-1950. Source: *see* **387**, 6s.6d.

Gunn-Russell, Linda 1953–

1953 born London
1971–75 studies ceramics at Camberwell School

389

	of Art and Crafts
1975–78	studio at 401½ Workshops, Lambeth, London
1978–82	studio in Clapham, London
1982–88	studio in East Dulwich, London
1988–	studio in Swiss Cottage, London

Linda Gunn-Russell's highly mannered work employs elaborate visual tricks of perspective to suggest volume in pieces that are near-flat. Earlier work was slip-cast, but from 1978 she began to develop complex handbuilt vessels, painted with slips. These explore the domestic forms of jugs and teapots, and later also sinuous, anthropomorphic female forms.

Linda Gunn-Russell, 'New Ceramicists', *Crafts*, 59 (1982)
Houston (1979), pp.98–9
Oxfordshire County Museum Services (1984), pp.32–3
Abigail Frost, exh. review, *Crafts*, 72 (1985)
Angel Row Gallery, *Linda Gunn-Russell: Sculptural Ceramics*, exh. pamphlet (Nottingham, 1993)
Pamela Johnson, 'Body Doubles', *Crafts*, 124 (1993)

389 Jug, 1980
Earthenware, slip-cast, masked and poured white glaze, raku-fired; h.26cm, d.26.8cm
C.117-1980. Source: British Crafts Centre, London (exhibition: *Raku and Saltglaze*, 1980, no.62), £47.90

Haile, Marianne *see* Marianne de Trey

Haile, Thomas Samuel (**Sam**)
1909–1948

1909	born London; leaves school at age 16; works in shipping firm; attends evening classes at Clapham School of Art
1931–35	wins scholarship to Royal College of Art, London, to study in School of Painting; transfers to School of Design in second year to escape its academicism, studying pottery under William Staite Murray (qv)
1935	teaches full-time at Leicester College of Art
1936–39	returns to London, teaching at Kingston and Hammersmith schools of art; shares workshop with Margaret Rey (qv) at Raynes Park, using small gas-fired kiln to make stoneware and earthenware
1937	exhibition at The Brygos Gallery, London, with James Dring (qv); joins Artists International Association and English Surrealist Group
1938	marries Marianne de Trey (qv)
1939	moves with de Trey to USA
1940	exhibits pots made in England at Rena Rosenthal's gallery on Madison Avenue, New York
1941–42	teaches at New York State College of Ceramics, Alfred University
1942–43	teaches pottery at College of Architecture, University of Michigan, Ann Arbor; inducted (drafted) into US Army
1944	transfers to British Army and returns to UK; becomes sergeant-instructor in the Army Educational Corps
1945	concussed in motorcycle accident and discharged from army; with de Trey sets up workshop at Bulmer Brickyard, near Sudbury, Suffolk, making slipware
1946–	pottery consultant to Rural Industries Bureau
1947	moves with de Trey to Shinners Bridge, Dartington, to cabin and studio previously occupied by Bernard Leach (qv)
1948	killed in motor accident at Poole, Dorset; memorial exhibitions at Southampton Art Gallery and Institute of Contemporary Arts, Washington, USA
1951	memorial exhibition, Crafts Centre of Great Britain, London

A profoundly original artist, Sam Haile was both a painter, whose work was allied to the English Surrealists, and a potter. As a student of painting at the Royal College of Art, he realized his unorthodox style would not earn him a diploma, and so transferred to the more enlightened pottery school under William Staite Murray (qv). Haile's small but vital oeuvre is associated with a series of short, distinct periods, the disruption of the Second World War forcing him to start from scratch on more than one occasion. After the war he took solace in the production of slipware, initially of traditional types, but increasingly exerting his personal expression. His tragically early death makes him a tantalizing figure in studio ceramics. He is credited with an important role in its development in the USA, and, had he lived, would likely have had a major influence on the post-war British scene. His surviving work powerfully demonstrates his ability to reinterpret traditional forms and techniques in a contemporary idiom and his mastery in integrating form and surface, revealing depths of space.

Arts and Crafts Exhibition Society (1935), (1938), (1946), (1948)
Brygos Gallery (1936)
— (1937b)
— *Stoneware Pottery by T.S. Haile and Decorated Plates and Tiles by C.J. Dring*, exh. cat. (London, 1937)
A.C. Sewter, 'T.S. Haile, Potter and Painter', *Apollo*, 44 (December 1946)
Cooper (1947), pp.*i–ii*, pls.9–14
'T.S. Haile, Ceramist', *Craft Horizons*, 9:2 (1949)
Patrick Heron, exh. review, *The Listener*, 46:1176 (1951)
Dartington Hall (1952)
Wingfield Digby (1952), pp.75–6, pls.36–40, 62
Rose (1955), pp.22–3, pls.62–5, (1970), pp.43–4, pls.64–7
Lewis (1956), pls.316, 331–2
Manchester Institute of Contemporary Arts, *The Surrealist Paintings and Drawings of Sam Haile*, exh. cat., text by A.C. Sewter (Manchester, 1967)
Garth Clark, 'Sam Haile: A Memorial', *Studio Potter*, 7:1 (1978)
Marianne de Trey, 'Sam Haile: Recollections', *Studio Potter*, 7:1 (1978)
Haslam (1984), p.65, pls.38–40
Paisley Museum and Art Galleries (1984), pp.40–1
Birch and Conran, *Sam Haile*, exh. cat. (London, 1987)
Marianne de Trey, 'Sam Haile – Painter and Potter', *CR*, 107 (1987)
Riddick (1990), p.38
Tanya Harrod, book review, *Crafts*, 123 (1993), reprinted in Harrod (2015), pp.241–3
Barry Hepton (ed.), *Sam Haile: Potter and Painter*, exh. publication, Cleveland Crafts Centre, texts by Paul Rice, Marianne Haile and others (London, 1993)
Paul Rice, 'Sam Haile', *Studio Pottery*, 2 (1993)
Michel Remy, *Surrealism in Britain* (Aldershot, 1999), pp.171–6, 310–12
Cooper (2003), p.230

390 Beer mug, *c.* 1937
Stoneware, grey glaze, painted in brown; inscribed 'NUNC / EST / BIBENDUM'; marks: 'SH' in monogram, impressed; h.16cm, d.13.5cm
C.50-2019. Source: Tattwa Gyani (daughter of Sam Haile), £750; acquired with funds raised in memory of Jonathan Nevitt
Probably made for the exhibition *Stoneware and Earthenware and Beer Sets*, The Brygos

390

392 / 391

393 / 394

395

397

398

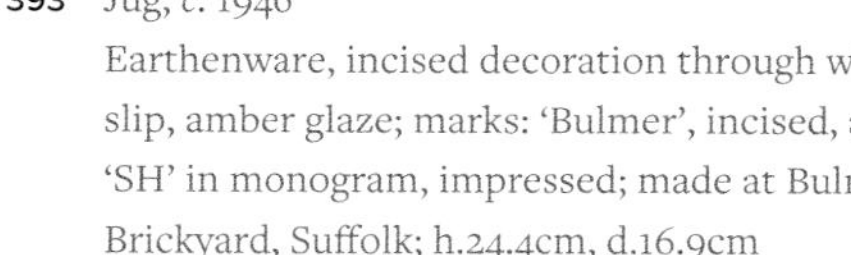

Gallery, London, 1937, and likely part of the consignment of Haile's work shipped to the USA in 1940. Similar mugs are visible in a photograph of Haile's exhibition at the University of Michigan, Ann Arbor, in 1943 (Hepton, 1993, p.43).

391 Jug, *c.* 1946
Earthenware, combed white over dark slip, amber glaze; marks: bull's head seal, impressed; made at Bulmer Brickyard, Suffolk; h.24cm, d.19.5cm
C.78-1986. Source: bequeathed by James Dring

392 Mug, *c.* 1946
Earthenware, combed white over dark slip, amber glaze; marks: bull's head seal, impressed; made at Bulmer Brickyard, Suffolk; h.10cm, d.12.4cm
C.79-1986. Source: *see* **391**

393 Jug, *c.* 1946
Earthenware, incised decoration through white slip, amber glaze; marks: 'Bulmer', incised, and 'SH' in monogram, impressed; made at Bulmer Brickyard, Suffolk; h.24.4cm, d.16.9cm
C.76-1986. Source: *see* **391**

394 Jug, *c.* 1946
Earthenware, dark slip with incised decoration and slip-trailing in white, amber glaze; marks: 'SH' in monogram, impressed; h.24.7cm, d.19.4cm
C.77-1986. Source: *see* **391**

395 Dish, *c.* 1946
Earthenware, slip-trailed in colours over white slip, amber glaze; marks: 'SH' in monogram, impressed; h.9.5cm, d.34.6cm
Circ.286-1951. Source: Marianne de Trey (from memorial exhibition, Crafts Centre of Great Britain, London, 1951), £9.9s.

396 Jug, *c.* 1946 (pl.31)
Earthenware, slip-trailed in white over dark slip, amber glaze; marks: bull's head seal, impressed; made at Bulmer Brickyard, Suffolk; h.32.7cm, d.16.5cm
Circ.287-1951. Source: *see* **395**, £5.5s.
Illustrated in Rose (1955), pl.64.

397 Loving cup, 1947
High-fired earthenware, slip-trailed in white, amber glaze; marks: 'SH' in monogram, impressed; inscribed: 'OLIVE & JAMES DRING / 29 MARCH 1947 / DRINK BE MERRY & MARRY'; h.21.1cm, d.20.6cm
C.80-1986. Source: *see* **391**
Made to commemorate the second marriage of Haile's friend James Dring (qv).

398 Jug, 1948
Earthenware, tin glaze, painted in blue and yellow; marks: 'SH' in monogram and acorn

seal, impressed; made at Shinners Bridge, Dartington; h.19.7cm, d.17.5cm
Circ.288-1951. Source: *see* **395**, £4.4s.

Hall, Morgen 1960–2016

1960	born Roseville, California, USA
1973–	moves with family to Scotland
1979–83	studies ceramics and jewellery at Grays School of Art, Aberdeen
1983–84	studies ceramics at South Glamorgan Institute of Higher Education, Cardiff
1984–	sets up studio at Chapter Arts Centre, Cardiff
1989–	solo exhibition at Godfrey and Twatt, Harrogate, North Yorkshire; exhibits widely thereafter
1998–2001	Senior Research Fellow, Centre for Ceramic Studies, University of Wales Institute, Cardiff

Morgen Hall's exuberant, yet finely detailed tableware celebrated food and the pleasures of dining. She primarily worked in thrown and turned tin-glazed red earthenware with cobalt slip, later introducing new processes such as the use of plotter-cut stencils and ram-pressing to produce embossed wares.

Morgen Hall, 'A Potter's Day', *CR*, 145 (1994)
— 'A Tea Cabaret', *CR*, 148 (1994)
— 'Playing with Pattern', *CR*, 194 (2002)
— **and Peter Castle**, 'Approaches to Re-inventing Studio Practice', *Ceramics Technical*, 11 (2000)
David Briers, *Morgen Hall*, Aberystwyth Arts Centre: Ceramic Series 29 (1988)
Nicole Swengley, 'Artists with Pots of Style', *The Times* (5 May 1990)
Oriel Cardiff, *Morgen Hall*, exh. pamphlet, text by David Briers (1992)
Potters/The Ceramics Book (1992) to (2012)
Llantarnam Grange Arts Centre, *The Breakfast, Lunch & Dinner Party*, exh. cat. (Cwmbran, 1994)
'Morgen Hall', *Ceramics Monthly*, 47:4 (1999)
Jeffrey Jones, *Morgen Hall*, Aberystwyth Arts Centre: Ceramic Series 97 (2000)
Godfrey & Watt, *Morgen Hall*, exh. cat. (Harrogate, 2006)
Ruthin Craft Centre (2006), pp.40–3, 76
— (2009), pp.24–5
Carlano (2010), pp.76–7

Exhibition reviews: Paul Vincent, *Studio Pottery*, 4 (1993); David Briers, *Crafts*, 133 (1995); Will Levi Marshall, *CR*, 159 (1996), and 173 (1998)

Obituaries: Jeffrey Jones, *The Guardian* (6 June 2016); Moira Vincentelli, *Interpreting Ceramics*, ejournal, 17 (2016)

399 'Tea cabaret set', 1997
Tin-glazed red earthenware, resist-decorated in blue slip, rutile glaze stain; the tray slab-built, the hollowware thrown, turned and rouletted; marks: 'Morgen Hall', sgraffito (tray); 'MORGEN HALL' in circular device, impressed (hollowware); h.16.9cm, d.23.3cm (teapot); d.50cm (tray); h.11.5cm, d.15.7cm (jug); h.12.6cm, d.10.2cm (sugar bowl); h.9.5cm (cups); d.15cm (saucers)
C.9 to 16-1998. Source: Crafts Council Shop at the V&A, £634.50

400 Spaghetti jar, 2003
Tin-glazed red earthenware, thrown and turned, resist-decorated in blue slip using computer-cut stencils, rutile glaze stain; marks: 'Morgen Hall', sgraffito; h.44.1cm, d.15.2cm
C.43:1,2-2004. Source: the artist, through an anonymous gift
The surface pattern is derived from digitally scanned cooked spaghetti, the image being used to produce stencils with the aid of a plotter-cutter.

399

400

Hall, William R. 1941–

1941	born Jerusalem
1959–61	studies at Lowestoft School of Art
1962–65	studies at Central School of Arts and Crafts, London
1966–74	teaches ceramics at School of Design and Furniture, High Wycombe, Buckinghamshire
1970–82	studio in High Wycombe
1974–	teaches ceramics at Sir John Cass School of Art, London
1977	wins Gold Medal at International Ceramics Competition, Faenza
1982–86	studio in Canterbury, Kent
1986–	studio in Winchester, Hampshire

William Hall's earlier work comprised slip-cast sculptural pieces, including model cars and aeroplanes. From about 1978 he focused on decorated porcelain tile plaques, developing techniques for inlaying colour analogous to printing, using low-relief plaster blocks in place of printing plates.

William Hall, 'Slipcasting', *CR*, 9 and 10 (1971)
— 'Ceramic Printing', *CR*, 158 (1996)
Crafts Advisory Committee (1976), p.98
Marigold Coleman, 'Painting on Clay', *Crafts*, 35 (1978)
Crafts Council (1980), p.58
Oxfordshire County Museum Services (1984), pp.34–5
Jane Waller, 'Colour in Clay – Part Three', *CR*, 147 (1994)
Yates-Owen and Fournier (2015)

Exhibition reviews: Emmanuel Cooper, '3 in Ceramics', *Art & Artists*, 14:8 (1979); Geoffrey Weston, '3 in Ceramics', *Crafts*, 43 (1980)

401 Wall plaque: *Future Man*, *c.* 1978
Porcelain, inlaid with coloured stoneware clays; h.22.5cm, w.11.3cm
C.111-1978. Source: the artist, £60

401

Halls, Susan 1966–

1966	born Gillingham, Kent
1984–88	studies ceramics at Medway College of Art and Design
1988–90	studies ceramics at Royal College of Art, London
1990–91	residency at Banff Centre for the Arts, Alberta, Canada
1991–94	workshop in Putney, London
1995–98	workshop in Balham, London
1998–2003	moves to USA; workshop in Southport, Connecticut
2003–17	workshop in Easthampton, Massachusetts
2017–	returns to UK, to the East Riding of Yorkshire, as artist-in-residence at University of York
2019–	moves to the Lizard, Cornwall, establishes studio

Susan Halls emerged as a new talent in the 1990s, her work contributing to the resurgence of figurative ceramics. Animals have provided her primary inspiration and subject matter, and her close observation and unsentimental treatment have produced compelling work concerned more with capturing the vitality of its subject than with detailed description. Her departure for the USA was prompted in part by frustration with the apparent lack of opportunities for ceramic artists.

Susan Halls, 'Animal Crackers', *CR*, 146 (1994)
— 'I've Had Enough. I'm Off', *Studio Pottery*, 32 (1998)
— *Ceramics for Beginners: Animals and Figures* (New York, 2011)
— *Pinch Pottery: Functional, Modern Handbuilding* (New York, 2014)
— 'The Conviction to Create', *CR*, 280 (2016)
Emmanuel Cooper, *Susan Halls*, Aberystwyth Arts Centre: Ceramic Series 63 (1993)
Museum of Modern Art, Oxford (1993), pp.40–1, 86, 94
Dormer (1994), pp.198–200
Peter Dormer, 'Emotion Transfigured', *Crafts*, 126 (1994)
Abigail Willis, 'Figurative Ceramics: Susan Halls and George Walker', *Studio Pottery*, 11 (1994)
Peter Beard, *Resist and Masking Techniques* (London, 1996), pp.96–9
Dormer (1997), pp.151–4
Nick Lees, 'Animal Behaviour', *CR*, 177 (1999)
Barbara Rittenberg, 'Infinite Re-creation', *Ceramics Monthly*, 51:5 (2003)
Alex McErlain, 'Drawing It Out', *CR*, 206 (2004)
Perryman (2008), pp.37–40

Exhibition reviews: Pamela Johnson, *Crafts*, 120 (1993); David Jones, *CR*, 165 (1997); Jane Perryman, *CR*, 172 (1998)

402 *Chunky Stiletto*, 1993
Paperclay, slab-built, colloidal slip, raku-fired; marks: 'SH 93', incised; h.20.7cm, d.24.8cm
C.258-1993. Source: Crafts Council Shop at the V&A, £130.50

403 Figure of a dog: *Little Horror*, 1997 (pl.107)
Paperclay, thrown and assembled, colloidal slip, raku-fired; h.28.7cm, d.43cm
C.70-1998. Source: the artist, £650

402

Hamada Shōji 1894–1978

1894	born Kawasaki, Japan
1913–16	studies ceramics at Tokyo Higher Technical School
1915	visits traditional pottery centres in Japan
1916–20	works at Kyoto City Ceramic Research Institute
1919	visits Bernard Leach (qv) at Abiko
1919–20	advises and assists Leach at Azabu, Tokyo
1920–23	accompanies Leach to St Ives, Cornwall, to establish Leach Pottery
1923	two solo exhibitions at Paterson's Gallery, London
1923–24	returns to Japan, via Europe
1924–	works in Okinawa and Mashiko
1929	visits England with Yanagi Sōetsu; solo exhibition at Paterson's Gallery, London
1930–	establishes own kiln at Mashiko
1931	exhibition at Paterson's Gallery, London
1952–53	with Yanagi, attends International Crafts Conference, Dartington Hall, Devon; tours USA with Leach and Yanagi
1955	designated Living National Treasure in Japan

Hamada Shōji is among the most revered and influential potters of the 20th century. He is associated with the development of the *mingei* (folkcraft) movement in Japan, yet his work has been a source of inspiration to potters of radically different schools. Hamada holds an important place in the history of studio ceramics in Britain. He helped Bernard Leach establish his pottery in St Ives and gave him support at critical moments in his career. He exhibited regularly in the UK, both while at the Leach Pottery and after returning to Japan. There is a relaxed quality to Hamada's throwing and decoration, yet the results are highly charged. These qualities are already apparent in his work from St Ives.

Hamada Shōji, *The Works of Shoji Hamada 1921–1969* (Tokyo, 1969)
— 'Hamada', in conversation with Bernard Leach, Victor Margrie and Michael Casson, *Crafts*, 4 (1973)
Arts and Crafts Exhibition Society (1926)
Colnaghi (1927)
'Some Modern Potters', *Artwork*, 5:19 (1929)
Paterson's Gallery, *Exhibition of Pottery by Shoji Hamada*, text by Bernard Leach (London, 1929)
Arthur Theodore Finch, 'The Craftsmanship of Shoji Hamada', *Parnassus*, 2:4 (1930)
Paterson's Gallery, *Exhibition of Pottery by Shoji Hamada*, text by Yanagi Sōetsu (London, 1931)

Dartington Hall (1952)
Wingfield Digby (1952), pp.69–70, pl.16
Rose (1955), pp.15–16, pls.B, 28–39, (1970), pp.31–2, pls.C, 28–39
Yoshiko Uchida, 'Hamada', *Craft Horizons*, 16:4 (1956)
Decorative Art (1964/65)
Susan Peterson, *Shoji Hamada: A Potter's Way and Work* (Tokyo/New York, 1974), revised (London, 2004)
Bernard Leach, *Hamada: Potter* (Tokyo/New York, 1975)
— and Janet Leach, 'Shoji Hamada', *CR*, 50 (1978)
Obituary, *The Times* (7 January 1978)
Susan Peterson, 'Reflections on Hamada', *Studio Potter*, 10:1 (1981)
Tate Gallery (1985), pp.231–32
Vincentelli and Hale (1986)
Birks and Wingfield Digby (1990), pp.95–119
Riddick (1990), pp.39–49
Edward Hughes, 'Clear Spring Water', *CR*, 171 (1998)
Timothy Wilcox (ed.), *Hamada Shōji: Master Potter*, exh. cat. (London, 1998)
Rupert Faulkner, 'A New Generation of Artist-Craftsmen', in Livingstone and Parry (2005), pp.312–27
Whybrow (2006), pp.60–3 and elsewhere
Victoria Oyama, 'Hamada Shoji on Making Teabowls', *Ceramics Technical*, 26 (2008)
Meghen Jones, 'Hamada Shōji, Kitaōji Rosanjin, and the Reception of Japanese Pottery in the Early Cold War United States', *Design and Culture*, 9:2 (2017)
Stair (2020)

Exhibition reviews: William McCance, *The Spectator* (26 May 1923); *The Times*, 'Anglo-Japanese Pottery' (1 November 1923), 'A Japanese Potter' (24 May 1929), 'Two Potters' (10 November 1931)

All works made at the Leach Pottery, St Ives. The V&A also holds later works made in Japan, not catalogued here.

404 Bowl, 1922–23 (pl.11)
Earthenware, incised decoration through white slip, amber glaze; marks: Hamada's seal and 'SI' in monogram, impressed; h.6.5cm, d.18.2cm
Circ.542-1923. Source: Paterson's Gallery, London (solo exhibition, May 1923), £2.5s.

405 Bowl, 1923
Stoneware, tenmoku glaze with black splashes; marks: Hamada's seal and 'SI' in monogram, impressed; h.5.4cm, d.17cm
Circ.992-1924. Source: given by W.W. Winkworth

405 / 407

406

William Winkworth recounted in a letter: 'Murray the potter admired it enormously at Hamada's first show [at Paterson's Gallery] and told Hamada to raise the price; which he was about to do when he found I had been there the day before and bought it.'

406 Bowl, 1923
Stoneware, wax-resist decoration, tenmoku glaze; marks: Hamada's seal and 'SI' in monogram, impressed; h.7cm, d.19.7cm
C.106-1924. Source: given by Sidney K. Greenslade
Shown in solo exhibition at Paterson's Gallery, London, November 1923.

407 Bowl, 1923
Stoneware, tenmoku glaze, painted in iron; marks: Hamada's seal and 'SI' in monogram, impressed; h.8.6cm, d.22.8cm
C.407-1934. Source: British Institute of Industrial Art (given by Bernard Leach, 1927)

408 Bottle, 1923 (pl.12)
Stoneware, greyish-white glaze, painted in grey-brown; marks: Hamada's seal and 'SI' in monogram, impressed; h.19.5cm, d.12.4cm
C.411-1934. Source: *see* 407

Hambling, Maggi 1945–

1945	born Sudbury, Suffolk
1962–64	studies at Ipswich School of Art
1964–67	studies at Camberwell School of Art and Crafts
1967–69	studies at Slade School of Fine Art, London
1992–93	experiments in clay one day a week at Royal College of Art, London
1993	solo exhibition, *Dragon Morning: Works in Clay*, CCA Galleries, London

Maggi Hambling – the celebrated and sometimes controversial artist and portraitist – began experimenting with clay in December 1992, working at the Royal College of Art with technical assistance from Matthew Groves. The resulting pieces developed the celestial symbolism and dreamlike imagery of her recent paintings. Hambling did not pursue ceramics further, but the experience encouraged her to continue exploring three-dimensional sculptural form.

CCA Galleries, *Dragon Morning: Works in Clay*, exh. pamphlet, text by George Melly (London, 1993)
Emmanuel Cooper, 'Maggi Hambling', *CR*, 143 (1993)
Iain Gale, 'Excursions into the Third Dimension', *The Independent* (25 June 1993)
Maggi Hambling: The Works (London, 2006), see esp. pp.125–32

409

An interview with Maggi Hambling, in which her work in clay is discussed, is in the Artists' Lives sound archive at the British Library, London (C466/48).

409 *Hermaphrodite Self Portrait*, 1993
White high-fired earthenware, handbuilt, painted in slips and enamels; made at Royal College of Art, London; h.39cm, d.33.6cm
C.248-1993. Source: CCA Galleries, London (solo exhibition: *Dragon Morning: Works in Clay*, 1993), £898.87

Hamilton, Cuthbert 1884–1958

1884	born London
1899–1903	studies at Slade School of Fine Art, a contemporary of Wyndham Lewis
1913	briefly joins Omega Workshops (qv), leaving with Lewis
1914	joins Rebel Art Centre, London, founded by Lewis
c. 1915–20	establishes Yeoman Pottery in Yeoman's Row, Kensington, London, working with William Staite Murray (qv)
1919	shows pottery at Arts League of Service *Exhibition of Practical Arts*, Twenty-One Gallery, London
1920	shows paintings, woodcuts and pottery at Group X exhibition, Mansard Gallery, London

Cuthbert Hamilton was a Vorticist artist, a member of the Camden Town Group and an associate of Wyndham Lewis. He served as a special constable during the First World War. By 1916 he had become preoccupied with ceramics and established Yeoman Pottery in Kensington, where he worked with William Staite Murray (qv). It is not clear whether Murray made pots for Hamilton to decorate. After the closure of Yeoman Pottery, Hamilton gradually abandoned his artistic career.

Arts League of Service, *Exhibition of Practical Arts*, exh. cat., Twenty-One Gallery (London, 1919)
Arts Council of Great Britain, *Vorticism and its Allies*, exh. cat. (London, 1974), p.31
Malcolm Haslam, 'Some Vorticist Pottery', *The Connoisseur* (October 1975)
Richard Cork, *Vorticism and Abstract Art in the Machine Age* (London, 1976), pp.545–6
Anthony d'Offay, *The Omega Workshops: Alliance and Enmity in English Art 1911–1920*, exh. cat. (London, 1984), no.144
Haslam (1984), pp.10–13

410 Dish, *c.* 1919 (pl.5)
Earthenware, painted in blue-black; marks: 'CH' in monogram, painted; h.3.6cm, d.17.7cm
C.120-1984. Source: Anthony d'Offay Gallery, London, £1500
A price of '£1.5.0' is marked in pencil on the base.

Hamlyn, Jane 1940–

1940	born London
1968–70	attends pottery classes at Battersea Adult Education Institute and Putney Art School
1972–74	Studio Pottery Course at Harrow School of Art
1975–	establishes Millfield Pottery, Everton, Nottinghamshire; builds oil-fired kiln
1976	first solo exhibition, Craftwork, Guildford, Surrey; exhibits widely thereafter
1999	saltglaze prize at *Westerwaldpreis*, Höhr-Grenzhausen, Germany
2000–	builds new gas-fired kiln

A pioneer of the revival of saltglaze, Jane Hamlyn is among the most creative potters to have focused on the production of domestic ware. Robust and eminently usable, her work displays a satisfying range of textures and colours on an inventive range of forms, which for a time incorporated decorative modelled handles and relief patterns. Since 2000 Hamlyn has concentrated on more austere and less overtly functional forms, notably tilted, cylindrical vessels with strongly sculptural qualities.

Jane Hamlyn, 'Paper Resist Decoration', *CR*, 55 (1979)
— 'Salt Glaze and Something Else', *Ceramics Monthly*, 37:4 (1989)
— 'Function, Context and Meaning', *CR*, 155 (1995)
— 'Making Sense', in Exeter City Museums and Art Gallery, *Making Sense: Crafts in Context*, exh. cat. (1995), reprinted in Stair (2000), pp.76–8
— contribution, in 'The First Decade of Harrow 1963–1974', *Ceramics in Society*, 41 (2000)
— 'Empty Vessels', *CR*, 204 (2003)
— 'If Only ...', *CR*, 224 (2007)
'CPA New Members', *CR*, 43 (1977)
Potters/The Ceramics Book (1977) to (2012)
Crafts Council (1980), p.58
Isabelle Anscombe, 'Put It on the Table', *Crafts*, 56 (1982)
Anne Leon, 'Jane Hamlyn at Millfield Pottery', *CR*, 74 (1982)
Crafts Council (1985), p.50
Peter Starkey, 'Jane Hamlyn – Potter', *CR*, 101 (1986)
Gibson (1987), pp.112–19
Sally Shrimpton, *Jane Hamlyn*, Aberystwyth Arts Centre: Ceramic Series 19 (1987)
Craft Centre and Design Gallery, *Jane Hamlyn: Saltglaze*, exh. pamphlet, text by Peter Dormer (Leeds, 1988)
Peter Dormer, 'Jane Hamlyn's Current Work', *Ceramics Monthly*, 37:4 (1989)
Emmanuel Cooper, 'Jane Hamlyn – Saltglaze Potter', *CR*, 127 (1991)
Rufford Craft Centre, *Jane Hamlyn: Saltglaze*, exh. cat., text by Alison Britton (1991)
Rosemary Cochrane, 'For Use and Ornament', *CR*, 139 (1993)
Ruth Weidmann (ed.), *Salzbrand Keramik '93*, exh. cat. (Koblenz, 1993), pp.36–7
Anna Douglas and Nicholas Wegner (eds), *Artists' Stories* (Sunderland, 1995), pp.56–9
Keramikmuseum Westerwald, *Europäische Keramik '99: Westerwaldpreis*, exh. cat. (Höhr-Grenzhausen, 1999)
Seisbøll (2000)
Cochrane (2001), pp.59–61
Rogers (2002), pp.148–52
Rufford Ceramic Centre, *Jane Hamlyn: Saltglazed Ceramics*, exh. cat., text by Tanya Harrod (Ollerton, 2002)
David Whiting, 'A Sense of Integrity', *Ceramics: Art and Perception*, 63 (2006)
Hanaor (2007), pp.152–3
Whiting (2009), pp.46–51
Nottingham City Museums and Galleries (2017), pp.46–7

Exhibition reviews: Peter Crotty and Rosemary Wren, *Crafts*, 20 (1976); Catherine Miller, *Crafts*, 49 (1981); W.A. Ismay, *Crafts*, 94 (1988); Emma Clegg, *CR*, 169 (1998); Kyra Cane, *CR*, 195 (2002); David Whiting, *Crafts*, 177 (2002)

411 Jug, 1980
Stoneware, brown saltglaze with decoration in green and blue; marks: 'JH' in monogram, impressed; h.20.1cm, d.14.2cm
C.44-1980. Source: Craftsmen Potters Association, London (*Jugs* exhibition, 1980, no.31), £9

412 Oval dish, 1988
Stoneware, blue and green-brown saltglaze, impressed decoration; marks: 'JH' in monogram, impressed; h.10.5cm, d.53.7cm
C.16-1989. Source: Contemporary Applied Arts, London, £145.80

411

412

413 Mug, 1996
Stoneware, blue and green saltglaze; marks: 'JH' in monogram and commemorative seal, impressed; h.9cm, d.11.5cm
C.92-1997. Source: given by V&A Enterprises
Produced for sale at the exhibition *William Morris*, V&A, London, 1996.

414 *Bell jar*, 1997 (pl.101)
Stoneware, blue and green saltglaze; marks: 'JH' in monogram, impressed; h.34cm, d.25.4cm
C.22:1,2-1998. Source: Contemporary Ceramics: Craft Potters Shop and Gallery, London (solo exhibition, 1997), £433.80

Hammond, Henry H. Fauchon
1914–1989

1914	born Croydon, Surrey
1929–34	Croydon School of Art, taught among others by Reginald Marlow (qv)
1934–37	awarded Royal Exhibition Scholarship to School of Design, Royal College of Art, London; studies mural painting and design under Eric Ravilious and Edward Bawden, and pottery under William Staite Murray (qv)
1939	appointed to Farnham School of Art as pottery instructor; war prevents him taking up the post
1940–46	war service
1946–80	teaches at Farnham School of Art (later West Surrey College of Art and Design), becoming Head of Ceramics
1946–51	works in slipware only
1947	spends two weeks at St Ives with Bernard Leach (qv)
1947–48	studio at Runwick House, Hampshire
1948–	studio at Bentley, Hampshire, shared from 1954 with Paul Barron (qv)
1959	solo exhibition, Primavera, London
1980	retires; awarded MBE

413

Henry Hammond was an accomplished potter and educator. His work shows the continuing influence of William Staite Murray (qv), most notably in its assured brush decoration, which also reflects Hammond's appreciation of the natural world. Like Murray, Hammond concentrated on individual pieces, but his forms were less demonstrative and more serviceable, bringing them closer in spirit to Bernard Leach (qv). A contemplative and spiritual man, Hammond held a profound belief in craft as a positive force, offering synthesis and harmony.

Henry Hammond, 'Tradition', *Athene*, 7:1&2 (1955)
— 'A Magnetic Teacher', *Crafts*, 14 (1975)
— 'A Visit to Kilmington Manor', in *Katharine Pleydell-Bouverie – A Potter's Life* (London, 1986)
— contribution, in 'Bernard Leach – A Living Tradition', *CR*, 108 (1987)
Arts and Crafts Exhibition Society (1938), (1946) to (1957)
British Council (1942)
Decorative Art (1942), (1950/51), (1960/61)
Cooper (1947), p.*ii*, pl.15
Dartington Hall (1952)
Wingfield Digby (1952), pp.76–7, pls.41–3, 58
Rose (1955), p.23, pl.66, (1970), p.44, pl.68
Lewis (1956), pls.335–7
Casson (1967), p.6, pls.125–8
Potters (1972) to (1989)
V&A (1972), p.110
Crafts Council (1980), p.59
Haslam (1984), pp.65–8, pls.44–6
Paisley Museum and Art Galleries (1984), pp.41–2
Crafts Council (1985), p.50
Bonhams, *Contemporary Ceramics*, sale of contents of Hammond's studio (London, 5 April 1990)
Tanya Harrod and James Hockey, 'A Tribute to Henry Fauchon Hammond', *Crafts*, 102 (1990)
Holburne Museum and Crafts Study Centre, *A Fine Line: Henry Hammond 1914–89* (Bath, 1992)
Sebastian Blackie, 'Henry Hammond', *Studio Pottery*, 8 (1994)
Carlano (2010), pp.78–9
Nottingham City Museums and Galleries (2017), p.48

Exhibition reviews: *Pottery Quarterly*, 6:22 (1959), pp.69–70, pls.5–10; David Hamilton, *Crafts*, 30 (1978); David Whiting, *Crafts*, 118 (1992)

Obituaries: Sebastian Blackie, *CR*, 120 (1989); Tanya Harrod, *The Independent* (16 August 1989); Victor Margrie, *Crafts*, 101 (1989); *Daily Telegraph* (21 August 1989)

The papers of Henry Hammond are at the Crafts Study Centre, Farnham (HAM).

415 Bowl, 1938 (pl.26)
Stoneware, yellowish-brown glaze, painted in black; marks: 'HH' in monogram, painted; h.10.5cm, d.26.8cm
Circ.93-1939. Source: The Brygos Gallery, London (joint exhibition with Robert Washington and Gwilym Thomas, 1938, no.72), £4.4s.

416 Jar, 1938
Stoneware, cream glaze, painted in brown; h.30cm, d.26.3cm
Circ.94-1939. Source: *see* **415** (no.96), £7.7s.

416 / 417

418

419 / 420

422

423

424

417 Bowl, 1938
Stoneware, yellow-brown glaze, painted in brown; h.14cm, d.33.5cm
Circ.95-1939. Source: *see* **415** (no.80), £6.6s.

418 Jar, 1939
Stoneware, oatmeal glaze, painted in brown; marks: 'HH' in square monogram, impressed; h.28.2cm, d.26cm
Circ.478-1939. Source: the artist (from Royal College of Art annual exhibition, 1939), £5.5s. Illustrated in Cooper (1947), pl.15.

419 Jug, 1950
Earthenware, slip-trailed in white on a dark ground, honey-coloured glaze; marks: 'HH' in monogram, impressed; h.27.3cm, d.21cm
Circ.274-1950. Source: Arts and Crafts Exhibition Society (Twenty-second Exhibition, V&A, 1950, no.182), £3.3s.
On seeing this jug in 1989, Hammond commented that he had never really felt happy as an earthenware potter, unlike his colleague Paul Barron (qv), but they had no stoneware kiln at Farnham at that date.

420 Jug, 1950
Earthenware, slip-trailed in white on a dark ground, greenish glaze; marks: 'HH' in monogram, impressed; h.29.7cm, d.20cm
Circ.275-1950. Source: *see* **419** (no.183), £3.3s.

421 Tall pot: *Cow Parsley*, 1959 (pl.44)
Stoneware, pale ash glaze, painted in brown; marks: 'HH' in monogram, impressed; h.38.1cm, d.14.8cm
Circ.129-1959. Source: Primavera, London (solo exhibition, 1959, no.4), £8.8s.

422 Bowl, *c.* 1977
Stoneware, grey ash glaze, painted in brown; marks: 'HH' in monogram, impressed; h.11.3cm, d.22.3cm
C.152-1980. Source: Paul Rice Gallery, London, £155.25
Shown in exhibition with David Leach, Casson Gallery, London, 1977.

423 Bowl, *c.* 1980
Stoneware, oatmeal glaze, painted in brown and green; marks: 'HH' in monogram, impressed; h.11.2cm, d.23cm
C.27-1990. Source: bequest of the artist

424 Dish: *Morning*, 1982–83
Stoneware, oatmeal glaze, painted in black and brown; marks: 'HH' in monogram, impressed; h.5.8cm, d.22.7cm
C.82-1984. Source: given by the Friends of the V&A (purchased at the Craftsmen Potters Association exhibition, *Studio Ceramics Today*, V&A, 1983, no.197, £135)

Hanna, Ashraf 1967–

1967 born El Minia, Egypt
1986–89 foundation studies at El Minia College of Fine Arts
1991–94 studies theatre design at Central Saint Martins College of Art and Design, London
1997– begins working with clay
1998 establishes studio in Hackney, London
2000– moves to Pembrokeshire, establishes studio
2001 solo exhibition, Mercer Art Gallery, Harrogate, North Yorkshire; exhibits widely thereafter
2009–11 studies ceramics and glass at Royal College of Art, London
2010 Welsh Artist of the Year, Applied Arts category
2013 receives Creative Wales Award
2015 awarded Best in Show at British Glass Biennale
2017 solo exhibition, *50 at 50*, Contemporary Ceramics Centre, London

Prior to study at the Royal College of Art, Ashraf Hanna concentrated on handbuilt, smoke-fired pots, decorated in 'naked raku' resist techniques or with carved surfaces. He has since developed more spacially complex sculptural vessels, often with softly curved surfaces of a single hue, interrupted by sharp edges. He is also recognized for his work in kiln-cast glass.

Ashraf Hanna, 'Smoked and Polished', *CR*, 187 (2001)
— 'A Potter's Day', *CR*, 216 (2005)
— statement, in Bendavid and Lalumia (2017), pp.19, 38
Potters/The Ceramics Book (2000) to (2012)
Andrews (2005)
Perryman (2008), pp.160–2
Amanda Fielding, 'Challenging Success', *CR*, 251 (2011)
Maggie Barnes, 'Forward Motion', *CR*, 285 (2017)
Amber Creswell Bell, *Clay: Contemporary Ceramic Artisans* (London, 2017), pp.48–51

A short film, *Form and Material: Ashraf Hanna*, was made by R&A Collaborations in 2015, with support from the Arts Council of Wales.

425 *Blue Undulating Vessel*, 2017
Earthenware, handbuilt, sprayed with blue terra-sigillata slip; h.35cm, d.24.5cm
ME.2-2018. Source: Cavaliero Finn at Collect 2018, £1800

426 / 425

426 *Grey Undulating Vessel*, 2017
Earthenware, handbuilt, sprayed with grey terra-sigillata slip; h.39cm, d.24.5cm
ME.3-2018. Source: *see* **425**, £1800

Hanssen, Gwyn *see* Gwyn Hanssen Pigott

Hanssen, Louis 1934–1968

1934 born Northwest Territories, Canada
1959 arrives in London, having dropped out of English course at University of British Columbia; marries Gwyn Hanssen (qv)
1960– learns pottery from Gwyn; shares studio at their home in Notting Hill, London
1962 joint exhibition with Gwyn at Primavera, London
1963– separates from Gwyn; sets up workshop in Hampstead, London
1965 solo exhibition, Primavera, London

Louis Hanssen, a poet, became a highly proficient potter in a very short time under the tutelage of his wife, Gwyn Hanssen. Initially making domestic stoneware, he increasingly also explored expressive sculptural forms. The accompanying notes to his solo exhibition at Primavera in 1965 describe it as 'one of the most challenging' the gallery had arranged. Louis' homosexuality resulted in his separation from Gwyn, but they nevertheless remained close, and he had made plans to join her in France shortly before his suicide. Louis Hanssen's later life became the subject of Nicholas Wright's play *The Reporter* in 2007.

Louis Hanssen, brief statement and biographical note, *Pottery Quarterly*, 8:30 (1963), p.6, pls.18–19
Primavera, *Stoneware by Louis Hanssen*, exh. notes with brief statement (London, 1965) – copy held in V&A Archive, nominal file MA/1/P2127
Decorative Art (1966/67)
Casson (1967), p.6, pls.31–4
Tanya Harrod, 'Portrait of an Artist as a Young Woman: Gwyn Hanssen Pigott 1935–1973', in Jason Smith, *Gwyn Hanssen Pigott: A Survey 1955–2005* (Melbourne, 2005), pp.9–13
Nottingham City Museums and Galleries (2017), p.50

Exhibition reviews: *Pottery Quarterly*, 7:28 (1962); *Pottery Quarterly*, 8:32 (1965)

427

427 'Footed bowl (goblet bowl)', 1961–62
Stoneware, combed, yellow-brown ash glaze; marks: square seal; h.19.5cm, d.27cm
Circ.454-1962. Source: Primavera, London (exhibition: *Stoneware Pots by Gwyn and Louis Hanssen*, 1962, no.55), £6.10s.

428 Pot, 1965 (pl.50)
Stoneware, moulded and coiled, with dark brown, blue and orange-brown glazes; h.67cm, d.49.5cm
Circ.304-1965. Source: Primavera, London (exhibition: *Stoneware by Louis Hanssen*, 1965, no.8), £31.10s.
Illustrated in *Decorative Art* (1966/67), p.129, and Casson (1967), pl.33.

Hanssen Pigott, Gwyn (née **John**, previously **Hanssen**) 1935–2013

1935 born Ballarat, Victoria, Australia
1955–57 trains with Ivan McMeekin, New South Wales

1958–59 comes to England; works with Ray Finch (qv) at Winchcombe, Bernard Leach (qv) at St Ives, and Michael Cardew (qv) at Wenford Bridge
1960 establishes studio in Notting Hill, London, with husband, Louis Hanssen (qv); works intermittently for Alan Caiger-Smith (qv) at Aldermaston
1962 joint exhibition with Louis at Primavera, London
1963–64 makes visits to France; buys house near Achères
1964–65 runs Wenford Bridge Pottery while Cardew is in Nigeria; visits Australia
1966–73 moves to Achères, establishes workshop making wood-fired pots
1969–71 visiting lecturer at Harrow School of Art
1971 solo exhibition, Crafts Centre of Great Britain, London
1973 returns to Australia
1975–80 establishes workhop in Tasmania with John Pigott, whom she marries in 1976
1980–81 tenancy at Jam Factory workshops, Adelaide
1981–88 Potter-in-Residence at Kelvin Grove campus of Brisbane College of Advanced Education, Queensland
1989–2000 moves to Netherdale, Central Queensland, establishes workshop with wood-fired kiln, making individual pieces and groups in porcelain
1992– solo exhibition, Galerie Besson, London, and in 2000, 2004 and 2010; regular solo exhibitions in Australia, New York and elsewhere
2000– moves studio to Ipswich, South East Queensland
2002 awarded Order of Australia Medal
2004 solo exhibition, *Caravan*, at Tate St Ives, Cornwall
2005 major retrospective at National Gallery of Victoria, Australia
2013 solo exhibition at Erskine, Hall & Coe, London; dies while in London

Gwyn Hanssen was Australia's most distinguished potter. She holds an important place in British ceramics through her training with leading British studio potters, her earlier career in London and her highly influential later exhibitions. In London she made elegant domestic stoneware fired in an electric kiln, but the lure of wood-firing drew her to work elsewhere. After a period in France, she returned to Australia, and worked increasingly in porcelain. Retaining the elegant simplicity of her domestic forms, she developed a new language for ceramics through the formation of still-life groups and nuanced linear installations of her pieces, informed by the paintings of Giorgio Morandi.

Gwyn Hanssen, brief statement and biographical note, *Pottery Quarterly*, 8:30 (1963), pp.5–6, pl.17
— 'The Potters of Haut-Berry', *Pottery in Australia*, 8:2 (1969)
— 'Gwyn Hanssen Talking', interview, *CR*, 11 (1971)
— statement, in Rothschild (1972)
— 'Clarity of Intention', *CR*, 124 (1990)
— 'Autobiographical Notes', *Studio Potter*, 20:1 (1991)
— 'Pulled-back Simplicity', *Studio Potter*, 26:1 (1997)
— 'The Rightness of Form', *CR*, 207 (2004)
Casson (1967), p.6, pls.129, 206–9
Paisley Museum and Art Galleries (1984), pp.42–3
Margaret Tuckson, 'Seeking Perfection', *CR*, 89 (1984)
Crafts Council (1985), pp.50–1
Galerie Besson, *Gwyn Hanssen Pigott: Still Lives*, exh. pamphlet, text by Victor Margrie (London, 1992)
Museum of Modern Art, Oxford (1993), pp.42–3, 86, 94
Neville French, 'Artist-in-Residence', *Ceramics: Art and Perception*, 17 (1994)
Gaze (1997), pp.642–4
Crafts Council (1999b), pp.26–9
Edmund de Waal, 'Gwyn Hanssen Pigott', *Revue de la Céramique et du Verre*, 112 (2000)
Galerie Besson, exh. pamphlet, text by Edmund de Waal (London, 2000)
Minogue and Sanderson (2000), pp.14–18
Galerie Besson, *Gwyn Hanssen Pigott: Still Lifes for Windows*, exh. pamphlet, text by David Whiting (London, 2004)
Tate St Ives, *Gwyn Hanssen Pigott: Caravan*, exh. cat., text by Emmanuel Cooper (St Ives, 2004)
Jason Smith, *Gwyn Hanssen Pigott: A Survey 1955–2005*, texts by Tanya Harrod, Alison Britton and others, with detailed chronology and bibliography (Melbourne: National Gallery of Victoria, 2005)
Clark, Strauss and others (2012), pp.72–3, 400, 455
Cooper (2012), pp.192–4
Adamson, Droth and Olding (2017), pp.366–7
Nottingham City Museums and Galleries (2017), p.49

Exhibition reviews: *Pottery Quarterly*, 7:28 (1962); Anthony Hepburn, *Craft Horizons*, 31:4 (1971); Emmanuel Cooper, *Crafts*, 120 (1993); Alison Britton, *CR*, 185 (2000); David Whiting, *Crafts*, 166 (2000); Nicholas Rena, *Crafts*, 190 (2004); Owen Rye, *Ceramics: Art and Perception*, 62 (2005)

Obituaries: David Whiting, *The Guardian* (11 July 2013); *The Times* (13 July 2013); Tanya Harrod, *The Independent* (17 July 2013); Tanya Harrod, *Crafts*, 244 (2013), reprinted in Harrod (2015), pp.283–7

An interview with Gwyn Hanssen Pigott is in the Crafts Lives sound archive at the British Library, London (C960/127).

429 Punch set (bowl, ladle and six cups), *c.* 1961 (pl.43)
Stoneware, thrown, incised decoration under a yellow-brown wood-ash glaze; marks: circular device, impressed; h.22cm, d.27.8cm (bowl); l.26cm (ladle); h.5.8cm, d.9.5cm (cups)
C.17 to 24-2000. Source: given by Janet Fielder, Cheltenham
Hanssen's punch sets were produced as a commission for Liberty's, London, from where this set was originally bought. A similar set is illustrated in *Pottery Quarterly*, 7:28 (1962), pl.5.

430 'Large pink/white bowl', 1970
Stoneware, thrown and coiled, flecked white

430

431

glaze to interior, porcelain slip to exterior, tinged pink from wood-firing with light additions of salt; marks: 'GH' in monogram, impressed; made at Achères, France; h.15.5cm, d.46.8cm
Circ.237-1971. Source: Crafts Centre of Great Britain, London (solo exhibition: *Stoneware and Porcelain*, 1971, no.168), £35

431 *Still Life, 2 bottles, goblet and beaker*, 1992
Porcelain, glazed, wood-fired; marks: circular device, impressed; h.27.1cm, d.7.6cm (bottle); h.23.5cm, d.7.8cm (bottle); h.13cm, d.8.9cm (goblet); h.8.9cm, d.8.6cm (beaker)
C.44:1 to 4-1993. Source: Galerie Besson, London (solo exhibition, 1992), £990

432 *Kinder Trail*, 2010 (pl.132)
Glazed porcelain; marks: circular device, impressed; h.16cm, l.128cm (installed)
C.16:1 to 14-2010. Source: Galerie Besson (solo exhibition, 2010, no.4), £11,250; acquired through the generosity of Gerard and Sarah Griffin

Harding, Deborah N. (later **Hard**) 1903–1992

1903 born Sheffield, Yorkshire
1909– moves with family to Letchworth, Hertfordshire
mid-1920s studies pottery at Central School of Arts and Crafts, London
c. 1925–30 studio in Meadow Way, Letchworth
1930–31 studies pottery at Royal College of Art, London
c. 1931–39 studio in The Wynd, Letchworth; dismantled when building requisitioned at outbreak of war
c. 1931–39 teaches pottery at the Cloisters, Letchworth, her students including pupils from neighbouring St Christopher School
1948– moves to Manor House, Bygrave, Hertfordshire; makes domestic pottery for private use only

Deborah Harding was active professionally as a studio potter in the later 1920s and 1930s. Her earlier work added lustre decoration to wares produced by other manufacturers, but by 1930 she was making her own boldly modern stoneware. She exhibited regularly with the Arts and Crafts Exhibition Society and Red Rose Guild. Her work was also shown in London at the The Three Shields gallery in Kensington and The Brygos Gallery, and elsewhere.

433

Arts and Crafts Exhibition Society (1926) to (1938)
Decorative Art (1930), (1935)
'A Letchworth Potter', *The Citizen* (3 July 1931)
V&A (1936), pls.42–3
Brygos Gallery (1937a), (1937b)
Vincentelli and Hale (1986)
'Potter's Funeral', obituary, *Letchworth & Baldock Comet* (August 1992)
Harrod (1999), pp.118, 133

Exhibition reviews: 'Englishwoman Exhibition', *The Times* (14 November 1930); 'Two Potters', *The Times* (10 November 1933); 'Beer Mugs on View', *The Times* (20 April 1937)

433 Vase, *c.* 1937
Stoneware, green spiral, whitish glaze; marks: 'D.N.H.', incised; h.18.6cm, d.10.7cm
Circ.311-1954. Source: given by the Council for Art and Industry, Department of Overseas Trade

Harrison, Keith 1967–

1967 born West Bromwich, Staffordshire
1987–90 studies ceramics at Cardiff Institute of Higher Education, switching courses from industrial design
2000–02 studies ceramics at Royal College of Art, London
2002– teaches ceramics at Bath Spa University; tutor in fine art from 2016; Research Professor from 2014
2002–13 studio at Flameworks, Plymouth, Devon
2003 Gasworks/Arts Council International Artists Fellowship, Khoj, New Delhi, India
2006 installations, *Last Supper* and *M25 London Orbital*, at V&A
2011 installation, *Float*, at Jerwood Makers Open, London
2012–13 ceramics residency at V&A, staging 'disruptions', *Lucie Rie vs Grindcore*, *Circulation* and *Moon: A public demonstration*
2013 performance, *Bustleholme*, at De La Warr Pavilion, Bexhill-on-Sea, East Sussex
2013– studio at KARST, Plymouth
2015 installation, *Mute*, at National Museum Cardiff
2016–17 awarded Jerwood Open Forest commission, staging *Joyride* performance at Cannock Chase, Staffordshire

The work of Keith Harrison offers a radical reimagining of ceramic practice. Embracing the possibilities of live performance, Harrison stages process-led experiments and happenings in which outcomes often remain uncertain. Earlier works explored the live firing of clay using industrial or domestic electrical systems. Since the early 2010s he has co-opted music or sound as a disruptive agent, colliding it with clay or other materials. Socially motivated, his practice works in response to specific sites and situations.

Keith Harrison, statement, in Aberystwyth Arts Centre (1990), supplement, p.6
— 'High Tension', *CR*, 229 (2008)
— interview by Matilda Pye, in Matilda Pye and Linda Sandino (eds), *Artists Work in Museums: Histories, Interventions, Subjectivities* (Bath, 2013), pp.187–99
— **and Richard Wentworth**, 'On the Lineage of Making', in Jerwood Charitable Foundation, *In Conversation* (London, 2008)
Richard Slee, 'Sleepers', *Ceramics in Society*, 48 (2002)
Jo Dahn, 'Think About It', *CR*, 206 (2004)
— 'Clay Rocks', *CR*, 223 (2007)
Hanaor (2007), pp.110–13
Twomey (2009), pp.13–15, 79–99, 125–6
Dahn (2011), pp.153–5, 165–6
Jerwood Visual Arts, *Jerwood Makers Open*, exh. cat. (London, 2011)
Crafts Council, *Sound Matters*, exh. cat. (London, 2013), pp.18–21
Josie Ensor, 'Art of Noise at the V&A', *Sunday Telegraph* (17 March 2013)
Tom Whipple, 'Heavy Metal Brings House Down at V&A', *The Times* (20 March 2013)
Dahn (2015), pp.11, 28–35

Alun Graves, 'Damaging the Historic Fabric: Keith Harrison at the Victoria and Albert Museum', in Brown, Stair and Twomey (2016), pp.31–44
Jerwood Visual Arts, *Jerwood Open Forest*, exh. cat. (London, 2016)
Elderton and Morrill (2017), pp.110–11
Agustina Andreoletti, 'Performative Raw Clay Practices and Ceramic Firing Techniques', *Culture Machine*, ejournal, 17 (2018)

Exhibition reviews: Glenn Adamson, *Crafts*, 232 (2011); Simon Olding, *CR*, 252 (2011); Catherine Roche, 'Fragile?', *CCQ Magazine*, 7 (2015); Daniel Dylan Wray, *The Guardian* (12 February 2019)

A film of Keith Harrison performing *Lucie Rie vs Grindcore* was made by Jared Schiller for the Crafts Council exhibition *Sound Matters* in 2013. A film, *Bustleholme*, documenting Harrison and the band Napalm Death's performance at De La Warr Pavilion, was made by Jared Schiller for The Vinyl Factory in 2013. A number of Harrison's other performances have also been documented on film.

434 *Resistor*, 2001
Domestic electric heater, Egyptian paste, video; h.26.5cm, w.37.5cm (heater)
C.68:1,2-2019. Source: the artist, £1125; acquired through the generosity of Gerard and Sarah Griffin
Resistor was fired and filmed in Harrison's grandmother-in-law's flat in Northolt, London. It was first shown in the exhibition *Sleepers*, curated by Richard Slee, at the Royal Cornwall Museum, Truro, as part of the *ceramica* festival, 2002.

435 *Transformer*, 2002 (pl.115)
Domestic electric heater, Egyptian paste, portable cassette player, cassette recording, timer switches; h.49.5cm, w.46cm (heater)
C.69:1 to 5-2019. Source: the artist, £1125
The three-bar heater was bequeathed to Harrison by his grandmother-in-law, Eileen Olive Hogg. The colours of the Egyptian paste represent, in electrical resistance code, the dates of her birth, marriage and death. As originally enacted, a recording of her family singing 'Auld Lang Syne' was played while the fire was switched on daily using timer switches. *Transformer* was first exhibited at Harrison's Royal College of Art degree show in 2002.

434

Henderson, Ewen 1934–2000

1934	born Cheddleton, Staffordshire
1964–65	foundation course at Goldsmiths' College, London, after seven years as branch manager of timber preservation company in Cardiff
1965–68	studies ceramics at Camberwell School of Art and Crafts
1968–73	studio in Camberwell, London
1970–	teaches at Camberwell School of Art and Crafts
1973–	studio in Camden, London
1986	retrospective exhibition, British Crafts Centre, London
1989	solo exhibition, Nationalmuseum, Stockholm
1995	touring solo exhibition, Midlands Arts Centre, Nottingham
1996	shortlisted for Jerwood Prize for Applied Arts

Ewen Henderson worked as a sculptor in fired clay – or in his words 'fluxed earth' – his radical and exploratory practice founded on an intense enquiry into material and process. Clays with differing properties were laminated and fired together, producing uncertain and dramatic results. Henderson's work is fundamentally concerned with landscape and natural forms. He developed increasingly rugged and earthy sculptural vessels, some ambitious in scale, though encompassing also an extended series of richly textured tea bowls. From the later 1980s he introduced more purely sculptural work, reminiscent of skulls and megaliths, turning finally to open, flattened and twisted forms in paperclay. In 1995 he curated the Crafts Council exhibition, *Pandora's Box*, a significant revisionist survey that proposed an alternative canon of post-war sculptural ceramics. Henderson was also active as a painter.

Ewen Henderson, 'Fancy is Fertile only when Futile', statement, in Crafts Council (1995b), p.3
— interview by David Whiting, in Crafts Council (1995b), pp.4–7
Fiona Adamczewski, 'Ewen Henderson and his Coiled Pots', *CR*, 35 (1975)
Amalgam, *Ewen Henderson at Amalgam*, exh. cat. (London, 1979)
Crafts Council (1980), p.59
Potters (1980), (1983), (1986)
Christopher Reid, 'Henderson Country', *Crafts*, 48 (1981)
Oxfordshire County Museum Services (1984), pp.36–7
Paisley Museum and Art Galleries (1984), p.43
Crafts Council (1985), p.52
Tony Birks, 'Ewen Henderson's Pots: A Marriage of Surface and Form', *American Ceramics*, 5:1 (1986)
British Crafts Centre, *Ewen Henderson: A Retrospective View 1970–1986*, exh. pamphlet (London, 1986)
Henry Pim, 'Creative Games', *CR*, 98 (1986)
Angus Suttie, 'Radstone and Henderson', in Anatol Orient Gallery, *Six Ways*, exh. pamphlet (London, 1988)
Tanya Harrod, *Ewen Henderson*, Aberystwyth Arts Centre: Ceramic Series 33 (1989)
Museum of Modern Art, Oxford (1993), pp.44–5, 86–7, 94
Crafts Council (1995b), pp.34–7
Ewen Henderson, texts by Roger Berthoud, David Whiting and Christopher Reid, published in association with Midlands Art Centre (Yeovil, 1995)
Deborah Norton, 'Ewen Henderson', *Studio Pottery*, 15 (1995)
Crafts Council (1996b), pp.24–5
Austin/Desmond Fine Art, *Ewen Henderson: Recent Work*, exh. cat., text by Michael Robinson (London, 1998)
London Institute (1998), pp.16–17, 26
Waller (1998), pp.146–8
Frankel (2000), pp.149–51
Red Gallery / London Institute Gallery, *Ewen Henderson: Paintings*, exh. cat. (Southsea/London, 2000)
Michael Robinson, 'Ewen Henderson and Kerstin Abraham: Crossing the Line', *Ceramics: Art and Perception*, 39 (2000)
Edmund de Waal, 'Ewen Henderson', *Crafts*, 170 (2001)
David Whiting, 'Ewen Henderson 1934–2000: The Tea Bowls', *Ceramics: Art and Perception*, 43 (2001)
— biography, in *Oxford Dictionary of National Biography* (Oxford, 2004)
Clark, Strauss and others (2012), pp.379, 438
Erskine, Hall & Coe, *Ewen Henderson*, exh. pamphlet (London, 2014)

Exhibition reviews: Lyn Colavecchia, *CR*, 15 (1972); Tanya Harrod, *Crafts*, 81 (1986), and 96 (1989); William Packer, *Crafts*, 108 (1991); Victor Margrie, *Crafts*, 119 (1992); Deborah Norton, *Studio Pottery*, 9 (1994); Marina Vaizey, *Crafts*, 129 (1994); Edmund de Waal, *CR*, 161 (1996); Alan Powers, *Crafts*, 143 (1996)

Obituaries: David Whiting, *The Guardian* (9 October 2000); *Daily Telegraph* (17 October 2000); *The Times* (30 November 2000); Emmanuel Cooper, *CR*, 187 (2001); Michael Robinson, *Crafts*, 168 (2001)

436 'Horizontally striped jar', 1979
Stoneware and porcelain, with body stains and oxides, handbuilt in layers, thin feldspathic glaze; h.24.7cm, d.22cm
C.139-1979. Source: Amalgam, London (solo exhibition, 1979, no.5), £50

437 Pot, 1982
Stoneware and porcelain, handbuilt, with orange, cream, grey and blueish glazes; h.59cm, d.35cm
C.82-1982. Source: Craft Shop, V&A, £283.50
Henderson considered this one of his best pieces to date.

438 Pot, 1984
Bone china and porcelain laminated to stoneware, handbuilt; h.44cm, d.22cm
C.152-1984. Source: British Crafts Centre, London (exhibition: *8 Ceramicists*, 1984, no.28), £256.50
One of a number of works by Henderson of the period that reference the human figure.

439 Pot, 1986
Bone china and porcelain laminated to stoneware, handbuilt, with bubbled cratered surface; h.71cm, d.30cm
C.176-1986. Source: British Crafts Centre, London (solo exhibition, 1986), £675

440 Tea bowl, 1987
Bone china and porcelain laminated to stoneware, handbuilt, with bubbled cratered brown glaze and red flashings; h.9.8cm, d.10cm
C.102-1987. Source: Paul Rice Gallery, London, £110

441 Sculpture from the series *Skull Mountain*, 1988 (pl.89)
Bone china and porcelain laminated to stoneware, handbuilt, with body stains and glazes; h.45cm, d.35.8cm
C.39-1989. Source: given by Ed Wolf, London

442 *Knot*, 1998
Paperclay on wire armature, slip, painted in green, pink and black; h.35.5cm, d.56cm
C.68-2002. Source: the Estate of Ewen Henderson, £4000; purchased through the James Yorke-Radleigh bequest and the Contemporary Ceramics Private Donors Fund

436

439

437

440

438

442

Hepburn, Anthony (Tony) 1942–2015

1942 born Stockport, Cheshire; schooled at Manchester High School of Art
1959–63 studies at Camberwell School of Art and Crafts, transferring from painting to ceramics
1963–65 teacher training at University of London
1965–68 shares studio in London with Ian Godfrey (qv) and Mo Jupp (qv); takes studio at Digswell Arts Trust, Hertfordshire
1968– moves to Leamington Spa, Warwickshire; teaches at Coventry College of Art; begins periodic visits to USA to work and teach; visits Japan with Bernard and Janet Leach (qv) in 1969
1969– touring exhibition, *Five Studio Potters*, organized by V&A
1970 wins Gold Medal at International Ceramics Competition, Faenza
1974–75 visiting artist, Art Institute of Chicago
1976–92 Professor of Ceramics, Alfred University, New York State
1992–2008 teaches ceramics at Cranbrook Academy of Art, Michigan

A pioneer of slab-built and slip-cast sculpture, Anthony Hepburn worked outside established ceramic traditions. His work explored materials and emphasized process, often capturing a sense of motion or of something about to occur. After a period of casting familiar household objects in the late 1960s, he turned to more abstract or conceptual work. Hepburn became a regular visitor to the USA, and his work in England reflected current developments in American ceramics. He eventually settled permanently in the USA, becoming an influential teacher. A vigorous commentator on the contemporary scene, Hepburn contributed a regular 'Letter from London' to the American journal *Craft Horizons* from 1969 to 1973.

Anthony Hepburn, 'Young Potters Reply', *Pottery Quarterly*, 9:33 (1967), pp.19–22, pl.15
— 'Discussion', *Pottery Quarterly*, 9:34 (1968), pp.63–5, pl.2
— 'American Ceramics 1970', *CR*, 7 (1971)
— 'Issues for American Ceramics for 1975', *CR*, 37 (1976)
— 'Aesthetics and Criticism', *Studio Potter*, 9:1 (1980)
— 'Drawing', *Studio Potter*, 14:1 (1985)
— 'Changing Channels', *Studio Potter*, 17:1 (1988)
— 'Some Thoughts on the Nature of Drawing', *American Ceramics*, 11:3 (1994)
— '24 Michigan Potters: Tony Hepburn', *Studio Potter*, 30:1 (2001)
Decorative Art (1968/69), (1973/74)
Tony Birks, 'Anthony Hepburn', *Craft Horizons*, 29:4 (1969)
Camden Arts Centre, *Tony Hepburn: Recent Work (Materials Pieces)*, exh. cat., text by Tony Hepburn (London, 1971)
Oxford Gallery (1974)
Birks (1976), pp.8–21
Crafts Advisory Committee (1976), p.99
Portsmouth City Museum and Art Gallery (1976), pp.4–9
'Tony Hepburn', *Ceramics Monthly*, 26:1 (1978)
'Economical Retrospection', *Ceramics Monthly*, 29:7 (1981)
Crafts Council (1985), p.53
Michael McTwigan. 'An Interview with Tony Hepburn', *American Ceramics*, 7:2 (1989)
Maria Porges, 'Towards Hybridity', *Ceramics: Art and Perception*, 30 (1997)
Vincent McGourty, 'Trivial Matters: Tony Hepburn at the ECWC', *Ceramics: Art and Perception*, 40 (2000)
Cooper (2012), pp.191–2

Exhibition reviews: John Berry, *CR*, 13 (1972); Garth Clark, 'Seven in 76', *Crafts*, 19 (1976); Gerry Craig, *Art in America*, 91:6 (2003)

An artist statement written for the *Five Studio Potters* exhibition is in the manuscripts collection, National Art Library, V&A, London (MSL/1969/3560).

443 *Large white double box*, 1967
Stoneware, slab-built, white dolomite glaze with enamel colours; h.56.2cm, d.41.3cm
Circ.1206&A-1967. Source: Crafts Centre of Great Britain, London (solo exhibition, 1967, no.26), £25

444 *Box with telephone and table leg*, 1968
Stoneware, slab-built and moulded, cream-brown dolomite glaze with red enamel; h.29.5cm, d.55cm
Circ.831-1968. Source: the artist, £45

445 *Box with tubes*, 1968 (pl.58)
Stoneware, slab-built and moulded, cream-white dolomite glaze with enamel colours; h.46.5cm, d.43.2cm
Circ.832-1968. Source: *see* 444, £30

443

444

Hinchcliffe, John 1949–2010

See 988 *under* Janice Tchalenko

Hine, Margaret 1927–1986

1927 born Derby
1946–48 studies painting at Derby School of Art
1948–49 trains as art teacher at Institute of Education, University of London, learning pottery under William Newland (qv); further pottery classes at Central School of Arts and Crafts, London, under Dora Billington (qv) and Newland
1950–54 shares studio in Bayswater, London, with Newland and Nicholas Vergette (qv)
1950–54 teaches ceramics at Barnet College of Further Education
1952 marries William Newland
1955– moves to Prestwood, Buckinghamshire, establishes workshop
1965–72 teaches at High Wycombe College of Art and Technology

447

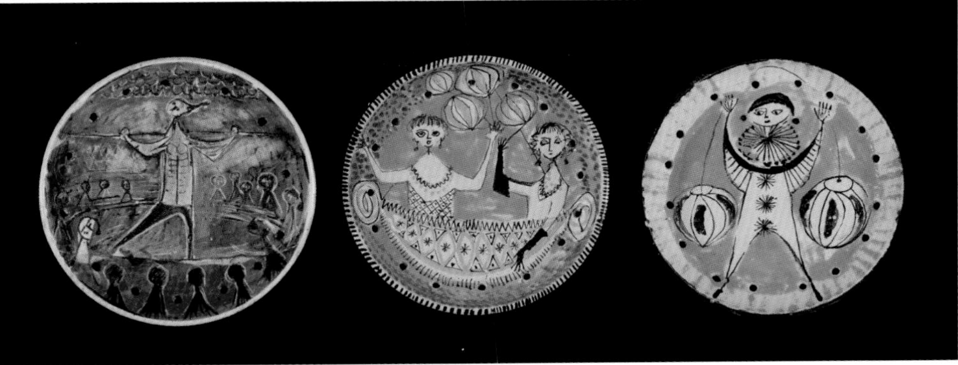

451 / 449 / 450

1972–85 teaches ceramics at Amersham College of Further Education and Art

Margaret Hine, along with her husband, William Newland (qv), was part of a group of artists who brought a 'new look' to ceramics in the 1950s, more in tune with contemporary taste. Hine concentrated on tin-glazed earthenware, making press-moulded dishes and thrown bowls with colourful and lively decoration, and spirited, stylized pottery figures and birds. She also worked to commission on murals for schools, and, with Newland and Nicholas Vergette (qv), on architectural elements for coffee bars and restaurants.

Arts and Crafts Exhibition Society (1952), (1954), (1957)
Decorative Art (1952/53)
Billington (1953), (1955)
Murray Fieldhouse, exh. review, *Pottery Quarterly*, 1:1 (1954)
Lewis (1956), pl.383
Smithsonian Institution (1959)
Paisley Museum and Art Galleries (1984), p.43
Partington (2005)

446 Figure of a mounted harlequin, *c.* 1953–54 (pl.36)
Earthenware, sgraffito through brown-black glaze over white tin glaze, with touches of yellow; marks: 'Margi / Hine', painted; h.19.6cm, w.10.8cm
C.46-2019. Source: Sally Nash (daughter of Margaret Hine), £300; acquired with funds raised in memory of Jonathan Nevitt
Illustrated in Billington (1955), p.20.

447 Pair of doves, 1954
Earthenware, sgraffito through purple-brown glaze over white tin glaze; marks: 'Margi Hine', painted; h.21cm, d.24.7cm
Circ.58&A-1954. Source: the artist, £10.10s.

448 Dish, *c.* 1954 (pl.35)
Earthenware, tin glaze, painted in colours; marks: 'Margi. Hine.', painted; h.4.6cm, d.34.5cm
C.47-2019. Source: Paul Rice, London, £1750; acquired with funds raised in memory of Jonathan Nevitt
Originally part of the decoration of the coffee bar La Ronde in Baker Street, London. Previously sold by Woolley & Wallis, Salisbury, in *British Art Pottery*, 30 November 2011, lot 481. *See also* **449** to **451** and **1012** to **1014**.

449 Plate, *c.* 1954
Earthenware, coloured glazes, painted in enamels; h.3cm, d.20.8cm
C.116-2011. Source: Woolley & Wallis, Salisbury (sale: *British Art Pottery*, 30 November 2011, lot 482), £863.80 (for group)
Originally part of the decoration of the coffee bar La Ronde in Baker Street, London. *See also* **448**, **450**, **451** and **1012** to **1014**.

450 Plate, *c.* 1954
Earthenware, coloured glazes, painted in enamel; h.2.7cm, d.21.3cm
C.117-2011. Source and remarks: *see* **449**

451 Plate, *c.* 1954
Earthenware, tin glaze, painted in colours; h.3.2cm, d.21.6cm
C.118-2011. Source and remarks: *see* **449**

Hirai, Akiko 1970–

1970 born Shizuoka, Japan
1989–93 studies psychology at Aichi Gakuin University, Japan
1999 moves to London
2000–03 studies ceramics at University of Westminster, transferring to Central Saint Martins, London, in 2002
2003– establishes studio at The Chocolate Factory, Hackney, London
2005–15 teaches ceramics at Kensington and Chelsea College
2012– regular solo exhibitions at New Craftsman Gallery, St Ives; Contemporary Ceramics Centre, London; The Scottish Gallery, Edinburgh; Flow Gallery, London; and elsewhere
2019 Loewe Foundation Craft Prize finalist

Akiko Hirai makes stoneware for domestic use, as well as individual pieces, including the large, rugged moon jars for which she has become well known. Her work reflects her Japanese cultural inheritance and explores the aesthetics of beauty associated with imperfection.

Akiko Hirai, 'Imperfection and Balance', *CR*, 267 (2014)
The Ceramics Book (2012)
Korean Cultural Centre UK, *Moon Jar: Contemporary Translations in Britain*, exh. cat. (London, 2013)
Adamson, Droth and Olding (2017), pp.178–81
Amber Creswell Bell, *Clay: Contemporary Ceramic Artisans* (London, 2017), pp.10–13
Imogen Greenhalgh, 'Surface Play', *Crafts*, 273 (2018)
Morris (2018), pp.84–7

452 Large moon jar: *Eclipse Night*, 2019 (pl.146)
Stoneware, cherry tree wood-ash glaze, 'landscape inclusions'; h.65cm, d.65cm
C.33-2019. Source: The Scottish Gallery, Edinburgh (solo exhibition: *Under the Cherry Tree*, 2019), £3400; purchase funded by Christopher M. Gorman-Evans

Homoky, Nicholas 1950–

1950	born Sárvár, Hungary
1956	family moves to Manchester, England
1970–73	studies ceramics at Bristol Polytechnic
1973–76	studies ceramics at Royal College of Art, London
1976–79	teaches ceramics at South Glamorgan Institute of Higher Education, Cardiff; studio in Penarth, South Glamorgan
1979–	teaches ceramics at Bristol Polytechnic; establishes studio in Bristol
1981	solo exhibition, Hetjens-Museum, Düsseldorf, Germany
1989–90	teaching exchange to Towson State University, Baltimore, USA
1992–	studio in Backwell, Somerset
1994	solo exhibition, Alpha House Gallery, Sherborne, Dorset
2000–	studio in Yatton, Somerset

Nicholas Homoky gained early acclaim for his elegant bowls and beakers in polished unglazed porcelain with inlaid black decoration. Approaching the vessel primarily as a visual entity, he evolved works as compositions of line and form through the deconstruction and reintegration of images and formal elements. He exchanged porcelain for inlaid red clay for a time from the mid-1980s, and before 1990 introduced abstract figurative sculptures and vessel forms in stoneware with black and white terra-sigillata slips.

Nicholas Homoky, 'Mixing Metaphors', *Crafts*, 52 (1981)
— 'Less is More', *CR*, 146 (1994)
— *Nicholas Homoky* (Marston Magna, 1997)
— 'Understanding Inspiration', *Kerameiki Techni*, 29 (1998)
'CPA New Members', *CR*, 58 (1979)
Lane (1980)
Potters (1980), (1983)
Hetjens-Museum, *Nicholas Homoky*, exh. cat. (Düsseldorf, 1981)
Crafts Council (1985), p.53
Adlin (1998)
Ian Wilson, 'Simply Sophisticated', *Keramik Magazin*, 2 (2003)
Carlano (2010), pp.80–1
Clark, Strauss and others (2012), pp.379, 438

Exhibition reviews: Emmanuel Cooper, *Art & Artists*, 13:1 (1978); Victor Margrie, *Studio Pottery*, 11 (1994); David Whiting, *Crafts*, 132 (1995); Emmanuel Cooper, *CR*, 170 (1998)

453 Pot, 1979
Porcelain, inlaid in black, unglazed; marks: 'NH' in monogram, impressed; h.9.8cm, d.15.8cm
C.119-1979. Source: Casson Gallery, London, £72

454 Handled bowl, 1979
Porcelain, inlaid in black, unglazed; marks: 'NH' in monogram, impressed; h.13.1cm, d.8.9cm
C.120-1979. Source: *see* 453, £76

455 'Coffee Pot', 1980
Porcelain, handbuilt, inlaid in black, unglazed and polished; h.13.5cm, d.12.1cm
C.26&A-1980. Source: Craftsmen Potters Association, London (exhibition with Gordon Baldwin, Ruth and Alan Barrett-Danes, and Peter Simpson, 1980, no.49), £80

453 / 454

455

Hopkins, Alfred George 1884–1940

1884	born Lambeth, London
until 1915	works for Doulton's, Lambeth, as a 'plasterer'
1915–39	teaches pottery classes at Camberwell School of Arts and Crafts
c. 1916–	with his brother, Henry Hopkins, establishes studio in Lambeth Road, London, later moving to Old Lambeth Pottery, Lower Kennington Lane
c. 1932–	moves to Broadstairs, Kent, establishes Stone Pottery

Alfred Hopkins came from a family of potters. Both he and his brother, Henry (1885–1951), worked for Doulton's before together establishing a workshop, making underglaze decorated pottery, supplying ceramic materials and machinery, and firing work by other potters. Moving to the Old Lambeth Pottery, they worked on stoneware and porcelain during the 1920s, and experimented with saltglaze. Alfred became a potter of some note, reputedly the first to ask a price of £100 for a pot –the 'first red salt-glaze porcelain ever produced', shown at the Fine Art Society, London, in 1927.

Arts and Crafts Exhibition Society (1912) to (1926), (1938)
Royal Academy of Arts (1923)
British Institute of Industrial Art (1927)
Ernest Marsh, *The Revival of Salt-glaze Stoneware Pottery*, pamphlet for the Fine Art Society (London, 1927)
Haslam (1984), pp.8, 30
Vincentelli and Hale (1986)
'Alfred George Hopkins', *Mapping the Practice and Profession of Sculpture in Britain and Ireland 1851–1951*, University of Glasgow History of Art and HATII, online database (2011)

Exhibition reviews: 'English Pottery', *The Times* (23 November 1929); 'London Stoneware', *The Times* (17 November 1932); 'London Saltglaze Stoneware', *Manchester Guardian* (3 December 1932)

Alfred Hopkins' correspondence with the collector Sydney Greenslade is in the Ealing Local History Centre, London (NRA 35881 Greenslade). A substantial collection of his pottery is at Aberystwyth University.

456 Dish, 1916
White earthenware, transparent glaze, painted in black, green and crimson enamels; marks: 'A. & H. HOPKINS / 208 LAMBETH RD / LONDON

456

457 / 458

SE', impressed, '1916', incised; d.30.5cm
C.61-1972. Source: T. Stainton, Beaconsfield, Bucks, £16.50
Made in partnership with Henry Hopkins.

457 Pot, 1927
Stoneware, saltglaze over mottled yellow-brown glaze; marks: 'A G Hopkins / Lambeth / 1927 / 3', incised; h.11cm, d.13.2cm
Circ.354-1958. Source: George Wingfield Digby, London, £1.15s. (with **458**)

458 Bowl, 1927
Stoneware, saltglaze over mottled yellow-brown glaze; marks: 'A G Hopkins Lambeth 1927', incised; h.6.4cm, d.16.7cm
Circ.355-1958. Source: *see* **457**

459 Jug, 1927
Stoneware, brown saltglaze; marks: '1927 / A G Hopkins', incised, and 'A G Hopkins LAMBETH', impressed; h.12cm, d.16.9cm

459

460 / 462 / 461

C.488-1934. Source: British Institute of Industrial Art (given by the artist)

460 Pot, 1927
Stoneware, saltglaze over bubbled muddy-green glaze; marks: '192? [probably "7"] A G Hopkins', incised; h.11.7cm, d.18.6cm
C.474-1927. Source: given by a group who attended lectures on modern pottery given at the V&A
Bernard Rackham, Keeper of the Ceramics Department, notes: 'This jar is an important piece of the stoneware being made by Alfred G. Hopkins at Lambeth and illustrates his limitations as an artist (apart from his skill in technique) as compared with such masters of present day pottery as W.S. Murray and B. Leach. ... The vase will be useful as a record specimen.'

461 Pot, 1931
Stoneware, mottled brown glaze; marks: 'A G Hopkins/I/Lambeth', incised; h.11.5cm, d.12cm
C.2-1933. Source: given by Miss A.J. Tufnell, London
Bought by the donor at the Fine Art Society, London, in December 1932. Described by the maker: 'Sea warm shell quality; madripore form: softened latitudinal ribs.' Bernard Rackham notes: 'He is not one of our best potters and much of his work is in my opinion bad, but the white pot ... is interesting as a revival of white salt glaze ware and the little pot which I picked out ... may serve to show Mr. Hopkins the direction he should take if he is to improve his output.'

462 Vase, 1931
Porcelain, saltglaze; marks: 'A G Hopkins/ Lambeth', incised, and '1931', painted; h.26.5cm, d.11.2cm
C.3-1933. Source: *see* **461**
Described by the maker: 'White saltglaze porcelain vase, translucent. Lily form; pitted.'

Hosono, Hitomi 1978–

1978	born Gifu Prefecture, Japan
1998–2002	studies ceramics at Kanazawa College of Art, Japan
2005–06	studies ceramic design at Danmarks Designskole, Copenhagen
2007–09	studies ceramics at Royal College of Art, London
2009–	studio in London; represented by Adrian Sassoon, London
2013	wins Perrier-Jouët Arts Salon Prize
2014	awarded Jerwood Makers Open commission
2017	solo exhibition, Daiwa Anglo-Japanese Foundation, London
2017–	artist-in-residence, Wedgwood, Stoke-on-Trent

Hitomi Hosono is known for her exquisite, botanically inspired porcelain vessels, each built up with hundreds of press-moulded 'sprigs' – ornament traditionally applied as relief decoration. The original sprig models follow close observation of the texture and structure of leaves and flowers, and each moulded sprig is carved with finer detail before being applied to an underlying thrown form.

Hitomi Hosono, 'Potters on Pots', *CR*, 295 (2019)
Caroline Clifton-Mogg, 'Hitomi Hosono', *House & Garden* (December 2012)
Kimberley Chandler, 'Caught in the Act', *CR*, 265 (2014)

463

Jerwood Visual Arts, *Jerwood Makers Open*, exh. cat. (London, 2014)
Teleri Lloyd-Jones, 'Take Five', *Crafts*, 249 (2014)
Dominique Corlett, 'The Delicate Touch', interview, *Homes & Antiques* (September 2015)
Grant Gibson, 'Art and Industry', *Crafts*, 274 (2018)
Tom Loxley, 'The Fossil Hunter', *Rakesprogress*, 7 (2018)
Morris (2018), pp.226–31
Scottish Gallery, *A Natural Selection*, exh. cat. (Edinburgh, 2019)

A short film, *Hosono Hitomi: Making Beauty*, was made by the British Museum, London, in 2017.

463 *Large Leaves Bowl*, 2010
Porcelain, moulded, carved and handbuilt, unglazed; h.26cm, d.30cm
FE.35-2010. Source: Adrian Sassoon at Collect 2010, £2750; purchase funded by the Friends of the V&A

The museum also holds a plate decorated with a pattern by Hitomi Hosono (C.141-2012), not catalogued here.

Hoy, Agnete (**Anita**) (née Blichfeldt) 1914–2000

1914	born Southall, London, of Danish parents
1921–	returns to Denmark following her father's death
1933–36	studies ceramics at Copenhagen School of Arts and Crafts
1937–39	works with Gerhard Nielsen at Holbaek pottery, then with Nathalie Krebs at Saxbo pottery, Herlev
1939	visits UK; outbreak of war prevents return to Denmark
1940–52	heads studio department at Bullers, Stoke-on-Trent; studio closes
1952–56	heads studio department at Royal Doulton, Lambeth, London, designing salt-glazed stoneware
1957–85	establishes own studio in Acton, London
1961–80	teaches at Hammersmith College of Art
1961–83	teaches at West Surrey College of Art and Design, Farnham

Agnete Hoy forms a bridge between industry and the studio potter. At Bullers – manufacturers of porcelain insulators – she ran a small workshop along studio lines within an industrial setting, a model of production more often associated with Scandinavia. The establishment of her own workshop followed the closure in 1956 of Doulton's Lambeth factory, after which she worked alone, producing mainly individual pieces in earthenware, stoneware and porcelain.

Agnete Hoy, 'Art Among the Insulators', *CR*, 69 (1981)
'An Adventure in Porcelain', *Pottery and Glass* (August 1947)
'The Work of Agnete Hoy', *Pottery Gazette and Glass Trade Review* (July 1952)
'New Stoneware from Lambeth', *Royal Doulton Magazine* (June 1953)
Arts and Crafts Exhibition Society (1957)
Biographical notes, *Pottery Quarterly*, 8:30 (1963), p.6, pl.20
Casson (1967), p.7, pls.130–1
Potters (1972) to (1997)
Crafts Advisory Committee (1976), p.100
Gladstone Pottery Museum, *Art Among the Insulators: the Bullers Studio 1932–52*, exh. cat. (1977)
Cheryl Buckley, *Potters and Paintresses: Women Designers in the Pottery Industry* (London, 1990), pp.143–8
Riddick (1990), p.51
Gaze (1997), pp.713–14
Emmanuel Cooper, obituary, *The Independent* (14 April 2000)
Desmond Eyles and Louise Irvine, *The Doulton Lambeth Wares* (Shepton Beauchamp, 2002)
Susan Taylor, *Bullers of Milton* (Leek, 2003)

An interview with Agnete Hoy is in the Recording the Crafts video archive at UWE Bristol (also held in the National Art Library, V&A, London, 704.AA.0025 to 704.AA.0029).

464 Bowl, 1960
Porcelain, 'wet on wet' slip decoration in green and pink; marks: 'Agnete / Hoy', incised; h.4.7cm, d.13.5cm
C.262-1983. Source: the artist, £50

464

The museum also holds pieces made by Agnete Hoy at Bullers (C.255 to 263-1983) and designed by her at Doulton (Circ.842 to 844-1956), not catalogued here.

Hughes, Amy Jayne 1985–

1985	born Dewsbury, West Yorkshire
2004–07	studies ceramics at Loughborough University
2008–10	studies ceramics at Royal College of Art, London
2010–	founding member, Studio Manifold, Haggerston, London
2015	ceramics and industry residency, V&A, in collaboration with 1882 Ltd; shortlisted for British Ceramics Biennial AWARD
2018–19	solo exhibition, *Garniture*, Croome Court, Worcestershire

Amy Jayne Hughes works in response to historic ceramics, reinterpreting 18th-century vases for a contemporary audience. A handbuilder and talented illustrator, she explores the relationship between form and decoration, capturing in her vessels the freedom and spontaneity of her drawing.

Amy Jayne Hughes, 'A Potter's Day', *CR*, 255 (2012)
Bornholm Art Museum, *European Ceramic Context 2014: New Talent*, exh. cat. (Gudhjem, 2014), pp.98–9
Olivier Dupon, *Encore! The New Artisans* (London, 2015), pp.12–15
Edith Garcia, 'Collectives: The Model for Success', *Ceramics Monthly* (March 2020)
Annie Le Santo, 'Modern Decadence', *CR*, 309 (2021)

465 Vase: *Tryst*, 2015
Bone china, slip-cast, painted in blue; marks:

465

'Amy Hughes/Tryst/Made in England', and '1882' and 'V&A' logos, printed in black; h.37cm, d.19cm
C.26-2016. Source: 1882 Ltd, £720; acquired through the generosity of Gerard and Sarah Griffin
Developed during her V&A residency, *Tryst* was designed by Hughes, who enhanced the original model for an edition of slip-cast vases using applied reliefs moulded from historic objects in the museum. The vases were made in Stoke-on-Trent by 1882 Ltd, and freely decorated according to Hughes' instruction, resulting in a series of individualized objects.

Hughes, Edward 1953–2006

1953	born Wallasey, Cheshire
1973–76	studies ceramics at Bath Academy of Art
1975	works briefly at Winchcombe Pottery, Gloucestershire
1977–79	scholarship to study ceramics at Kyoto City University of Arts, Japan
1979–	first solo exhibition at Azuchi Gallery, Osaka; establishes workshop in Shiga, Japan
1984	returns to England
1985–89	workshop at Renwick, Cumbria
1989–	workshop at Isel, Cumbria
2000	awarded full membership of arts association Kokugakai, Tokyo; solo exhibition at Brantwood, Cumbria

Edward Hughes was an accomplished potter whose work drew upon East Asian stoneware traditions and the vitality of English slipware. His reduction-fired stoneware and porcelain, often slip-decorated, shows admirable clarity of design and great subtlety in glaze effects. Hughes enjoyed much success in Japan, where he first became established and continued to exhibit following his return to England. His tragic death while mountaineering cut short his career at a time of great creativity.

Potters (1997)
Wheeler (1998), pp.36, 80, 157
Christian Dymond, 'Fiery Art', *Cumbria Life* (June 1999)
Alex McErlain, 'Putting Life in Clay', *CR*, 197 (2002)
Stephanie Boydell, Shizuko Hughes and Alex McErlain, *A Japanese Passion: The Pottery of Edward Hughes* (2012)
James Hake, 'Potters on Pots', *CR*, 294 (2018)

Exhibition reviews: Emmanuel Cooper, *CR*, 169 (1998); David Whiting, *Crafts*, 160 (1999); Liz Mitchell, *CR*, 244 (2010)

Obituaries: Emmanuel Cooper, *The Independent* (21 April 2006); *The Times* (29 April 2006); David Whiting, *Crafts*, 201 (2006)

466

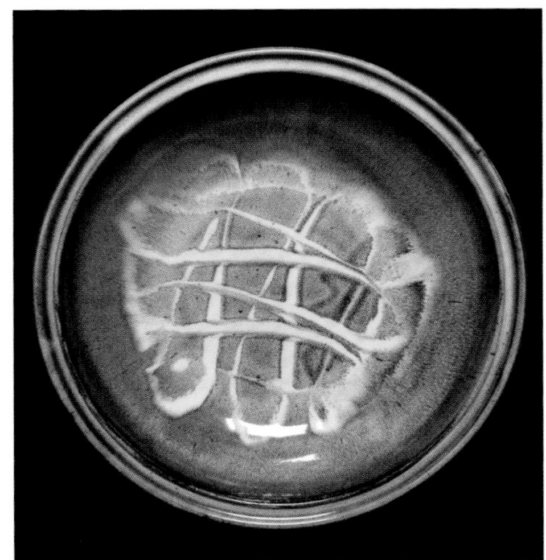

467

466 Lidded jar, 1999
Stoneware, oatmeal wood-ash glaze exterior, tenmoku interior; marks: 'EH' in monogram, impressed; h.24.4cm, d.17.8cm
C.123:1,2-1999. Source: given by Alan P. Sainer (from solo exhibition, Paul Rice Gallery, London, 1999)

467 Charger, 2001
Stoneware, ash glaze with slip-trailed decoration; marks: 'EH' seal, impressed; h.10.3cm, d.50cm
C.20-2005. Source: Joanna Bird Pottery, £1800
Made for the exhibition *The Japanese Craft Tradition: Kokten Korgei* at Blackwell, Cumbria, 2001. The 'hare's fur' glaze is derived from locally sourced wood ash, from Red How.

Illsley, Bryan 1937–

1937	born Surbiton, Surrey
1953	apprentice stonemason
1954–57	attends evening classes at Kingston School of Art
1963–	moves to St Ives, Cornwall
1964–66	works part-time at the Leach Pottery; makes roughly improvised slabbed clay vessels and first wooden sculptures
1966–82	works with Breon O'Casey, making jewellery
1978	makes first iron sculptures
1986–	moves to London
1989–	resumes occasional work in clay; establishes studio in Stamford Hill
2005|10|14	solo exhibitions (including ceramics), Barrett Marsden (later Marsden Woo) Gallery, London

Bryan Illsley's diverse practice encompasses jewellery, painting and sculpure in wood, iron and clay. His mature work in clay, strongly abstract but often with figurative allusions, followed his move to London, where he works in a studio adjacent to that of Alison Britton (qv).

Crafts Council, *Bryan Illsley: Work in Wood, Metal and Paint*, exh. cat., text by Janet Leach (London, 1984)
Contemporary Applied Arts, *Bryan Illsley: Souvenirs from St Ives*, exh. pamphlet, text by Alison Britton (London, 1988), reprinted in Britton (2013), pp.53–5
— *Clay Bodies*, exh. pamphlet, text by Alison Britton (London, 1989)
Museum of Modern Art, Oxford (1993), pp.50–1, 87, 94
Crafts Council (1995b), pp.38–9

468

David Whiting, 'Sources of Inspiration', *Crafts*, 144 (1997)
Emma Maiden, exh. review, *CR*, 243 (2010)

468 *Punk*, 1989
Earthenware, handbuilt, largely unglazed; marks: 'B.I.1989', painted; h.97cm, d.33cm
C.185:1 to 4-1991. Source: the artist, £1000
Shown in the group exhibition *Clay Bodies*, Contemporary Applied Arts, London, 1989.

See also **101** *under* Alison Britton.

Ions, Neil 1949–

1949	born Newcastle-under-Lyme, Staffordshire
1969–72	studies sculpture at Newport College of Art, South Wales
1972–75	studies ceramics at Royal College of Art, London
1975–81	founder member of Fosseway House Workshops, Stow-on-the-Wold, Gloucestershire
1981–91	establishes Kitebrook Workshop, Oxfordshire
1991–96	workshop in Little Compton, Warwickshire
1997–	workshop in Chastleton, Oxfordshire

Neil Ions is known for his sculptural pottery forms and animal figures, and in particular his clay wind instruments, made in earthenware with painted slip decoration. His work draws inspiration from the natural world, from music and from Native American ceramics.

469

470

Neil Ions, 'Ocarinas and Flutes', *Artists Newsletter* (September 1984)
— 'Playing with Clay', *CR*, 90 (1984)
Houston (1979), pp.158–61
'CPA New Members', *CR*, 66 (1980)
Potters (1980) to (1989)
Gibson (1987), pp.42–9
Wren (1990), pp.70–1

469 Pair of ocarinas in the form of birds, 1980
Earthenware, press-moulded and handbuilt, painted in coloured slips and burnished; marks: 'Neil Ions', incised; h.10.3cm, d.19cm
C.42&A-1980. Source: Craftsmen Potters Association, London, £25.20

470 Vase: *Let Me Take You Down*, 1982
Earthenware, handbuilt, painted in coloured slips and burnished; marks: 'Neil Ions 1982', painted; h.43.2cm, d.18.7cm
C.73-1984. Source: given by the Friends of the V&A (purchased at the Craftsmen Potters Association exhibition, *Studio Ceramics Today*, V&A, 1983, no.85, £90)

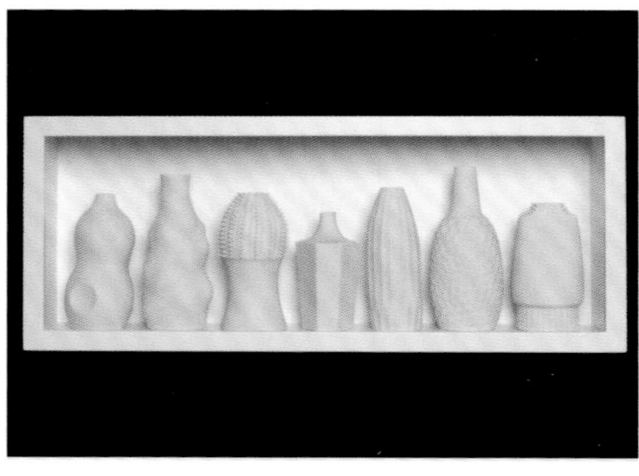

471

Iwamoto, Ikuko 1971–

1971	born Wakayama, Japan
1990–93	studies ceramics at Tezukayama College, Nara, Japan
1993–2000	teaches ceramics in Osaka and Nara, Japan
2002–04	studies ceramics at Camberwell College of Arts
2004–06	studies ceramics at Royal College of Art, London
2006–	sets up studio at Craft Central, Clerkenwell, London
2009	winner of Ceramic Review Prize for Innovation at Ceramic Art London
2013	solo exhibition, Snug Gallery, Hebden Bridge, West Yorkshire
2014–15	*A Common Ground*, exhibition with Junko Mori and Kayo Saito, Touchstones Rochdale, Lancashire
2017–	studio at The Chocolate Factory, Hackney, London

Ikuko Iwamoto makes quirky, tactile – or aggressively spiky – tableware, sculptural objects and framed assemblages in slip-cast porcelain with applied surface details. Her work draws upon nature, in particular the seemingly fantastical forms observed by microscopy.

Nicolette Loizou, 'Organised Chaos', *CR*, 242 (2010)
Olivier Dupon, *The New Artisans* (London, 2011), pp.104–5
The Ceramics Book (2012)
'Rising Stars of the CPA', *CR*, 293 (2018)

471 *Seven B*, 2012
Seven porcelain vessels, slip-cast, with additions, glazed wooden frame; marks: 'Seven B 1/7 Ikuko Iwamoto', pencilled; h.21cm, d.52cm
C.134-2013. Source: Contemporary Ceramics Centre at Collect 2013, £901.60; purchase funded by the Friends of the V&A

Jupp, Mo (Maurice) 1938–2018

1938	born Clapham, London
1960–64	studies at Camberwell School of Art and Crafts
1964–67	studies ceramics at Royal College of Art, London
1968	solo exhibition, Crafts Centre of Great Britain, London; exhibits widely thereafter
1968–2003	teaches variously at Harrow School of Art, West Surrey College of Art and Design, Hornsey College of Arts and Crafts, Bristol Polytechnic, Bath Academy of Art, Middlesex Polytechnic and Cardiff Institute of Higher Education
1972–76	workshop at Fawkham, Kent
1976–78	renovates Upper Tump Farm, English Bicknor, Gloucestershire
1978–82	workshop at Soilwell Manor, Lydney, Gloucestershire
1982–87	workshop at Symonds Yat, Herefordshire
1987–98	workshop in Bermondsey, London
1998–2011	workshop at Archway Ceramics, Limehouse, London
2011–	moves to France

Mo Jupp was an innovative and maverick ceramic sculptor. He is best known for his helmets, first made in the early 1970s after he inadvertently strayed onto the racetrack at Brands Hatch, Kent, and his long-term exploration of the female form, work that reflects the male gaze. Jupp was noted for his dextrous handling of clay, and used a range of ceramic materials and processes. On occasion he was wildly experimental, as in his series of temples housing silver genitalia, adorned with wire, feathers and beads. Generous and irreverent, Jupp was an inspirational teacher, his desire to give something back leading him to teach at numerous art colleges, where he also made work.

Mo Jupp, interview, in Cameron and Lewis (1976), pp.78–83, 166
— 'Solving Problems', *CR*, 109 (1988)
— 'Revelations', *CR*, 180 (1999)
'Evening Meeting: Training the Potter', transcript (Jupp erroneously named 'Judd'), in Craftsmen Potters Association (1966), pp.27–30
Decorative Art (1968/69), (1973/74)
Grabowski Gallery, *Pamela Hutchinson, Mo Jupp, Heather Leslie*, exh. pamphlet (London, 1969)
V&A (1972), p.111
Fiona Adamczewski, 'Maverick Potter', *CR*, 28 (1974)
Oxford Gallery (1974)
Crafts Advisory Committee (1976), p.100
Crafts Council (1980), p.59
— (1985), p.54
Contemporary Applied Arts, *Mo Jupp: Sculptor*, exh. pamphlet, text by Victor Margrie (London, 1988)
Tanya Harrod, 'Mo Jupp: New Work', *Crafts*, 91 (1988)
Wren (1990), pp.64–5
Galerie Besson, *Mo Jupp*, exh. pamphlet (London, 1992)
Crafts Council (1995b), pp.40–1
Peter's Barn Gallery, *Mo Jupp*, exh. cat. (Midhurst, 1997)
Hannah Wingrave, 'Mo Jupp', *Ceramics in Society*, 43 (2001)

472 / 473

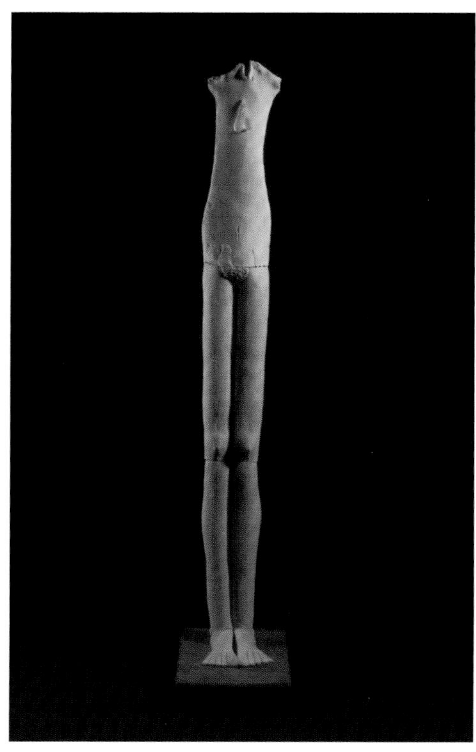

475

Perryman (2004), pp.48–54
Ruthin Craft Centre (2006), pp.48–51, 77
Where I Fell in Love Gallery, *Mo Jupp: 70th Birthday Celebration Show* (Shipston-on-Stour, 2008)
Oxford Ceramics Gallery, *Mo Jupp*, exh. pamphlet, text by David Whiting (London, 2013)
James Campbell, obituary, *Crafts*, 275 (2018)

Exhibition reviews: Anthony Hepburn, *Craft Horizons*, 29 (May 1969); J.D.H. Catleugh, 'Ten British Potters', *CR*, 17 (1972); Oliver Watson, *Crafts*, 116 (1992); Shane Enright, *Studio Pottery*, 3 (1993); David Jones, *CR*, 163 (1997); David Whiting, *Crafts*, 149 (1997); Jane Perryman, *CR*, 172 (1998); Nicholas Lees, *CR*, 193 (2002); Matthew Partington, *CR*, 205 (2004)

An interview with Mo Jupp is in the Crafts Lives sound archive at the British Library, London (C960/51).

472 'Small Pot on Pedestal', 1969
Stoneware, thrown in sections, white glaze, silver enamel; h.20.2cm, d.11.5cm
Circ.540-1969. Source: Primavera, London (group exhibition: *Craft Comprehensive 1 – Ceramics*, 1969, no.76), £9.9s.

473 'Small Pot on Pedestal', 1969
Stoneware, thrown in sections, white glaze, silver enamel; h.24.6cm, d.11.6cm
Circ.541-1969. Source: *see* **472** (no.77), £9.9s.

474 Helmet, 1972 (pl.64)
Stoneware, press-moulded, with black and white and green surface; h.23.9cm, d.29cm
Circ.290-1973. Source: the artist, £25

475 Figure, 1987–88
Low-fired porcelain, handbuilt, constructed from sections; h.108.6cm, d.33.4cm
C.41-1989. Source: Contemporary Applied Arts, London (solo exhibition, 1988), £1620

Kalan, Stephanie 1909–1978

1909	born Austria
1953–	establishes pottery workshop in Mitcham, Surrey
1962	exhibition with Anton Kalan at Cooling Galleries, London
1962–	moves to Newport, Essex, re-establishes workshop

Stephanie Kalan came to England as an émigré with her husband, Anton Kalan, before the Second World War. She turned to pottery after the war,

477 / 476

478

479

and together with Anton established a pottery studio where they worked alongside one another, signing their own work. Stephanie Kalan specialized in glazes, for which she carried out extensive research. She is notable for developing a crystalline glaze, of which the two items in the museum were acquired as examples. Her work was retailed by Liberty, London.

Stephanie Kalan, glaze recipes, *Pottery Quarterly*, 6:22 (1959), p.68, correction, 6:23 (1959), p.101
— notes on copper-red glazes, *CR*, 29 (1974)
— 'Chrome-tin Pink and Red Glazes', *CR*, 47 (1977)
— 'Matt Glazes', *CR*, 50 (1978)
Arts and Crafts Exhibition Society (1957)

476 Bowl, 1966
Stoneware, crystalline glaze; marks: 'S KALAN', incised; h.8.6cm, d.16.5cm
Circ.1219-1967. Source: given by the artist

477 Pot, 1966
Stoneware, crystalline glaze; marks: 'S KALAN', incised; h.11.4cm, d.10.9cm
Circ.1220-1967. Source: *see* 476

Kalindjian, Sona 1934–

1934	born Cyprus
1958	moves to UK
1969–73	studies at Hornsey College of Art, London
1973–79	teaches at Loughton College of Further Education
1974–	establishes workshop in Chiswick, London
1997–	moves workshop to Ford, Northumberland

Working under the name Chiswick Ceramics, Sona Kalindjian specialized in tile murals, sculptural tableware and commemorative wares, mostly slip-cast with painted or screen-print decoration.

Sona Kalindjian, letter, *CR*, 24 (1973)
J.D.H. Catleugh, 'Teapots', exh. review, *CR*, 31 (1975)
Editorial notice, *CR*, 39 (1976)

478 Tea set, 1979
Earthenware, slip-cast, with enamel decoration screen-printed in blue and red; marks: 'SK 79', painted, and 'Sona Kalindjian', incised; made at Chiswick Ceramics, London; h.26.6cm, d.22.7cm (teapot)
C.3 to D-1980. Source: the artist, £49

The museum also holds a slip-cast jewellery box in the form of Chiswick House, London, made for sale in the shop (C.4&A-1980).

Kattah, Mawuena 1975–

1975	born London
2007–	joins London collective and studio Intoart
2015–16	residency at V&A and at Studio Manifold, London, working with ceramicist Matthew Raw to develop ceramic works
2016	solo exhibition, Tenderbooks, London

Mawuena Kattah's practice encompasses paintings, prints, ceramics and textiles. Reflecting kinship and her love of pattern and colour, her exuberant work draws upon family photographs taken in Ghana and London. Kattah is a member of Intoart, a creative studio in London that works with artists with learning disabilities.

The Studio Project: Opening Art Practice (London: Intoart, 2007)
Whitechapel Gallery, *Intoart: See the Revolutionary Art Exhibit*, exh. cat. (London, 2009)
Michele Hanson, 'In a World of Fear and Loathing, We Need Art More than Ever', *The Guardian* (27 June 2016)
Mawuena Kattah: Ceramics, Textiles and Works on Paper (London: Intoart, 2016)
Imogen Greenhalgh, 'Breaking Down Barriers', *Crafts*, 272 (2018)
Yinka Shonibare, *Criminal Ornamentation*, exh. cat. (London: Hayward Publishing, 2018)
Isabella Smith, 'Signature Dishes', *Crafts*, 290 (2021)

A film, *Mawuena Kattah: Ceramics, Textiles and Works on Paper*, was made by Intoart in 2016.

479 Tile panel in nine sections: *Auntie, Mum and Me Talking About My Fabric Collection*, 2016
Glazed ceramic tiles, painted in colours; h.125cm, w.165cm
C.30:1 to 9-2020. Source: Intoart at Collect 2020, £6400

Keegan, Steven 1965–

1965	born Coventry, Warwickshire
1985–88	studies at Wolverhampton Polytechnic
1988–90	studies ceramics at Royal College of Art, London
1990	residency with The Grizedale Society, Cumbria
1991–2019	teaches at North Wales School of Art and Design, North East Wales Institute of Higher Education, Wrexham (later Wrexham Glyndŵr University)
1999–2008	visiting lecturer, Wetterhoff School of Art, HAMK University, Finland
1999–	studio in Cerrigydrudion, Conwy

Steven Keegan concentrated on figurative ceramics, notably animals, and had a particular

480

interest in raku. He later extended his practice to include photography.

Paul Greenhalgh, 'The Critic's Eye', *Crafts*, 113 (1991)

Exhibition reviews: Emmanuel Cooper, *Crafts*, 113 (1991); Robert S. Silver, '300 Tonnes of Clay', *Studio Pottery*, 27 (1997)

480 *Newby the Dog*, 1991
Earthenware, handbuilt, raku-fired, with stone base; h.41cm, d.23.5cm
C.196:1,2-1991. Source: Black Bull Gallery, London (exhibition: *Steven Keegan, Laurance Simon, Carole Windham*, 1991), £264.37

Keeler, Walter 1942–

1942	born Edgware, Middlesex
1958–63	studies ceramics at Harrow School of Art
1963	teacher training at Hornsey College of Art
1964	marries fellow potter Madoline Cansfield
1964–78	teaches at Harrow School of Art, where runs kiln site
1965–76	studio at Bledlow Ridge, Buckinghamshire
1976–	studio at Penallt, Monmouth, Gwent
1978–2002	teaches at Bristol Polytechnic; appointed Professor, 1998
2004–05	touring solo exhibition, The City Gallery, Leicester

Walter Keeler is one of the most consistently inventive potters. Based on the domestic forms of teapot, jug, dish and jar, and never departing from the possibility of function, his work shows a crisp precision in design and fluency in making, coupled with a striking and sometimes playful sculptural vision. He is best known for his work in salt-glazed stoneware, his thrown, altered and assembled forms often evoking objects made from plate metal. Since the mid-1990s he has developed a parallel strand of earthenware with coloured glazes, originally inspired by early industrial pottery, in particular Whieldon-type Staffordshire wares.

Walter Keeler, 'Young Potters Reply', *Pottery Quarterly*, 9:33 (1967), pp.19, 28–9
— 'Raku', *CR*, 1 (1970)
— 'Innovating Function', interview, *Studio Potter*, 19:2 (1991)
— interview, *Studio Pottery*, 14 (1995)
— interview by Martina Margetts, in Crafts Council (1996c), pp.22–5, see also pp.84, 135
— 'An Abstract Art', *CR*, 197 (2002)
— 'What If ...', *CR*, 227 (2007)
— 'Masterclass', *CR*, 294 (2018)
Potters/The Ceramics Book (1972) to (2012)
V&A (1972), p.111
Rosemary Wren and Peter Crotty, 'Walter Keeler', *CR*, 18 (1972)
Crafts Advisory Committee (1976), p.101
— 'Meet the Craftsmen: Walter Keeler', leaflet (London, 1976)
— (1977), p.14
Crafts Council (1980), p.59
Isabelle Anscombe, 'Put It on the Table', *Crafts*, 56 (1982)
Michael Casson, 'Creative Potter', *CR*, 77 (1982)
Cheryl McLean, 'Walter Keeler', *Ceramics Monthly*, 31:7 (1983)
David Briers, *Walter Keeler*, Aberystwyth Arts Centre: Ceramic Series 6 (1985)
Crafts Council (1985), pp.55–7
ICA (1985), p.43
Colin Voake, 'Salt of the Earth', *Crafts*, 81 (1986)
David Briers, 'Serious but not Solemn', *CR*, 112 (1988)
'Walter Keeler – Making a Lidded Jar', *CR*, 113 (1988)
Contemporary Applied Arts, *Walter Keeler*, exh. pamphlet, text by Alison Britton (London, 1989), reprinted in Britton (2013), pp.74–7
Emmanuel Cooper, 'Sources of Inspiration', *Crafts*, 101 (1989)
Tanya Harrod, 'Innovation and Function: Walter Keeler', in Northern Centre for Contemporary Art (1989), pp.70–3
Jeanne Kart, 'Walter Keeler Workshop', *Ceramics Monthly*, 37:9 (1989)
Aberystwyth (1990), supplement, p.7
Cooper (1990)
Emmanuel Cooper, 'The Grammar of Clay', *CR*, 152 (1995)
Rufford Craft Centre, *Walter Keeler*, exh. pamphlet (Nottinghamshire, 1995)
Contemporary Applied Arts, *Walter Keeler*, exh. pamphlet, text by Tanya Harrod (London, 1999)
Crafts Council (1999b), pp.34–7
Nicholas Lees, 'A Sense of Proportion', *CR*, 179 (1999)
Peter Saunders, 'Walter Keeler's New Challenge', *Ceramics: Art and Perception*, 35 (1999)
Cochrane (2001), pp.57–9
Crafts Council (2001), pp.20–1, 31
Rogers (2002), pp.162–6
Matthew Partington, 'The Whieldon-inspired Earthenwares of Walter Keeler', in Tom Walford and Hilary Young (eds), *British Ceramic Design 1600–2002* (Beckenham, 2003), pp.145–52
Emmanuel Cooper and Amanda Fielding, *Walter Keeler* (Ruthin, 2004)
Ruthin Craft Centre (2004), pp.46–9, 69
— (2006), pp.52–5, 78
Whiting (2009), pp.56–61
Carlano (2010), pp.84–5
Clark, Strauss and others (2012), pp.382, 440
Oxford Ceramics Gallery, *Walter Keeler*, exh. pamphlet (Oxford, 2013)
Philip Hughes, 'Walter Keeler', *Craft Arts International*, 92 (2014)
Goldmark Gallery, *Walter Keeler: Treasures of the Everyday*, exh. cat., text by Teleri Lloyd-Jones (Uppingham, 2017) – an accompanying documentary was released on DVD
Nottingham City Museums and Galleries (2017), p.53
Who's Who 2020 (2019)

Exhibition reviews: Audrey Blackman, *CR*, 5 (1970); Jerome Abbo, *CR*, 17 (1972); W.A. Ismay, *Crafts*, 49 (1981); Tony Birks, *Crafts*, 59 (1982); Peter Dormer, *Crafts*, 103 (1990); Peter Inch, *Studio Pottery*, 6 (1993); David Briers, *Crafts*, 135 (1995); Stephen Woodruff, *CR*, 166 (1997); Alison Britton, *Crafts*, 161 (1999); David Whiting, *Crafts*, 189 (2004); Teleri Lloyd-Jones, *Crafts*, 263 (2016)

An interview with Walter Keeler is in the Crafts Lives sound archive at the British Library, London (C960/27).

481 'Small jug with shimmied base', 1982
Stoneware, brown saltglaze with blue-grey interior; marks: circular device, impressed; h.21cm, d.16.5cm
C.109-1982. Source: Craftsmen Potters Association, London (solo exhibition, 1982, no.81), £19.35

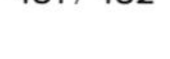

481 / 482

485

488

483

487

489

482 Mug, 1982
Stoneware, brown saltglaze with blue-grey interior; marks: circular device, impressed; h.9.6cm, d.12.3cm
C.108-1982. Source: *see* **481** (no.90), £6.45

483 'Large dish with pulled handles', 1982
Stoneware, brown saltglaze with blue-grey glaze interior; marks: 'WK' and a circular device, impressed; h.8.3cm, d.41cm
C.111-1982. Source: *see* **481** (no.175), £64.50

484 'Angular teapot', 1982 (pl.81)
Stoneware, brown saltglaze; marks: circular device, impressed; h.19.5cm, d.20cm
C.110&A-1982. Source: *see* **481** (no.207), £103.20

485 Carafe, 1982
Stoneware, blue saltglaze; marks: circular device, impressed; h.24.8cm, d.13.6cm
C.74-1984. Source: given by the Friends of the V&A (purchased at the Craftsmen Potters Association exhibition, *Studio Ceramics Today*, V&A, 1983, no.95, £86)

486 Teapot, 1984 (pl.81)
Stoneware, grey-brown saltglaze; marks: circular device, impressed; h.10.7cm, d.26cm
C.153-1984. Source: British Crafts Centre, London (exhibition: *8 Ceramicists*, 1984, no.38), £63.45

487 'Cache Pot', 1984
Stoneware, blue-grey saltglaze; marks: circular device, impressed; h.19.6cm, d.22.6cm
C.154-1984. Source: *see* **486** (no.42), £36.22

488 Jug, 1992
Stoneware, thrown and constructed, blue saltglaze with brown interior; marks: circular device, impressed; h.25.6cm, d.27cm
C.104-1992. Source: the artist, £300

489 Lidded jar, 1995
Stoneware, blue saltglaze; marks: circular device, impressed; h.27.1cm, d.16.4cm
C.73:1,2-1995. Source: Rufford Craft Centre, Nottinghamshire (solo exhibition, 1995), £135

490 *Toast Machine*, 1998
Earthenware, green and yellow glazes; marks: circular device, applied; h.14.8cm, d.15.6cm
C.16-1999. Source: the artist, £200; purchase funded by the Friends of the V&A
Shown in the University of the West of England student and staff exhibition, *Melt Down*, V&A, 1998.

491 Teapot, 1999
Earthenware, black and yellow glazes; marks:

circular device, applied; h.22.5cm, d.17.9cm
C.15-1999. Source: the artist, £230; gift of Adrian Sassoon, Esq.

492 'Cut branch dish', 2005 (pl.114)
Earthenware, grey-green and yellow glazes; marks: circular device, applied; h.28.2cm, d.52cm
C.141-2006. Source: Contemporary Ceramics at Collect 2006; gift of Nicholas and Judith Goodison through Art Fund

493 'Articulated jug', 2009
Stoneware, thrown and constructed, blue saltglaze; marks: circular device, applied; h.38.1cm, d.20.7cm
C.30-2009. Source: the artist, £500; acquired through the generosity of Gerard and Sarah Griffin

490 / 491

493 / 494 / 495

494 'Extruded jug with branches', 2014
Earthenware, extruded, green, black and yellow glazes; marks: circular device, applied; h.34.7cm, d.25.8cm
C.241-2014. Source: Ruthin Craft Centre at Collect 2014, £1184.40; purchase funded by the Friends of the V&A

495 'Extruded jug', 2015
Stoneware, extruded, blue saltglaze; marks: circular device, applied; h.50.8cm, d.25.3cm
C.67-2015. Source: Contemporary Ceramics Centre, London (solo exhibition, 2015), £1486.75; acquired through the generosity of Gerard and Sarah Griffin

---

Keenan, Chris 1960–

1960	born Gillingham, Kent
1978–81	studies drama at University of Hull
1982–95	works as professional actor
1995–97	apprenticed to Edmund de Waal (qv)
1998–	establishes own studio in Camberwell, London, shared with Georgina Frankel from 1999 to 2003, then Carina Ciscato (qv)
2001–	regular solo exhibitions, including at Beaux Arts, Bath (from 2004), and New Craftsman Gallery, St Ives (from 2012)
2014	residency at Mashiko Museum of Ceramic Art, Tochigi, Japan
2016	solo exhibition, *houseplace*, Blackwell, The Arts and Crafts House, Cumbria

Chris Keenan is perhaps the most accomplished maker of domestic porcelain to emerge in the 21st century. His work is refined, yet practical, with a certain playfulness. The first apprentice of Edmund de Waal – whose domestic porcelain provided an example – Keenan has developed his own distinctive range of unfussy shapes, complemented by celadon and tenmoku glazes and simple graphic decoration.

Chris Keenan, 'Artist and Industry', *CR*, 236 (2009)
— 'From There to Here', *CR*, 268 (2014)
— 'The Shape of Things to Come', *CR*, 281 (2016)
— 'Potter's Secrets', *CR*, 311 (2021)
Potters/The Ceramics Book (2000) to (2012)
Amanda Fielding, 'Classic Concerns', *CR*, 186 (2000)
Crafts Council (2003), pp.49–52
Harriet Smith, 'First Service', *Crafts*, 201 (2006)
Heidi Yeo, '60|40 Starting Point Series 2010: Linda Florence, David Gates, Chris Keenan', *Craft Research*, 2:1 (2011)
Oxford Ceramics Gallery, *Chris Keenan*, exh. leaflet, text by David Whiting (Oxford, 2013)
Scottish Gallery, *Chris Keenan: Familial Bonds*, exh. leaflet (Edinburgh, 2014)
Teleri Lloyd-Jones, 'The House Guest', *Crafts*, 261 (2016)

Exhibition reviews: Fiona Johnson, *CR*, 176 (1999); Harriet Smith, *Ceramics: Art and Perception*, 97 (2014)

496 Bowl, 2006
Porcelain, thrown, celadon glaze with tenmoku sgraffito edge; marks: 'C' within a diamond, impressed; h.11.5cm, d.29.1cm
C.145-2006. Source: the artist, £500; funded by the Royal Borough of Kensington and Chelsea Decorative and Fine Arts Society

497 *Family of rocking bowls*, 2007
Porcelain, celadon and tenmoku glazes; h.12.9cm, d.13.8cm (largest bowl)
C.29 to 36-2008. Source: the artist, £600; acquired through the generosity of Gerard and Sarah Griffin
Keenan noted: 'I think this is the best grouping from recent firings ... they work together very well in a familial kind of way.' His rocking bowls were featured in *Elle Decoration* (November 2007).

496

497

The museum also holds examples and prototypes of Keenan's *Sora* tableware, designed for the retailer Habitat, not catalogued here (C.188 to 216-2009 and C.352 to 358-2009).

Kemp, Dorothy 1905–2001

1930s	becomes interested in pottery while teaching at a school in Sheffield, Yorkshire, having previously studied history at Manchester University
1935–36	works with Bernard Leach (qv) at Shinners Bridge, Dartington, Devon, making slipware
c. 1940–49	works regularly at Leach Pottery, St Ives, during summer vacations, making Standard Ware and her own work; moves to teach in Saltash, Cornwall, to be within easier reach of the pottery
c. 1947–50	during vacations, works with Margaret Leach (qv), a fellow former student at St Ives, at The Barn Pottery, Brockweir, Gloucestershire, making slipware
c. 1950–	moves to Felixstowe, Suffolk; teaches pottery at Northgate Grammar School for Girls, Ipswich

A history teacher by profession, Dorothy Kemp became an accomplished maker of repetition slipware and stoneware in her spare time. Her book, *English Slipware: How to Make It*, was primarily intended as a guide for teaching in secondary schools.

Dorothy Kemp, *English Slipware: How to Make It*, introduction by Bernard Leach (London, 1954)
Arts and Crafts Exhibition Society (1944), (1946)
Cooper (1947), p.*ii*, pl.18a
Dartington Hall (1952)
Wingfield Digby (1952), p.83, pls.54, 59
Lewis (1956), pl.342
Decorative Art (1958/59)
Leach (1978), p.222
Whybrow (2006), pp.106–7

498 Jug: *Water Wheel* pattern, 1949
Stoneware, grey glaze, wax-resist decoration in brown; marks: 'DK' in monogram, impressed; made at Leach Pottery, St Ives; h.22.2cm, d.18cm
Circ.165-1950. Source: the artist, £2.2s.

499 Cider jug and two mugs, 1949
Stoneware, purple-brown glaze; marks: 'DK' and 'SI' in monogram, impressed; made at Leach Pottery, St Ives; h.28cm, d.15.2cm
Circ.166 to 168-1950. Source: *see* **498**, £2.2s. (jug); 7s.6d. (each mug)

498

499

500

500 Bowl, 1949
Earthenware, slip decoration in black, amber glaze; marks: 'DK' in monogram, impressed; made at The Barn Pottery, Brockweir; h.10.5cm, d.27.9cm
Circ.169-1950. Source: *see* **498**, £1.10s.

Keyes, Phyllis Marion 1880–1968

1880	born Marylebone, London
1931–	meets and collaborates with Duncan Grant and Vanessa Bell
1933–	establishes pottery studio, Warren Street, London
1936–	moves studio to Clipstone Street, London

The potter Phyllis Keyes was an associate of the Bloomsbury Group. She first met the painters Duncan Grant (1885–1978) and Vanessa Bell (1879–1961) in 1931, when they visited a kiln in Lambeth, London, with her, and began to experiment with colours and glazes. Keyes made pieces for Grant and Bell to decorate, including those exhibited in their Music Room interior shown at the Lefevre Galleries in 1932. Encouraged by the success of the collaboration, Keyes established her own studio in central London, working in tin-glazed earthenware, mostly slip-cast, often making pieces of Neo-Georgian style. Angelica Garnett, daughter of Grant and Bell, made occasional visits to her studio to assist with their decoration. Keyes was self-taught as a potter, having seemingly absorbed the rudiments as a child at a pottery in Devon.

'The Little Old Lady of the Vases', *Daily Mirror* (31 January 1944)
Frances Spalding, *Duncan Grant* (London, 1997)

501 Vase, *c.* 1932 (pl.21)
Earthenware, tin glaze, painted in colours; made by Phyllis Keyes, painted by Duncan Grant; h.31.1cm, d.19cm
Misc.2:135-1934. Source: given by Margaret Armitage (née Bulley)
The shape was copied from a two-handled vase bought by Grant in Tunisia in 1914. This vase is closely similar to one in the collection at Charleston, East Sussex (CHA/C/181), from Grant and Bell's Music Room interior.

502 Vase, *c.* 1932 (pl.21)
Earthenware, tin glaze, painted in colours; made by Phyllis Keyes, painted by Vanessa Bell; marks: 'P' between linked keys, incised, 'VB', painted; h.28.5cm, d.18.7cm
Misc.2:136-1934. Source: *see* **501**
A paper label on the base is inscribed: 'No 71 / 24/-'.

503 Vase, *c.* 1934
Earthenware, slip-cast, tin glaze with turquoise interior; marks: 'P' between linked keys, painted; h.19.7cm, d.19.6cm
C.227-1934. Source: given by the artist
Based on a Chinese vase lent to Keyes by the painter and critic Roger Fry, with the idea that she should copy it.

504 Wall pocket, *c.* 1934
Earthenware, tin glaze; made to a design by Stephen Tomlin; marks: 'TS' in monogram and 'P' between linked keys, painted; h.38.6cm, d.10cm
C.228-1934. Source: *see* **503**

505 Vase, *c.* 1937
Earthenware, tin glaze, painted in colours; made by Phyllis Keyes, painted by Duncan Grant; h.25.7cm, d.23.4cm
Circ.389-1954. Source: given by the Council for Art and Industry
See Crafts Council, *The Omega Workshops, 1913–19* (London, 1984), p.66, C25.

506 Vase, *c.* 1943
Earthenware, tin glaze, painted in turquoise and brown; marks: 'P' between linked keys, painted; h.21.3cm, d.15.9cm
Circ.1-1944. Source: Heal & Son Ltd, London, £2.15s.
Of the vase, Harry Trethowan of Heal's noted, 'The production including the decoration is entirely the work of Miss Keyes.'

King, Ruth 1955–

1955	born Enfield, Middlesex
1974–77	studies ceramics at Camberwell School of Art and Crafts, London
1978–81	workshops in Brixton, then Charlton, London
1981–	moves to Fulford, York, sharing workshop of David Lloyd Jones (qv)
1987–	workshop in Shipton-by-Beningbrough, North Yorkshire; continues firing work at Fulford until 1994; builds gas kiln in 1997 and resumes making
2016	solo exhibition, Contemporary Ceramics Centre, London

506 / 503

Ruth King makes handbuilt, non-functional vessels of strongly sculptural character. Earlier work was in oxidized stoneware, but she began concentrating on saltglaze while at Fulford, firing with wood. She has since continued with saltglaze, now fired in a gas kiln, introducing colour to her highly controlled forms through sprayed layers of oxide.

Ruth King, 'A Potter's Day', *CR*, 126 (1990)
— 'Connecting Threads', *CPA News*, 124 (2009)
— 'Potter's Secrets', *CR*, 310 (2021)
'CPA New Members', *CR*, 68 (1981)
Potters/The Ceramics Book (1983) to (1994), (2000) to (2012)
Sally Boyle, exh. review, *CR*, 220 (2006)
Lyn Wait, 'A Quiet Dynamic', *Ceramics: Art and Perception*, 65 (2006)
Jane Cox, 'Line and Body', *CR*, 254 (2012)
Alex McErlain, 'Focus and Form', *CR*, 279 (2016)

507 Tall pot, 1983
Stoneware, slab-built, mottled grey-green matt glaze; marks: 'RK', applied; h.41.7cm, d.38.2cm
C.75-1984. Source: given by the Friends of the V&A (purchased at the Craftsmen Potters Association exhibition, *Studio Ceramics Today*, V&A, 1983, no.97, £108)

504

505

507

Kneebone, Rachel 1973–

1973	born Oxfordshire
1994–97	studies ceramics at University of the West of England, Bristol
2002–04	studies ceramics at Royal College of Art, London
2006	solo exhibition, Madder Rose, London
2009	solo exhibition, *The Descent*, White Cube, London
2012	solo exhibition, *Regarding Rodin*, Brooklyn Museum, New York, USA
2012–	studio in Holloway, London
2017	solo exhibition, *Raft of the Medusa*, Foundling Museum, London; interventions including *399 Days*, V&A, London

Rachel Kneebone works in porcelain, drawing on art-historical and literary sources to create complex semi-figurative and architectonic sculptures that explore the human condition and experience. Her works are at once dreamlike and intensely physical, reflecting themes of mortality and sexuality and the possibilities of renewal and transformation. The softness of the porcelain clay, captured by Kneebone's deft modelling, contrasts with the deeply fissured forms of the fired sculptures, which reveal the material pushed to its limits.

White Cube, *Rachel Kneebone: Works 2007–2010*, exh. cat. (London, 2010)
— *Rachel Kneebone: 399 Days*, exh. cat. (London, 2014)
Rachel Kneebone: Regarding Rodin, exh. cat., published following an exhibition at the Brooklyn Museum (London, 2014)
Kathleen Whitney, 'Fusion: A Conversation with Rachel Kneebone', *Sculpture*, 34:2 (2015)
Elderton and Morrill (2017), pp.140–1
Serlachius Museums, *Rachel Kneebone: Punoutua*, exh. cat. (Helsinki, 2020)
Emily Spicer, 'Rachel Kneebone', interview, *Studio International*, ejournal (25 June 2021)

Exhibition reviews: Emma Clegg, 'The Way We Work Now', *CR*, 217 (2006); Simon Martin, *CR*, 238 (2009); Harry J. Weil, *Art Papers Magazine*, 36:4 (2012); Jack Tan, *CR*, 271 (2015); Colin Martin, *CR*, 288 (2017); Marina Warner, 'In Rochdale', *LRB* blog (5 February 2019)

508 *Raft of the Medusa I*, 2015 (pl.140)
Glazed porcelain, handbuilt, on Corian base; h.55.5cm, d.74.5cm (porcelain), h.9.8cm, d.80cm (base)
C.339:1,2-2018. Source: White Cube, £60,000; purchased with the support of Gerard and Sarah Griffin, and Christian and Florence Levett
Shown in solo exhibition *Raft of the Medusa*, Foundling Museum, London, 2017.

Koch, Gabriele 1948–

1948	born Lörrach, Germany
1967–73	studies English, history and political science at University of Heidelberg; studies Spanish at University of Zaragoza, travels in Spain
1974–77	attends pottery classes at Camden Institute, London
1977–	establishes studio in Highgate, London
1977–78	teacher training, King's College, London
1979–81	studies ceramics at Goldsmiths' College, London, under David Garbett (qv)
1984	first solo exhibition at Oliver and Pink, London; exhibits widely thereafter in UK and internationally
1993–2009	regular solo exhibitions at Alpha House Gallery, Sherborne, Dorset
2005	solo exhibition, Keramikmuseum Staufen, Karlsruhe, Germany

Gabriele Koch is known for her pared-down, handbuilt, burnished earthenware vessels, richly patterned through smoke-firing. During the 2010s she began to develop work in black stoneware, boldly decorated with bands of white porcelain.

Gabriele Koch, *Gabriele Koch* (Marston Magna, 1995), revised (2002)
— statement, in Bendavid and Lalumia (2017), pp.24, 39
Crafts Centre and Design Gallery, *Gabriele Koch*, exh. pamphlet, texts by Emmanuel Cooper and Cyril Frankel (Leeds, 1989)
Potters/The Ceramics Book (1989) to (2012)
Tony Birks, 'Low Tech: High Precision', *CR*, 144 (1993)
Andrews (1994), p.89, (2005), p.191
Crafts Council (1995a), p.44
Perryman (1995), pp.51–6, (2008), pp.55–60
Edmund de Waal, *Gabriele Koch*, Aberystwyth Arts Centre: Ceramic Series 83 (1997)
Frankel (2000), pp.183–6
Moira Vincentelli, 'Embodiments: Women's Ceramic Traditions and the Work of Gabriele Koch and Vilma Henkelman', in Stair (2000), pp.122–9
Tony Birks, 'Gabriele Koch', *Ceramics Monthly*, 53:10 (2005)
— 'Gabriele Koch', *Ceramics: Art and Perception*, 75 (2009)
— *Gabriele Koch: Hand Building and Smoke Firing* (Catrine, 2009)
Carlano (2010), pp.90–1
Game (2016), pp.34–5
Jochem (2018), pp.47, 118–19, 216–17, 280
Thormann (2018), pp.260–1, 475, 507
Taylor (2020), pp.14–15, 50, 64–5

Exhibition reviews: Victor Margrie, *Crafts*, 122 (1993); Lionel Phillips, *Studio Pottery*, 16 (1995); Emma Clegg, *CR*, 170 (1998), and 185 (2000); David Briers, *Crafts*, 184 (2003); Emmanuel Cooper, *CR*, 233 (2008); Tony Birks, *Ceramics: Art and Perception*, 91 (2013)

509 *Burnished Vessel*, 1994
Earthenware, handbuilt, burnished, smoked;

509

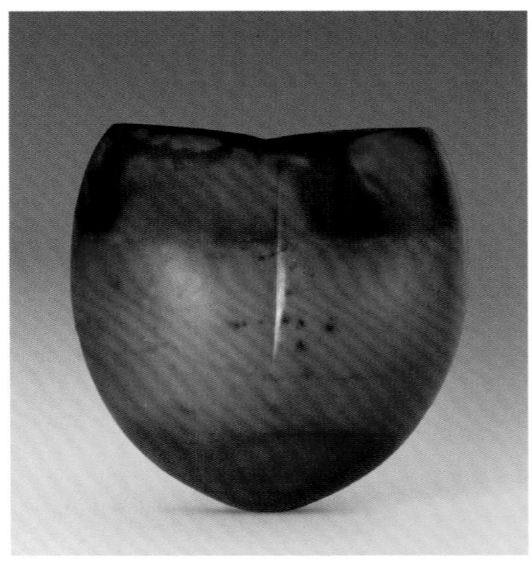

510

marks: 'Gabriele Koch', incised; h.38.4cm, d.40.4cm
C.60-1995. Source: Craft Potters Association, London (exhibition: *Studio Ceramics 94*, V&A, 1994), £600

510 *Red Pod Form*, 2009
Earthenware, handbuilt, burnished, smoked; marks: 'Gabriele / Koch', incised; h.36.1cm, d.36.3cm
C.106-2011. Source: anonymous gift

La Salle, Vivian Neil (Brother Damian) 1911–1994

1928–33	studies at Architectural Association School of Architecture, London
1935	becomes Associate Member of Royal Institute of British Architects
1946–47| 49–51	studies pottery at Central School of Arts and Crafts, London, under Dora Billington (qv)
1947–	joins teaching order of De La Salle Brothers, taking the name Brother Damian; teaches pottery at Roman Catholic schools, including Cardinal Langley RC School, Manchester
1972	retires

Vivian Neil La Salle took up pottery after working as an architect, and while considering joining a Roman Catholic teaching order. He made painted tin-glazed earthenware dishes and stoneware.

Arts and Crafts Exhibition Society (1946), (1948), (1950)

511 Dish, 1950
Earthenware, tin glaze, painted in green, yellow and blue; marks: 'Bro D', incised; made at Central School of Arts and Crafts; h.7.8cm, d.40.2cm
Circ.46-1951. Source: the artist (shown at the Twenty-second Exhibition of the Arts and Crafts Exhibition Society, V&A, 1950, no.497), £7.7s.

Law, Roger 1941–

See **261** and **262** *under* Dartington Pottery *and* **992** *under* Janice Tchalenko

511

Lax, Aimee 1977–

1977	born Bedford, Bedfordshire
1996–99	studies ceramics at Bath Spa University
2003–05	studies ceramics at Royal College of Art, London
2005–06	solo exhibition, *Artificial Nature*, Royal Over-Seas League, London
2007	residency, Banff Centre for the Arts, Alberta, Canada
2007–	studio at Stroud Valleys Artspace, Gloucestershire
2008	solo exhibition, *Confines and Mutations*, Stroud Valleys Artspace
2015	commission for Eden Project, Cornwall
2017	residency, Cove Park, Argyll and Bute
2019	solo exhibition, *Radioactive Boglach*, New Brewery Arts, Cirencester, Gloucestershire
2019–20	ceramics residency, V&A

At times collaborating with scientists, Aimee Lax creates sculptures and installations that explore relationships between nature, culture and the environment. Combining clay with synthetic materials, such as silicone or acrylic, her works suggest forms that are artificial or alien, generating feelings of attraction and repulsion.

Bornholms Kunstmuseum, *European Ceramic Context 2006: Young Ceramists*, exh. cat. (Gudhjem, 2006), pp.104–5
Jo Dahn, exh. review, *CR*, 231 (2008)
Eden Project, *Invisible You: The Human Microbiome*, exh. cat. (2015), pp.42–3
New Brewery Arts, *Aimee Lax: Radioactive Boglach*, exh. leaflet, interview by Beth Alden (Cirencester, 2019)

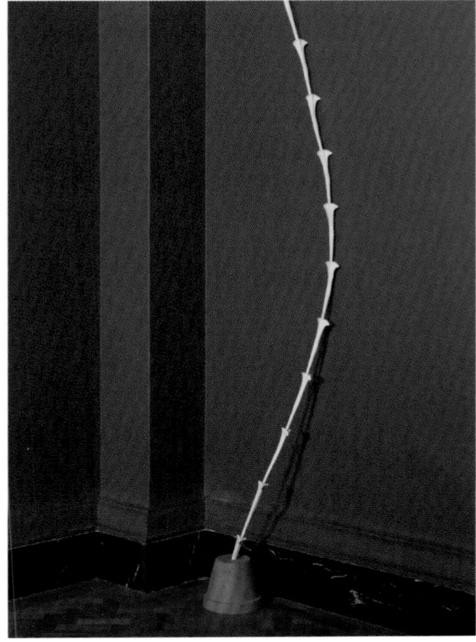

512

512 *Ready Grown*, 2004
Porcelain, slip-cast, with found terracotta flowerpot; made at Royal College of Art, London; dimensions variable
C.81:1 to 27-2007. Source: the artist, £1500; acquired through the generosity of Gerard and Sarah Griffin

Leach, Bernard Howell 1887–1979 *see also* Leach Pottery

1887	born Hong Kong; mother dies, taken by grandparents to Japan
1890	rejoins father in Hong Kong
1894	moves with father to Singapore
1897	moves to UK, to attend Beaumont Jesuit College, Windsor, Berkshire
1903	studies at Slade School of Fine Art, London, under Henry Tonks
1905	lives in Manchester with his uncle, William Hoyle, and aunt Edith
1906–07	joins Hong Kong and Shanghai Bank, as clerk
1907	studies at London School of Art, taking etching under Frank Brangwyn
1909	moves to Japan; builds house in Tokyo; marries cousin Muriel Hoyle
1910	meets the artist Tomimoto Kenkichi
1911	discovers pottery at raku party; meets Yanagi Sōetsu; learns pottery under Urano Shigekichi, who held the title 6th Kenzan, in a line of traditional potters;

	son David Leach (qv) born
1913	establishes small pottery workshop at his home, Urano building kiln; Leach and Tomimoto jointly receive title of 7th Kenzan; son Michael Leach (qv) born
1914	first solo exhibition in Tokyo
1914–16	travels to China to meet, and becomes in thrall to, Alfred Westharp, a philosopher
1916	returns to Japan; buys Kenzan's kiln and rebuilds it on Yanagi's land at Abiko
1918	visits Korea with Yanagi
1919	meets Hamada Shōji (qv); workshop burns down
1919–20	workshop at Azabu, Tokyo
1920	returns to England with Hamada and establishes Leach Pottery in St Ives, Cornwall, with support from Frances Horne, a local philanthropist
1922	solo exhibition, Cotswold Gallery, London, Leach's first since returning to England
1923–	first student, Michael Cardew (qv), joins pottery; Hamada returns to Japan
1923–24	Matsubayashi Tsurunosuke (qv) joins pottery and rebuilds kiln
1929	Yanagi and Hamada visit St Ives
1930	son David joins pottery as apprentice
1932–	begins teaching part-time at Dartington Hall, Devon, and builds pottery at Shinners Bridge; becomes interested in Baha'i faith through the American artist Mark Tobey
1933–	David takes over at Dartington
1934–35	visits Japan with Tobey at invitation of National Craft Society; travels and makes pots at various kilns; visits Korea
1934–37	David studies in Stoke-on-Trent; Harry Davis (qv) and Laurie Cookes left in charge of Leach Pottery; Bernard Forrester takes over at Dartington
1935	with Laurie, purchases caravan and lives itinerantly, visiting Ditchling and Winchcombe; settles at Dartington
1936	resumes teaching at Dartington; develops plans for production pottery, and possible relocation from St Ives; makes slipware at Shinners Bridge
1937–	builds 'cabin' at Shinners Bridge, living there with Laurie; writes *A Potter's Book*
1937–	David becomes manager at St Ives, embarking on modernization with £3000 funding from Dartington over three years; installs oil-fired kiln; discontinues earthenware production
1940	becomes Baha'i; publishes *A Potter's Book*
1941	returns to St Ives when David conscripted; bomb damages pottery
1944	marries Laurie Cookes
1946–55	takes David into partnership
1949	visits Sweden, Norway and Denmark
1950	lecture tour of USA, organized by Institute of Contemporary Art, Washington, DC
1952	International Crafts Conference, Dartington Hall; Yanagi and Hamada attend
1952–54	tours USA and Japan; meets Janet Darnell (later Leach) (qv)
1955	David and Michael Leach leave St Ives to establish own potteries
1956	Janet arrives and marries Bernard
1960	BBC film, *A Potter's World*, produced by John Read; visits Scandinavia
1961	retrospective exhibition, *Fifty Years a Potter*, Arts Council Gallery, London; lecture tour, USA; awarded Hon. D.Litt. from Exeter University
1961–62	visits Japan, Australia and New Zealand
1962	awarded CBE
1963	visits Paris, for exhibition with Hamada
1964	visits Japan, attending annual meeting of Japanese Association of Folk Craft, Okinawa
1966	visits Colombia, Venezuela, USA and Japan, where awarded Order of the Sacred Treasure, 2nd Class; retrospective exhibition, Tokyo
1967	visits Japan, with Janet
1968	awarded Freedom of the Borough of St Ives, with the sculptor Barbara Hepworth
1969	visits Japan, with Janet
1970	visits Denmark; Westward Television film, *The Potter's Art*, directed by Derek Fairhead
1971	visits Japan
1972	sight failing, largely ceases potting; awarded Honorary Doctorate, Royal College of Art, London
1973	visits Japan, records interviews with Hamada; made Companion of Honour
1974	visits Japan to receive Japan Foundation Cultural Award
1977	retrospective exhibition, *The Art of Bernard Leach*, V&A, London

Bernard Leach is undoubtedly one of the most important potters of the 20th century. Through his prodigious output of pots over more than 60 years, his extensive writings and frequent lecture tours, his regular exhibitions and many students, his influence has been far-reaching and profound. Throughout his life Leach positioned himself as an intermediary between East and West, a position shaped by a nostalgic and romantic view of East Asia, and mediated by his circle of friends in the Japanese *mingei* (folkcraft) movement, most notably Yanagi Sōetsu.

Having travelled to Japan with the idea of teaching etching, Leach became enthralled by the art of ceramics, and in 1920 returned to England with Hamada Shōji (qv) to establish the Leach Pottery in St Ives. Together they built the first East Asian-style climbing kiln in Europe, and set about producing reduced stoneware and slip-decorated earthenware, as well as some raku, fired in a separate small kiln. The pottery was founded on the principle of the individuality of the artist, and its economics – at least initially – were based on those of the studio rather than the country workshop or factory. In the early years at St Ives, Leach faced numerous technical challenges and struggled to keep the pottery afloat. Its later success and relative financial stability owe much to others, most particularly his son David, as well as to the patronage of Leonard and Dorothy Elmhirst of Dartington Hall.

Leach espoused the importance of functionality, though in his individual work – as opposed to the Standard Ware produced by his pottery (*see* Leach Pottery) – this manifested itself only in so far as he concentrated on recognizable, useful, ceramic forms, intended primarily as expressive artistic objects rather than for practical use. He was an accomplished graphic artist, and his most celebrated pots often explore the decorated surface using brushwork or sgraffito. Some of Leach's finest pots were made after 1956, when his third wife, Janet Leach, assumed the running of the pottery and encouraged him to focus on his own work. His larger pieces were thrown to his design by David and later by William Marshall (qv), and finished by Leach.

In the post-war era the work of the Leach Pottery and Leach's teachings and writings – most particularly *A Potter's Book*, published in 1940 – became hugely influential. As well as offering practical advice, *A Potter's Book* extolled the virtues of an independent artistic life, inspiring a new generation of studio potters. From its early years the Leach Pottery also provided an important training ground. Those who worked there include: Michael Cardew (qv), Katharine Pleydell-Bouverie (qv), Norah Braden (qv), Charlotte Epton (qv), Dorothy Kemp (qv), Michael Leach (qv), Margaret Leach (qv), Kenneth Quick (qv), Robin Welch (qv), Gwyn Hanssen Pigott (qv), Richard Batterham (qv), John Leach (qv) and Jason Wason (qv).

Meanwhile, Leach's promotion of certain values in making, alongside a particular canon of Chinese and Korean ceramics, has led to an identifiable 'Leach school' of potters, marked by his influence.

Bernard Leach, *A Review 1909–1914* (Tokyo, 1914)
— *An English Artist in Japan* (Tokyo, 1920)
— *A Potter's Outlook*, Handworkers' Pamphlets No.3 (London: New Handworkers' Gallery, 1928)
— *A Potter's Book* (London, 1940), 2nd edition (1945), 3rd edition (1975)
— 'Pottery', in John Farleigh (ed.), *Fifteen Craftsmen on their Crafts* (London, 1945), pp.44–51
— 'The English Potters', *The Listener* (2 January 1947)
— 'The Contemporary Studio-Potter', *Journal of the Royal Society of Arts* (21 May 1948)
— *A Potter's Portfolio* (London, 1951)
— 'Onda Diary', *Pottery Quarterly*, 1:4 (1954)
— 'The Contemporary Studio-Potter', *Pottery Quarterly*, 5:18 (1958)
— 'In Reply to Paul Brown', *Pottery Quarterly*, 6:24 (1959)
— *A Potter in Japan 1952–1954* (London, 1960)
— 'Looking Backwards and Forwards at 72', in Barrow (1960)
— *Kenzan and his Tradition* (London, 1966)
— *A Potter's Work* (London, 1967)
— 'Students and Hand-Made Standard Ware', *CR*, 9 (1971)
— statement, in Rothschild (1972)
— *The Unknown Craftsman*, translated and adapted from the work of Yanagi Sōetsu (Tokyo, 1972)
— *Drawings, Verse and Belief* (Bath, 1973), revised (London, 1977)
— *Hamada: Potter* (Tokyo, 1975), (London, 1976)
— *A Potter's Challenge* (London, 1976)
— 'A Message from Bernard Leach', *Studio Potter*, 5:2 (1977)
— *Beyond East and West: Memoirs, Portraits and Essays* (London, 1978)
— 'Shoji Hamada: A Tribute', *CR*, 50 (1978)
Cotswold Gallery, *Pottery and Etchings by Bernard Leach*, exh. pamphlet (London, 1922)
Arts and Crafts Exhibition Society (1923) to (1952)
British Institute of Industrial Art (1923), (1927), (1929)
Royal Academy of Arts (1923)
Guild of Potters (1924)
Michael Cardew, 'The Pottery of Mr Bernard Leach', *The Studio* (1925), pp.298–301
Decorative Art (1926) to (1931), (1933), (1937), (1952/53), (1956/57), (1958/59), (1962/63)
Colnaghi (1927), (1928), (1929)
Beaux Arts Gallery, *Stoneware Pottery by Bernard Leach*, exh. cat. (London, 1928)
— *Stoneware Pottery and Porcelain by Kenkichi Tomimoto (of Tokyo) and Bernard Leach*, exh. cat. (London, 1931)
John Gould Fletcher, 'The Pottery and Tiles of Bernard Leach', *Artwork*, 7:26 (1931)
'Leach and Tomimoto', *The Studio* (1931), pp.346–49
V&A (1936), pls.37, 39, 45–6
British Council (1942)
Ernest Marsh, 'Bernard Leach: Potter', *Apollo*, 37 (January 1943)
J.P. Hodin, 'The Art of Bernard Leach', *Design*, 48 (September 1946)
Cooper (1947), pp.*ii–iii*, pls.18b–25
J.P. Hodin, 'Bernard Leach and his Thirty Years in the Service of Ceramic Art', *The Studio* (March 1947), pp.89–92
John Farleigh, *The Creative Craftsman* (London, 1950), pp.60–74
Dartington Hall (1952)
David Lewis, 'Leach and Hamada', *The Studio*, 144 (October 1952), p.114–17
Wingfield Digby (1952), pp.18, 29–34, 66–9, pls.1–15, 53
Rose (1955), pp.9–13, pls.B, 10–23, (1970), pp.25–30, pls.A–B, 10–27
T. Barrow (ed.), *Bernard Leach: Essays in Appreciation* (Wellington, 1960)
Arts Council, *Bernard Leach: 50 Years a Potter*, exh. cat. (London, 1961)
Casson (1967), p.7, pls.37, 132–7
Janet Leach, 'Letter from Japan', *Pottery Quarterly*, 9:36 (1969)
Potters (1972) to (1977)
V&A (1972), p.112
David Smith-Greenwood, 'A Visit with Bernard Leach', interview, *Ceramics Monthly*, 22:9 (1974)
Hugh Wakefield, 'The Leach Tradition', *Crafts*, 6 (1974)
Lucie-Smith (1975), pp.32–49
Crafts Advisory Committee (1976), p.102
Carol Hogben, 'Towards a Standard', review of Bernard Leach Seminar, *Crafts*, 26 (1977)
V&A, *The Art of Bernard Leach*, exh. pamphlet, text by John Houston (London, 1977)
Geoffrey Whiting, 'Bernard Leach Retrospective Exhibition and Seminar', *Pottery Quarterly*, 12:48 (1977)
'Bernard Leach Potter', various authors, *CR*, 50 (1978)
Carol Hogben (ed.), *The Art of Bernard Leach* (London, 1978)
Michael Cardew, 'Bernard Leach', memorial address, *Crafts*, 39 (1979)
'Tribute to Bernard Leach', various authors, *CR*, 58 (1979)
Susan Peterson, 'Reflections: Leach at Alfred', *Studio Potter*, 9:2 (1981)
Barley Roscoe, 'Pots of Inspiration', *CR*, 77 (1982)
Paisley Museum and Art Galleries (1984), pp.49–51
Crafts Council (1985), pp.58–60
Barley Roscoe, 'Bernard Leach: The Sources of his Influence', in ICA (1985), pp.35–9
Tate Gallery (1985), pp.228–31
Watson (1985)
John Maltby, 'The Leach Tradition', *Crafts*, 80 (1986)
Vincentelli and Hale (1986)
'Bernard Leach', centenary supplement, various authors, *CR*, 108 (1987)
Breon O'Casey, 'Towards a Standard', *CR*, 114 (1988)
Brian Moeran, 'Bernard Leach and the Japanese Folk Craft Movement: The Formative Years', *Journal of Design History*, 2:2/3 (1989)
Birks and Wingfield Digby (1990), pp.11–93
Riddick (1990), pp.59–74
Ellen P. Conant, 'Leach, Hamada, Yanagi: Myth and Reality', *Studio Potter*, 21:1 (1992)
Whiting (1993)
Edmund de Waal, 'Beyond the Potter's Wheel', *Crafts*, 129 (1994)
Tanya Harrod, 'Traditionalist or Visionary', *CR*, 150 (1994)
— 'Writers and Thinkers', *Crafts*, 128 (1994)
Vivenne Browning, *St Ives Summer 1946: The Leach Pottery* (St Ives, 1995)
Edmund de Waal, *Bernard Leach* (London: Tate Gallery, 1997)
— 'Homo Orientalis: Bernard Leach and the Image of the Japanese Craftsman', *Journal of Design History*, 10:4 (1997)
— 'Homo Orientalis: Bernard Leach and the Japanese Soul', in Harrod (1997), pp.117–25
David Jeremiah, 'Beautiful Things: Dartington and the Art of the Potter and Weaver', in Harrod (1997), pp.163–76
Oliver Watson, *Bernard Leach: Potter and Artist*, exh. cat. (London: Crafts Council, 1997)
— 'Bernard Leach: Rewriting a Life', in Coatts (1997), pp.22–36
'Alternative Perspectives on Bernard Leach', various authors, *Studio Potter*, 27:1 (1998), and 27:2 (1999)
Jeffrey Jones, 'Listening to Bernard Leach: Exploring the Testimony of a Studio Potter', *Oral History*, 27:2 (1999)
Emmanuel Cooper, 'Leach and Cardew – The Early Years', *Interpreting Ceramics*, ejournal, 3 (2002)
Penlee House Gallery and Museum, *Bernard Leach: Concept and Form*, exh. cat., text by Emmanuel Cooper (Penzance, 2002)
Emmanuel Cooper, *Bernard Leach: Life and Work* (New Haven/London, 2003)
J.V.G. Mallet, 'The "Gentleman" Potters Part 1, Bernard and Janet Leach', *English Ceramic Circle Transactions*, 18:2 (2003)

Whybrow (2006)
Penelope Curtis, 'Support/Surface or Sculpture/ Craft: Considering Barbara Hepworth and Bernard Leach', *Journal of Modern Craft*, 2:1 (2009)
John Edgeler, *Slipware and St Ives: The Leach Pottery 1920–1937* (Winchcombe, 2010)
Simon Olding, *The Etchings of Bernard Leach* (Farnham: Crafts Study Centre, 2010)
Glenn Allison and others, *Thrown: British Columbia's Apprentices of Bernard Leach and their Contemporaries* (Vancouver, 2011)
Christie's, *Asobi: Ingenious Creativity and Ceramics from the Collection of Bernard Leach* (London, 15 October 2013)
W.K. Slater, 'Report on the Centralised Control of the Artist Craftsman', memorandum to Bernard Leach of 1935, with commentary by Simon Olding, *Journal of Modern Craft*, 6:3 (2013)
Paul Denison, 'Craft as Art: St Ives Through the Lens of Bernard Leach', in *Modern Art and St Ives: International Exchanges 1915–65*, exh. cat. (London: Tate Publishing, 2014), pp.64–9
Nottingham City Museums and Galleries (2017), pp.55–6
Simon Olding (ed.), *Bernard Leach: Discovered Archives* (Farnham: Crafts Study Centre, 2021)

Exhibition reviews: Frank Rutter, 'Potter and Etcher', *Sunday Times* (26 November 1922); *The Times* (14 November 1923), (21 April 1926), (23 March 1927), (6 December 1928), (12 May 1931), (29 October 1931), (5 December 1933), (25 April 1936) and (12 March 1958); Patrick Heron, *New English Weekly* (Summer 1946); *Pottery Quarterly*, 3:10 (1956), 5:17 (1958), and 7:26 (1961); George Wingfield Digby, *Museums Journal* (January 1961) and *Burlington Magazine*, review of Leach's personal collection, 121:915 (1979); Gordon Baldwin and Murray Fieldhouse, *Crafts*, 26 (1977); Geoffrey Whiting, *Pottery Quarterly*, 12:48 (1977); Janet Koplos, *Crafts*, 87 (1987); Tanya Harrod, *Crafts*, 152 (1998), and *Burlington Magazine*, 145:1205 (2003)

Obituaries: Alan Caiger-Smith, *Burlington Magazine*, 121:916 (1979); *The Telegraph* (7 May 1979); *The Times* (19 November 1979)

The papers of Bernard Leach (and associated archival holdings) are at the Crafts Study Centre, Farnham (BHL, BLE, ABL, BLS). A recorded interview with Bernard Leach, made by Marty Gross in 1975, is in the Potters of the Bernard Leach Legacy collection at the British Library, London (C1330/25).

All works made at the Leach Pottery, St Ives, unless stated otherwise.

513 Vase, 1913 (pl.3)
Raku, incised and decorated with slips, transparent glaze; marks: 'BHL' in monogram, incised; made in Tokyo; h.13.9cm, d.14.2cm
C.138-2013. Source: Christie's, London (sale: *Asobi: Ingenious Creativity*, 15 October 2013, lot 126), £11,700
Formerly in the collection of the artist.

514

515

516

517

519

520

514 Cup on three legs, 1919
Porcelain, painted in blue; marks: 'BL' in monogram, painted in blue; made in Tokyo; h.8.6cm, d.6.8cm
C.742-1921. Source: given by Lt-Col. K. Dingwall, DSO, through Art Fund

515 Vase, 1921–22
Stoneware, kaki on tenmoku glaze; marks: 'BL' and 'SI' in monogram, impressed; h.13.8cm, d.10cm
C.1040-1922. Source: given by Lt-Col. K. Dingwall, DSO, through Art Fund (from solo exhibition, Cotswold Gallery, London, November 1922, £2)

516 Drug jar, 1923
Earthenware, incised decoration through white slip, amber galena glaze; inscribed '1923'; marks: 'BL' and 'SI' in monogram, impressed; h.15.9cm, d.11.5cm
C.67-1976. Source: A. Landau, London, £200

517 Cup and saucer, *c.* 1920–24
Earthenware, slip-trailed in white, amber galena glaze; marks: 'BL' and 'SI' (on saucer), 'SI' in monogram, impressed (on cup); h.6.7cm, d.13.2cm
C.84&A-1972. Source: given by Dr Mildred Creak and Mrs Falchikov
Acquired from Bernard Leach by an aunt of Dr Creak, who had been an established artist in St Ives when Leach started his pottery, and had remained friends until her death in 1934. The dating was proposed by Leach.

518 Large dish, 1923 (pl.10)
Earthenware, painted in brown on white slip, amber galena glaze; marks: 'BL 1923', painted in slips; h.11.9cm, d.42cm
Circ.1278-1923. Source: the artist, £5
Shown at the British Institute of Industrial Art's *Exhibition of Industrial Art of To-Day* (1923) and selected for acquisition as 'a suitable addition to the case of modern pottery being formed in Circ [the Circulation Department]'. Bernard Rackham, Keeper of the Ceramics Department, commented that it represented 'a very interesting revival of an old technique'. Leach reduced his price from £7.10s. to £5. The design is taken from a stone carving on a Han dynasty (206 BC–AD 220) tomb that he may have seen in China. The 'Tree of Life' is a theme that Leach returned to frequently. In *A Potter's Portfolio* (1951) he commented that the motifs – tree, horse, fish, deer, the Plough (or Big Dipper) asterism and snails – 'may be seen as symbolic', but was not specific as to their meaning.

519 Lidded pot, 1923
Earthenware, incised decoration through white slip, amber galena glaze; marks: 'BL' and 'SI' in monogram, impressed; h.13.8cm, d.14.7cm
C.405&A-1934. Source: British Institute of Industrial Art (given by the artist, 1923)

520 Jar, 1923
Stoneware, pale grey-green glaze, painted in dark grey; marks: 'BL' and 'SI' in monogram, impressed; h.15.7cm, d.13.6cm
C.406-1934. Source: *see* **519**

521 Jar, 1923
Stoneware, mottled reddish-brown glaze; marks: 'SI' in monogram, impressed; h.15cm, d.16.5cm
C.408-1934. Source: *see* **519**
A paper exhibition label reads '31/£3'.

522 Jar, 1923–24
Stoneware, mottled greenish-brown glaze, painted in brown; marks: 'BL' and 'SI' in monogram, impressed; h.17.2cm, d.19.3cm
Circ.993-1924. Source: the artist; given by W.W. Winkworth

523 Bowl, 1925–26 (pl.14)
Stoneware, cut sides, discoloured celadon glaze; marks: 'BL' and 'SI' in monogram, impressed; h.9.8cm, d.13.8cm
C.148-1926. Source: given by Lt-Col. K. Dingwall, DSO, through Art Fund (selected with **524** by Bernard Rackham from 'the recent exhibition of the latest work of Mr. Bernard Leach')
In *A Potter's Work* (1967), pl.17, Leach commented: 'I like this cut-sided pot as well as anything I have made.' Its matt surface and warm discolouration were the unintended result of using railway-sleeper wood impregnated with salts as kiln fuel. Many other pots in the firing were ruined. Also illustrated in *A Potter's Book* (1940), pl.48. A paper label gives the price '£12'.

524 Bowl, 1925–26
Stoneware, kaki on rust-red tenmoku glaze; marks: 'BL' and 'SI' in monogram, impressed; h.8.5cm, d.12.9cm
C.149-1926. Source: *see* **523**
A paper label gives the price '£5'.

521

522

524 / 531

525 Jar, *c.* 1925–30
Stoneware, fluted sides, tenmoku glaze; marks: 'BL' and 'SI' in monogram, impressed; h.20.1cm, d.16.1cm
C.68-1976. Source: A. Landau, London, £220

526 Jar, 1926–27
Stoneware, pale blue 'Yuan' glaze; marks: 'BL'

525

526

527

528

529

and 'SI' in monogram, impressed; h.16cm, d.17cm
Circ.646-1927. Source: the artist, £4
Shown in the British Institute of Industrial Art exhibition *Recent Examples of British Pottery*, held at the V&A in 1927.

527 Three tiles, 1926–27
Stoneware, oatmeal glaze, painted in brown and blue; marks: 'BL' and 'SI' in monogram, painted; h.9.5cm, w.9.5cm (each)
C.402, 404 & 409-1934. Source: British Institute of Industrial Art (given by the artist, 1927)

528 Panel of nine tiles, 1927
Stoneware, oatmeal glaze, incised and painted in blue and brown; h.9cm, w.9cm (each)
C.403-1934. Source: *see* **527**

529 Bowl, 1927
Stoneware, grey glaze, painted in dark grey; marks: 'BL' and 'SI' in monogram, impressed; h.9.8cm, d.22.2cm
C.410-1934. Source: *see* **527**

530 Bowl, *c.* 1930
Stoneware, white slip, incised decoration, painted in blue and brown; marks: 'BL' and 'SI' in monogram, impressed; h.7.3cm, d.18.4cm
C.58-1973. Source: given by Dr Mildred Creak and Mrs Falchikov

531 Bowl, 1931 (illustrated p.277)
Stoneware, dark and light brown glazes; marks: 'BL' and 'SI' in monogram, impressed; h.10.7cm, d.13.2cm
C.963-1935. Source: given by the Pottery and Crafts Fund of the Contemporary Art Society (purchased from Beaux Arts Gallery, London, 1931 [exhibition with Tomimoto Kenkichi], £3.3s.)
A paper label inscribed '73.' refers to its Contemporary Art Society (CAS) collection number.

532 Bottle, 1931 (p.2)
Stoneware, matt white glaze, painted in brown; marks: 'BL' and 'SI' in monogram, impressed, and 'PK', incised; h.34.3cm, d.14cm
Circ.144-1931. Source: Beaux Arts Gallery, London (exhibition: *Stoneware Pottery and Porcelain by Kenkichi Tomimoto (of Tokyo) and Bernard Leach*, 1931), £21
This bottle is glazed with a celebrated, laboriously prepared, velvety-white bracken-ash glaze, which in subsequent years Leach was unable to replicate (Leach, *Hamada* (1976), p.48). The same glaze is used on the famous *Leaping Salmon* bottle in the Milner-White Collection now in York Art Gallery (Riddick, 1990, no.66). The V&A 'leaping fish' bottle is the original from which a series was derived in the post-war period. It was purchased together with **533**, **534**, a celadon-glazed stoneware bottle (Circ.146-1931; destroyed through enemy bombardment while on loan to the Sheffield College of Arts and Crafts, 1940–41) and a plate by Tomimoto (Circ.148-1931).

533 Jar, 1931 (fig.6)
Stoneware, incised decoration through grey pigment over an off-white slip; marks: 'BL' and 'SI' in monogram, impressed; h.26.3cm, d.21cm
Circ.147-1931. Source: *see* **532**, £15.15s.

534 Square dish, 1931
Porcelain, painted in blue and yellow, with firing cracks repaired with gold lacquer; marks: 'SI' in monogram, impressed, and 'BL', in script

on the interior; h.2.5cm, d.16.7cm
Circ.145-1931. Source: *see* **532**, £5.5s.

535 Bowl: *Korean washerwoman*, 1931 (pl.18)
Porcelain, stencilled design through a buff slip, with incised and inlaid decoration, and painting in iron pigment; marks: monograms 'BL' and 'SI', painted; h.12.9cm, d.34cm
Circ.22-1961. Source: given by Miss Madeleine Whyte
Although previously published as dating from 1936 or 1940, this bowl is probably that listed in the catalogue for Leach's exhibition of 1931 with Tomimoto Kenkichi at the Beaux Arts Gallery, London, as no. 135: 'Inlaid porcelain Bowl; "Korean washerwoman" pattern'. It was shown in Leach's Arts Council retrospective in 1961, having been recommended for inclusion by George Wingfield Digby, and was subsequently given to the museum. In a letter to the donor of 14 April 1961, Leach writes of the bowl: 'Yes I still like it: I only did one of that sort.' In *A Potter's Work* (1967), pl.26, he describes its decoration as 'the memory of a Korean woman beating her washing in the rocky bed of a stream'. The museum possesses a later ink-wash drawing by Leach of the same subject (E.1203-1978).

536 Dish, *c.* 1932
Earthenware, slip-trailed in white, amber glaze; marks: 'BL' and 'SI' in monogram, impressed; h.5.4cm, d.30.2cm
Circ.587-1968. Source: The Artist Potters Shop, Eastbourne, £40

537 Panel of nine tiles, 1938
Stoneware, oatmeal glaze, painted in brown and incised; marks: 'BL' and 'SI' in monogram, painted; h.15cm, w.15cm (each)
C.47-1946. Source: given by the artist
This and the following two panels were chosen for an exhibition of tiles held at the museum in 1939. Arthur Lane, Keeper of the Ceramics Department, recommending acceptance of the gift, noted: 'They are of good artistic & technical quality, and Mr Leach himself considers them worthy examples of his work. He recently called here to see whether he could offer anything superior to replace them, and decided not.'

538 Panel of nine tiles, *c.* 1939
Stoneware, oatmeal glaze, painted in blue and brown; marks: 'SI' interlaced and 'BL' monogram in lower corners, painted; h.10cm, w.10cm (each)
C.48-1946. Source: *see* **537**

530

536

534

537

538

539

540

542

545

541

543 / 544

539 Panel of nine tiles, *c.* 1939
Stoneware, oatmeal glaze, painted in brown and incised; marks: 'SI' and 'BL' in monogram in lower corners, painted; h.10cm, w.10cm (each)
C.49-1946. Source: *see* 537

540 Bowl, 1947
Stoneware, incised decoration through iron pigment, oatmeal glaze; inscribed '19' and '47'; marks: 'BL' and 'SI' in monogram, impressed; h.12.1cm, d.22.5cm
Circ.280-1950. Source: Arts and Crafts Exhibition Society (Twenty-second Exhibition, V&A, 1950, no.594), £7

541 'Tall Pot, olive and rust', 1950
Stoneware, olive glaze, painted in brown; thrown by David Leach, decorated by Bernard Leach; marks: 'DL' and 'SI' in monogram, impressed; h.40cm, d.20cm
Circ.281-1950. Source: Arts and Crafts Exhibition Society (Twenty-second Exhibition, V&A, 1950, no.548), £20
Bernard Leach was unenthusiastic about this pot. In a letter to Hugh Wakefield, Assistant Keeper of the V&A's Circulation Department, he wrote: 'I cannot help feeling rather sorry that you have got the big pot from the Arts & Crafts Society Exhibition. The history of it is David made the shape at this end, got stuck on the decoration and handed it over to me at that stage. Then it fired very nicely, but I still don't think the shape is a good one.' The museum subsequently considered returning it in favour of the two jars acquired in 1952 (543 and 544), though this evidently was not done.

542 Small pot, 1950
Porcelain, tenmoku glaze with kaki spots; marks: 'SI' in monogram, impressed; h.5.9cm, d.6cm
Circ.84-1951. Source: given by the artist
Bernard Leach offered this pot to the museum as he was particularly pleased with the glaze effect, writing: 'There is also a tiny bottle with the most beautiful combination of Tenmoku and Kaki in spots which I would be very glad to give to the Museum if you would care to have it.'

543 Jar, 1951
Stoneware, grey-white glaze, resist decoration in brown; marks: 'BL' and 'SI' in monogram, impressed; h.24.5cm, d.24cm
Circ.136-1952. Source: the pottery, £12

544 Jar, 1951
Stoneware, grey-white glaze, incised pattern through brown; marks: 'BL' and 'SI' in monogram, impressed; h.24.2cm, d.24.4cm
Circ.137-1952. Source: *see* 543, £12

545 Jar with flattened sides, *c.* 1952
Stoneware, oatmeal glaze, painted in blue-black and brown; marks: 'BL' and 'SI' in monogram, impressed; h.26.9cm, d.24.5cm
C.66-1976. Source: A. Landau, London, £150

546 Pot, *c.* 1955
Stoneware, yellow-brown mottled ash glaze; marks: 'BL' and 'SI' in monogram and 'England', impressed; h.35.6cm, d.30cm
C.29-1968. Source: given by Mr Paul Bester in memory of his son, Mr Gerald Bester

546

548

549

547 Pilgrim bottle, 1956 (pl.40)
Stoneware, thrown and assembled, tenmoku glaze, incised decoration; h.28cm, d.23cm
Circ.498-1956. Source: Liberty & Co., London (Leach Pottery exhibition, 1956), £30
Leach is reported to have thought this bottle one of the best pieces he had made for some time. See exh. review, *Pottery Quarterly*, 3:10 (1956), p.77. Illustrated in *A Potter's Work* (1967), pl.59.

548 Pot, *c.* 1957
Stoneware, tenmoku glaze, incised decoration; marks: 'BL' and 'SI' in monogram, impressed; h.34cm, d.26.9cm
Circ.115-1958. Source: Primavera, London (solo exhibition, 1958), £30

549 Pot, *c.* 1959
Stoneware, fluted, tenmoku glaze; marks: 'BL' and 'SI' in monogram and 'England', impressed; h.36.3cm, d.29.7cm
Circ.129-1960. Source: Primavera, London (exhibition: *Porcelain and Stoneware by Bernard Leach*, 1960, no.2), £30
The exhibition handlist lists this as 'Tenmoku fluted pot with cap'. A note on the acquisition papers, however, records: 'Leach felt at the exhibition that the piece was spoiled by the small cap which accompanied it, and the latter has therefore been excluded from this purchase.' The cap explains the small lugs, which would allow it to be tied on.

550 Tile, *c.* 1950–59
Stoneware tile of industrial manufacture, painted in brown and blue on a grey glaze; marks: 'SI' and 'BL' in monogram, painted, and '... NDY ENGLAND', moulded (probably for the firm of Candy & Co. Ltd, Newton Abbot, Devon); h.14.7cm, w.14.7cm
C.89-1997. Source: provenance unknown

551 Bottle, 1961–62
Stoneware, incised decoration through iron pigment, oatmeal glaze; marks: 'BL' and 'SI' in monogram and 'ENGLAND', impressed; h.40cm, d.16.7cm
C.157-1979. Source: given by George and Cornelia Wingfield Digby in memory of Bernard Leach
Purchased by the donors from Bernard Leach in St Ives in 1963.

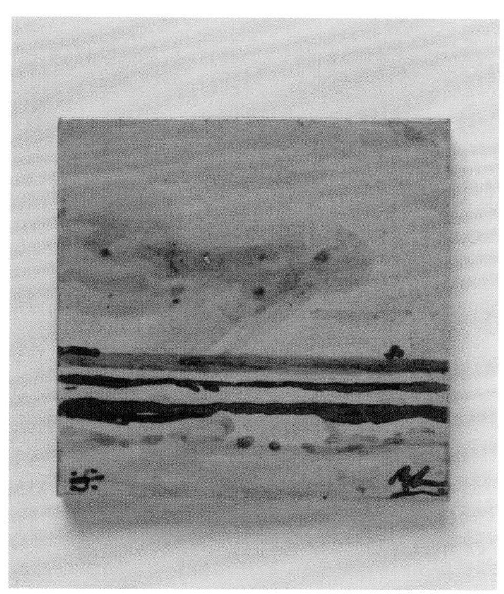
550

551

552 Lidded jar, 1963
Stoneware, cut sides, tenmoku glaze; marks: 'BL' and 'SI' in monogram, impressed; h.25.2cm, d.22.8cm
Circ.551&A-1963. Source: Primavera, London (solo exhibition, 1963, no.9), £35

553 Pot, 1967
Porcelain, fluted sides, white glaze; marks: 'BL' and 'SI' in monogram, impressed; h.28.7cm, d.19cm
Circ.1192-1967. Source: Crane Kalman Gallery, London, £85

552

554

553

554 Pot, 1972
Stoneware, dark green glaze, brown at rim; marks: 'BL' and 'SI' in monogram, impressed; h.28.9cm, d.25cm
Circ.332-1973. Source: the artist (following the exhibitions *International Ceramics 1972*, V&A, 1972, and *The Craftsman's Art*, V&A, 1973), £100

Leach, David 1911–2005 *see also* Leach Pottery

1911	born Tokyo, Japan; son of Bernard Leach (qv)
1920	family moves to St Ives, Cornwall
1930–	decides against university; joins Leach Pottery as apprentice
1933–34	teaches at Dartington Hall, Devon, and develops plans for a pottery
1934–37	attends pottery managers' course at North Staffordshire Technical College, Stoke-on-Trent
1937–	returns to Leach Pottery and embarks on reorganization; converts kiln to oil-firing, develops Standard Ware range in stoneware, trains team of apprentices
1938	plans for production pottery at Dartington Hall shelved
1939	son John Leach (qv) born
1941	son Jeremy Leach (qv) born
1941–45	war service
1946–55	partnership with Bernard Leach to run Leach Pottery
1950	initiates pottery evening classes at Penzance School of Art
1951	helps establish pottery at Sandefjord, Norway
1951	experiments with lower-firing porcelain body with the help of Edward Burke, chief chemist at Portland Cement Company
1953–54	takes over pottery department at Loughborough College of Art for one year; develops range of stoneware glazes for Podmores, Stoke-on-Trent
1954–55	establishes pottery for Carmelite Friars at Aylesford, Kent, taken over by Colin Pearson (qv)
1956–	establishes own pottery at Lowerdown Cross, Bovey Tracey, Devon, making slipware and tin-glazed earthenware
1961	builds two-chamber wood- and oil-fired kiln; abandons earthenware for stoneware and porcelain
1966	solo exhibition, Craftsmen Potters Shop, London
1967	Chairman of Craftsmen Potters Association; Gold Medal, International Academy of Ceramics, Istanbul; develops throwable translucent porcelain body, subsequently marketed as David Leach Porcelain by Podmores
1975	joins board of Dartington Pottery Training Workshop
1978	workshop tour, USA
1982	builds small gas-fired kiln; discontinues use of large kiln
1987	awarded OBE
2003	touring retrospective exhibition, Devon Guild of Craftsmen

David Leach played a crucial part in the survival of the Leach Pottery into the post-war era, using knowledge gained through his technical training in Stoke-on-Trent to reorganize the workshop and set it up as a production pottery. He brought in machinery, including a pug-mill for clay preparation, and converted the kiln to oil-firing. He also introduced a new stoneware body and with his father designed the range of Standard Ware shapes. Bernard Leach had strongly disapproved of his mixing with 'the industrial devils of Stoke', but was mollified when he saw the results. David developed real individuality as a potter only after leaving St Ives and establishing his own pottery in Devon. He produced there a distinctive body of work, but is important also for his technical interests, including his development of a porcelain suitable for the studio potter, and for his involvement in education.

David Leach, 'Porcelain Body', *CR*, 2 (1970)
— 'Lowerdown Pottery', *CR*, 21 (1973)
— interview, in Cameron and Lewis (1976), pp.84–95, 166
— 'Elegance and Strength', *Crafts*, 38 (1979)
— 'Making a Teapot', *CR*, 126 (1990)
— 'A Potter's Day', *CR*, 138 (1992)
— 'Dartington; The 30's and Beyond', in Whiting (1993)
— *David Leach*, Aberystwyth Arts Centre: Ceramic Series 76 (1996)
Arts and Crafts Exhibition Society (1948), (1950), (1952)
Dartington Hall (1952)
Wingfield Digby (1952)
Murray Fieldhouse, 'Workshop Visit to Loughborough College', *Pottery Quarterly*, 2:6 (1955)

Rose (1955), pp.13–14, pl.26A, (1970), pp.39–40, pl.72
Decorative Art (1961/62), (1968/69), (1975/76)
Casson (1967), p.7, pls.141–2, 213–16
Potters (1972) to (2000)
V&A (1972), p.112
Crafts Advisory Committee (1976), p.102
Edelman (1976), Part I
Crafts Advisory Committee (1977), p.17
Robert Fournier (ed.), *David Leach: A Monograph*, ed. from tapes made by Bernard and David Leach (Lacock, 1977)
Crafts Council (1980), p.60
Gary C. Hatcher, 'A Day in the Life: Apprenticing with David Leach', *Ceramics Monthly*, 28:6 (1980)
Paisley Museum and Art Galleries (1984), p.51
Crafts Council (1985), pp.60–1
Tate Gallery (1985), p.236
W.A. Ismay, 'David Leach – Sixty Years a Potter', *CR*, 125 (1990)
Riddick (1990), p.75
Peter Dormer, 'Sources of Inspiration', *Crafts*, 120 (1993)
Whiting (1993)
Emmanuel Cooper, 'An Unassuming Talent', *CR*, 149 (1994)
Anne-Carole Chamier, 'Ways of Seeing', *CR*, 158 (1996)
Gary Hatcher, 'A Conversation with David Leach', *Ceramics Monthly*, 45:1 (1997)
Emmanuel Cooper, 'A Dynasty of Potters', *Resurgence*, 209 (2001)
Cooper (2003)
Emmanuel Cooper and Kathy Niblett, *David Leach*, biography and exh. cat. (Shepton Beauchamp, 2003)
Kathy Niblett and Tim Andrews, 'David Leach', *CR*, 200 (2003)
Whybrow (2006)
Nottingham City Museums and Galleries (2017), pp.57–8

Exhibition reviews: Barbara Hepworth, *St Ives Times* (19 August 1949); 'Pottery from Loughborough College', *Pottery Quarterly*, 1:4 (1954); Elaine and Emanuel Benson, *Craft Horizons*, 26:6 (1966); W.A. Ismay, *CR*, 16 (1972), and 46 (1977); *CR*, 57 (1979); Paul Vincent, *Studio Pottery*, 1 (1993), and 15 (1995); Julian Stair, *Crafts*, 183 (2003)

Obituaries: Emmanuel Cooper, *The Independent* (25 February 2005); *The Times* (25 February 2005); Victor Margrie, *The Guardian* (26 February 2005); David Whiting, *Crafts*, 194 (2005)

An interview with David Leach is in the Recording the Crafts video archive at UWE Bristol (also held in the National Art Library, V&A, London, 704.AA.0030 to 704.AA.0042).

All works made at Lowerdown Pottery, Bovey Tracey, unless stated otherwise.

555 Jar, 1951
Stoneware, tenmoku glaze with brush decoration; marks: obscured seals; made at Leach Pottery, St Ives; h.16.8cm, d.22.5cm
Circ.138-1952. Source: the pottery, £10

556 Footed bowl, 1966
Stoneware, tenmoku and mottled greenish glaze; marks: 'DL' and 'L+' in monogram, impressed; h.16.2cm, d.39.5cm
Circ.880-1966. Source: Craftsmen Potters Association, London, £15.15s.

557 Bottle vase, 1972
Stoneware, tenmoku glaze with finger-wiped decoration; marks: 'DL' in monogram, impressed; h.60.5cm, d.26.5cm
Circ.163-1973. Source: the artist, £50

558 Round pot, 1972
Porcelain, speckled pink glaze with crackle; marks: 'DL' in monogram, impressed; h.18.5cm, d.20cm
Circ.293-1973. Source: the artist, £15

559 Coffee set, *c.* 1976
Stoneware, speckled matt oatmeal glaze, painted in iron; marks: 'L+', impressed; h.13.5cm, d.16.3cm (coffee pot); h.7.8cm, d.12.7cm (milk jug); h.6.2cm, d.8.4cm (sugar bowl); h.7cm, d.9.7cm (mug)
C.54:1,2, 55, 56 & 57-2004. Source: given by Robin Hildyard
From the standard range of tableware made at Lowerdown to David Leach's designs, largely by apprentices or students. The brushed foxglove motif was particularly favoured by David.

555

556

557

558

559

560

561

563 / 562

564

560 Large pot, 1980
Stoneware, tenmoku glaze, brush decoration in ilmenite; marks: 'DL' in monogram, impressed; h.42.1cm, d.31.8cm
C.172-1980. Source: Craftsmen Potters Association, London (solo exhibition, 1980, no.12), £162

561 Dish, 1980
Stoneware, wax-resist decoration in white over a tenmoku glaze; marks: 'DL' in monogram, impressed; h.5.3cm, d.29.5cm
C.173-1980. Source: *see* **560** (no.46), £60

562 Teapot, 1980
Porcelain, fluted, celadon glaze, cane handle; marks: 'DL' in monogram, impressed; h.15cm, d.18.2cm
C.174&A-1980. Source: *see* **560** (no.116), £28

563 Bowl, 1980
Porcelain, fluted, blue-grey 'gunmetal' glaze; marks: 'DL' in monogram, impressed; h.7.2cm, d.10.7cm
C.175-1980. Source: *see* **560** (no.127), £10
The 'gunmetal' glaze was a new experiment.

564 Lidded jar, 1997
Porcelain, thrown, fluted, celadon glaze; marks: 'DL' in monogram, impressed; h.15cm, d.13.9cm
C.20:1,2-1998. Source: Galerie Besson, London (joint exhibition with Jessamine Kendall, 1997, no.47), £260

See also 541 *under* Bernard Leach.

Leach, Janet (née **Darnell**) 1918–1997
see also Leach Pottery

1918	born Grand Saline, Texas, USA
1938–	moves to New York, enrols at art school, under sculptor Robert Cronbach; works as assistant to Cronbach and on Federal Art Project
1941–45	works as welder in Staten Island shipyard
1947–	becomes interested in pottery, studies at Inwood Pottery, New York; teaches pottery at Rockland State Hospital, New York, in occupational therapy department
1948–54	establishes pottery at Threefold Farm, an anthroposophic community in Spring Valley, New York State
1950	studies ceramics at Alfred University, New York State, on summer course
1952	meets Bernard Leach (qv) and Hamada Shōji (qv) at seminar at Black Mountain College, North Carolina, during their tour of USA
1954–55	travels to Japan to work with Hamada at Mashiko; travels in Japan with Leach; works at Ichino Pottery, Tamba
1956–	moves to St Ives, Cornwall, to marry Leach; gradually assumes management of Leach Pottery (qv)
1965–	founds gallery, New Craftsman, St Ives, with Mary 'Boots' Redgrave
1979–	Bernard Leach dies, leaving Janet his share of the pottery; phases out Standard Ware production; concentrates on own work, working alongside former apprentice Trevor Corser
2006	retrospective exhibition, Tate St Ives

Janet Leach was a vigorous potter, whose expressive, handbuilt and thrown work was informed by traditional Japanese pottery and the work of Hamada Shōji (qv). Freely rendered, her pots often exhibit contrasting textures, with flowing ash glazes on red stoneware, or slashes of white glaze animating black clay. Janet took over the running of the Leach Pottery (qv) following her marriage to Bernard Leach (qv), modifying and updating its Standard Ware, bringing in international students, and encouraging more individual work to be made. Despite Bernard's dominant position in studio pottery, Janet retained a distinctive and strongly individual voice, which showed little by way of direct influence.

Janet Leach, 'With Hamada in Mashiko', with biographical notes, *Pottery Quarterly*, 3:11 (1956)
— 'Tamba', *Pottery Quarterly*, 4:13 (1957)
— 'Korean Throwing', *Pottery Quarterly*, 4:14 (1957)
— 'A Letter from Japan', *Pottery Quarterly*, 9:36 (1970)
— 'Fifty One Years of the Leach Pottery', *CR*, 14 (1972)
— statement, in Rothschild (1972)
— 'Going to Pot', *CR*, 71 (1981)
— 'American Foreigner', *Studio Potter*, 11:2 (1983)
— 'Pots at the Tate!', *CR*, 92 (1985)
— 'A Potter's Day', *CR*, 146 (1994)
Decorative Art (1965/66)
Casson (1967), p.7, pls.38, 138–40
J.P. Hodin, 'Janet Darnell Leach', *Pottery Quarterly*, 9:33 (1967), pp.7–13, pls.4–5
Rose (1970), p.51, pls.86–9
Birks (1976), pp.104–17
Crafts Advisory Committee (1976), p.103
'Janet Leach – Recent Pots', *CR*, 39 (1976)
'Janet Leach – New Ceramics', *CR*, 51 (1978)
Crafts Council (1980), p.60
Potters (1980) to (1997)
Harriet Brisson, 'Janet Darnell Leach', *Ceramics Monthly*, 30:1 (1982)
Paisley Museum and Art Galleries (1984), pp.51–2
Crafts Council (1985), p.62
Christopher Reid, 'Something in the Air', *Crafts*, 73 (1985)
Tate Gallery (1985), pp.240
Emmanuel Cooper, 'Sculptural Potter', *CR*, 120 (1989)
— *Janet Leach*, Aberystwyth Arts Centre: Ceramic Series 44 (1990)
Paul Vincent, 'Interview with Janet Leach', *Studio Pottery*, 2 (1993)
Crafts Council (1995b), pp.42–3
'Janet Leach – New Pots', *CR*, 156 (1995)
Cooper (2003)
J.V.G. Mallet, 'The "Gentleman" Potters Part 1, Bernard and Janet Leach', *English Ceramic Circle Transactions*, 18:2 (2003)
Joanna Wason, 'Janet Leach', *CR*, 221 (2006)
David Whiting, 'The Life of Janet Leach', *Crafts*, 203 (2006)
Whybrow (2006), pp.45–53, 68–71 and elsewhere
Emmanuel Cooper, *Janet Leach: A Potter's Life* (London, 2007)
Bic Wood, letter, *CR*, 225 (2007)
Nottingham City Museums and Galleries (2017), p.59
Joanna Wason, *Janet Leach: Potter* (Cornwall, 2021)

Exhibition reviews: *Pottery Quarterly*, 6:24 (1959); W.A. Ismay, *CR*, 17 (1972); Tony Birks, *CR*, 33 (1975); Eileen Lewenstein, *Crafts*, 15 (1975); Ian Auld, *Crafts*, 26 (1977); William Edwards, *Crafts*, 32 (1978); W.A. Ismay, *Crafts*, 50 (1981); Jonathan Sidney, *CR*, 82 (1983); Tony Birks, *Crafts*, 63 (1983); Marilyn Walters, *Ceramics: Art and Perception*, 68 (2007)

Obituaries: Emmanuel Cooper, *The Independent* (13 September 1997); *Daily Telegraph* (16 September 1997); *The Times* (17 September 1997); Paul Vincent, *The Guardian* (18 September 1997); Tanya Harrod, *Crafts*, 149 (1997)

565

567

568

569

All works made at the Leach Pottery, St Ives.

565 Vase, 1963
Stoneware, ash glaze; marks: 'JL' and 'SI' in monogram, impressed; h.37cm, d.23.6cm
Circ.375-1963. Source: Primavera, London (solo exhibition, 1963, no.3), £18

566 Large vase, 1965 (pl.48)
Stoneware, slab-built, ash glaze over red body, tenmoku interior; marks: 'JL' and 'SI' in monogram, impressed; h.42cm, d.23cm
Circ.352-1965. Source: Primavera, London (exhibition: *Pottery by Janet Leach*, 1965, no.1), £30

567 Vase, 1975–76
Stoneware, ash glaze; marks: 'JL' and 'SI' in monogram, impressed; h.25cm, d.15.3cm
C.283-1976. Source: the pottery, £40

568 Vase, 1983
Stoneware, white glaze on unglazed stained black; marks: 'JL' and 'SI' in monogram, impressed; h.25.6cm, d.32.6cm
C.251-1983. Source: Craftsmen Potters

Association, London (solo exhibition, 1983, no.63), £450

569 Vase, 1983
Porcelain, painted in brown, brown glazed interior; marks: 'JL' and 'SI' in monogram, impressed; h.21.6cm, d.14.6cm
C.252-1983. Source: *see* **568** (no.109), £175

Leach, Jeremy 1941–

1941	born St Ives, the son of David Leach (qv)
1959–62	trains intermittently with father at Lowerdown Pottery, Bovey Tracey
1961–	studies at Central School of Arts and Crafts, London
1962–64	workshop in Southwark, London
1965	visits Lebanon, potting and exhibiting
1970–	works at Lowerdown Pottery for several years after a period teaching; pots elsewhere for short periods
1998–2001	establishes Moorlands Pottery, Haytor Vale, Devon
2001–13	returns to Lowerdown Pottery; continues potting there after his father's death in 2005
2014–	workshop at the Edgemoor Hotel, Bovey Tracey

The second son of David Leach (qv), Jeremy Leach produced domestic ware and individual pieces in stoneware and porcelain, working in the Anglo-Asian school of practice established by his grandfather Bernard Leach (qv).

Jeremy Leach, *Throwing: An Analysis of Centering for Hospitals, Colleges and Schools*, pamphlet (1979)
Val Barry, exh. review, *CR*, 27 (1974)
Crafts Advisory Committee (1976), p.103
Crafts Council (1980), p.60
Emmanuel Cooper, *David Leach* (Shepton Beauchamp, 2003), p.119

570

570 Bowl, *c.* 2000–10
Stoneware, celadon glaze; marks: 'M', 'JLJC' and an ichthus, impressed; made at Moorlands Pottery and Lowerdown Pottery; h.15.5cm, d.33cm
C.42-2011. Source: given by the artist
One of a number of unfinished pieces made at Moorlands that were fired following Leach's return to Lowerdown.

Leach, John 1939–2021

1939	born St Ives, the son of David Leach (qv)
1957–	works with father at Lowerdown Pottery, Bovey Tracey, also for short periods with Ray Finch (qv) and with Colin Pearson (qv) at Aylesford, Kent
1960–63	apprentice at Leach Pottery, St Ives
1963	sets up pottery with Harold Guilland in Mendocino, California, USA
1965–	establishes Muchelney Pottery, Somerset; works alone, making oil-fired domestic stoneware
1972–	takes on Nick Rees as an apprentice
1976–	begins wood-firing
1981–	begins making signed, individual work
1984	study tour of Nigeria
1985–98	regular workshops and lectures in USA, Canada, Denmark and Sweden
1997–98	builds new three-chambered wood-fired kiln
2002–	former apprentice Mark Melbourne returns full-time
2003–	opens John Leach Gallery at Muchelney Pottery
2018	Nick Rees retires
2021	solo exhibition, *John Leach: 65 Years A Potter*, Leach Pottery, St Ives

The grandson of Bernard Leach (qv) and son of David Leach (qv), John Leach achieved considerable success with his distinctive range of thrown domestic stoneware. His shapes are strong, robust and practical, their unglazed exteriors warmly flashed by the flame and ash of the wood-fired kiln. The range, which extended to more than 60 designs, was produced by a small team with Leach and the potters Nick Rees and Mark Melbourne at its core. Leach also developed individual work, most notably his striking, unpredictably marked, black pots, fired in sawdust-filled saggars.

John Leach, contribution, in 'Bernard Leach – A Living Tradition', *CR*, 108 (1987)
Potters/The Ceramics Book (1972) to (2012)
Decorative Art (1974/75), (1977)
'Working in Somerset', *Crafts*, 16 (1975), pp.11–12
Crafts Advisory Committee (1976), p.104
— (1977), p.18
Crafts Council (1980), p.60
'John Leach – Country Jugs', *CR*, 67 (1981)
'John Leach: Functional Ware', *Ceramics Monthly*, 31:6 (1983)
Crafts Council (1985), p.62
Tate Gallery (1985), p.241
Amanda Hare, 'Nigerian Journey', *Crafts*, 89 (1987)
Rufford Craft Centre, *John Leach, Potter*, exh. pamphlet (Nottinghamshire, 1988)
Richard La Trobe-Bateman, 'Working Potter', *CR*, 115 (1989)
Cooper (1990)
Perryman (1995), pp.81–2
Marian Edwards, 'Conservationist Potter', *Ceramics Monthly*, 45:7 (1997)
Lionel Phillips, 'John Leach', *Studio Pottery*, 25 (1997)
Paul Vincent, 'John Leach at Muchelney Pottery', *Studio Pottery*, 38 (1999)
Jim Robison, 'The Potters of Muchelney', *CR*, 198 (2002)
Andy Christian, 'Flame and Ash', *CR*, 256 (2012)
James Brinsford, 'A Potter's Flood', *CR*, 269 (2014)
Michael Jones, 'Visit to Muchelney Pottery', *CPA News*, 162 (2015)
Nottingham City Museums and Galleries (2017), pp.60–1
Martin Hesp, obituary, *Western Daily Press* (1 September 2021)

Exhibition reviews: W.A. Ismay, *CR*, 18 (1972), and *Crafts*, 93 (1988)

A recorded interview with John Leach is in the Potters of the Bernard Leach Legacy collection at the British Library, London (C1330/05).

571 Cider jar, 1981 (pl.79)
Stoneware, brown glazed interior, unglazed exterior with ash flashings; marks: 'MUCHELNEY', impressed; h.38.3cm, d.26.3cm
C.88-1981. Source: Muchelney Pottery, by mail order, £43 (with **572** and **573**)
No.28 in the Muchelney mail order catalogue.

572 'Large Hotpot', 1981
Stoneware, green glazed interior, unglazed exterior with ash flashings; marks: 'MUCHELNEY', impressed; h.22.8cm, d.26cm

573 / 572

574

C.89&A-1981. Source: *see* 571
No.2 in the Muchelney mail order catalogue.

573 Jug, 1981
Stoneware, brown glazed interior, unglazed exterior with ash flashings; marks: 'MUCHELNEY', impressed; h.20.6cm, d.18.2cm
C.90-1981. Source: *see* 571
No.24 in the Muchelney mail order catalogue.

574 'Fat vase, scratched', 1984
Stoneware, unglazed, fired in a sawdust-filled saggar; marks: 'JHL' and 'MUCHELNEY' in monogram, impressed; h.18.8cm, d.19cm
C.36-1985. Source: J K Hill, London (solo exhibition: *John Leach in a 'Black Mood'*, 1984, no.10), £200

Leach, Margaret (later Heron) 1918–2003

1918 born Cheshire
1936–40 studies at Liverpool City School of Art
1942–46 works with Bernard Leach (qv) at Leach Pottery, St Ives
1947–50 takes over and re-establishes the unoccupied The Barn Pottery, Brockweir, Gloucestershire, making slipware; Lewis Groves (qv) trains with her; Dorothy Kemp (qv) works with her during vacations
1950– joins Taena Community, Aylburton, Gloucestershire, working with Groves at the pottery he has established
1952– moves with Taena Community to Whitley Court, Upton St Leonards, Gloucestershire
1956 ceases potting on marriage

Margaret Leach – no relation of Bernard Leach (qv) – was recognized for her traditional domestic slipware. As a student at the Leach Pottery, she was welcomed for her co-operative spirit and competence in throwing. She established her own workshop in the Wye Valley – hence the 'WV' initials of her mark – before joining the Taena Community, a small Christian community engaged in farming and pottery, where she worked alongside Lewis Groves (qv).

Arts and Crafts Exhibition Society (1944), (1946)
Wingfield Digby (1952), p.83, pls.59–60
George Ineson, *Community Journey* (London, 1956), pp.153–4, 190
Lewis (1956), pl.363
Cooper (2003), pp.217–18, 225
Whybrow (2006), pp.108–9 and elsewhere

575 Dish, 1949
Earthenware, slip-trailed in black on white, amber glaze; marks: 'WV' in monogram, impressed; h.4cm, d.28.2cm
Circ.160-1950. Source: the artist, 17s.6d.

576 Quart jug, 1949
Earthenware, black slip, amber glaze; h.15.4cm, d.15.7cm
Circ.161-1950. Source: *see* 575, 12s.6d.

577 Soup bowl, 1949
Earthenware, black and white slips, amber glaze; marks: 'WV' in monogram, impressed; h.6.2cm, d.13.2cm
Circ.163-1950. Source: *see* 575, 5s.

578 Bowl, 1949
Earthenware, white slip over black, amber glaze; h.6.8cm, d.14.3cm
Circ.162-1950. Source: *see* 575, 6s.

579 Vase, 1949
Earthenware, painted black slip on white, amber glaze; marks: 'WV' in monogram, impressed; h.16.9cm, d.18.4cm
Circ.164-1950. Source: *see* 575, £2.10s.

577 / 575 / 576

579 / 578

Leach, William **Michael** 1913–1985

1913 born Japan, the son of Bernard Leach (qv)
1930–33 studies biology at University of Cambridge
1939 works at Leach Pottery, St Ives, after period of teaching
1940–46 serves in Pioneer Corps in East Africa, where sets up two potteries making tableware for troops
1946–48 works at Wrecclesham Pottery, Farnham, then Bullers, Stoke-on-Trent, with Anita (Agnete) Hoy (qv)
1949–55 returns to Leach Pottery
early 1950s teaches at Penzance School of Art, taking over from David Leach (qv)
1956– establishes Yelland Manor Pottery, North Devon
1983 retires, sells pottery

Following the Second World War, Michael Leach sought a position at the Leach Pottery (qv),

a proposition that met some resistance from his father, Bernard (qv), and older brother, David (qv), due to his lack of experience and his temperament. He nevertheless joined the pottery after working elsewhere, and participated in its management during periods when they were absent. He went on to establish his own pottery at Yelland Manor, making domestic ware and individual pieces, initially in slip-decorated earthenware and later reduction stoneware, selling primarily through the pottery's showroom.

Dartington Hall (1952)
Elmer Taylor, 'An Apprenticeship in England', *Ceramics Monthly*, 21:1 (1973)
Maggie Curtis, 'Michael Leach', letter, *CR*, 93 (1985)
Tate Gallery (1985), p.239
Emmanuel Cooper, exh. review, *Crafts*, 135 (1995)
North Devon Museum, *Michael Leach 1913–1985: A Memorial Exhibition*, exh. cat. (Barnstaple, 1995)
Paul Vincent, 'Michael Leach', *Studio Pottery*, 14 (1995)
Cooper (2003)
Whybrow (2006), pp.132–3 and elsewhere

580 Pot, *c.* 1961
Stoneware, mottled yellow and brown glaze; marks: 'ML' in monogram and 'Y', impressed; h.24cm, d.17cm
Circ.440-1962. Source: the artist, £6
This pot was put forward for acquisition by the potter. In correspondence he stated that he had made three further versions as people had wanted it – a practice he was not happy with and did not intend to repeat. This pot he described as 'the original'.

580

Leach Pottery *see also* Bernard Leach, David Leach *and* Janet Leach

The Leach Pottery was founded by Bernard Leach (qv) in St Ives, Cornwall, in 1920. In its earlier years its output was primarily of individual pieces made for exhibition, but about 1927, confronted with increasing financial pressures, Leach introduced a range of decorated tiles for fireplaces and furniture, and attempted a more regular production of earthenware for daily use, which he exhibited separately from his other work. Leach outlined his position regarding the production of domestic ware in his pamphlet, *A Potter's Outlook*, and found support in the philosophies of the Japanese *mingei* (folkcraft) movement, which saw such work as the basis for true artistic expression. With encouragement from Yanagi Sōetsu and Hamada Shōji (qv), Leach began working at Leonard and Dorothy Elmhirst's educational community at Dartington Hall, Devon, in 1932, gaining their financial support to explore plans for a production pottery there. This scheme was developed further by Bernard's son David Leach (qv), who took over his father's duties at Dartington while Bernard was in Japan (1934–35). Though the Dartington scheme was eventually shelved, David's work would benefit production at St Ives.

Realizing the limits of his technical knowledge, David, with backing from the Elmhirsts, enrolled on a pottery managers' course in Stoke-on-Trent. Returning to St Ives in 1937, he embarked on a reorganization of the Leach Pottery and arranged for local apprentices to be taken on, William Marshall (qv) being the first. With input from Bernard, David developed prototypes for a range of domestic stoneware, which became known as Standard Ware and was listed in a mail order catalogue. This comprised bowls, plates, jugs, mugs, coffee pots and other items. Some pieces were made in celadon porcelain, including a tea set available by special order. Four basic stoneware glazes were used: tenmoku; mottled grey-brown; celadon; and a creamy oatmeal with painting in blue and brown. Combining an attractive earthiness with practicality and ease of production, the range became the benchmark for domestic studio pottery. The ware was made by a team of potters under David's direction and marked with the Leach Pottery seal. Decoration, when added, was at first the responsibility of Bernard or David, and later also Marshall. By 1960 about 18,000 pieces of domestic stoneware and porcelain were produced annually, alongside 2000–3000 pieces of individual work.

Following David's departure and her arrival in 1956, Janet Leach (qv) took over the management of the pottery, overseeing Standard Ware production with Marshall. Modifications were made to certain shapes, and a more textured body introduced, using local clay from Doble's clay pit in St Agnes. Following Bernard's death in 1979 Janet discontinued the production of Standard Ware and the number of potters dwindled. The pottery eventually closed in 2005, but reopened as a museum and working studio three years later under the management of a charitable trust, after a major restoration. A range of soda-fired domestic ware was produced under its first Lead Potter, Jack Doherty. When the South African potter Roelof Uys was subsequently appointed to the role in 2013, he developed a new stoneware range, closer in concept and design to the original Leach Standard Ware. This was supplemented by a porcelain range, designed by Uys in 2015.

The Leach Pottery, pottery brochure (St Ives, 1928)
The Leach Pottery: Catalogue of Tiles, Fireplaces, Pottery (St Ives, *c.* 1930)
The Leach Pottery 1920–1946, with history by Bernard Leach, pamphlet (London: Berkeley Galleries, 1946)
Robert Richman, 'The Leach Pottery at St Ives', *Craft Horizons*, 10:3 (1950)
Murray Fieldhouse, 'Workshop Visit: The Leach Pottery', *Pottery Quarterly*, 1:1 (1954)
Rose (1955), pp.13–14, pls.24–5, (1970), pp.38–41
Casson (1967), pls.217–21
Janet Leach, 'Fifty One Years of the Leach Pottery', *CR*, 14 (1972)
Oliver Watson, 'The St Ives Pottery', in Tate Gallery (1985), pp.220–7
Alex Lambley, 'The Leach Pottery', *Ceramics Technical*, 36 (2013)
Roelof Uys, 'Behind the Kiln Door', *Ceramics Monthly*, 66:2 (2018)

Catalogues of Leach Pottery Standard Ware were issued regularly between 1946 and 1975.

For individual work made at the Leach Pottery, *see under* Bernard Leach, David Leach, Janet

581

of the Standard Ware range listed in the Leach Pottery catalogues. Though they are not marked with Bernard Leach's seal, David Leach indicated they were made by Bernard.

585 / 584 / 586

588 / 587 / 589

591 / 590

593 / 592

Leach, Hamada Shōji, William Marshall, Henry Bergen, Norah Braden, Michael Cardew, Charlotte Epton, Sylvia Fox-Strangways, Dorothy Kemp and Matsubayashi Tsurunosuke.

581 Tea bowl, *c.* 1925–29
Raku, painted in green, yellow and brown under a slightly opaque glaze; marks: 'SI' in monogram, impressed; h.8.7cm, d.8.9cm
C.133-2003. Source: given by Gillian Lee
The Leach Pottery gave demonstrations of the raku technique on Thursday afternoons during the summer, at which visitors could decorate pots and watch them being glazed and fired. This tea bowl is likely the product of one such demonstration.

582 Jug, 1940 (pl.30)
Stoneware, tenmoku glaze; marks: 'SI' in monogram, impressed; h.17.3cm, d.18cm
Circ.30-1940. Source: Heal & Son Ltd, London, 18s.9d.

583 Jug, 1940 (pl.30)
Stoneware, oatmeal glaze; marks: 'SI' in monogram, impressed; h.8.4cm, d.12cm
Circ.31-1940. Source: *see* **582**, 4s.6d.

584 Teapot, *c.* 1945
Porcelain, fluted spout, celadon glaze; marks: 'SI' in monogram, impressed; h.14.7cm, d.23.2cm
Circ.88&A-1964. Source: given by the Contemporary Art Society, having been acquired for their Pottery and Crafts Fund by Cecilia Sempill in 1945–46, together with **585** to **589** as a 'Celadon Tea Set' attributed to Bernard Leach. The gift was made as part of the Society's distribution of residual stock in 1963–64.
This teapot and accompanying fluted teacups and saucers (**585**) and bowl (**586**) are not part of the Standard Ware range listed in the Leach Pottery catalogues. Though they are not marked with Bernard Leach's seal, David Leach indicated they were made by Bernard.

585 Two cups and saucers, *c.* 1945
Porcelain, fluted, celadon glaze; marks: 'SI' in monogram, impressed; h.7.8cm, 7.3cm (cups), d.14cm, 14.3cm (saucers)
Circ.93&A, 94&A-1964. Source: *see* **584**

586 Sugar bowl, *c.* 1945
Porcelain, fluted, celadon glaze; marks: 'SI' in monogram, impressed; h.5.7cm, d.10cm
Circ.90-1964. Source: *see* **584**

587 Milk jug, *c.* 1945
Porcelain, celadon glaze; marks: 'SI' in monogram, impressed; h.9cm, d.11.5cm
Circ.91-1964. Source: *see* **584**
This milk jug design was later offered as no.87 in the Leach Pottery catalogue, part of a celadon tea set that included a teapot with engraved oakleaf design (*see* **590**). David Leach indicated that this particular milk jug and its accompanying basin and plate (**588** and **589**) were made by Bernard.

588 Sugar or slop basin, *c.* 1945
Porcelain, celadon glaze; marks: 'SI' in monogram, impressed; h.6.2cm, d.11.4cm
Circ.89-1964. Source: *see* **584**

589 Tea plate, *c.* 1945
Porcelain, celadon glaze; marks: 'SI' in monogram, impressed; h.2.5cm, d.14.9cm
Circ.92-1964. Source: *see* **584**

The item descriptions and numbers for **590** to **597** are as given in the 1949 Leach Pottery Catalogue, which was current at the time of their acquisition by the museum. The attributions were made by David Leach in 2004.

590 'Teapot, engraved oakleaf' (no.85), 1949
Porcelain, celadon glaze with incised decoration; made by David Leach, engraved by Bernard Leach; marks: 'SI' in monogram', impressed; h.15.9cm, d.27.2cm
Circ.170&A-1950. Source: the pottery, £1.15s.
This teapot is part of the 'Celadon Porcelain Teaset' offered in the 1949 Leach Pottery Catalogue. A note therein advises customers that, 'For technical reasons the production of porcelain teasets is limited and delivery may take longer than in other cases.' An equivalent

teapot with jam pot (*see* **591**) and milk jug (*see* **587**) is illustrated in Rose (1955), pl.25A.

591 'Porcelain lidded jampot' (no.32), 1949
Porcelain, celadon glaze with incised decoration; made by David Leach, engraved by Bernard Leach; marks: 'SI' in monogram, impressed; h.8cm, d.9cm
Circ.175&A-1950. Source: *see* **590**, 8s.6d.

592 'General purpose bowl' (no.82), 1949
Stoneware, celadon glaze interior; made by David Leach; marks: 'SI' in monogram, impressed; h.6.7cm, d.14.5cm
Circ.173-1950. Source: *see* **590**, 4s.

593 'Small decorated porringer' (no.10), 1949
Stoneware, oatmeal glaze with painted decoration in blue-brown; made by David Leach, decorated by Bernard Leach; marks: 'SI' in monogram, impressed; h.7cm, d.12.9cm
Circ.174-1950. Source: *see* **590**, 6s.

594 'Shallow decorated bowl' (no.9), 1949
Stoneware, tenmoku glaze with incised decoration through to a white glaze; made by David Leach or the team, decorated by Bernard Leach; marks: 'SI' in monogram, impressed; h.2.5cm, d.11cm
Circ.177-1950. Source: *see* **590**, 10s.

595 'Shallow decorated bowl' (no.9), 1949
Stoneware, oatmeal glaze with painted decoration in blue and brown; made by David Leach or the team, decorated by Bernard Leach; marks: 'SI' in monogram, impressed; h.2.8cm, d.11.3cm
Circ.178-1950. Source: *see* **590**, 10s.

596 'Glazed "pitcher" jug' (no.25), 1949
Stoneware, green and brown mottled glaze; marks: 'SI' in monogram, impressed; h.11cm, d.14cm
Circ.179-1950. Source: *see* **590**, 7s.

597 'Large beer tankard' (no.39), 1949
Stoneware, tenmoku glaze; made by David Leach; marks: 'SI' in monogram, impressed; h.12cm, d.13cm
Circ.176-1950. Source: *see* **590**, 7s.6d.

598 Jug, 1949
Stoneware, tenmoku glaze; made by David Leach; marks: 'SI' in monogram, impressed; h.26.4cm, d.16.6cm
Circ.172-1950. Source: *see* **590**, £3

599 Fruit bowl, 1949
Stoneware, painting in blue and brown in an oatmeal glaze, outside brown glaze; made by David Leach or the team, decorated by Bernard Leach; marks: 'SI' in monogram, impressed, 'BL', painted; h.12cm, d.30.3cm
Circ.171-1950. Source: *see* **590**, £3
This is a Standard Ware fruit bowl, decorated and initialled by Bernard Leach.

600 Lidded coffee jug, *c.* 1955
Stoneware, celadon glaze; marks: 'SI' in monogram and 'ENGLAND', impressed; h.19.3cm, d.15.3cm
C.29:1,2-1994. Source: B. & D. Kirk Antiques, Penzance, £35

Items **601** to **608** are part of the new Leach Pottery Standard Ware range designed by Lead Potter, Roelof Uys, in early 2014, and were made by the production team.

601 Large jug, 2018
Stoneware, greyish-white dolomite glaze; marks: 'SI' in monogram, impressed; h.28.4cm, d.18.2cm
C.14-2019. Source: the pottery, £243.54 (total for group); acquired through the generosity of Gerard and Sarah Griffin

602 Medium jug, 2018
Stoneware, green ash glaze; marks: 'SI' in monogram, impressed; h.20.5cm, d.15.3cm
C.15-2019. Source: *see* **601**

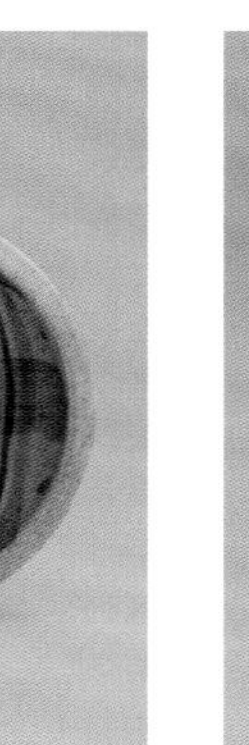

594 / 595

596

597 / 598

599

600

607 / 601 / 604 / 602 / 605 / 603 / 606 / 608

609

603 Small jug, 2018
Stoneware, tenmoku glaze; marks: 'SI' in monogram, impressed; h.10.4cm, d.12.5cm
C.16-2019. Source: *see* **601**

604 Large mug, 2018
Stoneware, tenmoku glaze; marks: 'SI' in monogram, impressed; h.9.7cm, d.10.7cm
C.17-2019. Source: *see* **601**

605 Small mug, 2018
Stoneware, green ash glaze; marks: 'SI' in monogram, impressed; h.7.7cm, d.9.3cm
C.18-2019. Source: *see* **601**

606 Medium general purpose bowl, 2018
Stoneware, greyish-white dolomite glaze; marks: 'SI' in monogram, impressed; h.7.3cm, d.16.2cm
C.19-2019. Source: *see* **601**

607 Honey pot, 2018
Stoneware, greyish-white dolomite glaze; marks: 'SI' in monogram, impressed; h.9cm, d.9cm
C.20:1,2-2019. Source: *see* **601**

608 Set of three mixing bowls, 2018
Stoneware, unglazed exterior, greyish-white dolomite glaze interior; marks: 'SI' in monogram, impressed; h.9.5cm, d.22.7cm (large bowl); h.7.4cm, d.17.3cm (medium bowl); h.5.5cm, d.13cm (small bowl)
C.21:1 to 3-2019. Source: *see* **601**

609 Small jug, small mug and small bowl, 2018
Porcelain, bluish Ying Ching glaze, brushed iron oxide rim; marks: 'SI' in monogram, impressed; h.10.1cm, d.11.7cm (jug); h.8.4cm, d.8.8cm (mug); h.5.9cm, d.12.5cm (bowl)
C.22 to 24-2019. Source: *see* **601**
Designed by Lead Potter, Roelof Uys, in early 2015, and made by the production team.

Lee, Jennifer 1956–

1956	born Ellon, Aberdeenshire
1975–79	studies ceramics and tapestry at Edinburgh College of Art
1979–80	travels in USA
1980–83	studies ceramics at Royal College of Art, London
1981–	solo exhibition, The Scottish Gallery, Edinburgh; exhibits widely thereafter
1983–87	studio at 401½ Workshops, London
1988–	studio in Peckham, London
1990–	regular solo exhibitions, Galerie Besson, London, and later Erskine, Hall & Coe, London
1991–	regular international solo exhibitions, Graham Gallery, New York, and later Frank Lloyd Gallery, Santa Monica; Liverpool Street Gallery, Sydney; Sokyo Gallery, Kyoto; and elsewhere
1993–94	retrospective exhibition, Röhsska Museet, Göteborg, and Aberdeen Art Gallery and Museum
2009	exhibition (with Lucie Rie and Ernst Gamperl), *U-Tsu-Wa*, 21_21 Design Sight, Tokyo, at invitation of the fashion designer Issey Miyake
2014–18	residencies in Shigaraki, Japan
2018	wins Loewe Foundation Craft Prize
2019	residency, Mashiko, Japan
2019	solo survey, *Jennifer Lee: the potter's space*, Kettle's Yard, Cambridge
2021	awarded OBE

Jennifer Lee is a leading exponent of the handbuilt vessel, making works of poise and refinement. Rising from narrow bases that lend a floating presence, her pots often present asymmetric disruptions to their profile or rims. Colour is explored with great subtlety using oxides and stains integrated into the clay body, creating bands and traces, haloes and speckles, in unglazed, burnished surfaces.

Jennifer Lee, 'Handbuilt Coloured Stoneware', *CR*, 95 (1985)
Amanda Fielding, 'Surfacing', *Crafts*, 87 (1987)
Jennifer Lee: Ceramics, text by David Queensberry (London: Woolley Dale Press, 1987)
Galerie Besson, *Jennifer Lee*, exh. pamphlet, text by David Attenborough (London, 1990)
Christopher Andreae, 'Graceful Tilting Contours of Clay', *Christian Science Monitor* (8 April 1991)
Jennifer Lee, text by Adam Levy (London: Atlas, 1993)
Adam Levy, 'The Anatomy of Things', *Revue de la Céramique et du Verre*, 76 (1994)
Galerie Besson, *Jennifer Lee*, exh. pamphlet, text by Edmund de Waal (London, 1997)
Karen Livingstone, 'Resonance', *Ceramics: Art and Perception*, 29 (1997)
Waller (1998), pp.67–8
Frankel (2000), pp.194–7
Danielle Pacaud, 'A Spirited Materiality', *Craft Arts International*, 52 (2001)
Galerie Besson, *Jennifer Lee*, exh. pamphlet, texts by Amanda Fielding and David Whiting, (London, 2003)
David Whiting, 'The Circumnavigation of Form', *Ceramics Monthly*, 51:8 (2003)
Perryman (2004), pp.138–43
Carole Andreani, 'Gres, la forme et l'infini', *Revue de la Céramique et du Verre*, 142 (2005)
Claudia Clare, 'Alive and Aware', *CR*, 231 (2008)
Galerie Besson, *Jennifer Lee*, exh. pamphlet, text by Alun Graves (London, 2008)

Whiting (2009), pp.78–83
Carlano (2010), pp.96–7
Liverpool Street Gallery, *Jennifer Lee*, exh. pamphlet, text by Edmund de Waal (Sydney, 2010)
Falls the Shadow: Jennifer Lee, text by Tanya Harrod (London: Atlas, 2012)
Erskine, Hall & Coe, *Jennifer Lee*, exh. pamphlets, text by Emma Crichton-Miller (London, 2013), (2016) and (2019)
Teleri Lloyd-Jones, 'A Journey from White to Red', *Crafts*, 262 (2016)
Isabella Smith, 'Balance and Poise', *CR*, 293 (2018)
Sokyo Gallery, *Jennifer Lee*, exh. cat., text by Tetsuro Degawa (Kyoto, 2018)
Sarah Griffin and Andrew Nairne (eds), *Jennifer Lee: the potter's space*, exh. cat. (Cambridge: Kettle's Yard, 2019)
Erskine, Hall & Coe, *Jennifer Lee: Ten Pots*, exh. cat., text by Robin Vousden (London, 2021)
Thorpe (2021), pp.39–45

Exhibition reviews: Arda Lacey, *Arts Review* (18 May 1990); Eileen Lewenstein, *Crafts*, 105 (1990); Karen S. Chambers, *American Ceramics*, 13:3 (2000); Amanda Fielding, *CR*, 187 (2001); Ellie Irons, *Ceramics: Art and Perception*, 62 (2005); Brett Ballard, *Ceramics: Art and Perception*, 83 (2011); Sara Roberts, *Crafts*, 235 (2012); Amy Sherlock, *Frieze*, 207 (2019)

610 Pot, 1985
Coloured stoneware, handbuilt; h.24.5cm, d.19cm
C.230-1985. Source: the artist (solo exhibition, Rosenthal Studio-Haus, London, 1985), £135
Artist's logbook number JL-401/200.

611 Pot, 1985
Coloured stoneware, handbuilt; h.15.2cm, d.12.6cm
C.231-1985. Source: *see* **610**, £80
Artist's logbook number JL-401/207.

612 *Pale, haloed granite traces, bronze specks*, 2007 (pl.123)
Coloured stoneware, handbuilt; marks: 'VII' in a circle, painted; h.27.5cm, d.19.3cm
C.67-2008. Source: Galerie Besson, London (solo exhibition, 2008), £3500; acquired through the generosity of Gerard and Sarah Griffin
Artist's logbook number JL735.

613 *Speckled shale, trace, haloed granite band, tilted olive rim*, 2019
Coloured stoneware, handbuilt; marks: 'XIX' in a circle, painted; h.24cm, d.16.8cm
C.53-2019. Source: the artist (exhibition: *Jennifer Lee: the potter's space*, Kettle's Yard, Cambridge, 2019), £20,000; acquired through the generosity of Gerard and Sarah Griffin
Artist's logbook number JL910. The museum also holds a pencil drawing by Lee of the finished pot (E.209-2020).

611 / 610

613

Lewenstein, Eileen (née Mawson) 1925–2005

1925	born London
1941–43	studies painting at West of England College of Art, Bristol
1943–44	studies at Beckenham School of Art
1944–45	teacher training at Institute of Education, University of London; teaches at Derby High School for Girls; attends pottery evening classes at Derby Art School, where much enthused by Robert Washington (qv), who teaches there
1946	becomes member of Artists International Association, serving on Central Committee 1947–49
1946–48	co-partner with Donald Mills (qv) and Brigitte Appleby in Donald Mills Pottery, London
1948	founds Briglin Pottery in Baker Street, London, with Appleby, producing Scandinavian-inspired domestic wares
1958	resigns from Briglin Pottery, leaving Appleby as sole partner
1959–63	studio in Camden, London; works alone making individual pieces
1960–69	teaches ceramics, Hornsey College of Art
1963–75	studio in Hampstead, London
1967	receives commission for large ceramic screen for the Convent of Our Lady of Sion, Chepstow Villas, London
1970–97	co-founder and co-editor with Emmanuel Cooper (qv) of *Ceramic Review*
1974	elected to the council of the International Academy of Ceramics
1976–	moves from London to Hove, Sussex; establishes workshop
2001	awarded MBE

Eileen Lewenstein was co-editor of *Ceramic Review* and a prolific writer, reviewer and lecturer. Politically motivated, and a member of the Communist Party from 1946 until the early 1960s, she had an international outlook, and was a supporter of the radical and innovative. As a potter she followed a range of interests, from rugged sculptural pieces to gentle forms with delicate surfaces and colouring.

Eileen Lewenstein, 'Ceramic Review', *Studio Potter*, 20:2 (1992)
— and Cooper (1974)
Arts and Crafts Exhibition Society (1954)
Decorative Art (1957/58), (1958/59), (1960/61) to (1963/64), (1965/66) to (1969/70), (1971/72) to (1974/75)
Biographical notes, *Pottery Quarterly*, 8:30 (1963), p.6, pl.23
Casson (1967), p.7, pls.39–40, 144
Rose (1970), p.50, pl.85
Potters (1972) to (2000)
Crafts Advisory Committee (1976), p.104

614

617

615

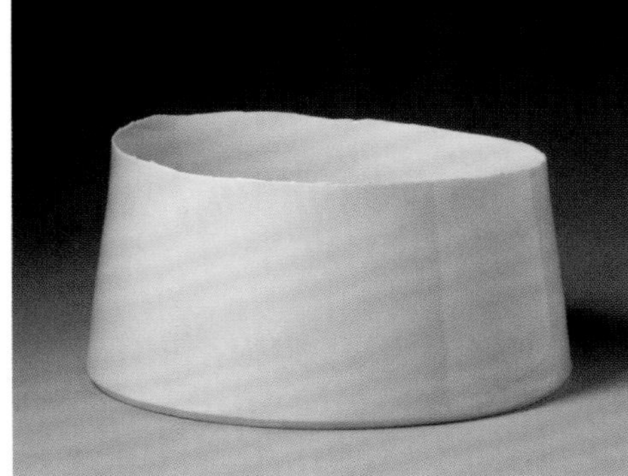

616

Sylvia Hyman, 'England's Eileen Lewenstein', *Ceramics Monthly*, 27:5 (1979)
Crafts Council (1980), p.60
Tanya Harrod, 'The Critic's Eye', *Crafts*, 107 (1990)
— *Eileen Lewenstein*, Aberystwyth Arts Centre: Ceramic Series 50 (1992)
— 'Potting and Editing', *CR*, 169 (1998)
Anthea Arnold, *Briglin Pottery 1948–1990* (Maidstone, 2002)
Tanya Harrod, 'Sources of Inspiration', *Crafts*, 175 (2002)
Sue Herdman, 'From our Archive', *CR*, 276 (2015)
Nottingham City Museums and Galleries (2017), p.62

Exhibition reviews: *Pottery Quarterly*, 7:28 (1962); Anthony Hepburn, *Craft Horizons*, 31:3 (1971), and *CR*, 9 (1971); Gordon Baldwin, *Crafts*, 7 (1974); Rosemarie Pitts, *Crafts*, 33 (1978), and 44 (1980); Emmanuel Cooper, *Art & Artists*, 15:2 (1980)

Obituaries: Emmanuel Cooper, *CR*, 213 (2005), and *The Independent* (26 March 2005); Tanya Harrod, *The Guardian* (30 March 2005); *The Times* (14 April 2005); Carolyn Trant, *Crafts*, 195 (2005)

614 Flower holder, 1971
Stoneware, handbuilt, metallic black glaze; marks: 'EL' in monogram, impressed; h.21.3cm, d.24.9cm
Circ.125-1971. Source: Pace Gallery, London, £30

615 Dish: *Wave Variations*, 1982
Stoneware, press-moulded, decoration in coloured slips; marks: 'EL' in monogram, impressed; h.4.6cm, d.30.6cm
C.76-1984. Source: given by the Friends of the V&A (purchased at the Craftsmen Potters Association exhibition, *Studio Ceramics Today*, V&A, 1983, no.110, £90)

Liao, Chun 1969–

1969	born Taichung, Taiwan
1993–96	studies ceramics at Bath Spa University College
1996–98	studies ceramics at Royal College of Art, London
1998–99	postgraduate research on Chinese raw glazes, Royal College of Art
2001–02	studio in Penfold Street, London
2002–15	regular solo exhibitions at Barrett Marsden (later Marsden Woo) Gallery, London
2003–18	studio in Finchley, London

Chun Liao is known for her exquisite, apparently simple, yet highly expressive, thrown pots: gently tapering cylinders of varying size, with untrimmed, fragile rims, and traces of fired metal. She is a meticulous student of glazes, which she applies raw to (unfired) porcelain pots that are once-fired in an electric kiln. Liao was among the first potters to meaningfully explore groupings and installations of vessels, often working with pieces of miniature, concentrated scale. She has also been influential in her development of arrays of vibrantly glazed pots.

Frankel (2000), pp.222–5
Barrett Marsden Gallery, *Chun Liao*, exh. pamphlet, text by Alison Britton (London, 2002)
Amanda Fielding, 'Chun Liao', *CR*, 194 (2002)
Alun Graves, 'Chun Liao', exh. essay, Barrett Marsden Gallery, London (2004)
Emmanuel Cooper, 'Rainbows of Light', *CR*, 238 (2009)

Exhibition reviews: Emma Clegg, *CR*, 211 (2005); David Whiting, *Crafts*, 192 (2005); Matthew Kangas, *Ceramics: Art and Perception*, 92 (2013)

Other essays issued alongside exhibitions at Marsden Woo (formerly Barrett Marsden) Gallery, London, offer further useful texts.

616 Pot, 2001
Porcelain, transparent glaze; marks: 'Chun Liao / 2001', incised; h.12.7cm, d.24.2cm
C.11-2002. Source: Barrett Marsden Gallery, London (solo exhibition, 2002, no.12); anonymous gift

617 Installation, 2008
Porcelain, coloured glazes, copper, gold; marks: 'Chun Liao / 2008', incised (variously with month or date); h.17.9cm, d.13.1cm (largest pot)
C.218:1 to 154-2009. Source: Barrett Marsden Gallery, £5869.57; acquired through the generosity of Gerard and Sarah Griffin

Lindo, Vicky 1980– and **William** (**Bill**) **Brookes** 1980–

1980	Vicky Lindo born Barnstaple, Devon; William Brookes born Chichester, West Sussex
1996–98	both study art and design at Petroc College, North Devon, where they meet
1999–2002	both study Design Crafts at Hereford College of Art and Design, Lindo specializing in textiles, Brookes in woodwork
2002–	Lindo works as independent maker in textiles and as museum assistant; Brookes works as cabinetmaker
2013–	together establish ceramic studio, The Pigeon Club, Bideford, Devon
2017	win Elle Decoration British Design Award in ceramics category
2019	win British Ceramics Biennial AWARD, Stoke-on-Trent, for *Dead Dad Book*
2019–20	solo exhibition, *Dead Dad Book*, The Burton, Bideford

Vicky Lindo and her partner, Bill Brookes, work collaboratively, making slip-cast earthenware with lively sgraffito decoration through vibrant underglaze colours. Lindo – whose name they predominantly work under – creates the graphic surfaces with their strongly illustrative qualities, fluently and deeply carved to give a relief effect. Brookes makes the plaster moulds and casts the wares, which they together design. Inspiration is drawn from a wide range of sources, including North Devon slipware.

Vicky Lindo, 'Dead Dad Book', *Ceramics: Art and Perception*, 115 (2020)
Annie Le Santo, 'Wild Cards', *CR*, 304 (2020)
Taylor (2020), pp.240–1

618 *Dead Dad Book*, 2019
12 works. All earthenware, slip-cast, with incised decororation through underglaze colours; most pieces inscribed with their titles, the artists' names and 'Made in Bideford', some also with narrative inscriptions
C.32 to 44-2020. Source: the artists, £51,000
Dead Dad Book is a narrative series of works commemorating the life of Vicky Lindo's father, Michael Anthony Lindo. Of West African and Chinese heritage, Lindo had travelled from Jamaica to England aged 11, as part of the Windrush generation (people who emigrated from the Caribbean to Britain after the Second World War). Settling in Devon, he married and started a family, but, experiencing alcohol addiction, he one day disappeared. Years later his family learned that he had died in Wexford, Ireland, where he had lived in a makeshift hut in the woods. The *Dead Dad Book* refers to a diary kept by his family on a journey to Ireland to discover his story.

618 A / B / C / D

618 E / F / G / H

A *Jug of the World*
h.38.6cm, d.28cm
C.32-2020

B Pot: *Chinoiserie Dragons*
h.33.3cm, d.23.5cm
C.33-2020

C Pot: *My English Heart*
h.33.6cm, d.23.4cm
C.34-2020

D Pot: *My DNA*
h.61cm, d.26.8cm
C.35-2020

E Pot: *Birth, Marriage and Death*
h.60.1cm, d.24.9cm
C.36-2020

F Pair of cat figures: *Mother and Father (Love and Kaos)*
h.33cm, d.20cm (*Mother*); h.33.1cm, d.18.3cm (*Father*)
C.37, 38-2020

G *Michael Anthony Lindo (Memory Pot)*
h.60.6cm, d.28cm
C.39-2020

H Jug: *My Dad*
h.35.7cm, d.32.3cm
C.40-2020

I Swimming in Coolree Reservoir (Platter) (pl.149)
h.7cm, l.54.1cm
C.41-2020

J Pot: *Yearning for some facts* (pl.149)
h.32.8cm, d.24.8cm
C.42-2020

K *The Green Man* (Platter) (pl.149)
h.6.4cm, l.54.1cm
C.43-2020

L Pot: *Wexford People* (pl.149)
h.34cm, d.23.3cm
C.44-2020

Lloyd Jones, David 1928–1994

1928 born Wimbledon, London
1946–48 serves in British Army in India
1951–52 studies fine art at Guildford School of Art, concentrating on sculpture, but learning to pot with Helen Pincombe (qv)
1962– sets up pottery in Fulford, York, making reduction-fired stoneware and porcelain
1980 solo exhibition, Craftsmen Potters Shop, London
1989 awarded Honorary Doctorate by University of York

David Lloyd Jones was an accomplished potter who concentrated on well-designed functional ware and strong individual pieces in stoneware and porcelain, working in a manner informed by Bernard Leach (qv). Although he was largely self-taught, his work nevertheless shows impressive technical control.

David Lloyd Jones, 'Plate Making', *CR*, 49 and 53 (1978)
Potters (1972) to (1992)
Rosemary Wren and Peter Crotty, 'Potters', *CR*, 13 (1972)
Crafts Advisory Committee (1977), p.19
'David Lloyd Jones', *CR*, 65 (1980)
W.A. Ismay, '20 Years a Potter', *CR*, 87 (1984)
Paisley Museum and Art Galleries (1984), p.53
Crafts Council (1985), p.63
W.A. Ismay, 'Practical Potter', *CR*, 157 (1996)
York City Art Gallery, *The Art of the Potter David Lloyd-Jones 1928–1994*, exh. cat., text by Emmanuel Cooper (York, 1996)
Nottingham City Museums and Galleries (2017), p.63

Exhibition reviews: Michael Casson, *Crafts*, 33 (1978); Mary Sara, *Studio Pottery*, 20 (1996)

Obituaries: Mick Casson, *Crafts*, 128 (1994); Emmanuel Cooper, *The Independent* (29 January 1994); W.A. Ismay, *CR*, 147 (1994)

619 Large jug, 1980
Stoneware, speckled grey celadon glaze; marks: 'LJ', impressed; h.31.4cm, d.25cm
C.124-1980. Source: Craftsmen Potters Association, London (solo exhibition, 1980, no.13), £40

620 Footed bowl, 1980
Stoneware, cream glaze, wax-resist decoration; marks: 'LJ', impressed; h.17.2cm, d.20.8cm
C.125-1980. Source: *see* **619** (no.75), £28

621 Dish, 1980
Stoneware, white glaze, iron decoration; marks: 'LJ', impressed; h.5.2cm, d.44.2cm
C.126-1980. Source: *see* **619** (no.123), £64

620 / 621 / 619

Locke, Donald 1930–2010

1930 born Stewartville, Guyana; family later moves to Georgetown
1954–57 awarded British Council Scholarship to Bath Academy of Art, Corsham, where studies painting under William Scott, sculpture under Bernard Meadows and ceramics under James Tower (qv)
1957–59 returns to Georgetown
1959–64 studies Fine Art at University of Edinburgh and Edinburgh College of Art, studying ceramics under Katie Horsman
1964–70 teaches at Queen's College, Georgetown
1969 takes leave from teaching for ceramic research at Edinburgh College of Art
1971–79 studio in London
1975 solo exhibition, Commonwealth Art Gallery, London
1976 guest artist at Haystack Mountain School of Crafts, Maine, USA
1978 exhibition with Siddig El Nigoumi (qv), Amalgam Gallery, London
1979–80 awarded Guggenheim Fellowship; artist-in-residence, Arizona State University, USA
1980– discontinues ceramics; works in bronze and mixed media
1981– granted permanent residency in USA
1990– moves to Atlanta, Georgia
2006– returns to ceramics

Donald Locke was a ceramic artist and sculptor. In the decade from 1969, during which he was active in the UK, he concentrated on biomorphic ceramic forms and mixed-media sculptures that combined ceramic elements with wood, steel and other materials. Many of his works of the period explicitly reference colonialism and slavery, including his *Plantation* series of mixed-media ceramic sculptures and the installation *Trophies of Empire*, now in the Tate collection. Locke sometimes used the pseudonym Issorosano Ite – a reference to a palm found in Guyana – and marked some pieces accordingly.

Donald Locke, *Out of Anarchy: Five Decades of Ceramics and Hybrid Sculptures (1959–2009): The Work of Donald Locke* (Newark, 2011)
Commonwealth Art Gallery, *Caribbean Artists in England*, exh. cat. (London, 1971)
V&A (1972), p.112
Commonwealth Art Gallery, *Donald Locke: Mixed-media Ceramics*, exh. cat. (London, 1975)
Claribel Cone, 'Donald Locke', *Artspace*, 5:1 (1980)
Barbara Cortright, 'An Interview with Donald Locke', *Artspace*, 5:4 (1981)
Hayward Gallery, *The Other Story: Afro-Asian Artists in Post-War Britain*, exh. cat. (London, 1989), pp.89–93

Obituary, *The Times* (5 February 2011)
Tate Britain, *Artist and Empire: Facing Britain's Imperial Past*, exh. cat. (London, 2015), p.229

Exhibition reviews: illustration, *CR*, 25 (1974); Guy Burn, *Arts Review* (14 April 1978); Holland Cotter, *New York Times* (20 May 2016)

Donald Locke's archive is at the Rose Library, Emory University, Atlanta, USA (Manuscript Collection No. 1440).

622 *Standing Bottle with Sternum*, 1976 (pl.65)
Stoneware, handbuilt, matt black oxide-saturated slip, Albany slip on lip; marks: 'ITE 76 HAYSTACK'; made at Haystack Mountain School of Crafts, Maine; h.30.7cm, d.16.6cm
C.68-1980. Source: Anthony Shaw, London (solo exhibition: *Ceramic Bottle Forms*, 1979, no.4), £125
Previously shown at the 6th International Biennial of Ceramic Art, Vallauris, France, 1978.

Lord, Andrew 1950–

1950	born Rochdale, Lancashire
1966–68	studies at Rochdale School of Art
1968–71	studies ceramics at Central School of Art and Design, London, under Gilbert Harding Green
1972	works at De Porceleyne Fles factory, Delft, Netherlands, in Architectural Department, later in Experimental Department
1974	travels to Mexico on British Council/ CONACYT scholarship, where attached to Museo Nacional de Antropología
1975–80	works in Rotterdam (supported by Rotterdam Art Foundation) and later Amsterdam; travels extensively in Europe
1976–80	visiting lecturer, Bath Academy of Art
1978	solo exhibition, *Pottery*, Anthony Stokes Gallery, London, travelling to Stedelijk Museum, Amsterdam
1980	solo exhibition, *Angled Pottery*, Art & Project, Amsterdam
1981	solo exhibition, Blum Helman Gallery, New York, USA; exhibits widely thereafter
1982–	moves to New York
1984–93	studio on the Lower East Side
1993–2013	studio on the Bowery
2010	retrospective exhibitions, Santa Monica Museum of Art, California, and MK Gallery, Milton Keynes
2014	residency, Cité Internationale des Arts, Paris
2015–21	works in studios in New York, New Mexico and the Netherlands
2017	solo exhibition, Art Institute of Chicago

Andrew Lord works predominantly with clay and bronze, making sculpture that is informed by his experience of looking at painting, exploring the senses and memory. Lord often develops works as groups of two or more vessels, these sometimes numbering more than 30. In the mid-1970s he began to explore the fall of light on objects, using this as a guide to deconstructing and reassembling forms in a Cubist or Constructivist manner. Subsequent work became more gestural, using bodily interactions as part of the making process. In the 2000s Lord moved from vessels to objects reflecting the natural world and the human figure, including work about his native Lancashire.

Andrew Lord, 'Only Connect', in Stair (2000), pp.25–7
V&A (1972), p.113
Birks (1976), pp.40–51
Frits Keers, 'Atelier 15', *Stedelijk Museum Bulletin* (September 1978)
Stedelijk Museum, *Ansuya Blom, Dineke Blom … Andrew Lord*, exh. cat. (Amsterdam, 1978)
'Andrew Lord: Angled Pottery', *Art & Project Bulletin*, 119 (1980)
Kasper Koenig (ed.), *Heute: Westkunst*, exh. cat. (Museen der Stadt Köln, 1981)
'Andrew Lord', *Art & Project Bulletin*, 143 (1985)
Blum Helman, *Andrew Lord: New Work*, exh. cat., text by Christopher Knight (New York, 1986)
Museum Haus Lange, *Anderer Leute Kunst*, exh. cat., text by Julian Heynen (Krefeld, 1987)
Gallery Bruno Bischofberger, *James Schuyler: Poems/ Andrew Lord: Sculptures* (Zurich, 1992)
Carnegie Museum of Art, *Andrew Lord*, exh. pamphlet, with interview (Pittsburgh, 1993)
Christopher Knight, *Last Chance for Eden: Selected Art Criticism 1979–1994* (Los Angeles, 1996), pp.131–4
Rijksmuseum Twenthe, *Andrew Lord: New Sculpture*, exh. cat. (Enschede, 2003)
Paul Kasmin Gallery, *Andrew Lord: Sculpture and Related Drawings*, exh. cat. (New York, 2004)
Emma Dean and Anthony Spira (eds), *Andrew Lord*, interview by James Rondeau, text by Dawn Adès (Santa Monica/Milton Keynes, 2010)
Elderton and Morrill (2017), pp.174–5

Exhibition reviews: Tony Birks, *CR*, 53 (1978); William Packer, *Crafts*, 34 (1978); John Russell, *New York Times* (18 December 1981); Emmanuel Cooper, *Crafts*, 106 (1990); Roberta Smith, *New York Times* (20 November 1992); Jerry Saltz, *Art in America*, 81:2 (1993); Janet Koplos, *Art in America*, 93:4 (2005); Robert Pincus-Witten, *Artforum International*, 47:10 (2009); Amanda Fielding, *Ceramics: Art and Perception*, 84 (2011); Ken Johnson, *New York Times* (15 May 2015)

623

623 *Box with figure*, 1972
Earthenware, hand-modelled, coloured slips, transparent glaze; marks: 'Andrew Lord 1972', incised; h.23.5cm, d.21cm
Circ.154&A-1973. Source: the artist, £15

624 *Vase and dish. Cubist black set*, 1978 (pl.70)
Earthenware, handbuilt, painted matt grey-black surface; marks: 'Andrew Lord 1978', incised; h.29.4cm (vase), d.31.9cm (dish)
C.172, 173-1984. Source: Anthony Stokes Gallery, London, £1897 (originally shown in solo exhibition: *Pottery*, 1978)

Lowerdown Pottery *see* David Leach

Lowndes, Gillian 1936–2010

1936	born West Kirby, Merseyside; grows up in Bombay (now Mumbai), India
1955–58	studies sculpture and pottery at Central School of Arts and Crafts, London
1958–60	briefly attends École des Beaux Arts, Paris; rents studio in Montparnasse
1960–	joins workshop of Robin Welch (qv) in Bloomsbury, London
1961–66	teaches at Central School, and later at Brighton College of Arts and Crafts and Harrow School of Art

1963	solo exhibition, Bristol Guild of Applied Art
1966–75	establishes studio at Grittleton, Wiltshire, with Ian Auld (qv); teaches at Bristol Polytechnic
1966	exhibition with Auld at Primavera, London
1969–	touring exhibition, *Five Studio Potters*, organized by V&A
1970–72	travels with Auld to Nigeria
1975–	joins Auld in Camberwell, London; establishes studio; begins teaching part-time at Central and Camberwell schools of arts and crafts
1977	exhibition with Auld at British Crafts Centre, London
1987	solo exhibition, Crafts Council, London
1988	moves with Auld to Toppesfield, Essex; establishes studio
1994	solo exhibition, Contemporary Applied Arts, London
1995	retires from Central Saint Martins College of Arts and Design
1996	marries Ian Auld
1997	retires from Camberwell College of Arts
2002	moves to Spitalfields, London, following Auld's death

Gillian Lowndes was among the most radical and innovative ceramic artists of the post-war era. Concerned primarily with form, Lowndes was in essence a sculptor. Her earlier work, handbuilt in stoneware, was based on hollow forms, yet looked beyond pottery for its inspiration. From the late 1970s, while others explored abstract vessels, Lowndes developed her practice as a bricolage artist, incorporating fibreglass, wire and found objects into her work. The formal radicalism of her sculpture belies the sensitivity with which her exploration of materials and processes was conducted. A respected outsider within the craft community, Lowndes was largely ignored by the fine-art world in her lifetime, but her work has since gained wider recognition.

Decorative Art (1965/66), (1967/68)
Birks (1967), pp.77–92, (1976), pp.134–45
Casson (1967), p.7, pls.41–2
Biographical notes, *Pottery Quarterly*, 9:33 (1967), p.33, pl.16
Potters (1972), (1974), (1975)
Sue Harley, 'Ian Auld and Gillian Lowndes', *CR*, 44 (1977)
Elisabeth Cameron, 'Gillian Lowndes', *CR*, 83 (1983)
Paisley Museum and Art Galleries (1984), p.55
Crafts Council (1985), pp.63–5
— *Gillian Lowndes: New Ceramic* Sculpture, exh. cat., introduction by Tanya Harrod (London, 1987)
Tanya Harrod, 'Transcending Clay', *Crafts*, 84 (1987)
Henry Pim, 'Uncertain Echoes', *CR*, 103 (1987)
Museum of Modern Art, Oxford (1993), pp.54–5, 88, 95
Victor Margrie, 'Gillian Lowndes', *Studio Pottery*, 9 (1994)
Crafts Council (1995b), pp.44–7
— (1996c), pp.110, 136
Gaze (1997)
London Institute (1998), pp.10–11, 24
Amanda Fielding, 'Bristling with Energy', *CR*, 181 (2000)
Carlano (2010), pp.98–9
Amanda Fielding, *Gillian Lowndes* (Ruthin, 2013)

Exhibition reviews: Elaine and Emanuel Benson, *Craft Horizons*, 26:6 (1966); Lavinia Learmont and Louise Collis, *Art & Artists*, 12:1 (1977); Angus Suttie, *Crafts*, 75 (1985); David Whiting, *Crafts*, 129 (1994); Amy Sherlock, *Frieze*, 185 (2017)

Obituaries: *The Times* (15 October 2010); Amanda Fielding, *The Guardian* (18 November 2010); Emmanuel Cooper, *The Independent* (20 November 2010) and *Crafts*, 228 (2011); Tony Birks, *Ceramics: Art and Perception*, 84 (2011)

An artist statement written for the *Five Studio Potters* exhibition is in the manuscripts collection, National Art Library, V&A, London (MSL/1969/3560).

625 Three standing pipes, 1967 (pl.51)
Stoneware, coil-built, buff titanium or grey nickel and cobalt glaze; h.72.8cm (tallest pipe), d.7.8cm
Circ.826 to 828-1968. Source: the artist, £15 (each)
Illustrated in Birks (1967), pl.62.

626 Pot with three necks, 1968
Stoneware, handbuilt, impressed decoration, blue glaze; h.38.3cm, d.28.8cm
Circ.829-1968. Source: *see* **626**, £15

627 Sculpture, 1968
Stoneware, slab-built, buff titanium glaze; h.34.3cm, d.58.5cm
Circ.830-1968. Source: *see* **625**, £25

628 Basket-like form, 1976
Stoneware, handbuilt rolled clay on a slab base, ochre glaze; h.26cm, d.30.7cm
C.11-2018. Source: David Zwirner, London, £4050; purchase funded by an anonymous donor
Pierced holes in the corners of the piece suggest that it was intended for wall-mounting.

626

627

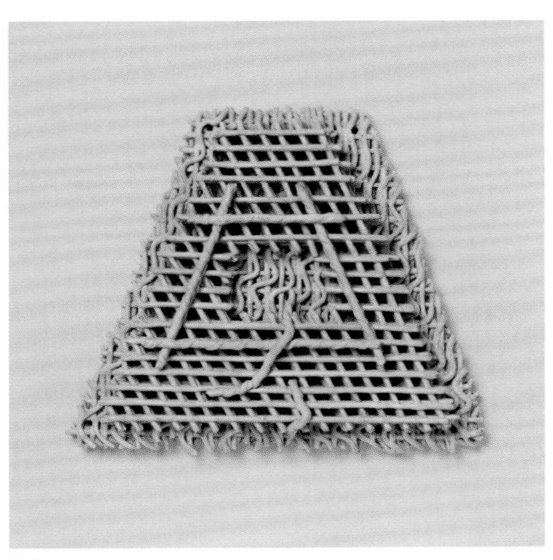

628

629

630

629 *Cup on Base*, 1986
Stoneware, handbuilt, with metal elements, and painted mottled yellow and white; h.18cm, d.23.3cm
C.39-1987. Source: Crafts Council, London (solo exhibition, 1987), £315

630 *Hook Figure*, 1994
Slip-dipped loofah, ceramic cone, metal clips and wire; h.145cm, d.39cm
C.75:1 to 3-2008. Source: the artist, £1500; acquired through the generosity of Gerard and Sarah Griffin
Shown in Lowndes' solo exhibition, Contemporary Applied Arts, London, 1994.

631 *Scroll*, 1996 (pl.95)
Bone china, fibreglass, stainless-steel rope; h.12.3cm, d.29cm
C.76-2008. Source: the artist, £1500; acquired through the generosity of Gerard and Sarah Griffin
Shown in the Crafts Council exhibition, *Objects of Our Time*, 1996–97.

Lunn, Dora E. (later **Hedges**)
1881–1970

1881	born Sheffield, Yorkshire; family later moves to London
1907	awarded Art Class Teacher's Certificate
1908	awarded diploma in design from Royal College of Art, London
1912	exhibits embroidery with Arts and Crafts Exhibition Society
1915	briefly attends pottery classes at Camberwell School of Arts and Crafts, under Alfred Hopkins (qv), leaving due to segregation of women students, who were taught pottery decoration but not throwing
1916–*c.* 1928	establishes The Ravenscourt Pottery in Ravenscourt Park, London, employing a small team of women potters; teaches part-time
1917–	exhibits regularly at British Industries Fair, London, the first woman potter to do so; Queen Mary and Queen Alexandra make purchases
1925	receives Honourable Mention at Paris International Exhibition
1931	publishes *Pottery in the Making*, a practical manual for pottery students and teachers; teaches at Froebel Educational Institute, London
1933–	establishes Dora Lunn Pottery in Chiswick, London, making individual work

A pioneer of studio pottery, Dora Lunn overcame technological challenges and the expectations of convention to establish herself as an independent woman potter as early as 1916. She gained knowledge of ceramics from her father, Richard Lunn, who taught pottery at the Royal College of Art and Camberwell School of Arts and Crafts. She appears to have envisaged working with him, but following his death in 1915 and a brief period of further study, she established The Ravenscourt Pottery in London. Working with a small team of women, she made both practical and decorative wares noted for their refined coloured glazes and restrained decoration, as well as figures. Initially all her pottery was made in moulds, but Lunn subsequently engaged professional throwers and later herself learned to throw. In its early years Ravenscourt Pottery achieved a measure of success and gained much press coverage. Personal and financial circumstances nevertheless forced Lunn to sell up in the late 1920s, following which she concentrated on teaching and writing, before later establishing a workshop in Chiswick.

Dora Lunn, *Pottery in the Making: A Handbook for Teachers and Individual Workers* (Leicester/London, 1931)
— *Life and the Crafts: A Talk Given to the Crafts Circle House of Arts*, pamphlet (1947)
— 'A Potter's Pot-Pourri' (unpublished, 1951)
Arts and Crafts Exhibition Society (1912), (1923), (1926), (1928), (1935), (1941), (1946), (1948)
Decorative Art (1919), (1926), (1927), (1950/51)
British Institute of Industrial Art (1922), (1923), (1927), (1929)
Royal Academy of Arts (1923)
Guild of Potters (1924), (1925), (1926)
Colnaghi (1927), (1928)
Exh. review, *Art News and Review* (21 October 1950)
Graham McLaren, 'A Complete Potteress – The Life and Work of Dora Lunn', *Journal of the Decorative Arts Society*, 13 (1989)
Bergesen (1991), pp.239–41
Vincentelli (2000), pp.226–31
Jones (2007), pp.38–40, 186–7, 209–10

Dora Lunn's papers are in the V&A Archive of Art and Design, London (AAD/1983/1). These include a typescript of her unpublished autobiography, 'A Potter's Pot-Pourri'.

632 Vase, *c.* 1919 (pl.6)
Earthenware, mottled blue glaze; marks: 'RAVENSCOURT', impressed; h.24cm, d.14.6cm
C.505-1919. Source: the artist; given by Lt-Col. K. Dingwall, DSO
A paper label gives the price '35/-'.

633 Bowl, *c.* 1920
Earthenware, turquoise glaze, painted in black; marks: 'RAVENSCOURT.', stamped in brown; h.6.9cm, d.18.2cm
C.402-1920. Source: the artist; given by Lt-Col. K. Dingwall, DSO, through Art Fund

633 / 637

634

634 Dish, *c.* 1916–28
Earthenware, painted decoration in black; marks: 'RAVENSCOURT', incised; h.7.7cm, d.35.8cm
C.287-1983. Source: Mrs Woronieki, London, £80 (for group)
Items **634** to **639** had been purchased by their vendor to the museum at a house sale in Chiswick, London. The house was thought to have been Dora Lunn's home.

635 Pot, *c.* 1916–28 (pl.6)
Earthenware, slip-cast, blue-grey glaze; marks: 'RAVENSCOURT', impressed; h.19cm, d.17.7cm
C.288-1983. Source: *see* **634**

636 Vase, 1920
Earthenware, with painted lines in blue and green; marks: '1920' and 'DL' in monogram, incised; h.13.3cm, d.9.2cm
C.289-1983. Source: *see* **634**

637 Bowl, *c.* 1916–28
Earthenware, yellow glaze interior, painted exterior in black; marks: 'RAVENSCOURT', incised; h.5.8cm, d.9.4cm
C.290-1983. Source: *see* **634**

636 / 638

639

638 Vase, *c.* 1933–40
Earthenware, green glaze and a blue rim; marks: 'DHL' in monogram, incised; h.14.9cm, d.6.4cm
C.291-1983. Source: *see* **634**

639 Pot, *c.* 1950–55
Stoneware, grey glaze with dark speckles; marks: 'DORA LUNN' in a rectangular frame, incised; h.9cm, d.10cm
C.292-1983. Source: *see* **634**

Magson, Mal (née Withers) 1950–

1950– born Sheffield, Yorkshire
1968–72 studies ceramics at Loughborough College of Art and Design
1973 workshop in Sheffield
1974–84 workshop in East Lutton, North Yorkshire
1984–89 workshop in East Ayton, Scarborough, North Yorkshire
1985 solo exhibitions, Bohun Gallery, Henley-on-Thames, Oxfordshire, and Candover Gallery, Alresford, Hampshire
1989–2001 workshop in Scarborough
1994–99 teaches ceramics at University College Scarborough
2002– workshop in Muston, North Yorkshire

640

Mal Magson became known for her decorative unglazed stoneware, made using an agate technique developed while she was at college. Layers of coloured clays were laminated, folded and rolled to achieve intricate patterns, from which her forms – predominantly bowls and dishes – were handbuilt. Since 2000 she has seldom made for exhibition and her work has become more personally motivated. It often takes the form of small sculptural pieces, not necessarily agate.

Chris Utley and Mal Magson, *Exploring Clay with Children* (London, 1997)
W.A. Ismay, exh. review, *CR*, 27 (1974)
'CPA New Members', *CR*, 61 (1980)
Potters (1980) to (1997)
Jane Waller, 'Colouring Clay', *CR*, 145 (1994)

640 Lotus bowl, 1983
Stoneware, coloured clays, unglazed; h.10.2cm, d.23.8cm
C.212-1983. Source: Henry Rothschild Associates, Cambridge (group exhibition, Kettle's Yard, no.244), £55

Mallalieu, Fenella 1956–

1956 born London
1985–86 studies ceramics part-time at Goldsmiths' College
1986–88 studies ceramics at Harrow College of Higher Education
1989–2001 studio in De Beauvoir Town, London
1995– teaches part-time at Camberwell College of Arts
1997 designs *Omega* tableware range for Poole Pottery, Dorset
2001–03 studio in Haggerston, London
2004–10 studio in De Beauvoir Town, London
2010 discontinues potting

641 / 642

Fenella Mallalieu's interest in pottery began as a hobby while she was working as a writer on antiques. After training at Harrow, she developed a range of lively, thrown domestic earthenware, decorated with coloured glazes.

Fenella Mallalieu, 'Pots for the Southern Hearted', *CR*, 143 (1993)
Nicole Swengley, 'Artists with Pots of Style', *The Times* (5 May 1990)
Potters/The Ceramics Book (1992) to (2006)
Crafts Council (1995a), p.48
David Whiting, *Fenella Mallalieu*, Aberystwyth Arts Centre: Ceramic Series 82 (1997)

641 Bowl, 1994
Earthenware, decorated with terracotta slip, wax resist and lead glazes; marks: 'Fenella Mallalieu', incised; h.10cm, d.36cm
C.61-1995. Source: Craft Potters Association, London (exhibition: *Studio Ceramics 94*, V&A, 1994), £72

642 Jug, 1994
Earthenware, decorated with terracotta slip, wax resist and lead glazes; marks: 'Fenella Mallalieu', incised; h.21.2cm, d.21cm
C.62-1995. Source: *see* **641**, £48

Malone, Jim 1946–

1946	born Sheffield, Yorkshire
1966–69	teacher training, Bangor, Caernarfonshire
1972–76	studies ceramics at Camberwell School of Art and Crafts
1975	trains briefly at Winchcombe Pottery, under Ray Finch (qv)
1976–82	workshop at Llandegla, Clwyd
1978–	solo exhibition at Craftwork, Guildford, Surrey; thereafter frequent UK solo exhibitions
1982–90	teaches ceramics at Cumbria College of Art, Carlisle
1984–2001	workshop at Ainstable, Cumbria
1997–98	retrospective exhibition, Bolton Museum and Art Gallery, and tour
2002–04	workshop at Burnby, Yorkshire
2005–	workshop at Lessonhall, Cumbria

Jim Malone stands among the most resolute potters of the Leach school, his work drawing upon the precepts and aesthetics proposed by Bernard Leach (qv). Responding to the forms of medieval English earthenware and early Korean and Chinese stonewares, he has developed an ongoing series of stoneware and porcelain bottles, jugs, bowls and jars – useful, unforced shapes, vigorously thrown and decorated with fluency. Malone places great value on the use of local materials, reflecting an empathy with the natural environment.

Jim Malone, 'CPA Membership', letter of resignation, *CR*, 85 (1984)
— 'A Point of View', *Real Pottery* (*Pottery Quarterly*), 14:56 (1985)
'CPA New Members', *CR*, 53 (1978)
Crafts Council (1980), p.60
Christopher Reid, 'Tradition and the Individual Talent', *Crafts*, 45 (1980)
Paisley Museum and Art Galleries (1984), p.60
Crafts Council (1985), p.65
Alex McErlain, 'Jim Malone', *Ceramics Monthly*, 39:8 (1991)
Rogers (1991), (2003)
Alex McErlain, 'Jim Malone Potter', interview, *CR*, 140 (1993)
Potters/The Ceramics Book (1994) to (2012)
Mike Dodd, 'Lasting Values', *CR*, 161 (1996)
Bolton Museum and Art Gallery, *Jim Malone: Artist Potter*, exh. cat. (1997)
'Jim Malone', exh. preview, *CR*, 209 (2004)
Goldmark Gallery, *Jim Malone: The Pursuit of Beauty*, exh. cat., text by David Whiting (Uppingham, 2008) – see also cats. from 2011 and 2016
Whiting (2009), pp.34–9
Carlano (2010), pp.100–1
John Foley, 'The Man and the Pot', *CR*, 243 (2010)
Ben Boswell, 'Country Life', *CR*, 267 (2014)
Alex McErlain, 'A Lifetime's Endeavour', *CR*, 295 (2019)

Exhibition reviews: Colin Pearson, *Crafts*, 32 (1978); Alex McErlain, *Crafts*, 112 (1991); Paul Vincent, *Studio Pottery*, 1 (1993); David Whiting, *Crafts*, 120 (1993); Robert Silver, *Studio Pottery*, 9 (1994); Emmanuel Cooper, *Crafts*, 150 (1998); Helen Phillips, *CR*, 169 (1998); Richard Gray, *CR*, 188 (2001); Jude Jelfs, *CR*, 194 (2002); Ann Head, *Ceramics: Art and Perception*, 88 (2012)

643

A recorded interview with Jim Malone is in the Potters of the Bernard Leach Legacy collection at the British Library, London (C1330/15). A documentary film, *Jim Malone: Potter*, was made by Goldmark and released on DVD in 2011.

643 Lidded jar, 1980
Stoneware, incised decoration, greenish ash glaze; marks: 'JM', impressed; h.21cm, d.21.5cm
C.183&A-1980. Source: Craftsmen Potters Association, London (exhibition with Jane Hamlyn and Gary Standige, 1980, no.103), £30

644 Bottle, 1998 (pl.99)
Stoneware, thrown, incised decoration, tenmoku and ash glazes; marks: 'JM' and 'A', impressed; h.38.6cm, d.19.9cm
C.72-1998. Source: the artist, £350
Shown with other new work at Birmingham Museum and Art Gallery alongside the retrospective *Jim Malone: Artist Potter*, 1998.

Malone, Kate 1959–

1959	born London
1979–82	studies ceramics at Bristol Polytechnic
1983–86	studies ceramics at Royal College of Art, London
1986–88	studio at South Bank Craft Centre, London
1988	first solo exhibition, The Orangery, Holland Park, London

1988–	establishes Balls Pond Studio, Culford Mews, London
1994–	represented by Adrian Sassoon, London
1998–2000	solo exhibition, *The Allotment*, Midlands Arts Centre, Birmingham, and tour
2001–	additional small workshop in Cotignac, France
2015	tiled façade, in collaboration with EPR Architects, 24 Savile Row, London
2018–	establishes compact new studio in Culford Mews; develops large workshop in Thanet, Kent
2019	awarded MBE
2020	launches FiredUp4 campaign to provide pottery studios for OnSide Youth Zones charity

Known for her colourful, exuberant vessels based on natural forms, Kate Malone is among the UK's most popular and celebrated ceramic artists. Inspiration for her earlier work came from aquatic life, then later plants – in particular gourds, pineapples, berries and seedpods – and in the late 2000s and 2010s, atomic and geological forms, playfully interpreted. Since 1992–93 she has concentrated on crystalline-glazed stoneware, having worked previously in earthenware with multiple fired glazes. In addition to her individual studio pieces, Malone has fulfilled various large-scale public commissions for hospitals, schools, libraries, other buildings and parks. She is also familiar from her role as a judge on the British television series *The Great Pottery Throw Down*.

Kate Malone, 'Fruits of the Earth', *CR*, 143 (1993)
— 'A Potter's Day', *CR*, 162 (1996)
— 'Crystalline Alchemy', *CR*, 164 (1997)
— 'What If …', *CR*, 234 (2008)
— 'Source or Sauce', *CR*, 246 (2010)
— **and Lesley Jackson**, *Kate Malone: A Book of Pots* (London, 2003)
Tanya Harrod, 'Potter of the New Spirit', *CR*, 106 (1987)
Pamela Johnson, 'Sub-Aquatic Ceramics', *Crafts*, 94 (1988)
Emmanuel Cooper, *Kate Malone*, Aberystwyth Arts Centre: Ceramic Series 38 (1989)
Manchester City Art Gallery, *Fruits of the Earth and Sea*, exh. pamphlet, text and interview by Lesley Jackson (1994)
Crafts Council (1995a), pp.45, 48
Alison Goddard, 'Crystal Glaze', *New Scientist* (1 July 1995)
Potters (1997), (2000)
Lesley Jackson, 'Sharp Urban Potters', *The Independent* (13 November 1998)
Midlands Arts Centre, *The Allotment: New Ceramics by Kate Malone*, exh. cat., text by Pamela Johnson, interview by Emmanuel Cooper (Birmingham, 1998)
Anatol Orient, 'Shake, Rattle and Roll', *CR*, 180 (1999)
Geffrye Museum, *Ceramic Rooms: At Home with Kate Malone and Edmund de Waal*, exh. pamphlet, text by Paul Vincent (London, 2002)
Julia Pitts, 'Opposites Attract', *CR*, 198 (2002)
Clare Beck, 'Kate Malone: Next to Nature', interview, *Ceramics: Art and Perception*, 62 (2005)
Emma Clegg, 'Nature and Nurture', *CR*, 215 (2005)
Pearson (2005)
Blackwell, The Arts and Crafts House, *Kate Malone: Next to Nature*, exh. cat., texts by Lesley Jackson and Kate Malone (Bowness-on-Windermere: Lakeland Arts Trust, 2010)
Carlano (2010), pp.102–3
Canary Wharf Group, *Kate Malone: A Celebration of Clay*, exh. pamphlet, text by Ann Elliott (London, 2014)
Grant Gibson, 'The Shape of Things to Come', *Crafts*, 252 (2015)
Isabel Andrews, 'From the Manor Drawn', *CR*, 280 (2016)
Adrian Sassoon, *Kate Malone: Inspired by Waddesdon*, exh. cat., text by Dame Rosalind Savill (London, 2016)
Paul Bailey, 'Moving in a New Direction', *Ceramics: Art and Perception*, 112 (2019)

Exhibition reviews: Pamela Johnson, *Crafts*, 126 (1994); Paul Vincent, *Studio Pottery*, 11 (1994); Will Levi Marshall, *CR*, 154 (1995); Malcolm Haslam, *Crafts*, 147 (1997); Deborah Norton, *Studio Pottery*, 27 (1997); Lesley Jackson, *Crafts*, 157 (1999), and *Ceramics in Society*, 50 (2002); Robert S. Silver and Paul Vincent, *Ceramics in Society*, 39 (2000); Kate McIntyre, *Crafts*, 180 (2003); Grant Gibson, *Crafts*, 262 (2016)

An interview with Kate Malone is in the Crafts Lives sound archive at the British Library, London (C960/83).

645 *Monster Lily Leaf*, c. 1986–87
Earthenware, handbuilt, with coloured glazes; h.15.5cm, d.57cm
C.137-2006. Source: given by Drs Deborah and Israel Doniach
Shown in the solo exhibition *Fruits de Mer*, The Orangery, Holland Park, London, 1988.

646 *Millennium Jug of Symbols*, 1999
Stoneware, press-moulded, with applied sprigs and crystalline glazes; marks: 'Kate / Malone', incised; h.32.2cm, d.33.5cm
C.10-2001. Source: the artist, £1100; gift of Adrian Sassoon, Esq.
The stamped inscription reads 'SHARING HOSPITALITY PROSPERITY FERTILITY FOR THE MILLENIUM 2000' [*sic*]. The applied sprigs (pineapple, pumpkin, gourd and jug) reference Malone's standard range of pottery forms, and are symbolic of the properties and values recorded in the inscription.

647 *Snow Lady Gourd*, 2008 (pl.127)
Stoneware, crystalline glazes; h.68cm, d.55cm
C.225-2009. Source: Adrian Sassoon at Collect 2009, £7500; acquired through the generosity of Gerard and Sarah Griffin

645

646

Maltby, John 1936–2020

1936 born Cleethorpes, Lincolnshire
1954–58 studies sculpture at Leicester College of Art
1958–59 trains as art teacher at Goldsmiths' College, London
1959–61 teaches painting at Caterham School, Surrey
1962–64 works with David Leach (qv)
1964– establishes Stoneshill Pottery near Crediton, Devon
1974 wins Gold Medal at International Ceramics Competition, Faenza
1996– turns to making small-scale handbuilt sculpture

John Maltby was inspired to become a potter after reading Bernard Leach's (qv) *A Potter's Book*, and subsequently trained with David Leach (qv). Initially he produced domestic stoneware following their example, but increasingly concentrated on individual pieces of more personal character. Known for his vivid decoration and use of enamel colour, Maltby for a time drew loosely upon Japanese traditions, but progressively he sought to express an English sensibility in his work, developing sloping, slab-built vessels decorated with sea and landscape motifs. He later turned to small figurative sculpture, after heart surgery left him unable to continue with strenuous work.

John Maltby, 'Overglaze Enamels', *Pottery Quarterly*, 11:42 (1974)
— 'On Decoration', *CR*, 78 (1982)
— 'Over Glaze Enamel', *Artists Newsletter* (September 1984)
— 'On Pots and Art', *CR*, 102 (1986)
— 'The Leach Tradition', *Crafts*, 80 (1986)
— 'In Reply to Breon O'Casey', *CR*, 115 (1989)
— *John Maltby*, Aberystwyth Arts Centre: Ceramic Series 36 (1989)
— 'Vitreous Slip Decoration', *Artists Newsletter* (July 1990)
— 'The Englishness of English Pots', *CR*, 122 (1990)
— 'Finding a New Reality', *CR*, 137 (1992)
— 'Heart to Art', *CR*, 166 (1997)
— **and Andy Christian**, *John Maltby*, Aberystwyth Arts Centre: Ceramic Series 95 (2000)
Casson (1967), p.7, pl.223
Potters/The Ceramics Book (1972) to (1992), (2012)
V&A (1972), p.113
Jeannie Lowe, 'A Potter of the Countryside', *CR*, 29 (1974)
Crafts Advisory Committee (1976), p.105
Crafts Council (1980), p.61

648

649

— (1985), p.65
Gibson (1987), pp.70–7
Rufford Craft Centre, *Aspects of Place: An Exhibition of New Ceramics by John Maltby*, exh. pamphlet (Nottinghamshire, 1992)
Hannah Wingrave, 'John Maltby: English Artist', interview, *Ceramics in Society*, 44 (2001)
Galerie Besson, *John Maltby: Variations on a Musical Theme*, exh. pamphlet (London, 2003)
Rufford Craft Centre, *John Maltby*, exh. pamphlet (Nottinghamshire, 2003)
Godfrey and Watt, *John Maltby*, exh. cat. (Harrogate, 2005) – see also cats. from 2007, 2009 and 2010
Andy Christian, 'Private Passions', *CR*, 237 (2009)
Carlano (2010), pp.104–5
Devon Guild of Craftsmen, *John Maltby, Breon O'Casey*, exh. cat. (Bovey Tracey, 2011)
Nottingham City Museums and Galleries (2017), pp.64–5
Andy Christian, 'A Life in the Making', *CR*, 300 (2019)
Nigel Dutt, obituary, *The Guardian* (15 January 2021)

Exhibition reviews: Eileen Lewenstein, *CR*, 16 (1972); David Leach, *CR*, 24 (1973); Jon Catleugh, *Crafts*, 45 (1980); Emmanuel Cooper, *Crafts*, 111 (1991); Paul Vincent, *Studio Pottery*, 1 (1993); Rudolf Strasser, *Studio Pottery*, 29 (1997); Ian Wilson, *Crafts*, 148 (1997); Andy Christian, *CR*, 250 (2011)

648 Square dish, 1981
Stoneware, wax-resist decoration with tenmoku and brown glazes; marks: 'Maltby', painted; h.3.7cm, d.38.2cm
C.70-1981. Source: Craft Shop, V&A, £62.01

649 Tankard: *Boat, White Moon and Stars*, 1990
Stoneware, handbuilt, white, matt blue and black glazes, inlaid black lines; marks: 'MALTBY', painted; h.16.2cm, d.24cm
C.56-1990. Source: Crafts Council Shop at the V&A, £77.40

Margrie, Victor 1929–

1929 born Highbury, London
1946–52 studies at Hornsey School of Art
1952–56 part-time teaching at various London art colleges
1954–71 workshop in London, and later Potten End, Hertfordshire
1956–71 Head of Ceramics, Harrow School of Art
1963 with Michael Casson (qv) founds Harrow Studio Pottery Course
1964|66|69 solo exhibitions at Crafts Centre of Great Britain, London
1971–77 Secretary, Crafts Advisory Committee
1977–84 Director, Crafts Council
1984 awarded CBE
1984–85 Professor, Royal College of Art, London
1985– workshop in Bristol
1988– moves to Doccombe, Devon
1993–2005 associate editor, *Studio Pottery* magazine
2012– moves to Shroton, Dorset

Victor Margrie had a considerable influence on the crafts through his role as Secretary of the newly established Crafts Advisory Committee (CAC) and his subsequent Directorship of the Crafts Council, as the CAC was renamed. Margrie is also notable for co-founding the influential vocational Studio Pottery Course at Harrow School of Art. As a potter, he concentrated on refined, individual work in porcelain, after a period making functional pieces in stoneware.

Victor Margrie, 'Sky Porcelain', *CR*, 2 (1970)
— 'Glaze Calculators', *Pottery Quarterly*, 10:38 (1971)
— 'The Work of the Crafts Advisory Committee', *Museums Journal*, 74:3 (1974)
— 'British Ceramics', *CR*, 71 (1981)
— 'Influence and Innovation', *CR*, 100 (1986)
— 'Aspects of Contemporary Ceramics', *CR*, 115 (1989)
— 'The Search for a Unified Theory of Craft', *Studio Potter*, 23:1 (1994)

650 / 651

— 'Talking About the Harrow Course', interview by John Houston, in Peters (2012), pp.14–31
Arts and Crafts Exhibition Society (1957)
Decorative Art (1963/64), (1965/66)
Casson (1967), p.7, pls.145–7
Potters (1972) to (1986)
Eileen Lewenstein and Emmanuel Cooper, 'Victor Margrie Talking', *CR*, 19 (1973)
Crafts Advisory Committee (1976), p.106
Walter Keeler, comments on Margrie's work, *Crafts*, 81 (1986), p.43
Harrod (1999), pp.380–1, 412–13
Who's Who 2020 (2019)

An interview with Victor Margrie is in the Crafts Lives sound archive at the British Library, London (C960/35).

650 Bowl, 1969
Porcelain, cut and applied decoration, celadon glaze; marks: seal, impressed; h.7.7cm, d.9.1cm
Circ.757-1969. Source: Crafts Centre of Great Britain, London (solo exhibition: *Porcelain Bowls*, 1969, no.18), £7
According to Margrie, the 'concept derived from sky patterns'.

651 Bowl, 1969
Porcelain, cut and applied decoration, celadon glaze; marks: seal, impressed; h.9.3cm, d.10.2cm
Circ.756-1969. Source: *see* **650** (no.26), £20

Marlow, Reginald 1903–1972

1903	born West Ham, Essex; grows up in Lowestoft, Suffolk
c. 1920–23	attends Lowestoft and Norwich schools of art
1923–27	studies pottery at Royal College of Art, London, under William Staite Murray (qv)
1930–32	assistant art master at Christ's Hospital, Horsham, West Sussex
1932–34	teaches in the Department of Industrial Design, Leicester College of Art; succeeded by Sam Haile (qv)
1935–	teaches design at Croydon School of Art, becoming Head of Department; part-time teaching at Central School of Art, London
1948–60s	Principal of Stoke-on-Trent College of Art
1959–67	President of the Society of Designer Craftsmen

In 1959 William Staite Murray (qv) cited Reginald Marlow, together with Henry Hammond (qv), as carrying on 'the tradition formed in those days', namely, when Murray had taught at the Royal College of Art (*see* bibliography for Heber Mathews (qv)). According to the critic A.C. Sewter, Marlow achieved his aesthetic expression through texture, colour and decoration combined with shape, rather than through basic form alone.

Reginald Marlow, *Pottery Making and Decorating* (London, 1957)
Arts and Crafts Exhibition Society (1938) to (1957)
British Council (1942)
Cooper (1947), p.*iii*, pl.26
A.C. Sewter, 'Reginald Marlow – Potter', *Apollo*, 46 (October 1947)
Decorative Art (1950/51) to (1953/54), (1955/56), (1957/58)
Society of Designer Craftsmen, *Exhibition 1962*, exh. cat. (London, 1962)
Casson (1967), p.7, pls.148–9

652

652 Vase, 1962
Stoneware, oatmeal glaze, painted in blue and brown; marks: 'RM' in monogram, painted; h.37cm, d.10.8cm
Circ.650-1962. Source: Society of Designer Craftsmen (Twenty-seventh Exhibition, Sanderson's, London, 1962, no.143), £10

Marshall, Ray 1913–1986

1913	born Warner, Alberta, Canada
c. 1940–45	serves in Royal Canadian Army Medical Corps
c. 1945	studies pottery at Guildford School of Art, under Helen Pincombe (qv), while stationed nearby
1946–47	works briefly with Ray Finch (qv) at Winchcombe; studies pottery at Royal College of Art, London, under Helen Pincombe
1947–48	works at Kingwood Design and Craftsmanship pottery workshop, Wormley, Surrey
1948–	establishes Milland Pottery, Milland, West Sussex, with Jane Aburrow
1954–	works in own workshop, Bridgefoot Pottery, Stedham, West Sussex

Ray Marshall established Milland Pottery with Jane Aburrow and initially also Lester Campion, together building the pottery from scratch at Aburrow's father's farm. There they worked as part of a small team making domestic earthenware, Marshall throwing and decorating most of the flatware. After leaving Milland, he worked alone, making domestic stoneware and individual pieces.

Murray Fieldhouse, 'Workshop Visit: Milland Pottery', *Pottery Quarterly*, 1:2 (1954)
Illustration, *Pottery Quarterly*, 7:26 (1961), pl.10
'Evening Meeting: Throwing', transcript, in Craftsmen Potters Association (1966)
Casson (1967), p.7, pls.150–1
Paisley Museum and Art Galleries (1984), p.60
Obituary, *The Times* (6 February 1986)
Avis M. Loshak, letter, *CR*, 103 (1987)

653 Dish, *c.* 1952–55
Earthenware, painted in black over blue-green slips, incised; marks: 'MILLAND / POTTERY / ENGLAND' enclosing a windmill, stamped in brown; h.2.7cm, d.17.1cm
C.188-1986. Source: bequeathed by Ray Marshall

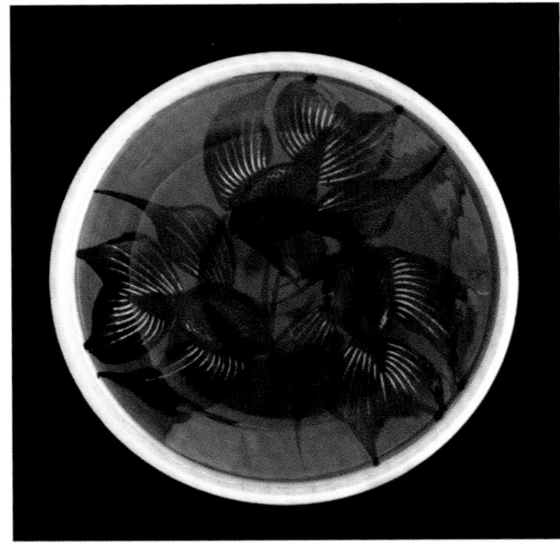

653

654 / 655

654 Pot with handles, *c.* 1960
Stoneware, unglazed, impressed and applied decoration, darkened with oxide; marks: 'Ray Marshall', incised; h.21.8cm, d.30.7cm
C.186-1986. Source: *see* 653

655 Bottle vase, 1961
Stoneware, oatmeal glaze, incised decoration, darkened with oxide; marks: 'Ray Marshall / 1961', incised; h.31cm, d.18.7cm
C.187-1986. Source: *see* 653

Marshall, William (Bill) 1923–2007

1923	born St Ives, Cornwall
1938–	joins Leach Pottery as an apprentice
1942	conscripted into army
1947–	rejoins pottery, becomes foreman and Bernard Leach's (qv) right-hand man
1977–	leaves to establish own pottery at Lelant; teaches at Cornwall Technical College, Redruth

William Marshall was the first of the apprentices taken on at the Leach Pottery (qv) as part of David Leach's (qv) reorganization. A local boy, he came straight from school and was trained as a thrower for the new Standard Ware range. He became the foreman of the pottery, and after David's departure in 1955 was responsible for throwing, to designs done on paper, all of Bernard Leach's larger vases. His own individual work developed strongly, in a style influenced by that of Hamada Shōji (qv), after he left the Leach Pottery and set up on his own.

Dartington Hall (1952)
Casson (1967), p.7, pl.152
Rose (1970), p.40, pls.74–5
Bernard and Janet Leach, letter, *CR*, 49 (1978)
Leach (1978), pp.155–6
Tate Gallery (1985), p.238
Watson (1985)
Birks and Wingfield Digby (1990), pp.157–69
Cooper (2003)
Whybrow (2006), pp.104–5 and elsewhere
Carlano (2010), pp.106–7
Nottingham City Museums and Galleries (2017), pp.66

Exhibition reviews: *Pottery Quarterly*, 3:10 (1956), and 6:24 (1959); W.A. Ismay, *CR*, 27 (1974); Eileen Lewenstein, *Crafts*, 8 (1974); Philip Rawson, *Crafts*, 52 (1981); Tanya Harrod, *Crafts*, 91 (1988); Paul Vincent, *Studio Pottery*, 4 (1993); Peter Lane, *CR*, 180 (1999)

Obituaries: *The Times* (7 May 2007); Emmanuel Cooper, *The Independent* (10 May 2007) and *Crafts*, 207 (2007); David Whiting, *The Guardian* (25 May 2007)

A recorded interview with William Marshall is in the Potters of the Bernard Leach Legacy collection at the British Library, London (C1330/26).

656 Vase, *c.* 1950
Porcelain, pale celadon glaze; marks: 'WM' and 'SI' in monogram, impressed; h.11.7cm, d.8.6cm
C.120-1977. Source: Richard Dennis, London (from the collection of Sir Edward Maufe), £10

657 Jug, *c.* 1985
Stoneware, ash glaze; marks: 'WM' in monogram, impressed; h.38.2cm, d.20.5cm
C.154-1991. Source: private sale, £200

658 Bottle, 1989
Porcelain, cut sides, matt blue glaze; marks: 'WM' in monogram, impressed; h.19.2cm, d.12cm
C.5-1990. Source: Amalgam, London, £135

656

657

658

Mathews, Heber 1905–1959

1905 born Lambeth, London
1927–31 enters School of Design, Royal College of Art, London, studying pottery under William Staite Murray (qv); acts as student-demonstrator in final year
1932– sets up workshop and builds oil-fired kiln in Lee, Kent; appointed pottery advisor to Rural Industries Bureau
1932–59 teaches at Woolwich Polytechnic, becoming Head of Art School
1958–59 President of the Arts and Crafts Exhibition Society

In his introduction to Heber Mathews' memorial exhibition catalogue, William Staite Murray (qv) placed his former pupil among the 'few students who sensed the inner meaning of potting, and saw that pots when infused with vitality could be an articulating art; they saw potting ... when imbued with feeling to have the moving power of sculpture'. Of his later works, Murray remarked: 'Their inspiration I thought to be classical, with a calm dignity that marks good breeding. They were in no way derivative, but were highly individual, and announced the work of a fine artist composing from within.' Mathews' strongest work explores form virtually to the exclusion of decoration. Impressive, even monumental, pots bear restrained, subtle glazes.

Heber Mathews, 'Artists' Training' and 'Artistic Poverty', letters, *Daily Telegraph* (2 and 7 August 1956)
Arts and Crafts Exhibition Society (1938) to (1957)
British Council (1942)
Cooper (1947), p.*iii*, pls.27–32
A.C. Sewter, 'Heber Mathews – Potter', *Apollo*, 46 (August 1947)
Wingfield Digby (1952), p.77, pl.44
Decorative Art (1954/55)
Lewis (1956), pls.322, 326–7
Crafts Centre of Great Britain, *Heber Mathews: Memorial Exhibition*, exh. pamphlet, text by W. Staite Murray (London, 1959)
Smithsonian Institution (1959)
J.H. Whitfield, obituary, *The Times* (11 February 1959)
Haslam (1984), pp.64–5, pls.35–7

The museum holds several tiles and tile-panels painted by Mathews (C.193 to 200-1985), not catalogued here. An archive of photographs and printed material is in the V&A Archive of Art and Design, London (AAD/1988/19). The dating of pieces acquired in 1985 was proposed by Monica Mathews, the potter's sister.

659 Jar, *c.* 1932
Stoneware, dark speckled brown glaze; marks: 'HM', incised; h.24.2cm, d.23.6cm
C.190-1985. Source: given by Mr R.D.C. Mathews

660 Jar, *c.* 1932
Stoneware, streaky brown glaze; marks: 'HM', incised; h.18.5cm, d.20.3cm
C.191-1985. Source: *see* **659**

661 Jar, *c.* 1934
Stoneware, painting in brown in a creamy-grey glaze; marks: 'HM', incised; h.24.4cm, d.23.5cm
C.185-1985. Source: *see* **659**

662 Pot, *c.* 1937
Stoneware, incised decoration through brown under a thin grey glaze; marks: 'HM', incised; h.26.7cm, d.20.7cm
C.189-1985. Source: *see* **659**

663 Cider jar and stand, *c.* 1938
Stoneware, oatmeal glaze, painted in brown; marks: 'HM', incised; h.58cm, d.22.8cm
C.184-1985. Source: *see* **659**
Illustrated in Cooper (1947), pl.32 and jacket, and Sewter (1947). Shown at the *Inn Crafts Exhibition*, RBA Galleries, London, 1948.

664 Bowl, *c.* 1940
Stoneware, yellow glaze; marks: 'HM', painted; h.16cm, d.33cm
C.187-1985. Source: *see* **659**

665 Bowl, 1950
Stoneware, oatmeal glaze, painted in brown; marks: illegible oval seal, impressed, and 'HM', incised; h.9cm, d.24cm
Circ.282-1950. Source: Arts and Crafts Exhibition Society (Twenty-second Exhibition, V&A, 1950, no.626), £3.3s.

666 / 663 / 662

661 / 659

664

667 / 660

665

668

669

666 Bowl, *c.* 1955
Stoneware, grey glaze, painted in brown; h.34.3cm, d.28cm
C.188-1985. Source: *see* **659**

667 Bowl, *c.* 1956
Porcelain, cut decoration; marks: indistinct seal; h.8.7cm, d.10.8cm
C.186-1985. Source: *see* **659**

668 Footed bowl, *c.* 1958
Stoneware, oatmeal glaze, yellow glaze interior; marks: 'HM', incised and painted in brown; h.26.5cm, d.44cm
Circ.518-1962. Source: Mr R.D.C. Mathews, £20
Shown in the Smithsonian Institution touring exhibition *British Artist Craftsmen*, 1959–60, no.87.

669 Pot, 1958
Stoneware, incised lines, oatmeal glaze; h.38.2cm, d.25cm
Circ.263-1959. Source: Crafts Centre of Great Britain, London, £20
In his recommendation for purchase Peter Floud, of the museum's Circulation Department, noted: 'For years we have tried to persuade ... Mathews, the pottery advisor to the Crafts Centre, to sell us one of his own pots. He always procrastinated on the grounds that he would do something better later. This spring he suddenly died. We have however been allowed to pick one pot from the few which he left.' Mathews' brother agreed the purchase.

Matsubayashi Tsurunosuke 1894–1932

1894 born Kyoto, Japan
1919–22 studies at Kyoto City Ceramic Research Institute, under Hamada Shōji (qv) and Kawai Kanjirō
1922–23 travels to UK to study art and ceramic engineering; briefly studies at Royal College of Art, London
1923–24 joins Leach Pottery, St Ives; rebuilds climbing kiln at invitation of Bernard Leach (qv)
1924–25 briefly studies at Exeter College, Oxford, and Académie Colarossi, Paris, then travels in Europe
1925– returns to Japan

Matsubayashi Tsurunosuke was a potter and ceramic engineer from a prestigious Japanese potting family: his father was the 12th head of the Asahi kiln at Uji, Kyoto. While studying in the UK, he was invited to the Leach Pottery (qv), where he designed and built a three-chambered climbing kiln, replacing Leach and Hamada's earlier kiln and transforming the success of their firings. He also built a small, round up-draught kiln at St Ives used for raku and galena ware, and designed a kiln for Katharine Pleydell-Bouverie (qv), built later at Coleshill, Berkshire. Bernard Leach (qv) greatly valued his help, but thought his pots terrible. The importance of his contribution to the Leach Pottery is nevertheless evident. His occasional evening lectures on ceramic technology were diligently recorded in note form by Pleydell-Bouverie, who recalled him with humour and affection in her later writing.

Katharine Pleydell-Bouverie, 'At St Ives in the Early Years', in Barrow (1960)
Leach (1978), pp.149–55 – includes Pleydell-Bouverie's 1960 text
Tate Gallery (1985), p.233
Cardew (1988), pp.34–40
Shinya Maezaki, 'A Legacy of Matsubayashi Tsurunosuke in St Ives', in Michelle Huang (ed.), *Beyond Boundaries: East and West Cross-Cultural Encounters* (Newcastle, 2011), pp.110–21
— 'Matsubayashi Tsurunosuke and the British Studio Pottery 1924–1928: Letters from Bernard Leach, Michael Cardew, Katharine Pleydell-Bouverie and Ada Mason', *English Ceramic Circle Transactions*, 22 (2011)
Harrod (2012)
Shinya Maezaki, 'Matsubayashi Tsurunosuke', in Hugh Cortazzi (ed.), *Britain and Japan: Biographical Portraits, Vol. VIII* (Leiden, 2013), pp.312–23

670

670 Bowl, 1924
Stoneware, marbled, with greenish glaze; marks: 'SI' and personal seal, impressed; made at Leach Pottery, St Ives; h.9.8cm, d.21.3cm
C.1370-1924. Source: given by the artist
The body contains one part native black Japanese clay (brought by Matsubayashi) to three parts white clay from Devon and near St Ives.

Matsunaga, Nao 1980–

1980 born Osaka, Japan
1993 moves to England to attend Summerhill School, Suffolk
1999–2002 studies 3D Crafts at University of Brighton
2005–07 studies ceramics at Royal College of Art, London
2008–14 studio in Hackney, London
2008 solo exhibition, Konstfack, Stockholm
2011– regular exhibitions, Marsden Woo Gallery, London; frequent solo exhibitions in UK and internationally
2013 winner, British Ceramics Biennial AWARD, Stoke-on-Trent
2014 ceramics residency, V&A
2014– studio in Tottenham Hale, London
2017– solo exhibitions, New Art Centre, Salisbury

Working with clay and wood, Nao Matsunaga makes abstract sculpture informed by an interest in ceremonial objects and spaces that transcend the everyday, becoming extraordinary or strange. Cultural references are diverse, reflecting his Anglo-Japanese experience and a part-nomadic practice based around international residencies, from Arizona in the USA to Norway. An intuitive and original artist, Matsunaga employs rapid or repetitive action in the making process in order to allow space for the unconscious, and for the material to guide the outcome.

Nao Matsunaga and James Rigler, 'Art and Friendship', *CR*, 260 (2013)
Ruthin Craft Centre (2010)
Alison Britton, 'Making, Drawing and Time', exh. essay, Marsden Woo Gallery (London, 2011), reprinted in Britton (2013), pp.220–3
Alun Graves, 'Nao Matsunaga: Stones and Bones', exh. essay, Marsden Woo Gallery (London, 2012)
Jerwood Visual Arts, *Jerwood Makers Open*, exh. cat. (London, 2012)
Nao Matsunaga, text by Terunobu Fujimori (2012)
Phoebe Cummings, 'Nao Matsunaga: Monster Rock Circle', exh. essay, Marsden Woo Gallery (London, 2015)
Adamson, Droth and Olding (2017), pp.184–7, 421
Imogen Greenhalgh, 'Going Underground', *Crafts*, 268 (2017)
Glenn Adamson, *Major Progression: Nao Matsunaga in the Studio*, published to accompany the exhibition *Nao Matsunaga: Raw Faces* (Farnham: Crafts Study Centre, 2018)
Anthony Shaw, 'Curator's Choice', *CR*, 303 (2020)
Thorpe (2021), pp.155–63

671 *Busy Signal*, 2012 (pl.137)
High-fired black earthenware, handbuilt, carved wood; h.62cm, d.66cm
C.133:1,2-2013. Source: Marsden Woo Gallery, London (solo exhibition: *Stones and Bones*, 2012), £3708.33; acquired through the generosity of Gerard and Sarah Griffin

McLean, Bruce 1944–

1944	born Glasgow
1961–63	studies at Glasgow School of Art
1963–66	studies at St Martin's School of Art, London
1985–2012	teaches at Slade School of Fine Art, London
1986–	collaborates with Fulham Pottery, London; exhibits ceramics at Bernard Jacobson Gallery, London, Anthony d'Offay Gallery, London, and The Scottish Gallery, Edinburgh
1988	works at Het Keramisch Werkcentrum, Heusden, Netherlands
2015	collaboration and exhibition, *Set in Stoke*, British Ceramics Biennial, Stoke-on-Trent, working also with Johnson Tiles
2016	solo exhibitions, *One Hundred Plates*, New Art Centre, Wiltshire, and *Out of Stoke*, Contemporary Ceramics Centre, London
2017	collaborates with 1882 Ltd, Stoke-on-Trent, on *Garden Ware* series, presented at London Design Festival, V&A
2018	solo exhibition, *Garden Ware Vessels*, New Art Centre, Wiltshire

A leading figure in contemporary art, Bruce McLean emerged as part of a radical generation of sculptors and conceptual artists whose work challenged academicism and formalist modernism. His work encompasses sculpture, performance, painting, printmaking, photography and ceramics. He first turned to clay in 1986 at the invitation of Douglas Woolf, owner of Fulham Pottery. There he worked with the potter Jean-Paul Landreau, painting and incising bold, figurative designs onto slip-cast bowls, press-moulded dishes and slab-built jugs, which he increasingly played a part in making. He has returned actively to ceramics since 2015, collaborating with the British Ceramics Biennial and later 1882 Ltd, while also making his characteristic slab-built jugs and vases in his London studio.

Bruce McLean, *A Lawnmower in the Loft* (London, 2017)
Mary Rose Beaumont, exh. review, *Arts Review*, 38 (25 April 1986), p.222
Mel Gooding, 'McLean's Pots', *Crafts*, 80 (1986)
'Bruce McLean: Painter Potter', *CR*, 100 (1986)
Manchester City Art Gallery, *Out of Clay: Creations in Clay by Artists, Potters and Sculptors*, exh. pamphlet (1988)
Museum voor Hedendaagse Kunst, Het Kruithuis, *Bruce McLean: Where do you Stand?*, exh. cat., text by Mel Gooding ('s-Hertogenbosch, 1988)
Oliver Watson, 'The Critic's Eye', *Crafts*, 100 (1989)
John Berry, 'Bruce McLean', *CR*, 124 (1990)
Mel Gooding, *Bruce McLean* (Oxford, 1990)
Museum of Modern Art, Oxford (1993), pp.56–7, 88–9, 95
Museum voor Hedendaagse Kunst, Het Kruithuis, *The Unexpected: Artists' Ceramics of the 20th Century*, text 'The Tangerine Test' by Jos Poodt ('s-Hertogenbosch, 1998)

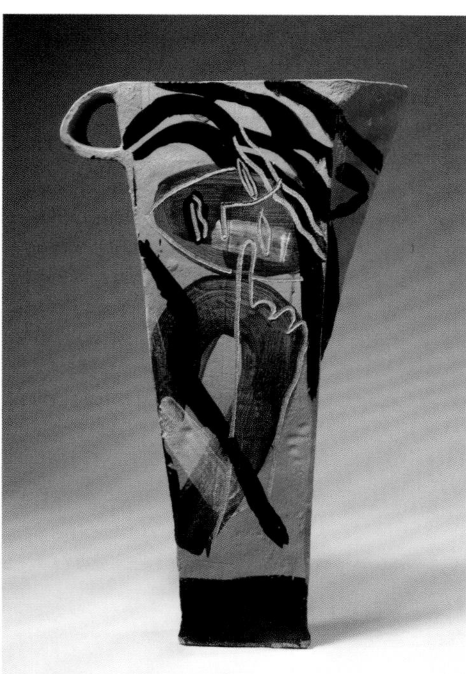

672

672 Jug, 1987
Earthenware, painted in slips and colours, and incised; made and decorated by Bruce McLean; h.94cm, d.54cm
C.98-1987. Source: Anthony d'Offay Gallery, London, £1863

McNicoll, Carol 1943–

1943	born Birmingham
1967–70	studies Fine Art at Leeds Polytechnic
1970–73	studies ceramics at Royal College of Art, London
1973–75	studio at 401½ Workshops, London, shared with Alison Britton (qv)
1976–83	studio in Kensington, London
1983–	studio in Kentish Town, London
1985	solo exhibition, Crafts Council, London
1985–86	designs giftware for Next Interiors
1986–2000	teaches at Camberwell College of Arts and Crafts
2001	shortlisted for Jerwood Applied Arts Prize
2003	touring retrospective exhibition, The City Gallery, Leicester (Crafts Council *Show 5* partnership)

Carol McNicoll is among the most radically inventive of potters. She emerged in the 1970s as part of the group of Royal College of Art graduates – including Jacqueline Poncelet (qv) and Alison

Britton (qv) – whose work underpinned the 'New Ceramics' movement. McNicoll has remained committed to the production of semi-functional pieces for the domestic realm, seeing this as a space for complex, multi-faceted and often subversive objects. She started out producing slip-cast wares in short runs, achieving considerable success. Tiring of production potting, she turned to collaboration with industry for the manufacture of her designs during the 1980s, and concentrated increasingly on one-off pieces in her own studio. Her work is mostly slip-cast and assembled, using moulds taken from figures and components modelled in clay after photographs or drawings, or models made from other materials. Increasingly it has developed as a form part of bricolage, with McNicoll casting from or appropriating found objects, and collaging surface imagery. Such processes provide her with an opportunity for social comment.

Carol McNicoll, 'A Potter's Day', *CR*, 161 (1996)
— 'The Real Craft Economy', in Harrod (1997), pp.379–82
— 'Off-centre', *CR*, 233 (2008)
Houston (1979), pp.56–61
Janet Street-Porter, 'Tea-time for the Nonconformist', *Crafts*, 47 (1980)
Oxfordshire County Museum Services (1984), pp.40–1
Paisley Museum and Art Galleries (1984), p.59
Crafts Council (1985), pp.65–6
— *Carol McNicoll Ceramics*, exh. cat., text by Richard Deacon (London, 1985)
ICA (1985), pp.43–4
Tanya Harrod, 'Bridging the Divide', *Crafts*, 80 (1986)
Henry Pim, 'Carol McNicoll – Ceramics', *CR*, 97 (1986)
Eileen Lewenstein, 'Slip-caster Extraordinary', *CR*, 117 (1989)
Houston (1991)
Museum of Modern Art, Oxford (1993), pp.58–9, 89–90, 95
Crafts Council (1995a), p.49
— (1996c), pp.81, 137
Tanya Harrod, 'Sources of Inspiration', *Crafts*, 161 (1999)
Yorkshire Sculpture Park, *Carol McNicoll: Knick-knacks*, exh. cat., text by Tanya Harrod (Wakefield, 2000)
Crafts Council (2001), pp.22–3, 31
Jonathan Bell, 'Pattern Crazy', interview, *Crafts*, 177 (2002)
Tanya Harrod and RoseLee Goldberg, *Carol McNicoll* (Aldershot, 2003)
Claudia Clare, 'Life and Art', *CR*, 205 (2004)
Hanaor (2007), pp.200–1
Whiting (2009), pp.24–9
Carlano (2010), pp.108–11
Veiteberg (2011), pp.98–9
Ian Wilson, 'Ornamentation with Attitude', *Craft Arts International*, 96 (2016)
Isabella Smith, 'Breaking the Mould', *Crafts*, 283 (2020)
Thorpe (2021), pp.46–55

Exhibition reviews: Diana Whelan, *Crafts*, 17 (1975); Piers Gough, *Crafts*, 78 (1986); Tanya Harrod, *Crafts*, 100 (1989), and *CR*, 260 (2013); David Briers, *CR*, 186 (2000); David Whiting, *Crafts*, 168 (2001); Lesley Jackson, *Crafts*, 186 (2004); Liz Hoggard, *Crafts*, 199 (2006)

An interview with Carol McNicoll is in the Crafts Lives sound archive at the British Library, London (C960/109).

673 'Ceramic piece', 1980
Earthenware, slip-cast and assembled, painted coloured slips; marks: 'Carol McNicoll', painted; h.40.2cm, d.28.5cm
C.53-1982. Source: Craft Shop, V&A, £232.87

674 Bowl, 1985 (pl.83)
Earthenware, slip-cast and assembled, painted coloured slips; marks: 'Carol McNicoll', painted; h.16.8cm, d.37.3cm
C.38-1987. Source: Crafts Council, London (solo exhibition, 1985), £427

675 Teapot and mug, 1988
Earthenware, slip-cast, painted coloured slips; marks: 'Carol McNicoll', painted; h.16.8cm, d.34cm (teapot); h.8.6cm, d.14.1cm (mug)
C.10&A, 11-1989. Source: Contemporary Applied Arts, London, £135.45
These pieces are examples of McNicoll's series production.

676 Planter, 1998
High-fired earthenware, slip-cast and assembled, coloured glazes and transfers; marks: 'Carol McNicoll', incised; h.20.5cm, d.29.5cm
C.30-1999. Source: given by Ed Wolf

677 *Home Sweet Home*, 2011 (pl.133)
Earthenware, slip-cast, transfer-printed and painted, found earthenware plate with additional transfers; marks: printed Myott factory mark and 'Carol / McNicoll / HOME SWEET HOME', painted; h.25.3cm, d.35.6cm
C.104-2012. Source: Marsden Woo Gallery, London (group exhibition: *Ideal Home*, 2011), £2311.67; acquired through the generosity of Gerard and Sarah Griffin

The museum also holds a glass jug made by Steven Newell in collaboration with McNicoll (C.144-1993).

675

673

676

Meanley, Peter 1944–

1944 born Huddersfield, Yorkshire
1962–65 studies painting at York School of Art
1965–68 studies ceramics at Royal College of Art, London
1969–2002 teaches at Belfast School of Art (later University of Ulster)
1972– studio in Bangor, County Down
1998 awarded DPhil, University of Ulster
2008 solo retrospective, *Past Gazing Future Glazing*, Ulster Folk and Transport Museum, Holywood, and Hunt Museum, Limerick

Peter Meanley has worked exclusively in saltglaze since 1986, notably as a maker of teapots of highly inventive form. Since the 2000s, he has concentrated on bellarmines, portrait jugs and later puzzle jugs in saltglaze. His earlier work proceeded in distinct phases. Objects in the form of blowtorches, rocking pots and flat irons in oxidized stoneware were followed from 1976 by slab-built or wheel-made clocks. Large earthenware bowls with metallic glazes were made from 1982.

Peter Meanley, 'Working with Saltglaze', *CR*, 130 and 131 (1991)
— 'Pigments, Salt and Glass', *Ceramics Technical*, 9 (1999)
— 'Making Teapots', *Ceramics Technical*, 10 (2000)
— 'Using Insulating Materials for the Construction of Salt Kilns', *Ceramics Technical*, 18 (2004)
— 'Transformations', *CR*, 216 (2005)
— 'What If ...', *CR*, 252 (2011)
— **and William Byers**, 'Something in the Air', *CR*, 157 (1996), and 167 (1997)
Potters/The Ceramics Book (1977) to (2012)
Timothy Malm, 'Ceramics in Northern Ireland', *Ceramics Monthly*, 43:1 (1995)
Woodhead (2005)
Liz Baird, 'Making Pottering Around into an Artform', *Belfast Telegraph* (8 July 2008)
Michael Moore, exh. review, *CR*, 232 (2008)
Henry Sandon, 'Pride of Place', *CR*, 256 (2012)

678 Teapot, 1994
Stoneware, blue saltglaze; marks: 'pm94', impressed; h.14.1cm, d.29.2cm
C.63:1,2-1995. Source: Craft Potters Association, London (exhibition: *Studio Ceramics 94*, V&A, 1994), £120

Mehornay, William 1945–

1945 born Kansas City, Missouri, USA
1967 comes to UK with US Air Force
1970–71 studies ceramics at Hammersmith College of Art
1972–73 works at Aldermaston Pottery with Alan Caiger-Smith (qv)
1974–75 workshop in Fen Ditton, Cambridgeshire
1975– successive workshops in Acton and Richmond, London
2013 ceases potting

William Mehornay initially specialized in fine, thrown porcelain with monochrome glazes, following the model of wares made for the Chinese imperial court. From 1981 until 2009 he worked primarily for the interior design market, producing large slip-cast porcelain vases, jars and lamps with lacquered, japanned and gilded finishes.

Lucie-Smith (1975), pp.86–91
Illustrations, *CR*, 57 (1979), p.14, and *CR*, 101 (1986), p.10
Potters (1980), (1983)
'Purity in Porcelain', *Collectors' Guide* (March 1981)

679 Teapot, 1976
Porcelain, transparent glaze; marks: 'WNM' in monogram, impressed; h.10.9cm, d.13.9cm
C.9&A-1979. Source: given by R.J. Charleston

Mellon, Eric James 1925–2014

1925 born Watford, Hertfordshire
1939–44 studies at Watford School of Art
1941–43 takes weekend pottery classes at Harrow School of Art
1945–50 studies printmaking at Central School of Arts and Crafts, London; part-time from 1947
1952–56 establishes artist community at Hillesden, Buckinghamshire, with Derek Davis (qv), John Clarke, Martina Thomas (whom he later marries) and others; works in slip-decorated earthenware; fulfils tilework commissions
1958– establishes workshop in Bognor Regis, Sussex; introduced to stoneware by Rosemary Wren (qv)
1965– begins experiments with ash glazes
1969– frequent solo exhibitions
1973–92 Head of Art at Slindon College, West Sussex
1982 introduced to raku by Jill Crowley (qv)
2000 retrospective exhibition, Yorkshire Museum, York

The work of Eric James Mellon is notable in combining ash-glazed stoneware or porcelain with lyrical figurative painted decoration based on life-drawing. Working in thematic series, he explored mythological and folkloric subjects, circus life, mermaids, and themes of tenderness or social comment. Mellon also worked extensively as a printmaker, painter and graphic artist.

Eric James Mellon, 'Ash Glazes', *CR*, 42 (1976), 43 (1977), and 65 (1980)
— 'Magic and Poetry', *CR*, 114 (1988)
— 'Burning Passion', *CR*, 172 (1998)
— *The Ceramicist as Artist*, privately published cat. for Yorkshire Museum retrospective (Chichester, 2000)
— 'Colour in Ash Glazes', *CR*, 183 (2000)
Decorative Art (1971/72)
Potters/The Ceramics Book (1972) to (2012)
V&A (1972), p.114
Commonwealth Art Gallery, *Eric Mellon*, exh. cat., text by R.H. Bowden (London, 1973)

Crafts Advisory Committee (1976), p.107
Crafts Council (1980), p.61
Oxfordshire County Museum Services (1984), pp.38–9
Eric James Mellon: Ceramics, Drawings, Paintings 1966–1986, artist's pamphlet, introduction by W.A. Ismay (1986)
Paul Foster (ed.), *Eric James Mellon: Ceramic Artist* (Chichester, 2000)
Dewar (2002), pp.65–7
Paul Foster (ed.), *Eric James Mellon: The Development of Glazes 1951–2012* (Chichester, 2012)
Nottingham City Museums and Galleries (2017), p.67

Exhibition reviews: R.H. Bowden, *Arts Review*, 18:12 (1966), and 19:21 (1967); Judith Brooke, *Arts Review*, 18:24 (1966); Eileen Lewenstein, *CR*, 1 and 4 (1970); Ian Bennett, *Crafts*, 36 (1979)

680

681

Obituaries: *The Telegraph* (5 February 2014); *The Times* (5 February 2014); Tanya Harrod, *The Guardian* (24 February 2014); David Whiting, *The Independent* (12 March 2014)

An interview with Eric James Mellon is in the Crafts Lives sound archive at the British Library, London (C960/98).

680 Dish, 1968
Stoneware, painted in blue and brown under a wood-ash glaze; marks: 'Eric James Mellon / Elm Ash / 1968', painted; h.5.9cm, d.30.1cm
C.59-1985. Source: Paul Rice Gallery, London, £280

681 Pot, 1984
Stoneware, painted in colours under a bush-ash glaze; marks: 'Eric James Mellon 1984 34 Philadelphus Ash Theme of Tenderness' and a fox, painted in brown; h.15.9cm, d.15cm
C.200-1984. Source: Paul Rice Gallery, London (solo exhibition, 1984), £330
The decoration comprises a mermaid in the forms of a flautist and a woman catching a fox, a moon-goddess and embracing lovers, and a bird-maiden. Mellon depicted mermaids as legged or tailed.

Milland Pottery *see* Ray Marshall

Mills, Donald 1922–1997 and Jacqueline (née Holder) 1927–1995

1922	Donald born London
1938–	studies at Croydon School of Art
1945	employed as a thrower at Fulham Pottery; teaches at the Central School of Arts and Crafts, London, and elsewhere
1946	becomes member of Artists International Association (AIA)
1946–48	establishes Donald Mills Pottery in the Borough, London, working in partnership with former students Eileen Lewenstein (qv) and Brigitte Appleby in the production of tablewares and refractory elements for electric fires; continues with own individual pieces
1947	marries Jacqueline Holder, who has studied painting at Willesden School of Art (1943–46); elected to AIA Central Committee as Vice Treasurer; exhibition of individual stonewares at AIA Gallery, London
1948	partnership of Donald Mills Pottery dissolved when firm driven bankrupt over non-payment for an order for 250,000 electric fire elements
1948–52	with Jacqueline, establishes Donald Mills Pottery Ltd, retaining Silvester Street premises in London
1952–74	abandons potting due to damage to hands; establishes Mills and Hubball Ltd, supplying pottery materials and equipment
1974–	resumes potting with Jacqueline, moving to Itchenor, West Sussex

For much of his career, Donald Mills worked in partnership with his wife, Jacqueline, Donald throwing, Jacqueline decorating. At Silvester Street they produced tableware and individual pieces in celadon-glazed stoneware, also experimenting with copper-red glazes and high-fired tin-glazed ware. After resuming potting in Sussex, they specialized in commemorative wares.

Arts and Crafts Exhibition Society (1941) to (1950)
Cooper (1947), p.*iii*, pl.33
Decorative Art (1949) to (1952/53)
'Donald Mills Pottery', *Pottery and Glass* (November 1949)
Ronald Wilson, exh. review, *Art News and Review* (1949)
A.W. Chapman, 'Jacqueline Mills', obituary, *Crafts*, 137 (1995)
Eileen Lewenstein, 'Donald Mills', obituary, *CR*, 167 (1997)
Anthea Arnold, *Briglin Pottery 1948–1990* (Maidstone, 2002), pp.7–8
Whybrow (2006), pp.114–15

682 Dish: *Evening Sky*, 1950
Stoneware, mottled copper-red glaze; h.6.2cm, d.27cm
Circ.279-1950. Source: Arts and Crafts Exhibition Society (Twenty-second Exhibition, V&A, 1950, no.593), £10.10s.

683 Teapot, 1951
Stoneware, tin glaze, painted in brown, yellow and blue; marks: 'DM', painted; h.16.4cm, d.23.6cm
Circ.18-1952. Source: Heal & Son Ltd, London, £1.15s.6d.

C.954-1935. Source: given by the Pottery and Crafts Fund of the Contemporary Art Society (purchased from Paterson's Gallery, London, 1929 (solo exhibition: *Stoneware Pottery*, no.87, 'Fauns' [*sic*]), £8.8s.)

705 Tall pot: *Madonna*, 1930
Stoneware, grey glaze, incised and painted in red; marks: 'M' in a pentagon, impressed; h.56cm, d.18.4cm
C.60-1976. Source: Richard Dennis, London, £312
Shown in solo exhibition, *Pottery, Paintings and Furniture*, Lefevre Gallery, London, 1930 (no.8, listed at 60 guineas).

706 Pot: *Spring Song*, 1930
Stoneware, grey glaze, painted in red and blue; marks: 'M' in a pentagon, impressed; h.27.8cm, d.17.4cm
Circ.425-1930. Source: Lefevre Gallery, London (solo exhibition: *Pottery, Paintings and Furniture*, 1930, no.27, listed at 30 guineas), £42 (with **707** and **708**)
Regarding the acquisition of **706** to **708**, Bernard Rackham, Keeper of the Ceramics Department, stated: 'These pieces will, in my opinion, well represent Mr. Murray's latest work, which shows him still to be the most able of the artist-potters working in England at this time.' He also recorded the combination of painting in copper-red and grey glaze as being a technique that Murray had not tried before.

707 Pot: *Vine*, 1930
Stoneware, cream glaze, painted in brown; marks: 'M' in a pentagon, impressed; h.18.7cm, d.19.8cm
Circ.426-1930. Source: *see* **706** (no.59, listed at 12 guineas)

708 Bowl: 'Unglazed. Brush Decoration', 1930 (pl.16)
Stoneware, painted in brown, glazed interior; marks: 'M' in a pentagon, impressed; h.10cm, d.12.8cm
Circ.427-1930. Source: *see* **706** (no.93, listed at 4 guineas)

709 Tea bowl, 1930
Porcelain, painted in blue and brown; inscribed 'Bernard Rackham his Tea Bowl – 1930'; marks: 'M' in a pentagon, impressed; h.6cm, d.8.4cm
C.140-2012. Source: given by Elizabeth Rackham
Made as a gift for Bernard Rackham, the V&A's Keeper of Ceramics and a long-standing supporter of Murray. The gift perhaps reflects Murray's gratitude for the three works bought by the museum in 1930 (**706** to **708**).

710 Tea bowl, *c.* 1930
Stoneware, mottled tenmoku glaze; marks: 'M' in a pentagon, impressed; h.7.7cm, d.10.8cm
Circ.276-1955. Source: given by Lady Russell, MBE, from the collection of the late Francis Moore

711 Tea bowl, *c.* 1930
Stoneware, brown glaze with purple flushes; marks: 'M' in a pentagon, impressed; h.8cm, d.11cm
C.114-1977. Source: Richard Dennis, London (from the collection of Sir Edward Maufe), £100

712 Pot: *Eterne* (later *Wheel of Life*), 1933–34 (pl.22)
Stoneware, grey glaze, painted in brown; marks: 'M' in a pentagon, impressed; h.62.8cm, d.30.5cm
Circ.352-1958. Source: Leicester Galleries, London (solo exhibition, 1958, no.18), £94.10s.
One of Murray's most impressive pots, *Eterne* was originally shown in his solo exhibition of *Pottery and Paintings* at the Lefevre Galleries in April–May 1934, listed as no.60 and priced at 125 guineas, equally the most expensive piece in the show. It was subsequently illustrated in Cooper (1947), pl.36, as *Eterne*. Presumably

706

707

709

710 / 711

713

714

unsold in 1934, it was included in his final exhibition in 1958, where it was exhibited as *Wheel of Life*. It was illustrated as such in *Pottery Quarterly*, 5:20 (1958), pl.1, and dated 1933. The pot has frequently, and erroneously, been assumed to date from the late 1930s.

713 Pot, 1934
Stoneware, tenmoku glaze with white mottling; marks: 'M' in a pentagon, impressed, and 'FRID', painted; h.21.8cm, d.21.7cm
Circ.352-1939. Source: given by the Pottery and Crafts Fund of the Contemporary Art Society (purchased from Lefevre Galleries, London, 1934, £10.10s.)
The pot bears the Society's paper labels inscribed: 'C.A.S.', '133' and 'W. Staite Murray'.

714 Bowl, *c.* 1930–35
Stoneware, grey glaze; marks: 'M' in pentagon, impressed; 'KI.D.F', incised, '59.' and 'P.', painted; h.11.5cm, d.20.4cm
C.180-2014. Source: bequeathed by Mme. Renée Collinson

Newland, William 1919–1998

1919	born Masterton, New Zealand
1942–45	prisoner of war in Italy and Germany; establishes art school at Stalag VIIIA prisoner-of-war camp, teaches and studies with fellow POWs
1945–47	studies painting at Chelsea School of Art, having received bursary from New Zealand government
1947–48	trains at Institute of Education, University of London; attends pottery classes under Dora Billington (qv) at Central School of Arts and Crafts in evenings
1948–	teaches ceramics part-time at Institute of Education and Central School
1949–55	establishes studio in Bayswater, London, shared with Margaret Hine (qv) and Nicholas Vergette (qv)
1952	marries Margaret Hine
1955–	moves to Prestwood, Buckinghamshire, establishes workshop
1962–	teaches full-time at Institute of Education; teaching eclipses making
c. 1965	ceases teaching at Central School
1982–	retires from teaching; returns to making at Prestwood

William Newland was the central figure in a group that emerged from the Institute of Education, where he taught pottery to artists training for the Art Teacher's Diploma. Margaret Hine (qv), James Tower (qv) and Nicholas Vergette (qv) were all introduced to pottery at the Institute, as Newland himself had been. Newland's circle rejected the Anglo-Asian stoneware school as out-of-step with contemporary trends in architecture and interior design, instead taking inspiration from Picasso's ceramics, shown in London for the first time in 1950. Accomplished in a wide range of pottery techniques, Newland was particularly drawn to slipware and tin-glazed earthenware, making vigorously decorated dishes and spirited wheel-thrown and assembled bulls and other figures. Together with Hine, who he married, and for a time Vergette, Newland also produced decorative ceramics for London's burgeoning coffee-bar scene. He returned to making after a committed career as an educator, producing a series of tin-glazed dishes painted with mythological subjects.

William Newland, 'Recent Ceramic Art', *World Review* (December 1952)
— review of 'The Work of the Modern Potter in England', *Journal of the Royal Society of Arts*, 101:4899 (1953), pp.445–6
— notes on work exhibited at the Crafts Centre of Great Britain, *Pottery Quarterly*, 1:3 (1954), pp.39–41
— 'The Modern Potter's Craft: A Conversation with William Newland', in ICA (1985), pp.40–2
— 'Tactile Knowing', in Anthony Dyson (ed.), *Art and Design Education: Heritage and Prospect* (London, 1986)
— 'A Handful of Clay', *CR*, 158 (1996)
Arts and Crafts Exhibition Society (1950) to (1957)
Decorative Art (1952/53), (1954/55)
Billington (1953), (1955)
Lewis (1956), pl.379
Smithsonian Institution (1959)
ICA (1985), p.44
Harrod (1989)
Daphne Carnegy, *Tin-glazed Earthenware* (London, 1993), pp.102–5
Aberystwyth Arts Centre, *William Newland: It's All There in Front of You*, exh. cat. (Aberystwyth, 1996)
Tanya Harrod, 'Sources of Inspiraton', *Crafts*, 139 (1996)
Jones (2000)
Partington (2005)
Nottingham City Museums and Galleries (2017), p.68

Exhibition reviews: Murray Fieldhouse, *Pottery Quarterly*, 1:1 (1954); David Whiting, *Studio Pottery*, 21 (1996)

Obituaries: Alison Britton, *CR*, 172 (1998); Tanya Harrod, *The Independent* (12 May 1998); David Reeves, *Crafts*, 153 (1998)

715

716

An interview with William Newland is in the Recording the Crafts video archive at UWE Bristol (also held in the National Art Library, V&A, London, 704.AA.0045 to 704.AA.0047).

715 Jar, 1950
Stoneware, tenmoku glaze; marks: 'W.N. 1950', incised; made at Central School of Arts and Crafts; h.34.8cm, d.23.2cm
Circ.283-1950. Source: Arts and Crafts Exhibition Society (Twenty-second Exhibition, V&A, 1950, no.574), £8.8s.

716 Figure of a bull, 1954
Earthenware, thrown and assembled, sgraffito through purple-brown glaze over white tin glaze; marks: 'William / NEWLAND / 54', incised; h.35.9cm, d.37.7cm
Circ.57-1954. Source: the artist, £10.10s.

717 Figure of a harlequin, 1954 (fig.9)
Earthenware, thrown and assembled, tin glaze, painted in colours; marks: 'WILLIAM / NEWLAND / 54', painted; h.83cm, d.48cm
C.24-2020. Source: private sale, £8000 (with **718**); acquired with funds raised in memory of Jonathan Nevitt
This figure, together with **718**, is believed to have formed part of the decor of the restaurant Le Pavillon, in Draycott Avenue, Chelsea, London. A comparable figure was exhibited at the Crafts Centre of Great Britain in 1954, illustrated in *Pottery Quarterly*, 1:3 (1954), p.39.

719

720

718 Figure on a donkey, *c.* 1954 (pl.37)
Earthenware, thrown and assembled, sgraffito through purple-brown glaze over white tin glaze; marks: 'NEWLAND', inscribed; h.50cm, d.45cm
C.25-2020. Source: see **717**

719 Pot, 1957
Earthenware, incised decoration, grey-white glaze; marks: 'William Newland 57' and 'WN 57', painted; h.31.6cm, d.36.9cm
Circ.95-1959. Source: the artist, £12

720 Four bottles, 1958–59
Earthenware, grey and matt brown glazes; marks: 'William Newland', painted in blue; h.36.8cm, d.15cm
Circ.96 to C-1959. Source: *see* **719**, £6
The tall bottles are dated 1958, the squat bottle 1959.

Newman, Bryan 1935–2019

1935	born London
1951–56	studies at Camberwell School of Arts and Crafts, specializing in pottery under Dick Kendall from 1953
1958–66	teaches part-time at Camberwell School of Arts and Crafts
1959–64	sets up workshop in Dulwich, London, shared with his wife, Julia, and others
1961–62	exhibition with Ian Auld (qv) at Primavera, London
1961–68	teaches part-time at Harrow School of Art
1965–	moves to Somerset, establishes Aller Pottery, near Langport, with Julia
1966–73	teaches part-time at Bath Academy of Art
2003	Julia dies; Bryan continues to pot at reduced rate

Bryan Newman worked for many years in partnership with his wife, Julia, producing domestic ware in considerable quantity alongside his ceramic sculpture. A potter of great energy and a pioneer of thrown and assembled and slab-built forms, he is particularly known for his cityscapes, arks and bridges, as well as his inventive sculptural teapots.

Bryan Newman, 'Ways of Working and Thinking', *Pottery Quarterly*, 8:29 (1963)
— statement, in Rothschild (1972)
— interview, in Cameron and Lewis (1976), pp.106–17, 167
— 'Slab-building', in Tony Birks, *Pottery* (London, 1979)
Biographical notes, *Pottery Quarterly*, 8:30 (1963), p.7, and 9:35 (1969), p.106
Decorative Art (1964/65), (1971/72)
Illustration of domestic ware, *Pottery Quarterly*, 8:32 (1965), pl.8
Birks (1967), pp.93–108, (1976), pp.52–69
Casson (1967), p.7, pls.43–6
Potters (1972) to (1986)
'Working in Somerset', *Crafts*, 16 (1975), pp.11–12
Crafts Advisory Committee (1976), p.108
Tony Birks, 'The Newmans at Aller', *CR*, 43 (1977)
Janet Kovesi, 'Teapot Maniac', *CR*, 51 (1978)
Crafts Council (1980), p.61
— (1985), pp.66–7

Exhibition reviews: *Pottery Quarterly*, 7:28 (1962); W.A. Ismay, *CR*, 13 (1972)

721 *Bobbin Tree*, *c.* 1966
Stoneware, thrown and assembled, dry ash

721

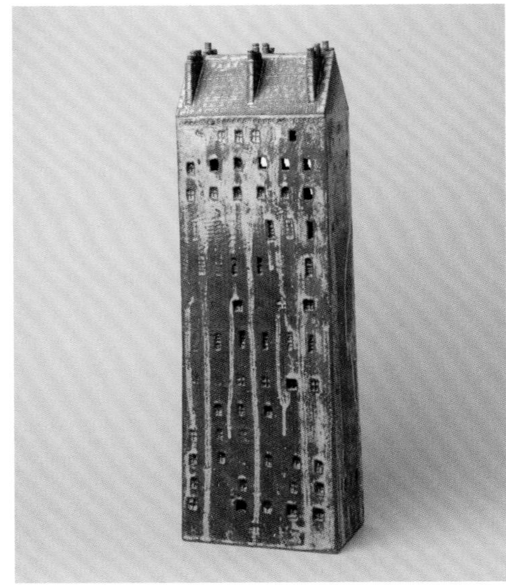

724

and china clay glaze; h.23.5cm, d.16.7cm
C.75-2004. Source: given by Michael Hall
Illustrated in Birks (1967), pl.76. Formerly in the collection of the gallerist Nicholas Treadwell.

722 Sculpture, 1969 (fig.1)
Stoneware, slab-built, with thrown elements, matt yellow-brown glaze; h.21.9cm, d.25.2cm
Circ.218-1972. Source: the artist, £15
Shown in the Smithsonian Institution touring exhibition *British Designer Craftsmen*, 1970–71, no.49.

723 *Houses with motorway*, 1973 (pl.61)
Stoneware, slab-built, vitreous slip; h.13.5cm, d.32.5cm
Circ.301-1974. Source: the artist, £18
Shown in the exhibition *The Craftsman's Art*, V&A, 1973, no.169.

724 *Tenement Block*, c. 1982
Stoneware, slab-built, ochre glaze; marks: 'A', impressed; h.52.3cm, d.16.4cm
C.19-2005. Source: given by Marianne Heller

Nisbet, Eileen (née Hull) 1929–1990

1929	born London
1950–53	studies at Hornsey School of Art
1960–63	studies ceramics at Central School of Arts and Crafts, London; subsequently teaches for a period at Harrow School of Art
1965–	studio in Holborn, London
1965–90	teaches ceramics at Central School of Art and Design, London
1977	solo exhibition, *Planes and Light*, Casson Gallery, London; awarded Crafts Advisory Committee (CAC) bursary to explore colour
early 1980s–	new studio in Holborn, London

Eileen Nisbet was a contemporary at Hornsey School of Art of Michael Casson (qv), who became a lifelong friend. Her earlier work comprised large press-moulded earthenware dishes with linear decoration, and handbuilt ceramic murals. From 1975 she developed distinctive abstract planar sculptures alluding to botanical, mechanical or ceramic forms, assembled after firing from wafer-thin porcelain slabs. Early examples were monochrome, exploiting the translucent qualities of porcelain; subsequent pieces incorporated painted or inlaid colour. For many years Nisbet taught at the Central School, her student and later colleague Rob Kesseler describing her as 'a wonderful unassuming teacher who opened a rich world of ceramic decoration'. Nisbet was the sister of the abstract painter James Hull.

Kenneth Clark, *Practical Pottery and Ceramics* (London, 1964), p.37, pls.9, 16–18, 88–90
Casson (1967), p.7, pls.47–51
David Canter, 'The Craftsman Potters Shop', *CR*, 6 (1970) – illustrates ceramic relief
Potters (1972) to (1986)
V&A (1972), p.114
Crafts Advisory Committee (1976), p.109
'In Brief: Eileen Nisbet', notice of CAC bursary, *Crafts*, 26 (1977), pp.10–11
Crafts Council (1980), p.61
Lane (1980)
Peter Lane, 'Eileen Nisbet's Porcelain', *CR*, 61 (1980)
Oxfordshire County Museum Services (1984), pp.42–3
Paisley Museum and Art Galleries (1984), p.63
Crafts Council (1985), p.68
Kesseler (2017), p.31

Exhibition reviews: *CR*, 33 (1975); Glenys Barton, *Crafts*, 27 (1977); *Arts Review* (February 1978), p.51; Emmanuel Cooper, *Art & Artists*, 14:8 (1979); Geoffrey Weston, '3 in Ceramics', *Crafts*, 43 (1980); Philip Rawson, 'Eight Ceramicists', *Crafts*, 68 (1984)

Obituaries: Mick Casson, *CR*, 125 (1990), and *Crafts*, 106 (1990)

Eileen Nisbet demonstrated decorating techniques in episode 3 of the BBC TV series *The Craft of the Potter*, 1976.

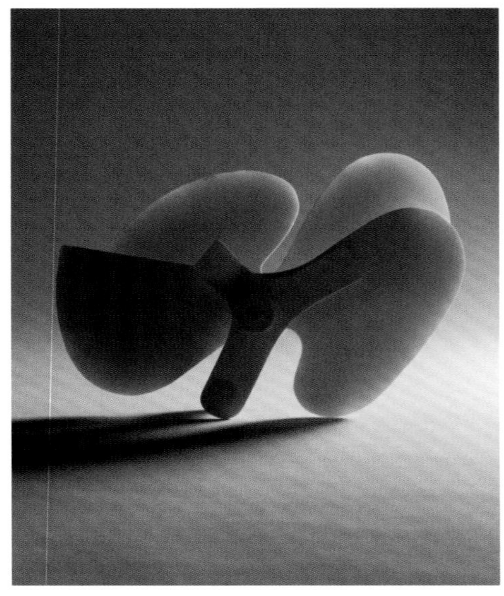

725

725 *Horizontal Flower Sculpture*, 1983
Porcelain, hand-modelled flat elements, assembled after firing; h.21.5cm, d.33cm
C.331-1983. Source: Craftsmen Potters Association, London (group exhibition: *Decorated Porcelain*, 1983, no.207), £315

OBrien, Michael 1930–

1930	born Edinburgh
1952–54	studies painting at Farnham School of Art
1959	attends 'Fundamental Pottery' course run by Michael Cardew (qv) at Wenford Bridge
1963–	joins Pottery Training Centre, Abuja (now Suleja), Nigeria, as student under Cardew
1965	takes over running of Pottery Training Centre
1973	returns to England to run Wenford Bridge Pottery in Cardew's absence; later works at Farnham School of Art
1979	returns to Nigeria to teach at Ahmadu Bello University, Zaria
1985–	establishes Maraba Pottery, near Kaduna, with Danlami Aliyu (qv)
1987–	returns to England, establishes pottery at Headley, Surrey; travels regularly to Nigeria
1997–	establishes pottery at Bwari, Nigeria, with Stephen Mhya
2019	exhibition, *Michael OBrien: In Nigeria*, Crafts Study Centre, Farnham

726

Michael OBrien played an important role at the Pottery Training Centre, Abuja (now Suleja), Nigeria, carrying out rationalization that for a time secured its financial viability, following Michael Cardew's (qv) departure. He has since continued to train potters and establish potteries in Nigeria, while maintaining his own workshop in Surrey. His own pots follow in the African-inflected stoneware tradition established by Cardew.

Michael OBrien, 'Abuja after Michael Cardew', *CR*, 34 (1975)
— interview by Jeffrey Jones, *Interpreting Ceramics*, ejournal, 3 (2001)
Ian Auld, 'Letter from Nigeria', *CR*, 11 (1971)
Harrod (2012), see esp. pp.295, 298, 355–6
Ozioma Onuzulike, 'The Making of National Ceramics Exhibitions of the Craft Potters Association of Nigeria', *Interpreting Ceramics*, ejournal, 17 (2016)
Anthony OBrien, 'Cardew and OBrien: Two Potters in Nigeria', *CR*, 287 (2017)

726 Beer mug, 1963
Stoneware, incised with a grass 'comb' and inlaid with porcelain under a transparent glaze; made at Abuja; h.12cm, d.13.2cm
C.56-2008. Source: given by Michael OBrien
OBrien made this mug after visiting the pottery village of Ushafa, and its decoration follows traditional local designs.

Odney Pottery *see also* John Bew

Odney Pottery was established in 1943 by John Bew (qv) at Grove Farm, Cookham, Berkshire, through an agreement with the retailer John Lewis Partnership, which the pottery was to supply. Suitable clay was dug locally at Fifield. The main throwers were Mervyn ('Reg') Davies, who had worked with Bew in Wales, and Frank Spindler. Others included Muriel Tudor-Jones and Reg Moon. Geoffrey Eastop (qv) also worked there for a time. Odney produced slipware, mostly using the local red clay, but also in a white body from about 1951. Bew's relationship with the Partnership was at times strained; in 1948 he gained agreement to sell more widely. A successful exhibition was held at the Cooling Galleries in New Bond Street, London, in 1949, and the pottery was well represented at the Festival of Britain in 1951. Odney nevertheless faced increased competition as restrictions on imports into Britain were lifted, this likely contributing to Bew's tragic death in 1954, apparently by suicide. The pottery closed early in 1956. Since 2013 the Grove Farm site has housed the archives of the John Lewis Partnership.

Item 731 was recorded as Frank Spindler's work at the time of its acquisition by the museum, and other items listed below may also be by Spindler. Spindler was notably adept at slip-decorating, a skill said to have been gained through earlier work in a bakery icing cakes. Later Spindler worked at the Chelsea Pottery (qv) and reportedly then presented as a woman (Geoffrey Eastop, British Library Crafts Lives sound archive, London, C960/680).

Cooper (1947), p.*iii*, pls.34–5
Arts and Crafts Exhibition Society (1950)
News of closure, *Pottery Quarterly*, 3:9 (1956), p.37
Frank Spindler, notes on making slipware, *Pottery Quarterly*, 4:13 (1957), p.42, pls.13–15
Utilitarian or Utopian?: The Odney Pottery 1942–1956, exh. pamphlet, The Parish Centre, Holy Trinity Church (Cookham, 2007)

727 Shallow bowl, 1949
Red earthenware, cobalt and black slip, tin glaze; h.3.4cm, d.16.2cm
Circ.193-1949. Source: the pottery (following exhibition at the Cooling Galleries, London, 1949), 15s.

728 Plate, 1949
Red earthenware, thrown, slip-trailed in black on a cobalt slip ground; marks: 'ODNEY', impressed; h.2.7cm, d.17cm
Circ.194-1949. Source: *see* 727, 10s.

729 Plate, 1949
Porcelain, press-moulded, sgraffito through cobalt slip; h.3cm, d.16.5cm
Circ.195-1949. Source: *see* 727, 12s.6d.

729 / 727 / 728

730

731

730 Dish, 1951
White earthenware, combed slip in white and orange on a black ground; marks: 'Odney', incised; h.3.5cm, d.29cm
Circ.185-1951. Source: the pottery, £3.13s.6d. Acquired with 731 after the Twenty-second Exhibition of the Arts and Crafts Exhibition Society, held at the V&A in 1950, where similar items were shown.

731 Plate, 1951
Earthenware, coloured slips; made by A.F. Spindler; marks: 'Odney', incised; h.4.5cm, d.32.2cm
Circ.184-1951. Source: *see* 730, £5.5s.

Odundo, Magdalene 1950–

1950	born Nairobi, Kenya
1968–71	studies commercial art part-time at Nairobi Polytechnic
1971–73	moves to UK; studies graphics at Cambridge College of Art
1973–76	studies ceramics at West Surrey College of Art and Design, Farnham
1974	three-month apprenticeship at Pottery Training Centre, Abuja (now Suleja), Nigeria
1976–79	museum educator, Commonwealth Institute, London
1979–82	studies ceramics at Royal College of Art, London
1982–85	workshop in Ripley, Surrey
1985–93	workshop in Bentley, Hampshire
1993–2007	workshop in Wrecclesham, Farnham, Surrey
1997–2014	teaches at University for the Creative Arts, Farnham (UCA); appointed Professor in 2000
2008	awarded OBE
2009–	workshop in Upper Hale, Farnham, Surrey
2014–	Professor Emerita, UCA; awarded Honorary Doctorate, University of Florida, Gainesville, USA
2016	awarded Honorary Doctorate, University of the Arts, London
2018–	Chancellor, UCA
2019	retrospective exhibition, *The Journey of Things*, The Hepworth Wakefield, West Yorkshire, and Sainsbury Centre, Norwich, Norfolk
2020	awarded DBE
2021	awarded Honorary Doctorate, Royal College of Art

Magdalene Odundo is recognized as one of the most significant ceramic artists of the late 20th and early 21st centuries. While first developed within the context of a British art-school training, her handbuilt and burnished vessels are informed by a broad range of ceramic traditions, including those of her native Kenya, as well as of Nigeria, New Mexico and elsewhere. Evolved and refined throughout her career, these increasingly sculptural pottery forms have strongly anthropomorphic characteristics, referencing in particular female bodies and body adornment.

Magdalene Odundo, statement, in Bendavid and Lalumia (2017), pp.28, 40
'CPA New Member', *CR*, 83 (1983)
Potters (1983) to (1992)
Megan Tressida, 'A Feat of Clay', *World of Interiors* (June 1984)
'Kenyan Heritage', *Crafts*, 67 (1984)
Crafts Council (1985), p.68
Glynn Vivian Art Gallery, *New Works: Magdalene Odundo*, exh. cat. (Swansea, 1987)
Louisa Buck, 'The Critic's Eye', *Crafts*, 119 (1992)
Yvònne Joris (ed.), *Magdalene Odundo*, exh. cat. ('s-Hertogenbosch, 1994)
Anthony Slayter-Ralph (ed.), *Magdalene Odundo* (Aldershot, 1994)
Marla Berns, *Ceramic Gestures: New Vessels by Magdalene Odundo*, exh. cat. (Santa Barbara, 1995)
Perryman (1995), pp.74–6, (2008), pp.88–92
Marla Berns, 'Magdalene Anyango N. Odundo', *African Arts*, 29:1 (1996)
Betty Blandino, 'Private Conversation', *CR*, 170 (1998)
Lakeland Arts Trust, *Magdalene Odundo: Clay Forms*, exh. cat. (Bowness-on-Windermere, 2001)
Hannah Wingrave, 'Magdalene Odundo: Physical Vessels', *Ceramics in Society*, 45 (2001)
Augustus Casely-Hayford, 'Forms and Forces', *Crafts*, 192 (2005)
Ashley Howard, 'Intimate Humanity', *CR*, 252 (2011)
Teleri Lloyd-Jones, 'True to Form', *Crafts*, 250 (2014)
National Glass Centre, *Magdalene Odundo: Tri-Part-It-Us*, exh. cat. (Sunderland, 2015)
Simon Olding, 'Magdalene Odundo's Untitled #10 (1995)', *Journal of Modern Craft*, 8:2 (2015)
Elsbeth Joyce Court, 'Magdalene A.N. Odundo: Pathways to Path Maker', *Critical Interventions*, 11:1 (2017)
Jennifer Zwilling, 'Magdalene Odundo', *American Craft Inquiry*, 1:2 (2017)
Andrew Bonacina (ed.), *Magdalene Odundo: The Journey of Things*, exh. cat. (London, 2019)
Charles Darwent, 'Catholic Taste', *Crafts*, 276 (2019)

732

Isabella Smith, 'Figuration and Abstraction', *CR*, 296 (2019)
Fitzwilliam Museum, *Magdalene Odundo in Cambridge*, exh. cat. (Cambridge, 2021)
Salon 94, *Magdalene Odundo*, exh. cat., texts by Augustus Casely-Hayford and Barbara Thompson (New York, 2021)

Exhibition reviews: David Briers, *Crafts*, 92 (1988), and 173 (2001); Victor Margrie, *Crafts*, 119 (1992); Robert Soppelsa, *African Arts*, 29:1 (1996); Emmanuel Cooper, *Crafts*, 151 (1998), and *CR*, 191 (2001); Robin Poynor and MacKenzie Moon, *African Arts*, 40:2 (2007); Haley Jones and Elizabeth Caris, *African Arts*, 52:1 (2019)

732 Pot, 1982
Earthenware, burnished, reduced black in the firing; h.19.1cm, d.15.5cm
C.58-2015. Source: given by David Queensberry
Bought by Queensberry – then Professor of Ceramics – at Odundo's Royal College of Art degree show.

733 *Symmetrical ribbed pot*, 1983 (pl.88)
Red earthenware, burnished, reduced black in the firing; marks: 'Odundo 83'; h.28.6cm, d.23.8cm
C.78-1984. Source: given by the Friends of the V&A (purchased at the Craftsmen Potters Association exhibition, *Studio Ceramics Today*, V&A, 1983, no.128, £315)

O'Malley, Peter 1917–1994

1917	born London
1945	marries Joan Warburton, a painter, after war service in East Asia

c. 1947	attends pottery evening classes at Camberwell School of Arts and Crafts
1948–52	studies ceramics at Royal College of Art, London
1951–52	spends year in France on Travelling Scholarship, drawing and working at pottery of Carlos Fernandez, Aix-en-Provence, and visiting potteries at Vallauris and Biot
1952–53	works briefly with Anita Hoy (qv) at Bullers, Stoke-on-Trent, then spends nine months at Wattisfield Pottery, Suffolk, a traditional country pottery
1953–69	teaches ceramics at Royal College of Art
1969	retires; establishes workshop in Stoke-by-Nayland, Suffolk
1970–79	teaches pottery part-time at Colchester Technical College

Peter O'Malley spent most of his working life as a tutor at the Royal College of Art, where he was engaged in industrial techniques. His studio pottery was made at the College, in his own time.

Lewis (1956), pls.370–1

Pottery Quarterly, 6:21 (1959), pls.4–5

Sally Hunter, 'Joan Warburton', obituary, *The Independent* (18 August 1996)

Sally Hunter Fine Art, *Joan Warburton: Portrait of a Life*, exh. pamphlet, with biographical notes on Peter O'Malley (London, 1996)

734 Pot, *c.* 1958
Stoneware, matt black glaze with abraded decoration, interior grey glaze; h.29.3cm, d.19cm
Circ.64-1959. Source: Foyles Art Gallery, London, £11.11s.

Omega Workshops

The Omega Workshops opened at 33 Fitzroy Square, London, in July 1913. The prime mover behind their formation was the critic and painter Roger Fry (1866–1934), who sought to bring freshness, spontaneity and artistic expression to interior decoration. Omega produced a range of domestic items designed and made by artists who worked anonymously, among them Vanessa Bell (qv) and Duncan Grant (qv). The first Omega ceramics were overpainted industrially produced wares, but in late 1913 Fry learned how to throw from George Schenck, a flowerpot maker in Mitcham, Surrey. Under his direction, Fry – and briefly Bell – threw a variety of vases and bowls, a number of which were decorated with painting on a white tin glaze. Late the following year, Fry was introduced to the firm of Carter & Co. in Poole, Dorset, and there began making a wide range of tableware. Although he envisaged his designs being repeated by others, almost all Omega pottery seems to have been made by Fry himself, and thrown on the wheel. Most pieces carry a monochrome grey-white tin glaze, with cobalt blue and black glazes later being introduced. The Omega Workshops closed in 1919.

Omega Workshops Ltd: Artist Decorators, cat. (London, 1914)

Rose (1955), p.7, (1970), pp.23–4

Quentin Bell, 'The Omega Revisited', *The Listener* (30 January 1964)

Isabelle Anscombe, *Omega and After: Bloomsbury and the Decorative Arts* (London, 1981)

Judith Collins, *The Omega Workshops* (London, 1983)

— 'Roger Fry and Omega Pottery', *CR*, 86 (1984)

Crafts Council, *The Omega Workshops, 1913–19: Decorative Arts of Bloomsbury*, exh. cat. (London, 1984)

Anthony d'Offay, *The Omega Workshops: Alliance and Enmity in English Art 1911–1920*, exh. cat. (London, 1984)

Bergesen (1991), pp.218–20

Julian Stair, 'The Employment of Matter: Pottery of the Omega Workshops', in Alexandra Gerstein (ed.), *Beyond Bloomsbury: Designs of the Omega Workshops 1913–19*, exh. cat. (London: Courtauld Gallery, 2009), pp.27–33

735 Vase, *c.* 1913
Painted in enamels on a commercial blank; probably painted by Roger Fry; marks: 'Ω' in a square, painted; h.21.2cm, d.9.5cm
Circ.202-1964. Source: Margaret Deneke, £5
See Crafts Council (1984), p.65, C9.

736 Plate, *c.* 1913
Painted in enamels on a commercial blank; painted by Duncan Grant; marks: 'Ω' in a square, painted; d.25.4cm
Circ.256-1964. Source: given by Mrs Beatrice Mayor
See Crafts Council (1984), p.65, C10.

737 Vase, *c.* 1914 (pl.4)
Earthenware, tin glaze, painted in blue and ochre; thrown by Roger Fry, painted by Vanessa Bell; marks: traces of 'Ω' in a square, painted in ochre; h.19.8cm, d.11.2cm

734

735

736

738

742 / 741 / 739 / 740

747 / 743 / 746

Circ.257-1964. Source: given by Miss H. Sollas
See Crafts Council (1984), p.65, C11.

738 Tea set, *c.* 1914–15
Earthenware, tin glaze; marks: 'Ω' in a square, incised; h.14.2cm, d.25.1cm (teapot); h.9.5cm, d.15.1cm (jug); h.6.3cm, d.9.5cm (sugar bowl); h.7cm, d.11cm (each of four cups); d.14.2cm (each of four saucers)
Misc.2:55 & B to G-1934. Source: given by Margaret Armitage (née Bulley)
By the time Margaret Bulley's collection of modern decorative art was given to the V&A, the various items of Omega tableware (**738** to **742**) had been conflated into a single group. However, records show that the tea set and one jam pot had been acquired by Bulley earlier, while the coffee pot, three plates and another jam pot had been in Roger Fry's possession until 1929. The pieces were made at the factory of Carter & Co., Poole, probably by Fry himself, with assistance. While Fry intended that his thrown pottery shapes be reproduced using moulds, there is no indication that moulds have been used in the manufacture of these pieces. Bulley illustrated the teapot in her 1933 book *Have You Good Taste?*, admiring its aesthetics, but noting that it would be a better teapot if it poured without dripping.

739 Jam pot, *c.* 1914–18
Earthenware, tin glaze; marks: 'Ω' in a square, incised; h.10.5cm, d.11.2cm
Misc.2:55A-1934. Source: *see* **738**

740 Coffee pot, 1918
Earthenware, tin glaze; marks: 'Ω' in a square, incised; h.18.5cm, d.18cm
Misc.2:55H-1934. Source: *see* **738**
A letter from Fry to Vanessa Bell of 18 September 1918 (Tate Archive, London) notes the coffee pot as a new shape. Its form is similar to that of jam pot **741**.

741 Jam pot, *c.* 1918
Earthenware, tin glaze; h.13.7cm, d.10.2cm
Misc.2:55I-1934. Source: *see* **738**

742 Three plates, *c.* 1914–15
Earthenware, tin glaze; marks: 'Ω' in a square, incised; h.4.3cm, d.28.9cm (each)
Misc.2:55/J,K,L-1934. Source: *see* **738**

743 Bowl, *c.* 1914
Earthenware, tin glaze, painted in lustre; made and decorated by Roger Fry; h.5.9cm, d.18cm
Misc.2:56-1934. Source: *see* **738**

744 Tureen and cover, *c.* 1914–15 (fig.4)
Earthenware, tin glaze; made by Roger Fry at the factory of Carter & Co., Poole; marks: 'Ω' in a square, incised; h.29.1cm, d.20.6mm
Circ.246&A-1958. Source: given by Pamela Diamand (daughter of Roger Fry)
Items **744** to **747** probably came from the home of Fry's sister Margery Fry, following her death.

745 Plate, *c.* 1914–15 (fig.4)
Earthenware, tin glaze; made by Roger Fry at the factory of Carter & Co., Poole; marks: 'Ω' in a square, incised; h.3.9cm, d.28.7cm
Circ.250-1958. Source: *see* **744**

746 Bowl, *c.* 1914–15
Earthenware, tin glaze with turquoise interior; made by Roger Fry at the factory of Carter & Co., Poole; marks: 'Ω' in a square, incised; h.7.5cm, d.14.8cm
Circ.248-1958. Source: *see* **744**

747 Bowl, *c.* 1916
Earthenware, brown-black glaze; probably made by Roger Fry at the factory of Carter

& Co., Poole; marks: 'Ω' in a square, incised; h.5.6cm, d.16.7cm
Circ.249-1958. Source: *see* 744

748 Sauce boat, *c.* 1914–15 (fig.4)
Earthenware, tin glaze; made by Roger Fry at the factory of Carter & Co., Poole; marks: 'Ω' in a square, incised; h.8.1cm, d.22.7cm
Circ.173-1964. Source: Angelica Garnett, £15
Following an approach from the V&A exploring the possibility of buying the sauce boat, Garnett – the daughter of Vanessa Bell and Duncan Grant – wrote, 'I feel reluctant to let it go as I love it – but for this very reason it would probably be better for you to have it as the risk of breakage would be so much less.' The sauce boat was illustrated and discussed by Quentin Bell (qv) in *The Listener* (30 January 1964).

Owen, Elspeth 1938–

1938	born Stony Stratford, Buckinghamshire
1957–60	studies modern history at Oxford University
1973	takes pottery evening classes at Cambridge School of Art under Zoë Ellison, while training as a psychotherapist, though largely self-taught as a potter
1975–76	works in Papua New Guinea
1976–	sets up workshop in Grantchester, Cambridge
1980–96	tutor in art and women's studies for Open University
1983–87	periods spent working in Devon, North Uist, Cornwall and South Wales
1986	solo exhibition, Crafts Council Shop at the V&A
1994	residency at Banff Centre for the Arts, Alberta, Canada; solo exhibition, Nancy Margolis Gallery, New York
1995–2012	regular solo exhibitions, Hart Gallery, London
1998	solo exhibition, Primavera, Cambridge
2000	solo exhibition, Helen Drutt, Philadelphia, USA
2012|14	solo exhibitions, Oxford Ceramics Gallery, Oxford

Elspeth Owen is a remarkable potter and experimental artist whose work encompasses a variety of media, including found objects, video and performance. Her practice is informed by feminist art and politics. Her fine handbuilt pots have a concentrated energy, with subtly textured surfaces and a softness of form and profile that reflects her intuitive handling of her material. Even her largest pots are formed by pinching, often with colour first added to the clay, before being burnished and fired.

Elspeth Owen, 'A Sense of Balance', *Crafts*, 42 (1980)
— 'Rural Ride', *Crafts*, 81 (1986)
— 'On Being a Potter', *CR*, 114 (1988)
— 'Clay and Words', *Studio Potter*, 35:2 (2007)
Tanya Harrod, *Elspeth Owen*, Aberystwyth Arts Centre: Ceramic Series 30 (1988)
Perryman (1995), pp.29–30
Primavera, *Coming Round Again*, exh. cat., texts by Tanya Harrod, Edmund de Waal and Gillian Beer (Cambridge, 1998)
Waller (1998), pp.58–9
Hannah Wingrave, 'Millennium Potter?', *Studio Pottery*, 38 (1999)
Ruthin Craft Centre (2002), pp.42–7, 79
Perryman (2004), pp.34–8
Oxford Ceramics Gallery, *Elspeth Owen*, exh. cat., text by Sebastian Blackie (Oxford, 2012)
Jeremy Theophilus, 'Pride of Place', *CR*, 263 (2013)
Oxford Ceramics Gallery, *Elspeth Owen*, exh. pamphlet, text by David Whiting (Oxford, 2014)
June Raby, 'Elspeth Owen', *Studio Potter*, 45:1 (2017)

Exhibition reviews: Amanda Fielding, *Crafts*, 84 (1987), and *CR*, 169 (1998); Edmund de Waal, *Crafts*, 136 (1995); Jaine Jackson, *CR*, 155 (1995); David Whiting, *Crafts*, 150 (1998), and 192 (2005); Ben Eldridge, *CR*, 209 (2004); Claudia Clare, *CR*, 223 (2007); Ian Wilson, *CR*, 268 (2014)

An interview with Elspeth Owen is in the Crafts Lives sound archive at the British Library, London (C960/134).

749 Pot, 1983
Earthenware, pinched, burnished and smoked; h.15.7cm, d.16cm
C.213-1983. Source: Henry Rothschild Associates, Cambridge (group exhibition, Kettle's Yard, no.284), £38

750 *Menopause Pot*, 1987 (pl.86)
Earthenware stained with vanadium oxide, pinched, fired with seaweed, with 13 slip-coated fired tampons; made in Zennor; h.29.5cm, d.29.8cm
C.340:1,2-2018. Source: the artist, £600; acquired through the generosity of Gerard and Sarah Griffin
The pot is one of four made by the artist in response to the onset of the menopause, created as containers for her last bloodied tampons, which were repeatedly dipped in slip and fired as a form of memorial. They are among the largest pinch pots she has made.

749

Oyekan, Lawson 1961–

1961	born Lambeth, London; grows up in Ibadan, Nigeria
1979–83	studies applied chemistry and, later, art at The Polytechnic, Ibadan
1985–88	studies ceramics at Central School of Art and Design, London
1988–90	studies ceramics at Royal College of Art, London
1993–2001	studio in Islington, London
1994–	numerous international solo and group exhibitions
1995	solo exhibition, The City Gallery, Leicester
1997–2003	solo exhibitions, Garth Clark Gallery, New York
1998|2011	solo exhibitions, One Canada Square, Canary Wharf, London
1999–2007	works from Tommerup Keramiske Værksted (Tommerup Ceramic Workshop), Denmark
2001	Grand Prix Award, World Ceramic Biennale, Korea
2005	solo exhibition, Maryland Institute College of Art, USA
c. 2010–	establishes workshop in Vosges, France

Lawson Oyekan is among the most original artists to have emerged in the 1990s and 2000s. His daring handling of clay serves metaphorical ends, expressing vulnerability and resilience. Perilously thin-walled thrown porcelain vessels were

followed by larger earthenware forms, handbuilt from clay 'patties', these sculptures sometimes bearing roughly incised text in English or Yoruba. Earthy and suggestive of natural formations, these upright forms also have a strong human presence. Pierced walls are characteristic, the admission of light offering a metaphor for healing. Oyekan's compelling art reflects his cultural experience. An international artist, he has sought opportunities to make work on residencies and in studios around the world.

Potters (1992)
Museum of Modern Art, Oxford (1993), pp.62–3, 90, 95
Pamela Johnson, 'Dimensions of Light', *Crafts*, 126 (1994)
Alison Britton, 'The Human Presence in Clay', *CR*, 156 (1995)
Crafts Council (1995b), pp.48–9
Barry Schwabsky, 'Lawson Oyekan', *American Craft*, 60:4 (2000)
Perryman (2004), pp.120–5
Maryland Institute College of Art, *Lawson Oyekan and the Spirit of Nature*, exh. cat. (Baltimore, 2005)
Clare Twomey, 'The Spirit of Nature', *Ceramics: Art and Perception*, 60 (2005)
Sarah Tanguy, 'Evolutionary Imagination: A Conversation with Lawson Oyekan', *Sculpture*, 25:6 (2006)
Carlano (2010), pp.116–17
Clark, Strauss and others (2012), pp.397–8, 452
Adamson, Droth and Olding (2017), pp.382–5, 423–4

Exhibition reviews: David Jones, *CR*, 153 (1995); Helen Talbot, *Studio Pottery*, 15 (1995); David Whiting, *Crafts*, 135 (1995); Nicki Jarvis, *Studio Pottery*, 24 (1996); Ken Johnson, *New York Times* (2 May 2003); Janet Koplos, *Art in America*, 91:11 (2003)

751 Sculpture: member of the *Coming Up For Air* series, 2001 (the series made 1999–2002) (pl.110)
Red earthenware mixed with cotton fibre, handbuilt, incised; made at Tommerup Keramiske Værksted ApS, Denmark; h.195cm, d.38cm
C.22-2005. Source: Barrett Marsden Gallery, London, £11,875

Park, Heather 1943–

1943	born Fulmer, Buckinghamshire
1962–65	studies painting at St Albans School of Art
1965–66	studies for teaching certificate, Goldsmiths' College, London
1967–69	studies stained glass and mural enamelling, Central School of Art and Design, London
1990–95	various part-time courses in ceramics at local colleges of further education in London
1997–2014	studio at Cockpit Arts, Holborn, London
2002	group exhibition, *Sleepers*, Royal Cornwall Museum, Truro, selected by Richard Slee (qv)
2007	solo exhibition, Gallery Terra Delft, Netherlands

Heather Park is known for her extraordinary, highly detailed handbuilt sculptural objects, reminiscent of coral and plant forms. Trained originally in painting, Park turned to ceramics after decades experiencing agoraphobia and living as a recluse. Her work gained recognition after attracting the attention of Richard Slee (qv), who selected it for a number of curated exhibitions in the 2000s. It has since been exhibited internationally by Joanna Bird Pottery and Gallery Terra Delft.

Emma Maiden, 'Late Blooming', *Crafts*, 189 (2004)
Ian Wilson, 'Heather Park', *Keramik Magazin* (March 2008)
Jerwood Visual Arts, *Jerwood Contemporary Makers*, exh. cat. (London, 2010)
Brandpunt Terra 2011 (Delft, 2011), pp.122–3

Exhibition reviews: Alun Graves, 'Slee Selects', *CR*, 197 (2002); David Whiting, 'Breakers', *Crafts*, 202 (2006)

752

752 *First Shoots*, 2004
Earthenware, handbuilt, oxides, underglaze colours, glazes and lustre; h.51cm, d.48cm
C.96-2007. Source: given by Heather Park and Joanna Bird Pottery

---

Parkinson, Susan (née Sanderson) 1925–2012 and Richard 1927–1985

Susan

1925	born Calcutta, India
1943–44	studies at Guildford School of Art
1945–49	studies sculpture at Royal College of Art, London, under Frank Dobson and John Skeaping
1949	marries Richard Parkinson
1952–63	with Richard, establishes pottery at Brabourne Lees, Kent
1963–85	teaches at Brickwall House, Northiam, East Sussex, a specialist dyslexia school
1992–	co-founds Arts Dyslexia Trust

Richard

1927	born London
c. 1948–50	studies pottery at Guildford School of Art, under Helen Pincombe (qv)
1949	marries Susan Sanderson
1950	works during summer with Harry and May Davis (qv) at Crowan Pottery, Cornwall
c. 1950–51	studies at Woolwich Polytechnic, under Heber Mathews (qv)
1952–63	with Susan, establishes pottery at Brabourne Lees, Kent
c. 1960–71	teaches ceramics at Hornsey College of Art
1966–68	pottery in Cambridgeshire, decorating industrial whitewares, mostly mugs, for National Trust charity and similar customers; designs by his third wife, Dorn Parkinson
1968–71	moves pottery to London
1971–82	moves to Wales; establishes pottery at Boncath, Pembrokeshire, casting and decorating mugs and lidded boxes

Susan and Richard Parkinson are best known for the quirky, stylized, slip-cast porcelain figures and dishes they produced together during the 1950s, operating as Richard Parkinson Ltd. Susan was the designer and principal decorator, Richard the technical manager. He developed a high-temperature porcelain for slip-casting and designed a kiln in which to fire it. He also made tableware using semi-industrial jiggering and jolleying

techniques, in which forms on or in a rotating mould are shaped using a profile tool. After they separated in the early 1960s and the pottery was dismantled, Susan became involved with teaching art to students with dyslexia and campaigned for recognition of their creative potential.

Richard Parkinson, 'Porcelain', *CR*, 3 (1970)
Arts and Crafts Exhibition Society (1954), (1957)
Exh. review, *Pottery Quarterly*, 4:13 (1957)
Margot Coatts, 'Sources of Inspiration: Susan Parkinson', *Crafts*, 172 (2001)
Carol Cashmore and Tim Smith-Vincent, *Susan Parkinson and the Richard Parkinson Pottery* (Burnham-on-Crouch/Radway, 2004)

753

754

Obituaries (Susan Parkinson): *The Times* (21 November 2012); *Daily Telegraph* (24 December 2012)

753 *Cock and Hen*, 1954
Porcelain, slip-cast, unglazed, incised decoration through brown pigment; h.30.1cm, d.16.2cm
Circ.266 & 267-1954. Source: Primavera, London, £3.15s.

754 *Golfer*, c. 1955–60
Porcelain, slip-cast, painted in black; marks: 'RICHARD / PARKINSON' enclosing 'PORCELAIN / MADE / ENGLAND', and seal, impressed; h.38.3cm, d.15.2cm
C.6-1998. Source: gift of Paul Atterbury, in memory of his mother, Audrey Atterbury

The V&A Theatre and Performance collection holds a set of theatrical figures produced by the Parkinsons for Briglin Pottery, London, not catalogued here (S.1009-1996).

Parnell, Gwendolen 1874–1957

1874	born Gibraltar; family later moves to London
1898–99	studies at Royal College of Art, London, then studies portraiture at Arthur Cope's art school, London, and in Munich, Germany
1901–	resident in Chelsea, London
1914–	works as an illustrator; retrains as a potter at Camberwell School of Arts and Crafts, under Richard Lunn
1916	first exhibited figure, *Henry VIII*, at Amateur Art Exhibition, London, bought by Queen Mary
1917	works at Glebe Place, Chelsea
1918–	establishes studio in Upper Cheyne Row, Chelsea; exhibits widely and holds annual exhibitions at studio (from 1919)
1921–	moves to larger studio in Paradise Walk, Chelsea
1925–26	President of Guild of Potters
1927	solo exhibition, Leicester Galleries, London
1936–41	employed by Royal Worcester Porcelain to model figures for mass production; moves studio to Trotshill Farm, near Worcester

Gwendolen Parnell was the first of the independent makers of pottery figures to become active in Chelsea, London, training and establishing her workshop during the First World War. She is known particularly for her imaginative modelling of shepherdesses, clowns, harlequins and theatrical figures. Parnell led a small studio supported by assistants, including for a time Madeline Raper (qv). Dora Lunn (qv), another pioneering studio potter, was a close acquaintance.

Decorative Art (1919)
A Catalogue of Further Pieces of the Chelsea Cheyne Figures from the original Designs of Gwendolen Parnell, exh. cat., text by Reginald Blunt (London, 1921)
British Institute of Industrial Art (1923), (1927), (1929)
Blunt (1924), pp.85–7, pls.36–7
Guild of Potters (1924), (1925), (1926)
Illustrated Souvenir of the Palace of Arts Wembley, British Empire Exhibition (London, 1924), p.148
Clara T. MacChesney, 'A Famous New Chelsea Potter', *Arts & Decoration*, 22 (January 1925)
Colnaghi (1927), (1928), (1929), (1932)
Forsyth (1927), p.134
Leicester Galleries, *Chelsea Cheyne figures by Gwendolen Parnell*, exh. cat. (London, 1927)
Beatrice Caroline Erskine, 'Gwendolen Parnell and her Chelsea Cheyne figures', *Apollo*, 9 (February 1929)
J.L.N., 'Gwendolen Parnell's China Figures', *Walker's Monthly* (July 1932)
Walker's Galleries, *An Exhibition of China Figures by Gwendolen Parnell*, exh. leaflet (London, 1932)
Obituary, *The Times* (4 December 1957)
Geoffrey Godden, 'Some Female Ceramic Artists and Modellers', *Apollo*, 73 (February 1961)
Hawkins Opie (1985), p.345
Vincentelli (2000), pp.227–8
Knott (2021)

Exhibition reviews: *The Times* (17 December 1920), (4 June 1924), (11 July 1925), (18 June 1927), (23 June 1928); *Illustrated London News* (11 June 1921), (21 January 1933); *The Sphere* (24 September 1921), (22 October 1924); *The Queen* (21 January 1922), (23 December 1922); *The Sketch* (26 April 1922), (27 December 1922); S.B.W., 'The Guild of Potters', *The Studio*, 91 (1926), p.35; *Apollo*, 12 (August 1930), pp.166–7

Two albums of press cuttings, photographs and illustrations concerning Gwendolen Parnell and her Chelsea Pottery, covering the period 1918–33, are in the National Art Library, V&A, London (96.N.81 and 96.N.82).

755 / 756

755 Figure of a shepherdess with infant satyr, *c.* 1918
Earthenware, painted in colours; marks: a rabbit enclosed by 'G P / CHEYNE', and '5' in a circle, incised; h.16.4cm, d.13.4cm
C.190-1918. Source: given by A.R.B. Parnell, Esq.

756 Basket of flowers, 1924
Semi-porcelain, glazed and painted; marks: 'Chelsea Cheyne / 1924', painted; h.3.4cm, d.4.7cm
C.436-1934. Source: British Institute of Industrial Art (given by H.M. The Queen)

Parr, Harry 1882–1966

1882	born Wolstanton, Staffordshire
1900s	studies at Burslem School of Art
c. 1911	teaches part-time at Woolwich Polytechnic
c. 1914–54	studio at 14A Cheyne Row, Chelsea, London
1918–	begins modelling pottery; exhibits regularly at Royal Academy of Arts Summer Exhibition and elsewhere
1930–40	teaches modelling at Camberwell School of Arts and Crafts
c. 1955–	recorded at Milman's Street, Chelsea

A sculptor, potter and medallist, Harry Parr was one of a number of independent makers of pottery figures active in Chelsea, London, after the First World War.

Arts and Crafts Exhibition Society (1923), (1926)
Royal Academy of Arts (1923)
Blunt (1924), p.88, pl.24
Florence Davies, 'British Handcraft in Detroit', *American Magazine of Art*, 15:2 (1924), p.75
British Institute of Industrial Art (1927), (1929)
M.C. Salaman, 'Harry Parr's Pottery Figures', *Creative Art*, 5 (November 1929)
Reginald Haggar, *A Century of Art Education in the Potteries* (Stoke-on-Trent, 1953), pp.32, 46
Royal Academy Exhibitors 1905–1970: Vol. 5 LAWR–SHER (Wakefield, 1981), pp.276–7
'Harry Parr', *Mapping the Practice and Profession of Sculpture in Britain and Ireland 1851–1951*, University of Glasgow History of Art and HATII, online database (2011)

Exhibition reviews: *Staffordshire Sentinel* (8 November 1927), (16 May 1929)

757 Figure group: *Boy and Turkey*, 1925 (introduced *c.* 1924)
Earthenware, slip-cast, painted in enamel colours, wooden base; marks: 'HY PARR / 1925 / CHELSEA', incised; h.26.5cm, d.15.5cm
C.41-1985. Source: Richard Dennis, London, £300

758 Figure group: *Boy and Toad*, 1927
Earthenware, slip-cast, painted in colours; marks: 'HY PARR / CHELSEA' and '1927', incised; h.14.9cm, d.9cm
C.430-1934. Source: British Institute of Industrial Art (given by H.M. The Queen, 1927)

759 Figure group: *Mother and Child*, 1927
Stoneware, slip-cast, white glaze; mark: 'HY PARR 1927 / CHELSEA', incised; h.30.5cm, d.11cm
C.429-1934. Source: British Institute of Industrial Art (given by Mr George Cross, 1927)

Partington, Claire 1973–

1973	born Wigan, Lancashire
1991–95	studies sculpture at Central Saint Martins, London
1995–2010	works in museums, including V&A
1999–2000	postgraduate museum studies, University of Leicester
2003–	resumes making, concentrating on ceramics
2003–08	takes evening classes in ceramics at Kensington and Chelsea College
2010–	studio at Kingsgate Workshops, London
2017	solo exhibition, James Freeman Gallery, London
2018	*Taking Tea* commission for Seattle Art Museum, USA
2019	solo exhibition, *The Hunting Party*, Winston Wächter, Seattle, USA

Trained as a sculptor, Claire Partington resumed making after a period working in museums. She has since steadily built a reputation for her figurative ceramic sculptures, which explore narrative, identity and status. Her work draws upon European applied art from 1600 onwards.

Garcia (2012), pp.58–60
Hey! Modern Art and Pop Culture Act III Art Show, exh. cat. (Paris, 2015), pp.234–8
James Freeman Gallery, *Claire Partington: A Cautionary Tale*, exh. cat. (London, 2017)
Imogen Greenhalgh, 'Sculptural Theatre', *CR*, 294 (2018)
Matthew Kangas, 'Tea and Postcolonial Retribution', *Ceramics: Art and Perception*, 115 (2020)

760 *Cub*, 2018 (pl.144)
Glazed earthenware, handbuilt, enamel, lustre,

757 / 758 / 759

777

778

David Fraser Jenkins and Hugh Fowler Wright, *The Art of John Piper* (London, 2015), see esp. pp.362–9

777 Dish, 1974
Earthenware, press-moulded, blue-black glaze with overglaze painting in white; marks: 'JP' and 'VI 74', painted; h.68cm, d.48cm
C.64-1976. Source: given by the artist
The dishes were made and decorated by Piper. The original moulds were made with the help of Geoffrey Eastop.

778 Dish, 1974
Earthenware, press-moulded, incised decoration through dark slip; marks: 'JP VIII 74', painted; h.40cm, d.61cm
C.65-1976. Source: *see* 777

Pleydell-Bouverie, Katharine
1895–1985

1895	born Coleshill, Berkshire
c. 1921	becomes interested in handmade pottery after seeing Roger Fry's work for the Omega Workshops (qv)
1921–23	studies pottery at Central School of Arts and Crafts, London, under Dora Billington (qv), first at evening classes, later full-time; taught throwing there by W. Askew, a professional potter
1922	meets Bernard Leach (qv) at his exhibition at Cotswold Gallery, London; requests to join Leach Pottery, St Ives (qv)
1924–25	after short trial period in 1923, joins Leach Pottery as paying pupil; Ada Mason ('Peter') joins her
1925	returns to Coleshill estate with Mason and establishes pottery at Mill Cottage; builds wood-fired kiln to Matsubayashi Tsurunosuke's (qv) design; experiments with wood-ash glazes
1927	Mason leaves for USA
1928–36	Norah Braden (qv) joins Pleydell-Bouverie for part of each year, working in partnership and experimenting with wood-ash glazes
1930|32	joint exhibitions with Braden at Paterson's Gallery, London
1940–46	war disrupts work
1946–	Coleshill estate sold by family; Pleydell-Bouverie moves to Kilmington Manor, Wiltshire; builds oil-fired kiln; Braden is a regular visitor during holidays
1960	installs electric kiln
1980	retrospective exhibition, Crafts Study Centre, Bath

Katharine Pleydell-Bouverie (known as 'Bina' to her family and 'Beano' to her friends) was one of Bernard Leach's (qv) first students at St Ives. She subsequently devoted herself to stoneware with wood-ash glazes, establishing a pottery on her family's estate at Coleshill, where she worked in partnership with Norah Braden. The wooded estate provided fuel for her wood-fired kiln and ash from a large range of trees for countless glaze experiments. Even when circumstances forced her to use an oil-fired kiln, and then an oxidizing electric kiln, she sought stonewares with the same qualities as those of her earlier work – soft natural colours on gentle forms. Writing to Bernard Leach in 1928, she stated: 'I want my pots to make people think, not of the Chinese, but of things like pebbles and shells and birds' eggs and stones over which moss grows. Flowers stand out of them more pleasantly, so it seems to me.' While their pots are similar, Pleydell-Bouverie was less inclined towards decoration than Braden, instead emphasizing the subtle beauty of their glazes. Often they are marked with numerals that refer to particular glaze and body recipes. Pleydell-Bouverie kept meticulous records and her glaze notebooks are preserved with other papers at the Crafts Study Centre, Farnham (KPB, KPG). She was always modest, and critical of her achievements. Not having to earn a living from her work, she charged low prices right to the end of her life.

Katharine Pleydell-Bouverie, 'The Preparation of Ash for Stoneware Glazes', *Pottery Quarterly*, 6:22 (1959)
— 'At St Ives in the Early Years', in Barrow (1960)
— 'Wood and Vegetable Ashes in Stoneware Glazes', *CR*, 5 and 6 (1970)
— statement, in Rothschild (1972)
— 'A Visit to Katharine Pleydell-Bouverie', interview, *CR*, 30 (1974)
— 'Early Days at St Ives', *CR*, 50 (1978)
— 'Ash Glazes', *CR*, 51 (1978)
British Institute of Industrial Art (1923), nos.94FF and 135SS, (1933), pp.80–1
Arts and Crafts Exhibition Society (1928), (1931), (1938)
Colnaghi (1928), (1929)
Decorative Art (1929), (1930)
Paterson's Gallery, *Stoneware by D.K.N. Braden and K. Pleydell-Bouverie*, exh. cat. (London, 1930)
W.A. Thorpe, 'English Stoneware Pottery by Miss K. Pleydell-Bouverie and Miss D.K.N. Braden', *Artwork*, 6:24 (1930)
Paterson's Gallery, *Stoneware by K. Pleydell-Bouverie and D.K.N. Braden*, exh. cat. (London, 1932)
Zwemmer (1933)
V&A (1936), pls.40, 42, 45, 49
Brygos Gallery (1937b)
British Council (1942)
Ernest Marsh, 'Studio Potters of Coleshill, Wilts', *Apollo*, 38 (December 1943)
Cooper (1947), p.*iv*, pls.41–2
Dartington Hall (1952)
Wingfield Digby (1952), pp.37, 78–9, pls.46–8
Rose (1955), pp.19–20, pls.56–7, (1970), pp.36–7, pls.54–5
Lewis (1956), pl.338
Casson (1967), p.8, pls.161–2
Potters (1972) to (1983)
Fiona Adamczewski, 'Katharine Pleydell-Bouverie', *Crafts*, 19 (1976)
Crafts Advisory Committee (1976), p.111
Leach (1978), pp.149–53
Crafts Council (1980), p.62
Crafts Study Centre, *Katharine Pleydell-Bouverie*, exh. cat., texts by Barley Roscoe, Michael Cardew, Henry Hammond and Katharine Pleydell-Bouverie (Bath, 1980)

Isabelle Anscombe, *A Woman's Touch* (London, 1984), pp.161–5
Paisley Museum and Art Galleries (1984), pp.66–7
David Leach, 'Katharine Pleydell-Bouverie', *CR*, 92 (1985)
Barley Roscoe and Michael Casson, 'Beano', *Crafts*, 75 (1985)
Obituary, *The Times* (17 January 1985)
Crafts Council, *Katharine Pleydell-Bouverie: A Potter's Life 1895–1985* (London, 1986) – includes transcripts of Pleydell-Bouverie's letters to Bernard Leach and of her edited glaze notebooks
Vincentelli and Hale (1986)
Cardew (1988), see esp. pp.34, 76–7, 155
Birks and Wingfield Digby (1990), pp.139–51
Riddick (1990), pp.103–5
Rogers (1991), pp.84–91
Barley Roscoe, 'Katharine Pleydell-Bouverie', *Studio Pottery*, 1 (1993)
Gaze (1997)
Vincentelli (2000), pp.143–7
Cooper (2003), p.153
Emmanuel Cooper, biography, in *Oxford Dictionary of National Biography* (Oxford, 2004)
J.V.G. Mallet, 'The "Gentleman Potters" Part 2: Michael Cardew and Katharine Pleydell-Bouverie', *English Ceramic Circle Transactions*, 18:3 (2004)
Harrod (2012), see esp. pp.59–61 – includes revised version of Pleydell-Bouverie's first meeting with Leach
Nottingham City Museums and Galleries (2017), pp.71–2
Richard Batterham, 'Katharine Pleydell-Bouverie', in Edgeler (2019), pp.38–41
Coll Minogue, 'Katharine Pleydell-Bouverie', *The Log Book*, 81 (2020)

Exhibition reviews: *The Times*, 'Stoneware Pottery' (22 May 1930), 'Stoneware Pottery' (23 May 1932), 'Pots for Bulbs' (30 September 1933), 'Christmas Art Shows' (16 December 1936), 'Narrative Pictures' (14 December 1937); *Journal of the Royal Society of Arts* (23 May 1930); *Pottery Quarterly*, 3:11 (1956); Murray Fieldhouse, *Pottery Quarterly*, 5:20 (1958); David Leach, *CR*, 28 (1974)

779 Dish, late 1920s
Stoneware, incised decoration, brownish ash glaze; marks: 'KPB' and 'COLE' in rectangular seals, impressed; h.5.5cm, d.16.5cm
C.72-1981. Source: Richard Dennis, London, £60

780 Bottle, *c.* 1929
Stoneware, grey ash glaze; marks: '40', incised, and '12, [?]', painted; h.19.6cm, d.10.5cm
C.962-1935. Source: given by the Pottery and Crafts Fund of the Contemporary Art Society (purchased in 1930, probably from Colnaghi, London, £2.2s.)
The *Contemporary Art Society Report 1930–1931* records the purchase of a ribbed vase by Norah Braden, but its attribution had been amended to Pleydell-Bouverie in the list of distributions in the 1934–35 *Report*. The bottle vase bears no seal, but its detailing suggests the latter

779

780

785

782

784 / 783

786

787

789

788

790 / 791

attribution is correct. It is perhaps the 'Bottle, grey, fluted' listed as no.H16 in Colnaghi (1929), where Braden and Pleydell-Bouverie's work is undifferentiated.

781 Bottle: *Roc's Egg*, 1929–30 (pl.20)
Stoneware, grey-green ash glaze; marks: 'KPB' in monogram, impressed; h.25.4cm, d.17.2cm
Circ.236-1930. Source: the artist, £5.5s. (following joint exhibition with Norah Braden, Paterson's Gallery, London, 1930, no.12)

782 Covered pot, 1930
Stoneware, cut sides, mottled cream-brown hawthorn-ash glaze; marks: 'KPB' in monogram, impressed, and 'XLIV', painted; h.16.7cm, d.14.6cm
Circ.237&A-1930. Source: the artist, £5.5s. (following joint exhibition with Norah Braden, Paterson's Gallery, London, 1930, no.2)

783 'Red octagonal stoneware jar', 1930–31
Stoneware, crystalline red-brown ash glaze; marks: 'KPB' in monogram, impressed, and '7-36.', painted; h.20.2cm, d.19.4cm
Circ.763-1931. Source: the artist (shown at the Fifteenth Exhibition of the Arts and Crafts Exhibition Society, Royal Academy, London, 1931, no.364c), £3.3s.
Illustrated in Rose (1955), pl.57.

784 Bottle, 1932
Stoneware, wood-ash tenmoku glaze; marks: 'KPB' in monogram, impressed, and '37', painted; h.34.3cm, d.19.2cm
C.324-1983. Source: given by the artist
Considering it a 'decent' example of her work, Pleydell-Bouverie gave this bottle in place of **789**, which she wanted destroyed or hidden. See Mallet (2004).

785 Bottle, 1931–32
Stoneware, whitish ash glaze, painted in brown; marks: 'KPB' in monogram, impressed, '103', incised, and 'LXXXV.2.A', painted; h.16.7cm, d.12.9cm
Circ.252-1932. Source: Paterson's Gallery, London (exhibition with Norah Braden, 1932, no.4), £2.2s.

786 Bottle, 1932
Stoneware, brown ash glaze, painted darker bands; marks: 'KPB' in monogram, impressed; h.17.3cm, d.14.8cm
C.414-1934. Source: British Institute of Industrial Art (purchased through the Spielmann Memorial Fund, 1932)

787 Bulb bowl, *c.* 1933–34
Stoneware, unglazed, incised decoration and ash flashings; marks: 'KPB' in monogram, impressed, and '134[?]', incised; h.6.4cm, d.14.5cm
C.73-1981. Source: Richard Dennis, London, £45

788 Bowl, *c.* 1935
Stoneware, grey ash glaze, painted brown bands; marks: 'KPB' in monogram, impressed, '120', incised, and '13' and '21', painted; h.7.8cm, d.10cm
C.115-1977. Source: Richard Dennis, London (from the collection of Sir Edward Maufe), £25

789 Pot, *c.* 1935
Stoneware, mottled oatmeal glaze with wax-resist decoration; marks: 'KPB' in monogram, impressed, and '187', incised; h.22cm, d.16.5cm
C.71-1981. Source: Richard Dennis, London, £150
Made for a friend who was a morris dancer, the pot carries decoration of interlocking swords. Following its purchase, Pleydell-Bouverie professed herself 'a bit horrified that you had acquired that awful folk-dance pot for the museum', offering instead **784**.

790 Dish, 1956
Stoneware, dark ash glaze, slip-trailed in white; marks: 'KPB' in monogram, impressed, and '199'[?], incised; h.7.3cm, d.33.8cm
Circ.649-1956. Source: Primavera, London (solo exhibition, 1956, no.15), £3.10s.

791 Dish, *c.* 1975
Stoneware, dark ash glaze with milky streaks; marks: 'KPB' in monogram, impressed, and '27' and further illegible code, painted; h.5.5cm, d.26.5cm
C.19-1981. Source: Paul Rice Gallery, London, £60

Poncelet, Jacqueline (Jacqui) 1947–

1947	born Liège, Belgium; grows up in West Midlands, UK
1965–69	studies ceramics at Wolverhampton College of Art
1969–72	studies ceramics at Royal College of Art, London
1972–77	studio in King's Cross, London, shared successively with Glenys Barton (qv), Tony Bennett and Alison Britton (qv); teaches part-time at Portsmouth Polytechnic
1977–2000	married to the sculptor Richard Deacon (qv)
1977–82	studio in Brixton, London; teaches part-time at West Surrey College of Art and Design, Farnham
1978–79	spends year in USA on British Council Bicentennial Arts Fellowship
1981	solo exhibition, *Jacqui Poncelet – New Ceramics*, Crafts Council, London, and tour
1982–86	collaborative project with Bing & Grøndahl, Denmark
1982–2001	studio in East Dulwich, London
1982–2006	teaches part-time at Camberwell College of Arts
1985	solo exhibition, Whitechapel Art Gallery, London
1986–	discontinues work in clay
2001–	studio in West Norwood, London
2010–	additional studio in Ogmore Vale, Bridgend; returns occasionally to clay

Jacqueline Poncelet – alongside Elizabeth Fritsch (qv), Alison Britton (qv), Carol McNicoll (qv) and Glenys Barton (qv) – was part of the progressive group of women artists who emerged from the Royal College of Art in the early 1970s, and whose work underpinned the 'New Ceramics' movement. In the years during which she worked actively in clay, Poncelet did more than perhaps any other artist to advance the sculptural language of ceramics. During this period the nature of her work changed dramatically. In 1976 she abandoned the fine cast bone-china vessels that had brought early success for larger slab-built earthenware forms, geometrical in shape and decoration. Her subsequent work became more organic in form, and more colourful and patterned. In the mid-1980s she abandoned references to the vessel and began placing sculptures – sometimes multi-part – on the gallery floor. Shortly after she discontinued ceramics and developed a multi-disciplinary art practice. Of this shift, she has written:

In the late eighties I somewhat eased out of the craft world, and although it seems to be documented that I had an abrupt re-think, it wasn't as simple as that. For me, the making of things has had continuity and that process has, in a way, had a life of its own; one thing has led to another. I found that I needed to progress from the form of the vessel, and I also wanted to work with materials other than clay. The change was gradual, with the inclusion of bronze, fabric, print, paint and canvas, found materials etc, and eventually I began to collaborate with architects and town planners through commissions.
(Email to the author, 12 November 2012)

Jacqueline Poncelet, statement and biography, in V&A (1977), pp.7–9
— 'Made for Whom? Made for What? Made for Where?', in Crafts Council (2001), pp.6–9
V&A (1972), p.116
Fiona Adamczewski, 'Outside Tradition', *Crafts*, 2 (1973)
Crafts Advisory Committee (1974), pp.13–16
Ulster Museum (1974)
Decorative Art (1974/75), (1975/76), (1977), (1978), (1980)
Lucie-Smith (1975), pp.76–84
Crafts Advisory Committee (1976), p.111
Portsmouth City Museum and Art Gallery (1976), pp.9–10
Crafts Council (1980), p.62
— *Jacqui Poncelet: New Ceramics*, exh. cat., text by Richard Deacon (London, 1981)
Rosemary Pitts, 'American Graffiti', interview, *Crafts*, 50 (1981)
Paisley Museum and Art Galleries (1984), p.67
David Briers, *Jacqui Poncelet*, Aberystwyth Arts Centre: Ceramic Series 5 (1985)
Crafts Council (1985), pp.71–4
Paul Filmer, 'Jacqui Poncelet', in ICA (1985), pp.28–32
Whitechapel Art Gallery, *Jacqueline Poncelet: Recent Work*, exh. cat. (London, 1985)
Martina Margetts, 'Bridging the Divide', *Crafts*, 80 (1986)
Griselda Gilroy, 'The Critic's Eye', *Crafts*, 115 (1992)
Museum of Modern Art, Oxford (1993), pp.68–9, 90–1, 95
London Institute (1998), pp.14–15, 25
Penelope Curtis, *Attending to the Barely Made*, interview with Jacqui Poncelet, Henry Moore Institute Essays on Sculpture 29 (Leeds, 2000)
Anatol Orient, 'The Pleasure of Stuff', *CR*, 185 (2000)
Jonathan Bell, 'Pattern Crazy', interview, *Crafts*, 177 (2002)
Crafts Council (2003), pp.17–20
Carlano (2010), pp.122–3
Clark, Strauss and others (2012), pp.400, 455

792

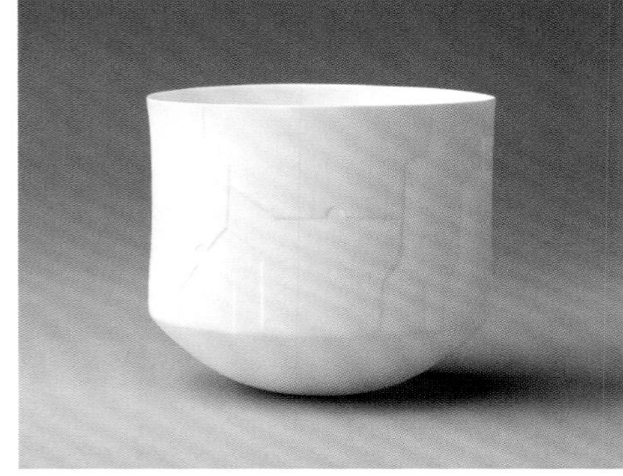
793

794 / 795

797 / 796

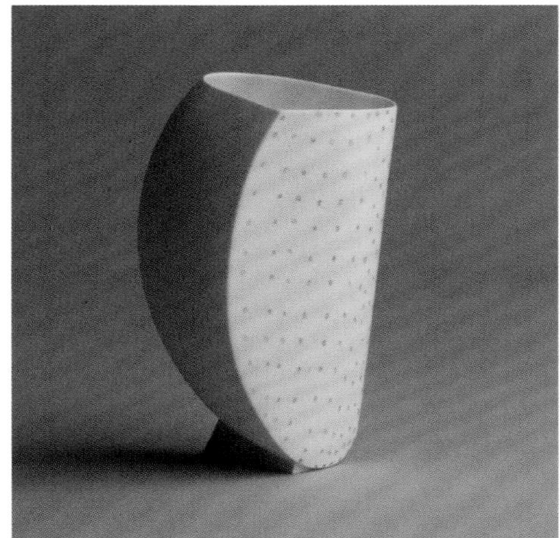

800

Nottingham City Museums and Galleries (2017), p.73
Emma Crichton-Miller, 'Artistic Expression', *CR*, 300 (2019)
New Art Centre, *Jacqueline Poncelet: Now and Then*, exh. e-cat. (Salisbury, 2020)
Interview, in Racz (2020), pp.75–83
Veronica Simpson, 'Jacqueline Poncelet', interview, *Studio International*, ejournal (14 September 2020)

Exhibition reviews: J.D.H. Catleugh, *CR*, 22 (1973), and 35 (1975); Garth Clark, 'Seven in 76', *Crafts*, 19 (1976); Paul Filmer, *Crafts*, 55 (1982); Emmanuel Cooper, *Crafts*, 137 (1995)

An interview with Jacqueline Poncelet is in the Crafts Lives sound archive at the British Library, London (C960/116).

792 Bowl, 1972
Bone china, slip-cast, with body stain spotted into the mould; h.8.7cm, d.13.4cm
Circ.276-1973. Source: the artist (following the exhibition *The Craftsman's Art*, V&A, 1973, no.180), £25

793 Bowl, 1974
Bone china, slip-cast, carved; h.8.7cm, d.9.9cm
Circ.366-1974. Source: the artist, £27

794 *Double circle form*, 1974
Bone china, slip-cast, with grey, green and yellow stains; h.10.2cm, d.11.6cm
Circ.501-1974. Source: the artist, £30

795 Pot, 1974
Bone china, slip-cast, with grey, green, blue-green and yellow stains; h.15.5cm, d.11cm
Circ.500-1974. Source: the artist, £30

796 *Bowl with rim*, 1976
Bone china, slip-cast, marbled blue stain; h.7.6cm, d.13.5cm
Circ.253-1976. Source: the artist, £35

797 *Bowl with rim*, 1976
Bone china, slip-cast, pierced and carved; h.8.1cm, d.14.5cm
Circ.254-1976. Source: the artist, £35

798 *Oval form with a half foot*, 1976 (pl.69)
Bone china, slip-cast in two parts; h.6.6cm, d.10.9cm
Circ.255-1976. Source: the artist, £30

799 *Tilted form*, 1976 (pl.69)
Bone china, slip-cast; h.10.3cm, d.13.4cm
Circ.256-1976. Source: the artist, £25

800 *Pot with foot*, 1976
Bone china, slip-cast, one side glazed and spotted with blue and yellow enamel; h.14.7cm, d.8.6cm
Circ.534-1976. Source: the artist, £30

801 Pot, 1978
Earthenware, slab-built, with inlaid coloured clays; h.29.4cm, d.35.6cm
C.30-1980. Source: Oxford Gallery, Oxford, £115.92

802 *Zig-Zag Pot*, 1979
Stoneware, slab-built, with brown slips and white glaze; made in Claremont, California, USA; h.32.6cm, d.39.3cm
C.54-1982. Source: the artist, £200

803 *Spoon and bowl*, 1980
Red stoneware, handbuilt, with volcanic black and yellow glazes, and orange enamel; h.4.4cm, d.20.5cm (bowl); l.17.1cm, d.9.5cm (spoon)
C.67:1,2-1998. Source: the artist, £500

804 Form, 1980–81
Stoneware, handbuilt, with inlaid coloured clays and low-temperature enamel; h.13cm, d.50cm
C.75-1981. Source: Crafts Council, London (solo exhibition: *New Ceramics*, 1981, no.2), £333

805 Dish, 1980–81
Stoneware, handbuilt, inlaid dark clay, turquoise glaze and overglaze enamels; h.9.4cm, d.35.6cm
C.76-1981. Source: *see* **804** (no.9), £166

801

802

803

804

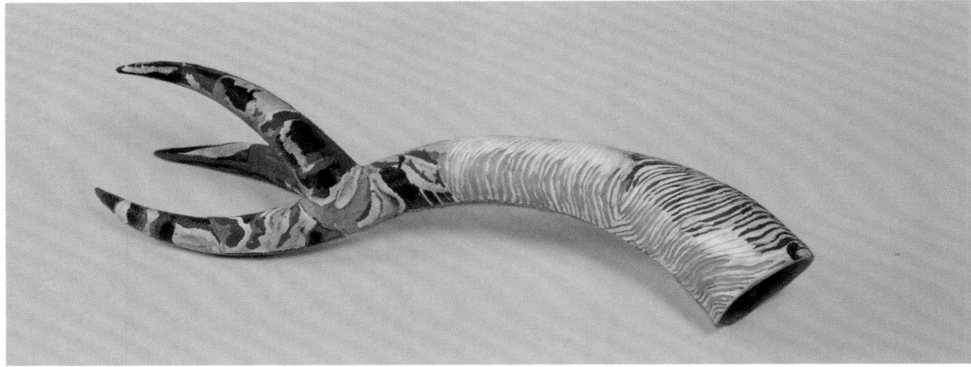

807

805

806

806 *Three legged form*, 1983
Stoneware, handbuilt, with inlaid coloured clays and low-temperature enamel; h.27.6cm, d.33.8cm
C.339-1983. Source: Craft Shop, V&A, £525.60

807 *Horn and Claw*, 1985
Earthenware, handbuilt from press-moulded relief-patterned sections, painted with slips and glazes; h.102.5cm, d.25.5cm
C.66-1998. Source: the artist, £1800
The work may be placed standing and leaning, or lying on the floor.

808 *Sculpture in 3 Parts*, 1986 (pl.84)
Earthenware, handbuilt from press-moulded relief-patterned sections, painted with slips and glazes, printed fabric; l.93.2cm (largest part), overall dimensions variable
C.58:1 to 4-2013. Source: the artist, £10,000; acquired through the generosity of Gerard and Sarah Griffin
Shown in *Aperto 86* at the Venice Biennale, 1986. The printed fabric ground is a later addition to the work.

The museum also holds three works produced in collaboration with Bing & Grøndahl, Denmark, not catalogued here (C.125 & 126-1987, C.68-1998).

Pope, Nicholas 1949–

1949	born Sydney, Australia
1970–73	studies at Bath Academy of Art
1974	British Council exchange scholarship, Institutul de Arte Plastice 'Nicolae Grigorescu', Bucharest, Romania
1980	represents Britain at Venice Biennale
1981–	studio in Much Marcle, Herefordshire
1982	British Council cultural visitor to Zimbabwe and Tanzania; contracts viral encephalitis, undiagnosed for several years
1987–91	temporarily ceases working
1993	solo exhibition, Art & Project, Slootdorp, Netherlands, showing porcelain
1994|95	residencies at European Ceramic Work Centre (EKWC), 's-Hertogenbosch, Netherlands
1996–97	solo exhibition, *The Apostles Speaking in Tongues*, Tate Gallery, London

Known previously for his sculpture in wood, chalk and stone, Nicholas Pope began working in clay and knitted fabric about 1992, following an enforced hiatus in making resulting from serious illness. His use of softer materials that could be worked additively reflected not only his reduced physical capacity but also a desire for a more personal sculptural language, and the possibility of colour. Pope's work addresses themes of ritual, belief, corporeality and community. Many of his ceramic works – including his series of fonts – have been conceived for an imagined non-denominational chapel, *The Oratory of Heavenly Space*.

Nicholas Pope with Kevin Mount, 'Off Balance', in Camila Maroja, Caroline Menezes and Fabrizio Augusto Poltronieri (eds), *The Permanence of the Transient: Precariousness in Art* (Newcastle upon Tyne, 2014), pp.135–47

Art & Project, *Nicholas Pope: Heavenly Space: Eight Works in Porcelain*, exh. cat. (Slootdorp, 1993)

Tate Gallery, *Nicholas Pope: The Apostles Speaking in Tongues*, exh. pamphlet, text by Frances Morris (London, 1996)

Lindsey Hoole, 'Speaking in Tongues', *CR*, 163 (1997)

Geitner and Klein (2002)

Jonathan Vickery, *Nicholas Pope: The Sacred and the Profane*, Henry Moore Institute Essays on Sculpture 43 (Leeds, 2003)

Nicholas Pope, texts by Adriaan van Ravesteijn, Penelope Curtis, Christopher Townsend, Andrew Sabin, and Nicholas Pope in conversation with Stephen Feeke (London, 2013)

Lily Crowther, 'One Man's Way', *CR*, 274 (2015)

Nicholas Pope: Drawings, texts by James Hamilton, and Nicholas Pope in conversation with Jon Wood (London, 2016)

Interview, in Racz (2020), pp.109–17

Exhibition reviews: Maud Milton, *Studio Pottery*, 26 (1997); Alison Britton, *CR*, 204 (2003); David Taylor,

Architects' Journal, 218:10 (2003); Lily Crowther, *CR*, 266 (2014); Isabella Smith, *Crafts*, 289 (2021)

809 *Hermaphroditic Font*, 1995 (fig.14)
Earthenware, handbuilt, coloured glazes; made at the European Ceramic Work Centre, 's-Hertogenbosch, Netherlands; h.125cm, d.115cm
C.1-2020. Source: The Sunday Painter, £22,500; acquired through the generosity of Gerard and Sarah Griffin

Priest, Frances 1976–

1976	born Wakefield, West Yorkshire
1995–99	studies ceramics at Edinburgh College of Art
1999–	establishes first Edinburgh studio
2001–05	teaches part-time at Edinburgh College of Art
2003	first solo exhibition, The Scottish Gallery, Edinburgh
2005–06	travels to Japan, Thailand, Cambodia and Laos
2008	residency, Cove Park, Argyll and Bute
2015	*Patterns of Flora* commission for Raasay House, Isle of Raasay
2018	*The Tiled Corridor* commission for Royal Edinburgh Hospital
2019	solo exhibition, *Influences of the East*, Bowes Museum, County Durham

Frances Priest became known for her slabbed sculptures with surfaces animated by drawing. She has since become increasingly preoccupied with the language of ornamentation, creating intricately decorated objects reflecting specific localities and cultural histories.

Scottish Gallery, *Line and Form*, exh. cat., text by Amanda Game (Edinburgh, 2003)
— *Surface and Shape*, exh. cat., text by Stuart Bennett (Edinburgh, 2005)
Bornholms Kunstmuseum, *European Ceramic Context 2006: Young Ceramists*, exh. cat. (Gudhjem, 2006), pp.104–5
Ellie Herring, 'Conversation Pieces', *Crafts*, 218 (2009)
Scottish Gallery, *Objects of Touch and Travel …*, exh. leaflet, text by Ellie Herring (Edinburgh, 2009)
Sarah Rothwell, 'Capturing Decorative Art – The Work of Frances Priest', *Journal of the Decorative Arts Society*, 45 (2021)

810

Exhibition reviews: Tony Franks, *CR*, 202 (2003); Sarah-Jane Selwood, *CR*, 216 (2005)

810 *Sliding Contour*, 2005
Stoneware, handbuilt, with inlaid glaze; h.27.5cm, d.52.5cm
C.140-2006. Source: The Scottish Gallery at Collect 2006; gift of Nicholas and Judith Goodison through Art Fund
Previously shown in the solo exhibition *Surface and Shape*, The Scottish Gallery, Edinburgh, 2005.

Quick, Kenneth 1931–1963

1931	born St Ives, the nephew of William Marshall (qv)
1945–	joins Leach Pottery, St Ives (qv), as apprentice, making Standard Ware
1955–	establishes Tregenna Hill Pottery, St Ives, with small electric kiln
1959	spends six months in USA, visiting potteries and teaching
1960–	rejoins Leach Pottery
1963	visits pottery of Hamada Shōji (qv) in Mashiko, Japan; dies while swimming
1964	work included in his memory at exhibition of Leach Pottery at Crafts Centre of Great Britain, London

Kenneth Quick was regarded as one of the most promising local apprentices to be trained at the Leach Pottery (qv). He left to set up his own one-man workshop, but was later persuaded to return. Seen as a potential pottery manager, he travelled to Japan on a trip supported by the Pottery, where tragically he drowned.

Dartington Hall (1952)
Illustrations of Tregenna Hill Pottery standard ware, *Pottery Quarterly*, 4:15 (1957), p.128, pls.9–10

811

Rose (1970), p.40, pl.73
Leach (1978), pp.259–60
Tate Gallery (1985), pp.238–9
Cooper (2003), pp.226, 277–8, 284, 309–10
Whybrow (2006), pp.120–1

811 Jar, 1963
Stoneware, incised decoration, green glaze; made at Hamada Shōji's pottery, Mashiko, Japan; h.18.3cm, d.18.3cm
C.81-1981. Source: Christopher Wood Gallery, London, £300
Made shortly before the potter's untimely death. The remains of a paper label on its base read: 'Made by Kenneth … at Mashiko'.

Radstone, Sara 1955–

1955	born London
1975–76	studies at Herefordshire College of Art and Design
1976–79	studies ceramics at Camberwell School of Art and Crafts
1979–84	studio at 401½ Workshops, London
1982–90	teaches at West Surrey College of Art and Design, Farnham
1984–97	teaches at Wimbledon School of Art
1985–95	studio at Arlingford Studios, Brixton, London, shared with Julian Stair (qv)
1988	wins Unilever Prize, Portobello Contemporary Art Festival
1993	awarded Arts Foundation Fellowship
1994–	teaches at City Lit, London
1995–	studio in Blackheath, London
1998–	gallery artist with regular exhibitions, Barrett Marsden (later Marsden Woo) Gallery, London
2017	retrospective exhibition, *More than Words*, York Art Gallery

Sara Radstone is one of an important group of ceramic sculptors trained at Camberwell in the late 1970s, which included her contemporaries Henry Pim (qv) and Angus Suttie (qv). Radstone's work explores the passage of time, conjuring this through forms and surfaces that appear eroded or decayed, faded or patinated. Her forms are ambiguous and elusive, but often refer to books and items that hold memories or suggest human narratives. After initially exploring vessels and then enclosed forms, Radstone expanded her practice to encompass wall installations and floor-based pieces.

Sara Radstone, 'Scratching the Surface', interview, *Crafts*, 270 (2018)
Houston (1979), p.144
Crafts Council (1982), p.16
Richard Deacon, 'Fragile Presences', *Crafts*, 62 (1983)
Paisley Museum and Art Galleries (1984), p.70
Crafts Council (1985), p.75
Angus Suttie, 'Sara Radstone', *CR*, 100 (1986)
Anatol Orient Gallery, *Six Ways*, exh. pamphlet, text by Angus Suttie (London, 1988)
Contemporary Applied Arts, *Sara Radstone, Angus Suttie*, exh. pamphlet, text by Alison Britton (London, 1990)
Museum of Modern Art, Oxford (1993), pp.70–1, 91, 95
Crafts Council (1995b), pp.54–5
An Lanntair, *Sara Radstone: Ceramics 79–97*, exh. cat. (Stornoway, 1997)
Emma Maiden, 'Sara Radstone', *Studio Pottery*, 28 (1997)
Barrett Marsden Gallery, *Sara Radstone: Hard Lines*, exh. pamphlet, text by Alison Britton (London, 1998)
Frankel (2000), pp.164–70
Perryman (2004), pp.28–33
Whiting (2009), pp.146–51
Ruthin Craft Centre (2010)
Julian Champkin, 'Leaves of Clay', *CR*, 271 (2015)
Sara Radstone: More than Words, text by Siobhan Feeney (London: Anthony Shaw Collection, 2018)
Thorpe (2021), pp.56–68

Exhibition reviews: Alison Britton, *Crafts*, 82 (1986); Tanya Harrod, *Crafts*, 104 (1990); Emmanuel Cooper, *CR*, 166 (1997); Lionel Phillips, *Studio Pottery*, 28 (1997); David Whiting, *Crafts*, 158 (1999); Emma Maiden, *Crafts*, 176 (2002); Oliver Watson, *CR*, 195 (2002); Shane Enright, *CR*, 212 (2005); Richard Stubbs, *CR*, 248 (2011)

Essays issued alongside exhibitions at Barrett Marsden (later Marsden Woo) Gallery, London, offer further useful texts.

812 Pot, 1983 (pl.93)
Stoneware, handbuilt, greyish glaze; h.34.7cm, d.34.1cm
C.333-1983. Source: Craft Shop, V&A (solo showcase exhibition), £170.10

813 Vessel, 1988
Stoneware, handbuilt, green and purple-brown glazes and incised markings; h.62cm, d.45.8cm
C.63-1988. Source: Michaelson and Orient, London, £450

814 *Nushu*, 2006
Stoneware, handbuilt from press-moulded slabs, painted with slip and grey stain; inscribed with text written upside down; h.28cm, w.17.5cm, d.4cm (each of five pieces)
C.90:1 to 5-2011. Source: anonymous gift
Shown in the exhibition *Sara Radstone and Partridge & Walmsley*, Barrett Marsden Gallery, London, 2007. The title refers to a script used to write a local dialect of Chinese that developed as a form of private communication between women.

813

815 *Ghost IV*, 2007
Stoneware, handbuilt from press-moulded slabs, painted with slip and dark stain; h.225cm, d.21cm
C.89:1,2-2011. Source: *see* **814**
Shown in the exhibition *Sara Radstone and Partridge & Walmsley*, Barrett Marsden Gallery, London, 2007.

Raeburn, Elizabeth 1943–

1943	born Little Bookham, Surrey
1968–73	works in publishing and teaching
1973–75	Studio Pottery Course at Harrow School of Art; works briefly with David Leach (qv)
1975–	establishes workshop in West Pennard, Somerset, with Rodney Lawrence
1981	first solo exhibition, Dan Klein Gallery, London; exhibits widely thereafter
1994|2000	mural commissions for Musgrove Park Hospital, Taunton, Somerset

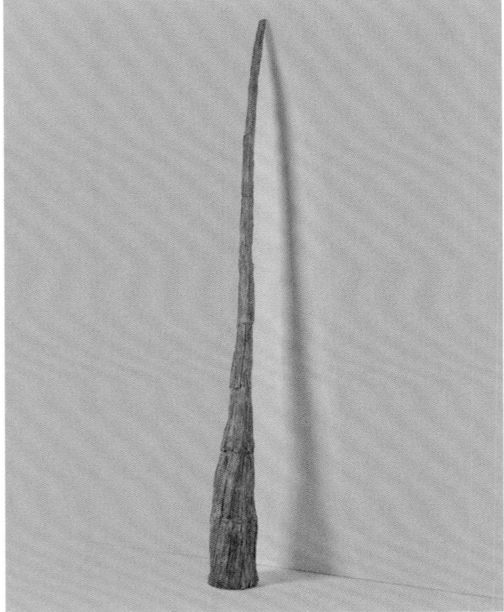
815

814

Elizabeth Raeburn has concentrated on raku-fired handbuilt forms since 1981, notably exploring sculptural vessels on pedestal bases. Following a commission for a raku landscape mural in 1994, she began developing further pictorial work in the form of curved, self-supporting tiles, composite panels and pots.

Elizabeth Raeburn, contribution, in 'The First Decade of Harrow 1963–1974', *Ceramics in Society*, 41 (2000)
Fischer Fine Art, *Nine Potters*, exh. cat. (London, 1986)
Galerie Besson, *Elizabeth Raeburn*, exh. pamphlet (London, 1989) – see also pamphlets from 1992, 1995, 2001, 2004 and 2010
Andrews (1994), (2005)
Lionel Phillips, 'Elizabeth Raeburn and Rodney Lawrence', *Somerset Magazine* (May 1996)

Exhibition reviews: Arda Lacey, *Arts Review*, 41 (21 April 1989); Eileen Lewenstein, *Crafts*, 119 (1992); Delphine Laurent, *Revue de la Céramique et du Verre*, 113 (2000); Sue Hoar, *London Potters Newsletter*, 83 (2001)

816 Pot, 1983
Raku, handbuilt; marks: 'ER' in a circle, and a quatrefoil in a circle, impressed; h.25.3cm, d.19.6cm
C.319-1983. Source: the artist, £30

Raper, Agnes **Madeline** 1874–1948

1874	born Murree, India (now in Pakistan)
1921	studies at Camberwell School of Arts and Crafts
1924–27	having previously worked with Gwendolen Parnell (qv), establishes Glebe Pottery, Upper Cheyne Row, Chelsea, London, with two assistants
1924	exhibits at *The Chelsea China and Pottery Exhibition*, Chelsea Town Hall; two pieces bought by Queen Mary
1924–26	exhibits with Society of Women Artists, London; at British Industries Fair, Birmingham; and at Paris International Exhibition
1927–37	studio at Lonsdale Road, Castlenau, London; works with three assistants
1929–33	solo exhibitions at Fine Arts Society, Graham Gallery and Walker's Galleries, London
1937	retires to Felixstowe, Suffolk

816

Madeline Raper was one of a number of independent modellers of figurative pottery active in London in the 1920s and '30s. She is known for her intricately detailed models of historic and vernacular buildings. Her work enjoyed the patronage of Queen Mary (consort of King George V), who owned more than 30 pieces.

Blunt (1924), p.89, pl.43
Guild of Potters (1925), (1926)
'A New Pottery Fashion', *Evening Telegraph* (Dundee, 16 February 1928)
British Institute of Industrial Art (1929)
Fine Art Society, *Catalogue of an Exhibition of Glebe Chelsea Models in Pottery by Madeline Raper*, exh. pamphlet (London, 1929)
John Booth, 'The Exhibition of Glebe Chelsea Pottery by A. Madeline Raper', *Walker's Monthly* (February 1932)
Walker's Galleries, *An Exhibition of Glebe-Chelsea Pottery by A. Madeline Raper*, exh. leaflet (London, 1932)
— *An Exhibition of Glebe-Chelsea Pottery Models by A. Madeline Raper*, exh. pamphlet (London, 1933)
Charles Baile de Laperrière (ed.), *The Society of Women Artists Exhibitors 1855–1996: Volume 3 L–R* (Calne, 1996)
Knott (2021)

Exhibition reviews: *The Times* (4 June 1924), (5 December 1925), (18 June 1929), (4 December 1930); *Daily Mail Atlantic Edition* (7 July 1924)

817 Perfume burner: *Round Thatched Cottage*, 1924 (pl.9)
Earthenware, slip-cast and modelled, painted in colours; marks: 'Glebe. Chelsea', and 'C' enclosing 'IMS', painted; h.12.9cm, d.11.8cm
C.435 to B-1934. Source: British Institute of Industrial Art (given by H.M. The Queen)

818

818 Model of a church, 1932
Earthenware, modelled, painted in colours; marks: 'GLEBE–CHELSEA / 1932', painted; h.4.6cm, w.6.7cm
C.228-2014. Source: given by David Beard

Rasmussen, Merete 1974–

1974	born Copenhagen, Denmark; grows up in Sweden
1997–99	studies ceramics at Östra Grevie Folkhögskola, Sweden
2000–05	studies ceramics at Designskolen Kolding, Denmark
2005–	moves to London, sets up studio in Camberwell
2010–	solo exhibition, The Scottish Gallery, Edinburgh; regular solo exhibitions in UK and internationally thereafter
2015	solo exhibition, Pangolin London, exhibiting work in bronze and ceramic
2017–	moves to Sussex, sets up studio

Merete Rasmussen is known for her complex abstract sculptures, often formed as an intertwined loop with a continuous surface. Handbuilt in stoneware, each is finished with matt slip glaze in a single, progressively more vibrant, colour. Since 2015 Rasmussen has also explored the use of other materials, including painted or patinated bronze.

Merete Rasmussen, statement, in Bendavid and Lalumia (2017), pp.30, 40
The Ceramics Book (2008), (2012)
Amanda Fielding, 'Turn, Twist, Flow', *CR*, 244 (2010)

819

Teleri Lloyd-Jones, 'A Ceramist who's Showing her Metal', *Crafts*, 257 (2015)
Pangolin London, *Merete Rasmussen: Bronze and Ceramic*, exh. cat. (London, 2015)
— *Merete Rasmussen: New Work*, exh. cat. (London, 2019)

819 *Red Twisted Form*, 2012
Stoneware, handbuilt, with sprayed matt red glaze; h.50cm, d.90cm
C.102-2012. Source: Contemporary Applied Arts at Collect 2012, £4250; purchase funded by the Friends of the V&A

Ravenscourt Pottery *see* Dora Lunn

Rena, Nicholas 1963–

1963	born London
1982–87	studies architecture at University of Cambridge
1992–93	studies ceramics at City Lit, London
1993–95	studies ceramics at Royal College of Art, London
1996–99	studio at 401½ Workshops, London
1999–	studio in Hammersmith, London
2000|02	solo exhibitions, Garth Clark Gallery, New York, USA
2001	shortlisted for Jerwood Applied Arts Prize
2001–10	solo exhibitions, Barrett Marsden (later Marsden Woo) Gallery, London
2009	exhibition (with Julian Schwarz), Musée des Arts Décoratifs, Paris
2015	solo exhibition, *After Matisse*, Holburne Museum, Bath

Nicholas Rena is known for his monumental vessel forms and use of intense colour. Rendered with architectural clarity, his work has a powerful sculptural presence, presenting jug and bowl forms as archetypes that function on a symbolic level. Rena's approach to colour is unorthodox, eschewing fired decoration for painted or ink-infused surfaces polished with wax – processes that achieve great depth of colour and preserve the precision of profile and edge.

Barrett Marsden Gallery, *Nicholas Rena*, exh. pamphlet, text by Garth Clark (London, 2001)
Frédéric Bodet, 'Distance Imposée', *Revue de la Céramique et du Verre*, 117 (2001)
Crafts Council (2001), pp.24–5, 31
Amanda Fielding, 'Making it Work', *CR*, 192 (2001)
Emma Maiden, 'Mass Appeal', *Crafts*, 170 (2001)
Perryman (2004), pp.39–43
Jerwood Contemporary Makers, exh. cat. (London, 2008)
Carlano (2010), pp.124–5
Janet McKenzie, 'Architecture + Ceramics = Sculpture', *Studio International*, ejournal (18 June 2010)
WCC-BF (2010), pp.86–9, 100
Browse and Darby, *Nicholas Rena: Deep in the Green Lilac Park*, exh. cat. (London, 2012)
Clark, Strauss and others (2012), pp.224–5, 402, 457
Bird (2013), pp.77–8
Liz Farrelly, 'Family, Home and Soane', *Crafts*, 241 (2013)
Grant Gibson, 'Polished Performance', *Crafts*, 253 (2015)
Holburne Museum, *Nicholas Rena: After Matisse*, exh. pamphlet (Bath, 2015)
Imogen Greenhalgh, 'Colourful Restraint', *CR*, 298 (2019)
Oxford Ceramics Gallery, *Nicholas Rena: Sunday Morning*, exh. cat. (Oxford, 2019)

Exhibition reviews: Emma Maiden, 'New Directions in Ceramic Sculpture', *Crafts*, 167 (2000); Jane Perryman, *CR*, 181 (2000); Felicity Aylieff, *CR*, 205 (2004); Bonnie Kemske, 'Jerwood Contemporary Makers', *CR*, 233 (2008); Nicholas Oddy, *CR*, 236 (2009); Shane Enright, 'Marking the Line', *Crafts*, 242 (2013); Colin Martin, 'Marking the Line', *Craft Arts International*, 88 (2013); *Studio International*, ejournal (26 June 2013)

820 *Vessel Made In Anticipation*, 2002
White earthenware, press-moulded, stained with blue ink and polished with beeswax; l.70cm, d.25.6cm
C.16-2003. Source: Barrett Marsden Gallery, £2880

820

821 *The Given's the Given*, 2008 (pl.128)
White earthenware, press-moulded, painted and polished; h.73.7cm, d.56.9cm
C.26-2008. Source: Barrett Marsden Gallery, London, £3480.85; acquired through the generosity of Gerard and Sarah Griffin

822 *Red Bowl*, 2009 (pl.128)
White earthenware, press-moulded, painted and polished; h.34.5cm, d.57.2cm
C.5-2010. Source: Marsden Woo Gallery, London, £3331.92; acquired through the generosity of Gerard and Sarah Griffin

Rey, Enid **Margaret** 1911–2010

1911	born Dinas Powys, Glamorgan; grows up in Bognor Regis, Sussex
1929–30	studies at Brighton School of Art
1930–33	studies at Royal College of Art, London, in School of Design, studying pottery under William Staite Murray (qv) in final year
1935–39	studio in Raynes Park, London, shared with Sam Haile (qv) from 1936
1938	solo exhibition, The Brygos Gallery, London
1961–	studio in Forest Green, Surrey; works mostly in clay sculpture, having largely ceased to pot

Margaret Rey gained recognition as a potter in the late 1930s, being singled out for praise in exhibition reviews. While many of William Staite Murray's (qv) pupils exhibited at The Brygos Gallery, she alone was afforded a solo exhibition. Her work shows Murray's influence. Reduction-fired, thrown stoneware pots, sometimes brush-decorated, range from small bowls to large, named pieces. Rey ceased potting during the Second World War and subsequently took a variety of jobs, only later re-establishing a studio.

Brygos Gallery (1937a), (1937b)
Arts and Crafts Exhibition Society (1938)
Brygos Gallery, *Stoneware by Margaret Rey*, exh. cat. (London, 1938)
Rice and Gowing (1989), pp.78–83, 240
Riddick (1990), p.106
Paul Rice, 'Margaret Rey, R.J. Washington', *Studio Pottery*, 7 (1994)
Barbara Wakefield, 'A Link through Time', *CR*, 203 (2003)
Obituary, *The Times* (21 August 2010)

Exhibition reviews: *The Times* (26 March 1938); Tanya Harrod, *Crafts*, 87 (1987)

An interview with Margaret Rey is in the Crafts Lives sound archive at the British Library, London (C960/17).

823 Bowl, 1936–37 (pl.25)
Stoneware, blue mottled glaze, brown rim; marks: 'RM' in triangular monogram, impressed, and 'R95', painted; h.7.2cm, d.10.5cm
C.27-1937. Source: The Brygos Gallery, London (exhibition: *Stoneware and Earthenware*, 1937); given by Lt-Col. K. Dingwall, DSO, through Art Fund

A further stoneware pot by Rey, entitled *Water Reeds*, was acquired by the museum at the *Fiftieth Anniversary Exhibition* of the Arts and Crafts Exhibition Society (exhibit no.98) in 1938 for £5.5s. (Circ.303-1938), but was subsequently written off, presumably due to damage.

Reychan, Stanislas 1897–1994

1897	born Vienna; childhood spent in Lwów (now Lviv, Ukraine)
1915–18	serves in Austrian Army
1940–49	arrives in London with Polish Army, working in an administrative capacity
1944	awarded MBE for services in the Allied cause
1949–51	studies sculpture at St Martin's School of Art, London, under Walter Marsden
1951–53	studies ceramics at Central School of Arts and Crafts, London, under Dora Billington (qv)
1953–85	studio in St John's Wood, London
1985	retires

Stanislas Reychan turned to art following his demobilization in 1949. For 33 years he produced lively, popular modelled figures and ornaments from his London studio. A regular exhibitor at the open-air shows of the Hampstead Artists' Council, Reychan also exhibited at the Royal Academy, London, and with the National Society of Painters, Sculptors and Printmakers.

Stanislas Reychan, 'Pottery Sculpture', *Pottery Quarterly*, 6:22 (1959)
— *Playing With Dolls: An Autobiography of a Potter* (London, 1993)
Arts and Crafts Exhibition Society (1954), (1957)
Exh. review, *Pottery Quarterly*, 3:10 (1956)
Peter Lewis, 'Stanislas Reychan', *The Studio* (March 1957)
'Potters Profile', *Pottery Quarterly*, 4:14 (1957), pl.13
Potters (1972) to (1986)
Arts Review (April 1974)
Crafts Advisory Committee (1976), p.112
Crafts Council (1980), p.62
'CPA News', *CR*, 95 (1985)
'Stanislas Reychan', *Ceramics Monthly*, 34:2 (1986), pp.73–5
Wren (1990), pp.58–61

824

825

824 *Prometheus*, c. 1980–85
Red earthenware, hand-modelled, tin glaze, painted in turquoise, blue and manganese; marks: 'REYCHAN' and device, impressed; h.31.8cm, d.25.5cm
C.205-1993. Source: given by the artist

Richards, Ceri 1903–1971

1903	born Dunvant, Swansea
1920–24	studies at Swansea School of Art
1924–27	studies at Royal College of Art, London

Ceri Richards was an accomplished painter and printmaker, whose work reflects a profound engagement with modern European painting. In the 1940s he began exploring themes from domestic and urban life in a lyrical and colourful manner. Costerwomen – based on London's pearly queens (known for their distinctive clothes covered with mother-of-pearl buttons) – became a favourite subject. Richards appears seldom to have turned his hand to ceramic painting.

Mel Gooding, *Ceri Richards* (Moffat, 2002)

825 Dish depicting a costerwoman, 1949
Earthenware, tin glaze, painted in colours; marks: 'CR49', painted; made at the workshop of John Erland, Brompton Square, London, and painted by Ceri Richards; h.6.4cm, d.40.5cm
Circ.476-1970. Source: Marlborough Fine Art, London, £135

Richards, Christine-Ann 1944–

1944	born Fulmer, Buckinghamshire
1971–73	Studio Pottery Course at Harrow School of Art
1973	apprenticed to Bryan and Julia Newman (qv)
1974	apprenticed to David Leach (qv)
1975–81	establishes workshop with Barbican Arts Group, London
1978	visits China with Craftsmen Potters Association
1979–89	undertakes Chinese studies, full- and part-time, at School of Oriental and African Studies, University of London

1982–92	workshop in King's Cross, London
1984–	travels regularly to China and Central Asia, organizing and leading cultural tours
1992	participates in International Workshop of Ceramic Art in Tokoname, Japan
1992–	workshop in Wanstrow, Somerset
1996	visits Japan on Churchill Fellowship, exploring use of water in landscape and architecture

Christine-Ann Richards has been much influenced by East Asian art and culture, a study trip to China in 1978 proving pivotal. She has worked in thrown porcelain throughout her career, specializing in crackle and monochrome glazes, at times adding splashed markings. Since 1989 she has also developed large vitrified earthenware pots and water features for gardens.

Christine-Ann Richards, 'Colouring Glazes', *CR*, 54 (1978)
— 'Early Northern Whitewares of Gongxian, Xing and Ding', *Transactions of the Oriental Ceramic Society*, 49 (1984/85)
— 'Travelling in China', *CR*, 91 (1985)
— 'China – Ten Years On', *CR*, 117 (1989)
— 'A Potter's Day', *CR*, 128 (1991)
— contribution, in 'The First Decade of Harrow 1963–1974', *Ceramics in Society*, 41 (2000)
— 'Getting Started', *CPA News*, 130 (2010)
— 'Commissioning Ceramics', *ClayCraft*, 14 (2018)
'CPA New Members', *CR*, 42 (1976)
Potters/The Ceramics Book (1977) to (2012)
Karin Hessenberg, *Ceramics for Gardens and Landscapes* (London, 2000), pp.62, 80–2

826 Long-necked bottle, 1982
Porcelain, crackled white glaze stained with red lustre; marks: 'car', impressed; h.25.6cm, d.13.6cm
C.79-1984. Source: given by the Friends of the V&A (purchased at the Craftsmen Potters Association exhibition, *Studio Ceramics Today*, V&A, 1983, no.139, £75.25)

826

Richards, Frances E. 1868/69–1931

Frances Richards was an early exponent of studio pottery. Relatively little is known about her, though she was considered by Dora Lunn (qv) as perhaps the first independent artist-potter. She seems initially to have produced mould-made pottery with painted decorative designs. By the 1920s, however, she was making thrown wares with a range of glazes, working from her home in Archway Road, Highgate, London, where she had a kiln in the garden. Richards exhibited with the Arts and Crafts Exhibition Society from 1912 onwards. She had a solo exhibition at The Three Shields gallery in Kensington in 1928, and sold through Heal's. She is nevertheless said to have lived an isolated life of poverty. The ceramics collection at Aberystwyth University includes 32 pieces of her work, acquired in the 1920s.

Arts and Crafts Exhibition Society (1912) to (1931)
Decorative Art (1917), (1927), (1928)
British Institute of Industrial Art (1923), (1927), (1929)
Royal Academy of Arts (1923)
Vincentelli and Hale (1986)
Riddick (1990), pp.107–8
Jones (2007), p.38

827 Pot, 1923
Earthenware, mottled green-brown glaze with brown bands; marks: 'FR' in square monogram surrounded by '1 9 2 III', incised; h.16.7cm, d.12.8cm
C.422-1934. Source: British Institute of Industrial Art (given by the artist)

828 Honey pot, 1924
Earthenware, white glaze, painted in blue; marks: 'FR' in square monogram surrounded by '1924', painted; h.9.8cm, d.12.5cm
C.423&A-1934. Source: *see* 827

829 Pot, 1924
Earthenware, incised lines, green glaze; marks: 'FR' in square monogram surrounded by '1924', incised; h.20.2cm, d.15.7cm
Circ.277-1955. Source: given by Lady Russell, MBE, from the collection of the late Francis Moore

830 Pot, 1927
Stoneware, mottled brown and green glaze; marks: 'FR' in square monogram and '192VII', incised; h.14.3cm, d.17cm
C.93-1927. Source: given by Mrs J Cochrane Shanks
In 1936 the same donor offered the museum another piece as a gift, which was refused by Bernard Rackham, Keeper of the Ceramics Department, as it did not seem '... to be so favourable an illustration of Miss Richards' skill as the vase by her you gave us some time ago. You told me, it is true, that Miss Richards herself thought very highly of it, but I sometimes think that artists are not always the best judges of their own work.'

830 / 827

829 / 828

Rie, Lucie (née **Gomperz**) 1902–1995

1902 born Vienna, Austria
1921–26 studies pottery at Kunstgewerbeschule, Vienna; her teachers include Michael Powolny
1925–37 work shown in international exhibitions in Paris, Brussels and Milan
1938 moves to London, following Hitler's annexation of Austria
1939– establishes workshop in Albion Mews, London
1945–53 designs and makes ceramic buttons for Bimini, London
1946– Hans Coper (qv) joins workshop
1947–58 shares workshop with Hans Coper, making tableware and individual work
1949–66 regular solo exhibitions at Berkeley Galleries, London, shared with Coper, 1950–56
1967 retrospective exhibition organized by Arts Council
1968 awarded OBE
1969 awarded Honorary Doctorate, Royal College of Art
1969– touring exhibition, *Five Studio Potters*, organized by V&A
1981 awarded CBE
1981–82 retrospective exhibition, organized by the Crafts Council, at Sainsbury Centre for Visual Arts, Norwich, Norfolk, and V&A
1989 solo exhibition in Japan, organized by the fashion designer Issey Miyake
1990 suffers stroke, ceases potting
1991 awarded DBE

Lucie Rie is one of the most important and celebrated potters of the post-war period. She achieved early success in Vienna, working in a manner informed by European modernism. Arriving in England as an émigré in 1938 and establishing a studio in London, she nevertheless effectively had to start anew. Rie's name is closely associated with that of her fellow émigré Hans Coper (qv), who came to work for her and subsequently shared her studio as an equal until 1958. Rie and Coper used comparable materials and processes, and shared a reluctance to discuss their work, but ultimately pursued different aims. While Coper developed overtly sculptural pots, Rie made highly individual and expressive ceramics based on the fundamental pottery forms of bowl, pot and bottle. Underpinned by a modernist sensibility, these respond to a wide range of historic sources. Rie's work is particularly remarkable in developing studio pottery as a modern, urban practice of contemporary relevance. Her rich and complex glazes, vibrantly coloured or deeply textured, were achieved while firing in an electric kiln.

Decorative Art (1932), (1954/55), (1961/62), (1965/66), (1967/68), (1973/74), (1974/75)
Cooper (1947), p.*iv*, pl.43
Arts and Crafts Exhibition Society (1950)
Berkeley Galleries, *Exhibition of Pottery by Lucie Rie and Hans Coper*, leaflet, text by Maurice Collis (London, 1951) – see also leaflets from later exhibitions
Dartington Hall (1952)
Wingfield Digby (1952), p.79, pls.49–52
Billington (1953)
A.C. Sewter, 'Lucie Rie – Potter', *Apollo*, 59 (February 1954)
Rose (1955), p.24, pls.D, 68–75, (1970), pp.45–8, pls.E, 90–103
Lewis (1956), pl.372
Exh. review, *Pottery Quarterly*, 3:12 (1956)
Smithsonian Institution (1959)
Arts Council, *Lucie Rie: A Retrospective Exhibition of Earthenware, Stoneware and Porcelain 1926–1967* (London, 1967)
Birks (1967), pp.15–28, (1976), pp.118–33
Casson (1967), p.8, pls.167–72, 231
Tarby Davenport, 'The Pottery of Lucie Rie', *Design*, 226 (1967)
Museum Boymans-van Beuningen, *Lucie Rie, Hans Coper*, exh. cat. (Rotterdam, 1967)
Museum für Kunst und Gewerbe, *Lucie Rie – Hans Coper: Keramik*, exh. cat. (Hamburg, 1972)
V&A (1972), p.118
Tarby Davenport, 'A Potter of Our Time', *CR*, 27 (1974)
Lucie-Smith (1975), pp.62–71
Crafts Advisory Committee (1976), p.113
Crafts Council (1980), p.62
Emmanuel Cooper, 'Lucie Rie – Potter', *CR*, 72 (1981)
John Houston (ed.), *Lucie Rie: A Survey of her Life and Work*, exh. cat. (London: Crafts Council, 1981)
Christopher Reid, 'Lucie Rie', *Crafts*, 53 (1981)
Paisley Museum and Art Galleries (1984), pp.71–3
Crafts Council (1985), pp.75–7
Michael Dunas and Sarah Bodine, 'In Search of Form: Hans Coper and Lucie Rie', *American Ceramics*, 3:4 (1985)
ICA (1985), p.44
Emmanuel Cooper, 'Lucie Rie – Artist Potter', *CR*, 100 (1986)
Tony Birks, *Lucie Rie* (London, 1987)
W.A. Ismay, 'Lucie Rie at 85', *CR*, 110 (1988)
Sainsbury Centre for Visual Arts (1990)
Shipley Art Gallery, *Lucie Rie and Hans Coper from the Eagle Collection*, exh. leaflet (Gateshead, 1990)
Tanya Harrod, 'Potted History of Modern Form and Function', *Independent on Sunday* (26 January 1992)
'Lucie Rie 1902–1995', various contributors, *CR*, 154 (1995)
Tony Birks, 'Lucie Rie and Her Work with Hans Coper', in Coatts (1997), pp.95–106
Alison Britton, 'Clay and Asphalt: The Metropolitan World of Rie and Coper', *CR*, 163 (1997)
Margot Coatts (ed.), *Lucie Rie and Hans Coper: Potters in Parallel*, exh. cat. (London: Barbican Art Gallery, 1997)
Gaze (1997)
Frankel (2000), pp.66–133
Emmanuel Cooper (ed.), *Lucie Rie: The Life and Work of Lucie Rie 1902–1995* (London, 2002)
Carlano (2010), pp.126–7
J.V.G. Mallet, 'Conversations with Lucie Rie', *English Ceramic Circle Transactions*, 21 (2010)
National Museum of Modern Art, *Lucie Rie: A Retrospective*, exh. cat. (Tokyo, 2010)
Emmanuel Cooper, *Lucie Rie: Modernist Potter*, detailed biography with bibliography and exhibitions list (New Haven/London, 2012)
Mienke Simon Thomas, *The Essential Potness: Lucie Rie and Hans Coper in Museum Boijmans Van Beuningen* (Rotterdam, 2014)
Ibaraki Ceramic Art Museum, *Lucie Rie: A Retrospective*, exh. cat. (2015)
Nottingham City Museums and Galleries (2017), pp.75–6
York Art Gallery, *Lucie Rie: Ceramics and Buttons* (York, 2018)

Obituaries: Margot Coatts, *Crafts*, 134 (1995); Emmanuel Cooper, *The Independent* (3 April 1995); Fiona MacCarthy, *The Guardian* (3 April 1995); *Daily Telegraph* (3 April 1995); *The Times* (3 April 1995)

The papers of Lucie Rie are at the Crafts Study Centre, Farnham (RIE).

The pots acquired from Lucie Rie in 1982 (**831** to **843**, **850**, **851**, **871** to **874** and **876**) had been included in the Crafts Council retrospective exhibition, shown at the Sainsbury Centre for Visual Arts and the V&A.

831 Pot, *c.* 1926
Earthenware, blue, orange, white and brown glaze splashes; marks: 'L.R.G. WIEN', painted in black; h.7.8cm, d.10.5cm
C.35-1982. Source: given by the artist

832 Bowl, 1930–38
Earthenware, blue and brown pitted glaze; marks: 'L.R.G. WIEN', painted in blue; h.9cm, d.27.6cm
C.36-1982. Source: *see* **831**

833 Pot, 1930–38
Earthenware, turquoise and black pitted glaze, unglazed interior; marks: 'L.R.G. WIEN', painted; h.15.8cm, d.18.3cm
C.37-1982. Source: *see* **831**

834 Tea set, *c.* 1936 (pl.29)
Earthenware, burnished, unglazed; marks: 'L.R.G. WIEN', painted in black; h.19cm, d.16.2cm (teapot); h.5.7cm, d.8.6cm (jug); h.4.6cm, d.7.1cm (jug); h.4cm, d. 13.4cm (cup); d.16.2cm (saucer)
C.34 to E-1982. Source: *see* **831**
Rie sought to achieve a terra sigillata-like surface on these pieces. Following a suggestion, she boiled the teapot in a solution of borax after the first firing. She said that the experiment was a failure – the surface was not that which she desired, and the tea tasted of borax and was undrinkable. The teapot is illustrated in Rose (1970), pl.90.

835 Lidded pot, 1936–37 (pl.28)
Earthenware, brown and white pitted glaze, unglazed burnished lid; marks: 'L.R.G. WIEN', painted in blue; h.11.5cm, d.12.5cm
C.38&A-1982. Source: *see* **831**
Rie commented on the glaze of this piece: 'too much tin oxide – which was a mistake to start with, but which I then repeated'. Illustrated in Cooper (1947), pl.43, and Rose (1970), pl.91.

836 Pot, 1936–37 (pl.28)
Earthenware, brown and white pitted glaze; marks: 'L.R.G. WIEN', painted in blue; h.17.4cm, d.12.5cm
C.33-1982. Source: *see* **831**

837 Bowl, 1940–42
Earthenware, mottled brown glaze; marks: 'L./R.', painted in black; h.8.3cm, d.15.5cm
C.39-1982. Source: *see* **831**
Rie made this piece soon after meeting Bernard Leach (qv) for the first time, and for a short while tried, against her own nature, to make 'weighty' pots.

838 Buttons, 1945–46
Stoneware, with various coloured glazes; w.5cm (largest)
C.105 to AA-1982 (illustrated); C.1 to 222-2017. Source: see **831**

839 Choker and bracelet, 1945–46
Stoneware, pale glaze with gold lustre; w.22cm (choker), d.10cm (bracelet)
C.102&A-1982. Source: *see* **831**
The choker bears a label including the words: 'C8/1418/1 LTE Theatre Leasure [*sic*] and fashion ware/Choker white and gold. £2/5/0'.

840 Buckle, 1945–46
Stoneware, gold lustre glaze; w.7.7cm
C.103-1982. Source: *see* **831**

841 Earrings, 1945–46
Stoneware, with gold lustre; w.2.4cm
C.104-1982. Source: *see* **831**

831

832 / 833

837

838

839

840 / 841 / 842

843

847

848

850

849

851

842 Mirror frame, 1945–46
Stoneware, unglazed red clay with white glaze and gilded border; w.19.8cm, d.2cm
C.106-1982. Source: *see* **831**

843 Umbrella handles, *c.* 1945–47
Earthenware, black, white and blue glazes; l.12.2cm, d.2.9cm
C.101 to B-1982. Source: *see* **831**
According to Rie, the handles had too small a hole for attaching to umbrellas and were never used.

844 Bowl, 1950 (pl.33)
Stoneware, incised decoration through manganese oxide, white glaze interior; marks: 'LR' in monogram, impressed; h.11.8cm, d.16.4cm
Circ.1-1951. Source: Berkeley Galleries, London (exhibition with Hans Coper, 1950), £3.3s.

845 Bowl, 1950 (pl.33)
Porcelain, white and manganese glazes; marks: 'LR' in monogram, impressed; h.8.1cm, d.19.2cm
Circ.2-1951. Source: *see* **844**, £3.3s.

846 Bowl, 1950 (pl.33)
Porcelain, white glaze, incised decoration through manganese oxide band; marks: 'LR' in monogram, impressed; h.8.4cm, d.12cm
Circ.3-1951. Source: *see* **844**, £2.2s.

847 Teapot, 1951
Stoneware, black glaze, white glaze interior; marks: 'LR' in monogram, impressed; h.16cm, d.22.7cm
Circ.20&A-1952. Source: the artist, £2.2s.

848 Jug and two beakers, 1950–55
Stoneware, manganese and white glazes; marks: 'LR' and 'HC' in monogram, impressed; h.26.6cm, d.17.3cm (jug); h.11.8cm, d.8.1cm (beakers)
C.57 to B-1982. Source: Lady Sempill, Sudbury, £300 (with **849**)
Made with Hans Coper, whose seal they also bear. According to Rie, they were probably glazed by Coper, as she would have applied a narrower band of white glaze.

849 Cruet set, 1950–55
Stoneware, manganese and white glazes; marks: 'LR' in monogram, impressed; h.10cm (salt); h.9.5cm (pepper); h.5.8cm (mustard pot)
C.58 to C-1982. Source: *see* **848**

850 Cup and saucer, *c.* 1955
Stoneware, white glaze, dark rims; marks: 'LR' in monogram, impressed; h.7.5cm, d.8cm (cup); d.13cm (saucer)
C.41&A-1982. Source: given by the artist

851 Cup and saucer, *c.* 1955
Stoneware, incised decoration through manganese oxide, white glaze interior; marks: 'LR' in monogram, impressed; h.6.9cm, d.7.6cm (cup); d.14cm (saucer)
C.40&A-1982. Source: *see* **850**

852 Bowl, 1955
Porcelain, incised decoration through manganese glaze, white glaze band; marks: 'LR' in monogram, impressed; h.9.6cm, d.25.5cm
Circ.336-1955. Source: the artist, £12

852

853

854

855

856

869 / 858 / 857

853 Bowl, *c.* 1958
Stoneware, even white glaze, unglazed ring in interior; marks: 'LR' in monogram, impressed; h.16cm, d.21.5cm
C.187-2014. Source: Dr J.W. Mann Bequest

854 Bottle, 1959
Stoneware, white glaze with brown flecks; marks: 'LR' in monogram, impressed; h.41.6cm, d.13.1cm
Circ.126-1959. Source: the artist, £18.18s.

855 Bottle, 1959
Porcelain, incised and inlaid lines, manganese glaze, incised lines through blue; marks: 'LR' in monogram, impressed; h.17.8cm, d.7.6cm
Circ.127-1959. Source: the artist, £6

856 Bottle, 1959
Porcelain, manganese glaze, incised and inlaid lines, incised lines through blue; marks: 'LR' in monogram, impressed; h.12.4cm, d.9.9cm
Circ.128-1959. Source: the artist, £5

857 Bowl, *c.* 1960
Stoneware, slightly squared form, off-white glaze flecked with brown, unglazed ring in interior; marks: 'LR' in monogram, impressed; h.7.8cm, d.19.5cm
C.183-2014. Source: Dr J.W. Mann Bequest

858 Bowl, *c.* 1960
Stoneware, oval form, off-white glaze flecked with brown, unglazed ring in interior; marks: 'LR' in monogram, impressed; h.9.2cm, d.23.6cm
C.184-2014. Source: *see* **857**

859 Bowl, *c.* 1964
Stoneware, compressed sides, cratered and pitted white glaze; marks: 'LR' in monogram, impressed; h.13.1cm, d.26.7cm
C.185-2014. Source: *see* **857**

860 Bowl, *c.* 1960–65 (fig.10)
Porcelain, incised decoration through manganese oxide; marks: 'LR' in monogram, impressed; h.8.7cm, d.22cm
C.21-2006. Source: bequeathed by Simon Cooper in memory of Ruth Wertheimer

861 Bottle, 1966
Stoneware, white glaze; marks: 'LR' in monogram, impressed; h.31.5cm, d.13.2cm
Circ.757-1966. Source: Berkeley Galleries, London (solo exhibition, 1966), £35

862 'Tall-necked bottle', 1967 (pl.55)
Stoneware, mauve-brown with white spiral; marks: 'LR' in monogram, impressed; h.38.1cm, d.15.4cm
Circ.1226-1967. Source: Arts Council of Great Britain (*Lucie Rie* retrospective exhibition, 1967, no.305), £38

863 'Square-sectioned pot', 1967
Stoneware, white with pink flush; marks: 'LR' in monogram, impressed; h.27.4cm, d.17.5cm
Circ.1227-1967. Source: *see* **862** (no.321), £48

864 'Cylindrical vase', 1967
Stoneware, turned-in rim, grey glaze over blue body; marks: 'LR' in monogram, impressed;

859

861

863

865 / 864

868

879 / 877 / 870

h.15.6cm, d.11.6cm
Circ.1228-1967. Source: *see* **862** (no.328), £19

865 'Oval bowl on conical foot', 1967
Stoneware, grey glaze over blue body; marks: 'LR' in monogram, impressed; h.14cm, d.14.6cm
Circ.1229-1967. Source: *see* **862** (no.331), £22

866 'Large bowl', 1967 (pl.54)
Stoneware, mauve-brown; marks: 'LR' in monogram, impressed; h.11.4cm, d.40cm
Circ.1230-1967. Source: *see* **862** (no.332), £38

867 'High bowl', 1967 (pl.54)
Stoneware, mauve-brown with green; marks: 'LR' in monogram, applied; h.14.3cm, d.30cm
Circ.1231-1967. Source: *see* **862** (no.336), £30

868 Planter and saucer, *c.* 1967
Stoneware, pitted white and grey glaze flecked with brown; marks: 'LR' in monogram, impressed; h.27.5cm, d.26.5cm (planter), h.4.5cm, d.25.7cm (saucer)
C.191:1,2-2014. Source: Dr J.W. Mann Bequest

869 Bowl, *c.* 1968
Stoneware, pitted white and buff glaze; marks: 'LR' in monogram, impressed; h.9.8cm, d.15cm
C.182-2014. Source: *see* **868**

870 Vase, *c.* 1975
Stoneware, abraded white and buff glaze streaked and flecked with brown; marks: 'LR' in monogram, impressed; h.18cm, d.9cm
C.188-2014. Source: *see* **868**

871 Bowl, *c.* 1976
Porcelain, bronze rim and foot, incised lines with pink inlay under a white glaze; marks: 'LR' in monogram, applied; h.12cm, d.23.8cm
C.43-1982. Source: the artist, £280
Rie considered this one of her most successful pink bowls – with an effect she had not been able to repeat satisfactorily.

872 Bottle, *c.* 1979
Stoneware, pink, green and grey spirals in a pitted glaze; marks: 'LR' in monogram, applied; h.38cm, d.17.6cm
C.42-1982. Source: the artist, £420

873 Bowl, 1978–80
Porcelain, bronze rim, yellow glaze; marks: 'LR' in monogram, applied; h.11.3cm, d.19.7cm
C.45-1982. Source: the artist, £220

874 Bowl, 1978–80
Porcelain, bronze rim, green glaze; marks: 'LR' in monogram, applied; h.10.8cm, d.20.7cm
C.44-1982. Source: the artist, £220

875 Bowl, 1979
Porcelain, metallic bronze, black, brown and turquoise glazes; marks: 'LR' in monogram, applied; h.9.9cm, d.22.3cm
C.118-1979. Source: Casson Gallery, London, £200

876 Bowl, *c.* 1980
Porcelain, incised lines with pink inlay under a white glaze; marks: 'LR' in monogram, applied; h.9.4cm, d.20.8cm
C.46-1982. Source: the artist, £280

877 Vase, *c.* 1980
Stoneware, oval rim, contrasting clays spiralled

871

872

873 / 874

875

876

878

by throwing, pink, buff and white glaze streaked and flecked with brown; marks: 'LR' in monogram, impressed; h.19.5cm, d.13.2cm
C.190-2014. Source: Dr J.W. Mann Bequest

878 Bowl, *c.* 1981
Porcelain, incised decoration through manganese glaze; marks: 'LR' in monogram, impressed; h.11cm, d.22.6cm
C.186-2014. Source: *see* 877

879 Vase, *c.* 1983 (illustrated p.347)
Stoneware, oval rim, pitted white and green glaze; marks: 'LR' in monogram, impressed; h.16.5cm, d.11.5cm
C.189-2014. Source: *see* 877

Rigler, James 1978–

1978	born Wellington, New Zealand
1998–99	studies at The Bartlett School of Architecture, University College London
1999–2002	studies 3D Crafts at University of Brighton
2002–05	works as model- and mould-maker for Lambs Terracotta and Faience, West Sussex
2005–07	studies ceramics at Royal College of Art, London
2011–17	regular exhibitions at Marsden Woo Gallery, London
2013–	moves to Glasgow; studio at Glasgow Sculpture Studios
2013–14	ceramics residency, V&A
2015	solo exhibition, Tramway, Glasgow

James Rigler creates sculptures and installations that explore the language of architectural ornament, using clay in combination with other materials. His forms are usually press-moulded in earthenware and decorated with monochrome glazes or sometimes metal leaf. Often appearing as isolated or dislocated fragments of architecture, his sculptures have a theatrical quality, hovering between the familiar and the strange, the real and the imagined, the genuine and the fake.

James Rigler, 'For Discussion', *CR*, 252 (2011)
— 'From Lego to Lutyens', *Crafts*, 256 (2015)
— **and Nao Matsunaga**, 'Art and Friendship', *CR*, 260 (2013)
Jerwood Visual Arts, *Jerwood Makers Open*, exh. cat. (London, 2012)
Marsden Woo Gallery, *James Rigler: The Fading City*, exh. leaflet, text by Glenn Adamson (London, 2013)
Bornholm Art Museum, *European Ceramic Context 2014: New Talent*, exh. cat. (Gudhjem, 2014), pp.100–1
Imogen Greenhalgh, 'Going Underground', *Crafts*, 268 (2017)
Morris (2018), pp.198–203

880 *The Severed Head*, 2013
Earthenware, handbuilt, coloured glaze; h.72.5cm, d.45cm
C.107-2013. Source: Marsden Woo Gallery, London (solo exhibition: *The Fading City*, 2013), £3475; acquired through the generosity of Gerard and Sarah Griffin

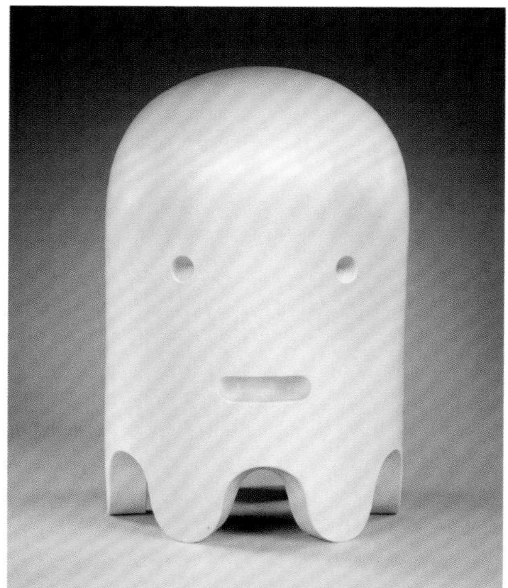

880

881

Roberts, David 1947–

1947	born Sheffield, Yorkshire
1966–70	teacher training at Bretton Hall College, Yorkshire, where introduced to ceramics
1970–81	works as art teacher; potting increasingly
1975–	moves to Holmfirth, Yorkshire; establishes workshop and begins work in raku in 1976
1981	begins full-time potting; receives Yorkshire Arts Association Travel Award to research raku in USA
1985–88	Chair of Craft Potters Association
2000–02	touring solo exhibition, *Painting with Smoke*, Huddersfield Art Gallery/ Cleveland Crafts Centre

David Roberts is a leading practitioner in raku techniques, known for his often substantial coil-built pots with bold, abstract markings that arise both through the raku process and by his own making. He is a pioneer of 'naked raku' – developed from the late 1980s – in which burnished clay surfaces are patterned by smoke penetrating cracked and incised layers of slip and glaze resist, which are subsequently flaked away from the pot.

David Roberts, 'Lightweight, Lift-off Raku Kiln', *CR*, 44 (1977)
— 'American Raku', *CR*, 76 (1982)
— 'Raku Now', *CR*, 118 (1989)
— 'Disentangling the Threads', *CR*, 186 (2000)
— 'Smoke Firing', *Studio Potter*, 29:1 (2000)
— 'What If ...', *CR*, 242 (2010)
— 'Painting with Smoke', *CR*, 296 (2019)

'CPA New Members', *CR*, 69 (1981)
Potters/The Ceramics Book (1983) to (2012)
Oxfordshire County Museum Services (1984), pp.48–9
Stephen Brayne, 'Raku Potter', *CR*, 105 (1987)
Emmanuel Cooper, *David Roberts*, Aberystwyth Arts Centre: Ceramic Series 23 (1987)
Tony Birks, 'David Roberts's Coiled Raku', *Ceramics Monthly*, 38:10 (1990)
Craft Centre and Design Gallery, *David Roberts: Raku*, exh. pamphlet, text by Tony Birks (Leeds, 1990)
W.A. Ismay, 'Pots of Striking Form', *CR*, 137 (1992)
Andrews (1994), (2005)
Jane Hamlyn, 'Raku Potter', *Ceramics: Art and Perception*, 20 (1995)
Perryman (1995), pp.109–11
Lynne Green, *Painting with Smoke: David Roberts: Raku Potter* (Otley, 2000), revised and expanded (Liversedge, 2009)
John Mathieson, *Raku* (London, 2002), p.86
Perryman (2004), pp.62–6
Carlano (2010), pp.128–9
Lemon Street Gallery, *David Roberts: The Colours of Black*, exh. pamphlet (Truro, 2016)
— *David Roberts and Andy Fullalove: Divergence Convergence in Response to Landscape*, exh. cat. (Truro, 2017)

Exhibition reviews: Stephanie Brown, 'Black Magic', *Crafts*, 88 (1987); Felicity Aylieff, *CR*, 154 (1995); David Briers, *Crafts*, 169 (2001); Fiona Hackney, *CR*, 268 (2014)

881 Vessel: *Cornucopia*, 1983
Raku, coil-built, sprayed glaze over masked lines, smoked; h.37cm, d.31.3cm
C.225-1983. Source: Queensberry Hunt, London, £150

Roberts, Hilary 1962–

1962	born London
1981–84	studies law at University of Kent at Canterbury
1991–94	studies ceramics at University of Westminster, Harrow
1994–97	establishes studio in London
1997–98	studio in Tackley, Oxfordshire
1998–2007	studio in Hebden Bridge, West Yorkshire
1999	three-person exhibition, Oxford Gallery, Oxford
2007–09	studies ceramics at University of Wales Institute, Cardiff
2009–	studio in Cardiff

Hilary Roberts gained early attention for her stylish domestic ware in white porcelain or black earthenware. She later concentrated on individual pieces in thrown or slab-built porcelain. During the 2010s she turned to making relief-decorated porcelain tiles.

882 / 883

Hilary Roberts, 'White Porcelain Tablewares', *Studio Pottery*, 18 (1995)
Gilles le Corre, 'White on White', exh. review, *CR*, 164 (1997)
Potters (1997), (2000)
V&A (1999)

882 Bowl, 1999
Porcelain, white and transparent glazes; marks: 'HR', impressed; h.15.3cm, d.49cm
C.124-1999. Source: the artist (from the exhibition *The New White: Contemporary Studio Porcelain*, V&A, 1999), £230 (with **883**)

883 Jug, 1999
Porcelain, white and transparent glazes; marks: 'HR', impressed; h.30.3cm, d.15cm
C.125-1999. Source: *see* **882**

Rogers, Mary (née Henley) 1929–

1929	born Derbyshire
1945–	joins firm of John Dickinson, printers and papermakers, working in graphics and illustration; studies part-time at Watford School of Art and St Martin's School of Art, London
1949	marries Bob Rogers, a sculptor
1960–64	studies ceramics part-time at Loughborough College of Art and Design
1960–87	pottery studio in Loughborough, Leicestershire
1966–70	teaches ceramics at Loughborough College of Education
1972	first solo exhibition, Peter Dingley Gallery, Stratford-upon-Avon, Warwickshire
1975	solo exhibition, British Crafts Centre, London
1987–	moves to Cornwall, establishes studio near Falmouth
1992–	ceases making ceramics due to allergic reactions to materials; paints and writes

Mary Rogers concentrated on small-scale handbuilt individual pieces, especially bowls, in porcelain and stoneware. Her work is based on close observation of natural forms, colours and textures.

Mary Rogers, 'Decoration through Form', *CR*, 9 (1971)
— statement, in Rothschild (1972)
— 'Hand Modelled or Pinched Pottery', *CR*, 38 (1976)
— interview, in Cameron and Lewis (1976), pp.126–35, 167
— *Mary Rogers on Pottery and Porcelain* (New York/Sherborne, 1979), revised (1984)
— 'Pinch-built Pottery', in Tony Birks, *Pottery* (London, 1979)
Decorative Art (1971/72), (1972/73)
Potters (1972) to (1986)
V&A (1972), p.118
Oxford Gallery (1974)
'Working in Leicestershire', *Crafts*, 13 (1975)
Crafts Advisory Committee (1976), p.114
Casson (1977)
'In Brief: Mary Rogers', notice of Crafts Advisory Committee (CAC) bursary, *Crafts*, 26 (1977)
Rosemarie Pitts, book review, *Crafts*, 41 (1979)
Rosemary Wren and Peter Crotty, book review, *CR*, 60 (1979)
Crafts Council (1980), p.62
Jon Catleugh, 'English Romantic', *CR*, 76 (1982)
Crafts Council (1985), pp.78–9
Nottingham City Museums and Galleries (2017), p.78

Exhibition reviews: J.D.H. Catleugh, *CR*, 15 (1972); Val Barry, *CR*, 20 (1973); W.A. Ismay, *CR*, 23 (1973), and 25 (1974); Victor Margrie, *CR*, 36 (1975); Angela Houghton, *Crafts*, 22 (1976); Emmanuel Cooper, *Art & Artists*, 14:5 (1979)

884 Bowl, 1979
Porcelain, handbuilt, matt glaze; marks: 'MER', incised; h.9.4cm, d.14.3cm
C.143-1980. Source: the artist, £70

885 Bowl, 1979
Porcelain, handbuilt, painted in blue and brown; marks: 'MER', incised; h.8.8cm, d.18.3cm
C.144-1980. Source: the artist, £80

886 Bowl, 1979
Porcelain, handbuilt, with oxide spots; marks: 'MER', incised; h.6.5cm, d.10.3cm
C.145-1980. Source: the artist, £50

Rogers, Phil (Philip) 1951–2020

1951	born Newport, Wales
1970–72	studies at Swansea College of Art
1972–73	teacher training at Swansea College of Education
1973–77	works as art teacher, Cambridgeshire
1978–84	establishes Marston Pottery in Rhayader, Powys
1978	solo exhibition, Quay Gallery, St Ives, Cambridgeshire; exhibits widely thereafter
1984–	moves to Lower Cefn Faes, Rhayader; re-establishes pottery and builds oil-fired kiln
1985	builds saltglaze kiln
1985–2000	runs annual summer schools at pottery
1991–95	Chair of Craft Potters Association
1993	visits Ethiopia to help establish a women's pottery in Gondar
1997	teaches salt-glazing and kiln-building at Chungnam University, Daejeon, South Korea
2004	completes build of two-chambered wood-fired kiln

Phil Rogers was among the most accomplished potters working within the school of practice established by Bernard Leach (qv), his work drawing particular influence from early Chinese and Korean ceramics. His production included both saltglaze and reduction-fired stoneware glazed using locally sourced wood-ash and other materials, firing with oil or wood. Most pots are concisely, yet fluently decorated, often with incised or combed marks, which his glazes enhance.

Phil Rogers, 'Mark of the Maker', *CR*, 108 (1987)
— contribution to 'Bernard Leach – A Living Tradition', *CR*, 108 (1987)
— 'A Potter's Day', *CR*, 123 (1990)

885 / 886 / 884

— *Ash Glazes* (London, 1991), see pp.92–9 for Rogers' own work
— 'The Lure of Wood Ash Glazes', *CR*, 131 (1991)
— 'An Autobiography', *Ceramics Monthly*, 41:5 (1993)
— 'Subtleties of Saltglaze', *CR*, 151 (1995)
— *Throwing Pots* (London, 1995)
— *Salt Glazing* (London, 2002), see pp.201–5 for Rogers' own work
— 'Now showing', *CR*, 201 (2003)
— 'A Potter's Kiln', *CR*, 223 (2007)
— 'What If ...', *CR*, 232 (2008)
— 'Potters on Pots', *CR*, 296 (2019)
Potters/The Ceramics Book (1986) to (2008)
David Briers, *Phil Rogers*, Aberystwyth Arts Centre: Ceramic Series 31 (1988)
David Whiting, *Phil Rogers*, Aberystwyth Arts Centre: Ceramic Series 74 (1995)
Josie Walter, 'The First Twenty Years', *CR*, 173 (1998)
Richard Busch, 'Phil Rogers', *Ceramics Monthly*, 51:5 (2003)
Goldmark Gallery, *Phil Rogers*, exh. cat., text by David Whiting (Uppingham, 2005) – see also cats. from 2008, 2014, 2017 and 2020
Pucker Gallery, *Phil Rogers: Potter* (Boston, 2007)
Whiting (2009), pp.52–5
Carlano (2010), pp.130–1
Christine Temin, 'Phil Rogers: Welsh Potter', *Ceramics: Art and Perception*, 85 (2011)
Goldmark Gallery, *Phil Rogers: A Portfolio* (Uppingham, 2012)

Obituaries: Isabella Smith, *The Guardian* (19 January 2021); Mike Goldmark and Josh Mansfield, *Ceramics: Art and Perception*, 117 (2021)

Exhibition reviews: Helen Talbot, *Studio Pottery*, 7 (1994); Ian Wilson, *Crafts*, 147 (1997); Emmanuel Cooper, *Crafts*, 157 (1999); Amanda Fielding, *CR*, 185 (2000); Jane Hamlyn, *CR*, 205 (2004); Andy Christian, *CR*, 267 (2014)

A recorded interview with Phil Rogers is in the Potters of the Bernard Leach Legacy collection at the British Library, London (C1330/17). Documentary films on Rogers were made by Goldmark and released on DVD in 2009 and 2014.

887 Bottle, 1999 (pl.102)
Stoneware, combed decoration, saltglaze with ash glaze on shoulder; marks: 'PR' monogram, impressed; h.38.3cm, d.22cm
C.14-2000. Source: the artist, £300
Considered by Rogers at the time of its acquisition by the museum to have been one of his most successful pots.

888

888 Tea bowl, 2006
Stoneware, tenmoku glaze, combed decoration; marks: 'PR' in monogram, impressed; h.8.2cm, d.12.6cm
C.70-2008. Source: Pucker Gallery, Boston, USA (solo exhibition, 2007); presented by Bernard and Suzanne Pucker in honour of Lady Judy Solomon

Rooke, Bernard 1938–

1938	born Ipswich, Suffolk
1955–59	studies painting and lithography at Ipswich School of Art
1959–60	studies printmaking and ceramics at Goldsmiths' College, London
1960–63	workshop in Forest Hill, London, shared with Alan Wallwork (qv)
1961–65	teaches part-time at Goldsmiths' College
1963–67	successive workshops in Greenwich, London
1967–	moves to Swilland, Suffolk, establishing pottery and painting studios, and later gallery
2004	pottery and gallery close; begins work on new painting studio

Concerned primarily with ceramics for interiors, Bernard Rooke produced stoneware vases, murals and lamp-bases of a sculptural character using a range of handbuilding and later also press-moulding and slip-casting techniques. From the mid-1970s he devoted himself increasingly to painting, his son Aaron eventually taking over the running of the pottery.

Biographical notes, *Pottery Quarterly*, 8:30 (1963), p.7, pl.30
Decorative Art (1964/65), (1968/69)
Casson (1967), p.8, pls.58–62
Potters (1972), (1974), (1975)
Paisley Museum and Art Galleries (1984), p.73
Crafts Council (1995b), pp.56–7
Paul Rice, 'Bernard Rooke', *Studio Pottery*, 15 (1995)
Carlano (2010), pp.132–3

Exhibition reviews: Joanna Constantinidis, *CR*, 7 (1971); Oliver Watson, *Crafts*, 106 (1990)

889

889 Pot, 1967
Stoneware, slab-built around a timber former, white slip, incised decoration with copper and iron pigments and matt black glaze; marks: 'BR', incised; h.34.5cm, d.19.5cm
C.28-1990. Source: Paul Rice Gallery, London (exhibition: *Bernard Rooke: Stoneware Pots 1960–1990*, 1990), £230

Ross, Duncan 1943–

1943	born Lahore, Pakistan
1962–65	studies ceramics at Farnham School of Art
1965–66	teacher training, Sussex University
1966–70	painting studio, north Devon
1966–88	teaches at various levels
1980–	establishes workshop in Hale, Surrey, making stoneware and porcelain
1988–	pots full-time, developing terra-sigillata carbonized earthenware
1990	first solo exhibition, Sheila Harrison Fine Art, London; exhibits widely thereafter

Duncan Ross is known for his fine burnished and smoked earthenware vessels, with dynamic linear markings and surface textures built up using layers of terra-sigillata slip.

890

Duncan Ross, 'Clay: Tenacious Earth', *Ceramics: Art and Perception*, 30 (1997)
— 'What If ...', *CR*, 244 (2010)
Emmanuel Cooper, 'Precise Vessels', *CR*, 129 (1991)
Potters/The Ceramics Book (1992) to (2012)
Peter Lane, 'Pots with Presence', *CR*, 155 (1995)
Perryman (1995), pp.70–4, (2008), pp.111–15
'Duncan Ross', *Ceramics Monthly*, 50:2 (2002)
Carlano (2010), pp.134–5
Masters: Earthenware: Major Works by Leading Artists (New York, 2010), pp.98–105
Brandpunt Terra 2011 (Delft, 2011), pp.132–3
Game (2016), pp.24–5, 94–5

Exhibition reviews: Sylvie Girard, *Revue de la Céramique et du Verre*, 61 (1992); Emmanuel Cooper, 'Earth and Fire', *Crafts*, 131 (1994)

890 Bowl, 1994
Earthenware, thrown, burnished, terra-sigillata slip, smoked; marks: 'DR' in monogram, incised; h.20.4cm, d.27.2cm
C.64-1995. Source: Craft Potters Association, London (exhibition: *Studio Ceramics 94*, V&A, 1994), £480

Russell, Christopher 1931–2018

1931 born Totnes, Devon
1945–51 studies pottery at Poole School of Art
1952–56 establishes Purbeck Pottery, Swanage, Dorset
1955 solo exhibition, Heal's, London
1956– travels to Barbados, intending to spend a year painting; establishes pottery at Bridgetown, with support from Barbados Development Board
1960– returns to UK, establishes studio in West Holme, Dorset

891

At his Purbeck Pottery, Christopher Russell made thrown pottery, decorating it with brushwork and wax-resist in combination with tin glaze, among other techniques. In Barbados he began fusing various kinds of glass onto the glazed surface of ceramic tiles. He continued exploring the process in Dorset, making brilliantly coloured tiles and panels for 50 years.

Christopher Russell, 'The Potters of Barbados', *Pottery Quarterly*, 4:16 (1957)
Decorative Art (1953/54), (1955/56)
Exh. review, *Pottery Quarterly*, 2:7 (1955), p.120, pl.9
Blanchett (2006), vol.3, pp.207–12

891 Pot, 1955
Red earthenware, tin glaze with wax-resist lines, painted in brown; marks: 'CR' in monogram, painted; h.21cm, d.20cm
Circ.340-1955. Source: Heal & Son Ltd, London, £12.12s.

St Leger, Sonia (later **Sally Willington**) 1931–2008

Sonia St Leger was born in Wembley, Middlesex, and schooled in north London. She studied at Willesden School of Art, and exhibited pottery made there with the Arts and Crafts Exhibition Society in 1950. About this time, she is reported to have made goblets and platters for The Gore Hotel, Kensington, London, for use in Elizabethan-style banquets. Known primarily as an activist and campaigner, Willington – as she became – founded the Association for Improvements in the Maternity Services (AIMS) in 1960 and was an early member of the Green Party. Having returned to London in the 1970s after periods living in Iraq and Cornwall, she established a small pottery in a shop in Battersea, which she ran throughout the 1980s. She subsequently moved to Nowra, Australia, returning to England in 2004.

892

Arts and Crafts Exhibition Society (1950)

Obituaries: Caroline Richmond and Christine Rodgers, *The Guardian* (26 November 2008); *AIMS Journal*, 20:3 (2008)

892 Pitcher, 1950
Earthenware, slip-trailed in white and black on a dark ground; marks: cross with four dots, impressed; made at Willesden School of Art; h.27.4cm, d.21.7cm
Circ.272-1950. Source: Arts and Crafts Exhibition Society (Twenty-second Exhibition, V&A, 1950, no.175), £2.2s.

Salazar, Fiona 1949–2017

1949 born Athens, Greece, of English parents; educated in England
1970–75 works in Radio Drama at BBC
1976–78 studies at Central School of Art and Design, London
1979–82 studies ceramics at Royal College of Art, London
1982–84 workshop in Wapping, London
1984–95 workshop at Kingsgate Workshops, Kilburn, London
1986|97 solo exhibitions, Crafts Council Shop at the V&A
1990 solo exhibition, Contemporary Applied Arts, London
1995– workshop in Muswell Hill, London

Fiona Salazar specialized in pots with unglazed burnished surfaces, usually black. Her forms, and the bold, coloured devices that decorate them, blend ancient Greek and Native American allusions.

Crafts Council (1985), p.79
Pamela Johnson, 'Individual Touch', interview, *Crafts*, 74 (1985)
John Gibson, 'Fiona Salazar', *CR*, 107 (1987)
Gibson (1987), pp.24–8
Potters (1989), (1992)
Contemporary Applied Arts, *Fiona Salazar*, exh. pamphlet, text by Alison Britton (London, 1990)

893 Pot, 1985
Earthenware, coil-built, terra-sigillata slip, burnished, painted with coloured slips; marks: 'Fiona / Salazar', painted in red; h.31.3cm, d.30.4cm
C.44-1985. Source: British Crafts Centre, London (group exhibition), £319.50

Schloessingk, Micki (also Micky Doherty) 1949–

1949	born London
1968–69	travels in India, encounters pottery-making
1970	workshop experience in Mayo, Ireland
1970–72	Studio Pottery Course at Harrow School of Art
1971–73	travels and works in potteries in France and Spain
1974–86	establishes pottery at Bentham, North Yorkshire, making wood-fired saltglaze tableware; works as Micky Doherty until early 1980s
1987–	moves to Cheriton, Gower, establishes workshop
1994|2004	solo exhibitions, Contemporary Ceramics, London
1998	travels to Australia, teaching and researching kilns
2001	builds new wood-fired kiln
2016–17	solo exhibition, Mission Gallery, Swansea, and tour
2017	builds new, smaller cross-draught kiln

893

Micki Schloessingk is a leading maker of wood-fired salt-glazed stoneware, producing pots for use. She obtains great richness of colour and depth of surface, and brings an inventive turn to deceptively simple shapes.

Micki Schloessingk, 'A Continuous Challenge', *The Log Book*, 33 (2008)
Potters/The Ceramics Book (1980) to (2012)
'CPA New Members', *CR*, 67 (1981)
Jane Hamlyn, 'An Apparent Simplicity', *Ceramics: Art and Perception*, 10 (1992)
Paul Vincent, 'Micki Schloessingk', *Studio Pottery*, 2 (1993)
John Nuttgens, *Micki Schloessingk*, Aberystwyth Arts Centre: Ceramic Series 66 (1994)
Andrew Webb, 'Saltglaze Potter', *CR*, 147 (1994)
Minogue and Sanderson (2000), pp.47–9
Cochrane (2001), pp.61–3
Rogers (2002), pp.206–10
Sarah Foster, 'The Holistic Approach', *CR*, 206 (2004)
Ruthin Craft Centre (2009), pp.30–1
Mission Gallery/Ruthin Craft Centre, *Micki Schloessingk: The Language of Clay* (Swansea/Ruthin, 2016)
Alex Reece, 'Earth, Salt and Fire', *Country Living* (November 2016)

Exhibition reviews: Jo Dahn, *Studio Pottery*, 11 (1994); David Whiting, *Crafts*, 131 (1994); Ellen Bell, *CR*, 284 (2017)

894 Jug, 1988
Stoneware, brown saltglaze with brushed decoration; marks: 'M', impressed; h.18cm, d.16.8cm
C.12-1989. Source: Contemporary Applied Arts, London, £38.70

895 Bowl, 1988
Stoneware, brown saltglaze with brushed decoration; marks: 'M', impressed; h.7.4cm, d.32.5cm
C.13-1989. Source: *see* **894**, £58.05

895 / 894

Scott, David 1950–

1950	born Yorkshire
1970–73	studies at North Staffordshire Polytechnic, Stoke-on-Trent
1973–76	studies ceramics at Royal College of Art, London
1976–83	teaches ceramics part-time at various colleges
1977–83	workshop in London
1983–	moves to Leicestershire, establishes workshop; teaches full-time at Loughborough College of Art and Design
1985	exhibition with Sabina Teuteberg, Craftsmen Potters Shop, London
2001–03	Chair of National Association for Ceramics in Higher Education (NACHE)

David Scott alternated between handbuilt sculptural pieces and thrown or handbuilt domestic objects, notably unglazed teapots, jars and jugs, which emphasized the decorative rather than the functional. He later concentrated on thrown vessel forms and experimented with 'anagama' firings.

David Scott, *Clays and Glazes in Studio Ceramics* (Marlborough, 1998)
— 'Ways with Anagama', *CR*, 182 (2000)
Potters/The Ceramics Book (1983) to (2006)
'CPA New Members', *CR*, 85 (1984)
Craftspace Touring (1993)

896

896 Teapot, 1982
Earthenware, unglazed, incised decoration, plastic handle; marks: 'DS', impressed; h.11.5cm (without handle), d.17.4cm
C.80-1984. Source: given by the Friends of the V&A (purchased at the Craftsmen Potters Association exhibition, *Studio Ceramics Today*, V&A, 1983, no.145, £25.80)

Scott, Paul 1953–

1953	born Darley Dale, Derbyshire
1972–77	trains as art teacher, St Martin's College, Lancaster
1977–85	works as art teacher in Solihull, West Midlands, then Carlisle, Cumbria
1985–	works as visual artist and author; studio in Blencogo, Cumbria
1987–98	Commissioning Editor, Ceramics, for *Artists Newsletter*
2001–11	Visiting Professor, Bergen National Academy of the Arts (KHiB), Norway
2010	awarded PhD, Manchester Metropolitan University
2011–18	Professor of Ceramics, Oslo National Academy of the Arts (KHiO), Norway
2012–14	Digital Research Fellow, Manchester Metropolitan University
2012–17	*Horizon* research project, with National Museum of Art, Architecture and Design, Oslo
2013–	*New American Scenery* research project

Paul Scott is a pivotal figure in the emergence of print-decorated ceramics as a major force within studio ceramic practice. Underpinned by detailed historical and technical research, his work draws upon the visual language of blue-and-white transfer-printed ware, using found historic objects, industrial whiteware or contemporary studio-made ceramics as grounds for his own collaged imagery. Exploring history, pattern, landscape and place – most notably Cumbria and the USA – his work often carries a strong political charge. In addition to his studio practice, Scott's importance lies in his advocacy for printed ceramics through his activities as a writer, curator and teacher.

Paul Scott, 'Ceramic Transfers', *Artists Newsletter* (July 1990)
— 'Printed Clay', *CR*, 140 (1993)
— *Ceramics and Print* (London, 1994), revised (2012)
— 'Pressing, Painting and Printing', *CR*, 160 (1996)
— *Painted Clay: Graphic Arts and the Ceramic Surface* (London, 2001)
— 'Hanoi Mosaic Mural', *CR*, 246 (2010)
— 'Willows, Windmills and Wild Roses: Recycling and Remediation', in Veiteberg (2011), pp.38–47
— 'From the Spode Archives', *CR*, 270 (2014)
— (ed.), *Hot off the Press: Ceramics and Print*, exh. cat., Tullie House City Museum & Art Gallery, Carlisle (London, 1996)
— and Knut Astrup Bull (eds), *Horizon: Transferware and Contemporary Ceramics* (Oslo and Stuttgart, 2015)
Orleans House Gallery, *Glazed Expressions: Contemporary Ceramics and the Written Word*, exh. cat., text by Paul Scott (Twickenham, 1998)
Collins Gallery, *The Plate Show*, exh. cat. (Glasgow, 1999)
Paul Mason, 'The Scott Collection: Cumbrian Blues', *Ceramics: Art and Perception*, 35 (1999)
Hatton Gallery, *Are You Sitting Comfortably? The Water-closet Workshop*, exh. cat. (Newcastle, 2002)
Tullie House Museum and Art Gallery, *Paul Scott: Cumbrian Blue(s)*, exh. cat. (Carlisle, 2003)
Manchester Metropolitan University Special Collections, *Confected Landscapes, Cultural Wallpaper and Contemporary Vignettes*, exh. pamphlet (2007)
Amy Gogarty, 'Paul Scott's Confected Landscapes and Contemporary Vignettes', *Ceramics: Art and Perception*, 75 (2009)
Andy Christian, 'The Wild and the Natural', *CR*, 244 (2010)
Winch (2010), pp.26–31
Scottish Gallery, *Paul Scott: Blue and White Horizons*, exh. cat. (Edinburgh, 2012)
Clare (2016), pp.102–3, 146–7
Scottish Gallery, *Paul Scott: Cuttings, Ruins, Refugees and Wild Roses*, exh. cat. (Edinburgh, 2016)
Exhibition reviews: Steve Ogden, *CR*, 203 (2003); Liz Mitchell, *CR*, 230 (2008); Teleri Lloyd-Jones, *Crafts*, 252 (2015)

897 *Scott's Cumbrian Blue(s), Foot and Mouth No. 5, after MacLeod, Darwell and May*, 2001, reworked 2012–13
In-glaze transfer collage on Royal Worcester bone-china platter; marks: signed 'Paul Scott' in blue; 'Foot & Mouth Nº:5 / (after Macleod [*sic*], Darwell & May)', and '01/07/01/13', painted in blue; 'BLENCOGO / SCOTT'S / CUMBRIAN BLUE(S) / ENGLAND', within an oval, 'REAL ART / A', within a circle, and a paintbrush bearing the words 'Scott's' and 'Scott's STANDARD', printed in blue; h.32.5cm, d.42.8cm
C.60-2013. Source: The Scottish Gallery, £1620; acquired through the generosity of Gerard and Sarah Griffin
Made in response to the 2001 outbreak of foot-and-mouth disease (a contagious disease of livestock) in Cumbria, Scott's image collaged press photos by Murdo MacLeod and others. A final set of plates with subtly reconfigured designs was made in 2012–13, after Scott rediscovered four of the original transfers in his studio.

898 *Cockle Pickers Willow Tea Service*, 2007
In-glaze transfer collage on porcelain or bone china, gold lustre; tea caddy handbuilt in porcelain by Jane Smith, cup early 19th-century pearlware, other pieces made by Royal Worcester or Royal Copenhagen; marks: signed 'Paul Scott' in blue; 'COCKLE PICKERS', enclosing a kneeling enslaved figure, 'SCOTT'S CUMBRIAN BLUE(S)', enclosing a flower, and 'REAL ART / A', within a circle, printed in blue; 'TP/03/06/03/07', inscribed in blue (teapot); other pieces with various similar printed marks including: 'SCOTT'S / CUMBRIAN BLUE(S)', enclosed by 'CUMBERLAND / ENGLAND', within an oval, and inscribed references: 'TC/01/06/03/07' (caddy); 'M/01/06/03/07' (milk jug); 'SB/01/06/03/07' (sugar bowl); 'S/05/06/03/07' (saucer); 'SP/01/06/03/07' (small plate); 'RC/02/06/03/07' (plate); h.14.6cm, d.19.8cm (teapot); h.13.2cm (caddy); h.9.6cm (jug); d.10.5cm (bowl); h.6.5cm (cup); d.13.5cm (saucer); d.17cm (plate); d.25cm (plate)
C.77:1 to 10-2008. Source: the artist, £1250
Scott's pattern refers to the tragic incident in 2004 in which a group of migrant workers from China were caught by the rising tide in

897

898

Morecambe Bay, north-west England, leading to more than 20 deaths.

899 *Spode Works Closed, Casserole 2*, 2009–10
In-glaze transfer and gold lustre on Spode *Blue Italian* porcelain casserole; marks: Spode factory marks; signed 'Paul Scott' in blue; 'BLENCOGO / SCOTT'S / CUMBRIAN BLUE(S) / ENGLAND', within an oval, 'SPODE WORKS CLOSED', within a decorative border, 'REAL ART / A', within a circle, 'BCB' logo (British Ceramics Biennial), and 'Object from closed Spode Factory - collected 15/07/09', printed in blue; '04/10/09/09', painted in blue; h.7.3cm, d.39.3cm
C.93-2011. Source: Bluecoat Display Centre at Collect 2011, £2094.30
In 2009 Scott was given limited access to the closed Spode factory in Stoke-on-Trent and allowed to collect a number of abandoned objects, including broken and unfinished tableware, to which he added printed details and gilding.

900 *Scott's Cumbrian Blue(s), Seascale Pigeon No. 14*, 2012
In-glaze transfer collage and gold lustre on Pountney and Co. earthenware platter, *c.* 1930; marks: Pountney factory mark; 'Seascale Pigeon No: 14' and 'Paul Scott' signature, inscribed in blue; printed artist's marks as **897**; '05/24/11/12', painted in blue; h.32.7cm, d.40.5cm
C.61-2013. Source: The Scottish Gallery (solo exhibition: *Blue and White Horizons*, 2012), £1350; acquired through the generosity of Gerard and Sarah Griffin
In 1998 pigeons roosting at Sellafield nuclear reprocesssing plant in Cumbria were found to carry 'significant' levels of radiation.

901 *Scott's Cumbrian Blue(s), Hedgerow No. 6*, 2012 (pl.134)

899

900

In-glaze transfer collage and gold lustre on Copeland earthenware platter, *c.* 1914; marks: Copeland Spode factory marks; 'Hedgerow Nº:6' and 'Paul Scott' signature, inscribed in blue; printed artist's marks as **897**; '04/24/11/12', painted in blue; h.28.2cm, d.37.8cm
C.62-2013. Source: *see* **900**, £1125

Selwood, Sarah-Jane 1969–

1969	born Edinburgh
1987–92	studies ceramics at Edinburgh College of Art, focusing on throwing in postgraduate year
1992–	establishes studio in Edinburgh
1993–2005	teaches ceramics at Edinburgh College of Art
1993–2007	solo and joint exhibitions at Candover Gallery, Alresford, Hampshire; The Scottish Gallery, Edinburgh; Galerie L, Hamburg, Germany; Contemporary Ceramics, London; Oxford Gallery, Oxford; and elsewhere
1997	residency in Takeo, Kyushu, Japan
2008	residency in Fuping, Shaanxi Province, China
2010–	discontinues professional making to pursue career as a radiographer

Sarah-Jane Selwood gained recognition for her precise, thrown and altered, celadon-glazed porcelain vessels inspired by Scotland's landscape. She later developed more complex, cut and reconstructed forms in porcelain and polished terracotta.

Sarah-Jane Selwood, profile and technical notes, *CR*, 148 (1994)
Will Levi Marshall, exh. review, *CR*, 166 (1997)
Potters (1997), (2000)
Christopher Andreae, 'Sarah-Jane Selwood's Porcelain Vessels', *Ceramics: Art and Perception*, 37 (1999)
Sarah-Jane Selwood, texts by Amanda Game and Christopher Andreae (Edinburgh, 1999)
V&A (1999)
Tony Franks, 'Measure for Measure', *CR*, 191 (2001)
Baird and Watban (2007), statement, pp.114–15

902

903

Scottish Gallery, *Sarah-Jane Selwood – New Ceramics*, exh. card, with artist statement (Edinburgh, 2007)

902 *Ribbed Matt White Bowl*, 1999
Porcelain, thrown and altered, matt bluish-white glaze; h.15.3cm, d.25.1cm
C.10-2002. Source: the artist (from exhibition: *The New White: Contemporary Studio Porcelain*, V&A, 1999), £210

Shaddock, Jill 1989–

1989	born Dewsbury, West Yorkshire
2007–08	foundation studies at Leeds College of Art and Design
2008–11	studies ceramics at Manchester Metropolitan University
2011–	establishes studio in Stockport, Greater Manchester
2013	selected for Crafts Council's Hothouse programme (providing support to emerging makers)
2014–	moves studio to Hebden Bridge, West Yorkshire

Jill Shaddock makes decorative, yet usable objects with great precision, using multi-layered slip-casting techniques. The resulting pieces, often assembled as groups, are of elegant minimal form and employ a refined colour palette.

'Craft Potters Association Members', *CPA News*, 165 (2016)
'Rising Stars of the CPA', *CR*, 293 (2018)

903 Coffee set for two, 2018
Parian porcelain, slip-cast in layers, body stains, transparent glaze, spalted beech plinth; h.8cm, d.8.6cm (cups); h.5.9cm, d.6cm (milk pourer); h.2.2cm, d.6cm (sugar pot); l.16.2cm, d.1cm (stirrers); l.35.6cm, d.11.6cm (wooden plinth)
C.30:1 to 7-2019. Source: the artist, £225; acquired through the generosity of Gerard and Sarah Griffin

Sharp, Alexander (Alex) 1918–2010

1918	born Barrhead, Renfrewshire
1948–51	trains under Bernard Leach (qv) at St Ives
c. 1951–60	establishes Morar Pottery, Inverness-shire, for Highland Home Industries
c. 1952–60	Pottery Officer, Scottish Country Industries Development Trust
c. 1960–61	part-time pottery adviser to Glasgow Corporation Education Department
c. 1961–84	establishes Bute Pottery in Rothesay, Isle of Bute
1984–	moves to Glasgow, sets up workshop at his home
2007	ceases potting

An accomplished, though lesser-known student of Bernard Leach (qv), Alexander Sharp first determined to be a potter after reading Leach's *A Potter's Book* while recovering in hospital from peritonitis. After a period in St Ives, he established Morar Pottery on the west coast of Scotland on behalf of Highland Home Industries, producing slipware, stoneware and porcelain, and providing training. His work was shown at the *Living Traditions* exhibition in Edinburgh as part of the Festival of Britain, 1951, and at the Dartington Hall exhibition, 1952. He later made domestic stoneware and individual pieces at his own pottery on the Isle of Bute.

Royal Scottish Museum, *Living Traditions: 1951 Festival Exhibition of Scottish Architecture and Crafts*, exh. cat. (1951)
Dartington Hall (1952)
Paisley Museum and Art Galleries (1984), pp.76–8
Robert Burns, obituary, *The Scotsman* (30 December 2010)

904 Pot, 1955
Stoneware, fluted sides, tenmoku glaze; marks: 'aS' in monogram and 'MP', impressed; h.16.3cm, d.15.2cm
Circ.240-1955. Source: Primavera, London, £3.5s.
A printed label reads 'MORAR / HIH / POTTERY'. The pot is said to have been one of two bought by Primavera's owner, Henry Rothschild, at a Highland Home Industries exhibition in London. The deep fluting was inspired by the cooling fins of a motorcycle engine.

Shelly, John 1907–1995

1907	born Newport, Shropshire, the son of a country parson; grows up near Salisbury, Wiltshire
1940s	attends pottery classes at Central School of Arts and Crafts under Dora Billington (qv) while serving in Royal Air Force and stationed in London
1949	trains at Winchcombe Pottery, under Ray Finch (qv)
1951–56	establishes The Bath Pottery, Bath, makes slipware and tin-glazed earthenware with two assistants; runs twice-yearly pottery courses; teaches at Bath Academy of Art, Corsham Court, for four years
1954	solo exhibition, Crafts Centre, London
1957–60	moves to Winterborne St Martin, Dorset, sets up Church Cottage Pottery, seeking to live and work in simpler way
1961–	moves to Old Manor, Littlehempston, near Totnes, Devon; runs pottery courses in summer, makes own pottery in winter

Primarily a slipware potter, John Shelly made domestic ware and individual pieces, particularly large dishes and cider jars. Initially following traditional designs, he soon evolved more individual decoration of fluid abstract patterns and fish. Shelly considered that slip, as a liquid medium, was especially suited to 'watery subjects'.

John Shelly, 'Sub Aqua', with biographical notes, *Pottery Quarterly*, 3:9 (1956)
Decorative Art (1953/54), (1954/55), (1955/56)
Arts and Crafts Exhibition Society (1954), (1957)
Lewis (1956), pls.345–6
News, *Pottery Quarterly*, 3:10 (1956), p.74
Biographical notes, *Pottery Quarterly*, 8:30 (1963)
Wheeler (1998), pp.54, 161

Exhibition reviews: *Pottery Quarterly*, 1:2 (1954), and 2:5 (1955)

905 Large bowl, 1958
Earthenware, slip-trailed decoration in white and brown, amber glaze; marks: 'Shelly / 1958', incised; h.6.2cm, d.40.7cm
Circ.43-1959. Source: the artist, £7.7s.

904

905

Shinners Bridge Pottery *see* Marianne de Trey

Shone, Patricia 1962–

1962	born Greenock, Scotland
1982–85	studies ceramics at Central School of Art and Design, London
1995	moves to the Isle of Skye
1998	resumes potting, sets up workshop at Ardvasar
2006	solo installation and exhibition, An Tuireann Arts Centre, Isle of Skye
2016	solo exhibition, 3Trees Ceramics, The Hague, Netherlands
2018	exhibition, *Fired Earth*, at The Scottish Gallery, Edinburgh, with Jennifer Hickey and Moyra Stewart
2020	solo exhibition, *Textures of the Land*, The Scottish Gallery, Edinburgh

Patricia Shone makes vessels with highly textured surfaces, informed by the rugged landscape of Skye and a sense of its past inhabitants. She has worked extensively in raku, and, from 2009, in wood-fired stoneware. Since 2015 she has also experimented with firing in saggars filled with combustible natural materials, within the wood-kiln.

'New Members', *CPA News*, 163 (2015)
Lindsay Oesterritter, *Mastering Kilns and Firing* (Stillwater, 2019), pp.182–4
Stephen Murfitt, *Contemporary Raku* (Ramsbury, 2022), pp.113–15

906 / 907

906 *Erosion Bowl 38 'light on a ridgeline'*, 2019
Stoneware, handbuilt, matt iron glaze interior, wood-fired; marks: 'PS', incised; h.19.2cm, d.22.5cm
C.28-2019. Source: given to the V&A as Winner of The Craft Pottery Charitable Trust Emmanuel Cooper Prize at Ceramic Art London 2019

907 *Erosion Bowl*, 2019
Stoneware, handbuilt, matt iron glaze interior, reduction-fired in a charcoal-filled saggar; marks: 'PS', incised; h.13.1cm, d.15.5cm
C.29-2019. Source: *see* **906**

Simon, Laurance 1959–

1959	born Paris
1978–79	studies English at Sorbonne Université, Paris
1982–85	studies ceramics at Camberwell School of Art and Crafts
1984	exchange, New York State College of Ceramics, Alfred University
1985–86	studies ceramics at South Glamorgan Institute of Higher Education, Cardiff
1990–94	studio in Southwark, London
1994	solo exhibition, Crafts Council Shop at the V&A
1994–2000	studio in Old Street, London
1999–2001	studio in Islington, London
2001–	studio in Kentish Town, London

Laurance Simon makes decorative handbuilt vessels and figurative sculptures, embracing elements of narrative and humour.

Laurance Simon, statement, in Bendavid and Lalumia (2017), pp.32, 41
Liz Hoggard, 'Lookout', *Crafts*, 117 (1992)
Elizabeth Esteve-Coll, 'Ways of Seeing', *CR*, 149 (1994)
Crafts Council (1995a), p.57
Carlano (2010), pp.140–1

Exhibition reviews: Emmanuel Cooper, *Crafts*, 113 (1991); Pamela Johnson, *Crafts*, 130 (1994); Will Levi Marshall, *CR*, 162 (1996); Amanda Fielding, *CR*, 177 (1999)

908

908 Candlestick, 1991
Earthenware, modelled, dry coloured glazes; h.32.2cm, d.26.8cm
C.195-1991. Source: Black Bull Gallery, London (exhibition: *Steven Keegan, Laurance Simon, Carole Windham*, 1991), £111.62

Simpson, Peter 1943–

1943	born Hillingdon, Middlesex
1959–64	studies sculpture with ceramics at Bournemouth and Poole College of Art
1965–70	teaches at Bournemouth and Poole College of Art
1970–	establishes studio in Sway, Hampshire
1970–74	teaches at Wimbledon College of Art
1974	exhibition with Gordon Baldwin (qv) at British Crafts Centre
1974–78	teaches ceramics at Bristol Polytechnic
1977–	studio in Brockenhurst, Hampshire
1979–94	teaches ceramics at Camberwell School of Art and Crafts; appointed Course Director in 1985
1994–99	Assistant Dean, School of Art and Design, University of Derby
1995–	studio in Melbourne, South Derbyshire
2000–	moves to Bristol, establishes studio
2003–	sets up studio in La Bourgeade, Champagnolles, France

Peter Simpson specialized in handbuilt, non-functional sculptural porcelain. Earlier work was inspired by organic forms such as fungi, seedpods or plants. He subsequently developed larger, more formal sculptures with totemic and ritual overtones, his work increasingly exploring the imprint of time. After 1990 he worked in mixed media and collage, returning to ceramics only occasionally.

909

910

Peter Simpson, 'Hand-built Porcelain', *CR*, 5 (1970)
— statement, in Rothschild (1972)
— statement, with text by John Dickerson, in Portsmouth City Museum and Art Gallery (1976), pp.10–11
— statement and biography, in V&A (1977), pp.9–10
— 'Subliminal Influences', *CR*, 121 (1990)
V&A (1972), p.119
Oxford Gallery (1974)
Ulster Museum (1974)
Crafts Advisory Committee (1976), p.116
Crafts Council (1980), p.63
Potters (1980)
Oxford Gallery, *Peter Simpson: Ceramics*, exh. pamphlet, text by John Russell Taylor (Oxford, 1981)
Oxfordshire County Museum Services (1984), pp.50–1
Michaelson and Orient, *Carcassonne Suite: Peter Simpson*, exh. cat. (London, 1990)
Matthew Partington, 'A Still-life Transposed', *CR*, 214 (2005)
Nottingham City Museums and Galleries (2017), p.79

Exhibition reviews: Emmanuel Cooper, *CR*, 4 (1970), and 25 (1974), and '3 in Ceramics', *Art & Artists*, 14:8 (1979); Lyn Colavecchia, *CR*, 15 (1972); J.D.H. Catleugh, *CR*, 28 (1974); Paul Clough, *Crafts*, 6 (1974); David Reeves, *Crafts*, 9 (1974), and 35 (1978); Garth Clark, 'Seven in 76', *Crafts*, 19 (1976); Geoffrey Weston, '3 in Ceramics', *Crafts*, 43 (1980); J.V.G. Mallet, *Crafts*, 104 (1990)

911

912

913

909 *Split form*, 1974
Porcelain, handbuilt, grey-brown glaze; marks: impressed device; h.15cm, d.18.4cm
Circ.484-1974. Source: British Crafts Centre, London (exhibition with Gordon Baldwin, 1974, no.40), £31.50

910 *Fungi form*, 1974
Porcelain, handbuilt, brown and yellowish matt glaze; marks: impressed device; h.14.3cm, d.40cm
Circ.485-1974. Source: *see* **909** (no.51), £40.95

911 *Open Spinner*, 1975
Porcelain, handbuilt, green-brown glaze; marks: impressed device; h.10.5cm, d.20cm
Circ.269-1975. Source: the artist, £37

912 *Small bowl form*, 1975
Porcelain, handbuilt, blue-grey glaze; marks: impressed device; h.4.7cm, d.12.1cm
Circ.286-1976. Source: the artist (from exhibition: *Seven in 76*, Portsmouth City Museum and Art Gallery, 1976), £25

913 *Fossil form*, 1975
Porcelain, handbuilt, metallic copper and white glazes; marks: impressed device; h.17.9cm, d.48cm
Circ.287-1976. Source: *see* **912**, £100

Slee, Richard 1946–

1946	born Carlisle, Cumberland
1964–65	studies at Carlisle College of Art and Design
1965–70	studies ceramics at Central School of Art and Design, London
1973–75	teaches at Hastings College of Further Education
1975–90	teaches at Harrow School of Art, Central School of Art and Design, and Brighton Polytechnic
1975–	studio in London
1980–	studio in Brighton
1986–88	degree by project, Royal College of Art, London
1990–2011	teaches at Camberwell College of Arts; Professor from 1992
1998–2008	regular exhibitions, Barrett Marsden Gallery, London
2003	solo exhibition, *Panorama*, Tate St Ives
2003	touring retrospective exhibition, The Potteries Museum and Art Gallery, Stoke-on-Trent (Crafts Council *Show 5* partnership)
2010–	represented by Hales Gallery, London and New York
2010–11	solo exhibition, *From Utility to Futility*, V&A
2014	touring solo exhibition, *Work and Play*, Tullie House, Carlisle
2020	touring solo exhibition, *Mantelpiece Observations*, Bolton Museum and Art Gallery

Richard Slee is among the most influential British ceramic artists of his generation, his finely crafted, richly conceptual work straddling the worlds of craft and contemporary art. During the 1980s Slee carved out his own niche, making work that was slick, colourful and highly glazed. Embracing Postmodern strategies of quotation and subversion, he borrowed variously from historical ceramics through to animated cartoons, creating vessels of surreal and witty character. A series of Toby jugs in the early 1990s marked a shift towards figurative or more overtly sculptural work. Slee then innovated by incorporating ready-mades in the form of found ceramic figurines, affording these works a disarming emotional resonance. He has since developed work using newly manufactured components gleaned from DIY and hardware stores.

Richard Slee, 'Richard Slee', *CR*, 79 (1983)
— 'Reinventing the Familiar', in Scott (1996), pp.63–5
— 'A Potter's Day', *CR*, 165 (1997)
— curator's foreword, in London Institute (1998), p.4
— 'What If …', *CR*, 230 (2008)
Janet Street-Porter, 'Slee Notes', *Design*, 293 (1973)
British Crafts Centre, *Richard Slee, Katherine Virgils*, exh. pamphlet, text by Richard Deacon (London, 1984)
Peter Dormer, 'Routes of Exchange', *Crafts*, 68 (1984)
Crafts Council (1985), p.79
ICA (1985), p.44
City Gallery, *Richard Slee – Recent Works*, exh. cat., text by Sean Hetterley (Leicester, 1989)
John Berry, 'Richard Slee – Craft Potter', *CR*, 125 (1990)
John Houston, *Richard Slee: Ceramics in Studio* (London, 1990)
Jeremy Myerson, 'A Test of Time', *Crafts*, 104 (1990)
John Houston, *Richard Slee*, Aberystwyth Arts Centre: Ceramic Series 46 (1991)
Paul Greenhalgh, 'Richard Slee', *Studio Pottery*, 1 (1993)
Museum of Modern Art, Oxford (1993), pp.74–5, 91–2, 95
Crafts Council (1995a), pp.52, 57–9
— (1996b), pp.26–7
Barbican Centre (1998)
Barrett Marsden Gallery, *Richard Slee: Grand Wizard of Studio Ceramics*, exh. pamphlet, text by Oliver Watson (London, 1998)
— *Richard Slee*, exh. pamphlet, text by Grayson Perry (London, 2000)
Paul Vincent, 'Slee is King!', *Studio Pottery*, 40 (2000)
Crafts Council (2001), pp.26–7, 31
Paul Vincent, 'Slee Crowned King', *Ceramic in Society*, 45 (2001)
Emma Maiden, 'A Career in Clay', *AN Magazine* (October 2002)
Tessa Peters and Janice West (eds), *The Uncanny Room*, exh. cat. (London, 2002), pp.44–57, 79
Garth Clark and Cathy Courtney, *Richard Slee* (Stoke-on-Trent/Aldershot, 2003)
Nicholas Rena, 'Wonderland', *CR*, 203 (2003)
Tate St Ives, *Richard Slee: Grand Wizard*, exh. cat., text by Oliver Watson (St Ives, 2003)
Lesley Jackson, 'Impossible to Pigeonhole', interview, *Ceramics in Society*, 57 (2004)
David Redhead, 'Hans Stofer and Richard Slee', conversation, *Crafts*, 203 (2006)
Adamson (2007), pp.134–7
Hanaor (2007), pp.60–3
Carlano (2010), pp.142–3
Amanda Fielding, 'Richard Slee: From Utility to Futility', online essay, V&A website (2010)
Veiteberg (2011), pp.112–13
Clark, Strauss and others (2012), pp.332–3, 406–7, 460
Mark Jones and Emily King, *Richard Slee: Means of Production* (London, 2014)
Teleri Lloyd-Jones, 'Play and Pessimism', interview, *Crafts*, 249 (2014)
Elderton and Morrill (2017), pp.272–3
Matthew Watson (ed.), *Mantelpiece Observations: Richard Slee*, exh. cat. (Bolton, 2020)
Thorpe (2021), pp.15–26

Exhibition reviews: Victor Margrie, *Crafts*, 102 (1990); Paul Vincent, *Studio Pottery*, 8 (1994); Alison Britton, 'Glazed Ceramics', *Crafts*, 149 (1997); Malcolm Haslam, *Crafts*, 165 (2000); Michael Wilson, *CR*, 183 (2000); Lesley Jackson, *Crafts*, 184 (2003); David Whiting, *Crafts*, 187 (2004); Emmanuel Cooper, *Crafts*, 225 (2010); Jefford Horrigan, *CR*, 257 (2012); Lesley Jackson, *Crafts*, 250 (2014); Julia Stephenson, *CR*, 270 (2014)

914 Bowl, 1971
Stoneware, press-moulded and handbuilt, ash glaze; made at Dan Arbeid's (qv) studio, Wendens Ambo, Essex; h.21.4cm, d.24.4cm
C.1-2011. Source: Jeffrey Pine, £2700
One of a series of four bowls with rims that suggest the idea of containment. The rim of

914

915

916

918

919

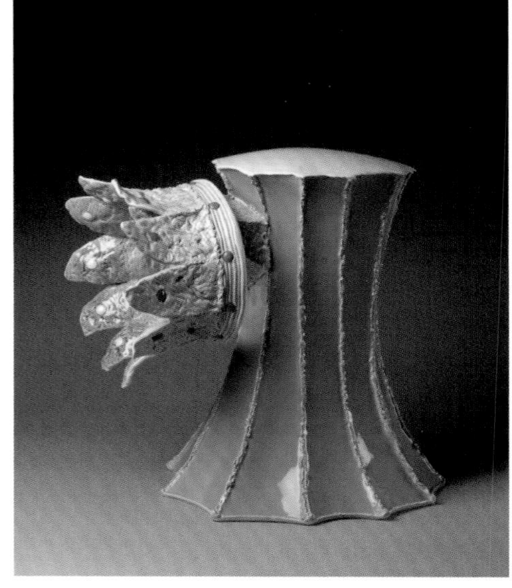
920

this bowl is formed as a picket fence, while the others are trees, a garden wall, and doors used as building-site hoardings. The materials used were those available at Arbeid's studio and contrast with Slee's later work.

915 Lidded jar, 1981
Earthenware, handbuilt, coloured glazes; marks: 'RICHARD SLEE', incised; h.26.8cm, d.27cm
C.110&A-1981. Source: the artist, £60

916 Lidded jar, *c.* 1981
Earthenware, handbuilt, coloured glazes; h.27.6cm, d.15.8cm
C.111&A-1981. Source: the artist, £60

917 *Cornucopia*, 1983 (pl.82)
Earthenware, handbuilt, coloured glazes; marks: 'RICHARD SLEE', incised; h.23.4cm, d.35.5cm
C.253-1983. Source: Craft Shop, V&A, £113.40

918 *Corral Dish*, 1984
Earthenware, handbuilt, coloured glazes; marks: 'RICHARD SLEE', incised; h.8.6cm, d.34.9cm
C.185-1984. Source: British Crafts Centre, London (exhibition with Katherine Virgils, 1984, no.5), £172.80

919 Dish, 1988
Earthenware, press-moulded, printed in black; marks: 'RICHARD SLEE', painted; h.5.2cm, d.52.5cm
C.15-1989. Source: Contemporary Applied Arts, London, £337.50
The clay body and printing technique were developed by Slee at the Royal College of Art.

920 *Crown and Anvil*, 1988
Earthenware, handbuilt, coloured glazes; marks: 'RICHARD SLEE', incised; h.39.5cm, d.37cm (anvil); h.13.6cm, d.14.3cm (crown)
C.143:1,2-1991. Source: Crafts Council, London (group retrospective exhibition, *Three Ways of Seeing*, 1990), £580.50

921 *Frond*, 1991
Earthenware, handbuilt, coloured glazes; marks: 'RICHARD SLEE', in underglaze crayon; h.54cm, d.24cm
C.233-1991. Source: Contemporary Applied Arts, London, £1113.50 (with **922**)

922 *Flower*, 1991
Earthenware, handbuilt, coloured glazes; marks: 'RICHARD SLEE', in underglaze crayon; h.58cm, d.21cm
C.234-1991. Source: *see* **921**

923 *Drunk Punch*, 1991 (fig.15)
Earthenware, handbuilt, painted in underglaze blue and on-glaze colours; marks: 'RICHARD SLEE', painted; h.52.5cm, d.50.5cm
C.15:1 to 5-1992. Source: Contemporary Applied Arts, London, £1215

924 Maquette for *Drunk Punch*, 1991
Earthenware, modelled, biscuit-fired; h.14cm, d.13.5cm
C.11:1 to 3-2000. Source: given by the artist

925 *Landscape with Hippo*, 1997
Earthenware, handbuilt, coloured glazes, found object; marks: 'RICHARD SLEE', inscribed; h.23.7cm, d.38cm
C.90-1997. Source: the artist, £300; gift of Adrian Sassoon, Esq.

926 *Siphoned Modernism*, 2001
Earthenware, handbuilt, white glaze, polythene pipe; marks: 'RICHARD / SLEE', written in blue; h.47cm, d.45.5cm
C.67-2005. Source: given by the artist
Shown in the *Jerwood Applied Arts Prize* exhibition, Crafts Council, London, 2001.

927 *Sausage*, 2006 (pl.117)
Earthenware, handbuilt, white glaze, workbench, elastic straps; marks: 'RICHARD SLEE', inscribed; h.16.5cm, d.53.3cm (sausage); h.78.4cm (workbench)
C.78:1 to 5-2007. Source: Barrett Marsden Gallery, London, £2827.66; acquired through the generosity of Gerard and Sarah Griffin

928 *Saws*, 2009
Earthenware, handbuilt, coloured glazes, found steel blades and bolts; marks: 'RICHARD SLEE', in black marker; h.16–28cm, d.53–90cm (each of ten saws)
C.2 to 11-2011. Source: Hales Gallery, London, £20,000; purchase supported by Richard Greenfield and the Covo Foundation
Shown in the exhibition *Richard Slee: From Utility to Futility*, V&A, 2010–11.

929 *Fly swat*, 2009
Plastic fly swat, glazed earthenware; h.3cm, d.47cm
C.12-2011. Source: Hales Gallery, London
Shown with *Saws* (**928**) in the exhibition *Richard Slee: From Utility to Futility*, V&A, 2010–11.

The museum also holds works by Slee in non-ceramic materials: *Spade*, 2006 (C.102-2007), and *Stadium*, 2013 (C.1-2019).

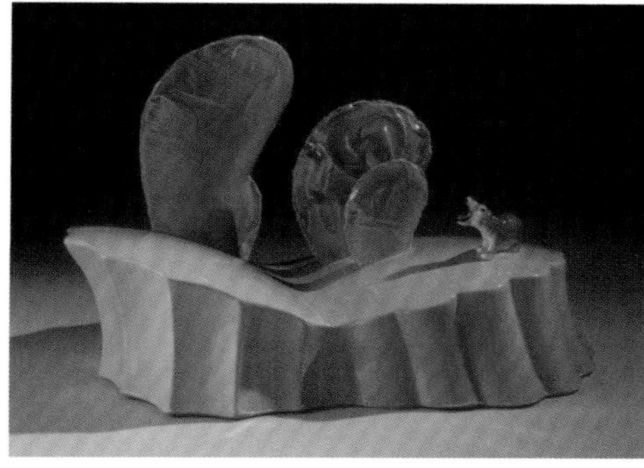
925

921 / 922

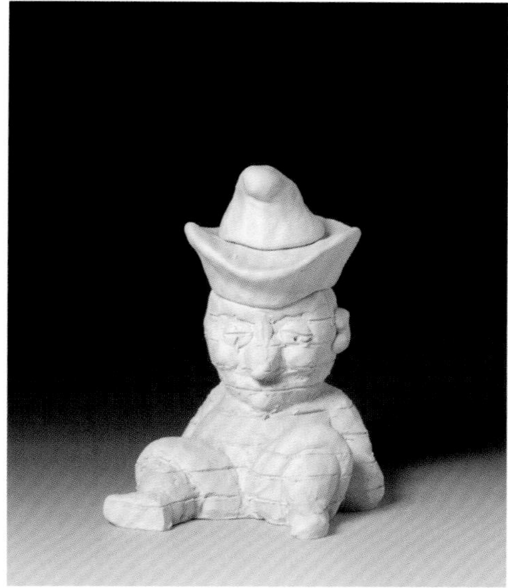
924

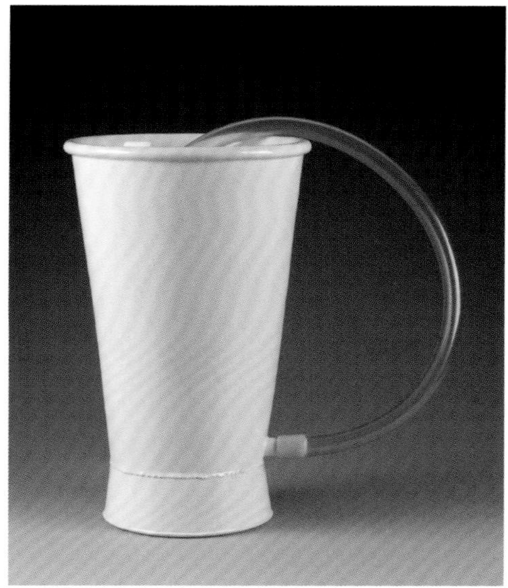
926

928

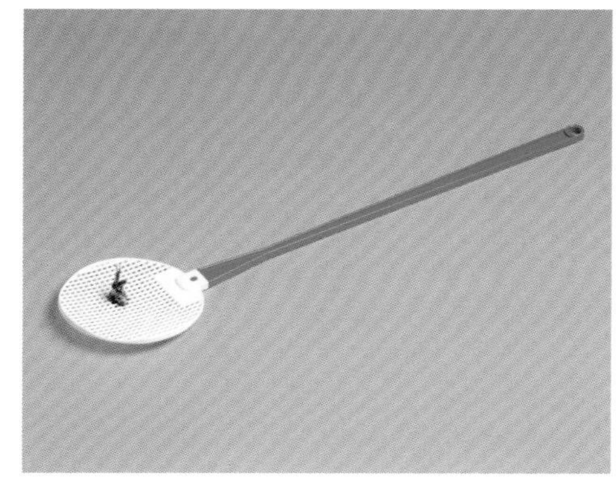
929

Smith, Martin 1950–

1950	born Braintree, Essex
1971–74	studies ceramics at Bristol Polytechnic
1974–78	workshop in Buxhall, Suffolk
1975–77	studies ceramics at Royal College of Art, London
1977–85	teaches at Loughborough College of Art and Design
1978–84	workshop in Rotherhithe, London
1978–	solo exhibition, Atmosphere, London; thereafter regular exhibitions at Galerie de Witte Voet, Amsterdam; Garth Clark Gallery, New York; and elsewhere
1980–83	teaches at Brighton Polytechnic
1981–82	touring solo exhibition, *Forms Around a Vessel*, Leeds Art Galleries
1984–2001	workshop in St John's Wood, London
1986–89	teaches ceramics at Camberwell School of Art and Crafts
1989–2018	teaches ceramics at Royal College of Art; Professor, 1999–2015; Senior Research Fellow, 2015–18
1996	shortlisted for Jerwood Prize for Applied Arts
1999–	regular solo exhibitions, Barrett Marsden (later Marsden Woo) Gallery, London
2002–	workshop in Camden, London

Martin Smith is one of the leading ceramic artists to have focused on formal, sculptural concerns, developing abstract pieces that emphasize geometry and construction, and explore space, colour, surface texture and reflected light. He gained early acclaim for his work in raku, his precise forms and controlled geometric decoration defying expectations of the technique. His subsequent work in red earthenware established his future direction, exploring the geometry of the vessel through precise, composite pieces of architectonic character, cutting, grinding and polishing elements after firing. Smith developed his ideas through successive series, extending his formal language to include wall pieces in 2007. His interest in linear and geometric pattern subsequently found expression in wall-mounted installations of printed plates in the early 2010s, and later that decade in small-scale Parian sculptures with digitally printed enamel decoration, developed through research with Steve Brown at the Royal College of Art.

Martin Smith, 'Raku Techniques', *Crafts*, 11 (1974)

— 'Forms Around a Vessel', *Ceramics Monthly*, 31:10 (1983)

— 'Revelations', *CR*, 189 (2001)

Crafts Advisory Committee (1976), p.116

Crafts Council (1980), p.63

Martina Margetts, 'Into The Red', *Crafts*, 42 (1980)

Leeds Art Galleries, *Martin Smith: Forms Around a Vessel*, exh. cat., texts by Martin Smith and Anthony Wells-Cole (1981)

'Forms Around a Vessel', *CR*, 75 (1982)

Oxfordshire County Museum Services (1984), pp.52–3

Paisley Museum and Art Galleries (1984), p.79

British Crafts Centre, *Martin Smith: New Ceramics*, exh. pamphlet, text by Anthony Wells-Cole (London, 1985)

Crafts Council (1985), p.80

Tanya Harrod, 'Martin Smith', *American Ceramics*, 5:3 (1987)

Contemporary Applied Arts, *Diversions on a Theme*, exh. pamphlet, text by Alison Britton (London, 1988)

— *Martin Smith*, exh. pamphlet (London, 1992)

Pamela Johnson, 'View from the Edge', *Crafts*, 119 (1992)

Museum of Modern Art, Oxford (1993), pp.76–7, 92, 95

Crafts Council (1996b), pp.28–9

— (1996c), pp.109, 140–1

Museum Boijmans Van Beuningen, *Martin Smith: Ceramics, Balance and Space 1976–1996*, exh. cat. (Rotterdam, 1996)

Deborah Norton, 'Perceptions and Illusions', *Studio Pottery*, 31 (1998)

Felicity Aylieff, 'Space Odyssey', *CR*, 176 (1999)

Barrett Marsden Gallery, *Martin Smith*, exh. pamphlet, text by Tessa Peters (London, 1999)

— *Martin Smith*, exh. pamphlet, text by John Pawson (London, 2001)

Tate St Ives, *Martin Smith: Wavelength*, exh. cat. (St Ives, 2001)

Carlano (2010), pp.144–5

Clark, Strauss and others (2012), pp.407, 460

Siobhan Feeney, 'The Work of Martin Smith', *Ceramics: Art and Perception*, 106 (2017)

Isabella Smith, 'Perfectly Formed', *Crafts*, 269 (2017)

Natalie Baerselman le Gros, 'Unfamiliar Forms', *CR*, 311 (2021)

Thorpe (2021), pp.123–31

Exhibition reviews: Jeremy Rees, 'Lucky Dip', *Crafts*, 10 (1974); Emmanuel Cooper, *Art & Artists*, 13:1 (1978); Richard Deacon, *Crafts*, 53 (1981); Emma Maiden, *Crafts*, 171 (2001); Julia Pitts, *CR*, 190 (2001); Shane Enright, *Crafts*, 195 (2005); Fiona Sibley, *CR*, 214 (2005); Amanda Fielding, *CR*, 230 (2008)

An interview with Martin Smith is in the Crafts Lives sound archive at the British Library, London (C960/151). Essays issued alongside exhibitions at Barrett Marsden (later Marsden Woo) Gallery, London, offer further useful texts.

930 Bowl, 1978
Raku, geometrical pattern in white glaze, unglazed areas reduced black; h.20.5cm, d.35cm
C.27-1978. Source: British Crafts Centre, London, £90

931 *Baroque Wall Piece No.1*, 1981
Red earthenware, press-moulded, cut, polished and assembled, with terra sigillata and slate; h.21cm, d.28.8cm
C.15-1982. Source: the artist (from exhibition: *Forms Around a Vessel*, Leeds Art Gallery, 1981), £500

930

931

932 Form, 1986
White earthenware, press-moulded, cut, polished and assembled, with slip and incised patterns; h.56.8cm, d.21cm
C.278-1986. Source: British Crafts Centre, London, £935

933 *Fact & Expectation No.1*, 1992 (pl.96)
Red earthenware, press-moulded, copper leaf; h.12cm, d.43.1cm
C.166-1992. Source: Contemporary Applied Arts, London (solo exhibition, 1992), £1980

934 *Presence & Absence No.2*, 1998
Red earthenware, thrown and assembled, aluminium leaf, concealed blue surfaces; h.17.3cm, d.52.5cm
C.20-1999. Source: Barrett Marsden Gallery, London, £2700

935 *Cord & Discord No.1*, 2006
White earthenware, thrown and assembled, underglaze colour and platinum leaf; h.18cm, d.57.7cm
C.1-2006. Source: gifted to the V&A as Winner of the Sotheby's Award at Collect 2006

936 *Cord & Discord No.9*, 2007
White earthenware, thrown and assembled, underglaze colour and platinum leaf; h.13.9cm, d.57.3cm
C.11-2009. Source: given by the artist

937 *Serial Dialogue in Fifteen Parts*, 2007 (pl.129)
Earthenware, press-moulded and polished, platinum leaf; h.101.5cm, w.170.5cm, d.6cm
C.20:1 to 15-2008. Source: Barrett Marsden Gallery, London (solo exhibition: *Wall Works*, 2007), £23,563.83; purchased with the support of Art Fund

932

934

935

936

Smith, Matt 1971–

1971	born Cambridgeshire
1996–98	undertakes Museum Studies at University of Leicester
2003–05	studies ceramics at City Lit, London
2005–06	studies ceramics at University of Westminster
2006–18	studio in Hove, East Sussex
2009–15	jointly founds Unravelled Arts, commissioning artists to respond to historic houses
2010–11	solo exhibition, *Queering the Museum*, Birmingham Museum and Art Gallery
2015–16	ceramics residency, V&A
2016	awarded practice-based PhD, University of Brighton: *Making Things Perfectly Queer: Art's Use of Craft to Signify LGBT Identities*
2016–22	teaches at Konstfack, Stockholm; appointed Professor of Craft in 2017
2018	solo exhibition, *Flux: Parian Unpacked*, The Fitzwilliam Museum, Cambridge
2018–	new studios in Hove and in Graiguenamanagh, Ireland

Working as both artist and curator, and often through interventions in museums and historic houses, Matt Smith questions dominant historical and institutional narratives, and seeks to give space to marginalized viewpoints and identities. His studio practice in ceramics often takes the form of bricolage, using processes of appropriation, juxtaposition and reinterpretation.

Matt Smith, 'The Art of Unravelling the Past', *Engage: The International Journal of Visual Art and Gallery Education*, 31 (2012)
— 'On Histories and Hierarchies', interview by Teleri Lloyd-Jones, *Crafts*, 253 (2015)
— 'Queering the Museum', in Brown, Stair and Twomey (2016), pp.196–208, reprinted in Livingstone and Petrie (2017), pp.363–72
— 'Queering the Historic House', in Brent Pilkey, Rachael M. Scicluna, Ben Campkin and Barbara Penner (eds), *Sexuality and Gender at Home* (London, 2017)
— *Losing Venus*, exh. cat. (2020)
— 'Remolding the Museum: In Residence at the V&A', in Joshua Adair and Amy Levin (eds), *Museums, Sexuality and Gender Activism* (London, 2020)
— **and Catherine Flood**, 'Disobedient Curating', *Art Journal*, 76:3–4 (2017)
— **and Richard Sandell**, 'Bringing Queer Home', in Richard Sandell, Rachael Lennon and Matt Smith (eds), *Prejudice and Pride: LGBTQ Heritage and its Contemporary Implications* (Leicester, 2018)

939 / 940

Unravelled Arts, *Unravelling The Manor House*, exh. cat. (2010), pp.7–11, 32–3
Garcia (2012), pp.100–1
The Stanley and Audrey Burton Gallery, *Other Stories: Queering the University Art Collection*, exh. cat. (Leeds, 2012)
Unravelled Arts, *Unravelling Nymans*, exh. cat. (2012), pp.8–13, 38–9
— *Unravelling The Vyne*, exh. cat. (2013), pp.4–6, 40–1
— *Unravelling Uppark*, exh. cat. (2014), pp.4–10, 44–5
Janet Marstine, *Critical Practice: Artists, Museums, Ethics* (Abingdon, 2017), pp.83–118
Fitzwilliam Museum, *Flux: Parian Unpacked*, exh. cat. (Cambridge, 2018)
Imogen Greenhalgh, 'Remaking the Museum', *Crafts*, 271 (2018)
Priya Khanchandani, exh. review, *Crafts*, 272 (2018)

938 *Wunderkammer 2*, 2017 (pl.145)
Black Parian porcelain, slip-cast and assembled; h.30.9cm, d.19.5cm
C.425-2017. Source: Cynthia Corbett Gallery at Collect 2017, £1600; purchase funded by the Friends of the V&A

Smith, Peter 1941–

1941	born Bristol
1960s	works as research chemist specializing in high-temperature chemistry, following study at University of London
1967–72	attends pottery evening classes at Chaucer Institute, London, under Robert Fournier
1973–	establishes pottery at Higher Bojewyan, Cornwall
1983–87	teaches part-time at Cornwall College of Further Education
1987–2002	teaches part-time at Falmouth College of Arts

Peter Smith's work reflects an intense engagement with materials and processes. He remains best known for the freely thrown, slip-decorated domestic earthenware that he developed in the first decade after establishing Bojewyan Pottery, firing it in a coal-burning kiln. From the mid-1980s he produced sculptural pieces in unfired clay stabilized with cement, applying paint as a glaze substitute and attaching ready-made handles. He later created mixed-media assemblages with factory- and self-made ceramic elements, and has continued to reinterpret his functional earthenware in sculptural ways.

Peter Smith, 'Reduced Glazes in Electric Kilns', *CR*, 24 (1973), and 25 (1974)
— 'Controlled Uncontrol', *Artists Newsletter* (September 1984)
— 'Iron Oxides', *CR*, 96 (1985)
— *Peter Smith*, Aberystwyth Arts Centre: Ceramic Series 13 (1985)
— 'A Visit to California', *CPA Newsletter* (1987)
— 'Fired with Coal', *CR*, 130 (1991)
— 'Bonfire Brilliance', *CR*, 163 (1997)
— 'The First Leach Climbing Kiln', *The Log Book*, 47 (2011), and 68 (2016)
— 'Vapour Production in the Wood Burning Kiln', *The Log Book*, 54 (2013)
'CPA New Members', *CR*, 64 (1980)
Potters/The Ceramics Book (1980) to (1994), (2006), (2008), (2012)
Isabelle Anscombe, 'Put It on the Table', *Crafts*, 56 (1982)
John Christian, 'A Marriage of Art and Science', *CR*, 266 (2014)

939 Dish, 1981
Earthenware, slab-built, slip and glaze; marks: 'PS' in monogram and two seals, impressed; h.5cm, d.29.4cm
C.177-1981. Source: Craftsmen Potters Association, London (exhibition with Sarah Walton, and Andrew and Joanna Young, 1981, no.29), £21

940 Jug, 1981
Earthenware, slip decoration; marks: 'PS' in monogram and two seals, applied; h.29.6cm, d.20.2cm
C.178-1981. Source: *see* **939** (no.59), £20

Solly, John 1928–2004

1928	born Maidstone, Kent
1943–49	studies pottery and sculpture at Maidstone School of Art under Percy Brown and Gwilym Thomas (qv); work experience at Rye Pottery, Sussex, in summer 1949
1946–48	National Service in Royal Air Force
1950–51	studies letter cutting part-time at Camberwell School of Arts and Crafts, alongside pottery at Central School of Art, London, under Dora Billington (qv)
1951	works at Winchcombe Pottery during summer; sets up workshop at parents' home; begins part-time teaching at Medway School of Art and elsewhere
1953–	establishes workshop and showroom in former basket factory, Maidstone
1960–	runs summer schools at his pottery
1965–68	teaches repetition throwing at Harrow School of Art
1986–	moves to Peasmarsh, East Sussex; largely abandons repetition production in favour of individual pieces

John Solly was a respected potter and teacher, whose well-made functional slipwares brought a contemporary sensibility to the medium. He was among the first to run summer courses, which proved highly successful, at his pottery. He continued potting until shortly before his death.

John Solly, 'The First Five Years', *Pottery Quarterly*, 6:23 (1959)
— 'Why I Make Earthenware', *CR*, 5 (1970)
— 'Slipware Potter', *CR*, 166 (1997)
'Modern and Practical Tableware – from a Kentish Pottery', *Pottery and Glass* (May 1954)
Lewis (1956), pls.352–3
'A Kentish Potter', *Pottery Gazette and Glass Trade Review* (May 1958)
'John Solly – Potter', *Kent Life* (December 1963)
Casson (1967), p.8, pls.234–5
Potters (1972) to (2000)
Crafts Advisory Committee (1976), p.117
Crafts Council (1980), p.63
Emmanuel Cooper, obituary, *The Independent* (17 August 2004)

941 Teapot, 1951
Earthenware, calligraphic decoration incised through a dark slip; marks: 'WJS', painted in blue; h.10.3cm, d.18.7cm
C.126:1,2-2006. Source: given by Clare Purves and Jackie Solly

942 Mug, *c.* 1953–55
Red earthenware, trailed slip decoration; marks: 'JOHN / SOLLY' enclosed by 'MAIDSTONE / KENT', impressed; h.11.4cm, d.13.5cm
C.127-2006. Source: *see* **941**

943 Tea set, *c.* 1953
Red earthenware, trailed decoration over buff and dark brown slips; marks: 'JOHN / SOLLY' enclosed by 'MAIDSTONE / KENT', stamped; h.11cm, d.17.4cm (teapot); h.6.9cm, d.8.5cm (sugar bowl); h.7cm (cup); d.13.5cm (saucer); d.23.8cm (plate); d.17.1cm (tea plate)
C.128:1,2, 129, 130:1,2, 131 & 132-2006. Source: *see* **941**

944 Plate, 1975
Red earthenware, trailed decoration on white slip under a honey glaze; marks: 'John Solly / 1975', incised; h.2.7cm, d.19.5cm
C.133-2006. Source: *see* **941**

945 Plate, *c.* 1975–86
Red earthenware, slip decoration in turquoise, blue and white; marks: 'JOHN / SOLLY' enclosed by 'MAIDSTONE / KENT', impressed; h.2.4cm, d.19.7cm
C.134-2006. Source: *see* **941**

Spindler, Frank *see under* Odney Pottery

Spira, Rupert 1960–

1960	born London
1978–80	studies ceramics at West Surrey College of Art and Design, Farnham, under Henry Hammond (qv)
1980–82	trains with Michael Cardew (qv) at Wenford Bridge
1984–	establishes workshop at Lower Froyle, Hampshire
1988–	sets up tilemaking workshop
1992	tile commission for 100 New Bridge Street, City of London
1996–	establishes workshop at More, Shropshire
2003	fire destroys workshop
2003–04	touring solo exhibition, Japan
2004	major solo exhibition, Sainsbury Centre for Visual Arts, Norwich, Norfolk
2013	closes workshop

At first enriched by the earthier traditions of the studio pottery movement, Rupert Spira gradually evolved his own refined and minimalist style. Alongside potters such as Julian Stair (qv) and Edmund de Waal (qv), he played a part in the resurgence of throwing, making functional wares and individual pieces, often employing luminous monochrome glazes. A master of the quiet and contemplative, he became increasingly concerned with bowl forms, as well as the integration of text into his work, inscribing or embossing poems by the poet Kathleen Raine, the poet and mystic Rumi, or himself. He has since ceased potting, turning instead to writing and spiritual teaching.

Rupert Spira, 'Idealism, Enthusiasm and Realism', *CR*, 137 (1992)
— 'A Potter's Day', *CR*, 153 (1995)
Amy Shelton, 'Rupert Spira', *Studio Pottery*, 12 (1994)
Potters (1997)
Oxford Gallery, *Rupert Spira*, exh. pamphlet (Oxford, 1998)
Frankel (2000), pp.204–21
Setagaya Art Museum, *Rupert Spira: Ceramics*, exh. cat. (Tokyo, 2003)
Emmanuel Cooper, 'Signature Pieces', *CR*, 208 (2004)
Ruthin Craft Centre (2004), pp.62–5, 71
Sainsbury Centre for Visual Arts, *Rupert Spira: Bowl*, exh. cat. (Norwich, 2004)
Pearson (2005), p.212
Carlano (2010), pp.146–9
Andy Christian, 'Finding the Words', *CR*, 273 (2015)
Teleri Lloyd-Jones, 'Rupert Spira', *Crafts*, 254 (2015)

941

942

943

944 / 945

946

Oxford Ceramics Gallery, *Rupert Spira: A Life in Ceramics*, exh. cat., texts by Caroline Seymour and Rupert Spira (Oxford, 2015)

Exhibition reviews: Robert Silver, *Studio Pottery*, 10 (1994); Margot Coatts, *Crafts*, 143 (1996); Lionel Phillips, *Studio Pottery*, 21 (1996); Julia Pitts, *CR*, 178 (1999); David Whiting, 'Contemporary Pots', *Crafts*, 156 (1999); Emma Maiden, *Crafts*, 191 (2004); Giles Sutherland, *CR*, 229 (2008)

946 *Poem Bowl*, 2003
Stoneware, text incised through black pigment over a white glaze; marks: 'RS', impressed seal; h.20.9cm, d.53.7cm
C.24-2005. Source: the artist, £2587.23; purchase funded by Anthony Weldon
The inscribed poem was written by Spira.

Spragg, Katie 1987–

1987	born Reading, Berkshire
2006–07	foundation course, Camberwell College of Arts
2007–10	studies 3D Materials Practice, University of Brighton, specializing in ceramics and plastics
2011–13	studio in Battersea, London, producing commercially focused work
2012	residency at Guldagergaard International Ceramic Research Center, Denmark
2013–17	studio at Iliffe Yard, Southwark, London
2014–16	studies ceramics at Royal College of Art, London
2016	residency at Scottish Sculpture Workshop, Aberdeenshire
2016–17	forms Collective Matter artist group with Eva Masterman and Mary O'Malley; together run community engagement project with Tate Exchange
2017–	with Collective Matter sets up studio with public engagement space at Sugarhouse Studios, Bermondsey, London
2018	solo exhibition, Blackwell, The Arts and Crafts House, and Abbot Hall Art Gallery, Cumbria
2018	solo exhibition, *Glasshouses*, Garden Museum, London

Katie Spragg creates immersive environments in clay, sometimes in combination with animation.

947

These range from boxed works containing landscapes in miniature to larger installations. Informed by detailed botanical study, her work offers a commentary on our experience of nature and its place in an environment increasingly shaped by humans.

Grant Gibson, 'Back to the Land', *Crafts*, 262 (2016)
Scottish Gallery, *A Natural Selection*, exh. cat. (Edinburgh, 2019)

947 Peephole box: *Hedgerow*, 2017
Hand-modelled porcelain, fumed oak, glass, plastic, battery-powered LEDs, switch; made at Iliffe Yard, London; box made by Geoffrey Hagger; h.29.2cm, d.28.7cm
C.424-2017. Source: Flow Gallery at Collect 2017 (solo spotlight display), £3300
One of three boxed works representing hedgerow, forest and meadow, based on observations made during a residency at the Scottish Sculpture Workshop in September 2016. The box form with viewfinder recalls kinetoscopes and stereoscopic viewers.

Stair, Julian 1955–

1955	born Bristol
1974–78	studies ceramics at Camberwell School of Art and Crafts
1975–76	works with Scott Marshall, Boscean Pottery, Cornwall
1978–81	studies ceramics at Royal College of Art, London
1981–85	studio at 401½ Workshops, Lambeth
1985–95	studio at Arlingford Studios, Brixton, shared with Sara Radstone (qv)
1987–98	teaches part-time at Roehampton Institute of Higher Education
1995–2006	studio at Vanguard Court, Camberwell, London, shared with Edmund de Waal (qv)
1998–99	Fellow in Craft and Criticism, University of Northumbria
2002	awarded PhD, Royal College of Art: *Critical Writing on English Studio Pottery 1910–1940*
2002–11	Senior Research Fellow, Camberwell College of Arts
2007–	studio in East Dulwich, London
2008	joins Cape Farewell (an arts organization that promotes cultural responses to climate change) expedition to Greenland
2012–14	solo exhibition, *Quietus*, mima, Middlesbrough, and tour

2012–14 Principal Research Fellow, University of Westminster

Julian Stair is a leading figure in contemporary British craft. A potter and writer, he has asserted the importance of function, of the haptic, and of the role of the body in relation to craft objects. As a researcher, he has investigated the early years of studio pottery, exploring its origins and critical reception. As an artist, he has played a key role in the revitalization of thrown ceramics. In the 1980s he made individual pots in porcelain with inlaid decoration, and later in red earthenware. Stair developed a focused interest in tableware by 1990, working in porcelain and fine red stoneware, and later also in a distinctive, muted stoneware palette. In 2001 he began elevating pieces by placing them on ceramic 'grounds'. Preoccupied also by the containment of the body after death, Stair embarked in the 2000s on a series of cinerary urns, monumental jars and sarcophagi: a tour de force of making by an individual artist.

Julian Stair, 'New Ceramicists', *Crafts*, 59 (1982)
— 'New Directions', *CR*, 104 (1987)
— 'Language Difficulties', comment, *Crafts*, 92 (1988)
— 'White Porcelain Tablewares', *Studio Pottery*, 18 (1995)
— 'Studio Ceramics: Ghetto or Ghetto Mentality', in Harrod (1997), pp.157–62
— 'A Sense of Place', *CR*, 191 (2001)
— 'Re-inventing the wheel – The Origins of Studio Pottery', in Paul Greenhalgh (ed.), *The Persistence of Craft* (London, 2002), pp.49–60
— 'Hybridity, Interpretation and Consumption: New Ceramics and Glass in Britain Today', in WCC-BF (2010), p.20
— *Julian Stair* (London, 2010)
— 'From Precepts to Praxis: The Origins of British Studio Pottery', in Adamson, Droth and Olding (2017), pp.29–55
— 'The Spark that Ignited the Flame: Hamada Shōji, Paterson's Gallery, and the Birth of English Studio Pottery', in Meghen Jones and Louise Allison Cort (eds), *Ceramics and Modernity in Japan* (Abingdon, 2020), pp.109–27
— (ed.) *The Body Politic: The Role of the Body and Contemporary Craft*, conference papers, introduction by Julian Stair (London: Crafts Council, 2000)
Brown, Stair and Twomey (2016)
Crafts Council (1985), p.81
Cooper (1990)
Craftspace Touring (1993)
Edmund de Waal, 'Personal Possession', *CR*, 163 (1997)
Shillam + Smith 3, *English Urban, American Rural*, exh. cat. (London, 1997)
Windsor (1997)
Rob Barnard, 'Julian Stair and Edmund de Waal', interview, *Ceramics: Art and Perception*, 38 (1999)
Pamela Johnson, 'Fellow to Fellow', *Crafts*, 159 (1999) – and letter from Stair in reply, *Crafts*, 160 (1999)
Shipley Art Gallery, *Hand to Hand: Ceramics by Julian Stair Painted by Eileen Cooper*, exh. cat. (Gateshead, 1999)
V&A (1999)
Claire Wilcox, 'English Urban, American Rural', *Ceramics Monthly*, 47:6 (1999)
Frankel (2000), pp.156–63
Emmanuel Cooper, 'Julian Stair's Urban Rituals', *Ceramics: Art and Perception*, 45 (2001)
Sarah Howell, 'Please Touch', *World of Interiors*, 21:9 (2001)
David Whiting, 'Movable Feasts', *Crafts*, 171 (2001)
Ruthin Craft Centre (2006), pp.56–9, 78
Carlano (2010), pp.150–1
Scottish Gallery, *Julian Stair: Ceramics*, exh. cat., text by Marina Vaizey (Edinburgh, 2010)
Marina Vaizey, 'Absorbing and Inescapable Presences', *CR*, 245 (2010)
Emma Crichton-Miller, 'Stair's Way to Heaven', *Crafts*, 237 (2012)
mima, *Julian Stair: Quietus: The Vessel, Death and the Human Body*, exh. cat. (Middlesbrough, 2012)
Nicole Mueller, 'Julian Stair and his Vessels', *New Ceramics*, 6 (2012)
Nigel Atkins, 'Julian Stair: Retour à l'essentiel', *Revue de la Céramique et du Verre*, 193 (2013)
Michael Tooby, 'Life and its End', *CR*, 267 (2014)
— (ed.), *Julian Stair: Quietus Reviewed: Archaeology of an Exhibition* (Bath, 2013)
'Table Manners', *Crafts*, 252 (2015)
Oxford Ceramics Gallery, *Re-naturing the Vessel: Julian Stair and Simone ten Hompel*, exh. pamphlet (Oxford, 2016)
Corvi-Mora, *Julian Stair: Equivalence*, exh. cat. (London, 2018)
Thormann (2018)
Roland Held, 'The Multivalence of Utility Ceramics', *Art Aurea*, 37 (2019)
Inner Lives: Cinerary Jars, published in conjunction with an exhibition at the Branch Museum, Richmond, Virginia (2020)

Exhibition reviews: Peter Dormer, *Crafts*, 70 (1984); Jane Warren Larson, *Ceramics Monthly*, 36:6 (1988); Paul Vincent, *Studio Pottery*, 23 (1996), and 28 (1997); Emmanuel Cooper, *Crafts*, 149 (1997); David Whiting, 'The New White', *Crafts*, 160 (1999); Amanda Fielding, CR, 181 (2000); Shane Enright, *Crafts*, 238 (2012); Stephen Knott, *Ceramics: Art and Perception*, 101 (2015)

An interview with Julian Stair is in the Crafts Lives sound archive at the British Library, London (C960/122).

948 Vase, 1984
Porcelain, incised and inlaid; marks: 'JS' in a circle, impressed; h.26.8cm, d.20.3cm
C.122-1984. Source: Oxford Gallery, Oxford, £213.30

949 Cup and saucer, 1992
Porcelain, blue glaze with sgraffito; marks: 'JS', impressed; h.7.7cm (cup), d.15.5cm (saucer)
C.14:1,2-2014. Source: acquired from the artist's collection

950 Place setting: dinner plate, side plate and bowl, 1993
Porcelain, copper and manganese underglaze decoration; marks: 'JS', impressed; d.25.9cm (dinner plate); d.20.6cm (side plate); h.6.7cm, d.16.5cm (bowl)
C.1 to 3-2014. Source: *see* **949**
Shown in the Craftspace Touring exhibition *High Table*, 1993, and the British Council touring exhibition *Dish of the Day*, 1997.

951 Cup and saucer, *c.* 1997
Porcelain, copper and manganese underglaze decoration; marks: 'JS', impressed (saucer); h.7.5cm (cup), d.15.1cm (saucer)
C.4:1,2-2014. Source: *see* **949**

952 Coffee cup and saucer, 1994
Red stoneware, grey glaze to interior and

948

949

950 / 951

953 / 952 / 955 / 954

956

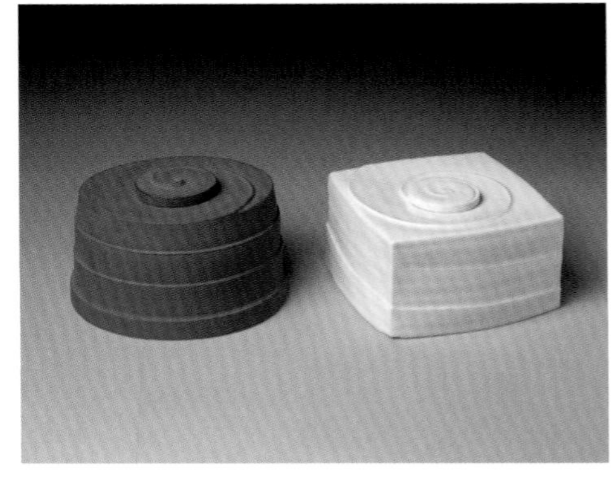
958 / 957

959

within footring; marks: 'JS', impressed (saucer); h.8.5cm (cup), d.15.3cm (saucer)
C.12-2014. Source: *see* **949**

953 Coffee pot, 1996
Red stoneware, faceted, clear glaze to interior and underside of lid, and within footring; marks: 'JS', impressed; h.20.3cm, d.20cm
C.11:1,2-2014. Source: *see* **949**

954 Teapot, 1996
Red stoneware, faceted, grey glaze to interior and underside of lid; marks: 'JS', impressed; h.19.9cm, d.18.9cm
C.13:1,2-2014. Source: *see* **949**

955 Jug, 1996
Porcelain, faceted; marks: 'JS', impressed; h.15.1cm, d.12.9cm
C.10-2014. Source: *see* **949**

956 Place setting: dinner plate, side plate, bowl, beaker, can and saucer, 1998
Porcelain, or red stoneware, with grey glaze within footring and to can interior; marks: 'JS', impressed; d.27.3cm (dinner plate); d.19.1cm (side plate); h.4.7cm, d.10.8cm (bowl); h.12.4cm (beaker); h.4.9cm (can); d.13.2cm (saucer)
C.5 to 8 & 9:1,2-2014. Source: *see* **949**
Shown in solo exhibition, Ingleby Gallery, Edinburgh, 1998.

957 Cinerary jar, 1999
Porcelain, thrown and constructed, semi-transparent glaze; marks: 'JS', impressed; h.9.4cm, d.17.5cm
C.15:1,2-2000. Source: the artist (from exhibition: *The New White: Contemporary Studio Porcelain*, V&A, 1999), £350; gift of Adrian Sassoon, Esq.

958 Cinerary jar, 2000
Red stoneware, thrown and constructed, black glazed interior; marks: 'JS', impressed; h.11.1cm, d.18.5cm
C.16:1,2-2000. Source: the artist, £350; gift of Adrian Sassoon, Esq.
Made as a companion to **957**.

959 Teapot and six cups, 2007
Basalt and stoneware, wisteria handle; marks: 'JS', impressed; h.21.2cm, d.15.9cm (teapot); h.6.4cm, d.7.7cm (tallest cup); h.4.8cm, d.27.4cm ('ground')
C.66:1 to 11-2008. Source: The Scottish Gallery at Collect 2008, £2748.94; gift of Nicholas and Judith Goodison through Art Fund

960 *Infant Sarcophagus I*, 2011
Reduced stoneware, wood, lead; made in Stair's studio, London, fired at Ibstock's Atlas factory, Walsall, West Midlands; h.20cm, d.84cm
C.194:1,2-2014. Source: the artist, £8750; acquired through the generosity of Gerard and Sarah Griffin
Shown with **961** to **964** in the solo exhibition *Quietus: The Vessel, Death and the Human Body*, mima, Middlesbrough, 2012, and tour.

961 *Floating Cinerary Jar I*, 2011–12
Red stoneware, thrown and squared, Venetian plaster ground; marks: 'JS', impressed; h.15.5cm (jar); h.40.5cm, d.40.5cm ('ground')
C.195:1 to 3-2014. Source: *see* **960**, £3437.50

962 *Floating Cinerary Jar V*, 2011–12
Porcelain, thrown and squared, Venetian plaster ground; marks: 'JS', impressed; h.21.2cm, d.17cm (jar); h.40.5cm, d.40.5cm ('ground')
C.196:1 to 3-2014. Source: *see* **960**, £3437.50

963 *Floating Cinerary Jar VI*, 2011–12
Reduced stoneware, Venetian plaster ground;

960

961

marks: 'JS', impressed; h.20.3cm, d.18.5cm (jar); h.40.5cm, d.40.5cm ('ground')
C.197:1 to 3-2014. Source: *see* **960**, £3437.50
This plaster ground was originally shown with Stair's *Cinerary Jar II*.

964 *Monumental Jar IX*, 2012 (pl.126)
Red stoneware, coiled and thrown; made at Ibstock's Cattybrook factory, Bristol; h.174cm, d.91cm
C.193:1,2-2014. Source: *see* **960**, £21,250

Standige, Gary 1946–2016

1946	born Blackpool, Lancashire
1964–67	studies ceramics at Stoke-on-Trent College of Art
1967–70	studies ceramics at Royal College of Art, London
1970	scholarship to study computer-aided art and design in USA and Canada
1972–74	teaches ceramics at Southend College of Technology
1974–81	teaches ceramics full-time at Medway College of Design, Kent
1976–81	workshop in Charing, Kent
1980	exhibition with Jane Hamlyn (qv) and Jim Malone (qv), Craftsmen Potters Association, London
1981–89	workshop in Aylesford, Kent
1981–89	teaches ceramics at West Surrey College of Art and Design, Farnham
1995–	workshop in Lindale, Cumbria

962 / 963

Gary Standige produced individual work in stoneware and porcelain, responding to Chinese and Korean sources. Later work reflected his interests in geometry and science, and he employed computer technology for modelling and drawing alongside traditional ceramic techniques.

'CPA New Members', *CR*, 51 (1978)
Potters/The Ceramics Book (1980) to (1989), (2012)
Catherine Miller, exh. review, *Crafts*, 49 (1981)

965 Lidded jar, 1980
Porcelain, cut sides, incised decoration, yellow ash glaze; marks: 'GS' in monogram, impressed; h.16cm, d.15.2cm
C.184&A-1980. Source: Craftsmen Potters Association, London (exhibition with Jane Hamlyn and Jim Malone, 1980, no.177), £30

Starkey, Peter 1945–

1945	born Widnes, Lancashire
1963–65	studies fine art at Portsmouth College of Art
1967–70	teacher training at Cardiff College of Education
1971–73	Studio Pottery Course at Harrow School of Art
1973–75	establishes Hunworth Pottery, Norfolk, making saltglaze
1975–79	first manager of Dartington Pottery Training Workshop, Devon
1979–2003	teaches ceramics at University of Wales Institute, Cardiff
1985–	workshop at Whitchurch, Herefordshire

Peter Starkey was a leader in the revival of saltglaze in studio pottery. He also played a significant role in the establishment of the Dartington Pottery Training Workshop (*see* Dart Pottery). His own work comprised domestic ware and individual pieces of robust, functional character.

Peter Starkey, 'Cameras and Craftsmen', *Crafts*, 15 (1975)
— interview, in Cameron and Lewis (1976), pp.136–43, 167
— *Saltglaze* (London, 1977)
— *Songs in Salt: New Lines in British Saltglaze*, exh. cat. (Leeuwarden: Keramiekmuseum het Princessehof, 1997)
'CPA New Members', *CR*, 31 (1975)
Potters/The Ceramics Book (1975) to (1989), (2008), (2012)
Crafts Advisory Committee (1977), p.21
Crafts Council (1980), p.63
— (1985), p.81
Whiting (1993), p.74
Cochrane (2001), pp.67–8
Nottingham City Museums and Galleries (2017), p.80

965

966

Exhibition reviews: Emmanuel Cooper, *Crafts*, 16 (1975); Paul Barron, *Crafts*, 36 (1979)

966 Lidded jar, *c.* 1970
Stoneware, brown saltglaze; h.29.5cm, d.22.1cm
C.18:1,2-1991. Source: the artist, £200
Illustrated in Starkey (1977), pp.72, 77.

Stofer, Hans 1957–

1957	born Baden, Switzerland
1972–76	trains as precision engineer and toolmaker, Brown Boveri Technical College, Baden
1981–84	studies jewellery and design, Zurich School of Art
1987–	moves to London
1994–99	teaches silversmithing and metalwork, Camberwell College of Arts
1999–2017	teaches at Royal College of Art, London; Professor of Goldsmithing, Silversmithing, Metalwork and Jewellery from 2006
2017–	Professor of Jewellery, Burg Giebichenstein University of Art and Design Halle, Germany; divides time between London and Halle

Hans Stofer is a progressive figure in jewellery and metalwork, his witty and surreal works exploring ideas of function, design and the domestic. He is particularly associated with the use of found objects, re-presenting seemingly mundane and sometimes fragmentary items in surprising and thought-provoking ways. His frequent appropriation of ceramics has given his work an importance within ceramic practice. Items or shards of domestic pottery are framed within wire structures to form new objects, or manipulated and reconstructed in ways that reflect specific narratives.

Marcus Field, 'Lookout', *Crafts*, 132 (1995)
Lesley Jackson, 'Mind Games', *Crafts*, 170 (2001)
Tessa Peters and Janice West (eds), *The Uncanny Room*, exh. cat. (London, 2002), pp.48–51, 80
Crafts Council, *Jerwood Applied Arts Prize 2005: Metal*, exh. cat. (London, 2005)
Lesley Jackson, 'Pieces of Eight', *Crafts*, 196 (2005)
Galerie S O, *Hans Stofer's Design Wilderness*, exh. cat., text by Linda Sandino (Solothurn, 2006)
David Redhead, 'Hans Stofer and Richard Slee', conversation, *Crafts*, 203 (2006)
Hanaor (2007), pp.180–1
Sarah Weir, 'Top Ten', *Crafts*, 206 (2007)
Veiteberg (2011), pp.122–3
Teleri Lloyd-Jones, 'How Long is a Piece of String?', *Crafts*, 247 (2014)

Exhibition reviews: Ralph Turner, *Crafts*, 161 (1999); Jivan Astfalck, *Crafts*, 168 (2001); David Whiting, 'Breakers', *Crafts*, 202 (2006); Fiona Rattray, *Crafts*, 224 (2010)

967 *Jane'scupreallybadlygluedtogether*, 2004
Broken bone-china cup and saucer, reassembled; marks: 'hans 03/4', engraved; h.7cm, d.8.2cm (cup); d.13.7cm (saucer)
C.79:1,2-2007. Source: Barrett Marsden Gallery, London, £1049.63; acquired through the generosity of Gerard and Sarah Griffin

968 *Robin Day*, 2006 (pl.118)
Porcelain bowl, gold leaf, removeable porcelain figure, steel, magnets; h.14.2cm, d.23.8cm
C.80:1,2-2007. Source: *see* **967**, £1949.31

969 *Espresso set*, 2007
Found ceramic, metal and plastic objects, altered and gilded; marks: 'HANS.STOFER', stamped (metal spoons); h.5.5cm, d.5.9cm (cups); d.10.4cm (saucers); l.11.1cm (metal spoons); h.7.8cm, d.8.5cm (jug); h.4.9cm, d.8cm (bowl); l.11.6cm (plastic spoon)
C.74:1 to 22-2007. Source: Galerie S O at Collect 2007, £1350
Stofer made this set for his own use, but showed it at Collect 'as a prototype for future work that looked at the notion of "art applied"'.

967

Stokes, Ann (née Mellis) 1922–2014

1922	born Gullane, East Lothian
1940–41	lives in St Ives; trains as a ballet dancer
1947	marries writer and painter Adrian Stokes
1956–	moves to Church Row, Hampstead, London
1957–	learns to pot with Christopher Magarshack at Well Walk Pottery, Hampstead; constructs pottery wheel at Church Row
1962	buys first pottery kiln
1967–2004	annual pre-Christmas sales at Church Row
1973–	divides time between Hampstead and Cortona, Italy

After leaving school, Ann Stokes lived in St Ives with her sister, the painter Margaret Mellis, there becoming friendly with the artists Ben Nicholson, Barbara Hepworth, Naum Gabo and Adrian Stokes, the last of whom she later married. She was an inventive and largely self-taught potter. Her output consisted of earthenware plates and tableware with painterly decoration, and modelled sculptural pieces of animal form, sometimes combining clay with fretwork.

Tanya Harrod, 'Lyrical Touch', *Crafts*, 77 (1985)
Hayward Gallery, *A Journey through Contemporary Art*

969

971 / 970

972

with Nigel Greenwood: The Hayward Annual 1985 (London, 1985)
Rebecca Hossack Gallery, *Ann Stokes: A Retrospective*, exh. pamphlet, text by John Golding (London, 1998)
Tanya Harrod (ed.), *Ann Stokes: Artists' Potter* (Farnham, 2009)
— obituary, *The Guardian* (14 May 2014)

An interview with Ann Stokes is in the Crafts Lives sound archive at the British Library, London (C960/13).

970 Plate, 1988
Red earthenware, stencilled and painted, transparent glaze; d.25.5cm
C.5-1995. Source: the artist, £40

971 Plate, 1994
Red earthenware, painted, transparent glaze; marks: 'W 7/94', incised; d.25.5cm
C.6-1995. Source: the artist, £40

Suttie, Angus 1946–1993

1946	born Tealing, Angus
1976–79	studies ceramics at Camberwell School of Art and Crafts
1979–80	teacher training, Whitelands College, Putney, London
1981–84	shares studio with Sara Radstone (qv) at 401½ Workshops, Lambeth, London
1983|87	solo exhibitions, Crafts Council Shop at the V&A
1984–	studio in Clerkenwell, London
1985	solo exhibition, Anatol Orient, London
1986–	teaches at Camberwell School of Art and Crafts
c. 1991–92	ceases making due to illness
1994	retrospective including last works, Contemporary Applied Arts, London

Angus Suttie was a contemporary of Sara Radstone (qv) and Henry Pim (qv) at Camberwell during an especially fertile period. An imaginative and intuitive artist, articulate both in his practice and his writing, Suttie addressed humanist concerns through his ceramics, seeking to reflect his life as a gay man. Although his career spanned little more than a decade, he left a rich legacy of highly inventive work. He explored apparently ordinary objects, in particular teapots, with a playful vision. Lively, extravagantly coloured forms in earthenware were followed by more sombre, architectonic and increasingly monumental works in stoneware. A final series of sculptures reflects his experience of living with AIDS.

Angus Suttie, 'New Ceramicists', *Crafts*, 59 (1982)
— 'Views on the Vessel', *Crafts*, 91 (1988)
— 'On Traditions', *CR*, 117 (1989)
— letter, *CR*, 119 (1989)
Anatol Orient, *The Whole Works*, exh. pamphlet (London, 1985)
Emmanuel Cooper, 'Teasing the Imagination', *CR*, 94 (1985)
Crafts Council (1985), pp.81–2
Peter Dormer, 'Structural Logic', *Crafts*, 88 (1987)
Contemporary Applied Arts, *Sara Radstone, Angus Suttie*, exh. pamphlet (London, 1990)
Museum of Modern Art, Oxford (1993), pp.78–9, 92, 95
Contemporary Applied Arts, *Angus Suttie 1946–1993*, exh. cat., texts by Jeffrey Weeks, Emmanuel Cooper and others (London, 1994)
Martina Margetts, 'The Last Pots', *CR*, 149 (1994)
Crafts Council (1995b), pp.58–9
Carlano (2010), pp.152–3
Ruthin Craft Centre, *Angus Suttie*, exh. cat., texts by Alison Britton and others (Ruthin, 2018)

Exhibition reviews: Griselda Gilroy, *Crafts*, 77 (1985); Paul Rice, *Studio Pottery*, 12 (1994); Eileen Lewenstein, *Crafts*, 132 (1995); Gregor White, *CR*, 187 (2001); Ellen Bell, *CR*, 292 (2018)

Obituaries: Emmanuel Cooper, *The Independent* (19 June 1993); Deborah Norton, *Studio Pottery*, 5 (1993); Sara Radstone, *Crafts*, 124 (1993)

The papers of Angus Suttie are at the Crafts Study Centre, Farnham (SUT).

972 Ladle, 1985
Earthenware, handbuilt, with coloured overglaze enamels and lustre; h.5.7cm, d.37.5cm
C.100-1987. Source: Anatol Orient, London, £37.60

973 *Large Blue Form*, 1988 (pl.91)
Earthenware, handbuilt, matt and vitreous glazes; marks: 'Suttie', incised; h.61cm, d.55.5cm
C.50-1990. Source: Contemporary Applied Arts, London (exhibition: *Sara Radstone, Angus Suttie*, 1990), £1080

Swindell, Geoffrey 1945–

1945	born Stoke-on-Trent
1960–67	studies painting and later ceramics at Stoke-on-Trent College of Art
1967–70	studies ceramics at Royal College of Art, London
1970–75	teaches at York School of Art; establishes studio in York
1972	solo exhibition, British Crafts Centre, London
1975–	teaches ceramics at Cardiff College of Art (later University of Wales Institute, Cardiff); establishes studio in Cardiff
1980–	studio in Dinas Powys, Vale of Glamorgan
1980–2006	regular solo exhibitions, James Graham & Sons Gallery, New York

2002	retrospective exhibition, Newport Museum and Art Gallery
2003–	retires from teaching, concentrates on making full-time

Geoffrey Swindell is recognized for his precisely engineered, intricately decorated miniature porcelain pots, which draw inspiration from sea creatures, fossils, tin-plate toys and science fiction. Early work was press-moulded and more overtly organic in form. Later vessels are thrown and crisply turned, their complex, richly chromatic surfaces suggesting human-made objects overtaken by nature.

Geoffrey Swindell, interview, in Cameron and Lewis (1976), pp.144–55, 168

— statement, with text by Jeannie Lowe, in Portsmouth City Museum and Art Gallery (1976), p.12

— 'Precise Porcelain', *CR*, 186 (2000)

— 'Imaginary and Personal Landscapes', *Ceramics Technical*, 20 (2005)

— 'Glaze Recipe', *CR*, 303 (2020)

Decorative Art (1971/72)

Jeannie Lowe, 'Geoffrey Swindell – Press Moulded Forms', *CR*, 18 (1972)

V&A (1972), p.119

Crafts Advisory Committee (1974), pp.25–8

Jeannie Lowe, 'Pressmoulding – The Technique Used by Geoffrey Swindell', *CR*, 27 (1974)

Oxford Gallery (1974)

'CPA New Members', *CR*, 34 (1975)

Crafts Advisory Committee (1976), p.118

Potters/The Ceramics Book (1977) to (1986), (2000) to (2012)

Crafts Council (1980), p.63

Lane (1980)

Gordon Elliott, 'Geoffrey Swindell', *Ceramics Monthly*, 29:7 (1981)

Peter Lane, 'The Precise Forms of Geoffrey Swindell', *CR*, 67 (1981)

Crafts Council (1985), pp.82–3

Moira Vincentelli, *Geoffrey Swindell*, Aberystwyth Arts Centre: Ceramic Series 25 (1988)

Newport Museum and Art Gallery, *Geoffrey Swindell: Passed and Present*, exh. cat., text by David Briers (Newport, 2002)

Carlano (2010), pp.154–5

Oxford Ceramics Gallery, *Geoffrey Swindell*, exh. cat., text by David Whiting (Oxford, 2013)

Nottingham City Museums and Galleries (2017), p.81

Exhibition reviews: Eileen Lewenstein, 'Diploma Students', *CR*, 4 (1970); J.D.H. Catleugh, *CR*, 19 (1973); Garth Clark, 'Seven in 76', *Crafts*, 19 (1976); David Briers, *Crafts*, 148 (1997); Jeffrey Jones, *CR*, 200 (2003); Emma Maiden, *Crafts*, 181 (2003)

974 Bowl, 1978
Porcelain, thrown and turned, sprayed coloured glazes; marks: 'S', impressed; h.7.6cm, d.11.2cm
C.116-1978. Source: Craftsmen Potters Association, London (exhibition with Delan Cookson and Geoffrey Eastop, 1978, no.151), £76.14

975 Pot, 1978
Porcelain, thrown and turned, sprayed coloured glazes; marks: 'S', impressed; h.9.1cm, d.8.6cm
C.115-1978. Source: *see* 974 (no.190), £84.60

Sykes, Steven 1914–1999

1914	born Formby, Lancashire
1933–36	studies at Royal College of Art, London, in School of Design, specializing in stained glass and mosaics
1937–39	assistant to Herbert Hendrie, Head of Design at Edinburgh College of Art, who ran a stained-glass business from his college studio
1940	marries Jean Judd, former Royal College of Art student, from whom he later learns pottery
1940–45	serves in Royal Engineers as camouflage officer
1946–79	teaches at Chelsea School of Art, London
1947–60	workshop in Kew, Surrey, making ceramics
1960–68	workshop in Fulham, London, making sculpture
1968–	workshop at Hopkiln, Bepton, West Sussex, where creates elaborate garden with decorative architectural features

Steven Sykes played a part in the post-war revival of tin glaze, coloured decoration and figural modelling, explored also by William Newland (qv), Margaret Hine (qv) and Nicholas Vergette (qv). He produced tableware, thrown and assembled figures and flower holders, and tiles richly decorated with both stamped and applied ornament inspired by popular art. His work was shown in the South Bank pavilions of the 1951 Festival of Britain, and he made tiles for the Dorchester Hotel, London. His most important works are his large architectural commissions produced in other materials, notably his concrete and mosaic mural for the Gethsemane Chapel, Coventry Cathedral; a reredos for the War Memorial Chapel, National Cathedral, Washington, DC; and a large fibreglass fountain outside the British Pavilion at Expo 67, Montreal, Canada.

974 / 975

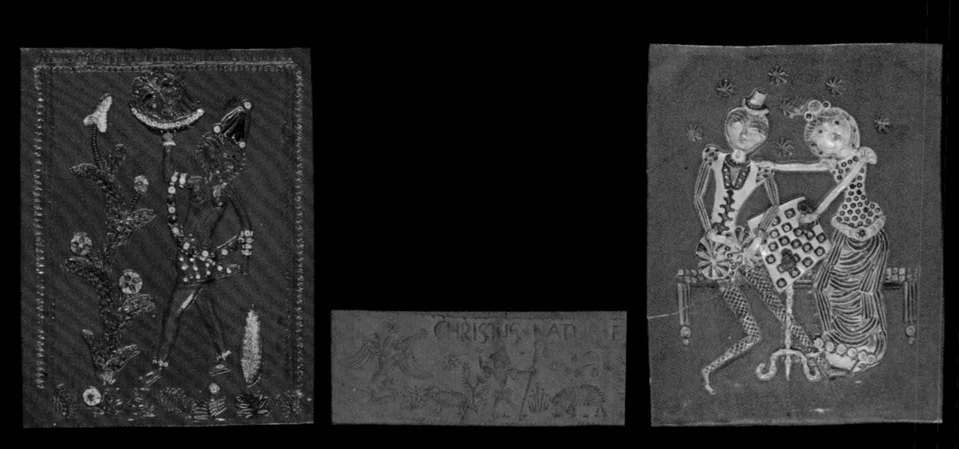

976 / 978 / 977

979

981

983

980

982

984

Steven Sykes, *Deceivers Ever: Memoirs of a Camouflage Officer* (Speldhurst, 1990)

Hugh Wakefield, 'The Ceramics of Stephen Sykes', *Image*, 6 (Spring 1951)

C.G. Tomrley, 'An English Potter', *Graphis*, 8:44 (1952)

Billington (1953)

Lewis (1956), pls.386–8

Louise Campbell (ed.), *To Build a Cathedral: Coventry Cathedral 1945–1962* (Warwick, 1987)

Tanya Harrod, 'An Un-English Country Garden', *Crafts*, 107 (1990)

Harrod (1999)

Exhibition reviews: *Architectural Review*, 53:665 (May 1952), pp.338–9; *Pottery Quarterly*, 1 (1954), pl.15; *Pottery Quarterly*, 2 (1954), pls.11–12

Obituaries: *The Telegraph* (26 January 1999); Tanya Harrod, *The Independent* (24 February 1999)

976 Tile: *Salome*, 1949
Earthenware, applied and impressed decoration, painted; marks: 'SALOME / Steven Sykes / Oct 49 / 369', incised; h.25.1cm, w.18.9cm
C.137-2001. Source: given by Caroline Dear

977 Tile, 1950
Earthenware, applied and impressed decoration, painted, backed with plaster; marks: 'Steven Sykes / 1950', incised; h.24.6cm, w.18.8cm
C.138-2001. Source: *see* **976**

978 Tile: *Christus Natus Est* (*Christ is Born*), *c.* 1950
Earthenware, applied and impressed decoration; marks: 'CHRISTUS NATUS EST', incised; h.7.7cm, w.21.3cm
C.139-2001. Source: *see* **976**

979 Dish, 1950
Earthenware, relief decoration, lustre, transparent glaze; h.7.6cm, d.30.5cm
Circ.180-1950. Source: the artist, £4.10s.

980 Dish: *Signs of the Zodiac*, 1950
Earthenware, relief decoration, tin glaze, painted in green; marks: 'Steven Sykes / 15.2.50', incised; h.7.3cm, d.29.5cm
Circ.181-1950. Source: the artist, £4.4s.

981 Dish: *Trumpeting Angel*, 1950
Earthenware, relief decoration, tin glaze, painted in green; marks: 'Steven Sykes / 1950', incised; h.4.6cm, d.30cm
Circ.182-1950. Source: the artist, £4

982 *Tripod Bird*, 1951
Earthenware, tin glaze, painted in black and green; marks: 'Steven Sykes 51', incised; h.33.9cm, d.40cm
Circ.75-1952. Source: the artist, £12.12s.

983 *Daphne*, 1951
Earthenware, unglazed with tin-glazed details, painted in green, black and blue; h.43cm, d.30cm
Circ.74 to B-1952. Source: the artist, £12.12s.

984 Panel of four tiles, 1955
Earthenware, relief decoration, blue-green glaze; h.44.5cm, w.41.5cm
Circ.97 to C-1963. Source: the artist, £35

Tacon, Pamela E. 1916–2006

1916– born Lambeth, London
1938–47 studies pottery at Royal College of Art, initially in London, 1938–39, then Ambleside, Cumbria, 1940–42, during the College's wartime evacuation; gains diploma in 1942; returns to the College for further study, 1946–47
early 1950s teaches pottery at Bath Academy of Art, Corsham Court, Wiltshire
c. 1955– teaches pottery at Kingston School of Art and Woolwich Polytechnic

Pamela Tacon studied pottery at the Royal College of Art around the time of the Second World War. The jug in the museum's collection was purchased from the College's annual exhibition of 1939, together with work by Henry Hammond (qv), Helen Pincombe (qv) and Gwilym Thomas (qv). Tacon taught ceramics after the war, but is not known to have exhibited work.

985 Jug, 1939
Stoneware, mottled cream and brown glaze; h.38cm, d.18cm
Circ.481-1939. Source: the artist (from Royal College of Art annual exhibition, 1939), £4.4s.

Taylor, Sutton 1943–

1943 born Keighley, Yorkshire
1964–69 teaches in Manchester and Kingston, Jamaica, during which time he discovers clay; becomes a self-taught potter
1971–76 studio at Temple Newsam, Leeds
1976–78 studio at The Almshouses, Aberford, Leeds
1978–90 studio at Lotherton Park, Aberford, Leeds
1980 first solo exhibition, Temple Newsam, Leeds
1984 Grand Prix, International Biennial of Ceramic Art, Vallauris, France
1990–96 studio at Robin Hood's Bay, North Yorkshire
1996 shortlisted for Jerwood Prize for Applied Arts
1997– studio in West Penwith, Cornwall
2010–11 touring solo exhibition

985

Sutton Taylor is among the most accomplished potters to have concentrated on decoration in polychrome reduced lustre – a complex and difficult technique. His vessels, often large open bowls, are adorned with rich all-over patterns that give full play to the brilliant metallic reflections and shimmering iridescence of combinations of copper, silver and gold lustres.

Sutton Taylor, 'Lustred Earthenware', *CR*, 82 (1983)
— 'A Potter's Day', *CR*, 159 (1996)
— 'Colour and Location', *Ceramics: Art and Perception*, 25 (1996)
— 'A Lustre Potter', *Studio Potter*, 25:2 (1997)
Leeds Art Galleries, *Sutton Taylor: Lustreware*, exh. pamphlet, text by Sutton Taylor (Leeds, 1980)
Oxfordshire County Museum Services (1984), pp.54–5
Crafts Council (1985), p.83
Craft Centre and Design Gallery, *Sutton Taylor: Lustreware*, exh. pamphlet (Leeds, 1988)
Potters (1989), (1992), (1997)
Margot Coatts, 'The Midas Touch', *Crafts*, 117 (1992)
Crafts Council (1995a), p.60
— (1996b), pp.30–1
Hart Gallery, *Sutton Taylor*, exh. pamphlet (London, 1996)
Marina Vaizey, *Sutton Taylor: A Lustrous Art* (London: Hart Gallery, 1999)
Hart Gallery, *Sutton Taylor: An Art of Happy Accidents*, exh. cat. (London, 2008)
Carlano (2010), pp.158–9
Hart Gallery, *Sutton Taylor: Lustre*, exh. cat., text by Moira Vincentelli (London, 2010)
Lemon Street Gallery, *Sutton Taylor*, exh. cat. (Truro, 2015) – see also cats. from 2016, 2017, 2018 and 2019
Oxford Ceramics Gallery, *Sutton Taylor*, exh. pamphlet (Oxford, 2018)

986

Exhibition reviews: Rowena Gardiner, *Arts Review* (21 April 1989); Gilles Le Corre, *CR*, 154 (1995)

986 Bowl, 1982–83
Earthenware, gold and red lustre on pale red-speckled ground; marks: 'ST' and 'L.H', impressed; h.15.2cm, d.37.8cm
C.224-1983. Source: Queensberry Hunt, London, £225

Tchalenko, Janice 1942–2018

1942 born Rugby, Warwickshire
1965–67 attends pottery classes at Putney School of Art
1969–71 Studio Pottery Course at Harrow School of Art
1971–2014 establishes studio in East Dulwich, London, making reduction-fired stoneware
1972–87 teaches part-time at Camberwell School of Art and Crafts
1980 receives Crafts Council/Guild of St George John Ruskin Craft Award, to develop range of tableware with pattern and colour
1981–96 teaches part-time at Royal College of Art, London
1984–2010 designer for Dart Pottery (qv)
1987 made Fellow of Royal College of Art
1992 retrospective exhibition, Ruskin Craft Gallery, Sheffield, and tour
1993 collaborates with Spitting Image workshop on *Seven Deadly Sins* sculptures, exhibited at V&A
2014– studio in Forest Hill, London, firing in electric kiln

Janice Tchalenko holds an important place in the history of studio ceramics as an innovator in domestic ware, as well as through her role as designer, forming a bridge between the individual potter and industry. A skilled thrower, Tchalenko initially produced domestic stoneware with muted single-coloured glazes, but in 1979 began exploring brightly coloured pattern and decoration on stoneware, a move seen as revolutionary and which had lasting influence. She is especially known for her highly decorative large thrown bowls and flared jugs, and press-moulded dishes. In 1984 she began working with Dartington Pottery Training Workshop (*see* Dart Pottery), which produced colourful tableware to her designs, to great acclaim. Work with larger manufacturers and retailers followed, including Next Interiors and Poole Pottery. More unexpectedly, Tchalenko collaborated with Roger Law and the Spitting Image workshop, making witty, grotesque sculptures representing the *Seven Deadly Sins*, and a further series of historically informed ceramics. Tchalenko meanwhile continued her own output of vividly decorated individual pots, eventually switching from reduction-fired stoneware to earthenware fired in an electric kiln.

Janice Tchalenko, 'Talking Pots', interview by Jane Hamlyn, *CR*, 135 (1992)
— 'What If ...', *CR*, 243 (2010)
'CPA New Members', *CR*, 30 (1974)
Potters (1975) to (1989)
Crafts Advisory Committee (1976), p.119
— (1977), p.22
Crafts Council (1980), p.64
Isabelle Anscombe, 'Put It on the Table', *Crafts*, 56 (1982)
Crafts Council (1982), pp.8–10
Emmanuel Cooper, 'Janice Tchalenko', *CR*, 80 (1983)
— *Janice Tchalenko*, Aberystwyth Arts Centre: Ceramic Series 2 (1984)
Oxfordshire County Museum Services (1984), pp.56–7
Paisley Museum and Art Galleries (1984), p.81
Crafts Council (1985), pp.84–5
Peter Dormer, 'Tchalenko, Eclectic', *Crafts*, 72 (1985)
ICA (1985), p.44
Tanya Harrod, 'Bridging the Divide', *Crafts*, 80 (1986)
Cooper (1990)
John Tchalenko and Oliver Watson, *Janice Tchalenko: Ceramics in Studio* (London, 1992)
Whiting (1993), pp.47–51, 86
Anna Douglas and Nicholas Wegner (eds), *Artists' Stories* (Sunderland, 1995), pp.108–11
'Potted History', *Crafts*, 143 (1996)
Gaze (1997)
Lesley Jackson, 'Sources of Inspiration', *Crafts*, 165 (2000)
Vincentelli (2000), pp.100–2
Crafts Council (2003), pp.45–8
Scottish Gallery, *Janice Tchalenko*, exh. pamphlet (Edinburgh, 2011)
Clark, Strauss and others (2012), pp.410, 464
Nottingham City Museums and Galleries (2017), p.82
Tanya Harrod, obituary, *The Guardian* (16 August 2018)

Exhibition reviews: Rachael Sherratt, *Crafts*, 87 (1987); Emmanuel Cooper, *Crafts*, 108 (1991), and 116 (1992); Pamela Johnson, *Crafts*, 125 (1993); Felicity Aylieff, *CR*, 169 (1998)

An interview with Janice Tchalenko is in the Crafts Lives sound archive at the British Library, London (C960/59).

987 Jug, 1980 (pl.72)
Stoneware, painted in blue, yellow and green glazes; h.29.2cm, d.20.3cm
C.43-1980. Source: Craftsmen Potters Association, London (*Jugs* exhibition, 1980, no.27), £18

988 Dish, 1982
Stoneware, press-moulded, painted in black, green and red glazes; h.5.8cm, d.49.5cm
C.91-1982. Source: Craft Shop, V&A (showcase exhibition: *Janice Tchalenko and John Hinchcliffe in Collaboration*, 1982, no.16), £80
One of a group of pieces made with the weaver John Hinchcliffe (1949–2010). It was subsequently shown in the 1982 Crafts Council exhibition *Making It*.

989 Bowl, 1983
Stoneware, painted in red, yellow, blue and green glazes; h.18.1cm, d.38.3cm
C.312-1983. Source: Bohun Gallery, Henley-on-Thames (solo exhibition, 1983), £200

990 Bowl, 1983
Stoneware, painted in red, green, yellow and blue glazes; h.11.8cm, d.35.3cm
C.313-1983. Source: *see* **989**, £110

991 Teapot, 1983
Stoneware, painting in coloured glazes; h.13cm, d.20.5cm
C.314&A-1983. Source: *see* **989**, £50

988

990

989

991

992 G / F / C / A / D / E / B

992 *Seven Deadly Sins*, 1993
C.364 to 370-1993. Source: the artist, £8000
Made by Janice Tchalenko in collaboration with Roger Law and Pablo Bach of the Spitting Image workshop, who modelled the forms. The series was shown in the exhibition *Seven Deadly Sins: Ceramics by Janice Tchalenko, with Roger Law and Pablo Bach*, V&A, 1993.

A *Lust*
Porcelain, modelled, reduction-fired, lustre glaze; h.14.6cm, d.25.1cm
C.364-1993

B *Anger*
Stoneware, modelled, reduction-fired; h.20.7cm, d.28.5cm
C.365-1993

C *Sloth*
Earthenware, thrown and altered, terra sigillata, with modelled glazed figure of a cat in interior; h.16.8cm, d.18.7cm
C.366:1,2-1993

D *Envy*
Earthenware, modelled, coloured glazes; h.12.9cm, d.26.8cm
C.367-1993

E *Gluttony*
Stoneware, modelled, saltglazed; h.15.9cm, d.25.8cm
C.368-1993

F *Pride*
Stoneware, thrown and modelled, reduction-fired; h.19.6cm, d.21.4cm
C.369:1,2-1993

G *Avarice*
Earthenware, modelled, lustre glaze; h.18.3cm, d.18.2cm
C.370-1993

See also Dart Pottery (**257** to **259** and **261**).

Thomas, Gwilym E. 1914–1995

1914	born Swansea, Glamorganshire
c. 1931–33	wins scholarship to Swansea School of Art, studies drawing and graphics
1935–38	studies pottery at Royal College of Art, London, under William Staite Murray (qv)
1946–	teaches part-time at Bromley and Maidstone schools of art, Kent
c. 1946–56	studio at Bromley, Kent
1951–	teaches part-time at Hammersmith College of Art
1956–	moves to Orpington, Kent, establishing studio with gas-fired kiln
1973–75	Head of Ceramics at Hammersmith College of Art

Gwilym Thomas was a contemporary of R.J. Washington (qv) and Henry Hammond (qv) at the Royal College of Art, and exhibited with them at The Brygos Gallery, London, in 1938. He was a conscientious objector during the Second World War and later devoted much time to teaching. Though a noteworthy potter, he only seldom showed his work, on occasion doing so alongside his wife, Margaret Kissack, also a potter.

Gwilym Thomas, *Step-by-step Guide to Pottery* (London, 1973)
Commonwealth Institute Art Gallery, *Margaret Connor, Hazel Shaw, Simone Troy, Margaret Kissack, Gwilym Thomas*, exh. cat. (London, 1970)
Graham Whitham, obituaries, *Crafts*, 137 (1995), *Studio Pottery*, 18 (1995), and *CR*, 158 (1996)
Glynn Vivian Art Gallery, *Gwilym Thomas: A Retrospective Exhibition*, exh. pamphlet (Swansea, 1997)
Malcolm Haslam, exh. review, *Crafts*, 162 (2000)
Rice (2002), pp.66, 246–7

993 Bowl, 1938
Stoneware, oatmeal glaze, painted in brown; h.11.7cm, d.16cm
Circ.98-1939. Source: The Brygos Gallery, London (exhibition with Henry Hammond and R.J. Washington, 1938, no.105), £1.5s.

994 Bowl, 1938
Stoneware, grey-green glaze, painted in brown; marks: 'G', incised; h.7.6cm, d.10.5cm
Circ.99-1939. Source: *see* **993** (no.148), 7s.6d.

995 Teapot, 1939
Stoneware, mottled green-brown glaze; h.15.4cm, d.19.5cm
Circ.482&A-1939. Source: the artist (from Royal College of Art annual exhibition, 1939), £1.11s.6d.

996 Bowl, 1965
Stoneware, incised, painted with iron and copper oxides; marks: 'GT 65', incised; h.23.5cm, d.30.4cm
C.8-2000. Source: given by Mrs Margaret Thomas

993 / 994

995

996 / 997

997 Goblet, 1976
Porcelain, incised, painted with manganese and copper oxides over wax resist; marks: 'GT 76', incised; h.17.5cm, d.8.5cm
C.9-2000. Source: *see* **996**

Tower, James 1919–1988

1919	born Sheerness, Kent
1938–40	studies painting at Royal Academy Schools, London
1940–46	war service, works on camouflage and mapping
1946–48	studies painting at Slade School of Fine Art, London
1948–49	trains as an art teacher at Institute of Education, University of London, where studies pottery under William Newland (qv); attends evening classes at Central School of Arts and Crafts under Dora Billington (qv)
1949–66	teaches and establishes pottery workshop at Bath Academy of Art, Corsham Court, Wiltshire
1951–63	regular solo exhibitions at Gimpel Fils, London
1959–	discontinues making decorated ceramics, turns to unglazed sculpture
1965–	moves to Barcombe, Sussex, sets up own workshop
1966–86	appointed Head of Fine Art, Brighton College of Art, sets up sculpture department
c. 1976–	resumes making ceramics
1978–86	regular solo exhibitions of ceramics at Gimpel Fils

James Tower was introduced to ceramics while training as an art teacher at the Institute of Education, where he was taught pottery by William Newland (qv). Together they developed a distinct method of tin-glaze decoration, drawing through an unfired contrasting glaze laid over a fired glaze, a technique Tower returned to throughout his career. Tower aligned himself with the world of fine art, exhibiting at the London gallery Gimpel Fils and teaching at Corsham alongside painters of the English avant-garde. From the mid-1950s he developed flattened sculptural vessel forms, often heavily ribbed. After a period concentrating on purely sculptural forms in unglazed white earthenware, some of which were cast in bronze, Tower returned to tin-glazed ceramics about 1976, making fine large vessels and dishes with decoration that evoked vegetation or water currents.

James Tower, 'Making Good', *CR*, 73 (1982)
Arts and Crafts Exhibition Society (1952)
Dartington Hall (1952)
Billington (1953)
Smithsonian Institution (1959)
Peter Lane, 'James Tower – Artist Potter', *CR*, 88 (1984)
Oxfordshire County Museum Services (1984), pp.58–9
Paisley Museum and Art Galleries (1984), p.81
Hove Museum and Art Gallery, *James Tower 1919–1988*, exh. pamphlet (1989)
David Whiting, 'James Tower', *Studio Pottery*, 3 (1993)
Frankel (2000), pp.178–80
Timothy Wilcox, *The Ceramic Art of James Tower*, foreword by Antony Gormley, includes cat. of works 1978–86 (Farnham, 2012)
Tony Birks, 'James Tower: Painter/Sculptor', *Ceramics: Art and Perception*, 98 (2014)
Erskine, Hall & Coe, *James Tower*, exh. pamphlet, text by Antony Gormley (London, 2014)
Nottingham City Museums and Galleries (2017), p.83
Timothy Wilcox (ed.), *James Tower: Ceramics, Sculptures and Drawings*, with artist statements, published on the occasion of an exhibition at Victoria Art Gallery, Bath (Stuttgart, 2019)

Exhibition reviews: Murray Fieldhouse, *Pottery Quarterly*, 1:1 (1954); *The Times* (11 December 1958) and (7 February 1963); Paul Atterbury, *Crafts*, 37 (1979); Eileen Lewenstein, *Crafts*, 98 (1989)

Obituaries: *The Times* (15 April 1988); Jasper Jewett, *The Independent* (29 April 1988); Emmanuel Cooper, *Crafts*, 93 (1988); Sean Hetterley, *CR*, 112 (1988)

998 Form, 1955
Earthenware, press-moulded, ribbed, black and white tin glazes; marks: 'J. Tower / 55.', incised;

998

1000

1001

h.41.5cm, d.69.5cm
C.135-2013. Source: Mallams, Oxford, £5120; acquired through the generosity of Gerard and Sarah Griffin
Given by the artist to Paul Gell, and subsequently bequeathed to Kenneth Clark (qv).

999 'Grey Blue Form', 1957 (pl.38)
Earthenware, sgraffito through white tin glaze over black; marks: 'James Tower / 57', incised; h.38cm, d.46.5cm
Circ.7-1958. Source: Gimpel Fils, London (solo exhibition, 1957, no.C.26), £18
Illustrated in Birks (1967), pl.1.

1000 'Red and White Oblong', 1958
Earthenware, sgraffito through white tin glaze over black; marks: 'James Tower / 58', incised; h.6.8cm, d.46.3cm
Circ.16-1959. Source: Gimpel Fils, London (solo exhibition, 1958, no.F.27), £22.9s.6d.

1001 *Glacier 2*, 1982
Earthenware, dark manganese over white tin glaze; marks: 'James Tower 82', incised; h.53.5cm, d.54cm
C.328-1983. Source: Gimpel Fils, London (exhibition with Michael Vaughan, 1982, no.132), £450

Trim, Judith (Judy) 1943–2001

1943	born Cambridge
1961–64	trains as an art teacher at Bath Academy of Art, specializing in painting and ceramics
1964–74	works as an art teacher at various London schools
1969–75	married to Roger Waters, founder member of rock band Pink Floyd; sets up studio in Islington, London
1979–85	works as part-time or visiting lecturer at various art schools
1982	solo exhibition, British Crafts Centre, London
1985	solo exhibition, Westminster Gallery, Boston, USA
1986	solo exhibition, Anatol Orient, London
c. 1986–	moves to Shepherd's Bush, London, sets up studio
1991	solo exhibition, Oxford Gallery, Oxford

Judy Trim combined a passion for low-tech firing methods with meticulous attention to detail, both in the handbuilding of her pots and in their decoration. Favouring the warmth and immediacy she found in unglazed surfaces, she made extensive use of burnished slips and smoke-firing, and, from the mid-1980s, metallic lustres.

1002

1003

1004

1005

Judy Trim, 'Mud into Magic', *CR*, 102 (1986)
Paisley Museum and Art Galleries (1984), p.81
Crafts Council (1985), p.86
'Judy Trim', *Ceramics Monthly*, 33:10 (1985)
Gibson (1987), pp.12–17
Potters (1989), (1992), (1997)
Paul Greenhalgh, exh. review, *Crafts*, 106 (1990)
Roy Miles Gallery, *Anna Dickinson, Judy Trim*, exh. cat. (London, 1990)
Margot Coatts, 'The Midas Touch', *Crafts*, 117 (1992)
Andrews (1994)
Nottingham City Museums and Galleries (2017), pp.84–5

Obituaries: Margot Coatts, *Crafts*, 170 (2001); Emmanuel Cooper, *The Independent* (25 January 2001); John Gibson, *CR*, 188 (2001)

1002 Pot, *c.* 1980
White earthenware, coil-built, painted and smoked; h.16.8cm, d.19.2cm
C.12-2005. Source: given by Theo Hessing

1003 *Small Sun Bowl*, 1985
Ceramic ('T Material'), coil-built, with burnished and painted coloured slips; h.12.3cm, d.36.6cm
C.13-2005. Source: *see* **1002**

1004 *Tear Jar*, *c.* 1986
Red earthenware, coil-built, sgraffito decoration, lustred and smoked; h.47cm, d.12.2cm
C.14-2005. Source: *see* **1002**

1005 Bowl: *Swaddled Mauve*, 1992
Ceramic ('T Material'), coil-built, painted and lustred; marks: 'JT' within a circle, and '92', incised; h.15.5cm, d.64.3cm
C.15-2005. Source: *see* **1002**

Turner, Annie 1958–

1958	born Gillingham, Kent, grows up in Waldringfield, Suffolk
1976–79	studies ceramics at Bristol Polytechnic
1980–83	studies ceramics at Royal College of Art, London
1984–	establishes studio at 401½ Workshops, London
1997–	studio in Camberwell, London
2004	solo exhibition, Galerie Besson, London
2007	solo exhibition, RBSA Gallery, Birmingham
2012	solo exhibition, Galerie Hélène Porée, Paris
2012–	moves studio to near Orford, Suffolk
2014	exhibition with Hervé Jézéquel, Erskine, Hall & Coe, London
2019	Loewe Foundation Craft Prize finalist

Annie Turner grew up beside the River Deben in Suffolk, and she has returned to this landscape to live and work. Her intricate handbuilt sculptures echo the structures and objects found in and around the river, such as ladders and nets. Their surfaces suggest processes of change and transformation, through erosion, decay or accretion.

David Whiting, 'A River Runs Through It', *Crafts*, 167 (2000)
Katy Bevan, 'Waterscapes', *CR*, 191 (2001)
Galerie Besson, *Annie Turner*, exh. leaflet, text by David Whiting (London, 2004)
RBSA Gallery, *River: Ceramics by Annie Turner*, exh. leaflet, text by David Whiting (Birmingham, 2007)
Whiting (2009), pp.116–21
WCC-BF (2010), pp.88–9, 100
Corinne Julius, 'The Ceramics of Annie Turner', *Craft Arts International*, 90 (2014)
Charlotte Dew, 'Still Flows the Deben', *CR*, 272 (2015)
Thorpe (2021), pp.111–16

Exhibition reviews: Richard Gray, *CR*, 186 (2000); David Whiting, *Crafts*, 166 (2000); Ben Eldridge, *CR*, 208 (2004)

Annie Turner was the subject of a short film in the BBC television series *Contemporary Visions* in 2003.

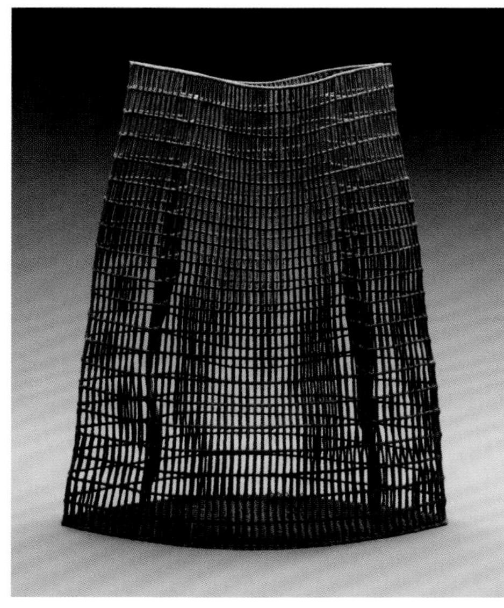

1006

1006 *Oyster Net*, 2013
Stoneware, handbuilt, lithium glaze; h.60.5cm, d.49cm
C.77-2013. Source: Joanna Bird at Collect 2013, £2800; purchase funded by the Friends of the V&A

Twomey, Clare 1968–

1968	born Ipswich, Suffolk
1991–94	studies ceramics at Edinburgh College of Art
1994–96	studies ceramics at Royal College of Art, London
1996–2001	studio in Brixton, London
1998–2000	teaches part-time at Edinburgh College of Art
2000–05	teaches at University College for the Creative Arts, Farnham
2001–09	studio in Camberwell, London
2004	installation, *Heirloom*, Mission Gallery, Swansea
2005–	Research Fellow at University of Westminster; Professor from 2017
2006	installation, *Trophy*, V&A, London
2008–	founds applied arts group 60|40, with David Clarke and Tracey Rowledge
2009–16	studio in Southwark, London
2010	installation, *Forever*, Nelson-Atkins Museum of Art, Kansas City, USA
2011–12	residency, V&A, London
2016–	studio at Thames Barrier, Charlton
2017	installation, *Factory: the seen and the unseen*, Tate Modern, London

Among the most groundbreaking and influential ceramic artists of her generation, Clare Twomey is a defining figure of the 'expanded field' of ceramics. Her practice encompasses site-specific installation and performance; she frequently collaborates with institutions, and embraces audience participation and temporality. Twomey uses these strategies to explore themes of social responsibility, often creating scenarios in which her audience are encouraged to make conscious decisions that determine their engagement with the work. Other installations explore aspects of craft skill and values in making, sometimes choreographing process as performance. Her work is invariably concerned with serial production: enacted in her studio; in the public realm; or for conceptual reasons, outsourced from industrial manufacturers. Twomey is also actively engaged in research in the applied arts at the University of Westminster.

Clare Twomey, 'A Potter's Day', *CR*, 199 (1999)
— 'Conscious Endeavours', *CR*, 193 (2002)
— 'Sculpture: Nine Voices', *Studio Potter*, 34:1 (2005)
— *Clare Twomey 1999–2006* (London, 2006)
— 'Clare Twomey', *Ceramics Monthly*, 55:9 (2007)
— 'Contemporary Clay', in Hanaor (2007), pp.26–37
— 'On the Cusp', *CR*, 229 (2008)
— 'Audience and the Museum', *NCECA Journal*, 34 (2013)
— 'Intangible Tools', *Ceramics Monthly*, 61:1 (2013)
— '10,000 Bowls', *CR*, 275 (2015)
— 'Ceramics in a Place of Cultural Discourse', in **Brown, Stair and Twomey** (2016), pp.1–4
— (**ed.**), *Possibilities & Losses: Transitions in Clay*, exh. cat. (London, 2009), see pp.15–19, 101–23, 126 for Twomey's own work
Crafts Council, *Approaching Content*, exh. cat. (London, 2003)
Shipley Art Gallery (2003b), pp.55–6
Tony Franks, 'From the Real to the Unreal', *Ceramics: Art and Perception*, 60 (2005)
Jo Dahn, 'Clare Twomey and David Cushway', in conversation, *Crafts*, 207 (2007)
Hanaor (2007), pp.132–5
Jerwood Contemporary Makers, exh. cat. (London, 2008)
Veronica Simpson, 'A World Beyond Art and Craft', *Crafts*, 215 (2008)
Zuiderzee Museum, *Monument: Clare Twomey*, texts by Amy Dickson and Liesbeth den Besten (2009)
David Buckland and Chris Wainwright (eds), *Unfold: A Cultural Response to Climate Change* (Vienna, 2010), pp.96–7
Dahn (2011), pp.155–7, 163–5
Gustavsbergs Konsthall, *60|40: David Clarke, Tracey Rowledge, Clare Twomey*, exh. cat. (Gustavsberg, 2011)
Veiteberg (2011), pp.128–9
Clare Twomey: Plymouth Porcelain: A New Collection, exh. pamphlet (Plymouth, 2012)
Bird (2013), pp.76–8
Liz Farrelly, 'Family, Home and Soane', *Crafts*, 241 (2013)

Virginia Jones, 'Clare Twomey', interview, *Journal of Australian Ceramics*, 52:3 (2013)
Gardiner Museum, *Piece by Piece: Clare Twomey*, exh. cat., text by Rachel Gotlieb (Toronto, 2014)
Dahn (2015), pp.78–82, 88–9
Teleri Lloyd-Jones, 'After Hours', *Crafts*, 255 (2015)
Clare (2016), pp.110–12
William Morris Gallery, *Clare Twomey: Time Present and Time Past*, exh. cat., text by Amy Dickson (London, 2016)
Mark Brown, 'All Fired Up: Tate Modern to Play Host to a Working Ceramics Factory', *The Guardian* (17 August 2017)
Elderton and Morrill (2017), pp.284–5
Emma Crichton-Miller, 'Statements in Clay', *CR*, 289 (2018)
Maria Balshaw. 'Art in Sensitive Times', in Jochen Volz and Gabi Ngcobo (eds), *We Are Many: Art, the Political and Multiple Truths*, Verbier Art Summit series (Cologne, 2019)

Exhibition reviews: Will Levi Marshall, *CR*, 174 (1998); Jo Dahn, *CR*, 211 (2005), and 'Clay Rocks', *CR*, 223 (2007); Liz Hoggard, 'Jerwood Contemporary Makers', *Crafts*, 213 (2008); Bonnie Kemske, 'Jerwood Contemporary Makers', *CR*, 233 (2008); Teleri Lloyd-Jones, 'Possibilities and Losses', *Crafts*, 219 (2009); Emma Shaw, 'Possibilities and Losses', *CR*, 240 (2009); Helen Carnac, 'The House of Words', *Journal of Modern Craft*, 3:2 (2010); Glen R. Brown, *Ceramics: Art and Perception*, 85 (2011), and 'Overthrown', *Ceramics: Art and Perception*, 87 (2012); Shane Enright, 'Marking the Line', *Crafts*, 242 (2013); Colin Martin, 'Marking the Line', *Craft Arts International*, 88 (2013); Emma Crichton-Miller, 'Centre of Ceramic Art', *Crafts*, 256 (2015); Gil McElroy, *Ceramics: Art and Perception*, 101 (2015)

1007 50 birds from *Trophy*, 2006 (*see also* fig.16)
Wedgwood blue jasper, cast and hand-finished; marks: 'ct', 'W' and 'V&A', impressed; l.5–8cm (each)
C.108:1 to 50-2007. Source: given by the artist
Trophy was an installation of 4000 birds, produced for the V&A Friday Late event *Clay Rocks!* in 2006. Visitors were invited to walk among the birds, which were freely installed in the V&A Cast Courts. The tacit understanding that visitors might each take one bird away resulted in the work's gradual diminution. These 50 birds were removed from the installation before the event opened to the public.

1007

Uusman, Beatrice (née Bötker) 1900–1984

Little is known of this Estonia-born potter. Active in London in the late 1920s, she exhibited at the Fourteenth Exhibition of the Arts and Crafts Exhibition Society in 1928, from where this pot was purchased by the Contemporary Art Society, together with work by Bernard Leach (qv) and Amy Leeming. Uusman showed two pots and three animal figures (a frog and two fish) in both stoneware and earthenware, and is listed at an address in Queen's Gate, London SW7. A label affixed to the pot reads 'MRS UUSMAN / CAMBERWELL / LONDON'. Uusman may have moved, or may have been a pupil at Camberwell School of Arts and Crafts. She died in Stockholm, Sweden, in 1984.

Arts and Crafts Exhibition Society (1928)
Contemporary Art Society, *Report 1928*, p.33

1008

1008 Pot, 1928
Earthenware, mottled brown glaze, blue-green glaze interior; h.11.7cm, d.15.6cm
C.958-1935. Source: given by the Pottery and Crafts Fund of the Contemporary Art Society, having been purchased from the Fourteenth Exhibition of the Arts and Crafts Exhibition Society, Royal Academy, London, 1928, £3.3s.

Uys, Roelof *see under* Leach Pottery

van der Beugel, Jacob 1978–

1978	born London
1997–2001	studies history of art at University of York
2001–02	apprenticed to Rupert Spira (qv)
2003–04	assistant to Edmund de Waal (qv)
2004–	establishes studio in Great Asby, Cumbria
2008–	moves to Devon, sets up studio in Bampton in 2010, after brief period in Filleigh
2014	commission, *The North Sketch Sequence*, Chatsworth, Derbyshire
2018–19	residency at The Wallace Collection, London
2019	commission, *The DNA Room*, Paleis Huis ten Bosch, Netherlands
2020	solo exhibition, Museum Beelden aan Zee, Netherlands

An accomplished maker of thrown domestic stoneware and vessels, Jacob van der Beugel sought to develop a more conceptual basis for his work, presenting groups as themed installations from 2008. He has since developed a practice based around substantial site-specific architectural commissions.

1009

1010

Shane Enright, 'Still Centre', exh. review, *Crafts*, 196 (2005)
Edmund de Waal, 'Still Alive', *CR*, 230 (2008)
Teleri Lloyd-Jones, 'An Air of Shelf Satisfaction', *Crafts*, 225 (2010)
Ian Wilson, 'Meditations on Still Lifes in Clay', *Craft Arts International*, 78 (2010)
Joanna Bird (ed.), *The North Sketch Sequence Chatsworth* (London, 2014)
Teleri Lloyd-Jones, 'The Gene Home Project', *Crafts*, 246 (2014)
Ian Wilson, 'Chatsworth House DNA Commission', *Craft Arts International*, 91 (2014)
Paleis Huis ten Bosch, *Jacob van der Beugel: The Green Room* (2019)
John Day, 'Under the Microscope', *Crafts*, 288 (2021)
Museum Beelden aan Zee, *Jacob van der Beugel: A Mutating Story*, exh. cat. (The Hague, 2021)

1009 Three lidded jars, 2008
Stoneware, with inclusions; marks: 'Jv', impressed on underside of lids; h.30.3cm, d.30.7cm; h.27.2cm, d.27.7cm; h.20.5cm, d.22.3cm
C.78:1,2; 79:1,2; 80:1,2-2008. Source: Contemporary Applied Arts, London (solo focus), £1767.81; acquired through the generosity of Gerard and Sarah Griffin
From an installation of 30 progressively larger and rougher-textured jars, *From Here to There – Is Man no more than This?*.

Vegas, Johnny (Michael Pennington) 1970–

1970	born St Helens, Lancashire
1990–93	studies ceramics at Middlesex Polytechnic
1995–	begins performing stand-up comedy as Johnny Vegas
1999	collaborates with Roger Law (qv) on the film *Pot Shots*
2000	performs at the V&A

After studying ceramics, Michael Pennington became a highly successful entertainer – known as Johnny Vegas – incorporating pottery demonstrations into his stand-up comedy routine. Since 2001 he has concentrated on an acting and television career.

Johnny Vegas, 'Revelations', *CR*, 178 (1999), p.66
— *Becoming Johnny Vegas* (London, 2013)
— 'Standing up for Pottery', interview, *CR*, 275 (2015)
Liz Hoggard, 'Viva Johnny Vegas', *Crafts*, 152 (1998)
May Ling Beadsmoore, 'Balls of Clay', review, *CR*, 171 (1998), p.55
Robert S. Silver, 'Ceramics as Performance: A Comic Turn of the Wheel with Johnny Vegas', *Studio Pottery*, 31 (1998)
'Night Class', review, *CR*, 198 (2002), p.65
'Expert Eyes', *CR*, 285 (2017)

1010 Teapot, 1999
Earthenware, thrown and assembled; h.12cm, d.17.5cm
C.2-2000. Source: given by Johnny Vegas
Made in under 60 seconds during a performance at the *Ceramic Millennium* conference, Amsterdam, and subsequently fired by Babs Haenen.

Vergette, Nicholas 1923–1974

1923	born Market Deeping, Lincolnshire
1941–46	serves as pilot in Royal Air Force in Europe and East Asia
1946–50	studies painting at Chelsea School of Art
1950–51	trains as art teacher at Institute of Education, University of London, studying pottery under William Newland (qv)
1951–58	teaches at Central School of Arts and Crafts, London
1958–59	visiting artist at School for American Craftsmen, Rochester, New York; mural commission for Cathedral of the Immaculate Conception, Syracuse
1959–	teaches at Southern Illinois University, Carbondale

Nicholas Vergette was introduced to ceramics by William Newland (qv) at the Institute of Education, and subsequently shared a studio with him and Margaret Hine (qv) in Bayswater, London, in the early 1950s. The three exhibited together, and worked to commission producing architectural decoration. Vergette made tin-glazed plates and bowls painted with colourful designs, and developed small-scale sculptures of animals and figures, and mosaic murals. After a year as a visiting artist in Rochester, New York, Vergette chose to remain in the USA, noting that the country invited innovation, experiment and daring. From then on he concentrated on ceramic sculpture, making totemic or eroded forms, sometimes of great size and destined for civic spaces.

Nicholas Vergette, 'Ceramics in the United States', with biographical notes, *Pottery Quarterly*, 8:32 (1965)
— 'The Place of the Crafts in Education', *Pottery in Australia*, 10:2 (1971)
Arts and Crafts Exhibition Society (1952), (1954), (1957)
Billington (1953), (1955)
Fennemore (1953)
Decorative Art (1954/55), (1956/57)
Lewis (1956), pls.389–91
Smithsonian Institution (1959)
Helen Vergette, 'The Architectural Mural/Mixed Media: Nicholas Vergette', *Craft Horizons*, 22:4 (1962)
Lawrence Alloway, 'The Plastic Reliefs of Nicholas Vergette', *Craft Horizons*, 28:2 (1968)
'Monumental Ceramic Sculpture for Southern Illinois Campus', *Ceramics Monthly*, 19:4 (1971)
John Gardner, 'Nicholas Vergette', *Craft Horizons*, 33:5 (1973)
— eulogy, *Craft Horizons*, 34:2 (1974)
Mitchell Museum, *Nicholas Vergette*, exh. cat. (Mount Vernon, 1974)
Robert A. Walsh (ed.), *Nicholas Vergette: His Work and His Ideas* (Carbondale, 1977)
Partington (2005)

Exhibition reviews: Murray Fieldhouse, *Pottery Quarterly*, 1:1 (1954); *Craft Horizons*, 16:2 (1956);

1011

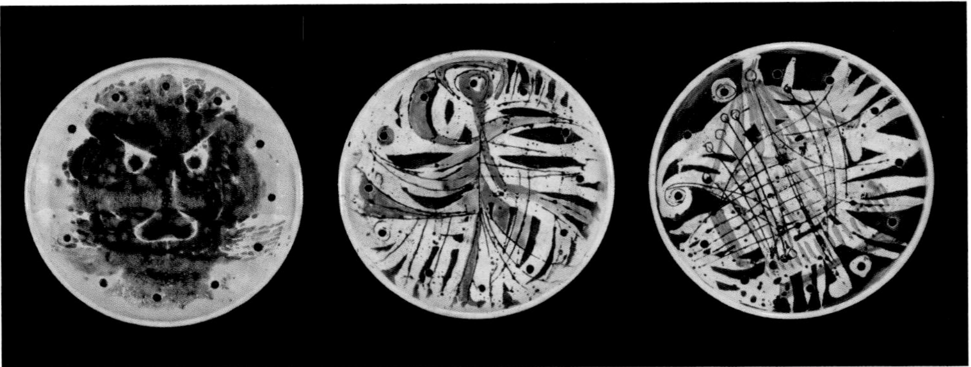

1014 / 1013 / 1012

Michael Higgins, *Craft Horizons*, 23:5 (1963); Jim Crumrine, *Craft Horizons*, 29:5 (1969)

1011 Bowl, 1954
Earthenware, sgraffito through white tin glaze over black, painted in colours; marks: 'N 54', painted; h.16.8cm, d.20cm
Circ.278-1954. Source: Crafts Centre of Great Britain, London, £3.3s.

1012 Plate, *c.* 1954
Earthenware, tin glaze, painted in colours; h.2.4cm, d.21.6cm
C.119-2011. Source: Woolley & Wallis, Salisbury (sale: *British Art Pottery*, 30 November 2011, lot 482), £863.80 (for group)
Originally part of the decoration of the coffee bar La Ronde in Baker Street, London. *See also* **448** to **451**, **1013** and **1014**.

1013 Plate, *c.* 1954
Earthenware, tin glaze, painted in colours; h.2.4cm, d.21cm
C.120-2011. Source and remarks: *see* **1012**

1014 Plate, *c.* 1954
Earthenware, tin glaze, painted in colours; h.2.6cm, d.21.1cm
C.121-2011. Source and remarks: *see* **1012**

Vyse, Charles 1882–1971 and **Nell** (née Edwards) 1892–1967

1882	Charles born Milton, Staffordshire
1894–1905	studies at Hanley School of Art
1896–	apprenticed to Doulton & Co., Burslem, as modeller
1905–10	wins scholarship to study sculpture at Royal College of Art, London
1909	travelling scholarship to Italy
1912	marries Sarah (Nell) Winmill Bullin Edwards
1919–	establishes pottery studio, Cheyne Row, Chelsea
1923–30	teaches modelling at Camberwell School of Arts and Crafts
1928–38	annual exhibitions at Walker's Galleries, London (also 1951–61)
1940	studio damaged in air raid; separates from Nell
1940–46	appointed modelling and pottery instructor at Farnham School of Art; leaves London; Nell ceases potting, remains in London
1946–	returns to Chelsea studio; works in collaboration with Barbara Waller
c. 1957–	Waller leaves to establish own studio in Hampshire
1963	retires to Deal, Kent

Charles and Nell Vyse worked in partnership, Charles drawing upon his training as a sculptor and in the pottery industry, Nell using her skills as a painter and developing knowledge of glaze chemistry. They became known for their slip-cast and assembled figures depicting street vendors and other local subjects, gaining early success with *The Balloon Woman* and *The Lavender Girl*, introduced in 1920 and produced in editions of 100. Subsequent figures were made in smaller numbers. In the mid-1920s they began the faithful emulation of Chinese stonewares, reproducing the effects of celadon, tenmoku and Jun glazes, and experimenting with ash glazes. In the 1930s they also produced stoneware with painted calligraphic and figurative decoration in a contemporary style. After the Second World War, Charles collaborated with his former student and fellow sculptor Barbara Waller (1923–1974), reproducing animal figures that she had modelled.

Charles Vyse, 'The Craftsman in Pottery', in Blunt (1924), pp.108–14
Bernard Rackham, 'The Pottery Figures of Mr Charles Vyse', *The Studio*, 81 (1921), pp.184–6
British Institute of Industrial Art (1923), (1929)
Guild of Potters (1924), (1925), (1926)
Colnaghi (1927)
Walker's Galleries, *Pottery, Stoneware and Hard Porcelain by Mr. and Mrs. Charles Vyse*, exh. cat. (London, 1928) – and subsequent annual catalogues
Arts and Crafts Exhibition Society (1931)
British Council (1942)
Ernest Marsh, 'Charles and Nell Vyse, Studio Potters of Chelsea', *Apollo*, 38 (July 1943)
'The Chelsea Potters', *The Sphere* (30 June 1951)
Wingfield Digby (1952), p.81, pl.55
Obituary (Charles Vyse), *The Times* (11 June 1971)
Blunt (1973), with account of former employee Bertha White, pp.*xviii–xxiii*, 87–8, pl.41
Figures and Stoneware Pottery by Charles Vyse, exh. cat., arranged by Richard Dennis at the Fine Art Society (London, 1974)
Marigold Coleman, 'Charles Vyse', *Crafts*, 12 (1975)
Vincentelli and Hale (1986)
Riddick (1990), pp.112–16
Vincentelli (2000), pp.141–3
Terence Cartlidge, *Charles and Nell Vyse: A Partnership* (Shepton Beauchamp, 2004)
Knott (2021)

Exhibition reviews: Ernest Marsh, *Walker's Monthly*, annually (December 1928) to (1938); *The Times* (23 November 1929), (28 November 1930), (2 December 1931), (30 November 1932), (6 December 1933), (19 December 1935), (5 December 1936), (10 December 1938); *Pottery Quarterly*, 3:9 (1956); Malcolm Haslam, *Connoisseur* (December 1974); Emmanuel Cooper, *CR*, 32 (1975)

1015 *The Balloon Woman*, 1920 (pl.7)
Earthenware, slip-cast and assembled, painted in colours; marks: 'CV' in monogram enclosed by '19 20 / CHELSEA.', painted; h.23cm,

d.14.7cm
C.656-1921. Source: given by Lt-Col. K. Dingwall, DSO, through Art Fund (following exhibition organized by the British Institute of Industrial Art)

1016 *The Balloon Woman*, 1921 (introduced 1920; see pl.7 for comparable image)
Earthenware, slip-cast and assembled, painted in colours; marks: 'CV' in monogram enclosed by '19 21. / CHELSEA.', painted; h.22cm, d.15cm
C.432-1934. Source: British Institute of Industrial Art

1017 *The Lavender Girl*, 1920 (pl.7)
Earthenware, slip-cast and assembled, painted in colours; marks: 'CV' in monogram enclosed by '19 20 / CHELSEA.', painted; h.22.5cm, d.17cm
C.428-1934. Source: British Institute of Industrial Art (given by the artist, 1920)

1018 Vase, *c.* 1929
Stoneware, incised decoration through slip, grey-white glaze; marks: 'CV' in monogram, incised; h.17.1cm, d.16.8cm
C.955-1935. Source: given by the Pottery and Crafts Fund of the Contemporary Art Society, having been presented by Ernest Marsh in 1929

1019 Bowl, 1931
Stoneware, incised decoration through white slip, celadon glaze; marks: 'TO EM FROM THE A-M SOCY FEB 1931.', incised; h.7.4cm, d.25.2cm
C.83-1984. Source: given by Mr Christopher Marsh, son of Ernest Marsh
The inscibed motto 'ADSUM PENE ADEMALL' is a mock-Latin phrase: 'had some, almost had them all'. The bowl was presented to Ernest Marsh by his friend and rival collector of Martinware, Francis Berry, who styled himself the Anti-Marsh Society in recognition of their good-humoured competition.

1020 Small vase, 1931
Stoneware, lavender-blue glaze with purple flushes; marks: 'C.V. 1931', incised; h.11.3cm, d.11cm
C.285-1976. Source: D.M. Booth, £60

1021 Bowl, *c.* 1931
Stoneware, mottled rust glaze, interior with pale lavender glaze; marks: 'C. VYSE', incised; h.6.7cm, d.13.3cm
C.284-1976. Source: *see* **1020**, £60

1022 Bowl, *c.* 1932
Stoneware, greyish glaze, painted in brown; marks: 'CHARLES VYSE CHELSEA', incised; h.13.4cm, d.21.5cm
C.132-1977. Source: Richard Dennis, London (from the collection of Sir Edward Maufe), £100

1023 Bowl, 1934 (illustrated p.384)
Stoneware, oatmeal glaze, painted in brown; marks: 'VYSE 1934', incised; h.11.5cm, d.21.7cm
C.61-1976. Source: Richard Dennis, London, £69

1024 Jug, 1934
Stoneware, speckled grey glaze, painted in brown; marks: '19 VYSE 34', incised; h.24.5cm, d.24.4cm
C.63-1980. Source: Richard Dennis, London, £300 (with **1025**)

1018

1019

1021 / 1029

1027 / 1020 / 1028

1022

1030 / 1023

1026

1032

1024 / 1025

1031

1033

The inscription reads: 'THIS IS THE JUG / THAT HOLDS THE BEER / TO FILL THE MUG / AND BRING US CHEER'.

1025 Mug, 1936
Stoneware, grey glaze, painted in blue; marks: 'VYSE 1936', incised; h.15cm, d.15.3cm
C.64-1980. Source: *see* **1024**
The inscription reads: 'ALL THE FUN OF THE FAIR'.

1026 Bowl, *c.* 1935
Stoneware, cut decoration, celadon glaze; marks: 'CHARLES VYSE, CHELSEA', incised; h.13.7cm, d.14.4cm
C.116-1977. Source: Richard Dennis, London (from the collection of Sir Edward Maufe), £50

1027 Bowl, *c.* 1935 (illustrated p.383)
Stoneware, blue and purple glaze; marks: 'CHARLES VYSE, CHELSEA', incised; h.8.5cm, d.13.5cm
C.117-1977. Source and provenance: *see* **1026**, £40

1028 Bowl, 1939 (illustrated p.383)
Stoneware, blue mottled glaze; marks: 'VYSE 1939' and 'SW', incised; h.11.6cm, d.17.8cm
C.118-1977. Source and provenance: *see* **1026**, £70

1029 Bowl, *c.* 1950 (illustrated p.383)
Stoneware, incised decoration, pale blue glaze, interior brown; marks: 'CHARLES VYSE, CHELSEA', incised; h.11.6cm, d.17.5cm
Circ.16-1951. Source: Walker's Galleries Ltd, London, £10.10s.

1030 Jug, *c.* 1950
Stoneware, grey glaze, painted in brown; marks: 'CHARLES VYSE, CHELSEA', incised; h.18.1cm, d.22.5cm
Circ.17-1951. Source: *see* **1029**, £6.6s.

1031 Figure of a shire stallion, *c.* 1950
Stoneware, slip-cast, tenmoku glaze; made by Charles Vyse and Barbara Waller; marks: 'CHARLES VYSE / BARBARA WALLER / CHELSEA', incised; h.25.8cm, d.28cm
C.287-1976. Source: bequeathed by Barbara Joan Waller

1032 Figure of a fighting cock, *c.* 1950
Earthenware, slip-cast, tin glaze, painted in colours; made by Charles Vyse and Barbara Waller; marks: 'CHARLES VYSE / BARBARA WALLER / CHELSEA', incised; h.25.5cm, d.18.5cm
C.288-1976. Source: *see* **1031**

1033 Figures of two fighting cocks, *c.* 1950
Glazed stoneware, slip-cast, oatmeal glaze, painted in brown, wooden base; made by Charles Vyse and Barbara Waller; h.24cm, d.19cm; h.18cm, d.26cm
C.289&A-1976. Source: *see* **1031**

1034 / 1035

1034 Figure of a genet, *c.* 1950
Stoneware, slip-cast, celadon glaze, wooden base; made by Charles Vyse and Barbara Waller; marks: 'CHARLES VYSE / BARBARA WALLER / CHELSEA'; h.16cm, d.15.5cm (without base)
C.290-1976. Source: *see* **1031**

1035 Figure of a genet, *c.* 1950
Stoneware, slip-cast, painted decoration in a tenmoku glaze; made by Charles Vyse and Barbara Waller; marks: 'CHARLES VYSE / BARBARA WALLER / CHELSEA'; h.16cm, d.16cm
C.291-1976. Source: *see* **1031**

Wade, Constance E. *see* Constance E. Dunn

Wadsworth, Philip (P.S.) 1910–1991

1910	born Staffordshire; son of John Wadsworth, former Art Director at Minton and Royal Worcester
1929–31	studies at Chelsea School of Art
1931–35	studies at Royal College of Art, London, studying pottery under William Staite Murray (qv) from 1932
1935–36	teaches part-time at Kingston School of Art, Surrey
1937	group exhibition, *Stoneware and Earthenware*, The Brygos Gallery, London
1937–40	teaches at Leicester School of Art
1940–45	serves in Royal Artillery; long period as prisoner of war in Thailand
1946–49	teaches at Leeds College of Art
1949–66	teaches at Southern College of Art, Poole, becoming Head of School; suffers from ill health; little time for his own work
1966	retires from teaching
1967–70	lives in France
1970–	returns to England, living in Malvern, Worcestershire; works on history of Minton with his wife, Zillah

Philip Wadsworth was drawn to pottery while at the Royal College of Art, through the teaching and influence of William Staite Murray (qv). Like Murray, he came to see pottery as a fine art. His work of the later 1930s shows Murray's stylistic influence, while exhibiting its own characteristics. He later devoted increasing time to teaching, making little of his own work.

Philip and Zillah Wadsworth, unpublished typescript history of Minton, The Minton Archive, Stoke-on-Trent City Archives (SD1705 / MS4520–MS4524)
Brygos Gallery (1937a)
Arts and Crafts Exhibition Society (1938), (1941)
Cooper (1947), p.*iv*, pl.44
Dartington Hall (1952)
Riddick (1990), p.117
Bernard Charles, obituary, *Crafts*, 115 (1992), pp.15–17
Phillips, *The Ceramic Art and Painting of John and Philip Wadsworth*, auction cat., with biographical notes by Zillah Wadsworth (London, 8 April 1992)

1036 Lidded jar, *c.* 1939
Stoneware, crackled transparent glaze; marks: 'PSW', incised; h.16.8cm, d.11.4cm
Circ.170&A-1939. Source: the artist, £1.1s.

1037 Lidded jar, *c.* 1939
Stoneware, oatmeal glaze; marks: 'PSW', incised; h.15cm, d.12.7cm
Circ.171&A-1939. Source: the artist, £1.10s.

1038 Lidded jar, *c.* 1939
Stoneware, mottled grey glaze flecked with brown; marks: 'PSW', incised; h.11.7cm, d.12.8cm
Circ.172&A-1939. Source: the artist, £2.2s.

1037 / 1038 / 1036

1039 Pot, *c.* 1939
Stoneware, grey glaze with dark bands; marks: 'PSW', incised; h.15.7cm, d.22.3cm
Circ.173-1939. Source: the artist, £5.5s.

1040 Bottle, *c.* 1939
Stoneware, thin grey glaze; marks: 'PSW', incised; h.19.7cm, d.10.8cm
Circ.174-1939. Source: the artist, 15s.6d.

1041 Pot, *c.* 1939
Stoneware, tenmoku glaze; marks: 'PSW', incised; h.30cm, d.25cm
Circ.175-1939. Source: the artist, £6.6s.

1042 Jug, *c.* 1939
Stoneware, reddish glaze; marks: 'PSW', painted; h.19.8cm, d.17.2cm
Circ.176-1939. Source: the artist, £1.1s.

1040 / 1039 / 1042

1041

Walford, James 1913–2001

1913 born Paris
1931–32 studies painting at Slade School of Fine Art and Royal College of Art, London
1945– attends pottery evening classes at Kingston School of Art under Dora Billington (qv), then Woolwich Polytechnic under Heber Mathews (qv)
1947 buys gas kiln from Bernard Leach (qv)
1948– begins potting at South Nutfield, Surrey
1951–57 solo exhibitions, Berkeley Galleries, London
1958 founder member of Craftsmen Potters Association
1959– moves to Steep Park, Crowborough, Sussex; abandons potting due to illness
1977– resumes potting on limited scale

James Walford concentrated on high-temperature glazes emulating those of Song dynasty and other Chinese wares, working alone, through repeated experiment. His particular success with celadon and blueish-white (*qingbai*) glazes was noted by Arthur Lane, the V&A's Keeper of Ceramics, in the 1950s. An early exponent of porcelain in studio ceramics, Walford made both pots and small-scale animal figures.

James Walford, 'Fuller's Earth', *CR*, 60 (1979)
Arts and Crafts Exhibition Society (1950), (1954), (1957)
Berkeley Galleries, *Celadon Pottery and Porcelain by James Walford*, exh. pamphlet, text by Arthur Lane (1953)
Domenic Leo, 'Looking East', *CR*, 124 (1990)

Exhibition reviews: *Pottery Quarterly*, 2:8 (1955); *The Times* (19 October 1955) and (8 November 1957)

1043 Bowl, 1951
Porcelain, white glaze; marks: 'JW' in monogram, impressed; h.6.9cm, d.10.9cm
Circ.310-1951. Source: Berkeley Galleries, London (solo exhibition, 1951), £3.3s.

1044 Vase, 1954
Stoneware, mottled brown ash glaze; marks: 'JW' in monogram, impressed, and '543', in black; h.11.3cm, d.10.5cm
C.7-1954. Source: the artist, £4.4s.
Described by Walford as 'protoporcelain specimens', **1044** to **1046** represent his experiments to reproduce the earliest Chinese stoneware glazes. The glaze on **1044** contains 45% red clay, 45% elm ash and 10% limestone, reduction-fired to 1230°C, whereas **1045** contains 25% blended red and ball clay, 45% elm ash, 10% limestone and 20% feldspar, similarly fired. **1046** has the same glaze as **1045**, but fired in oxidation.

1045 Vase, 1954
Stoneware, mottled brown ash glaze; marks: 'JW' in monogram, impressed, and '549', in black; h.12cm, d.10.7cm
C.6-1954. Source: the artist, £4.4s.

1046 Pot, 1954
Stoneware, mottled brown ash glaze; marks: 'JW' in monogram, impressed, and '549 / O', in black; h.9.2cm, d.12.2cm
C.5-1954. Source: given by the artist

1047 Bowl, 1957
Stoneware, blueish-white glaze; marks: 'JW' in monogram, impressed; h.11cm, d.23.8cm
Circ.203-1957. Source: Berkeley Galleries, London (solo exhibition, 1957), £15.15s.

1048 Vase, 1957
Stoneware, slip decoration, green glaze; marks: 'JW' in monogram, incised; h.19cm, d.16.7cm
Circ.204-1957. Source: *see* **1047**, £16.16s.

1049 Bottle, 1996
Porcelain, handbuilt, slip decoration, copper-red glaze; marks: 'JW' in monogram, impressed; h.28.5cm, d.14.7cm
C.119-1996. Source: given by the artist

1047 / 1043

1044 / 1046 / 1045

1048

1049

Waller, Barbara 1923–1974

See **1031** to **1035** *under* Charles Vyse

Wallwork, Alan 1931–2019

1931 born Watford, Hertfordshire
1954–55 teacher training at Newland Park Training College, Buckinghamshire, where self-taught in ceramics
1955–56 studies at Goldsmiths' College, London, taking pottery classes under Kenneth Clark (qv) and Gordon Baldwin (qv)
1957–62 establishes workshop and gallery – Alan Gallery – in Forest Hill, London, selling work by other potters and own domestic ware, tiles and sculptural stoneware; Bernard Rooke (qv) joins him in 1960
1962– moves to larger workshop and gallery in Greenwich, subletting space to Rooke, and Robert and Sheila Fournier (qv); makes earthenware tiles and handbuilt stoneware with team of assistants
1964– establishes large workshop in Marnhull, Dorset; moves tile production and by 1970 all production from Greenwich
1980– scales down production and works with fewer assistants due to increasing costs and desire for quieter life; discontinues tilemaking, concentrates on individual work in stoneware
1984– moves to Uplyme, near Lyme Regis, Dorset, working alone
1989– moves to nearby Rocombe
2004– moves to Missègre, France, later returning to Bere Regis, Dorset

Alan Wallwork developed handbuilt sculptural stoneware alongside more commercial activities, largely centred on tilemaking. At his studios in Greenwich, London, and at Marnhull, Dorset, he worked with teams of assistants; his tiles were endorsed by the Design Council's Design Centre through listing on their Design Index, and his pottery was sold in London through Heal's, the Craftsmen Potters Shop and Briglin Pottery, among other outlets. His individual work explored textural surface qualities, and responded to natural as well as ancient and totemic forms. After moving to the Dorset coast, he concentrated on smaller, organically inspired pieces, suggestive of pebbles and seedpods.

Alan Wallwork, 'Workshop', *CR*, 8 (1971)
— 'A Potter's Day', *CR*, 115 (1989)
— 'Destined for the Deep', *CR*, 156 (1995)
— 'A Touch of the Vapours', *CR*, 160 (1996)
— 'Getting it Right', on early years of Craftsmen Potters Association, *Interpreting Ceramics*, ejournal, 12 (2010)

1050

1052 / 1051

Decorative Art (1965/66)
Casson (1967), p.8, pls.64–70
Potters (1972) to (1992)
Oxford Ceramics Gallery, *Alan Wallwork: A Retrospective Exhibition*, exh. cat., with texts by Alan Wallwork and David Whiting (Oxford, 2012)
David Whiting, obituary, *The Guardian* (20 November 2019)

1050 Pot, 1965
Stoneware, handbuilt, mottled blue-brown glaze; marks: 'W', roughly incised; h.43.7cm, d.31.7cm
Circ.353-1965. Source: the artist (from exhibition: *Hand and Machine*, Design Centre, London), £14.14s.

1051 Tall pot, *c.* 1965
Stoneware, handbuilt, impressed decoration, partial yellowish glaze; h.83cm, d.31.5cm
C.7-2019. Source: given by David and Jean Richardson

1052 Stele form, *c.* 1965–70
Stoneware, handbuilt, relief decoration; h.84cm, d.33cm
C.8-2019. Source: *see* **1051**

Walsh, Andrea 1974–

1974 born Stockport, Greater Manchester
1995–98 studies fine art at Staffordshire University
1999–2000 studies glass techniques at International Glass Centre, West Midlands
2000–01 studies glass at Edinburgh College of Art
2004|06 solo exhibitions, Open Eye Gallery, Edinburgh
2005– establishes studio at The Drill Hall, Edinburgh
2007 residency, Cove Park, Argyll and Bute
2009 British Ceramics Biennial residency at Staffordshire University and Wedgwood factory, Stoke-on-Trent
2009 solo exhibition, Beaux Arts, Bath
2009–13 studio at Coburg House, Edinburgh
2011|13|15 shortlisted for British Ceramics Biennial AWARD
2013– studio at Wasps, Patriothall, Edinburgh
2014 travels to Japan
2017 Woman's Hour Craft Prize finalist
2018 solo exhibition, The Scottish Gallery, Edinburgh
2019 Loewe Foundation Craft Prize finalist

Andrea Walsh combines bone china and glass in her exquisite, highly considered box and vessel forms. While training in glass, she began using bone-china vessels as containers for pooled glass. She has since used the materials as separate elements, initially in a series of bone-china boxes with cast-glass lids. She has received particular recognition for her contained boxes: delicate lidded bone-china boxes – sometimes stained black or gilded – each cradled within an open glass vessel.

Harriet Smith, 'Cool, Calm and Confident', *CR*, 229 (2008)
Amanda Game, 'Boxing Clever', in Visual Arts Scotland, *vas:t 2015*, exh. cat. (Edinburgh, 2015), pp.20–3
Scottish Gallery, *Fine Lines*, exh. cat. (Edinburgh, 2015), pp.46–51
Imogen Greenhalgh, 'Box Office', *Crafts*, 267 (2017)

1054 / 1053

1055

'Woman's Hour Craft Prize', supplement, *Crafts*, 268 (2017)
Scottish Gallery, *Andrea Walsh*, exh. cat., texts by Alun Graves and Rose Watban (Edinburgh, 2018)

1053 *Small Square Faceted Box*, 2009–11
Bone china, slip-cast, with 22ct burnished gold, clear glass lid; marks: 'AW / 2009', impressed; h.4.1cm, d.7.2cm
C.127:1,2-2012. Source: the artist, £2250 (with **1054**); acquired through the generosity of Gerard and Sarah Griffin

1054 *Small Square Faceted Box*, 2009–11
Bone china, slip-cast, aqua glass lid; marks: 'AW', impressed; h.4cm, d.7cm
C.128:1,2-2012. Source: *see* **1053**

1055 *Contained Box – Pale Yellow and Black*, 2015
Lost-wax cast glass, bone china; marks: 'AW', impressed (on box); h.7.5cm, d.10.7cm
C.51:1 to 3-2015. Source: the artist at Collect 2015, £1750

1056 *Collection of Contained Boxes*, 2018, comprising *Contained Box (Soft Oval) – White and Platinum*; *Contained Box (Soft Oval) – Warm White and White*; *Contained Box (Long) – Clear and Gold* (pl.136)
Lost-wax cast glass, bone china, 22ct burnished gold and platinum; marks: 'AW', impressed (on boxes); h.7.5cm, d.11.5cm (*Soft Oval*); h.7.8cm, d.13.7cm (*Long*); l.65cm (installed as *Collection*)
C.25:1 to 3, 26:1 to 3, 27:1 to 3-2019. Source: Oxford Ceramics Gallery at Collect 2019, £12,500; purchase funded by Christopher M. Gorman-Evans

---

Walton, Sarah 1945–

1945	born Kent, grows up in London
1960–64	studies painting at Chelsea School of Art
1965–71	trains and works as a nurse
1971–73	Studio Pottery Course at Harrow School of Art
1973–74	works briefly for David Leach (qv) and Zelda Mowat
1975–	establishes workshop at Alciston, East Sussex
1990	receives Crafts Council/Guild of St George John Ruskin Award, to develop monumental forms for outside locations

Sarah Walton works in salt-glazed stoneware. She initially concentrated on thrown tableware, and gained recognition for its restraint and assured quality. In 1985 she began developing large handbuilt and press-moulded forms for outdoors, notably birdbaths. She is known for her series of birdbaths reminiscent of square boulders, set on timber bases.

1057

1059 / 1058

Sarah Walton, 'Salt-glaze', *Crafts*, 23 (1976), pp.12–13
— 'Nursing the Kiln', *Crafts*, 36 (1979)
— 'Salt and Form', *Ceramics Monthly*, 31:9 (1983)
— *Sarah Walton*, Aberystwyth Arts Centre: Ceramic Series 14 (1986)
— 'Saltglaze', *CR*, 104 (1987)
'CPA New Members', *CR*, 50 (1978)
Crafts Council (1980), p.64
Potters/The Ceramics Book (1980) to (2012)
Gwyn Hanssen Pigott, 'Domestic Pots – Domestic Potters', *CR*, 92 (1985)
Margot Coatts, 'Sarah Walton', *Studio Pottery*, 24 (1996)
Frankel (2000), pp.190–3
Cochrane (2001), pp.63–5
Hannah Wingrave, 'Sarah Walton', *Ceramics in Society*, 47 (2002)
Bonnie Kemske, 'Life Unfolding', *CR*, 256 (2012)

1057 Tea caddy, 1981
Stoneware, grey body, incised decoration, saltglaze; marks: 'SW', impressed; h.17.7cm, d.18.3cm
C.180&A-1981. Source: Craftsmen Potters Association, London (exhibition with Peter Smith and Andrew and Joanna Young, 1981, no.168), £40

1058 Jug, 1988
Stoneware, pink-brown saltglaze, green-grey interior; marks: 'SW' in monogram, impressed; h.22.6cm, d.16.7cm
C.6-1989. Source: Contemporary Applied Arts, London, £67.72

1059 Dish with handles, 1988
Stoneware, saltglaze with pink flushes; marks: 'SW' in monogram, impressed; h.9cm, d.29.7cm
C.9-1989. Source: *see* **1058**, £68.40

Ward, John 1938–

1938	born London
1965–66	studies ceramics part-time at East Ham Technical College, London, while working as a cameraman for the BBC
1966–70	studies ceramics at Camberwell School of Art and Crafts
1970–79	teaches ceramics part-time at Sydenham and Forest Hill Adult Education Institute, London

1971–76	first workshop in Anerley, London
1976–79	workshop in Charlton, London
1979–	moves to Cilgwyn, Pembrokeshire, establishes workshop
1982–	solo exhibition, Peter Dingley Gallery, Stratford-upon-Avon; thereafter regular solo exhibitions in UK and internationally

John Ward has gained a devoted following for his subtle pots, which combine refined shapes with subdued matt surfaces, sometimes with strikingly bold markings. While responding to both ancient and modern sources, Ward's work is in essence contemporary, and forms part of an ongoing vessel-making tradition associated with ideas of fine craft.

John Ward, 'What If ...', *CR*, 241 (2010)
Crafts Advisory Committee (1976), p.120
'CPA New Members', *CR*, 65 (1980)
Crafts Council (1980), p.64
Potters/The Ceramics Book (1983) to (2012)
Paisley Museum and Art Galleries (1984), pp.82–3
Stephen Brayne, 'The Pottery of John Ward', *CR*, 96 (1985)
Bonhams, *Contemporary Ceramics*, including the Sharman Collection (London, 27 February 1989), lots 110–37
David Sexton, 'John Ward', *Telegraph Weekend Magazine* (25 March 1989)
'John Ward', *Ceramics Monthly*, 38:3 (1990)
Bluecoat Display Centre, *John Ward*, exh. pamphlet, text by Emmanuel Cooper (Liverpool, 1996)
Frankel (2000), pp.146–8
Carlano (2010), pp.166–7
Moira Vincentelli, 'Cupped Hands', *CR*, 271 (2015)
Nottingham City Museums and Galleries (2017), pp.87–8
Emma Crichton-Miller, *The Pottery of John Ward* (London, 2022)

Exhibition reviews: illustration, *CR*, 30 (1974); Rosemarie Pitts, *Crafts*, 33 (1978); David Whiting, *Crafts*, 145 (1997)

1060 'Green and white banded oval bowl with double groove', 1985 (pl.87)
Stoneware, handbuilt, painted in a matt glaze; marks: 'JW' in monogram, impressed; h.20.3cm, d.21.3cm
C.25-1986. Source: Henry Rothschild, Cambridge (from exhibition: *European Ceramics and Wall Textures*, The Fitzwilliam Museum), £120

1061

1062

1061 Large collared bowl, 1987
Stoneware, handbuilt, matt black-brown and blue-green glazes; marks: 'JW' in monogram, impressed; h.26.7cm, d.35.5cm
C.34-2019. Source: Erskine, Hall & Coe, London (solo exhibition, 2019), £4500; acquired with funds raised in memory of Jonathan Nevitt
Originally supplied to the Craftsmen Potters Shop, London, in November 1987. Formerly in the collection of Patricia Ingleton and Elspeth Fyfe.

1062 Pot, 1994
Stoneware, handbuilt, black and white glazes; marks: 'JW' in monogram, impressed; h.38.2cm, d.30.5cm
C.69-2005. Source: given by Dasha Shenkman

Washington, Robert Johnson (**R.J.**) 1913–1997

1913	born Lambeth, London
1930–33	studies painting at Goldsmiths' College, London
1933–36	studies painting at Royal College of Art, London
1936–38	takes Art Teacher's Diploma at Goldsmiths' and Royal College of Art, studying pottery under William Staite Murray (qv); attends evening classes at Central School of Arts and Crafts with Dora Billington (qv)
1938–46	teaches painting and pottery at Derby School of Art; work interrupted by war service in Royal Air Force
1946–48	Deputy Principal, Thanet School of Art, Margate, Kent
1948–49	Principal, Dewsbury School of Art, West Yorkshire
1949–74	Inspector for Art Education, Essex Education Committee
1954–79	sporadically returns to potting in studio at his home in Little Baddow, Essex
1979–	retires, resumes making full-time

A student of painting, R.J. Washington was drawn to pottery while training as an art teacher at the Royal College of Art, and stayed on to study ceramics. He also benefited from Dora Billington's (qv) technical instruction at the Central School, which he passed onwards in his own years of teaching. Washington is particularly known for his tall, brush-decorated stoneware pots, made first in the 1930s. During his sporadic returns to potting, he gave these pots anthropomorphic profiles and painted them with Cubist figures. Exhibitions at the London galleries of Paul Rice and Anatol Orient brought renewed interest in his work during the 1980s. Increasingly inclined towards experimentation, Washington applied painting techniques to ceramics and mixed media in a late outpouring of work.

Robert J. Washington, autobiographical essay, *Ceramics Monthly*, 47:3 (1999)
Arts and Crafts Exhibition Society (1938), (1946)
Wingfield Digby (1952), pp.77–8, pl.45
Haslam (1984), pp.65–6, pls.41–3
Paul Rice, 'Margaret Rey, R.J. Washington', *Studio Pottery*, 7 (1994)
Brenda Pegrum, 'Body and Soul', *CR*, 174 (1998)
David Whiting, 'Late Celebration', *Crafts*, 155 (1998)
J.V.G. Mallet, 'R.J. Washington and his memories

1065 / 1067 / 1066

1068

1069

of William Staite Murray', *English Ceramic Circle Transactions*, 19:2 (2006)
Robert Cooper, exh. review, *CR*, 231 (2008)
Carlano (2010), pp.170–1

Obituaries: Paul Rice, *The Guardian* (26 November 1997) and *Crafts*, 151 (1998); Emmanuel Cooper, *The Independent* (28 November 1997); *The Times* (13 December 1997)

1063 Tall pot, 1938 (pl.27)
Stoneware, grey-brown glaze, painted in brown; marks: 'RJW', impressed; h.50.7cm, d.16.5cm
Circ.96-1939. Source: The Brygos Gallery, London (joint exhibition with Henry Hammond and Gwilym Thomas, 1938, no.225), £7.7s.

1064 Tall pot, 1938 (pl.27)
Stoneware, mottled yellow and brown glaze; marks: 'RJW', impressed; h.58.8cm, d.17.2cm
Circ.97-1939. Source: *see* **1063** (no.150), £5.5s.

1065 Tall pot, 1964
Stoneware, cream glaze, painted in brown; marks: 'RJW' and '64', incised; h.79.8cm, d.14cm
C.49-1979. Source: given by the artist

1066 Tall pot: *Uranus*, *c.* 1965
Stoneware, yellow glaze, painted in brown; h.70.6cm, d.16cm
C.48-1979. Source: *see* **1065**
Washington noted that the glaze 'owes its colour to uranium oxide (obtained before the war and hoarded carefully ever since)'.

1067 Pot: *Satyr and Dryad*, from a short series, *Satyrnalia*, 1981
Stoneware, cream glaze, painted in brown; marks: 'RJW 81', incised; h.49.1cm, d.21.1cm
C.32-1985. Source: the artist, £350
The profile of the pot is intended to evoke the outline of a woman's torso.

1068 Wall platter, 1986
Stoneware, handbuilt, painted with slips and enamels and incised; marks: 'RJW 86', incised; h.39.9cm, d.46.6cm
C.115-1998. Source: given by Su Washington

1069 Bowl, 1995–96
Earthenware mixed with ceramic fibre, handbuilt, turquoise and volcanic black glazes; h.8.8cm, d.18cm
C.116-1998. Source: *see* **1068**

Wason, Jason 1946–

1946 born Liverpool
1964–74 travels in Europe, North Africa, Middle East, Asia
1974–76 establishes crafts community in Dumfriesshire; builds kick-wheel and learns to throw
1976–81 works at Leach Pottery, St Ives
1981– establishes own studio, St Just, Cornwall
1990– solo exhibitions at Austin/Desmond Fine Art, London; Vincent Gallery, Exeter; and elsewhere
1995 solo exhibition, Museum Boijmans Van Beuningen, Rotterdam
1998 travels to New Mexico, USA, to study Mimbres pottery
2000|02|05 residencies in Seto, Aichi, Japan
2007– regular solo exhibitions at Lemon Street Gallery, Truro, Cornwall
2011 solo exhibition, Mashiko Museum of Ceramic Art, Tochigi, Japan

Jason Wason is recognized for his individual sculptural vessels, which suggest ancient ceremonial forms. Often of substantial size, these are marked by strong profiles and richly textured surfaces reminiscent of patinated metal. Before establishing his own workshop, he worked at the Leach Pottery, where he was among the last makers of its Standard Ware.

Paul Vincent, *Jason Wason*, Aberystwyth Arts Centre: Ceramic Series 61 (1993)
— 'Jason Wason', *Studio Pottery*, 1 (1993)
Austin/Desmond Fine Art, *Jason Wason: Ceramics*, exh. cat., text by David Archer (London, 1998)
Anthony Fagin, 'From Mimbres to Mashiko', *CR*, 220 (2006)
Whybrow (2006), pp.218–19
Lemon Street Gallery, *Jason Wason: The Circle is Unbroken*, exh. cat., text by David Whiting (Truro, 2007) – see also cats. from 2008, 2010, 2012 and 2014

1070

Pangolin, *Burnt Offerings: Jason Wason*, exh. cat., text by Anthony Fagin (London, 2010)
Austin/Desmond Fine Art, *Janet Leach, William Marshall, Jason Wason*, exh. cat., text by Michael Bird (London, 2011)
Andy Christian, 'Jason Wason', *Ceramics: Art and Perception*, 101 (2015)
Lemon Street Gallery, *Jason Wason: A View from the Edge*, exh. cat., text by Simon Olding (Truro, 2019)

Exhibition reviews: Jo Dahn, *Studio Pottery*, 6 (1993); Felicity Aylieff, *CR*, 173 (1998); Ian Wilson, *Crafts*, 167 (2000); Simon Martin, *CR*, 226 (2007)

1070 *Metallic Gold and Red Vessel*, 2019
High-fired earthenware, metallic oxides; h.54.7cm, d.52.5cm
C.54-2019. Source: given by Marie Louise Jones, Lemon Street Gallery, Truro (from solo exhibition: *A View from the Edge*, 2019)

Waters, James 1968– and **Tilla** (née Anderson) 1967–

James

1968	born Redditch, Worcestershire
1987–91	studies painting at Slade School of Art, London
1998–2000	apprentice and assistant to Rupert Spira (qv); meets Tilla

Tilla

1967	born Haslemere, Surrey
1986–90	studies painting at Bath Academy of Art
1993–94	trains as art teacher at Goldsmiths' College, London
1995–97	teaches art in Redbridge, London; takes evening classes in ceramics
1998–2000	apprentice and assistant to Rupert Spira; meets James
2002–	together set up workshop at Llansadwrn, Carmarthenshire
2007	solo exhibition, Aberystwyth Arts Centre, Ceredigion

James and Tilla Waters' practice is rooted in the production of precise, yet playful, functional wares in porcelain and stoneware. Since 2012 they have also made a number of individual pieces. Their partnership combines James' refined making skills with Tilla's sensibility towards design and colour.

Ruthin Craft Centre (2009), pp.32–3
Jo Dahn, 'Ideas and Visions', *CR*, 243 (2010)
The Ceramics Book (2012)
Paul McAllister, 'Enigmatic Tableware', *Ceramics Monthly*, 63:2 (2015)
Grant Gibson, 'Still Waters Run Deep', *Crafts*, 272 (2018)

1071

1071 Teapot, breakfast mug and pourer, 2018
Stoneware, stencilled decoration under a white glaze; marks: 'J & / T W', impressed; h.13.7cm, d.19.8cm (teapot); h.8cm, d.12.2cm (mug); h.10.9cm, d.7.6cm (pourer)
C.341:1,2, 342, 343-2018. Source: the artists, £284; acquired through the generosity of Gerard and Sarah Griffin

Welch, Robin 1936–2019

1936	born Nuneaton, Warwickshire
1952–53	studies at Nuneaton School of Art
1953–56	studies sculpture, and pottery under Michael Leach (qv), at Penzance College of Art; works part-time at Leach Pottery, St Ives
1959	studies ceramics at Central School of Arts and Crafts, London; subsequently appointed technical assistant
1960–	sets up workshop in Bloomsbury, London, with Gillian Lowndes (qv) and Kate Watts
1962	solo exhibition, Crafts Centre of Great Britain, London; exhibits widely thereafter
1962–65	moves to Australia, establishes pottery workshop near Melbourne with Ian Sprague
1965	returns to England, establishes workshop at Stradbroke, Suffolk
c. 1968–86	produces domestic ware alongside individual pieces
1979–80	residency in Victoria, Australia
1985	commission for monumental candleholders for Lincoln Cathedral
1990–91|96	visits to New South Wales, Australia, to study outback landscape

For many years Robin Welch made an acclaimed range of domestic stoneware based on simple cylindrical shapes, produced using semi-industrial 'jolleying' techniques, and part-glazed in distinctive matt colours. Alongside this, he made individual sculptural pieces in a similar, austere style. Welch later evolved looser, individual vessel forms with encrusted, painterly surfaces achieved through successive firings, drawing inspiration from the Australian landscape.

Robin Welch, 'Ceramic Textures', *Pottery Quarterly*, 8:29 (1963)
— 'Workshop', *CR*, 7 (1971)
Decorative Art (1962/63), (1963/64), (1965/66), (1966/67), (1969/70)
Biographical notes, *Pottery Quarterly*, 8:30 (1963), pp.8–9, pl.37, and 9:35 (1969), p.106, pls.14–15
Birks (1967), pp.125–40, (1976), pp.182–93
Jeremy Fisher, 'Pottery as Sculpture', *Design*, 239 (1968)
Potters (1972) to (1992)
Crafts Advisory Committee (1976), p.120
Crafts Council (1980), p.64
Peter Lane, 'Robin Welch', *CR*, 69 (1981)
Oxfordshire County Museum Services (1984), pp.60–1
Paisley Museum and Art Galleries (1984), p.83
John Colbeck, 'Robin Welch', *CR*, 136 (1992)
Greg (1995), p.34 and appendices
David Whiting, 'Robin Welch', *Craft Arts International*, 48 (2000)
Dewar (2002), pp.119–21
Simon Olding and Vivienne Light, *Robin Welch: Ceramic Artist*, exh. cat., Maltby Contemporary Art (Winchester, 2002)
Neil Bennison, 'Maverick Maker', *Craft Arts International*, 71 (2007)
Carlano (2010), pp.174–5
'65 Years in Clay', *CR*, 288 (2017)

Exhibition reviews: *Pottery Quarterly*, 7:28 (1962); *The Guardian* (16 June 1969); Anthony Hepburn, *Craft Horizons*, 29:5 (1969); Geoffrey Eastop, *CR*, 23 (1973), and 37 (1976); Peter Lane, *CR*, 101 (1986); Shane Enright, *Studio Pottery*, 3 (1993); David Whiting, *Crafts*, 148 (1997); Felicity Aylieff, *CR*, 178 (1999); Judy Adams, *CR*, 228 (2007)

Obituaries: David Whiting, *The Guardian* (27 December 2019) and *Crafts*, 283 (2020); Peter Wilson, *Ceramics: Art and Perception*, 116 (2020)

1072

1075 / 1074

An interview with Robin Welch is in the Crafts Lives sound archive at the British Library, London (C960/85).

1072 'Large Dish, Blue glaze, rust rim', 1962
Stoneware, blue, yellow and brown matt glazes; marks: 'Robin Welch', painted; h.6.5cm, d.33.6cm
Circ.648-1962. Source: Crafts Centre of Great Britain, London (solo exhibition, 1962, no.51), £4.15s.

1073 'Cylinder with Split Centre', 1968 (pl.53)
Stoneware, thrown in two sections and turned, with white matt ash glaze, copper oxide, matt black glaze and blue acrylic; marks: 'ROBIN WELCH / 68', painted; h.63cm, d.12.7cm
Circ.529-1969. Source: Crafts Centre of Great Britain, London (exhibition: *Robin Welch – Sculpture*, no.9, 1969), £25

1074 Bowl, 1983
Stoneware, reduction-fired, with low-temperature coloured glazes; marks: 'ROBIN WELCH', impressed; h.17cm, d.22.5cm
C.329-1983. Source: J K Hill, London (solo exhibition: *Pots and Paintings*, 1983, no.45), £79

1075 'Pod pot', 1983
Stoneware, reduction-fired, with low-temperature coloured glazes; marks: 'ROBIN WELCH', impressed; h.11.7cm, d.9cm
C.330-1983. Source: *see* 1074 (no.3), £38

Wells, Reginald Fairfax (**R.F.**)
1877–1951

1877	born Rio de Janeiro, Brazil
late 1890s	studies sculpture at Royal College of Art, London; later studies pottery at Camberwell School of Arts and Crafts
c. 1907–	establishes pottery at Coldrum Farm, near Wrotham, Kent
1909–14	moves pottery to Chelsea, London, working from addresses in Keppel Street and Elystan Street; continues using 'COL'DRUM' name on mark; employs Edward Baker as a thrower during this period
1914–18	pottery closes due to war; establishes aircraft manufacturing business on same site; re-launches as Wells Aviation Company in 1916 and production expands
1919–24	resumes potting, establishes London Pottery Company, King's Road, Chelsea, marking ware 'SOON'
1923	exhibition with William Staite Murray (qv) and Henry Wyse, Gieves Art Gallery, London
1925	solo exhibition, Fine Art Society, London
1925–51	moves to Storrington, Sussex, where establishes Tiles and Potteries Ltd; continues potting using 'SOON' mark
1926|27	solo exhibitions, Beaux Arts Gallery, London
1927–	designs and builds houses at West Chiltington, Sussex

Reginald Wells was a sculptor and potter, who at times worked also as a manufacturer and designer of aircraft, and as an architect. He is the earliest potter recorded in this catalogue, and his interest in English slipware and Chinese stoneware reflected the dominant concerns of the pioneers of studio pottery. Trained first as a sculptor, he modelled and cast in bronze small-scale, realist figurative sculpture from about 1899. He began making slipware about 1907 at Coldrum Farm near Wrotham in Kent, using local clay and drawing on local traditions. At Chelsea he continued with slipware but increasingly concentrated on the production of stoneware of Chinese inspiration, a preoccupation that he returned to after the First World War, both at Chelsea and at Storrington. These later wares were named and marked 'SOON', apparently a personal reference to his return to pottery and profitability, rather than an invocation of Song dynasty ceramics. Wells also modelled ceramic figures in this period, some based on earlier bronzes. He was highly regarded in the 1920s, though his reputation has since ebbed.

Reginald F. Wells, 'The Lure of Making Pottery', *Arts and Crafts*, 2:1 (May 1927)
Decorative Art (1913), (1927), (1928)
Arts and Crafts Exhibition Society (1923)
British Institute of Industrial Art (1923), (1927), (1929)
Royal Academy of Arts (1923)
Guild of Potters (1924)
Ernest Marsh, 'R.F. Wells – Sculptor and Potter', *Apollo*, 1:5 (May 1925)
Bernard Rackham, 'The Pottery of Mr. Reginald Wells', *The Studio*, 90 (December 1925)
Frederick Lessore, 'The Art of Reginald F. Wells Sculptor and Potter', *Artwork*, 8:2 (1926/27)
Obituary, *The Times* (18 July 1951)
Rose (1955), pp.7–8, pl.9, (1970), p.24, pl.8
Blunt (1973), pp.*xviii–xxiii*, 87, pls.38–40
Vincentelli and Hale (1986)
Riddick (1990), p.118
Bergesen (1993), pp.76–81
Luton Museum Service, *Reginald Fairfax Wells: Sculptor, Potter, Designer*, exh. cat., text by Paul Hyman (1998)
Jones (2007), pp.34–7

Exhibition reviews: Frank Rutter, *Sunday Times* (23 September 1923), (22 November 1925), (21 November 1926), (15 May 1927), (20 November 1927); *The Times* (13 November 1925)

1076 Handled bowl, 1909 (pl.2)
Earthenware, slip decoration in white, applied relief, greenish glaze; inscribed 'COL'DRUM. 1909'; marks: 'R.F.W', incised; made at Coldrum Farm, Wrotham, Kent; h.7.3cm, d.14.9cm
C.952-1917. Source: given by Herman Hart in memory of his wife

1077 Handled pot, *c.* 1909 (pl.2)
Earthenware, slip decoration in white, greenish glaze; inscribed 'COL'DRUM.'; made at Coldrum Farm, Wrotham, Kent; h.12.7cm, d.17.5cm
C.743-1923. Source: given by W. Ridout

1078

1083

1085 / 1086 / 1087

1079 / 1080 / 1081 / 1082

1084

1090 / 1089 / 1088

1078 Jug, 1909
Earthenware, slip-trailed in white on red clay, transparent glaze; inscribed 'COL'DRUM / CHELSEA / 1909'; h.20.9cm, d.24cm
C.82-1981. Source: Christopher Wood Gallery, London, £250

1079 Jar with three handles, *c.* 1910–14
Earthenware, greenish glaze with brown mottling; marks: 'COL'DRUM', impressed; h.29.9cm, d.19.2cm
Circ.517-1919. Source: given by Victor Ames
Ames was a friend of Wells. The group of pots he gifted (**1079** to **1092**) was supplied directly to the museum by Wells, who was yet to resume potting.

1080 Jar with three handles, *c.* 1910–14
Earthenware, greenish glaze with brown flecks; h.23.3cm, d.15.6cm
C.521-1919. Source: *see* **1079**
A paper label gives the price '15/6d'.

1081 Jar with two handles, *c.* 1910–14
Earthenware, green mottled glaze streaked brown; h.13.9cm, d.13.5cm
Circ.515-1919. Source: *see* **1079**

1082 Jar with three handles, *c.* 1910–14
Earthenware, transparent glaze with green streaks over a red body; h.29.4cm, d.18.8cm
C.530-1919. Source: *see* **1079**

1083 Bottle, *c.* 1910–14
Stoneware, mottled brown and green glaze; h.19.7cm, d.14cm
C.522-1919. Source: *see* **1079**

1084 Jar, *c.* 1910–14
Stoneware, mottled grey glaze; marks: 'COL'DRUM', impressed; h.28cm, d.24.4cm
C.531-1919. Source: *see* **1079**

1085 Jar, *c.* 1910–14
Stoneware, mottled greenish-grey and black glaze; h.18.7cm, d.14.6cm
C.526-1919. Source: *see* **1079**

1086 Jar, *c.* 1910–14
Stoneware, mottled grey and black glaze; h.10.6cm, d.12.7cm
C.523-1919. Source: *see* **1079**
The price '6/6d' is written in ink on the base.

1087 Jar, *c.* 1910–14
Stoneware, pale blue streaked glaze;

1093 / 1091 / 1092

1102 / 1095

1099 / 1100 / 1101

1094

1106 / 1096 / 1105

1103

h.14.4cm, d.10.3cm
C.525-1919. Source: *see* **1079**

1088 Jar, *c.* 1910–14
Stoneware, streaked blue and plum-red glaze; h.19.7cm, d.14.4cm
C.527-1919. Source: *see* **1079**

1089 Jar, *c.* 1910–14
Stoneware, plum-red glaze with blue streaks; h.18.9cm, d.14.3cm
C.524-1919. Source: *see* **1079**

1090 Jar, *c.* 1910–14
Stoneware, opaque glaze mottled blue and red; marks: 'COL'DRUM', impressed; h.20cm, d.15.1cm
Circ.516-1919. Source: *see* **1079**

1091 Jar, *c.* 1910–14
Stoneware, crackled white glaze; marks: 'COL'DRUM', impressed; h.19.4cm, d.16cm
C.528-1919. Source: *see* **1079**

1092 Pot, *c.* 1910–14
Stoneware, pale grey-white glaze with turquoise flecks; marks: 'COL'DRUM' and 'CHELSEA', impressed; h.31cm, d.16.9cm
C.529-1919. Source: *see* **1079**

1093 Jar, *c.* 1910–14
Stoneware, opaque white glaze with black crackle; marks: 'COL'DRUM CHELSEA', impressed; h.20.3cm, d.22.1cm
Circ.907-1967. Source: given by Miss Prunella Clough

1094 Jar, *c.* 1910–14
Stoneware, black glaze; marks: 'COL'DRUM', impressed; h.32.2cm, d.26cm
Circ.908-1967. Source: *see* **1093**

1095 Pot, *c.* 1910–14
Stoneware, streaked blue glaze; h.7.1cm, d.7.6cm
C.12-1924. Source: given by Victor Ames

1096 Pot, *c.* 1924
Stoneware, blue glaze with purple mottling; marks: 'SOON', impressed; h.7.7cm, d.7.8cm
Circ.991-1924. Source: given by W.W. Winkworth

1097 Pot, *c.* 1924 (pl.15)
Stoneware, opaque white glaze with crackle; marks: 'S', incised; h.15cm, d.10cm

C.60-1925. Source: Beaux Arts Gallery, London; given by Sir Amherst Selby-Bigge, Ernest Marsh and Bernard Rackham (purchased by the donors for £7.7s.)
Marsh wrote of this piece in 1925 (p.286) as follows: 'The horizontal ribbings running well down over the shoulder of the vase give the necessary distinction to a simple shape, and the glaze, with its delicate crackle, completes a very perfect little vase.'

1098 Bowl, *c.* 1925 (pl.15)
Stoneware, opaque white glaze; marks: 'SOON', incised; h.6cm, d.9.3cm
Circ.513-1925. Source: given by Bernard Rackham

1099 Jar, *c.* 1925
Stoneware, white glaze with crackle and green speckles; marks: 'SOON', incised; h.26.8cm, d.19.5cm
C.791-1925. Source: given by A.E. Anderson through Art Fund

1100 Jar, *c.* 1925
Stoneware, yellow-green glaze; marks: 'SOON', incised; h.20.8cm, d.17.3cm
C.790-1925. Source: *see* **1099**

1101 Jar, *c.* 1925
Stoneware, grey-cream crackled glaze; marks: 'SOON', incised; h.22.5cm, d.17.3cm
C.339-1926. Source: Fine Art Society, London; given by A.E. Anderson

1102 Bowl, *c.* 1925
Stoneware, mottled blue glaze; marks: 'SOON', incised; h.7cm, d.21.5cm
Circ.274-1955. Source: given by Lady Russell, MBE, from the collection of the late Francis Moore

1103 Vase (with wooden stand), *c.* 1925
Stoneware, grey glaze mottled black; marks: 'SOON', incised; h.26.8cm, d.17.7cm
Circ.273&A-1955. Source: *see* **1102**

1104 Jar, *c.* 1926
Stoneware, pale opaque green glaze; h.24.2cm, d.18.9cm
Circ.11-1927. Source: Beaux Arts Gallery, London; given by A.E. Anderson

1105 Vase, 1928
Stoneware, white glaze mottled black; marks: 'SOON', impressed; h.20.9cm, d.13.4cm
Circ.108-1959. Source: given by Wing-Commander H.D. Wells
This piece was lent to the British Institute of Industrial Art (then housed in the V&A) in 1928. It was given to the museum after Wells' death by his son. Illustrated in Rose (1955), pl.9.

1106 Vase, 1928
Stoneware, copper-red mottled glaze; marks: 'SOON', impressed; h.20.4cm, d.15.5cm
Circ.109-1959. Source: *see* **1105**

1107 Figure of a runner duck, 1923
Stoneware, press-moulded, painted in blue, yellow and green; h.18.9cm, d.12cm
C.438-1934. Source: British Institute of Industrial Art (given by the artist)

1108 Figure: *Motherhood*, 1924
Stoneware, press-moulded, brownish glaze; h.39.5cm, d.16.5cm
Circ.272-1955. Source: given by Lady Russell, MBE, from the collection of the late Francis Moore

1109 Figure of a horse, 1926
Stoneware, press-moulded, mottled blue-grey glaze; marks: 'SOON' (twice) and 'R. F. Wells', incised; h.29.6cm, d.35.8cm
Circ.10-1927. Source: given by R. Mond

1104

1107

1108

1109

White, Mary (née Rollinson) 1926–2013

1926	born Croesyceiliog, Monmouthshire
1943–	studies at Newport College of Art
1946–48	studies at Hammersmith College of Art

1949–50	Art Teacher's Diploma at Goldsmiths' College, London
1950–61	teaches in schools and art colleges
1951	marries artist Charles White
1962–73	teaches typography and ceramics at Atlantic College, St Donats, Glamorgan
1969–75	studio in Llantwit Major, Glamorgan; begins concentrating on ceramics
1975–80	studio in Malmesbury, Wiltshire
1980–	moves to Germany, establishes studio in Wonsheim
1982	awarded Staatspreis für das Kunsthandwerk Rheinland-Pfalz

Mary White worked mostly in porcelain, making delicate thrown vessels and small sculptures inspired by landscape forms. Also a trained and practising calligrapher, White experimented with calligraphy on pots prior to her move to Germany, and again from 1990 onwards.

Mary White, 'A Potter in Paradiesgarten', *CR*, 84 (1983)
— *Lettering on Ceramics* (London, 2003)
Commonwealth Art Gallery, *Mary White*, exh. cat. (London, 1973)
'CPA New Members', *CR*, 30 (1974)
Colin Murry, 'A Welsh Potter', *Ceramics Monthly*, 23:7 (1975)
Potters/The Ceramics Book (1975) to (2008)
Crafts Advisory Committee (1976), p.121
John Houston, exh. review, *Crafts*, 39 (1979)
Crafts Council (1980), p.65
Handwerkskammer Rheinhessen, *Mary White*, exh. pamphlet (Mainz, 1991)
Lily Crowther, 'To the Letter', *CR*, 269 (2014)

1110

1110 Bottle, 1977
Porcelain, coloured glazes, inscription in silver lustre; h.16cm, d.18.4cm
C.181-1977. Source: given by the artist
Presented following exhibition in the V&A Jubilee Celebration, 1977. Selected by Lady Casson.

Whiting, Geoffrey 1919–1988

1919	born Stocksfield, Northumberland
1937–39	trains at Birmingham School of Architecture
1940–48	army service in Burma (now Myanmar) and India; encounters and works with Indian village potters
1949–	establishes Avoncroft Pottery at Stoke Prior, Worcestershire; teaches at Stoke House, Bletchley, Buckinghamshire
1953	marries Anne Heath
1955–	moves Avoncroft Pottery to Hampton Lovett, Worcestershire; Anne initially assists with domestic ware range
1971	travels to Lesotho to establish pottery
1972–	moves workshop to St Augustine's College, Canterbury, Kent
1976–	pottery becomes attached to King's School, Canterbury; teaches part-time at King's School and Medway College of Design

Geoffrey Whiting made domestic ware and individual pieces, working in reduction-fired stoneware and some porcelain, after a short period making slip-decorated earthenware. He was particularly noted for his teapots. Self-taught with the aid of Bernard Leach's *A Potter's Book*, Whiting was a maker of discipline and integrity, who placed great value on craft skill and the provision of good, affordable handmade pottery.

Geoffrey Whiting, 'Making Teapots', with biographical notes, *Pottery Quarterly*, 2:7 (1955)
— 'Avoncroft Pottery', *Pottery Quarterly*, 5:20 (1958)
— 'Quality in Glazes', *Pottery Quarterly*, 10:37 (1971)
— 'Workshops and the Future of Potting', *CR*, 15 (1972)
— 'Off Centre', *CR*, 41 (1976)
— 'Quo Vadis?', *CR*, 84 (1983)
— 'Showman Potter', *CR*, 106 (1987)
— contribution to 'Bernard Leach – A Living Tradition', *CR*, 108 (1987)
Lewis (1956), pls.354–5
Casson (1967), p.8, pls.174, 242–3
Rose (1970), p.49, pls.78–9

1111

'Craftsman Potters Association: News of Members', *CR*, 8 (1971)
John M. Anderson, 'Geoffrey Whiting Film', letter, *CR*, 16 (1972)
Potters (1972) to (1986)
Crafts Advisory Committee (1977), p.23
'Geoffrey Whiting – Recent Work', *CR*, 59 (1979)
W.A. Ismay, 'Geoffrey Whiting – Potter', *CR*, 100 (1986)
Aberystwyth Arts Centre, *Geoffrey Whiting: Potter*, exh. cat. (1989)
David Whiting, 'A Personal View', *CR*, 120 (1989), and letter, *CR*, 121 (1990)
— 'Geoffrey Whiting', *Studio Pottery*, 11 (1994)
— 'Family Values', letter, *Crafts*, 135 (1995)
— 'Pride of Place', *CR*, 258 (2012)
— 'Anne Whiting', obituary, *The Guardian* (17 February 2017)
Nottingham City Museums and Galleries (2017), p.90

Exhibition reviews: *Pottery Quarterly*, 6:23 (1959); W.A. Ismay, *CR*, 29 (1974); Emmanuel Cooper, *Art & Artists*, 14:5 (1979), and *Crafts*, 115 (1992); Tanya Harrod, *The Spectator* (2 December 1989); Arda Lacey, *Arts Review* (18 May 1990); Moira Vincentelli, *Crafts*, 103 (1990); *The Cantuarian*, 56:1 (1991)

Obituaries: Emmanuel Cooper, *The Independent* (5 January 1988); *The Times* (15 January 1988); *CR*, 110 (1988); *Ceramics Monthly*, 36:6 (1988)

1111 Teapot, 1959
Stoneware, tenmoku glaze; marks: 'A' in a circle and 'GW' in monogram, impressed; h.12.1cm, d.20.3cm
Circ.328&A-1959. Source: the artist, £2.2s.

1112 Vase, 1959
Stoneware, grey and brown mottled glaze;

1112 / 1113

1114

marks: 'A' in a circle and 'GW' in monogram, impressed; h.23cm, d.17.8cm
Circ.327-1959. Source: the artist, £4

1113 Vase, 1973
Stoneware, deep blue glaze with poured brown glaze decoration; marks: 'GW' in monogram and 'A' in a circle, impressed; h.17.5cm, d.14cm
C.284-1987. Source: given by the artist

1114 Bottle, 1987
Stoneware, thrown, squared and cut, with grey and brown glazes; marks: 'A' and 'G' in circles, impressed; h.21.5cm, d.13.5cm
C.16-1988. Source: Craftsmen Potters Association, London (exhibition: *The Leach Tradition – A Creative Force*, 1987, no.139), £85.50

1115

Whittall, Eleanor E. 1900–1990

1900	born London
c. 1930s	studies at Central School of Arts and Crafts, London, under Dora Billington (qv)
c. 1944–65	studio in St Pancras, London
1953–58	President of the Arts and Crafts Exhibition Society
1954|56	solo exhibitions, The Cooling Galleries, London

Eleanor Whittall was engaged with ceramics by 1938, when she wrote to Bernard Leach (qv) enquiring about a summer school at Dartington Hall, Devon, and the purchase of a kick-wheel (Crafts Study Centre, Farnham, Bernard Leach archive, MSS 3405-7). By 1944 she was established in a studio in St Pancras, London, where she was later captured in David Gladwell's documentary *28b Camden Street* (1965), filmed at the time of its demolition. Whittall made individual thrown and altered pieces in stoneware and later also porcelain, decorating with brushwork or exploring the effects of ash glazes. A member of the Oriental Ceramic Society, she had a keen interest in Chinese art.

Eleanor Whittall, 'Clay on the Wheel', *Journal of the Association of Occupational Therapists*, 11:34 (1948), pp.23–5
— 'Vegetable Ash Glazes', *Pottery Quarterly*, 1:2 (1954)
Arts and Crafts Exhibition Society (1944), (1946), (1950) to (1957)
Decorative Art (1950/51) to (1957/58), (1959/60), (1963/64)
Billington (1953)

Exhibition reviews: *Pottery Quarterly*, 1:1 (1954), and 3:12 (1956), p.158, pl.9

1115 'Ice blue bowl on feet', 1956
Stoneware, reduced ash glaze; h.10.3cm, d.25cm
Circ.108-1957. Source: the artist, £15.15s. (following solo exhibition, The Cooling Galleries, London, 1956, no.92)

Wickham, Helen 1884–1982

1884	born Shepton Mallet, Somerset
1900s	studies at St John's Wood School of Art, London
1920s	studio in West Hampstead, London
1922–29	exhibits regularly in London

Helen Wickham was a maker of pottery figures, known in particular for her representations of women and children.

British Institute of Industrial Art (1923), no.134P, (1927), (1929), p.94
Arts and Crafts Exhibition Society (1926), (1928)
Exh. review, *Sheffield Independent* (21 May 1931)
Knott (2021)

Papers relating to Helen Wickham's career are in the Ternan Family Papers (MS915/2), Senate House Library, University of London.

1116 Figure: *Mischief*, 1923
Glazed earthenware, painted in colours; marks: 'HW' in monogram, within a circle, painted; h.14.2cm, d.9.7cm
C.487-1934. Source: British Institute of Industrial Art (given by the artist, 1923)

1116

Willington, Sally *see* Sonia St Leger

Winchcombe Pottery *see* Michael Cardew *and* Ray Finch

Wine, Jesse 1983–

1983	born Chester, Cheshire
2004–07	studies sculpture at Camberwell College of Arts
2008–10	studies sculpture at Royal College of Art, London
2010	exchange to Hunter College, New York, USA, where discovers clay
2011–16	studio in Elephant and Castle, London
2013–14	Ceramics Fellowship, Camden Arts Centre, London
2014–15	solo exhibition, *Young Man Red*, BALTIC Centre for Contemporary Art, Gateshead, Tyne and Wear
2016–	moves to New York, establishes studio in Brooklyn

A sculptor who primarily works in ceramics, Jesse Wine is a leading figure in a movement that has seen artists from fine-art backgrounds increasingly adopt clay. Marked by humour and generosity of spirit, his sculpture explores biographical and art-historical themes using elements of self-portraiture, and the depiction and reinterpretation of objects of personal or historical significance.

Jesse Wine and Nicolas Party, 'Apples and Pairs', conversation, *Frieze*, 175 (2015)
— **and Sam Thorne**, 'In Conversation', in Matson and Thorne (2016), pp.116–22
Camden Arts Centre, *Jesse Wine*, File Note 89 (London, 2013)
Matthew McLean, 'Botched Temporalities and Ceramic Selves', *Frieze*, 166 (2014)
Oriel Mostyn, *Jesse Wine: Uprisings*, exh. pamphlet, interview by Adam Carr (Llandudno, 2014)
Fanny Singer, 'Studio Visit: Jessie Wine', interview, *Art Papers*, 38:4 (2014)
Anna Colin and Lydia Yee (eds), *British Art Show 8*, exh. cat. (London, 2015)
Rob Sharp, 'Up and Coming: Ceramist Jesse Wine on Making Art Accessible', *Artsy*, online (7 October 2015)
Kettle's Yard, *Sludgy Portrait of Himself*, exh. pamphlet, interview by Guy Haywood (Cambridge, 2016)
Aaron Peasley, 'Bright Young Artists', *Interview* (December 2016)

1118

Claire Shea, 'Throwing Shapes', *Elephant*, 26 (2016)
Elderton and Morrill (2017), pp.290–3
Kathy Noble, 'A Sculpture Looking at You Whilst Touching Itself', interview, *Mousse*, 74 (2021)
Cassie Packard, 'Open to Possibility', interview, *Bomb*, ejournal (15 January 2021)

Exhibition reviews: Paul Kneale, *Frieze*, 152 (2013); Mark Harris, *Artforum*, online (2015); Kristen Tauer, *WWD*, ejournal (24 September 2020); Aaron Bogart, *Flash Art*, ejournal (14 January 2021); Elaine Y.J. Zheng, *This Is Tomorrow*, ejournal (26 February 2021)

1117 *Jesse show passion III*, 2014 (pl.138)
Earthenware, handbuilt, glaze; h.29.2cm, d.33.9cm
C.30-2016. Source: Mary Mary, Glasgow, £4000; acquired through the generosity of Gerard and Sarah Griffin
Shown in the solo exhibition *Chester Man*, Mary Mary, Glasgow, 2014.

1118 *Well nice. Proper nice I*, 2014
Earthenware, handbuilt, coloured glazes; h.19cm, d.46.9cm; h.19.3cm, d.48.6cm
C.31:1,2-2016. Source: *see* **1117**, £4400
Shown in the solo exhibition *Young Man Red*, BALTIC Centre for Contemporary Art, Gateshead, 2014–15.

Wolstencroft, Barbara *see* Barbara Cass

Wondrausch, Mary (née Lambert) 1923–2016

1923	born Battersea, London
1968–	studies ceramics part-time at Farnham School of Art
1974–	establishes Wharf Pottery, Godalming, Surrey
1976–	moves Wharf Pottery to Farncombe, Surrey
1984–	establishes workshop at Brickfields, Compton, Surrey
2000	awarded OBE

Mary Wondrausch turned to pottery after practising as a self-taught painter. She is known for her lively interpretations of traditional slipwares, in particular commemorative plates.

Mary Wondrausch, 'Down to Earth', *Crafts*, 48 and 49 (1981)
— 'Slip Decorated Earthenware', *CR*, 79 (1983)
— *Mary Wondrausch on Slipware* (London, 1986), revised (2001)
— 'Off Centre', *CR*, 184 (2000)
— 'Potter's Day', *CR*, 188 (2001)
— *Brickfields: My Life at Brickfields as a Potter, Painter, Gardener, Writer and Cook* (2004)
— 'What If ...', *CR*, 228 (2007)
Potters/The Ceramics Book (1986) to (2012)
Josie Walter, 'Slip into Action', *CR*, 164 (1997)
Eden and Eden (1999), pp.64–8

Interviews with Mary Wondrausch are in the Crafts Lives sound archive at the British Library, London (C960/77), and the Recording the Crafts video archive at UWE Bristol (also held in the National Art Library, V&A, London, 704.AA.0053 to 704.AA.0057).

1119 Figure: *Rampant Lion*, 1997
Earthenware, thrown and assembled, slip-trailed decoration; h.47.3cm, d.25.5cm
C.191-1997. Source: the artist (from the University of the West of England student

1119

and staff exhibition, *Smash and Grab*, V&A, 1997), £350

Wren, Denise K. (née **Tuckfield**) 1891–1979

1891 born Albany, Western Australia
1899–1900 family leaves for England, settling in East Molesey, Surrey
1907–12 studies at Kingston School of Art under Archibald Knox, takes up pottery
1911 learns to throw from Mr Mercer, flowerpot maker at Norbiton Potteries, Surrey
1912 with fellow students establishes Knox Guild of Design and Craft, sharing studio in Kingston; buys kick-wheel from Mercer
1915 marries Henry Wren
1920 with Henry buys plot in Oxshott, Surrey, builds house and workshop and buys American Drakenfeld gas-fired kiln; briefly attends pottery evening classes at Camberwell School of Arts and Crafts under Henry Hopkins
1922 daughter Rosemary Wren (qv) born
1922–50 runs two-week summer courses at Oxshott
1925–68 designs and builds coke-fired kilns, offering kiln plans for sale
1932–38 teaches at Hall School, Weybridge, Surrey
1937– designs textiles
1941–45 ceases potting due to war
1947 Henry Wren dies
1950 first saltglaze firing for Rosemary's diploma show; Rosemary joins pottery full-time
1954 Rosemary converts one of coke-fired kilns to gas
1958–59 designs and builds larger coke-fired kiln for salt-glazing
1968 saltglaze abandoned due to unavailability of suitable coke
1969–75 makes handbuilt smoke-fired elephants
1979 dies in Devon

Denise Wren was much influenced by the ideas and principles of the designer Archibald Knox, who taught her at Kingston School of Art. After Knox resigned his post following criticism of his unconventional teaching, Wren and fellow students left the School in solidarity, establishing a craft guild in his name. Among the earliest studio potters, she made pottery at the guild's workshop in Kingston before the First World War, and with her husband, Henry Wren, established Oxshott Pottery in Surrey in 1920, there making earthenware pots and figures decorated experimentally with commercially available glazes. She was a pioneer of handbuilding, promoting the technique at a time when it lay outside the mainstream. Her work remained little appreciated until after the Second World War, when she gained recognition for her contribution to the revival of salt-glazing. Wren also played an important role in the formation and development of the Craftsmen Potters Association.

Denise and Henry Wren, *Oxshott Hand-made Pottery*, exhibited at the Central Hall, Westminster, London (1924)
— *Handcraft Pottery, for Workshop and School* (London, 1928)
— *Pottery: The Finger-built Methods* (London, 1932)
Denise K. and Rosemary D. Wren, *Pottery Making: Making Pots and Building and Firing Small Kilns* (London, 1952)
— 'Coke and Pottery', *Gas Coke News* (October 1959)
British Institute of Industrial Art (1927)
Decorative Art (1927), (1928), (1963/64), (1966/67)
Exh. review, *Pottery Quarterly*, 6:24 (1959)
Casson (1967), p.8, pls.175–7
Commonwealth Institute Art Gallery, *An Exhibition of Batiks and Ceramics: Robin Anderson, Audrey Blackman, Noel Dyrenforth, Denise K. Wren*, exh. cat. (London, 1967)
Rose (1970), pp.20–1, pl.9
Potters (1972) to (1977)
Rothschild (1972)
Rosemary Wren, 'Denise K. Wren: Sixty-one Years a Potter', *CR*, 15 (1972)
Eileen Lewenstein, obituary, *CR*, 59 (1979)
Margot Coatts, 'Denise and Henry Wren – Pioneer Potters', *CR*, 87 (1984)
Crafts Study Centre, *The Oxshott Pottery: Denise and Henry Wren*, exh. cat., texts by Margot Coatts and Rosemary Wren (Bath, 1984)
Barley Roscoe, 'The Oxshott Pottery – Denise and Henry Wren', *Studio Pottery*, 5 (1993)
Rosemary D. Wren, *The Knox Guild and Its Background* (Strathpeffer, 1998)
Vincentelli (2000), pp.186, 225–6
Stephen A. Martin, *Archibald Knox* (London, 2001)
Nottingham City Museums and Galleries (2017), p.91

The papers of Denise Wren are held at Kingston History Centre (KHC/2017/020) and the Crafts Study Centre, Farnham (OXP).

1120 Pot, 1913 (pl.1)
Earthenware, handbuilt, incised decoration through dark slip over a white body, honey glaze; marks: 'DKT / 1913', incised; made at the Knox Guild of Design and Craft, Kingston, and fired at Kingston tobacco pipe works; h.11.3cm, d.9.5cm
C.102-1980. Source: Rosemary Wren, £500
The pot depicts the view from Wren's family home by Molesey Lock on the Thames. It shows her younger brother Charlie fishing.

1121

1122

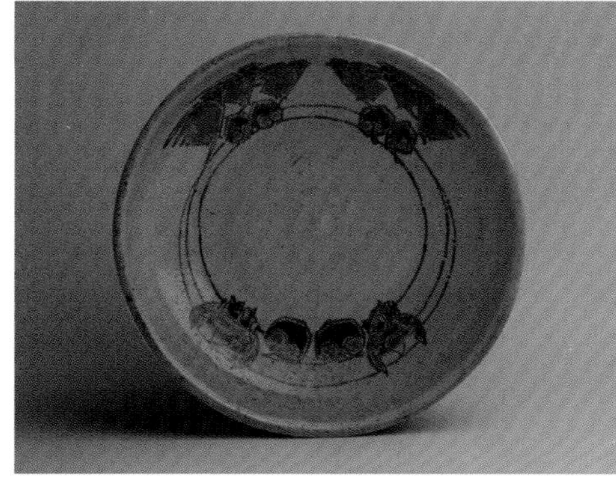
1123

1121 Dish, 1927
Earthenware, slip-trailed in white on a red body, unglazed; marks: 'D. K. WREN OXSHOTT 1927', incised; h.7cm, d.30cm

1124

1125

1127 / 1126

C.49-1981. Source: *see* **1120**, £200
A photograph of this dish being decorated is in Wren (1928), p.23.

1122 Covered jar, *c.* 1925–35
Earthenware, mottled blue glaze; marks: 'OXSHOTT', incised; h.15.5cm, d.14.7cm
C.50&A-1981. Source: *see* **1120**, £500

1123 Dish, *c.* 1928–32
Earthenware, painted in colours; marks: 'DENISE WREN' and 'M:M:' with a bird, painted, and 'OXSHOTT', incised; h.7cm, d.26.7cm
C.48-1981. Source: *see* **1120**, £250

1124 Jar, *c.* 1930–35
Earthenware, handbuilt from moulded slabs, blue-green glaze; marks: 'Denise K. Wren Oxshott', incised; h.33.2cm, d.21cm
C.51-1981. Source: *see* **1120**, £350
The jar reflects Wren's love of birds. The macaws depicted would have been based on those she kept.

1125 Jar, *c.* 1960
Stoneware, saltglaze, greenish ash glaze; marks: 'DKW Oxshott', incised; h.13.7cm, d.6cm
C.52-1981. Source: *see* **1120**, £45

1126 *Ikebana pot*, 1960–61
Stoneware, mottled green and brown saltglaze; marks: 'DKW Oxshott', incised; h.7.5cm, d.19.4cm
C.53-1981. Source: *see* **1120**, £150
Shown at one of two exhibitions of saltglaze shared with Rosemary Wren at Berkeley Galleries, London, in 1960 and 1961. A paper label bears the price '£10'.

1127 Jar, 1967
Stoneware, grey saltglaze, mottled brown; marks: 'DKW Oxshott', incised; h.25.4cm, d.12.3cm
Circ.1221-1967. Source: Commonwealth Institute Art Gallery (group exhibition of batiks and ceramics, 1967, no.46), £5

1128 Elephant, 1971 (pl.63)
Stoneware, handbuilt, unglazed, smoke-fired; h.25.5cm, d.29.8cm
Circ.238-1971. Source: Briglin Studio, London, £32

The museum also holds two items by Henry Wren, not catalogued here: a sherd of a tobacco jar, dated 1921 (C.54-1981), and a plant pot of about 1938 (C.133-1985).

Wren, Rosemary D. 1922–2013

1922	born Oxshott, Surrey; daughter of Henry and Denise Wren (qv)
1945–47	studies at Guildford School of Art, taking pottery under Helen Pincombe (qv)
1947–50	studies ceramics at Royal College of Art, London
1950	establishes own workshop at Oxshott Pottery, installs powered wheel
1953	Francine Delpierre and Albert Diato work briefly at Helen Pincombe's pottery in Oxshott; from them Rosemary learns technique of handbuilding hollow animal forms from flattened coils
1970–	Peter Crotty joins pottery, becomes Wren's partner
1979	together move Oxshott Pottery to Hittisleigh, Devon; Crotty takes over painted decoration of Wren's figures
1983	pottery moves to Lustleigh, Devon
1990	pottery moves to Strathpeffer, Ross and Cromarty
1996	abandons ceramic work due to macular degeneration, following period of simplification of techniques

Rosemary Wren is best known for her handbuilt raku and stoneware bird and animal figures. She worked alongside her mother, Denise Wren (qv), at Oxshott Pottery, eventually taking over its running in partnership with Peter Crotty. Rosemary Wren was instrumental in the establishment of the Craftsmen (now Craft) Potters Association in 1958 and was elected as its first Chair.

Rosemary Wren, 'Why Raku?', *CR*, 1 (1970)
— *Animal Forms and Figures* (London, 1990)
— 'Salt-glaze at The Oxshott Pottery', *Ceramics: Art and Perception*, 28 (1997)
— 'The Early Years [of the CPA]', in Cooper (2007b), pp.6–13
— and Peter Crotty, 'Potters' Aches and Pains', *CR*, 93 (1985)
— 'All Creatures Great and Small', *CR*, 98 (1986)
Arts and Crafts Exhibition Society (1950), (1957)
Decorative Art (1951/52), (1952/53), (1955/56), (1957/58), (1959/60), (1961/62), (1963/64), (1966/67), (1967/68)
Casson (1967), p.8, pls.178–9
Potters (1972) to (2000)

1129

Lyn Colavecchia, 'Peter M. Crotty', *CR*, 19 (1973)
Commonwealth Art Gallery, *Rosemary D. Wren*, exh. pamphlet (London, 1973)
Crafts Advisory Committee (1976), p.123
'Rosemary Wren: Animals and Birds', *CR*, 67 (1981)
Paisley Museum and Art Galleries (1984), p.83
Peter M. Crotty, 'A Day in the Life of Two Potters', *CR*, 113 (1988)
Margot Coatts, 'Sources of Inspiration', *Crafts*, 129 (1994)
Marshall Anderson, 'Rosemary Wren: Oxshott in Exile', *Studio Pottery*, 27 (1997)

Exhibition reviews: *Pottery Quarterly*, 4:14 (1957); Audrey Blackman, *CR*, 5 (1970); Robert Fournier, *CR*, 10 (1971); Lyn Colavecchia, *CR*, 16 (1972); W.A. Ismay, *CR*, 22 (1973)

An interview with Rosemary Wren is in the Crafts Lives sound archive at the British Library, London (C960/50). A film documenting her working methods, *Creatures in Clay*, was made by Robert Fournier and John Anderson in 1969.

See also bibliography for Denise Wren.

1129 Pot, 1957
Stoneware, grey-green glaze with resist decoration; h.32.6cm, d.17.5cm
Circ.126-1957. Source: Heal & Son Ltd, London (solo exhibition), £15.15s.

1130 Figure of a hen, 1957
Stoneware, slip-cast, painted in black and vitrified white slip; h.21.7cm, d.21.3cm
Circ.127-1957. Source: *see* **1129**, £3.13s.6d.

1130

1131

Made in response to Heal's interest in quantity production. Wren, however, soon discarded slip-casting in favour of individual handbuilding.

1131 *Nanny goat*, 1969
Raku, handbuilt, coloured glazes; marks: a wren in a square, impressed, and 'OXSHOTT', incised; h.24.7cm, d.20cm
Circ.754-1969. Source: Briglin Studio, London, £8

1132 *Woodpigeon*, 1980 (pl.74)
Stoneware, handbuilt, incised decoration, painted coloured glazes; marks: a wren in a square, impressed; h.21.2cm, d.29.4cm
C.191-1980. Source: Casson Gallery, London, £49

Wynn Reeves, Ann (later **Clark**)
1929–2017

1929	born London
1948–51	studies at Willesden School of Art
1951–54	studies ceramics at Central School of Arts and Crafts, London
1953–	joins Kenneth Clark (qv) at his studio in central London; marries Clark in 1954; increasingly works in partnership, producing designs for Kenneth Clark Pottery
1980–	pottery moves to Lewes, Sussex

Ann Wynn Reeves worked in a contemporary style in the 1950s, making press-moulded dishes and other individual pieces in tin-glazed earthenware with colourful, strongly graphic decoration. She went on to become the main designer for Kenneth Clark Pottery, producing decorative designs for tiles and dishes, and working on architectural commissions.

Arts and Crafts Exhibition Society (1954), (1957)
Decorative Art (1954/55), (1958/59), (1959/60), (1961/62)
Lewis (1956), pl.376
Casson (1967), p.8, pls.98–100, 195

Exhibition reviews: 'Potters from the Central School', *Pottery Quarterly*, 1:3 (1954); *Pottery Quarterly*, 2:8 (1955)

See also bibliography for Kenneth Clark.

1133 Bowl, 1957
Earthenware, sgraffito through white over brown-black glaze, painted in green; h.7.7cm, d.13.3cm
Circ.280-1958. Source: Kenneth Clark Pottery, £2

1134 Triangular dish on feet, 1958
Earthenware, press-moulded, incised through white over black glaze, painted in blue and green; marks: paper label: 'HANDMADE & DECORATED / By ANN WYNN REEVES'; h.8.8cm, d.36.5cm
Circ.279-1958. Source: *see* **1133**, £7.10s.

1135 Bowl, 1957
Earthenware, pinched, incised and painted with black and brown pigments, the interior glazed red; h.7cm, d.11cm
C.83-2014. Source: given by Ann Clark

1136 Figure of a chicken, 1958
Earthenware, slip-cast, tin glaze, painted in greenish-black; marks: 'AWR '58', painted; h.11.5cm, d.8.2cm
C.78-2014. Source: *see* **1135**

1137 Miniature dish, *c.* 1955–60
Earthenware, tin glaze, sgraffito through

1133

1138 / 1137

1139 / 1135

1134

1136

purplish-black pigment; h.3.8cm, d.9.9cm
C.79-2014. Source: *see* **1135**

1138 Miniature dish, *c.* 1955–60
Earthenware, tin glaze, sgraffito through purplish-black pigment; marks 'AWR', painted; h.2.1cm, d.7.7cm
C.80-2014. Source: *see* **1135**

1139 Vase, 1959
Earthenware, incised and painted in black, yellow and turquoise on a tin glaze; made by Kenneth Clark, decorated by Ann Wynn Reeves; marks: 'AWR / 59', painted; h.18cm, d.8.2cm
C.82-2014. Source: *see* **1135**

Yarrow, Catherine 1904–1990

1904	born Harpenden, Hertfordshire
c. 1924–26	travels widely; lives for a time in Paris; learns to draw
c. 1926–28	lives in south of France
1929–30	lives in London
early 1930s	returns to Paris; learns pottery from Josep Llorens Artigas; begins printmaking at Atelier 17
1940	leaves Paris for Lisbon
1941–	moves to New York
1943	exhibition (ceramics), Julien Levy Gallery, New York; possibly shares Carol Janeway's studio
1948–	returns to UK; buys large house in St John's Wood, London, sets up studio and ceramic workshop
1950	exhibition (paintings and ceramics) with Renato Guttuso, Hanover Gallery, London
1955	exhibition (ceramics) with Gudrun Krüger and Janet Murray, Archer Gallery, London
early 1960s–	sells house, converting its mews garage into studio flat and workshop
1969	exhibition (ceramics) with Thetis Blacker, Marjorie Parr Gallery, London
1988	ceases potting

Catherine Yarrow was a ceramicist, painter and printmaker. She is recognized for her inventive, handbuilt sculpture and stoneware pottery, which show aspects of Surrealism and Symbolism. Her biography is extraordinary. Seeking escape from conventional society, she settled in France during the 1920s and '30s, becoming acquainted with the poet Pierre Reverdy, and Surrealist artists including Alberto Giacometti, Jean (Hans) Arp, Max Ernst and Stanley William Hayter. Ahead of the German occupation in 1940, she fled France together with her partner, Michel Lukacs, and the painter Leonora Carrington, reaching New York the following year. There she renewed contact with the Surrealists, encountering also the artist Louise Bourgeois and the writer Anaïs Nin. She showed paintings and ceramics in London during the 1950s, following her return to England, but in later decades exhibited rarely. She taught private students at her workshop and was an important influence on Ewen Henderson (qv), whose inclusion of her work in his survey exhibition *Pandora's Box*, held at the Crafts Council in 1995, helped re-establish her reputation.

Hanover Gallery, *Renato Guttuso, Catherine Yarrow*, exh. pamphlet (London, 1950)
Fennemore (1953)
Exh. review, *Pottery Quarterly*, 2:5 (1955)
Crafts Council (1995b), pp.62–3
Austin/Desmond Fine Art, *Catherine Yarrow: Not What I Want*, exh. cat., text by Philip Wright (London, 2012)
Erskine, Hall & Coe, *Catherine Yarrow*, exh. pamphlet (London, 2013)

1140

1141

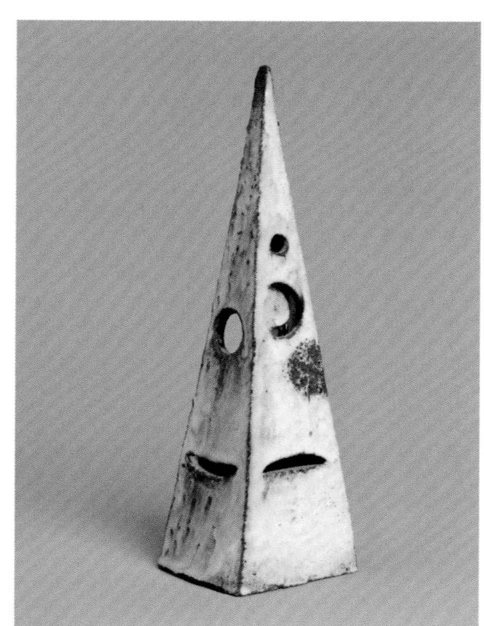
1142

1140 Bowl, *c.* 1965
Stoneware, press-moulded, painting in blue, red and iron in a grey glaze; marks: 'C.Y.', incised, h.6.4cm, d.9.4cm
C.105-2011. Source: given by Catherine Yarrow Estate

1141 *Bird's nest*, *c.* 1965
Stoneware, handbuilt, greenish glaze; h.20.7cm, d.25cm
C.104-2011. Source: *see* **1140**

1142 *Tower with Symbols*, *c.* 1986
Stoneware, slab-built, ash glaze; marks: 'C.Y.', incised, h.36.2cm, d.11.8cm
C.103-2011. Source: *see* **1140**

Yasuda, Takeshi 1943–

1943	born Tokyo, Japan
1963–66	trains at Daisei-Gama Pottery, Mashiko
1966–73	establishes own workshop at Mashiko
1973	moves to UK
1973–75	workshop at Monk Sherborne, Hampshire, shared with Sandy Brown (qv)
1975–93	workshop near South Molton, Devon, shared with Sandy Brown
1977	marries Sandy Brown
1978–85	teaches at West Surrey College of Art and Design, Farnham
1980–91	teaches at Kunsthåndværkerskolen, Kolding, Denmark
1984–86	residency, Cleveland Crafts Centre, Middlesbrough
1984–86	teaches at Camberwell School of Art and Crafts
1992–2001	Professor of Applied Art, University of Ulster
1993–	moves to Bath, Somerset; establishes studio
2000–20	studio in Larkhall, Bath, shared with Felicity Aylieff (qv)
2003	marries Felicity Aylieff
2005–10	Director, The Pottery Workshop, Jingdezhen, China
2011–	co-founds Red House Ceramics Studio, Jingdezhen, with Felicity Aylieff and Baixu Xiong

Takeshi Yasuda makes objects for use, approaching this more in terms of satisfying sensory needs rather than utility. His tableware and centrepieces suggest ritual and celebration, reflecting his love of food culture. His approach to material is direct, intuitive and often maverick. Powerfully and expressively thrown, his work is notable in retaining the plastic qualities of soft clay in the finished pots. Until the mid-1980s he worked in ash-glazed, reduction-fired stoneware; he then developed his *sancai* (three-colour) ware, fired in an electric kiln, and subsequently 'creamware', using porcelain clay fired to earthenware temperature. He has since concentrated on celadon porcelain, sometimes decorating it with precious metal.

Takeshi Yasuda, *Takeshi Yasuda* (Yeovil, 2004)
— statement, in Bendavid and Lalumia (2017), pp.35, 41
Potters/The Ceramics Book (1983) to (2012)
Sandy Brown, 'The Sensuous Pots of Takeshi Yasuda', *CR*, 93 (1985)
'Japanese Treasure', *Crafts*, 76 (1985)
Cleveland Crafts Centre, *Takeshi Yasuda: Ceramics*, exh. pamphlet, text by Oliver Watson (Middlesbrough, 1987)
Tony Birks, 'Sandy Brown and Takeshi Yasuda', *Ceramics Monthly*, 40:5 (1992)
Ruark Lewis, 'Takeshi Yasuda – Visitant', *Ceramics: Art and Perception*, 14 (1993)
Patrick Sargent, 'Sandy Brown and Takeshi Yasuda', *Studio Pottery*, 1 (1993)
Alpha House Gallery, *Takeshi Yasuda*, exh. pamphlet, text by Alison Britton (Sherborne, 1994)
Paul Vincent, 'Takeshi Yasuda Interviewed', *Studio Pottery*, 10 (1994)
Fenella Mallalieu, 'A Visit to Takeshi Yasuda', *CR*, 151 (1995)
Derek Topp Gallery, *The Cream of Takeshi Yasuda*, exh. cat., text by David Whiting (Rowsley, 1997)
Paul Mathieu, 'Pushing Boundaries', *Ceramics: Art and Perception*, 28 (1997)
Paul Vincent, '2 Careers in Parallel', *Studio Pottery*, 34 (1998)
Felicity Aylieff, 'Basic Form', *CR*, 180 (1999)
Rufford Gallery, *Takeshi Yasuda and the Expression of Clay*, exh. cat. (1999)
'Takeshi Yasuda', *Ceramics Monthly*, 48:8 (2000)
Yuko Kikuchi, 'Sources of Inspiration', *Crafts*, 173 (2001)
Sally Boyle, 'Opening Up', *CR*, 197 (2002)
Crafts Council of Ireland, *Peter Ting – Takeshi Yasuda*, exh. pamphlet, text by Alun Graves (Kilkenny, 2002)
Penny Smith, 'Consuming Passions', *Ceramics: Art and Perception*, 50 (2002)
Ruthin Craft Centre (2006), pp.60–3, 79
Carlano (2010), pp.178–81
Porcelain City – Jingdezhen, exh. cat. (London, 2011)
Andrew Buck, 'Takeshi Yasuda', interview, *Ceramics Technical*, 36 (2013)
Goldmark Gallery, *Takeshi Yasuda*, exh. cat., text by Prue Venables (Uppingham, 2013) – an

accompanying documentary, *Takeshi Yasuda: Made in China*, was released on DVD
Colin Martin, 'Producing Porcelain Tableware in Jingdezhen, China', *Ceramics Technical*, 37 (2013)
Nottingham City Museums and Galleries (2017), pp.92–3
Goldmark Gallery, *Takeshi Yasuda*, exh. cat., text by Sebastian Blackie (Uppingham, 2019)
Isabella Smith, 'Fluid Dynamism', *CR*, 297 (2019)
Sebastian Blackie, 'Working in China', *Ceramics: Art and Perception*, 115 (2020)

Exhibition reviews: Frances Bugg, *Crafts*, 87 (1987); Patrick Sargent, *Studio Pottery*, 1 (1993); Paul Vincent, *Studio Pottery*, 12 (1994); Emmanuel Cooper, *Crafts*, 143 (1996), and 144 (1997); Paul Vincent, *Studio Pottery*, 24 (1996); Alison Britton, *CR*, 213 (2005); Andy Christian, *CR*, 266 (2014); Colin Martin, *Craft Arts International*, 91 (2014)

An interview with Takeshi Yasuda is in the Crafts Lives sound archive at the British Library, London (C960/100).

1143 Dish, 1984
Stoneware, celadon glaze with white splashes; made in Devon; h.10cm, d.60cm
C.228-1985. Source: British Crafts Centre, London, £337.50

1144 Cream jug, 1996 (pl.97)
Earthenware, honey glaze; marks: crossed oval seal, impressed, and maker's paper label: 'CREAM JUG / Light Honey / Creamware / TY1645 Takeshi Yasuda'; h.13.3cm, d.18cm
C.86-1996. Source: Contemporary Applied Arts, London (exhibition: *Soft Clay*, 1996), £60.30

1145 Small dish with a handle, 1996 (pl.97)
Stoneware, cream slip, clear and coloured glazes; marks: crossed oval seal, impressed, and maker's paper label: 'SMALL DISH WITH A HANDLE / Sansai / Oxidised stoneware / TY1555 Takeshi Yasuda'; h.9.2cm, d.19.4cm
C.87-1996. Source: *see* **1144**, £60.30

1146 Two goblets, 1998
Earthenware, honey glaze; marks: '3500' and '3557' on maker's paper labels; h.13.8cm, d.8cm; h.11.5cm, d.9.5cm
C.134 & 135-2003. Source: given by Claire Thorn
Originally given as gifts to attendees of Contemporary Applied Arts' 50th anniversary party in 1998.

1143

1146

Yeoman Pottery *see* Cuthbert Hamilton

Youll, Dawn 1977–

1977–	born Sunderland, Tyne and Wear
1996–99	studies ceramics, Glasgow School of Art
1999	exchange, Maryland Institute of Art and Design, Baltimore, USA
2000–02	set crafts apprenticeship, Scottish Screen; subsequently works for a period in film and television
2003–09	teaches at Glasgow School of Art
2005–07	studio at Fireworks Studio, Glasgow
2007–08	studies ceramics, University of Wales Institute, Cardiff
2009	residency, Cove Park, Argyll and Bute
2010–	Crafts Programme Producer, Cove Park
2010–15	studio at Glasgow Sculpture Studios
2011	awarded Arts Foundation Fellowship
2011–	regular exhibitions, Marsden Woo Gallery, London
2016–	studio in Glasgow

Dawn Youll creates concentrated, tabletop-scale ceramic sculptures that typically juxtapose distinct, individually made elements with vibrant glazes or pronounced textures. Distilled and abstracted from familiar everyday forms and materials, these act as signs and signifiers, reflecting her interest in visual language and semiotics.

Bornholms Kunstmuseum, *European Ceramic Context 2010*, exh. cat. (Gudhjem, 2010), pp.124–5
Jerwood Visual Arts, *Jerwood Contemporary Makers*, exh. cat. (London, 2010)
Fife Contemporary Art & Craft/Oriel Davies, *Placement: Ceramic Connections: Wales and Scotland*, exh. cat., interview by Natasha Mayo (St Andrews/Newtown, 2011)
Ellie Herring, 'Sign Language', *Crafts*, 229 (2011)
Richard Slee, 'Introducing: Dawn Youll', exh. essay, Marsden Woo Gallery (2011)
Alexia Holt, 'A Sense of Place', essay for the exhibition *Dawn Youll: Locale*, Marsden Woo Gallery (2013)
Matthew Kangas, 'Toys in the Attic', *Ceramics: Art and Perception*, 92 (2013)

Exhibition reviews: Alun Graves, 'Slee Selects', *CR*, 197 (2002); Teleri Lloyd-Jones, 'Crafting Narratives', *Crafts*, 251 (2014); Linda Sandino, *CR*, 265 (2014)

1147 *National Trust*, 2010
Earthenware, slip-cast, red glaze and black slip; h.28.5cm, d.26cm
C.12:1,2-2010. Source: Marsden Woo Gallery at Collect 2010, £900; acquired through the generosity of Gerard and Sarah Griffin

1147

A. & J. Young Pottery

1949	Andrew Young born Cambridge
1950	Joanna Young (née Heseltine) born Farnham, Surrey
1970–73	both study ceramics at West Surrey College of Art and Design, Farnham, where they meet
1972–73	work for Gwyn Hanssen (qv) in France for several months
1973–74	art teacher training at Goldsmiths' College, London
1975	take over workshop at Hunworth, Norfolk, from Peter Starkey (qv); Andrew and Joanna marry
1981–	new workshop at Lower Gresham, Norfolk
1988	design wares for Next Interiors, produced in Stoke-on-Trent; receive Crafts Council/Guild of St George John Ruskin Craft Award, to explore industrial techniques
1990	redevelop workshop
1993	pots featured in the cookery writer and presenter Delia Smith's *Summer Collection* book and TV series
1998	commission for large bowls for Ely Cathedral, Cambridgeshire
2016	retire from potting

Andrew and Joanna Young are known for their elegant but eminently practical domestic ware. Their characteristic shapes, precisely turned and finished after throwing, show the influence of early industrial pottery. Their original, highly successful range of thinly glazed brown stoneware was, from 1994, complemented by white stoneware with coloured glazes and stamped, sprigged or rouletted decoration. The pottery supplied various retailers, including David Mellor and Bettys, but increasingly concentrated on direct sales from its own shop.

'CPA New Members', *CR*, 51 (1978)
Potters (1980) to (2000)
Gwyn Hanssen Pigott, 'Domestic Pots – Domestic Potters', *CR*, 92 (1985)
Stephen Brayne, 'Andrew and Joanna Young – Country Potters', *CR*, 104 (1987)
Barbara Taylor, *A & J Young: Country Potters*, Aberystwyth Arts Centre: Ceramic Series 24 (1987)
Cooper (1990)
British Council (1991), p.18
Crafts Council (1991)
Carol Marsh, 'Pottery with a Practical Air', *Country Homes and Interiors* (August 1992)
Archer (1995), p.86
Nottingham City Museums and Galleries (2017), p.94

1148 Jug, 1981
Stoneware, incised decoration, green glazed interior; marks: 'A & J YOUNG 1981', impressed; h.24.9cm, d.16.7cm
C.179-1981. Source: Craftsmen Potters Association, London (exhibition with Peter Smith and Sarah Walton, 1981, no.101), £20

1149 Bowl with handles, 1982
Stoneware, dog-tooth and sprigged decoration, pale orange glazed interior; marks: 'A & J YOUNG', impressed; h.11.6cm, d.21.6cm
C.81-1984. Source: given by the Friends of the V&A (purchased at the Craftsmen Potters Association exhibition, *Studio Ceramics Today*, V&A, 1983, no.182, £34.50)

1150 Lemon squeezer, 1988
Stoneware, thin brown glaze; marks: 'A & J YOUNG GRESHAM', impressed; h.7.5cm, d.13.6cm
C.17&A-1989. Source: David Mellor shop, London, £12.96

1151 Tureen and ladle, 1988
Stoneware, thin brown glaze with ash flashings, glazed interior; marks: 'A & J YOUNG GRESHAM', impressed; h.18.2cm, d.28.3cm
C.19 to B-1989. Source: *see* **1150**, £24.11

1148 / 1149

1150 / 1151

BIBLIOGRAPHY

Aberystwyth Arts Centre, *In the First Place: Work from Wales*, exh. cat. with 'Exhibitors Supplement', introduction by David Briers (Aberystwyth, 1990)

Adamson, Glenn, *Thinking Through Craft* (Oxford/New York, 2007)

— '... And Into the Fire: Post-studio Ceramics in Britain', in Carlano (2010), pp.199–203

—, Martina Droth and Simon Olding (eds), *Things of Beauty Growing: British Studio Pottery*, exh. cat. (New Haven/London, 2017)

Adlin, Jane, *Contemporary Ceramics: Selections from the Metropolitan Museum of Art* (New York, 1998)

Andrews, Tim, *Raku: A Review of Contemporary Work* (London, 1994), revised (2005), (2019)

Archer, Chloë, *Teapotmania: The Story of the British Craft Teapot and Teacosy*, exh. cat. (Norwich: Norfolk Museums Service, 1995)

Arts and Crafts Exhibition Society, *Catalogue of the Tenth Exhibition* (London, 1912) and catalogues of subsequent exhibitions: (1916), (1923), (1926), (1928), (1931), (1935), (1938), (1941), (1944), (1946), (1948), (1950), (1952), (1954), (1957)

Backemeyer, Sylvia (ed.), *Making Their Mark: Art, Craft and Design at the Central School, 1896–1966* (London, 2000)

Baird, Catriona and Rose Watban (eds), *The Cutting Edge: Scotland's Contemporary Crafts*, texts by Philippa Swann, Simon Olding and others (Edinburgh: National Museums Scotland, 2007)

Barbican Centre, *Atlantic Crossings: American Influence in the Work of Five British Ceramics Artists. Robert Cooper, Stephen Dixon, James Evans, Sean Henry, Richard Slee*, exh. pamphlet, text by Tessa Peters (London, 1998)

Barker, Janine, 'Henry Rothschild: Émigré Networks and European Connections', in Wadsworth-Boyle (2016), pp.33–43

— and Cheryl Buckley, 'The Primavera Story: 1946–67', in Christopher Breward, Fiona Fisher and Ghislaine Wood (eds), *British Design: Tradition and Modernity after 1948* (London, 2015), pp.25–39

Barrow, T. (ed.), *Bernard Leach: Essays in Appreciation* (Wellington, 1960)

Bendavid, Kochevet and Christine Lalumia (eds), *Home from Home: Ceramics by International Artists Working in Britain*, exh. cat. (London: Contemporary Applied Arts, 2017)

Bennett, Ian, *British 20th Century Studio Ceramics*, exh. cat. (London: Christopher Wood Gallery, 1980)

Bergesen, Victoria, *Encyclopaedia of British Art Pottery 1870–1920* (London, 1991)

— 'The Baker Family: Six Generations of Potters', *Journal of the Northern Ceramic Society*, 10 (1993)

Billington, Dora M., *The Art of the Potter* (London, New York and Toronto, 1937)

— 'The Younger English Potters', *The Studio*, 145:720 (March 1953)

— 'The New Look in British Pottery', *The Studio*, 149:742 (January 1955)

Bird, Joanna (ed.), *Marking the Line: Ceramics and Architecture. Christie Brown, Carina Ciscato, Nicholas Rena and Clare Twomey in response to Sir John Soane*, texts by Eric Parry, Alun Graves and others (London, 2013)

Birks, Tony, *The Art of the Modern Potter* (London, 1967), revised and enlarged as *Art of the Modern Potter* (1976)

— 'Britain', in Lewenstein and Cooper (1974), pp.23–51

— and Cornelia Wingfield Digby, *Bernard Leach, Hamada and their Circle: From the Wingfield Digby Collection*, introduction by Michael Webb (Oxford, 1990)

Blackie, Sebastian, 'Smoke and Fire', *CR*, 297 (2019)

Blanchett, Chris, *20th Century Decorative British Tiles* (Atglen, 2006)

Blandino, Betty, *Coiled Pottery: Traditional and Contemporary Ways* (London, 1984), revised (1997), (2003)

— *The Figure in Fired Clay* (London, 2001)

Blunt, Reginald (ed.), *The Cheyne Book of Chelsea China and Pottery* (London, 1924), published with an introduction by J.V.G. Mallet (Wakefield, 1973)

Breen, Laura, 'Productive Friction: Ceramic Practice and the Museum Since 1970', in Brown, Stair and Twomey (2016), pp.7–16

— *Ceramics and the Museum* (London, 2019)

British Council, *Exhibition of Modern British Crafts*, exh. cat., with text 'Modern British Pottery' by Lady Sempill (New York, 1942)

— *Colours of the Earth*, exh. cat., with texts by Oliver Watson, Michael Casson and Alison Britton (London, 1991)

British Institute of Industrial Art, *Exhibition of Present Day Industrial Art*, exh. cat., V&A (London, 1922)

— *Exhibition of Industrial Art of To-Day*, exh. cat., V&A (London, 1923)

— *Report on the Work of the British Institute of Industrial Art 1919–1924*, with list of works in the permanent collection (London, 1924)

— *Recent Examples of British Pottery*, exh. cat., V&A (London, 1927)

— *Catalogue of the British Institute of Industrial Art Autumn Exhibition Illustrating British Industrial Art for the Slender Purse*, V&A (London, 1929)

— *Catalogue of the Exhibition of Industrial Art in Relation to the Home*, Dorland Hall (London, 1933)

Britton, Alison, 'Overthrowing Tradition', *Interpreting Ceramics*, ejournal, 2 (2001), reproduced in Dahn and Jones (2013), pp.36–43

— *Seeing Things: Collected Writing on Art, Craft and Design* (London, 2013), revised (2022)

— and Simon Olding (eds), *Three by One: A Selection from Three Public Craft Collections by Alison Britton*, exh. cat., Crafts Council/Crafts Study Centre (London, 2009)

Brown, Christie, Julian Stair and Clare Twomey (eds), *Contemporary Clay and Museum Culture: Ceramics in the Expanded Field* (London/New York, 2016)

Brygos Gallery, *Under £10 English Pottery*, exh. cat. (London, 1936)

— *Stoneware and Earthenware*, exh. cat. (London, 1937a)

— *Stoneware and Earthenware and Beer Sets*, exh. cat. (London, 1937b)

Cameron, Elizabeth and Philippa Lewis, *Potters on Pottery* (London, 1976)

Cardew, Michael, *A Pioneer Potter: An Autobiography* (London, 1988)

Carlano, Annie (ed.), *Contemporary British Studio Ceramics: The Grainer Collection* (New Haven/London, 2010)

Casson, Michael, *Pottery in Britain Today* (London, 1967)

— 'Ceramics and Education', *Ceramic Review*, 21 (1973)

— 'British Ceramics Today', *Ceramics Monthly*, 30:2 (1982)

— with Anna Jackson (ed.), *The Craft of the Potter*, published to accompany the BBC television series (London, 1977)

Casson Henry, Pan, interviewed by Moira Vincentelli in 1994 about the Craftsmen Potters Shop and Casson Gallery, London, *Interpreting Ceramics*, ejournal, 6 (2005)

The Ceramics Book, previously published as *Potters*, ed. Emmanuel Cooper (London: Craft Potters Association, 2006), 2nd edition (2008), 3rd edition, ed. Bonnie Kemske (2012)

Clare, Claudia, *Subversive Ceramics* (London, 2016)

Clark, Garth, *Shards: Garth Clark on Ceramic Art* (New York, 2003)

— (ed.), *Ceramic Art: Comment and Review 1882–1977: An Anthology of Writings on Modern Ceramic Art* (New York, 1978)

— *Ceramic Millennium: Critical Writings on Ceramic History, Theory, and Art* (Halifax, Nova Scotia, 2006)

—, Cindi Strauss and others, *Shifting Paradigms in Contemporary Ceramics: The Garth Clark and Mark Del Vecchio Collection* (New Haven/London, 2012)

Coachworth, David, 'Studio Pottery', in Arts Council of Great Britain, *Thirties: British Art and Design before the War*, exh. cat. (London, 1979), pp.97–8

Coatts, Margot (ed.), *Pioneers of Modern Craft* (Manchester/New York, 1997)

Cochrane, Rosemary, *Salt-Glaze Ceramics* (Marlborough, 2001)

P. & D. Colnaghi & Co., *Catalogue of an Exhibition of the Work of Present-day Potters* (London, 1927) and catalogues of further similarly named exhibitions (1928), (1929)

— *Catalogue of an Exhibition of the Work of Michael Cardew, William B. Dalton, Lord Dunsany, Lily and Wilfred Norton, Gwendolen Parnell, Phyllis Simpson* (London, 1932)

Contemporary Art Society, *Report* (London, 1927) and subsequent annual or biennial reports (1928), (1929), (1930–31), (1932–33), (1934–35), (1936–37), (1938–39), (1940–41), (1942–43), (1944–45), (1946–47), (1947–48).

From (1928) to (1946–47), includes a Report of the Contemporary Art Society Pottery and Crafts Fund
Cooper, Emmanuel, *A Handbook of Pottery* (Harlow, 1970)
— *A History of Pottery* (London, 1972a)
— *Taking Up Pottery* (London, 1972b)
— *Pottery* (London, 1976)
— *The Potter's Book of Glaze Recipes* (London, 1980), revised (2004)
— *A History of World Pottery* (London, 1981), revised (1988)
— *Electric Kiln Pottery* (London, 1982)
— *Cooper's Book of Glaze Recipes* (London, 1987)
— 'Table Talk', *Crafts*, 107 (1990)
— *Glazes* (London, 1992)
— *Ten Thousand Years of Pottery* (London, 2000)
— 'Ends and Beginnings', *Interpreting Ceramics*, ejournal, 2 (2002)
— *Bernard Leach: Life and Work* (New Haven/London, 2003)
— 'Industrial Devil – The Relationship between the Ceramic Industry and the Studio Potter', *English Ceramic Circle Transactions*, 19:3 (2007a)
— *Contemporary Ceramics* (London, 2009)
— *Lucie Rie: Modernist Potter* (New Haven/London, 2012)
— (ed.), *The Pot, the Vessel, the Object: Fifty Years of Change and Diversity in the Craft Potters Association*, exh. cat., Aberystwyth Arts Centre (London, 2007b)
— and Derek Royle, *Glazes for the Studio Potter* (London, 1978)
Cooper, Ronald G., *The Modern Potter* (London, 1947)
Cowley, David, 'The Closure of Ceramics at Goldsmiths', *Studio Pottery*, 4 (1993)
Crafts Advisory Committee (CAC), *The Craftsman's Art*, exh. cat., published on the occasion of an exhibition at the V&A (London, 1973)
— *Ceramic Forms: Work Made by Seven British Potters between 1973 and 1974*, exh. cat. (London, 1974)
— *Craftsmen of Quality*, selected from the CAC's Index of Craftsmen (London, 1976)
— *Domestic Pottery*, exh. cat. (London, 1977)
Crafts Council, *Makers: An Illustrated Guide to the Work of More than 350 Artist Craftsmen* (London, 1980)
— *The Maker's Eye*, exh. cat., with texts by Alison Britton, Michael Cardew, Emmanuel Cooper and others (London, 1981)
— *Making It: An Exhibition in which David Poston, Pauline Solven and Janice Tchalenko Review their Careers in the Crafts and Introduce the Work of Eighteen Young Makers*, exh. cat. (London, 1982)
— *Crafts Council Collection 1972–1985*, complete cat., introduction to 'Ceramics' by Peter Dormer (London, 1985)
— *Beyond the Dovetail: Craft, Skill and Imagination*, exh. cat. (London, 1991)
— *Out of this World: The Influence of Nature in Craft and Design 1880–1995*, exh. cat. (London, 1995a)
— *Pandora's Box and the Tradition of Clay*, exh. cat., curated by Ewen Henderson (London, 1995b)
— *Guide: 50 Collections of Contemporary Crafts* (London, 1996a)
— *The Jerwood Prize for Applied Arts 1996: Ceramics*, exh. cat., text by John Houston (London, 1996b)
— *Objects of Our Time*, exh. cat., with text and interviews by Martina Margetts (London, 1996c)
— *Twenty-five Years: Crafts Council Shop at the Victoria and Albert Museum*, with text by Michael Robinson and list of exhibitions (London, 1999a)
— *(Un)limited: Repetition and Change in Contemporary International Craft*, exh. cat. (London, 1999b)
— *Ceramics: Jerwood Applied Arts Prize 2001*, exh. cat., text by Jacqueline Poncelet (London, 2001)
— *30/30 Vision: Creative Journeys in Contemporary Craft*, exh. cat. (London, 2003)
Craftsmen Potters Association, *Year Book 1966* (London, 1966)
— *Studio Ceramics Today. Potters 6th Edition*, exh. cat., V&A (London, 1983) – see also *Potters*
Craftspace Touring, *High Table: British Studio Pottery of the 1990s*, exh. cat., text by Oliver Watson (Birmingham, 1993)
Dahn, Jo, 'Elastic/Expanding: Contemporary Conceptual Ceramics', in Maria Elena Buszek (ed.), *Extra/Ordinary: Craft and Contemporary Art* (Durham/London, 2011), pp.153–71
— *New Directions in Ceramics: From Spectacle to Trace* (London, 2015)
— and Jeffrey Jones (eds), *Interpreting Ceramics: Selected Essays*, published in association with Interpreting Ceramics Research Collaboration (Bath, 2013)
Dartington Hall, *Catalogue of an Exhibition of Pottery and Textiles, 1920–1952, Made in Great Britain by Artist-craftsmen* (Dartington, 1952)
de Waal, Edmund, *20th Century Ceramics* (London, 2003)
— with Claudia Clare, *The Pot Book* (London, 2011)
Decorative Art: The Studio Year Book (London). Published annually with this or similar titles (1926) to (1960/61). Until (1925) titled *'The Studio' Year-Book of Decorative Art*. From (1961/62) titled *Decorative Art in Modern Interiors*
Del Vecchio, Mark, *Postmodern Ceramics* (London, 2001)
Dewar, Richard, *Stoneware* (London, 2002)
Dormer, Peter, *The New Ceramics: Trends and Traditions* (London, 1986), revised (1994)
— 'The Appearance of Craft', *Craft History*, 1 (1988), pp.73–81
— (ed.), *The Culture of Craft: Status and Future* (Manchester, 1997)
Edelman, Bacia, 'British Studio Potters', Parts I to III, *Ceramics Monthly*, 24:2–4 (1976)
Eden, Michael and Victoria Eden, *Slipware: Contemporary Approaches* (London/Philadelphia, 1999)
Edgeler, John, *Cardew's Craft Circle: Essays on Cotswolds Art and Crafts of the 1920s and 1930s* (Winchcombe, 2019)
Elderton, Louisa and Rebecca Morrill (eds), *Vitamin C: Clay and Ceramic in Contemporary Art*, introduction by Clare Lilley (London, 2017)
Fennemore, T.A., 'Potters as Artists', *House and Garden* (October 1953), pp.55–7, 101
Fielding, Amanda, 'Embodying Femininity', in Stair (2000), pp.89–95
Fitch, Doug, 'The Ceramic Heritage of Devon', in Sam Smiles (ed.), *Going Modern and Being British: Art, Architecture and Design in Devon c. 1910–1960* (Exeter, 1998), pp.79–92
Floud, Peter, 'The Crafts Then and Now', *The Studio*, 145 (1953), pp.126–35
Flynn, Michael, *Ceramic Figures: A Directory of Artists* (London, 2003)
Ford, Simon, 'Plastic Art in its Most Abstract Essence: Pottery and Art in the Interwar Years', in Penelope Curtis and Keith Wilson (eds), *Modern British Sculpture*, exh. cat. (London: Royal Academy of Arts, 2011), pp.136–40
Forsyth, Gordon M., 'Pottery', in *Reports on the Present Position and Tendencies of the Industrial Arts as Indicated at the International Exhibition of Modern Decorative and Industrial Arts, Paris, 1925* (London, 1927), pp.127–35
Fournier, Robert and Sheila Fournier, *A Guide to Public Collections of Studio Pottery in the British Isles* (London, 1994)
Frankel, Cyril, *Modern Pots: Hans Coper, Lucie Rie & their Contemporaries: The Lisa Sainsbury Collection* (Norwich: University of East Anglia, 2000)
Game, Amanda, *Contemporary British Crafts: The Goodison Gift to The Fitzwilliam Museum* (London, 2016)
Garcia, Edith, *Ceramics and the Human Figure* (London, 2012)
Gaze, Delia (ed.), *Dictionary of Women Artists* (London, 1997)
Geitner, Amanda and Christhilde Klein, *Slip: Artists in the Netherlands and Britain working with Ceramic*, exh. cat. (Haarlem/Norwich, 2002)
Gibson, John, *Pottery Decoration: Contemporary Approaches* (London, 1987)
Gilbert, John, 'Notes on Pottery Overseas', *Pottery in Australia*, 10:1 (1971), reprinted as 'Discussion', *Pottery Quarterly*, 11:42 (1974)
Godden, Geoffrey, *Encyclopaedia of British Pottery and Porcelain Marks* (London, 1964)
— *Encyclopaedia of British Porcelain Manufacturers* (London, 1988)
Gotlieb, Rachel, 'Vitality in British Art Pottery and Studio Pottery', *Apollo*, 127 (March 1988)
Gray, Laura, *Contemporary British Ceramics and the Influence of Sculpture: Monuments, Multiples, Destruction and Display* (New York/Abingdon, 2017)
Greenhalgh, Paul, *Ceramic, Art and Civilisation* (London, 2021)
Greg, Andrew (ed.), *Primavera: Pioneering Craft and Design 1945–1995*, exh. publication (Newcastle: Tyne and Wear Museums, 1995)
Guild of Potters, *Catalogue of the Guild of Potters*, exh. cat., Gieves Art Gallery (London, 1924)
— *Catalogue of the Second Exhibition of the Work of Members*, P. & D. Colnaghi & Co. (London, 1925)
— *Catalogue of the Third Exhibition of the Work of Members*, P. & D. Colnaghi & Co. (London, 1926)

Hanaor, Cigalle (ed.), *Breaking the Mould: New Approaches to Ceramics* (London, 2007)

Harris, Margaret, 'Domestic Pottery in England', *New Zealand Potter*, 18:1 (1976)

Harrod, Tanya, 'The Forgotten 50s', *Crafts*, 98 (1989), pp.30–3

— 'From "A Potter's Book" to "The Maker's Eye": British Studio Ceramics 1940–1982', in Northern Centre for Contemporary Art (1989), pp.17–42

— *The Crafts in Britain in the 20th Century* (New Haven, 1999)

— 'Six Exhibitions, Six Identities', in Britton and Olding (2009), pp.17–28

— 'The Everyday and the Numinous: British Studio Pottery 1980–2009', in Carlano (2010), pp.11–28

— *The Last Sane Man: Michael Cardew, Modern Pots, Colonialism and the Counterculture* (New Haven/London, 2012)

— *The Real Thing: Essays on Making in the Modern World* (London, 2015)

— 'Out of the Studio', in Brown, Stair and Twomey (2016), pp.45–54, reprinted in Matson and Thorne (2016), pp.88–106

— (ed.), *Obscure Objects of Desire: Reviewing the Crafts in the Twentieth Century*, conference papers (London: Crafts Council, 1997)

— (ed.), *Craft* (London: Whitechapel Gallery, 2018)

Haslam, Malcolm, *William Staite Murray*, exh. cat., published in association with Cleveland County Museum Service (London: Crafts Council, 1984)

Hawkins Opie, Jennifer, 'Twenty Years of Ceramic and Glass Design: The Collections of the British Institute of Industrial Art and Industry', *V&A Album*, 2 (1983)

— 'Art and Deco: The Problems of British Ceramics in the International Exhibition, Paris 1925', *V&A Album*, 4 (1985)

Houston, John (ed.), *Artists Craftsmen of 401½ and Fosseway House Workshops 1970–1980*, exh. cat. (London: Commonwealth Institute, 1979)

— *The Abstract Vessel* (London, 1991)

Hove Museum and Art Gallery, *Contemporary Craft Collection* (Hove, 1998)

Howard, Morris, 'Nation, Land and Heritage', in Christopher Breward and Ghislaine Wood (eds), *British Design from 1948: Innovation in the Modern Age* (London: V&A Publishing, 2012), pp.96–117

ICA (Institute of Contemporary Arts), *Fast Forward: New Directions in British Ceramics*, exh. cat. (London, 1985)

Jeremiah, David, 'Beautiful Things: Dartington and the Art of the Potter and Weaver', in Harrod (1997), pp.163–76

— 'Dartington: A Modern Adventure', in Sam Smiles (ed.), *Going Modern and Being British: Art, Architecture and Design in Devon c. 1910–1960* (Exeter, 1998), pp.43–78

Jochem, Marlene, *Ceramic Horizons: The Lotte Reimers Foundation Collection at Friedenstein Castle in Gotha* (Stuttgart, 2018)

Johnson, Pamela (ed.), *Ideas in the Making: Practice in Theory*, collected papers (London: Crafts Council, 1998)

Jones, Jeffrey, 'In Search of the Picassoettes', *Interpreting Ceramics*, ejournal, 1 (2000)

— *Studio Pottery in Britain 1900–2005* (London, 2007)

— *A Rough Equivalent: Sculpture and Pottery in the Post-War Period*, Henry Moore Institute Essays on Sculpture 62 (Leeds, 2010)

— 'English Pottery by Rackham and Read: A Question of Attribution', *Journal of Modern Craft*, 6:3 (2013), pp.275–91

Kemske, Bonnie, *The Tea Bowl: East and West* (London, 2017)

Kesseler, Rob, 'Beyond Billington: A Brief Personal Reflection on a Lifetime at the Central, 1970–2016', in Quinn and Sorrell (2017), pp.30–5

Knott, Rebecca, 'Chelsea Figurines and Studio Ceramics: The Overlooked Women Modellers of the Inter-war Period', *Journal of the Decorative Arts Society*, 45 (2021)

Lane, Peter, *Studio Porcelain* (London, 1980)

— *Studio Ceramics* (London, 1983)

— *Contemporary Porcelain: Materials, Techniques and Expressions* (London, 1995), revised (2003)

Leach, Bernard, *A Potter's Book* (London, 1940), revised (1945), (1975)

— *Beyond East and West: Memoirs, Portraits and Essays* (London, 1978)

Lewenstein, Eileen, 'Ceramics in Britain Today', *New Zealand Potter*, 18:1 (1976)

— and Emmanuel Cooper (eds), *New Ceramics* (London, 1974)

Lewis, Griselda, *A Picture History of English Pottery* (London, 1956)

Livingstone, Andrew and Kevin Petrie (eds), *The Ceramics Reader* (London, 2017)

Livingstone, Karen and Linda Parry (eds), *International Arts and Crafts*, exh. cat. (London: V&A, 2005)

London Institute, *Off the Wall On the Floor*, exh. cat., curated by Richard Slee (London, 1998)

Lucie-Smith, Edward, *World of the Makers: Today's Master Craftsmen and Craftswomen* (New York, 1975)

Lynn, Martha Drexler, *Clay Today: Contemporary Ceramists and Their Work*, a cat. of the Howard and Gwen Laurie Smits Collection at the Los Angeles County Museum of Art (Los Angeles/San Francisco, 1990)

MacCarthy, Fiona, 'The Inheritance of Diffidence: Crafts in Britain between the Wars', *Craft History*, 1 (1988), pp.31–48

Martin, Simon, 'Pop Goes the Art School: Design and Education', in Christopher Breward and Ghislaine Wood (eds), *British Design from 1948: Innovation in the Modern Age* (London: V&A Publishing, 2012), pp.156–75

Matson, Sara and Sam Thorne (eds), *That Continuous Thing: Artists and the Ceramics Studio, 1920 – Today*, exh. publication (Tate St Ives, 2016)

Meşher, *Beyond the Vessel: Myths, Legends, and Fables in Contemporary Ceramics around Europe*, exh. cat. (Istanbul, 2019)

Minogue, Coll and Robert Sanderson, *Wood-fired Ceramics: Contemporary Practices* (London, 2000)

Morris, Tom, *New Wave Clay: Ceramic Design, Art and Architecture* (Amsterdam, 2018)

Museum of Modern Art, Oxford, *The Raw and the Cooked: New Work in Clay in Britain*, exh. cat., curated by Alison Britton and Martina Margetts (Oxford, 1993)

Northern Centre for Contemporary Art, *The Harrow Connection*, exh. cat., texts by Patrick Nuttgens, Tanya Harrod, Danny Killick and others (Sunderland, 1989)

Nottingham City Museums and Galleries, *The Ballantyne Collection of 20th Century Studio Ceramics*, ed. Pamela Wood (Nottingham, 2017)

Oxford Gallery, *Towards Ceramic Sculpture*, exh. cat., introduction by Edward Lucie-Smith (Oxford, 1974)

Oxfordshire County Museum Services, *Artist Potters Now*, exh. cat. (Oxford, 1984)

Paisley Museum and Art Galleries, *The Studio Ceramics Collection at Paisley Museum and Art Galleries*, foreword by Robert A. Saunders (Paisley, 1984)

Partington, Matthew, 'Espresso, Exoticism and Earthenware: The London Coffee Bar Ceramics of the Picassoettes (William Newland, Margaret Hine and Nicholas Vergette) 1952–1966', *Interpreting Ceramics*, ejournal, 6 (2005), reproduced in Dahn and Jones (2013), pp.90–9

Pearson, Lynn, *Tile Gazetteer: A Guide to British Tile and Architectural Ceramics Locations* (Shepton Beauchamp, 2005)

Perryman, Jane, *Smoke-fired Pottery* (London, 1995)

— *Naked Clay: Ceramics without Glaze* (London, 2004)

— *Smoke Firing: Contemporary Artists and Approaches* (London, 2008)

Peters, Tessa (ed.), *Tradition and Innovation: Five Decades of Harrow Ceramics* (London: University of Westminster, 2012)

— and Janice West (eds), *Memoranda*, published to accompany an exhibition at the Crafts Study Centre (London, 2011)

Portsmouth City Museum and Art Gallery, *Seven in 76: Recent Work by Seven Contemporary Ceramists*, exh. cat. (Portsmouth, 1976)

Potters: An Illustrated Directory of the Work of Full Members of the Craftsmen Potters Association of Great Britain, ed. Emmanuel Cooper and Eileen Lewenstein (London: Craftsmen Potters Association, 1972) with 11 further editions: (1974), (1975), (1977), (1980), (1983), (1986), (1989), (1992), (1994), (1997), (2000). Titles vary slightly: from 3rd edition it includes *A Guide to Pottery Training in Britain*; 6th edition published as *Studio Ceramics Today* and combines exh. cat., V&A; from 9th edition the institution was renamed the Craft Potters Association; 12th edition ed. Emmanuel Cooper only; subsequently published as *The Ceramics Book*

Quinn, Anthony and Carla Sorrell, *Craftsmanship Alone is Not Enough: 100 Years of Ceramics at Central Saint Martins* (London, 2017)

Racz, Imogen, *British Art of the Long 1980s: Diverse Practices, Exhibitions and Infrastructures* (London, 2020)

Reed, Wyn, 'English Studio Pottery Today', *New Zealand Potter*, 12:1 (1970)

Rice, Paul, *British Studio Ceramics* (Marlborough, 2002)
— and Christopher Gowing, *British Studio Ceramics in the 20th Century* (London, 1989)
Riddick, Sarah, *Pioneer Studio Pottery: The Milner-White Collection*, published in association with York City Art Gallery (London, 1990)
Robinson, Michael, 'Studio Ceramics since 1945: Pandora's Box or a Gift from the Gods', in Crafts Council (1995b), pp.8–13
Rogers, Phil, *Ash Glazes* (London, 1991), revised (2003)
— *Salt Glazing* (London, 2002)
Rose, Muriel, *Artist-Potters in England* (London, 1955), revised and enlarged (1970)
Rothschild, Henry (ed.), *More British Potters*, exh. cat., Kettle's Yard (Cambridge, 1972)
Royal Academy of Arts, *Exhibition of Decorative Art*, includes Arts and Crafts Section arranged in collaboration with the Arts and Crafts Exhibition Society (London, 1923)
Ruthin Craft Centre, *Diaspora Cymreig: Makers of Welsh Origin Working Outside Wales*, exh. cat. (Ruthin, 2002)
— *Hands Across the Border*, exh. cat. (Ruthin, 2004)
— *Collecting Contemporary Ceramics*, exh. cat., in collaboration with National Museum Wales (Ruthin, 2006)
— *Welsh Table*, exh. cat. (Ruthin, 2009)
— *Studio: Photographs by Phil Sayer of 18 Influential Ceramicists' Studios*, exh. cat. (Ruthin, 2010)
Rutter, Frank, 'Modern English Pottery and Porcelain', *Apollo*, 2 (1925), pp.133–9
Sainsbury Centre for Visual Arts, *Lucie Rie, Hans Coper, and their Pupils: A Selection of Contemporary Ceramics Illustrating their Influence*, texts by Cyril Frankel and Tony Birks (Norwich, 1990)
Scott, Paul, *Ceramics and Print* (London, 1994), revised (2012)
— (ed.), *Hot off the Press: Ceramics and Print*, exh. cat., Tullie House City Museum & Art Gallery, Carlisle (London, 1996)
— and Knut Astrup Bull (eds), *Horizon: Transferware and Contemporary Ceramics* (Oslo/Stuttgart, 2015)
Seisbøll, Lise (ed.), *British ceramics. 2000.dk*, exh. cat. (Middelfart: Keramikmuseet Grimmerhus, 2000)
Sempill, Cecilia, *English Pottery and China* (London, 1944)
Shipley Art Gallery, *Contemporary Craft Collecting at the Shipley Art Gallery, Gateshead*, text by Tanya Harrod (Gateshead, 2003a)
— *Tell Tale: Narratives in Contemporary Craft*, exh. cat., text by Clare Phillips (Gateshead, 2003b)
Smithsonian Institution, *British Artist Craftsmen: An Exhibition of Contemporary Work* (London, 1959)
Speight, Charlotte F., *Images in Clay Sculpture: Historical and Contemporary Techniques* (New York, 1983)
Stair, Julian, 'Studio Ceramics: Ghetto or Ghetto Mentality', in Harrod (1997), pp.157–62
— 'Re-inventing the wheel – The Origins of Studio Pottery', in Paul Greenhalgh (ed.), *The Persistence of Craft* (London, 2002), pp.49–60
— 'From Precepts to Praxis: The Origins of British Studio Pottery', in Adamson, Droth and Olding (2017), pp.29–55
— 'The Spark that Ignited the Flame: Hamada Shōji, Paterson's Gallery, and the Birth of English Studio Pottery', in Meghen Jones and Louise Allison Cort (eds), *Ceramics and Modernity in Japan* (Abingdon, 2020), pp.109–27
— (ed.), *The Body Politic: The Role of the Body and Contemporary Craft*, conference papers, introduction by Julian Stair (London: Crafts Council, 2000)
Stephens, Chris, 'Ben Nicholson: Modernism, Craft and the English Vernacular', in David Peters Corbett, Ysanne Holt and Fiona Russell (eds), *The Geographies of Englishness: Landscape and the National Past 1880–1940* (New Haven, 2002), pp.225–47
Sunderland Arts Centre, *State of Clay*, exh. cat. (Sunderland, 1978)
Tate Gallery, *St Ives 1939–64: Twenty Five Years of Painting, Sculpture and Pottery*, exh. cat. (London, 1985)
Tate Liverpool, *A Secret History of Clay: from Gauguin to Gormley*, exh. cat. (Liverpool/London, 2004)
Taylor, Louisa, *Ceramics Masterclass: Creative Techniques of 100 Great Artists* (London, 2020)
Thormann, Olaf (ed.), *Vessel/Sculpture: German and International Ceramics since 1946: Grassi Museum of Applied Art Leipzig* (Stuttgart, 2008), vol.2 (2013), vol.3 (2018)
Thorpe, Ashley, *Contemporary British Ceramics: Beneath the Surface* (Marlborough, 2021)
Twomey, Clare, 'Contemporary Clay', in Hanaor (2007), pp.26–37
— (ed.), *Possibilities & Losses: Transitions in Clay*, exh. cat., with texts by Glenn Adamson and Jorunn Veiteberg, published by the Crafts Council in partnership with mima, Middlesbrough Institute of Modern Art (London, 2009)
Ulster Museum, *New Ceramics*, exh. cat., introduction by Michael Robinson (Belfast, 1974)
Vacher, Jean (ed.), *Muriel Rose: A Modern Crafts Legacy* (Farnham: Crafts Study Centre, 2006)
Veiteberg, Jorunn, 'The Postmodern Pot', in Clark, Strauss and others (2012), pp.122–42
— (ed.), *Thing Tang Trash: Upcycling in Contemporary Ceramics*, exh. cat., with texts by Jorunn Veiteberg, Alison Britton, Paul Scott, Anne Britt Ylvisåker, Ezra Shales and Heidi Bjørgan (Bergen, 2011)
Victoria and Albert Museum (V&A), *English Pottery Old and New*, picture book of an exhibition arranged in collaboration with the Council for Art and Industry held in 1935 (London, 1936)
— *International Ceramics 1972*, exh. cat. (London, 1972)
— *Six Studio Potters*, exh. leaflet (London, 1977)
— *The New White: Contemporary Studio Porcelain*, exh. leaflet, text by Alun Graves (London, 1999)
Vincentelli, Moira, *Aberystwyth Ceramics: A Selection of Ceramics from the Collection of the University College of Wales, Aberystwyth*, exh. cat. (Aberystwyth, 1979)
— *Women and Ceramics: Gendered Vessels* (Manchester/New York, 2000)
Vincentelli, Moira and Anna Hale, *Catalogue of Early Studio Pottery in the Collections of University College of Wales Aberystwyth* (Aberystwyth, 1986)
Wadsworth-Boyle, Morgan (ed.), *Shaping Ceramics: From Lucie Rie to Edmund de Waal*, exh. cat. (London: Jewish Museum, 2016)
Waller, Jane, *Colour in Clay* (Marlborough, 1998)
Walsh, Helen, *Centre of Ceramic Art: An Introduction* (York: York Museums Trust, 2016)
— *The Yorkshire Tea Ceremony: W.A. Ismay and His Collection of British Studio Pottery* (London, 2021)
Watson, Oliver, 'The St Ives Pottery', in Tate Gallery (1985), pp.220–7
— 'Justification and Means: The Early Acquisition of Studio Pots in the Victoria and Albert Museum', *Burlington Magazine*, 132:1046 (May 1990), pp.358–60
— *Studio Pottery: Twentieth Century British Ceramics in the Victoria and Albert Museum Collection* (London, 1993), originally published as *British Studio Pottery: The Victoria and Albert Museum Collection* (Oxford, 1990)
Wells-Cole, Anthony, 'Fifty Years of New Ceramics in Leeds', *Leeds Art Calendar*, 87 (1980)
Wheeler, Ron, *Winchcombe Pottery: The Cardew–Finch Tradition* (Oxford, 1998)
Whiting, David, *Modern British Potters and their Studios* (London, 2009)
— (ed.), *Dartington: 60 Years of Pottery 1933–1993*, published to accompany an exhibition at Dartington Cider Press Centre (Dartington, 1993)
Whybrow, Marion, *Leach Pottery St Ives: The Legacy of Bernard Leach*, originally published as *The Leach Legacy: St Ives Pottery and its Influence*, revised and expanded, with introductory essay by John Bedding (St Ives, 2006)
Winch, Dinah, '"Canvas-free Artists": Studio Pottery in Britain', in Stephen Whittle, Adrian Jenkins and others, *Creative Tension: British Art 1900–1950*, exh. cat. (London, 2005), pp.85–96
— (ed.), *Fired Up: Ceramics and Meaning*, exh. cat. (Oldham: Gallery Oldham, 2010)
Windsor, John, 'A Fine Romance', *The Independent – Magazine* (15 November 1997)
Wingfield Digby, George, *The Work of the Modern Potter in England* (London, 1952)
Woodhead, Steve, *The Teapot Book* (London, 2005)
World Crafts Council – Belgique francophone (WCC-BF), *European Triennial for Ceramics and Glass*, exh. cat. (Mons, 2010)
Wren, Rosemary, *Animal Forms and Figures* (London, 1990)
Yates-Owen, Eric and Robert Fournier, updated by James Hazelwood, *British Studio Potters' Marks*, 3rd edition (London/New York, 2015)
York City Art Gallery, *Michael Cardew and Pupils*, exh. cat., introduction by Tessa Sidey, contributions from Michael Cardew, Svend Bayer, Clive Bowen, Seth Cardew, Peter Dick and Ray Finch (York, 1983)
Zwemmer Gallery, *Artists of To-Day*, exh. cat. (London, 1933)

ACKNOWLEDGMENTS

A great many people have in various ways contributed to this book. First and foremost are the artists themselves, many of whom have supplied detailed information about their work, often on more than one occasion. My thanks go to them all, and also to the estates, relatives, partners, colleagues and friends of artists no longer with us, who have similarly provided details of lives and works. Many others have shared knowledge and information, supplied publications, or assisted in making contacts: Helen Bent, Helen Brown, Louise Chennell, David Cursons, Kitty Douglas-Hamilton, Andrew and Lisa Dowden, John Edgeler, John Faithfull, Philip Hughes, Christopher Jordan, Ruth Lloyd, Philippa Parker, Matthew Partington, Tessa Peters, Simon Olding, Jennifer Opie, Roger Stewart, Helen Walsh, David Whiting, Ben Williams and Chris Yeo have all been most helpful. Neil Parkinson, Archives & Collections Manager at the Royal College of Art, deserves particular thanks for his generous help in confirming dates of study and other details of former students of the College. I am especially grateful to Alison Britton, who read the introductory essay and made many helpful suggestions, and to Tanya Harrod for her kind foreword. My curatorial colleagues in the V&A, past and present, have provided invaluable support, and I would like to thank them all. In particular, I would like to acknowledge Claire Thorn, who gathered information from living artists in the collection during the 2000s when a new catalogue was first discussed; this material has provided an essential foundation for this new study. Rebecca Knott researched and drafted the entries on the figure-makers of the 1920s. Terry Bloxham, Eloise Donnelly, Rebecca Luffman and Simon Spier oversaw the lengthy photography programme. The wonderful object photographs were meanwhile taken by Ian Thomas, Mike Kitcatt, Christine Smith, Kieron Boyle, Sara Hodges, Sarah Duncan and others. Reino Liefkes has been a trusted voice over many years in all matters related to the collection. A number of ceramic installations and displays, outcomes from which are reflected on these pages, could not have been realized without the work of Kate Quinlan and Florence Tyler. I would also like to give special thanks to Sarah Griffin, whose engagement with and detailed knowledge of the discipline has made her counsel among my most valued, and to recognize all those whose generosity has supported the development of the collection. In making this book a reality, my sincere thanks go to my colleagues in V&A Publishing, in particular Jane Ace, Hannah Newell and Coralie Hepburn, and also to Julian Honer, Melissa Mellor and Rosalind Horne at Thames & Hudson. I would also like to thank Sarah Yates for her admirable attention to detail with the text, and Peter Dawson for his elegant design. I am especially grateful to Helen Ritchie for her support throughout the writing of this book, and for her insight. Above all, I would like to thank Oliver Watson for his encouragement and generosity. This book will always in part be his.

PICTURE CREDITS

All photography is © Victoria and Albert Museum, London, unless otherwise stated.
All works included in the illustrated catalogue, 'A–Z of Artists' (pp. 156–405), are © the Artist, unless otherwise stated.

pp.2, 14, 35, 40, 42, 47, 66, 72 (left), 95 (right) © The Bernard Leach Family. All rights reserved, DACS 2022
pp.4, 406–7 Photo © Ben Boswell
p.27 Photo: Dan Prince
pp.28, 127 (bottom) Courtesy of the artist and David Gill Gallery
p.29 Photo: Sylvain Deleu
pp.32–3, 156–7 Photo: Phil Sayer
p.34 (top) © The Estate of Denise Wren
p.36 (bottom) © The Estate of Cuthbert Hamilton
p.37 © The Estate of Dora Lunn
p.38 © The Estate of Charles and Nell Vyse
p.39 (left) © The Estate of Stella R Crofts
p.39 (right) © The Estate of Madeline Raper
p.41 © The Estate of Hamada Shōji
pp.42, 52–3, 67 © The Estate of Michael Cardew
pp.45–6, 51 © The Estate of William Staite Murray
p.48 © The Estate of Norah Braden
p.49 © The Estate of Katharine Pleydell-Bouverie
p.50 (left) © Estate of Duncan Grant. All rights reserved, DACS 2022
p.50 (right) © Estate of Vanessa Bell. All rights reserved, DACS 2022
p.54 (left) © The Estate of Margaret Rey
pp.54 (right), 69 © The Estate of Henry Hammond
p.55 © The Estate of RJ Washington
pp.56–7, 60, 76–7 © The Estate of Lucie Rie
p.59 (bottom) © The Estate of Marianne de Trey
pp.61, 65, 78–9 © The Estate of Hans Coper
p.63 © The Estate of William Newland
p.64 © The Estate of James Tower
p.68 (top) © The Estate of Alan Caiger-Smith
p.70 © The Estate of Helen Pincombe
pp.71 (left), 72 (right) © The Estate of Ruth Duckworth
p.71 (right) © The Estate of Dan Arbeid
p.72 © The Estate of Louis Hanssen
pp.72, 109 (top) © The Estate of Gillian Lowndes
p.73 (right) © The Estate of Ian Auld
p.73 (left) © The Estate of Robin Welch
p.80 © The Estate of Anthony Hepburn
pp.81, 105 © Gordon Baldwin
p.82 © The Estate of Ian Godfrey
p.83 © The Estate of Bryan Newman
p.84 © Ruth Barrett-Danes
p.85 (left) © The Estate of Denise K Wren
p.85 (top) © The Estate of Mo Jupp
p.85 (below right) Courtesy of the Donald Locke Estate
p.86 © The Estate of Colin Pearson
p.87 © The Estate of Michael Casson
p.88 (top) © Glenys Barton
pp.88 (bottom), 99 © Jacqueline Poncelet
p.89 © Andrew Lord
pp.90, 108 (left), 122 (top) © Alison Britton
p.90 (right) © Janice Tchalenko. All Rights Reserved, DACS 2022
p.91 © Elizabeth Fritsch
p.92 © The Estate of Rosemary Wren
p.93 © The Estate of Siddig El Nigoumi
p.94 © The Estate of Richard Batterham
p.95 (top) © Clive Bowen
p.95 (bottom left) © The Estate of Ray Finch
p.96 © The Estate of Joanna Constantinidis
pp.97, 123 (bottom) © Walter Keeler
p.98 (left) © Richard Slee
pp.98 (right), 126 Courtesy the artist and Hales, London and New York. Copyright the artist.
p.100 © Sandy Brown
p.101 © Elspeth Owen
p.102 © John Ward
p.103 © Magdalene Odundo
p.104 © The Estate of Ewen Henderson
p.106 © The Estate of Angus Suttie
p.107 (left) © Henry Pim
p.107 (right) © Sara Radstone
pp.109 (bottom), 136 © Martin Smith
p.110 © Takeshi Yasuda
p.111 © Edmund de Waal
p.112 (left) © Jim Malone
p.112 (right) Courtesy of Mike Dodd
p.113 (left) © Jane Hamlyn
p.113 (right) © The Estate of Phil Rogers
pp.114, 149 © Neil Brownsword
p.150 © Claire Partington
pp.115, 154 © Grayson Perry. Courtesy the artist and Victoria Miro
p.116 © Philip Eglin
p.117 Courtesy of Stephen Dixon
p.118 © Susan Halls
p.119 © Christie Brown
pp.120, 132 © Felicity Aylieff
p.121 © Lawson Oyekan
p.122 (bottom) © Ken Eastman
p.123 (top) © The Estate of Emmanuel Cooper
p.124 © Keith Harrison
p.125 © Laura Ford
p.126 Images courtesy the artist and Hales, London and New York. Copyright the artist.
p.127 (top) Courtesy of Hans Stofer
p.128 (top) © The Estate of Simon Carroll
p.128 (bottom) © The Estate of Danlami Aliyu
p.129 © Svend Bayer/ Photo: Chris Chapman
p.130 © Jennifer Lee
p.131 © Halima Cassell
p.132 © Julian Stair
p.134 © Kate Malone
p.135 © Nicholas Rena
p.137 © Richard Deacon; Courtesy Lisson Gallery
p.138 © Edmund de Waal/ Photo: Hélène Binet
p.139 © The Estate of Gwyn Hanssen Pigott/ Photo: Brian Hand
p.140 © Carol McNicoll
p.141 © Paul Scott
p.142 © Edmund de Waal/ Photo: Ian Skelton
p.143 © Andrea Walsh
p.144 © Nao Matsunaga
p.145 (top) © Jesse Wine
p.145 (bottom) © Aaron Angell
p.146 © Rachel Kneebone
p.147 Photo: Dewi Tannatt Lloyd
p.148 © Sam Bakewell
p.151 © Matt Smith
p.152 © Akiko Hirai
p.153 © Fernando Casasempere
p.155 © Vicky Lindo
p.185 Photo: Nick Moss, Todd-White Art Photography, Courtesy of the Crafts Council
p.369 (left, middle) Photo: Jan Baldwin

INDEX

This index relates only to the essay 'Studio Ceramics in Britain'.

Page numbers in *italic* refer to illustrations.

To all potters and lovers of pots

IMAGES:
pp.32–3: Alison Britton in her studio in Stamford Hill, London, 2003
pp.156–7: Philip Eglin in his studio in Shelton, Stoke-on-Trent, 2003
pp.406–7: Katharine Pleydell-Bouverie in her workshop at Kilmington Manor, Wiltshire, *c.* 1982–83

First published in the United Kingdom in 2023 by
Thames & Hudson Ltd, 181A High Holborn, London, London WC1V 7QX,
in association with the Victoria and Albert Museum, London

First published in the United States of America in 2023 by
Thames & Hudson Inc., 500 Fifth Avenue, New York, New York 10110

Designed by Peter Dawson, www.gradedesign.com

British Library Cataloguing-in-Publication Data
A catalogue record for this book is available from the British Library

Library of Congress Control Number 2022944833

ISBN 978-0-500-48089-2

Printed and bound in China by C & C Offset Printing Co. Ltd